JEWISH EVERY DAY
THE COMPLETE HANDBOOK
FOR EARLY CHILDHOOD TEACHERS

Maxine Segal Handelman
Musical Contributions by Julie Jaslow Auerbach

A.R.E. PUBLISHING, INC.
Denver, Colorado

Published by:
A.R.E. Publishing, Inc.
Denver, Colorado

Library of Congress Catalog Number 00-101924
ISBN 0-86705-048-9

© A.R.E. Publishing, Inc. 2000

Printed in the United States of America
10   9   8   7   6   5   4   3   2

DEDICATION

To Sharon Morton, Judy Aronson, and Renatta Cooper —
I have been blessed with three mentors, and my life is richer because of each.

ACKNOWLEDGEMENTS

From Max Segal Handelman

This book would not have been possible without the partnership and support of the Jewish Community Centers of Chicago. I am indebted to the Central staff for the time, understanding, kindness, and interest that was shown to me in the process of writing this book. Thank you to my fellow directors and teachers, who provided me with ideas, feedback, and classrooms in which to experiment. I am especially thankful to Avrum Cohen, Sheila Goldman, Fern Batchko, and Rabbi Yehiel Poupko, who supported me as a JCC employee and as a trusted colleague.

The faith, support, and encouragement I received from my publishers, Audrey Friedman Marcus and Rabbi Raymond A. Zwerin, carried me through the months of research and writing, and for this I am most grateful.

I would also like to thank Roberta Louis Goodman, Rhonda Mlodinoff, Ann and Mike Luban, and Ilene Vogelstein for their critical readings and helpful contributions.

Sincere appreciation to Nachama Skolnik Moskowitz for her contribution of activities to Chapters 6 and 19.

Sincere thanks to the models who grace the cover of *Jewish Every Day*: Sadie Parris, Reuben Roth, and Jacob Lazear, students in the early childhood program at Temple Sinai, Denver, and their teacher, Amy Musler.

Special thanks to Julie Jaslow Auerbach for her wonderful music activities and lists of songs for the holidays, her thorough list of music resources and discography (see the bibliography at the end of this volume), and for her generosity in allowing us to reprint the music for her wonderful songs.

And of course the biggest thank-you goes to Jacob, who proved to be more loving and patient than I ever imagined a person could be.

From Julie Jaslow Auerbach

My thanks and appreciation to the following:

To Lynne Yulish for her matter-of-fact, consistent, and generous support in transcribing and encouraging the transcription of my songs, and for her friendship.

To Velvel Pasternak, for his incredible knowledge of the field of Jewish music, and for his help in verifying sources.

To Alice Weinstein, for walking with me through the eleventh-hour research at such a busy time.

To my family: my husband, Irv, for his encouragement through the years and for jumping in when he was needed, and to my children — Marisha, Jessi, and Nate — who were always my reason for the music.

CONTENTS

INTRODUCTION

During the Chanukat HaGan *(Dedication of the Preschool) at a school where I was the Jewish Educator, we said the blessing and hung a* mezuzah *on every classroom door at child-height, sang the* Shema, *and practiced kissing the* mezuzah *as we walked in and out of the classrooms. Many of the children made* mezuzot *to take home and hang on their own doorposts. Afterward, parents came up to me and told me, "Now my child won't go to bed until we have gone around and kissed every* mezuzah *in the house." "My child had a* mezuzah *on her bedroom door already, but she made us move it down to where she could reach it." I knew I had gotten my message across.* (Maxine Segal Handelman, reflections on 1995)

Jewish early childhood education today must be many things: excellent education providing the best that developmental theory and brain research can prescribe, the foundation of a strong, positive Jewish identity, a pathway into Jewish life for families, and a support system for busy parents. In order to do this, Jewish early childhood educators must keep abreast of all the latest research. The media is overflowing with conflicting information about brain research, classroom management techniques, tips for working with troubled children and difficult families, using computers in the early childhood classroom, and so much more.

What the media is not overflowing with, however, is information about how to integrate Judaism into everything else that is going on in an early childhood classroom. That is where *Jewish Every Day: The Complete Handbook for Early Childhood Teachers* comes in. This book demonstrates an awareness that in order to help children build the foundation of a warm, meaningful Jewish identity, Judaism must be a meaningful part of every day, not just an addition to the curriculum on Shabbat and holidays. This book also recognizes that in order to create a loving, Jewish atmosphere at school, teachers must reach out to families and help them create a loving, Jewish atmosphere at home.

Jewish Every Day seeks to enable teachers to make their classrooms Jewish on a daily basis by integrating Jewish values and a Jewish frame of mind. This can only be accomplished effectively if the Jewish elements of the curriculum are developmentally appropriate. Early childhood education can only approach excellence when it prepares children to stand up to injustice. For Jewish children in a Jewish classroom, this requires some special considerations. These issues are all addressed in Part I of this book.

Central to Judaism are the three concepts of God, Torah, and Israel. Each of these concepts must inform the rest of the curriculum, throughout the entire year. Part II of this book is devoted to exploring each of these concepts and guiding teachers to integrate them in their daily class activities.

The pace of Jewish life is set by the Jewish calendar, and no guide for Jewish teachers would be complete without an extensive holiday section. In *Jewish Every Day*, Jewish early childhood teachers are recognized as adult learners as well as early childhood teachers. Each holiday chapter in Part III contains a significant amount of background information and resource listings to help teachers pursue further learning. Each of these chapters also contains, among other things, concepts for every age group infant through five, ideas for integrating Judaism into every area of the curriculum, and strategies for involving and teaching families. A glossary and Hebrew vocabulary list is also provided for each holiday.

Part IV of the book takes a brief look at many issues faced by today's Jewish early childhood teachers: dealing with secular holidays, working with non-Jewish families, keeping kosher, and making the summertime Jewish, among others. There are guides to making Hebrew, storytelling, and music integral parts of the classroom, and there is even a complete *mezuzah* curriculum.

The bibliography at the end of this book contains a wealth of resources. While most chapters have their own specfic bibliography, this final bibliography contains general Jewish and secular resources in the form of books, publishers, toys, materials, recordings, organizations, web sites and more.

It would be ideal if every early childhood teacher would take the time to sit down and read *Jewish Every Day* cover to cover. The reality is that this won't happen. So here are a few suggestions for which chapters will help various types of readers. The chapters in Parts I and II are filled with material meant to enrich your classroom all year, indeed meant to transform your classroom. Savor these chapters, but don't try to integrate everything at once. The holiday chapters in Part III will greatly enhance the holiday celebrations in your classroom, and will serve as excellent resources as you prepare for each holiday. Part IV should serve as a reference — turn to these chapters as the circumstances arise.

Excellent Jewish early childhood education can be achieved only through the dedication of Jewish early childhood teachers and directors. *Jewish Every Day: The Complete Handbook for Early Childhood Teachers* is an exceptional guide for those who have embarked on the journey.

INTRODUCTION TO PART I:
TOWARD EXCELLENCE

When Rabbi Joshua was an infant, his mother carried him in his cradle to the Bayt Midrash, the House of Study, so "his ears would become accustomed to the sounds of the Torah." (Jersualem Talmud)

Jewish early childhood education has existed in one form or another through the ages. Not too long ago in North America, this education consisted of synagogue nursery schools geared toward three and four-year-olds for a few hours a day or a week. Recently, such education has expanded well beyond nursery school. Jewish preschools and day-care centers serve infants through kindergarten and host parent/child classes as well. Jewish early childhood programs have also begun to focus on the Jewish education of families as well as children.

The field of Jewish early childhood education is constantly evolving. Changes come from within, from our own needs as early childhood educators constantly to evaluate and improve on the experiences we provide to young children and their families, as well as from the world around us. Jewish institutions across America were jolted into action by the 1990 Jewish Population Study, which shocked the Jewish community with its startling 52% rate of intermarriage statistic. Jewish education at all levels was looked to for solutions, and Jewish early childhood education in particular was seen as a prime resource for refocusing the American Jewish community.

The field of Jewish early childhood education is also in flux. Gone are the days when teachers were plentiful, and each came with a deep understanding of *yiddishkeit*. More often then not, our best teachers were mothers of graduating preschool students. State licensing standards prevent untrained parents from becoming teachers, and now, when their children reach school age, by and large, these mothers return to the courtroom or to the operating room. Good teachers are simply more difficult to find. And good teachers are harder to retain. Early childhood education overall is a low paying field. In 1999, New York teachers averaged $20,000 per year with no benefits.[1] Is it any wonder that many potential teachers are lost to higher paying fields?

Too frequently, teachers who do enter the field of Jewish early childhood education come with weak or non-existent Jewish backgrounds. In 1993, a report by the Council for Initiatives in Jewish Education revealed that fewer than half of Jewish early childhood educators had continued their Jewish education past the age of 13.[2] It is extremely difficult to teach what one does not know. Even so, such teachers can and do become excellent Jewish early childhood educators when they make a commitment to their own Jewish education. The path toward excellent Jewish early childhood education is fraught with stumbling blocks, but it is possible to navigate it and succeed.

Many communities are taking the initiative to overcome these stumbling blocks. In the face of teacher shortages and the deteriorating state of Jewish educational backgrounds among teachers

---

[1] Julie Wiener, "Bringing Jews in through the Nursery: Educators Rethink the Teaching of Tots." *JTA Daily News Bulletin* 77 (161), August 26, 1999: 1.

[2] Ibid.

in the field, there exists a strong movement toward professionalization of Jewish early childhood educators. Initiatives exist to upgrade the Jewish knowledge level of both teachers and parents. For example, the Jewish Community Centers Association of North America is piloting a multimedia curriculum headed up by Ruth Pinkenson Feldman that will teach children and their families key concepts from *Pirke Avot* (Ethics of the Fathers). In Baltimore, a program called *"Machon L'Morim: B'reshit"* is making major inroads in developing the Jewish knowledge base of the community's Jewish early childhood educators (more about this program in Chapter 2). In 1999, the Reform movement's Union of American Hebrew Congregations hired its first full-time staff person to assist the growing number of preschools at Reform congregations.[3] In 1998, the Bureau of Jewish Education of Greater Los Angeles published criteria for Accreditation in Jewish Education for Early Childhood Centers, to be used in conjunction with the accreditation process of the National Association for the Education of Young Children (NAEYC). There now exist national professional organizations for Jewish Early Childhood Educators, such as the National Association of Jewish Early Childhood Specialists, and the National Jewish Early Childhood Network, as well as a strong early childhood presence at the Coalition for the Advancement of Jewish Education (CAJE).

A major goal of Jewish early childhood education is to nurture in children the development of a strong, positive, warm Jewish identity and a love for Judaism. We strive to foster in them the desire and the ability to grow into Jewish adults who are proud of their heritage and happy and able to participate in Jewish life. This is not something achieved in a vacuum, with children alone. Our work includes the families of the young children in our care. If the family is not involved in its own process of Jewish education and development, then the Jewish growth of the child will have no foundation on which to stand and no basis from which to continue growing once the child leaves the Jewish early childhood educational setting.

To achieve this goal — the foundation of a Jewish identity that will sustain the child, indeed the family, through an entire lifetime — the Jewish education made available to the child and family must be absolutely the best education possible. The curriculum, defined as everything that happens while the child is at school and then some, must be tailored to offer each and every child the best access to a warm, positive Jewish world. Teachers who strive to reach this goal must be able to balance, on a day-to-day basis, what they know about teaching and how children learn with what they know about their particular students. Teachers must also be able to bring to the classroom a wealth of secular and Jewish knowledge and then weave these areas together.

Judaism does not happen separately from the rest of a child's life. Children are busy learning about the entire world. It is as easy for a child to go from observing a worm slithering on the ground to wondering about God as it is for that child to pick a couple berries off of a bush and declare them to be a pair of eyes. For Jewish early childhood education to be effective, it must integrate everything in the child's world. Separating Jewish concepts and experiences from secular concepts and experiences builds the foundation of a fragmented Jewish identity. An excellent Jewish education strives to make connections between Jewish events and everyday events. The excellent Jewish early childhood classroom is a model of Jewish living, one in which the atmosphere and the environment is Jewish every day.

This first section of this book lays the foundation upon which everything in an excellent Jewish early childhood classroom can be built. Chapter 1 explores developmentally appropriate practices in the Jewish early childhood setting. Chapter 2

---

[3]Ibid.

provides strategies for making the Jewish early childhood classroom Jewish every day. Chapter 3 enables teachers to integrate anti-bias education into the Jewish classroom. These topics do not pertain only to this section of the book; rather, each of the three — developmentally appropriate practices, ways to make the classroom Jewish every day, and an anti-bias approach – underlie and support every chapter in this book.

Excellent Jewish early childhood education is completely dependent on educators who invest themselves in Judaism and in the best ways to invite children into the joyful world of being Jewish. Teachers in these settings must be lifelong learners, continually striving to increase their knowledge and understanding of Judaism and developments in the field of early childhood education. This book seeks to teach and guide, but this is only one book. The many resources in the bibliographies will help you expand your Jewish knowledge.

CHAPTER 1

DEVELOPMENTALLY APPROPRIATE PRACTICE

On Lag B'Omer, Sharon told her four and five-year-olds the story of a teacher named Simeon Bar Yohai, who hid from the Romans in a cave, where he would study in secret with his students. Her children became very excited by the story, and during free play, they built caves from sheets and blocks. When the children asked, "What did Bar Yohai study in the cave?" Sharon told them about the Torah. The children posted lookouts, and dragged Hebrew and English books into the "caves" to study and discover for themselves just what was so important to Bar Yohai.

Many of the two-year-olds at the daycare were welcoming siblings into their families. Their teachers, Taaron and Linda, building on the excitement, designed the curriculum around all the babies. The children took a trip to the infant room of the Center to see the babies and to "help out." They went to see the kindergarten teacher who was pregnant. And they invited to class pregnant mommies and new baby brothers and sisters. The children practiced holding dolls with ahavah *(love)* and chesed *(kindness). Capitalizing on continuing interest, the teachers turned the focus onto these children and when they themselves were babies.*

It was almost Simchat Torah. Joann and Anna marched their class of three and four-year-olds into the synagogue's sanctuary to observe the Torahs firsthand. The children thought the Aron Kodesh was nice. They happily took turns kissing the Torah, but when the teachers took out a yad *(the pointer used to read a Torah), it felt as if an electric current ran through the group. "Let me see that yad," someone said. "I like that. I want one," exclaimed another. Joann and Anna nodded at each other. They knew how their Torah*

study would begin. Their initial "Torah topic" had just emerged.[1]

As Joan's four-year-old class approached Thanksgiving, she introduced the topic of coming to America. Families were solicited for stories of how they or their ancestors had come to this country. Joan webbed the topic with her class, which piqued the children's interest in the types of transportation used and the reasons people came. With the children, and after input from the parents, Joan created a bulletin board illustrating where each child's family had come from. One night, a father, a recent immigrant from Russia, saw the board and noticed the name of a town where one of the children's forebears had originated several generations before. He exclaimed, "Who's from there? That's the town I'm from!"

In recent years, the field of early childhood education has buzzed around concepts such as Developmentally Appropriate Practice, emergent curriculum, Reggio Emilia, webbing, and the Project Approach. Each of these approaches signifies a move away from "arts and crafts education" toward strategies that take into consideration all we have learned about how children develop. Today's early childhood educators recognize children as active learners, not jugs waiting to be filled or blank slates waiting to be written upon. In light of recent discoveries in brain development research, we know that the early years are critical in the development of connections in the brain. Because these connections impact on children's ability to think and process, we cannot waste these

---

[1]Thank you to Joann Dardick for this vignette.

years by simply "babysitting" children or allowing them to languish in front of the television.

WHAT IS DAP?

Developmentally Appropriate Practice (DAP) is, in the simplest terms, the philosophy of doing the right thing for each child at the right time. The "right thing" is making the decision that will best help each child to learn, grow, and develop into the most well adjusted, secure person he/she can be. DAP was originally defined as incorporating two dimensions: age appropriateness and individual appropriateness.

Age appropriateness acknowledges the universal predictable sequences of growth and change that occur in children in all areas — physical, emotional, social, cognitive, and spiritual. Knowledge of typical development provides a framework for creating a learning environment and for planning appropriate experiences for young children.

Individual appropriateness addresses the unique qualities of the individual — each child's personality, pattern and timing of growth, learning style, and family background. The experiences provided for each child should match his/her developing abilities while challenging his/her interests and understanding (Bredekamp, 1987).

The National Association for the Education of Young Children (NAEYC) expanded the definition of Developmentally Appropriate Practice in their 1996 "Position Statement on Developmentally Appropriate Practice in Early Childhood Programs Serving Children from Birth through Age 8." Recognizing the importance of the context in which children live NAEYC broadened the definition. DAP is now defined as, "the outcome of a process of teacher decision making that draws on at least three critical, interrelated bodies of knowledge: (1) what teachers know about how children develop and learn, (2) what teachers know about the individual children in their group, and (3) knowledge of the social and cultural context in

which those children live and learn" (Bredekamp, 1997, p. vii).

It is clear that what is developmentally appropriate for one child, one classroom, one school, or one year is not necessarily appropriate for another child in another class in another year. Consequently, there is no one set curriculum or pre-set method that could be labeled "Developmentally Appropriate Practice." Rather, DAP is a strategy to guide teachers in providing the best possible education to their students and families. NAEYC has been working for over a decade to guide the field of early childhood education with programs designed to help each child gain the most from the early years. Since 1986, NAEYC has published several editions of *Developmentally Appropriate Practice in Early Childhood Programs,* edited by Sue Bredekamp. Each edition reflects a developing knowledge of how children learn and an increased sensitivity to cultural differences.

EMERGENT CURRICULUM

Children learn best through play. Children play at the things that interest them the most. Acknowledging this, early childhood educators have begun to move away from pre-set themes and curriculum units toward topics and classrooms that are based on children's and teachers' interests. In a developmentally appropriate classroom, the curriculum is not directed by children or teachers alone. Rather, the curriculum results from interactions between teachers and children, with both providing ideas and developing them to create attractive and worthwhile themes (Cassidy, 1993). Emergent curriculum is a strategy designed to guide teachers through the process of DAP. While it is essential that teachers formulate and strive toward long-range goals and objectives for each child and for the group as a whole, emergent curriculum helps teachers balance long-range objectives with moment to moment opportunities based on child-teacher interactions and interests

(Kostelnik, 1992). Webbing (see p. 11) can be used to guide and expand the themes that emerge from the interests of the members of the class.

In the Foreword to *Emergent Curriculum* by Elizabeth Jones and John Nimmo, Carol Copple stresses that "each word in the phrase *emergent curriculum* has an important point to make. *Emergent* emphasizes that planning needs to emerge from the daily life of the children and adults in the program, particularly from the children's own interests. Yet, as the word *curriculum* conveys, there *is* also teacher planning in such settings, there *is* a curriculum" (p. vii). Written curriculum plans document the children's involvement with materials, questions, and discoveries, rather than document activities which teachers plan to direct.

Many teachers fear that using an emergent curriculum means waiting for the children to request topics of study, and being ready at a moment's notice to supply a week's worth of activities based on what the children encounter on the way to school. But emergent curriculum incorporates the interests of the adults as well as the children in the class. As early childhood educators, we are entitled to introduce the things we are interested in into the life of the classroom. We can plant the seed of a topic that supports a larger goal, and allow the seed to grow in ways determined by children's interests and input.

REGGIO EMILIA

In the schools of Reggio Emilia, Italy, home to possibly the finest example of Developmentally Appropriate Practice in the world, emergent curriculum is part of the overall philosophy. Reggio Emilia is not a model which we can replicate, but rather a set of principles from which we can extract useful hints. Reggio Emilia takes its cues from some of the same theorists who have been influential in the United States (including John Dewey, Jean Piaget, and Lev Vygotsky). Their ideas are not

necessarily new, just very well thought out, well funded, and well implemented (Gandini, 1993).

In Reggio Emilia, the child is viewed as competent and full of potential — a capable partner in his/her own education. A triad of child, teacher, and family is deemed necessary to the success of the experience. Indeed, parents built the first school, and family involvement remains essential to the education of the child. Following from the importance placed on this triad, children are viewed as growing and learning within the context of relationships — with other children, their teachers, their families, as well as with members of their larger community. Learning is a cooperative adventure.

Teachers act as partners with the children, and serve in a resource role. Teachers ask questions, listen to children, collaborate with children, and document the children's work. Documentation is an essential part of Reggio Emilia. Using photos, drawings, written explanations and transcripts of children's remarks, and examples of children's thinking and explorations in various media, teachers record the children's work and the process of their learning. This serves as a communication with families to help them understand the children's experiences. The documentation also serves to help teachers learn about children and understand them better, and to enable children to reflect on their own work and know their work is valued.

Finally, every school benefits from an *atelierista*, a visual arts specialist. In Reggio Emilia, art is viewed as a form of communication. Indeed, the many different media and art forms used by children in Reggio Emilia are referred to as the "100 languages of children." Art is not a separate part of the curriculum, but is considered inseparable from the whole cognitive/symbolic expression in the process of learning (Gandini, 1993). There is no time limit set on children's artistic explorations. The children engage in projects which may last a few days to a few months. The children's projects fall into three broadly defined categories: "those resulting from a child's natural encounter with the environment, those reflecting mutual interests on the part of the teacher and children, and those based on teacher concerns regarding specific cognitive and/or social concepts" (New, p. 7, 1990). Thus the curriculum itself is derived from the relationships the child has with the surrounding world.

SOURCES OF CURRICULUM

In the Reggio Emilia approach, the curriculum is drawn from the three broad sources listed above (a child's natural encounter with the environment, mutual interests on the part of the teacher and the children, and teacher concerns regarding specific cognitive and/or social concerns). In more American forms of emergent curriculum, there are many sources of curriculum. Betty Jones (1994, p. 127) lists nine of these: children's interests; teacher's interests; developmental tasks; things in the physical environment; people in the social environment; curriculum resource materials; serendipity: unexpected events; living together: conflict resolution, caregiving, and routines; values held by the school and community, family, and culture.

By culling the curriculum from these sources and others, teachers who employ emergent curriculum seek to engage children in-depth. By creating the classroom environment based on interactions between the interests of children and adults, teachers can support children's growth in more developmentally appropriate, personal ways. The goals of an emergent curriculum include encouraging creativity and cognitive growth via thorough investigations. Overall, the goal is to nurture creative, curious children who have a good sense of who they are and of the world around them.

As adult learners, we know that we tune into topics that catch our attention, pique our curiosity, speak to us personally. So much the more so for children, who have not yet learned to pay attention solely to be polite. When a teacher prepares for the year, a decision is made regarding long-range goals for the children, including empathy and sharing. If the teacher decides that these will be achieved through the themes of "All about Me"

and "Teddy Bears," chances are that some of the students will be engaged for some of the time. Alternatively, if this same teacher decides on the same long-range goals (caring and sharing), but does not map out her entire year, the results may be quite different. This teacher begins the year with "All about Me" and discovers, through observations of the children during this unit, that the majority of the children in the class have either recently gained or are anticipating the birth of a new sibling. The next unit in the class, "Babies," emerges from these observations, engaging most of the children most of the time, and expanding in many directions as different children ask questions. For example, the question "Was I a baby?" might lead to the compilation of a class album of all the children's baby pictures. "What do you do with a dirty baby?" may lead to providing dolls and sponges at the water table, along with soft towels and baby powder. Allowing the curriculum to emerge from a teacher's knowledge of the children is likely to connect more closely and deeply to the experiences and issues in the children's lives.

DAP IN A JEWISH EARLY CHILDHOOD SETTING

As incorporation of DAP and emergent curriculum have begun to change the face of early childhood education, Jewish teachers have found themselves in a quandary. Traditionally, Jewish preschools have followed a time bound curriculum based on the framework of the Jewish calendar. In the fall, we study apples for Rosh HaShanah, we plant in the middle of winter for Tu B'Shevat, we bake *matzah* and tell the story of Moses in the springtime. Every Friday, we light candles, drink grape juice, and eat *challah*.

Emergent curriculum is not a time bound strategy. Topics in a developmentally appropriate classroom are studied as the interests of teachers and children make them relevant. We study apples when a child comes back from picking apples in grandma's back yard. We plant when children notice the trees beginning to bud. We bake and tell stories to support what the teachers and children bring to the classroom. We create classroom rituals based on the members of the classroom. Judaism imposes a calendar on us — a calendar based on the moon, the sun, and our rich tradition, pre-set by generations and unbending to the whims of young children and their teachers.

Idie Benjamin (1998) points out that too often Jewish teachers who do an incredible job making the secular aspects of their curriculum developmentally appropriate fall flat when it comes to the Jewish aspects of their curriculum. For the Jewish curriculum, many teachers revert to an overemphasis on teacher-directed lessons and art projects. While DAP does not rule out teacher-directed lessons, it does seek a balance between teacher-directed and child-directed activities.

How then does one go about a Jewish curriculum in a developmentally appropriate way? It is important to remember that one of the sources of curriculum listed by Betty Jones (see above) is "values held by the school and community, family, and culture." This includes the values and content imbedded in each of the Jewish holidays. It is developmentally appropriate for a teacher to introduce a holiday into the curriculum in its proper season, so long as he/she does not forget to address it in a developmentally appropriate manner.

Implementing Jewish developmentally appropriate curriculum requires a leap of faith. It requires the belief that children can and should be allowed to play with and absorb Judaism the way we allow them to play with and absorb other concepts in the curriculum. We want young children to grasp number concepts — to recognize numerals, master number concepts, love math. Do we sit children down and lecture them about the rubrics of addition and subtraction, make them recite the numbers one to 20 three times a day, give them cutout numbers, and stand guard to make sure they paste the numbers on their paper in the right order? Of course not! We give children objects to sort and classify. We count the children sitting at the table. We graph the children's favorite foods.

Judaism can be part of the life of the classroom in the same natural way as math. Children can be given the opportunity to paint with Jewish symbol shapes, to wear the costumes of the biblical characters whose stories they have heard, and to experiment with different Jewish candles. Many teachers are wrapped up in minutia. They fear that children won't develop the strong Jewish identity their parents sent them to preschool to obtain unless, for example, they impart every single bit of information about each holiday, unless all the stripes on the children's Israeli flags are straight, and unless there are exactly eight branches plus a *shamash* on every *chanukiah*.

These fears are unfounded. In reality, there are two kinds of learning that people need: vertical and horizontal (Kostelnik 1992). Vertical learning is the hierarchical acquisition of skills and facts, somewhat akin to climbing a ladder. Horizontal learning, on the other hand, is conceptually based. Picture a net being spread out. When it is dragged in, some things slip through the holes, but the net still manages to capture a wide range of things. This is like many experiences occurring at the same time. The job of the learner is to make connections between the experiences. Both kinds of learning are essential to ensure both a *quantity* of knowledge and skills and a *quality* of understanding. Developmentally Appropriate Practice seeks a balance, with both types of learning being addressed and valued. Horizontal learning is important to give children a rich, quality, conceptual foundation on which all future learning is based.

When we make the Jewish aspects of the curriculum developmentally appropriate and embrace horizontal learning as much as vertical learning, we give our children this broad base, this foundation of knowledge which is, in essence, the foundation of their Jewish identity. If children one year can not remember the name of Antiochus and instead refer only to "the bad king," the next year, with enough opportunities to explore and play with the concepts, the children will not only remember the name, but they will compare Antiochus to Haman and Pharaoh.

In a developmentally appropriate Jewish classroom, there is a balance between the Jewish calendar and the everyday lives and interests of the members of the class. Teachers in such a classroom carefully consider the concepts of a Jewish holiday or topics and go with those that most closely connect to the lives of the children. Teachers in such a classroom are careful to engage children in the concepts of the theme or holiday at hand with both open-ended art experiences and art experiences that result in recognizable ritual objects. Teachers in such a classroom employ strategies that will engage their students in the story and rituals of each Jewish holiday in a way which will best connect with each child. When this balance is struck and when the Jewish areas of the curriculum are truly developmentally appropriate, then children can begin the process of building a strong, deep foundation of Jewish learning, a love for being Jewish, and the foundation for a positive Jewish identity which will serve them their entire lives.

This is a tall order. Developmentally appropriate Jewish education involves (1) what teachers know about how children develop and learn; (2) what teachers know about the individual children and families in their group; and (3) knowledge of the social and cultural context, namely the Jewish religious and cultural specifics, in which those children live and learn. In addition to the theories and experience we gained as we prepared to become teachers, this requires ample observation of the children in the class, and an effort to get to know the families of the children in the class, for they are students too.

A Jewish early childhood educator must make an effort to learn as much as he/she can about Jewish values, holidays, culture, and rituals. If the learner's job is to make connections between experiences, then the teacher's job is to plant the seeds and lay the groundwork for those experiences. Teachers who have a deep understanding and knowledge of Judaism will be that much more able to plant the seeds for meaningful experiences for their students. Seek out opportunities for Jewish learning. Check local JCCs, synagogues, and universities for classes on Jewish topics and Hebrew. The Internet contains a wealth of information on any Jewish topic (see the bibliography at the end of this volume, p. 378, for some suggested web sites), and many Jewish communities have their own web sites. Several colleges and universities offer Jewish learning opportunities over the Internet. Explore Jewish life. If Jewish observance is not part of your daily life, find ways to experience Jewish moments. Visit a friend's *sukkah*, get invited to Shabbat dinner at someone's house, crash a Jewish wedding, light Chanukah candles with a family with young children. Take a trip to Israel. The more you, as an adult, experience firsthand and the more you indulge in the joys of Jewish learning and living, then the more you, as a teacher, can give this love of Judaism to your children.

How does one begin to achieve these goals of Developmentally Appropriate Practice in the Jewish classroom? There are broad strategies and areas of focus that can facilitate DAP in a classroom. These include (1) close attention to the environment in a classroom, (2) webbing, and (3) continuous observation and evaluation. Each of these is described below.

THE ENVIRONMENT

The environment of the classroom is truly the unspoken curriculum. Walk into another teacher's classroom when no one is in the room. What do the walls tell you? Can you tell this is a Jewish classroom? What can you learn from the books on the shelf, the way the art supplies are stored, the food in the house corner? How do you feel, standing there in the middle of the room? Are you enticed to jump in, play, and explore? Do you get "hands off" vibes? Does this room belong to the teachers or to the children who gather there? What messages do the colors convey? Would a child with Attention Deficit Disorder (ADD) feel too over-stimulated? Would a curious child have enough to capture his/her interest? Is the message "Jewish Life Happens Here" conveyed by more than just one bulletin board with Shabbat symbols hanging in the same place since the beginning of the school year?

Begin the quest for developmentally appropriate Jewish practice with the physical environment of your room. There are ways to support the Jewish curriculum through every area of your room. Making good use of the walls, the supplies, and the materials will enable you to achieve balance and excellence.

The Walls

The walls of your classroom let people know who gathers there, what is going on, and what is important. There should be a balance of teacher-made or store-bought visuals and children's art-work and creations. Posters should reflect different kinds of children and families, Jewish, Israeli, and secular scenes. Photographs of children and families in the class engaged in Jewish and secular activities can be photocopied in color and enlarged into posters at any office supply or copy store. Laminate the best ones — it's cheaper than buying posters and more relevant to the children. Do the walls reflect the emerging Jewish aspects of the curriculum? Make sure what is on the walls changes often to reflect the ongoing life of the class, and that the walls serve to teach parents what their children are learning Jewishly. After a few weeks, we tend no longer to "see" visuals that have been in place for a long time.

Balance the visual atmosphere of the room with the needs of the children. Make sure you have simple, uncluttered areas to balance the crowded, busy display areas. Make sure every child has work displayed at some time. Even if children don't say anything, they know whose work is "good enough" to hang on the wall. If every

child's project comes out looking the same, reconsider the goals of the project. Was the child able to put himself/herself in the project, or did the teacher usurp all creative opportunities? Don't forget the ceiling, floor, windows, and hallways. These areas are included in this category and are spaces that can be used to communicate.

For more on the use of walls, see Chapter 2, "Jewish Every Day," p. 21.

The Supplies

The range of supplies, and the way supplies are stored gives a loud message as to what is supposed to happen in the classroom. Is a wide range of supplies available to children, or do children need a teacher's help or permission to obtain them? This includes art, building, writing, scientific exploration, and math supplies. Be creative in the breadth of supplies you offer. Include in the large range of supplies items such as catalogs from Judaica stores and old New Years cards to cut up, glitter in Jewish shapes from a party store, Hebrew newspapers, and stumps of different Jewish candles, etc. Work with children and other teachers to determine what this cache of supplies might include. Change the available supplies often. Remove supplies that are abused or unused. Add new supplies to expand and extend children's play, exploration, and understandings.

To introduce a curriculum theme which is based on teacher interests or outside demand, "plant" strategic tidbits or props to pique children's curiosity. When children "discover" a strategic prop that you have planted before an especially time-bound curriculum requirement (i.e., a holiday), the holiday becomes part of the life of the class in a more natural fashion. Add different kinds of *shofrot* to the science table before Rosh HaShanah, bring the *chanukiah* the children made in their class last year to circle time and see what discussion develops, place camels and people in the sand table before Pesach. Observing children with a strategic prop may lead the curriculum in directions not previously planned, while still providing specific holiday concept experiences and achieving larger, predetermined goals.

Keeping safety as the first priority, make sure that children have access to all the things they need to investigate their world creatively. Make sure there is a neat, clearly marked place for everything, and encourage children to return things to their proper spots.

The Materials

Fill the room with books, puzzles, games, props, plants, live animals, magnifying glasses, sorting bins, sensory items, music tape, and instruments — as much as space and budget and safety will allow. Make sure that a good percentage of the books, puzzles, games, music, etc., in the classroom support Jewish content. This can include overtly Jewish books, as well as "secular" books that illustrate Jewish values, such as *Rainbow Fish* by Marcus Pfister *(Tikkun Olam* and *Tzedakah) and Old Turtle* by Douglas Wood (God).

Be sure to include real Jewish ritual objects for the children to use as well. Do the children have a way of knowing what's available to them and what's off limits? Rotate materials to support specific themes and individual interests, and to prevent boredom. Store the materials so children can easily find what they are looking for and can easily return it to its place.

When considering how to ensure that the children share in the responsibility for the care of their room, plants, and animals, rely on Jewish values. These might include *Tikkun Olam* (repair of the world), *Tza'ar Ba'alay Chayim* (preventing the pain of animals) and *Bal Tashcheet* (do not destroy or waste) to engage the children in the respective helpful behaviors. Make sure that the materials change to reflect the development of the children over the course of the year.

WEBBING AND WEBBING JEWISHLY

A key strategy of DAP is webbing. Creating a curriculum web is similar to having a huge brainstorm on paper, a stream of consciousness with some structure. Picture a large construction of Tinker Toys, with spokes radiating from the wheels and connecting with other wheels in many directions. That is a three-dimensional model of a web. A written curriculum web presents to teachers and students the opportunity to collaborate on areas of interest and to explore and expand children's understandings. It allows teachers and children to make connections between topics.

Webbing is also the key to making sure that Jewish aspects of the curriculum are treated in a developmentally appropriate manner along with the rest of the curriculum. Webbing Jewish themes such as the holidays, biblical stories, or Jewish life cycle events, reveals the vast range of concepts related to any given theme (see the web in each holiday chapter). Too often, teachers plan curriculum by deciding what art projects they want to do to "cover" a topic. Approaching a holiday or other Jewish theme via a web helps you think about what concepts you want children to learn. Webbing can reveal strategies for tying Jewish concepts into those secular concepts already happening in the class. Webbing Jewish themes helps make connections between many Jewish and secular concepts, and provides direction for exploration and expansion, and allows for new possibilities to emerge.

There is no one right way to make a web. Any web strategy must be designed to let the web flow smoothly and quickly, to make opportunities to highlight key points of interest and expand on those. There should be room for group process (teacher with students, or several teachers together), as well as individual refinement (one or two teachers). The more people collaborating on a web, the richer the ideas will be, and the broader the related topics and interests will become. A web should be a usable tool that is instrumental in curriculum planning as well as in evaluation. A web is a tentative plan, and nothing about a web should be written in stone. A web is a way to encourage strands of curriculum to emerge naturally. All the strands of well-done web will be impossible to complete.

All of this said, how does one go about creating a web? One strategy is to start with a large pad of paper. Put the main topic word (determined either by observation of children's interests or by a time-bound holiday demand, or by another one of the sources of curriculum) in the middle of the paper in a circle. Then let the ideas fly! See figure 1 below. Draw a line from the main center word and write a related word. Draw lines from the new word and write more related concepts at the end of those lines. Allow the web to continue growing in this fashion through word association. At this point, edit nothing. Some concepts may grow into large "bouquets"; others may not produce more than a word or two. Circle the secondary words that seem the most interesting.

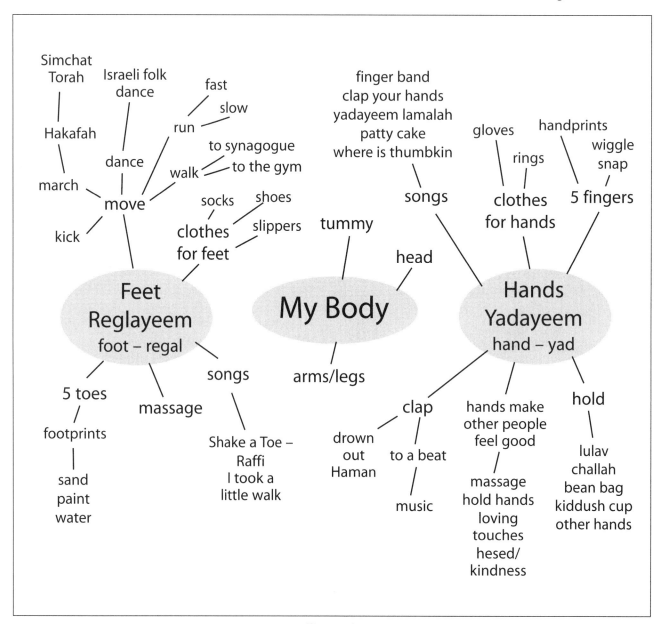

Figure 1

Another webbing strategy (Chard, 1998) requires pads of the smallest Post-it notes. Write down as many words as you can related to the topic at hand, one word per note. Make the words as specific and concrete as possible. Sort the words into groups that fit together. Label the categories you have made with a word or short phrase for each grouping. Arrange the categories around the main topic, and look for connections between the categories. Once you feel satisfied that all the ideas you have for now are on the table, transcribe the web to a large sheet of paper.

Webbing with children requires a little more creativity. With a large group, ask the children what they know about, and what they would like to know about, the topic at hand. As they volun-

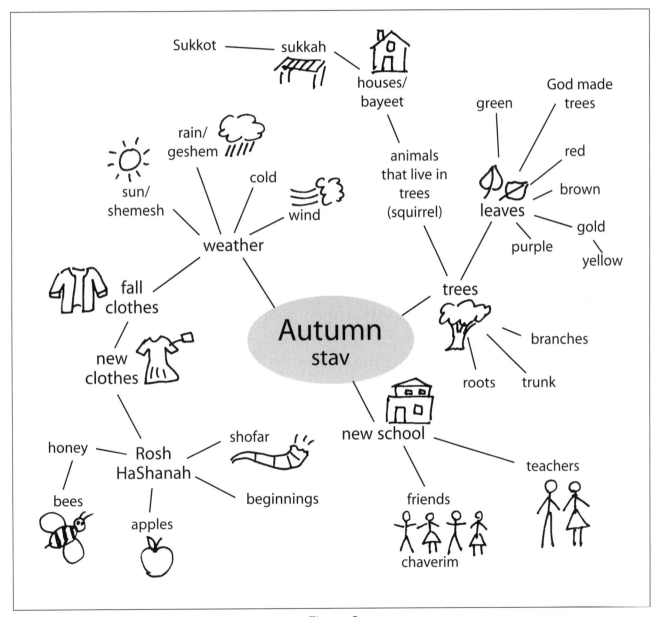

Figure 2

teer information, record it on a blackboard or large pad of paper, web fashion. This structure will enable you to ask more questions and develop the concepts that prove most interesting. A web is a useful tool to use directly with children. Creating a web together lets children know they have some control over the day-to-day happenings in their class and over what they are learning. It helps children make connections to other things going on in their lives, which in turn helps them make sense of their world. But, you say, young children do not read! When webbing with children, it is important to use a combination of words and pictures (see figure 2 on p. 13). This will encourage children to use the web for reference and evaluation. It will also empower children to create their own webs.

A web is a good place to include the interests and needs of individual children. When webbing with children, it may be useful to include children's names next to the things they suggest. This fosters ownership over the curriculum and may inspire more children to become involved in the process. Labeling the web with children's names may also help teachers gain a better understanding of the needs of specific children.

When you web a secular theme, look for places to add Hebrew vocabulary, Jewish songs and stories, Jewish values and concepts, holidays, related blessings, and Jewish rituals. Including the Jewish aspects of a subject in a web helps integrate Judaism into the entire curriculum (see figures 1 and figure 2). Webbing is the perfect tool to foster this integration, because webbing allows natural connections to suggest themselves. Judaism is not something we do only on Shabbat and holidays. Judaism is a way of life and a part of our being. Webbing with a Jewish frame of reference helps to make evident all the connections to Jewish themes that exist in the day-to-day curriculum.

Webbing is also instrumental in weaving together secular themes and Jewish themes. As you web a topic, expanding your thinking to include a very wide range of connected and related con-

cepts, you will discover links between topics and themes that may not have occurred to you otherwise. Using these links, it might be possible to create a continuum in which one web flows into another. As an example, one class might web Sukkot and decide to focus heavily on the topic of houses. When they web "houses," they may naturally move on to "families" because families live in houses. As they web and develop the topic "families," they may include in their "families" web "family celebrations," which leads them neatly into Chanukah (see figure 3 on p. 15). And so on through the year. While it is not necessary, or even always preferable, to develop each curricular unit from the web of the last unit, there is some value in providing these kinds of connections for children.

Webbing curriculum does not mean that you must throw away every curriculum book you own, and file every unit you have ever planned and done before. There is no need for every teacher constantly to reinvent the wheel. Use those resources! Adapt them to your classroom, your teaching style, and your children's interests (Jones, 1994). In fact, it is useful to investigate and become familiar with different curriculum sources, so that you have materials to rely on when the subject arises in your class.

Keep the webs you make. Develop your classroom curriculum from the most intriguing or interesting concepts in the web, using the web to guide you through different aspects of the chosen concepts, and to related concepts. Mark the web with different colors to signify which things you did, the things you tried that didn't go over well, and those things you might like to try again or come back to later. Feel free to continue expanding the web as you move through the curriculum. Remember, don't feel that you have to cover everything in the web. It won't happen, and it is probably counterproductive to try.

Webbing the Jewish themes and integrating Jewish concepts into every web in your curriculum will make your classroom a place in which there is always something interesting going on. Webbing every part of the curriculum results in children and teachers who are invested in the learning which is taking place. Further, the needs of individual children are addressed and woven into the curriculum so that the construction of strong Jewish identities become a natural part of every day.

Webbing will enable both teachers and children to see the wider context of everything that's happening, and the connections between the many parts of the curriculum. Webbing helps teachers make the best decisions for their particular students, based on long-range goals and the day-to-day lives of each person in the classroom.

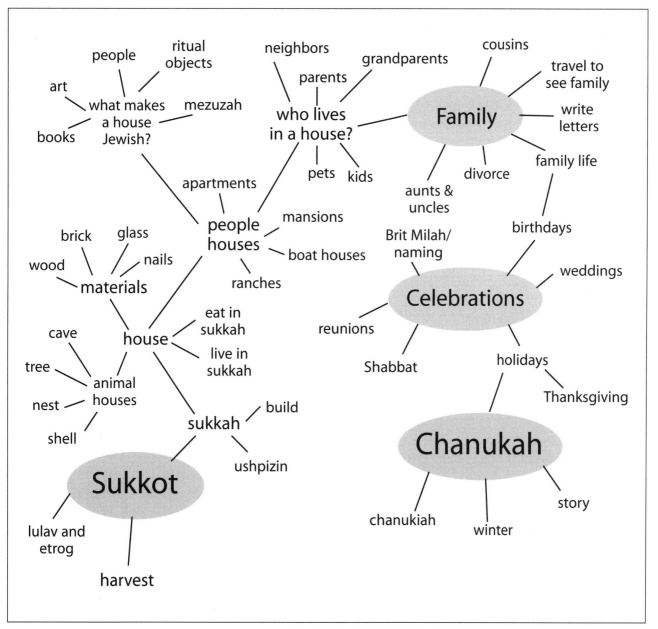

Figure 3
Expanding One Web through Several Units

OBSERVATION AND EVALUATION

An important part of the definition of Developmentally Appropriate Practice is that educational decisions are based on "what teachers know about the individual children in their group." To make the best decisions possible, teachers must find out everything they can about each of their children. Families are the teacher's partner for part of this investigation. Parents or guardians fill out forms with information about their child and family when the child is enrolled. Teachers should read these forms. But doing so is only a beginning, a jumping-off point. Teachers should make sure to talk with families about anything they don't understand or when they need more information to deal with a situation.

It is especially important for teachers to get to know not only their students, but also the children's families well. The building of a Jewish identity is not something teachers do alone. There must be a partnership between school and home. This partnership assures parents that what is taught at school will not denigrate how they observe at home, and it assures teachers that what the children learn at school will be supported at home. It is important for teachers to talk with families about such topics as the ways that Judaism is a part of the home. How do these ways compare to the ways in which Judaism is a part of the school? Are they similar, or will the child find school life disorienting? In what ways is the family interested in growing and evolving with their child?

As the year progresses, teachers may want to go beyond the information required on the form filled out at the beginning of the year, in order to meet each child's needs appropriately. At several points during the year, teachers and families should use either written or verbal methods for exchanging information about how the child is growing and developing. Teachers might seek to increase their understanding of certain children

by asking about a wide range of areas, including about extended family members living in the home, how parents talk to their children about being adopted, or about other extraordinary circumstances. This type of information helps teachers to be sensitive to differences in their class, and to make sure the curriculum supports the development and success of each child.

The best source of information about each child is the child himself/herself. Daily observation of children is a necessary part of Developmentally Appropriate Practice. Through the observation of children's play, through careful attention to children's questions, by listening to conversations between children, and by engaging in conversations with individual children, a teacher can gauge each child's needs, interests, strengths, and weaknesses. Often, keeping a journal documenting each child's behavior and activities can be a crucial tool in getting to know each child, and in assuring that the curriculum is engaging each child and supporting each child's development. These observations should serve as the fodder for the development of the curriculum. As the teacher observes each child, he/she can get a feel for Jewish values that come from each home, and how relevant Jewish themes are to each child's daily life. This observation is essential in being able to meet each child where he/she is, and in going on from there together.

Just as observation must be ongoing, so, too, must evaluation be continuous. Teachers must constantly evaluate the curriculum. Do the children look at the Hebrew books? Are the children motivated to give *Tzedakah* on their own? How can the teacher find out if the children know which blessing goes with which action? Ongoing evaluation, as opposed to summative evaluations (evaluations conducted at the end of a unit), can help a teacher fine tune a unit while it is in progress and determine the best courses of action. Some examples of useful evaluative questions are: What is still holding children's attention? Which puzzle hasn't been played with in two weeks? What materials or support can the teacher provide to expand the investigation the children have been purusing? How can the teacher help two other children work through a difficult challenge before they get frustrated and give up? Did that activity achieve the desired goals? Did it achieve some unexpected goals? Is it a good, natural time to conclude this unit, or do the children need more time to explore other related avenues?

Families should be solicited for ongoing feedback and evaluation as well. Observation and evaluation go hand in hand to enable teachers to make the best decisions they can for the children, and to ensure that the Jewish themes are part of the developmentally appropriate curriculum.

CREATING AN EXCELLENT JEWISH EARLY CHILDHOOD CLASSROOM

How do you know if you have mastered developmentally appropriate Jewish education? A group of top Jewish early childhood educators in Chicago joined together to answer this question.[2] They developed a list of "Guidelines for Creating an Excellent Jewish Early Childhood Classroom." Think about your own classroom and curriculum as you read the guideline questions below:

1. Can my classroom be immediately identified as a Jewish classroom by both children and families?
2. Does my classroom atmosphere provide a safe, nurturing climate in which children are free to grow and develop?
3. Can children of all abilities involved in this activity participate and feel a sense of accomplishment?
4. Have I used my knowledge about how children learn to ensure that the activity is child-focused rather than teacher-directed?

5. Have I incorporated Jewish values into the learning process and curriculum? Are Jewish elements integrated into the entire curriculum?
6. Are Jewish practices identified as such during the program? Are daily *mitzvot* and Jewish practices incorporated into the activity?
7. Have I provided the children with the opportunity to do projects, use materials, solve problems, explore, and investigate? Have they had a rich variety of experiences which involve "hands-on" learning?
8. Do the activities which are planned around this topic include various curriculum areas (e.g., language arts, math, social studies, science, art, music, physical education)?
9. Have I emphasized "sensory" learning in the experience?
10. Have I provided for social skill development during the activity through opportunity for peer interaction?

A Jewish early childhood school seeks to enable children to become learners, curious and creative, with strong Jewish identities and a sense of belonging to the Jewish community. The goals for Jewish children in a Jewish early childhood setting are, in many ways, the same goals teachers have for children everywhere — they all want their children to feel safe, to develop positive self-images, to love learning, to grow to be happy, productive adults. But, in Jewish schools, we strive for even more. We seek to give our children the gift of their Jewish heritage. As Jewish early childhood educators, we have the ability to nurture within children a love for Jewish learning, a fascination with Jewish holidays and life cycle events, and a passion for approaching the world in a Jewish way. When we design the entire curriculum, secular and Jewish aspects alike, to be genuinely suited to the specific children and families we serve, we enhance their lives, and indeed enhance the life of the Jewish people.

Andrea Rich, Elizabeth Shapiro, Sandy Shoichet, and Marci Sperling.

---

[2]The committee included Nina Chaitin, Diane Gould, Maxine Segal Handelman, Elizabeth Lassner, Rhonda Mlodinoff, Evie Wexler-Mylan, Candice Percansky,

BIBLIOGRAPHY

Benjamin, Idie. "Doing Early Childhood Education Appropriately and Jewishly." *Jewish Education News*, 19(3), 25-26, 1998.

Benjamin defines the current trend toward developmentally appropriate practice — a stage-based, child-sensitive approach to early childhood education — and shows how it may be applied to the Judaic program. She suggests ways to make the Jewish curriculum more experiential and sensory, and less concrete and factual.

Bredekamp, Sue, ed. *Developmentally Appropriate Practice in Early Childhood Programs Serving Children from Birth through Age Eight: Expanded Edition.* Washington DC: National Association for the Education of Young Children, 1987.

Guidelines to help teachers, parents, program administrators, policy makers, and others make informed decisions about the education of young children.

Bredekamp, Sue, and Carol Copple, eds. *Developmentally Appropriate Practice in Early Childhood Programs.* rev. ed. Washington DC: National Association for the Education of Young Children, 1997.

The most up-to-date guide to developmentally appropriate practice.

Cadwell, Louise Boyd. *Bringing Reggio Emilia Home: An Innovative Approach To Early Childhood Education.* New York: Teachers College Press, 1997.

The first book to integrate the experience of a year-long internship in the preschools of Reggio Emilia with a four-year adaptation effort in one American school in St. Louis, Missouri. Foreword by Lella Gandini.

Cassidy, Deborah, and Camille Lancaster. "The Grassroots Curriculum: A Dialogue between Children and Teachers." *Young Children*, 48 (6), 47-51, 1993.

Follows the development of an emerging curriculum, covering the teacher's role in the planning process and patterns of emergent curriculum.

Chard, Sylvia. *The Project Approach: Practical Guide 1: Developing the Basic Framework.* New York: Scholastic, 1998.

Includes information on the benefits of teaching with the Project Approach, classroom setup and techniques that support the approach, the phases of the Project Approach, and the role of teachers, parents, and children.

———. *The Project Approach: Practical Guide 2: Developing Curriculum with Children.* New York: Scholastic, 1998.

Includes information on how to prepare for a project, strategies and techniques to use in project fieldwork, how to keep a project going, how to conclude a project, and tips on classroom organization and management.

Edwards, Carolyn; Lella Gandini; and George Forman, eds. *The Hundred Languages of Children: The Reggio Emilia Approach To Early Childhood Education.* Norwood, NJ: Ablex, 1993.

The definitive work on the Reggio Emilia approach.

———. *The Hundred Languages of Children: The Reggio Emilia Approach — Advanced Reflections.* Norwood, NJ: Ablex, 1998.

Five years of reflection and essays on the Reggio Emilia approach.

Gandini, Lella. "Fundamentals of the Reggio Emilia Approach to Early Childhood Education." *Young Children*, 49 (1), 4-8, 1993.

A succinct description of the fundamental principles of the Reggio Emilia approach, which provides a framework for understanding Loris Malaguzzi's philosophy.

Gestwicki, Carol. *Developmentally Appropriate Practice: Curriculum and Development in Early Education.* 2d ed. Albany, NY: Delmar Publishers, 1995.

This book spells out the needs of each age group, infant through primary.

Hendrick, Joanne, ed. *First Steps toward Teaching the Reggio Way.* Upper Saddle River, NJ: Merrill, 1997.

A hands-on guide that examines how actual teachers in actual schools are working to grasp the principles of the Reggio Emilia approach and apply them in their everyday classroom settings. Written for presently practicing and future teachers by leading advocates of the Reggio philosophy.

Jones, Elizabeth, and John Nimmo. *Emergent Curriculum.* Washington, DC: National Association for the Education of Young Children, 1994.

An ongoing discussion among teachers in one program as they and the children move through the year, weaving the curriculum as they go along. Webs illustrate every unit.

Katz, Lilian, and Bernard Cesarone, eds. *Reflections on the Reggio Emilia Approach.* Urbana, IL: ERIC Clearinghouse on Elementary & Early Childhood Education, 1994.

A collection of seven papers representing a variety of perspectives on the implications of the Reggio Emilia approach to early education.

Kostelnik, Marjorie. "Myths Associated with Developmentally Appropriate Programs." *Young Children,* 47(4), 17-23, 1992.

Debunks nine of the most widely held myths about developmentally appropriate practice.

New, Rebecca. "Excellent Early Education: A City in Italy Has It." *Young Children,* 45(6), September 1990, 4-10.

An early, introductory article about the schools of Reggio Emilia and their innovative approach to early childhood education.

Perry, Gail, and Mary Duru, eds. *Resources for Developmentally Appropriate Practice: Recommendations from the Profession.* Washington, DC: National Association for the Education of Young Children, 2000.

Compilations of more than 1200 annotated resources for best practices in early childhood education.

BRAIN RESEARCH

Bransford, John D., Ann L. Brown, and Rodney R. Cocking, eds. *How People Learn: Brain, Mind, Experience, and School.* Washington, DC: National Academy Press, 1999.

This book presents a contemporary account of principles of learning based on recent research.

Brierley, John. *Give Me a Child Until He Is Seven: Brain Studies and Early Childhood Education.* London: Falmer Press, 1994.

A thorough study of the effects of brain research on early childhood education.

Kotulak, Ronald. *Inside the Brain: Revolutionary Discoveries of How the Mind Works.* Kansas City, MO: Andrews and McMeel, 1996.

The brain and how it works has long been one of life's more intriguing mysteries. Ronald Kotulak, a reporter for the *Chicago Tribune,* explores some of the secrets of the human brain through the work of the leading researchers in the field.

Shore, Rima. *Rethinking the Brain: New Insights into Early Development.* New York: Families and Work Institute, 1997.

An outstanding, thorough, and highly accessible review of new research on the development of children from birth to age five. This book was the source of inspiration, along with Carnegie Corporation's Starting Points report issued in 1994, for the recent explosion in interest in young children's healthy development.

CHAPTER 2

JEWISH EVERY DAY

On a walk around the neighborhood, Melissa finds a coin on the sidewalk. "Look Susan!" she says to her teacher, displaying the coin proudly. "That's wonderful, Melissa. Do you know a good place for 'found money'?" Susan asks. Melissa shakes her head, and Susan tells her, "It's chesed to give money you find to Tzedakah." Melissa smiles and clutches the coin tightly in her hand. When the class returns to their room, Melissa drags a chair over to the shelf by the Tzedakah box, and drops her coin in. She picks up the container, shakes it a few times, listening to the clink of the coins, then joins the rest of her class.

After going to the school Shabbat celebration a few times, 20-month-old Sarah sees the song leader in the hall and says, "This," balling her hands into fists and banging her fists, one on top of the other. The song leader is confused until Sarah's teacher translates, "Sarah is asking you for 'David Melech.' We sing that song every day for her – she just loves it."

In the four-year-old room, Hebrew and English magnetic letters are mixed together in one box. Three children are working with the letters on a large metal chalkboard. They call the teacher over to show her that they have formed their names in English. "Now can you show us how to make our names in Hebrew?" they ask the teacher.

An excellent Jewish early childhood classroom is Jewish every day. As the words of a Billy Joel song go, "I'm in a Jewish state of mind." Okay, he didn't exactly sing *that*, but it does take a Jewish state of mind to make a classroom feel like a Jewish place all the time, especially when it's not Shabbat or a holiday. Jewish is not something we do only when we go to synagogue or to grandma's house for *Seder*. Jewish is who we are all the time; it is a part of every decision we make and every activity we choose. A young child does not divide experience into compartments until he/she is taught to do so. If we compartmentalize the Jewish experience for children, if we have one circle time a week in which we sing Jewish songs and make Shabbat, but do not include anything Jewish in the rest of the circle times that week, then we do our children a disservice. This teaches the children that Judaism is just another thing to do, and that is not honest. Judaism is not something else to do; it is a way of life. Judaism needs to flavor everything that happens with children. In other words, Judaism must inform every aspect of the curriculum.

"PROVIDE YOURSELF WITH A TEACHER"

An excellent Jewish Early Childhood classroom is one in which the total curriculum, Jewish and otherwise, is tailored to fit the needs of each child and family, and one in which being Jewish is part of the day-to-day experience. Just as it is not expected that each teacher come to the classroom with a Master's Degree worth of knowledge in early childhood education, it is not expected that each teacher possess a Rabbi's wealth of Jewish information. But an excellent early childhood educator is someone who is constantly learning. *Pirke Avot* (Ethics of the Fathers) tells us, "Provide yourself with a teacher, and acquire a friend" (Mishnah 1:6).

Take an honest look at what you don't know, and find ways to learn more. Don't aim to learn it all this week; savor the process of learning. Make it a habit. Find a friend to teach you the *alef-bet*. Join a Jewish current events discussion group. Ask your School Director or Rabbi to suggest a list of good Jewish books or authors, and set a reasonable reading goal. Pair up with a friend and read the same Jewish book; do lunch and discuss it. Do something for each holiday that will help you learn as you do it, for example, go to synagogue or get invited to someone's home celebration. Research enough to write your classroom newsletter. Read the weekly Torah portion, regardless of whether you plan to go to synagogue to hear it read. Join a *Parashat HaShavua* (weekly Torah portion) study group. If your Jewish background is weak, attend a Basic Judaism or conversion class (these often welcome all learners, not just those planning to convert). Visit a Jewish museum or Jewish exhibit. Take a Jewish cooking class. Search the word "Jewish" on the Internet. Call up a Jewish friend who is more observant than you, and ask questions about his/her observance. Ask the families of the children in your class about the Jewish things they do in their family, and the reasons for doing them. Start lighting Shabbat candles at home. Pick a charity, and involve your whole family in collecting *Tzedakah* for that cause. Go to Israel. As stated in Chapter 1, the more a teacher knows about and feels for Judaism, intellectually and emotionally, the more easily he or she can make the classroom a place in which Judaism is a natural, daily occurrence.

THE UNSPOKEN CURRICULUM: THE WALLS

Many of the strategies which help make a room Jewishly developmentally appropriate (see Chapter 1, "Developmentally Appropriate Practice," p. 11) will also help integrate Jewish life into the daily life of the classroom. The walls are an important place for Jewish curriculum to develop and happen for at least two reasons. First and foremost,

anybody who walks into the school, or the classroom, should know immediately that this is a Jewish place. While we stop short of a sign announcing that "Jewish Life Happens Here," we do want this to be the conclusion anyone can easily reach. The evidence of Jewish life must be as much a part of the classroom as anything else. It should not be limited to one or two Jewish books on the bookshelf and a bulletin board in the corner with pictures of the Jewish holidays. Photographic documentation of the Rosh HaShanah apple picking trip should hang alongside the "Look How Many Teeth We've Lost!" poster. The walls should influence the Jewish life in the classroom, and Jewish life in the classroom should influence the walls.

The second important reason for including the walls in the Jewish curriculum is that kids learn from walls. Once, when I was teaching Sunday School, second grade, one of my most difficult students was having a classically bad day. I sat next to him in the school assembly, where the principal was teaching Jewish concepts, in Hebrew and English, using the mnemonic strategy of "placing" words all over the *bimah* where she stood. She stationed the word "friendship" over the Rabbi's head, and my difficult student who never seemed focused in my class said, "*Yedidut.*" I stared at him. How did he know the Hebrew word for friendship? Nonchalantly, he reminded me of the alphabetical border of Jewish concepts and values, in Hebrew and English, on the tops of the walls of every classroom in the school. This student who never seemed to learn from me was learning from the walls.

Of course, very young children cannot read words from the walls. But these children can "read" all sorts of images from the walls. And no need to stop with the walls. The ceiling, the floor, around the changing table, in the bathroom, under tables — all these areas can serve as locations for curriculum. Of course, this is not to say that every inch of space in the classroom should be jammed with stimulating visuals. Who could stand such an attack on the eyes? And who would be able to discern any one thing from the jumble?

An excellent Jewish early childhood educator carefully considers the messages he/she wants conveyed, and balances that with the desired visual environment of the room. The area for parent information must be eye-catching and clear, because conveying to families all the information they need is a daunting task. The walls of the classroom should not be overstimulating; yet, occasionally, the excitement of the children must manifest itself on the walls or other surfaces. A conscious effort must be made to consistently include Jewish images in the general visual culture. The walls must change to match the ongoing life of the classroom. Any visual display has a shelf life, after which it is no longer "seen."

Visuals and props that can supplement the ongoing, changing Jewish life of the classroom might include:

- Signs on the door in Hebrew and/or transliteration which say *Shalom* or *Barucheem HaBa'eem* (welcome)
- A Jewish/Hebrew name for the class, posted prominently
- Information/explanations for families about what their children are doing and learning Jewishly
- Posters of Jewish life cycle events, Jewish holidays, scenes of Israel, map of Israel, Noah's ark, Hebrew *alef bet,* number chart with Jewish pictures, etc. The posters should be laminated and rotated among rooms
- Pictures of Jewish values and *mitzvot,* such as *Bikur Choleem* (visiting a person in the hospital), *Shalom* (a child helping two other children to stop fighting), or *Tikkun Olam* (children recycling)
- Photos of the children in the class engaged in Jewish activities (eating *challah,* looking at a *lulav,* touching the *mezuzah*), enlarged, laminated, and mounted at eye level. These pictures can also be collected into a photo album for children to look at and even share with their families.
- Israeli flag
- Pictures from Jewish calendars and Jewish catalogs, cut out and mounted with Contact paper at eye level
- Jewish calendar for the teachers to use, hung in the classroom at adult eye level
- Children's art work, related to Jewish things happening in the room (e.g., body outlines with Hebrew and English labels, apple prints, *mitzvah* tree leaves, handmade *Tzedakah* box, Bible scenes created by children)
- Signs to explain what is happening in the classroom (e.g., "On Fridays, we eat *challah* for Shabbat"; "At naptime, we listen to Jewish lullabies"; "We are carrying flags for Simchat Torah!"). Signs can be laminated and used from year to year.

Some visuals that set the stage for Jewish life can remain in place all year. Frequently used blessings, Hebrew room labels, and a *mezuzah* on the door are some examples. A poster (or posters) with everyday *brachot* (blessings) for snack and lunch, for example, serve to ensure that everyone knows the words, and act as a reminder to include *brachot* in the rhythm of daily life. The more accessible a visual is, the more useful it is. Posting *brachot* in Hebrew, English, and transliteration will make the words of the *brachot* accessible to all the adults in the room. Illustrating the *brachot* with pictures of the appropriate foods (or actions) will give the *brachot* meaning to the children.

Many early childhood educators pepper their classrooms with labels (e.g., chair, table, clock, door) to foster reading readiness skills. Especially in classrooms of older children, we strive to create "print rich" environments, utilizing written language in ways that are relevant to young children. Adding Hebrew to room labels (שָׁעוֹן, שֻׁלְחָן, כִּסֵּא, דֶּלֶת, etc.) integrates the written Hebrew language into the daily classroom life. The addition of transliteration (e.g., *keesay, shulchan, sha'on, delet*) enables any teacher to integrate relevant spoken Hebrew vocabulary into the daily life of the classroom. Appendix B, page 359 contains many English, Hebrew, and transliterated labels for all areas of the room. Most likely, there are more labels in the list than any teacher would or could use in one classroom. It is appropriate in younger classrooms (infants to twos) to use far fewer labels than in an older classroom (threes to kindergarten). The older children have already developed connections to written language and are actively interested in pursuing more experience. Photocopy and enlarge the labels in Appendix B to whatever size is needed.

THE UNSPOKEN CURRICULUM: CLASSROOM SUPPLIES AND MATERIALS

As with the curriculum that happens on the walls, the suggestions for Jewish aspects of the room environment for a developmentally appropriate Jewish classroom (see Chapter 1, pp. 9-11) will also help integrate Jewish life into the daily life of the classroom. It is essential both that supplies and materials of a Jewish nature are plentiful in the classroom, and that these Jewish materials and supplies are integrated into the general inventory of materials. Here are some standard supplies and materials that can be a permanent or regular part of the classroom stock:

- Sponges and cookie cutters in the shape of Jewish objects for painting
- Cookie cutters in the shape of Jewish objects mixed in with the other playdough toys
- Hebrew newspaper for covering the tables during art projects
- Jewish foods (plastic *challah, matzah,* etc.) and kosher/Jewish ethnic food boxes in the house corner
- Stuffed Torahs
- Jewish stamps mixed in with other stamps and stamp pads

- Jewish star pasta, Jewish stickers, and Jewish glitter shapes (obtain from a party store)
- Punches for cut-outs in the shape of Jewish objects
- Real Jewish objects for children to see and touch. Metal *Seder* plate, *graggers,* large *dreidels, chanukiah,* candlesticks, *Kiddush* cup, spice box, etc.
- Israeli scarves for dress up
- Jewish holiday cloth napkins and tablecloths for the house corner
- Stencils of Hebrew letters and Jewish objects
- Jewish software for schools with computers
- Jewish puzzles – a good percentage of the puzzles in the classroom should be Jewish in nature or support the Jewish elements of the curriculum. These can rotate through the year to keep them fresh and relevant.
- Jewish games – games such as *Lotto,* matching games, and *Dominoes* are commercially available with Jewish themes and graphics. Board games, such as *Torah Slides and Ladders* or *Magical Mitzvah Park,* may also be appropriate for your classroom.
- Music – a high percentage of the music available in the classroom should be Jewish in nature. The Jewish cassette tapes or CDs should be chosen frequently and mixed in with secular tapes or CDs.
- Books – The children's bookshelf should contain a high percentage of Jewish books, which are rotated frequently (just as all the books should be). There are many Jewish board books for younger children, and many popular English children's books are available in Hebrew. Favorite English stories printed in Hebrew help to familiarize children with Hebrew writing in a relevant and fun way.
- Props for block play to facilitate synagogue, Jewish life, and Israel play, such as camels, stained glass blocks, Jerusalem stone blocks, people with *kipot,* castle blocks, etc.
- Blocks with Hebrew letters and Jewish pictures

- Magnetic Hebrew letters mixed in with magnetic English letters
- Catalogs from Judaic stores and old New Years cards to cut up

Materials and supplies can also be useful in integrating Jewish elements into secular topics. For an example, a unit on construction might include blueprints for a synagogue or *Aron HaKodesh*. The community helper unit could be supplemented by adding a "Rabbi uniform" — *tallit*, robe, *kipah*, *Siddur* — to the dress-up corner. A unit on dinosaurs could include the book *. . . And Then There Were Dinosaurs* by Sari Steinberg. Seeking out ways to integrate Jewish elements into the unspoken, seemingly secular curriculum will ensure that the whole curriculum is truly integrated.

For a list of sources for posters and materials, see the bibliography at the end of this book.

JEWISH FOUNDATION — VALUES AND MITZVOT

Of course, a physical environment which integrates Judaism into the whole curriculum is only the first step toward establishing a classroom which is Jewish every day. We must go beyond the unspoken curriculum and examine what really makes us Jewish. Certainly, it is not only Shabbat and the holidays, for being Jewish is far more than sharing in a common religion. Judaism is a culture, and for all our differences, Jews are One People — *K'lal Yisrael*. We are united in our commitments to God, Torah, and Israel (both the people and the country). We are bound by common values, language, stories, music, food, and traditions. Judaism even guides us in our treatment of other people, and in our relationship with God.

If we are serious about giving children a foundation for Jewish life and an identity that will last their whole lives, all of these factors are essential in the Jewish early childhood classroom. Employing Jewish values, Jewish culture, and Jewish "ways of being" as aspects underlying everything that happens in the classroom will create an environment which serves the whole Jewish child.

To allow one's teaching to be guided by Jewish values and principles, one must be familiar with and understand these values and principles. Reading this book only will not make an early childhood educator an expert on Jewish values. Provided in these pages is but a taste of — a brief introduction to — some Jewish values which are especially relevant and useful in the Jewish early childhood setting. Also included are some strategies for integrating Jewish values and principles into the warp and woof of daily classroom life. It is hoped that any Jewish early childhood educator seriously committed to becoming the best teacher he or she can be will be inspired by the taste presented here to pursue further study (See the resources in the bibliography at the end of this volume for suggestions on where to begin.)

Jewish values, and the rituals and behaviors to which they lead, serve to make us *kadosh* — distinct, special, holy. Anyone can go to visit someone who is sick in the hospital. In and of itself, that is not a Jewish behavior. But when one considers that *Bikur Choleem*, the *mitzvah* of visiting the sick is just that, a *mitzvah* — a commandment, visiting the sick takes on a unique significance. It's not just a nice thing to do, it's something we are expected to do, commanded to do. Visiting the sick is part of what makes us Jewish, because when we visit the sick, we model our behavior after God's behavior when God visited Abraham as he recuperated from his circumcision. Modeling our behavior after God's behavior makes our behavior and, in turn, us, holy.

Some of the values discussed here are *middot* (Jewish virtues), but many are actually *mitzvot* — commandments. There are 613 *mitzvot* listed in the Torah, including 248 positive *mitzvot* (things we should do) and 365 negative *mitzvot* (things we should not do). In general, *mitzvot* are divided into two categories: *Mitzvot Bayn Adam l'Makom*, those between a person and God, and *Mitzvot*

Bayn Adam l'Chavero, those between one person and another. We will focus mainly on the latter category here, because these are most relevant to the lives of young children. The values and *mitzvot* explored here are essential elements of how Judaism mandates we treat other people. When we bring explicitly Jewish values and *mitzvot* into the classroom, our children begin to learn how to approach the world with Jewish eyes. When a child understands and bases his/her behavior on Jewish values, and not just human decency, the child is building a Jewish vocabulary and a Jewish foundation which will serve the child throughout his/her life.

"Machon L'Morim: B'reshit," a professional development program for Jewish early childhood educators in Baltimore, MD, has been addressing this issue for several years. The program and its implications will be discussed at greater length later in this chapter (see p. 29), but reprinted below is a chart produced for this program (see Figure 4 on the following page) of some Jewish *mitzvot* and *middot*, their definitions, and examples of ways these values can be referred to in the classroom. This chart can be hung in the classroom and used as a resource every day. There are 22 *mitzvot/middot* listed, and, of course, the chart is not exhaustive. Still, even the most veteran of teachers would be wise to go slow. Pick a few *mitzvot/middot*, and focus on incorporating those into the life of the classroom. As you and the children master each, you can add another.

TOP TEN EARLY CHILDHOOD JEWISH VALUES

Following is a tutorial of the "top ten" early childhood Jewish values. This list does not include all the values and *mitzvot* one might bring into an early childhood classroom; that would require a separate volume. But these ten represent the essence of the Jewish view on human relationships.

1. *Mitzvah* – commandment. A *mitzvah* is not simply a good deed, although many *mitzvot* are good deeds. Because a *mitzvah* is something we are obligated to do, *mitzvot* take on additional meaning. It is not just a nice thing to

give *Tzedakah*. Rather, we are obligated to give *Tzedakah* and help the needy. Judaism does not teach us how to be good people by offering suggestions; we are *required* to do good things and be good people. It is this obligation which makes us distinct, which makes us *kadosh* (holy). In the early childhood classroom, we must be careful not to label every good deed a *mitzvah*, although there is indeed a long, yet specific list of good deeds that are *mitzvot*. *Mitzvot* are "God's rules." Many of the behaviors we do engage in with children are *mitzvot*, such as giving *Tzedakah*, saying blessings before we eat, etc., and we should certainly point this out to children. For example, you might say, "We give *Tzedakah* because it's a *mitzvah* to help other people. It is one of God's rules to give *Tzedakah*."

2. *Shalom* – Peace, Completeness. According to the Talmud, "The whole Torah exists only for the sake of *shalom*" (*Tanhuma, Shoftim* 18). Jewish prayer is filled with supplications for *shalom*, for example, "Grant us peace, your most precious gift, O Eternal Source of peace . . . " One of the names for God is *Oseh Shalom* — Maker of Peace. In the *Kaddish*, an integral part of daily liturgy, we pray, "May the Maker of Peace in high places let peace descend on us, and on all of Israel." We are a people with a history full of tumult and destruction that seeks serenity and security, not only for ourselves, but for the whole world. "*Shalom*" is even the salutation we use when greeting each other or taking our leave. In the early childhood classroom, the value of *shalom* takes us beyond another way to get the children quiet. Psalms 34:15 tells us, "Seek peace and pursue it." Children can become *rodfay shalom* (pursuers of peace), finding ways to bring calm and community to their own classroom (one child is a *rodayf/rodefet shalom*). Peace requires action. Children can practice the *mitzvah* of *Hava'at Shalom Bayn Adam l'Chavayro* (bringing

	MITZVAH	TRANSLITERATION	HEBREW TERM	WHEN YOU CAN REFER TO IT
1	Bringing Peace Between People	Hava'at Shalom Bayn Adam L'Chavayro	הבאת שלום בין אדם לחברו	when children are arguing after settling an argument
2	Clothing the Naked	Malbish Arumim	מלביש ערומים	clothing drive
3	Common Courtesy – Respect	Derech Eretz	דרך-ארץ	When children show respect for each other as in letting a child get in line
4	Do Not Destroy Needlessly	Bal Tashcheet	בל תשחית	ecology, destroy property, toys, nature
5	Feed the Hungry	Ma'achil Re'ayvim	מאכיל רעבים	food drive
6	Kindness to Animal	Tza'ar Ba'alay Chayim	צער בעלי חיים	feeding the class pet putting a bug outside instead of stepping on it
7	Repairing the World	Tikkun Olam	תקון עולם	recycling
8	Honoring the Elderly	Hiddur P'nay-Zakayn	הדור פני זקן	making cards for senior citizens
9	Return of Lost Articles	Hashavat Avaydah	השבת אבדה	when a child finds something that is not theirs and returns it to owner
10	Study	Talmud Torah	תלמוד תורה	telling Bible or holiday stories
11	Truth	Emet	אמת	when a child tells the truth
12	Visiting the Sick	Bikur Choleem	בקור חולים	calling on or making cards for sick friend, classmates, or relatives
13	Welcoming Guests	Hachnasat Orchim	הכנסת אורחים	Shabbat Ema & Abba invite guests (i.e., another class)
14	Cheerfulness	Sayver Panim Yafot	סבר פנים יפות	greet someone with a smile when kids are smiling and happy, especially after an incident when a child was sad.
15	Comforting Mourners	Nihum Avaylim	נחום אבלים	visiting a shiva house
16	Do Not Covet	Lo Tachmode	לא תחמד	hoarding toys
17	Guard Your Tongue	Shmirat HaLashon	שמירת הלשון	not calling other kids names
	Watching what you say			
a	Gossip	Lashon HaRa	לשון הרע	
b	Polite Speech	Dibur B'Ninus	דבור בנמוס	
c	Shaming	Boshet	בשת	
d	Slander	Rachilut	רכילות	
18	Honor Parents and Teachers	Kibbud Horim u'Morim	כבוד הורים ומורים	doing something special for parents and/or teachers
19	Peace in the Home/Classroom	Sh'lom Bayit/Keetah	שלום בית/כתה	sharing toys/markers
20	Righteous Deeds	Gemilut Chasadeem	גמילות חסדים	when a child goes out of his/her way to help another
21	Righteous Justice (Charity)	Tzedakah	צדק	weekly tzedakah food and clothing drives
22	Respecting the Poor	K'vod HeAhnee	כבוד עני	give money to homeless

* For each of these *middot* and *mitzvot*, you can simply say: [child's name], what a wonderful example of [*mitzvah*]
©"*Mchon L'Morim B'reshit*"; Reprinted with permission of "*Machon L'Morim B'reshit*," Irene Vogelstein, Director.

Figure 4

peace between people), by learning to mediate their own arguments. Children can also learn the value of *Sh'lom Bayit* (creating peace in the home). Songs such as *"Oseh Shalom"* and *"Sim Shalom"* can be regular features in the classroom song repertoire. For a lesson plan for Grades K-2 on *Sh'lom Bayit,* see Appendix 1 in *Teaching Jewish Virtues: Sacred Sources and Arts Activities* by Susan Freeman (A.R.E. Publishing, Inc.).

3. *Tza'ar Ba'alay Chayim* – Compassion To Animals (literally, preventing the pain of animals). "A righteous person knows the needs of one's beast" (Proverbs 12:10). According to Jewish law, we are allowed to use animals for our benefit, but they must be treated kindly because they, too, are God's creatures. Even when we kill animals for food or other uses, we must do everything within our ability to minimize the animal's pain. In the classroom, children are observing *Tza'ar Ba'alay Chayim* when they help to take care of the class pet, or when they guide a fly outside rather than swatting it.

4. *Tikkun Olam* – Repair of the World. In the *"Alaynu"* prayer, we place our hopes in God that the world will be perfected through God's reign. Yet, it is not up to God alone. We are God's partners in the improvement of creation. This *mitzvah* illustrates the reciprocal relationship which God established with human beings. It is our obligation to take care of the earth, and in turn, it takes care of us. Major Jewish social action efforts are based on the value *Tikkun Olam*. *Tikkun Olam* includes the *mitzvah* of *Bal Tashcheet* (preserving the earth). In the early childhood classroom, *Tikkun Olam* is embodied in efforts not to be wasteful with supplies and resources. It is present in the way the children care for the live things, plants and animals in their classroom, and in the way they care for their playground and other outdoor spaces. We are partners with God in the completion and repair of the world. Children will rise to opportunities to act as God's partner and take care of their world if they are given the vocabulary of the Jewish values and *mitzvot* to go along with their actions.

5. *Bikur Choleem* – Visiting the Sick. This *mitzvah* is found in the Talmud (*Shabbat* 127a): "These are the deeds which yield immediate fruit and continue to yield fruit in the time to come: honoring parents, doing deeds of kindness, attending the house of study, visiting the sick . . . " *Bikur Choleem* is a way to model our own behavior after God's behavior, to act *B'tzelem Elohim*, in the image of God, because God visited Abraham when he was sick (Genesis 18:1). In the early childhood classroom, *Bikur Choleem* is an important Jewish behavior to teach, especially when a child in the class, teacher, or family member is sick. You can share the song *"Mi Sheberach"* by Debbie Friedman (on the albums *And You Shall Be a Blessing* and *Renewal of Spirit*), the prayer for the ill, and find ways to connect the children with those who are sick. This can be done through visits, phone trees, and sending letters, artwork, and photos.

6. *Hachnasat Orcheem* – Hospitality to Strangers (literally, bringing in guests); an important act of kindness. This *mitzvah* is also found in the Talmud (*Shabbat* 127a): "Rabbi Judah said in Rab's name, 'Hospitality to strangers is greater than welcoming the presence of the *Shechinah*.'" It is a Jewish behavior to extend hospitality, because of the way Abraham opened his home to the three strangers who came to his tent (Genesis 18:2), and because of the lesson of the Exodus — that we were strangers in the land of Egypt. In the early childhood classroom, *Hachanasat Orcheem* dictates relationships the children have with each other and with the wider world. It provides a reason for inviting the child with whom you didn't really want to play into the house corner with you. *Hachnasat Orcheem* is also present when

we bring different classrooms together, visiting each other's rooms for special occasions or simply for snack time.

7. *Kavod* – Respect, Honor. The fifth of the Ten Commandments (Exodus 20:12) is *Kibbud Av v'Aym* (Honor Your Father and Mother). Basic human relations are based on *Kavod*, showing respect to the people with whom we interact. By honoring other people, we honor God. In the early childhood classroom, it is essential that *Kavod* be a two way street. Teachers must show their children *Kavod*, and children must give teachers *Kavod* as well. One form of *Kavod* is *Derech Eretz*, meaning the right way to behave (literally, "the way of the land," also translated as good manners or common courtesy).

8. *Gemilut Chasadim* – Acts of Loving-kindness or Good Deeds. In *Pirke Avot* 1:2 we learn: "The world stands on three things: Torah, worship, and acts of loving-kindness." The Talmud (*Peah* 1:1) details: "These are the things whose fruit a person enjoys in this world and whose reward is attained in the world to come: honoring parents, doing deeds of kindness, making peace, but the study of Torah is equal to them all [because it leads to them all]." *Chesed*, kindness, is encompassed in *Gemilut Chasadeem*. There have been entire curricula developed around the notion of kindness (e.g., *The Kindness Curriculum* by Judith Anne Rice).

In the Jewish early childhood classroom, it is important for children to learn that being nice and kind to other people is not just a good thing to do, it's a *Jewish* thing to do. *Gemilut Chasadeem* is a collection of acts which detail the way we as Jews are to take care of fellow Jews, by caring for the needy, visiting the sick, comforting the mourner, and burying the dead, among others. *Gemilut Chasadeem* goes beyond simple acts of kindness. This *mitzvah* spells out for us the times when we need to take care of each other, and describes how to go about doing so. Emphasizing *Gemilut*

Chasadeem in your classroom can imbue ordinary obligations with a greater sense of kindness. Children can learn that is it the Jewish way to help each other willingly and with care. They should be rewarded for their acts of loving-kindness, perhaps through a *"Gemilut Chasadeem* Tree," which continues to bloom throughout the year.

9. *Tzedakah* – from the root *tzedek*, meaning Justice and Righteousness. In Torah we are taught, *"Tzedek, tzedek tirdof – Justice, justice shall you pursue"* (Deuteronomy 16:20). Although *Tzedakah* is often translated as "charity," it has the wider connotation of giving back, or doing justice. Giving *Tzedakah* is a *mitzvah*; the Rabbis determined specific percentages of our income which we are obligated to give for *Tzedakah*. We give because as Jews we are commanded to help, not just because it is a nice thing to do. Giving *Tzedakah* is the just and right thing to do, and includes giving money, clothing, food, and time.

In the early childhood classroom, *Tzedakah* should take many forms, so that children are not limited to the "penny in the *pushke*" definition of *Tzedakah*. Food drives, collecting gently used clothing, and toy drives, etc., are and should be considered as acts of *Tzedakah*.

10. *K'lal Yisrael* – All Jews Are Part of One People. There is diversity among Jews. We identify ourselves as Orthodox, Reform, Conservative, Reconstructionist, Sephardic, Ashkenazic, Israeli, American, etc. Jews have different beliefs, customs, foods, languages. Yet, we are bound together as one people by God, Torah, and Israel. The value of *K'lal Yisrael* can be instrumental in instilling in children an appreciation of and a tolerance for differences. Exposing children to differences among Jews, through dress, food, language, songs, and stories opens children up to an appreciation for variety, and will lay the foundation for acceptance of other people in the world, Jewish and non-Jewish, who are different from them.

"MACHON L'MORIM: B'RESHIT"

Incorporating Jewish values and *mitzvot* into the daily life of the early childhood classroom requires a commitment to learning and integration by each teacher. *"Machon L'Morim: B'reshit"* is presented here an as outstanding example of one community's efforts to improve dramatically the quality of Jewish early childhood education. The program *"Machon L'Morim: B'reshit,"* directed by Ilene C. Vogelstein, began in Baltimore in 1995 with the realization that Jewish early childhood education could only be dramatically enriched if the Jewish knowledge level of early childhood teachers was dramatically raised. Program designers assumed that "a knowledgeable and committed Jewish teacher would naturally create learning opportunities and classroom settings that would foster the fullest development of each youngster and, thus, with the child's parents, build a strong and positive Jewish identity" ("In the Beginning . . . ," *Machon L'Morim: B'reshit Newsletter* 1(2), Winter 1997, p. 1).

"Machon L'Morim: B'reshit," through the generosity of the Children of Harvey and Lyn Meyerhoff Philanthropic Fund, set out to change the face of Jewish early childhood education in Baltimore through intensive Jewish learning and training in early childhood development. "The primary goal of the program is to develop personnel and environments that model integrated Jewish early childhood education" (Dr. Chaim Y. Botwinick, B'RESHIT: Retrospect and Prospect, *Machon L'Morim: B'reshit Newsletter* 1(2) Winter 1997, page 2). The program requires the commitment of the entire staff of a school for a period of several years. Teachers who participate are paid a stipend. Through intensive adult Jewish education, educational leadership training, professional dialogue, and demonstration classrooms, the teachers and directors of the program seek to instill in the participating teachers and schools increased Jewish literacy and spirituality, and greater comfort with

and increased use of Jewish concepts and Hebrew vocabulary in the classrooms.

After five years, change becomes more evident in the participating schools (conversation with Ilene C. Vogelstein, July, 1999). It can take five years to make change really happen and gain its own momentum. Still, once that kind of hard earned change happens, it become integral to the culture of the school. This is the kind of change the program seeks to engender.

The first two years of the program were devoted to *Torah Lishmah* — the study of Torah for its own sake. During the third year, the teachers began to examine some of what they had learned and to explore how to use their newfound knowledge to enrich their classrooms. They wrote curriculum units for "secular" themes such as "All about Me," "Firefighters," and "Chicks," complete with Jewish concepts, Jewish values, and Hebrew vocabulary, which integrated Jewish and secular objectives and activities throughout. During the fourth year, the teachers focused on implementation of the curricula in their classrooms. Intensive study was ongoing, as was constant evaluation and reflection.

The directors of *"Machon L'Morim: B'reshit"* discovered the great value of peer dialogue for support. They found that change was greatest when the entire staff of the school participated, including the director, and so they began to scaffold the aides and part-time teachers into the program. In the fifth year, beginning in the fall of 1999, the participants continued to study and create curriculum and teach, and began to work on their mentoring skills.

Teachers who participated in *"Machon L'Morim: B'reshit"* reflected on the excitement of raising the level of their Jewish consciousness. They became more aware of how Judaism plays a role in their daily lives, and how to think Jewishly about everyday activities. The program has helped them put Jewish flavor into their teaching, and made them more comfortable talking about aspects of religion with children. In their newsletter, Paula Berger, one of the participating teachers, commented about her *"Machon L'Morim: B'reshit"* experience: "Observing like this, I now realize how Shabbat is truly a pause in a week of activity. My only regret is that it took me 50 years to experience Shabbat in this way, but I can assure you that this experience will live in my heart forever." Another teacher, Talia Aaron observed, "One of the things we discovered and shared with our groups is that even if we're not teaching the *parashah* (weekly Torah portion), we're still teaching Torah."

"Machon L'Morim: B'reshit" is not just a tool for the early childhood community in Baltimore; it is also a resource that can be made available to every community. Although it is evident that the change achieved by the schools in Baltimore cannot simply be transferred to other places with a lesson plan — this change requires dedication, commitment and time — there is still something to be gained by attending a short-term workshop with a leader of *"Machon L'Morim: B'reshit."* The curriculum units they have produced include themes such as "All about Me," "Fall," "World around Us," and "Firefighter." All are available from *Machon L'Morim* (for address, see bibliography at the end of this volume). While most useful to teachers who have a wide understanding of the Jewish concepts included in each unit, these can provide inspiration and guidance to teachers with a less thorough background. Best of all, *"Machon L'Morim: B'reshit"* has dreams of "taking it on the road," and branching out to other cities. When that happens, other communities should jump at the chance to engage in such a dramatic opportunity for change. (Contact information for *"Machon L'Morim: B'reshit"* is on p. 364 of the bibliography at the end of this volume.)

AVIRAH — JEWISH ATMOSPHERE: ACTIVITIES

A room environment that is Jewish in feeling and appearance is essential, as is a milieu characterized by Jewish values. However, it is the daily activities — the music, stories, and play opportunities — that are the key to integrating Jewish and secular themes every day. Successful integration of these basic activities requires keeping in mind the whole Jewish child.

The children in our classes are not only Jewish on Shabbat and holidays; being Jewish is part of who they are all the time. With this in mind, it becomes a logical and preferable course of action to play Jewish music in the middle of the week, to bring a Jewish story to any circle time, to reinforce Jewish values at each appropriate moment, and to use *dreidels* to sort and classify, even in the middle of March.

There are many children's picture books which contain Jewish folktales and stories of life cycle events, which can easily fit into the day-to-day, non-holiday life of the classroom (see the bibliography below for some suggestions). Reading holiday related books out of their proper season also serves a great function. Reading a Pesach book in February serves as a preview for the upcoming holiday. For older children, previewing a holiday in this fashion can serve to revive memories they have of the holiday from years past. Doing so can also give teachers a preview of children's interests to concentrate on as the holiday draws closer. Reading a Sukkot book in April serves as a great review. What do the children remember about the holiday? This kind of review can help teachers evaluate how much their children absorbed during the holiday unit, and might also make apparent to teachers areas of interest to revisit before the school year is up.

Music can also provide a daily infusion of Jewish culture into the daily life of the class. Holiday music provides great preview and review, just as stories do. Non-holiday Jewish and Hebrew music such as on the albums *Aleph Bet Boogie* by Rabbi Joe Black or *My Jewish Discovery* by Craig Taubman, can be interspersed with secular music such as that by Raffi and Ella Jenkins. At naptime or quiet times, *Return To Pooh Corner* by Kenny Loggins can be alternated with a Jewish lullaby tape or Jewish instrumental music, such as Jon's Simon's jazz piano interpretations of traditional Jewish music, or Itzhak Perlman's *Tradition*. (See the bibliography at the end of this book, pp. 368-370 for more suggestions.) Jewish music needs to be as readily available as all other music, and teachers should make the choice to play it on a regular basis.

The same applies to singing Jewish songs — at circle time, during transitions, on a walk, while waiting for snack to be served. Holiday songs serve as preview and review, and general and non-holiday Hebrew songs breathe Jewish life into the curriculum. Many classrooms have a "song jar" full of songs, each song written on its own card, often illustrated and with all the words included for easy reference. Make sure that a good percentage of the songs in your song jar are Jewish songs. As you or your children draw out cards, deciding what songs to sing, the Jewish songs will become a natural part of your repertoire.

For more on integrating music into your classroom, see Chapter 22, "A Guide To Music in the Early Childhood Classroom," p. 282.

Of course, children do most of their learning as they play, exploring their world and investigating the way things are and the way things can be. As excellent early childhood educators, we take great care to structure the classroom environment to stimulate the richest play possible. Ways to make this environment more Jewish have already been addressed at some length earlier in this chapter. Still, we know that we do not just set up the environment and stand back to see what will happen. Our role as teacher during play is actively to observe children, to find ways to expand their play and help them build connections, without actually directing their play. We do this by asking probing, open, leading questions; by providing new props as they become crucial to further exploration; by intervening just in time to prevent frustration or a fight between children. We can do this in a Jewish way as well. By keeping Jewish themes and values in mind, we can introduce

these to the children's play, so that the Jewish themes and values become a part of the children's natural repertoire as well. When a child says, "Teacher, I'm going to the store," you might say, "Oh, are you going to buy the things you need for Shabbat dinner?" "Yes, I need seven chicken soups." "My goodness! Are you having lots of guests for Shabbat?" Or, in another transaction, you might ask a child, "Sarah, what are you building with these blocks?" She responds, "I made the hospital." "Who's inside the hospital?" you ask. "My mommy. She's getting my baby brother." "Are you going to visit her? That's *Bikur Choleem*. It's a *mitzvah*, and it will make your mommy so happy to see you!"

Hebrew is the language of Jews. Using Hebrew on a daily basis makes it a natural part of being Jewish. Extensive lists of Hebrew words and phrases may be found in Chapter 19 pp. 264-266, but one does not need an extensive Hebrew vocabulary to make it a natural part of the classroom life. A hearty *"Boker tov"* (good morning) as the children enter, and *"Shalom"* or *"L'hitra'ote"* (see you again) as they leave each day frame the day with a Hebrew feeling. Then, get into the Hebrew habit. Substitute *Z'man l'nakote* for "clean up time," *Naylaych* for "Let's go," *Todah* for "thank you," *Bevakashah* for "please" and also for "you're welcome," and *Yofee* or *Tov m'ode* for "good job." Pick a few favorite phrases and make them part of your working, natural vocabulary. Learn to count to five or ten or 20 in Hebrew, and count the children as they line up or sit down at circle. Learn the words to Hebrew songs such as *"David Melech"* and *"Hinay Mah Tov."* Look at the translation word for word, so you really understand the song.

David Melech Yisrael (David, King of Israel)
Chai, chai, v'kayam (He lives, lives forever).

Hinay mah tov u'mah na'eem (How good and nice it is)
Shevet (to sit) *acheem* (as brothers) *gam yachad* (all together).

Choose to sing these songs on a regular basis. Do the same thing with blessings. Knowing what the blessings really mean will facilitate actually being able to use them. Keep a Hebrew/English dictionary (or a book such as *The First Thousand Words in Hebrew* by Heather Amery and Yaffa Haron) on hand so that you can look up a word when a child asks for a definition.

(For more on integrating Hebrew into the everyday life of the class, see Chapter 19, "Integrating Hebrew Every Day," p. 262.

CONCLUSION

Make the commitment to integrate Judaism into every day. It may require an attitude adjustment or a restructuring or revision of your physical environment, but the rewards that both teachers and children will reap from a naturally, comfortably integrated Jewish classroom will far surpass any discomfort that may be experienced getting there. A classroom that integrates Judaism into the entire curriculum is surely addressing the whole Jewish child, and paving the way for a positive, warm Jewish identity.

BIBLIOGRAPHY

ADULTS

Artson, Bradley Shavit. *It's a Mitzvah! Step-by-Step To Jewish Living*. West Orange, NJ: Behrman House, 1995.

> Each chapter in this textbook for Grades 8 to adult explains a *mitzvah* and explores ways to put it into action.

Feinberg, Miriam P., and Rena Rotenberg. *Lively Legends — Jewish Values: An Early Childhood Teaching Guide*. Denver, CO: A.R.E. Publishing, Inc., 1993.

> Stories from Jewish lore that teach important Jewish values, and accompanying activities in various modalities. For teachers of PK-3.

Freeman, Susan. *Teaching Jewish Virtues: Sacred Sources and Arts Activities*. Denver, CO: A.R.E. Publishing, Inc., 1999.

> A helpful introduction to *middot* (Jewish virtues) and how to become a mensch. For teachers of K-adult.

Kadden, Barbara Binder, and Bruce Kadden. *Teaching Mitzvot: Concepts, Values and Activities*. Denver, CO: A.R.E. Publishing, Inc., 1996.

> Provides teachers of Grades K-12 with an overview of *mitzvot* and with many creative activities that can be adapted for preschool children.

Regosin, Ina, and Naomi Towvim, eds. *Milk and Honey: Five Units Integrating Jewish and General Curricula in the Early Childhood*. Newton, MA: The Early Childhood Institute, Board of Jewish Education of Greater Boston, 1990.

> Each of these five curriculum units helps teachers of young children to integrate Jewish values with general curriculum areas such as music, math, science, art, language arts, and dramatic play. Units include: Reading Plus – Children's Books with Jewish Themes and Values (ages 3-5), Noah and the Flood (age 3), Noah's Art (ages 4-5), The Mishkan – Building Community from Biblical Bases (ages 3-5), and Familiar Games the Jewish Way (ages 3-5).

Rice, Judith Anne. *The Kindness Curriculum: Introducing Young Children To Loving Values*. St. Paul, MN: Redleaf Press, 1995.

> Helps teachers create opportunities for kids to practice kindness, empathy, conflict resolution, and respect.

Schiller, Pam, and Tamera Bryant. *The Values Book: Teaching 16 Basic Values To Young Children*. Beltsville, MD: Gryphon House, 1998.

> Offers techniques and activities for teaching basic values.

Note: For story collections, see the bibliography for Chapter 21, "The Art of Storytelling," p. 281.

CHILDREN
Infant To 2 Years

Bogot, Howard I. *Becky and Benny Thank God*. New York: CCAR Press, 1996. (Ages infant-2)

> A "Pat the Bunny"-type book that lists all the things for which we are thankful to God. (Board Book)

Edwards, Michelle. *Blessed Are You*. New York: Lothrop, Lee & Shepard Books, 1993. (All ages)

> Traditional everyday Hebrew prayers.

Eisenberg, Ann. *I Can Celebrate!* Rockville, MD: KarBen Copies, 1988. (Ages infant-2)

> A spin through the Jewish year. (Board Book)

Feder, Harriet. *What Can You Do with a Bagel?* Rockville, MD: KarBen Copies, 1991. (Ages 1-4)

> Hang it, bang it, bite it, chew it! (Board Book)

Gold-Vukson, Marji. *The Colors of My Jewish Year*. Rockville, MD: Kar-Ben Copies, 1998. (Ages infant-2)

> Jewish symbols in every color. (Board Book)

Groner, Judye. *You Can Do a Mitzvah*. Rockville, MD: Kar-Ben Copies, 1999. (Ages infant-2)

> You're never too young to start helping others and doing *mitzvot*. (Board Book)

Lemelman, Martin. *My Jewish Home*. New York: UAHC Press, 1988. (infant-2)

> Symbols in the home. (Board Book)

Wells, Rosemary. *Forest of Dreams*. New York: Dial Books for Young Readers, 1988. (Ages 2-6)

> Beautiful illustrations tell the story of all the things in us that God made.

Wikler, Madeline, and Judye Groner. *In the Synagogue*. Rockville, MD: KarBen Copies, 1991. (Ages 1-4)

> Holidays and their symbols in the synagogue. (Board Book)

———. *Thank You God!* Rockville, MD: KarBen Copies, 1993. (All ages)

> A Jewish child's book of prayers.

3 Years

Brichto, Myra Pollak. *The God around Us: A Child's Garden of Prayer*. Rev. ed. New York: UAHC Press, 1999. (Ages 3-7)

> Blessings for the wondrous experiences of everyday life, for mountains, blooming trees, and different kinds of people, to list a few.

Gilman, Phoebe. *Something from Nothing*. New York: Scholastic, Inc., 1992. (Ages 3-7)

> Joseph's grandpa makes him a wonderful baby blanket. When the blanket wears out, Joseph's grandpa makes a wonderful jacket. What will happen when Joseph outgrows the jacket?

Mellonie, Bryan. *Lifetimes*. New York: Bantam Books, 1983. (Ages 3-8)

> A beautiful way to explain death to children.

Polacco, Patricia. *The Keeping Quilt*. New York: Simon & Schuster Books for Young Readers, 1988. (Ages 3-8)

> A quilt follows Anna's family through many generations and life cycle events.

Rosenfeld, Dina. *A Tree Full of Mitzvos*. New York: Merkos L'inyonei Chinuch, 1985. (Ages 3-7)

> The little maple tree seaches for *mitzvot* even it can do.

Sose, Bonnie L. *Designed by God So I Must Be Special*. Winter Park, FL: Character Builders for Kids, 1988. (Ages 3-8)

> Details all of the ways God made each of us special.

Zalben, Jane Breskin. *Pearl's Marigolds for Grandpa*. New York: Simon & Schuster Books for Young Readers, 1997. (Ages 3-8)

> When Pearl's grandpa dies, Pearl finds a way to remember him.

Zemach, Margot. *It Could Always Be Worse*. New York: Farrar, Strans and Giroux, 1976. (Ages 3-8)

> When the house gets too noisy, the Rabbi has a creative solution.

4 To 5 Years

Aroner, Miriam. *Kingdom of Singing Birds*. Rockville, MD: KarBen Copies, 1993. (Ages 4-8)

> When his collection of rare and exotic brids refuse to sing, the king calls wise Rabbi Zusya for help.

Berkeley, Laura. *The Seeds of Peace*. Briston, UK: Barefoot Books, 1999. (Ages 4-12)

> A thought provoking book about the value of happiness over riches.

Davis, Aubrey. *Bone Button Borscht*. Toronto: KidsCan Press, Inc., 1995. (Ages 4-9)

> A Jewish version of the folktale "Stone Soup."

Ginsburg, Marvell. *The Tattooed Torah*. New York: UAHC Press, 1983. (Ages 4-8)

> The story of a Torah scroll saved from the Holocaust.

Grode, Phyllis A. *Sophie's Name*. Rockville, MD: Kar-Ben Copies, 1990. (Ages 4-8)

> Sophie considers changing her name until she learns about all the people she is named for.

Karkowsky, Nancy. *Grandma's Soup*. Rockville, MD: KarBen Copies, 1989. (Ages 5-8)

> A young girl confronts her grandmother's growing confusion and disability from Alzheimer's disease.

Lamstein, Sarah Mavil. *I Like Your Buttons!* Morton Grove, IL: Albert Whitman & Co., 1999. (Ages 4-8)

> Kind words can be contagious.

Lanton, Sandy. *Daddy's Chair*. Rockville, MD: KarBen Copies, 1991. (Ages 5-10)

When Michael's father dies, his family observes *shivah*, the Jewish week of mourning.

Levine, Arthur. *Pearl Moscowitz's Last Stand*. New York: Tambourine Books, 1993. (Ages 4-8)

Pearl Moscowitz takes a stand when the government tries to chop down the last ginko tree on her street. A wonderful story of cooperation between different ethnic groups. Out of print, but worth looking for.

Miller, Deborah Uchill. *Fins and Scales*. Rockville, MD: KarBen Copies, 1991. (Ages 4-8)

A rhyming explanation of what's kosher.

Oberman, Sheldon. *The Always Prayer Shawl*. New York: Puffin Books, 1984. (Ages 4-8)

Adam's grandfather tells him the long family history of his *tallit*.

Podwal, Mark. *Golem: A Giant Made of Mud*. New York: Greenwillow Books, 1995. (Ages 4-8)

A retelling of the traditional Jewish folktale of the Golem.

Polacco, Patricia. *The Bee Tree*. New York: Putnam & Grosset Group, 1993. (Ages 4-8)

Mary Ellen's grandpa teaches her about the sweetness of learning.

Pomerantz, Barbara. *Bubby, Me and Memories*. New York: Union of American Hebrew Congregations, 1983. (Ages 3-8)

A photographic remembrance of Bubby, and an exploration of what it is to die.

———. *Who Will Lead Kiddush?* New York: UAHC Press, 1995. (Ages 4-8)

Mommy and Daddy divorce. Who will say *Kiddush* when Daddy's not there?

Prose, Francine. *You Never Know: A Legend of the Lamed-vavniks*. New York: Greenwillow Books, 1998. (Ages 4-8)

Though mocked by the rest of the villagers, poor Schmuel the Shoemaker turns out to be a very special person.

Rael, Elsa Okon. *What Zeesie Saw on Delancey Street*. New York: Simon & Schuster Books for Young Readers, 1996. (Ages 4+)

When Zeesie goes to her first "package party" (a party to raise funds to bring others to America), she learns a valuable lesson about *Tzedakah*.

Rice, David. *Because Brian Hugged His Mother*. Nevada City, CA: Dawn Publications, 1999. (Ages 4-12)

Brian sets in motion a series of unselfish acts when he gives his mother a great big hug.

Rothenberg, Joan. *Matza Ball Soup*. New York: Hyperion, 1999. (Ages 4-8)

Rosie's grandma tells Rosie of the family tradition behind needing four kinds of *matzah* balls in the soup. Recipes for tasty, delicate, hard, and fluffy *matzah* balls are included.

———. *Yettele's Feathers*. New York: Hyperion Paperbacks for Children, 1995. (Ages 4-8)

What happens when Yettele's gossiping gets out of control?

Sandfield, Steve. *Bit by Bit*. New York: Philomel Books, 1995. (Ages 4-8)

Zudel loved his warm winter coat so much he wore it out. With the remaining cloth, he made a jacket, and so on and so on. A delightful telling of a classic story.

Sasso, Sandy Eisenberg. *In God's Name*. Woodstock, VT: Jewish Lights Publishing, 1994. (Ages 5-10)

Everyone and everything in the world has a name. What is God's name?

Shulevitz, Uri. *The Treasure*. New York: Farrar, Straus and Giroux, 1978. (Ages 4-10)

Isaac has a dream that leads him to a treasure.

Silverman, Erica. *Raisel's Riddle*. New York: Farrar, Straus and Giroux, 1999. (Ages 4-8)

A Jewish Cinderella story, with a strong heroine and a positive emphasis on learning.

Steinberg, Sari. *. . . And Then There Were Dinosaurs*. St. Helier, NJ: Yellow Brick Road Press, 1993. (Ages 4-8)

A Jewish creation story of the dinosaurs.

Tabak, Simms. *Joseph Had a Little Overcoat.* New York: Viking Childrens Books, 1999. (Ages 4-8)
> When Joseph's overcoat gets too old and shabby, he makes it into a jacket. Die-cut holes in the pages allow children to guess what Joseph will make next.

Wing, Natasha. *Jalapeño Bagels.* New York: Atheneum Books for Young Readers, 1996. (Ages 5-8)
> For international day, Pablo wants to bring something that reflects the cultures of his Jewish father and Mexican mother.

Wood, Douglas. *Old Turtle.* Duluth, MN: Pfeifer-Hamilton Publishers, 1992. (Ages 4+)
> The animals try to figure out what God is. Beautiful illustrations.

MUSIC

For a complete listing of music resources and a discography of recordings on cassette tape and CD, see the bibliography at the end of this volume, pp. 366-370.

CHAPTER 3

AM YISRAEL: ANTI BIAS EDUCATION IN THE JEWISH PRESCHOOL

Who is wise? One who learns from everyone. (Pirke Avot 4:1)

*A*m Yisrael – the People of Israel — come in so many varieties. We believe differently, we live our lives in different ways, we speak many languages, we dwell in many lands. Our skin may be different colors, we have different ranges of abilities. Some of us create families with 13 children, others create families with two parents of the same sex. Yet, we are One People: *Am Yisrael.* It requires an incredible amount of tolerance and understanding, more than we have been able to achieve so far across the board, to get along with each other, and to appreciate and value all of the differences that make up *Am Yisrael.*

This chapter gives Jewish early childhood educators the tools to help Jewish children understand and appreciate differences, both among fellow Jews, and in their greater world as well. The chapter discusses the importance of anti-bias education for children in Jewish schools. Provided are tools to approach anti-bias education in a Jewishly appropriate way, and to integrate it into Jewish preschool programs.

A JEWISH RATIONALE FOR ANTI-BIAS EDUCATION

Our commitment to Judaism is more evident in our actions than in our words. We are called upon to be partners with God in *Tikkun Olam* — the perfection of the world. We are called upon to question what is unfair, to fight injustice. The prophet Isaiah bade us to observe what is right and do what is just (56:1).

Our Tanach gives us mixed messages about our relationship to the rest of the world. In our travels from Egypt to the Promised Land, we are instructed again and again by God to remain separate from the peoples around us. We are enjoined not to worship their gods, take their women for wives, or eat the food they eat. At the same time, we are repeatedly reminded to treat the stranger with the utmost hospitality and kindness, for we were strangers in the land of Egypt. Further, our tradition treasures diversity. From the tractate *Brachot* in the Talmud we learn, "The wise one blesses those who have opinions which are different from others', and who have outlooks which are not the same as the outlooks of others'," and "Blessed is God who discerns secrets, for the mind of each is different from the other, as is the face of each different from the other."

We therefore teach our children that to be a Jew is to be separate from other peoples. But we are also called upon to teach our children about their responsibility to the stranger, their obligation to *Tikkun Olam,* and to learn from all people. Our children need to be taught to notice differences, and to be aware that differences are beneficial to their world. Then children need to recognize stereotypes, to question them, and to correct them. And they need the tools to fight injustice in their world, to be able to act.

WHAT IS ANTI-BIAS EDUCATION?

Anti-bias education is more than a matter of adding some dolls, pictures, and books to a classroom which reflect peoples of different colors, ages, and abilities. Anti-bias is a philosophy of education which seeks to revolutionize a classroom, educating teachers and parents, and empowering children to grow up fighting injustice and standing up for what is right. The goals of an anti-bias approach are:

1. To foster the self-esteem and group identity of children, families, and staff.
2. To foster the appreciation of human diversity.
3. To enable each child to identify unfair treatment.
4. To empower each child to take action against unfair treatment.

Anti-bias education may start small, with environmental changes and some added activities. With nurturing, anti-bias will become a lens through which everything in the curriculum is viewed (Hohensee and Derman-Sparks).

In a homogeneous setting, educators might question the necessity of bringing up issues of differences and prejudice. The worry exists that discussing such topics will bring to children's attention differences that may have otherwise gone unnoticed. This "color blind" approach, the attitude that everyone is the same, despite color or ethnicity, actually works against children growing up free of racial and ethnic prejudice. Byrnes (1992) asserts that children begin developing attitudes about race and ethnicity as early as three or four years old, and that they notice skin color at an even younger age. In fact, skin color shapes a child's experience more than any other except possibly gender. Byrnes stresses the importance of talking about these things so that children can learn to avoid stereotypes and fight actively against prejudice.

Just as white children in all white classrooms need anti-bias education, so, too, do Jewish children in Jewish schools. The main task of an anti-bias education in an all white classroom is to thwart the belief that the dominant European-American culture is superior to other ways of life (Derman-Sparks, 1989). So, too, do Jewish chil-

dren. Jewish parents choose a Jewish school most often so that their children will begin to build a strong Jewish identity. Educators must walk a fine line, surrounding children with Jewish culture and influences, while actively dispelling a belief that this way of life is better than other people's. It is essential that preschoolers are not taught that being "chosen" means being "superior." An anti-bias education in a Jewish school should, for example, enable children to give *Tzedakah* without pitying and stereotyping "those poor people," to honor and keep Shabbat while acknowledging that other people have different, valid ways of celebrating and resting. The task to empower Jewish children to question stereotypes and combat injustice is a challenging one. Yet, as we prepare the children for leadership roles in tomorrow's world, it is essential to meet this challenge and to fulfill our partnership with God in creating a better world.

CONCEPTS AND GOALS

Following is a list of developmental attributes, concepts, and goals, which are appropriate for children of various ages. While most of these are appropriate for children in any school, some concepts are more specific to Jewish children. Some of the concepts listed here are adapted from Whaley, 1990; York, 1991; and Derman-Sparks, 1989.

Infant To 24 Months

1. Infants between two and four months begin to distinguish people and voices, and later, faces.
2. At seven months, babies can tell friendly from unfriendly voices.
3. By eight months, infants have formed a mental image of a face, and attend to differences from their model with interest.
4. By 13 months, babies show preferences for certain people.

5. Altruistic behavior has been noted in infants as young as 11 months. By 21 months, the ability to sympathize with others is emerging.

6. Between 15 and 18 months, toddlers develop a sense of self as a unique individual. Once self-awareness reaches this level, toddlers become vulnerable to shame and embarrassment, that feeling that "there's something wrong with me" or "I am bad." Children who feel shamed may feel the need to put others down in order to feel good about themselves as they get older.

7. Toddlers are becoming aware of others' feelings and attitudes, and connect feelings to specific situations. They engage in imitative play, and will mimic the attitudes of parents and caregivers.

8. Teachers help infants develop a secure sense of trust and a strong self-image by responding to infants' needs in a loving and timely manner.

9. Teachers help infants feel safe and comfortable in their own culture.

10. Empathy should be encouraged and supported in babies' behavior.

11. Labeling and validating emotions for infants and toddlers helps them in the process of self/ other differentiation. This will later lead to the development of altruistic and prosocial behaviors.

2 Years

1. Behavior is affected by the emotional reactions of parents and caregivers.

2. Fear is learned from significant adults. Children will become aversive to those things and people to which their significant adults are aversive.

3. Two-year-olds are beginning to balance self-identity with social conformity. If parents and caregivers are not careful, the ground is ripe for the planting of seeds of prejudice.

4. Exposing children to a wide range of emotional expressions can enhance the development of empathy.

5. Twos are becoming very aware of gender differences. Use diapering and changing times to reinforce positive gender attitudes.

6. Twos notice skin color. Use their questions to reinforce positive attitudes.

7. Twos are becoming aware of cultural aspects of gender and ethnic roles. Twos need lots of role models for the different roles men and women play in Judaism and in other aspects of their lives.

8. Twos can begin to be aware of cultural diversity if appropriate activities are a part of their daily environment. Make Hebrew and diverse Jewish rituals a part of every day.

9. Twos are especially curious. When curiosity is supported with honesty, warmth and acceptance, children learn tolerance.

10. Twos begin to define themselves and others by physical characteristics such as skin color and anatomy.

3 Years

1. Encourage children to ask about their own and other's physical characteristics.

2. Answer with honesty, developmentally appropriate information, warmth and acceptance.

3. Enable children to feel pride, but not superiority, about being Jewish.

4. Enable children to develop ease and feel comfort with physical differences. We are all made *B'Tzelem Elohim* – in God's image.

5. People are alike.

6. People are different.

7. Help children appreciate what all people share that makes us human.

8. There are many different kinds of families.

9. Support curiosity with honesty, warmth, and acceptance, in order to teach tolerance.

10. Young children may have fears about people with disabilities. Address their fears in a calm, accepting manner.

11. Threes are not yet sure of what makes them a boy or girl, and they are not yet sure if they will remain the same gender as they grow.

Listen to their questions, and answer simply and briefly.
12. Connect Jewish activities to individual children's families, to create cultural pride.

4 To 5 Years
1. Encourage children to ask about their own and other's physical characteristics.
2. Answer with honesty, developmentally appropriate information, warmth, and acceptance.
3. Enable children to feel pride, but not superiority, about being Jewish.
4. Enable children to develop ease and feel comfort with physical differences. We are all made *B'Tzelem Elohim* – in God's image.
5. All people are worthy, loveable, capable, equal, and *B'Tzelem Elohim*.
6. All people are important and deserve *Kavod* (respect).
7. People are alike. People are different.
8. Some physical attributes stay the same; some physical attributes change.
9. Help children appreciate what all people share that makes us human.
10. There are many different kinds of families.
11. Families live in different ways.
12. Culture comes from parents and families.
13. Support curiosity with honest, warmth, and acceptance, in order to teach tolerance.
14. Everyone has feelings.
15. It is important to try new experiences.
16. Young children want to know how they got their color, hair and eye characteristics.
17. Children may reject another child with a disability because of fear or stereotyping. Handle such rejection immediately.
18. Four-year-olds are strongly influenced by societal norms for gender behavior. Work to widen children's narrowing gender definitions by providing many non-stereotypical role models.
19. Connect Jewish activities to individual children's families, to create cultural pride.
20. Prevent the belief that white, Jewish culture is superior to other ways of life.

21. Work to expand children's concept of fairness and feelings of empathy.
22. Empower children to change things that seem unfair or make them uncomfortable.
23. Reward children when they stand up for themselves and each other against biased ideas and discriminatory behavior.

BRINGING ANTI-BIAS EDUCATION INTO YOUR CLASSROOM

Children with strong self-identities are best equipped to stand up and fight bias against themselves and others (Derman-Sparks, 1989). Anti-bias education for Jewish children should go beyond instilling a strong self-identity. Children must be exposed to all of the varying customs, languages, and characteristics of Jews all over the world, and even in North America. And, of course, there are also Jews with disabilities, gay and lesbian Jews, divorced families, Jews old and young, rich and poor. Jewish children who embrace the diversity within their own people will be that much more able and willing to embrace the diversity in the larger community.

What are some ways to accomplish anti-bias education for Jewish children? You might begin with small additions to the curriculum, such as showing an oil *chanukiah* or counting to five in Hebrew, Yiddish (a mixture of Hebrew and German), and Ladino (a mixture of Hebrew and Spanish). Eventually, the scope of world Judaism must come to pervade every holiday celebration, every discussion of "what do Jews do?" Begin by tapping the diversity of cultures and backgrounds of the families in your program from Israel, South Africa, Russia, Iran, South America, and so on. All children need to have their families' traditions acknowledged and celebrated, and the other children will benefit from exposure to the different traditions of their friends.

In time, the range should be expanded to communities which are not directly included in the school's population. Care should be taken to include all the faces of Judaism, just as care is taken to include all the faces of your community. In Chapter 2, "Jewish Every Day," pp. 25-28, there is a list of Jewish values and *mitzvot*, such as *Gemilut Chasadeem* and *Kavod*. We teach our children to do kindnesses not only for people like themselves, but for all people. This is one aspect of implementing the concept of anti-bias education.

THE TEACHER'S ROLE

The first step in integrating anti-bias education into a Jewish school is for the entire staff to understand the benefits of anti-bias education to their children, who are in the main members of a white majority and a Jewish minority. Teachers who understand the relevance of tolerance and a global concern to a Jewish education will be more willing and able to take the time to incorporate anti-bias philosophy into their classrooms.

The next — and perhaps the most difficult — step for teachers is to examine their own biases. There are many important questions to ask. How do I define myself? What things or people make me uncomfortable? Are there people I feel are not as worthy as I for a high quality of life? How do I treat people with skin color that is different from mine? people whose language is different from mine? people whose abilities are different from mine? people whose beliefs are different from mine? How did I come to hold the beliefs I hold about people who are different from me? Self-examination is difficult and time-consuming. Changing our attitudes and long-held beliefs also takes time.

It is not necessary for teachers to be "bias free" in order to create an anti-bias environment in their classrooms! Indeed, none of us is completely unbiased or free from prejudice. The goal is to become aware of biases and to understand how these affect your work with children. The more you know, the more comfortable you will be. Work with your Director to create a school climate that encourages and motivates all teachers to expand their awareness of bias. Work together as a staff, or team up with a few other teachers, to pool resources and share information and support while learning about other Jews, or examining your own attitudes and biases.

Dr. Jill Rosenzweig, Director of Early Childhood Services at the Tucson Jewish Community Center, describes how she got her teachers involved and invested in creating an anti-bias environment (personal communication, January 2000). She videotaped and shared with teachers vignettes showing teachers responding poorly to children's questions about skin color, gender, and other areas of potential bias. Soon, teachers were coming to her with their own tapes, eager to improve their own teaching and demonstrate their mastery of the philosophy of anti-bias education. Examining the vignettes also helped the teachers evaluate how anti-bias was affecting the children themselves as well as their families.

Once a teacher, or indeed an entire school staff, has begun to own the process of anti-bias education, and has been allowed and encouraged to examine their own biases, and how those biases affect their work with children, then teachers can embark on the journey of incorporating anti-bias education into their classrooms. In simplistic terms, this means bringing in and emphasizing diversity in the classroom, and then working with children to appreciate and value differences, to question injustice, and to make right what is wrong.

In every Jewish school, clear definitions must be set out and understood by all with regard to the philosophy of the community. For example, if a school is part of a community in which only boys wear *kipot*, and only girls light Shabbat candles, then these boundaries must be respected, and gender equality must be reinforced in other ways. If a school is in a community in which intermarriage is not condoned, then teachers need to present Jewish marriage as an option between two Jewish people. In a school that enforces *kashrut*, teachers must respect this by not bringing in food from non-kosher restaurants. The establishment of clear understandings up front will prevent limits from appearing as prejudices. Teachers must embody the ideals of tolerance in order to teach children this value.

GETTING STARTED

Anti-bias education cannot be accomplished in a two-week unit. Rather, it is an attitude, a belief, a motto. It begins with the environment of the room and the class. It continues with "teachable moments" that arise from the children's lives and the environment teachers have established in the classroom. There is no set curriculum that would be appropriate for every classroom, but there are many activities and strategies that can be used for consciousness-raising. There are also many excellent secular guides for anti-bias education (see the bibliography for this chapter). Below are suggestions for incorporating anti-bias activities into some aspects of the Jewish early childhood curriculum, including environment, consciousness-raising, and *Klal Yisrael*.

ENVIRONMENT

When introducing anti-bias education to your classroom, start with the environment. Through visual displays, book choices, and materials, you can convey a message of acceptance and diversity. Posters and other wall decorations should include the faces and cultural objects from different communities of Jews. Gender myth busters, such as photos of fathers lighting candles and women wearing *tallitot*, should be as prevalent as posters of Ethiopian Jews in the Israeli army and Jews in Santa Monica, California doing *tashlich* on the beach (especially if you live in a place with no beaches!). Of course, there should be plenty of visual representations of the Jewish experiences with which the children in your class are familiar. Enlarged photos of the children and their families doing Jewish things serve this purpose well.

Examine the books in the classroom. Do all the Jewish books portray the Ashkenazic experience, or are there stories and folktales from other Jewish cultures? Do all Jewish books have mother lighting the candles and father making *Kiddush*, or do books and pictures show women wearing *tallitot* and dancing with the Torah, and fathers cleaning the house for Pesach? Are there books and puzzles with Jews in wheelchairs participating in Jewish life? Do your books include stories about Jews interacting with people from other cultures and religions? Exposure (through books and pictures and one-to-one contact) to Jews with different skin color, different abilities, and different customs will help the children to become accepting of these differences.

The materials in the classroom can also contribute to an accepting tone. Both boys and girls will feel invited to practice all the Shabbat rituals if the Shabbat ritual objects are in the house corner for them to play with, and if they have seen role models demonstrate that both males and females may make *Kiddush* or light candles. Even in the most traditionally observant home, in which the woman normally lights the candles for Shabbat and the man usually says *Kiddush*, the man is obligated to light Shabbat candles if there are no women present. The same is true for a woman saying *Kiddush* in the absence of men.

Markers, crayons, and paint should be available in all colors of the rainbow, and all shades of skin tones. Provide ritual objects such as *tallitot, kipot,* and *tefillin* for children to explore with a teacher or to play with (remove the *tzitzit,* and use non-kosher *tefillin*). Exposure to these kinds of objects gives children the opportunity to ask questions and learn, "This is what some Jews do."

CONSCIOUSNESS-RAISING ACTIVITIES

Once a teacher has set the stage for anti-bias education by making the physical environment of her/his room accepting of differences, there are many consciousness-raising activities which can be added to the curriculum, to stimulate awareness of differences, and foster children's ability to fight injustice.

Physical Characteristics and Skin Color: B'Tzelem Elohim

1. In small groups of three to five children, hand each child a piece of fruit (the same kind of fruit to each child). Ask the children if they all have the same thing (they should agree that they do). Tell the children to examine their piece of fruit and get to know it very well (they should look at it from all sides with their eyes, fingers, noses). After a few minutes, collect all the fruit in a basket. Then ask the children, one by one, to find *their* piece of fruit. If the children have done a good job with the first part of the activity, they should each be able to find their own fruit, because each piece is unique. Like the fruit, we are all made *B'Tzelem Elohim*, and we need to look for the qualities that make each one of us special and unique.

2. There are many ways to help children examine skin color. The goal such activities should be to discover that each of us has a different color skin, even though some of us are labeled "white," "brown," or "black." Also, such activities should strip skin color of any value judgments. Our society is full of messages that assign positive value to white skin and negative values to every other color skin. The preschool is a good place to dispel these stereotypes.

   Invite all the children to place their hands in the middle of the circle. Talk about skin color as children wash their hands. Use the dolls in the classroom to talk about skin color. Assure children that skin color does not wash off, that brown skin is brown, not dirty. Admire each child's skin color. Give children paint so they can mix and create their own skin color with paint. Put some paint directly on a child's hand, and let the child direct which other colors need to be added to create his/her exact skin color. Let each child name her special, unique color, to foster ownership

and pride. Help children learn that they are not "white" — compare their skin to a piece of white paper to show the difference — but they are peach, pink, ivory, or whatever they name themselves (Teaching Tolerance Project, 1997, "Starting Small: Teaching Children Tolerance" video, 1997). "White" is a power label — it serves to divide people. Help children create labels for themselves that unite, not divide.

3. Help the children make fingerprints. Provide magnifying glasses so they can examine prints closely. Make two sets of each print, and see if the children can match them up. We all have fingers, but even our fingers are made *B'Tzelem Elohim*. The differences make us special and unique (York, 1991).

4. Make photo masks. Take close-up photos of the faces of people the children know, representing diversity in appearance, age, and gender. Also use photos or magazine pictures of Jews from around the world. Enlarge the pictures in color to the size of a real face, mount them on tag board, and then laminate them. Cut out eye and mouth holes, and mount each on a tongue depressor or paint stick. Introduce the masks at circle time, and put them out for the children on a discovery table or in the dramatic play area, along with a mirror. Listen to the conversations as children "try on" different faces. Look for anti-bias attitudes and lurking stereotypes (York, 1991).

Similarities and Differences

1. Have a bread snack. Serve breads from many different cultures: cornbread, *challah*, tortillas, pita, black bread, *matzah*, piki bread, steamed buns, white bread, multi-grain bread, scones, and so on. As you taste, talk about the name of the bread and where it comes from. Follow up with books like *Bread Bread Bread* by Ann Morris, *Bread Is for Eating* by David and Phyllis Gershator, and *Jalapeño Bagels* by Natasha Wing. You can also do this with rice (*Everybody Cooks Rice* by Nora Dooley), soup, and other

foods made differently in different cultures (York, 1998).

2. Children can notice differences even with their ears. Tape record individual children speaking. Also, record the voices of other significant people in the school or building. Record people speaking in different languages. Be sure to include Hebrew, the languages of the caregivers of the children, and, of course, all the home languages of children other than English (including accents, such as South African English). For younger children, limit the tapes to people in the room and familiar animals. Play the tapes for the children and let them figure out who the speaker is, or what language is being spoken (York, 1991).

3. Collect many pictures of people in all their diversity: people from different cultures, ethnic groups, physical abilities, religious groups (Hasidic Jews), Jews wearing and not wearing *kipot,* Jews doing Jewish things but not wearing any traditional Jewish garb, different family configurations (two parents, one parent, multigenerations, two parents of the same sex, parents and children whose skin colors don't all match). Be sure to have a few pictures from each "group." Mount the pictures on tagboard and laminate them. Make "People Cards" which can be used in many different activities. Encourage children to sort the pictures. Let them decide on which similarities determine a group, or provide suggestions.

4. Provide a large assortment of buttons to sort. For children under three, be sure to use only large, non-choking buttons! Make sure there are many ways to sort the buttons by similarities: number of holes, size, color, texture, etc. Encourage children to sort by a different characteristic each time.

Social Skills: Fairness and Finding Friends

1. Establish a "Peace Table" in your classroom (Teaching Tolerance Project, 1997; McGovern, 1997). This is a space with a small table and two chairs, some puppets, and pictures of children being friends/working things out. It is a neutral space and serves as a vehicle to teach children to work out their difficulties and relationships.

2. Use the "People Cards" (see Similarities and Differences, #3, above) to talk about friendship possibilities. Talk about which people might be friends with which other people. Help children think about questions such as: Can you be friends only with people who are like you? Might someone be so different you could never be friends with them? (York, 1998)

3. At snack or lunch, give seconds only to the girls (or to brown-eyed children, or to children wearing white shirts, etc.). When the children catch on and begin to protest, begin a discussion. Ask: Is this fair? What would make it more fair? Why is it unfair for some people to get something, but not everyone? How can we make our world more fair?

4. To foster understanding and empathy, not fear or pity, give children chances to experience physical disabilities. Use blindfolds, earplugs, wheelchairs, and so on. "Blind art" can be a regular feature in the classroom. Using different media, such as paint or playdough, children work with a blindfold. When two or three children, all blindfolded, work together on a project, the result can be increased cooperation as well as an increased focus on perception (Teaching Tolerance Project, 1997, p. 123; McGovern, 1997).

Daily Culture

1. Say "good morning" in different ways. Use different languages, including Hebrew, the languages of the children's caregivers, and the children's home languages, as well as sign language. Try this for "thank you" and "goodbye" as well.

2. Make a classroom scrapbook with photos, dictations, and pictures. Keep adding to it all year. Keep it on the bookshelf, so that the

children can review their past experiences and retell their own stories. Let families check out the book so they can look at it at home. Be sure to include multicultural experiences and rituals from different Jewish cultures that have become part of the classroom's holiday celebrations.

3. Collect pictures of apartment buildings, houses, tents, *sukkot*, houseboats, trailers, and so on. Chart the children who live in each kind of dwelling. Talk about why different people live in different kinds of homes. (York, 1991)

4. Explore different cultures through scents. Make spice jars (using film canisters or baby food jars) with spices, incense, and essential oils from different cultures. Be sure to include Israeli spices, such as *zatar* (hyssop). Encourage the children to find familiar smells and new scents. Talk about how people all over the world like to cook with different spices, and how homes all over the world smell different, depending on the kinds of food cooked in them (York, 1991).

Care for Animals: Tza'ar Ba'alay Chayim

1. Just as we care for other people, it is our responsibility to care for animals. Teach the children how to care for a classroom pet. This teaches children about interdependence, caring for others, and gentleness — all skills which are important in human relationships as well. Let the children take responsibility for making sure the animal is cared for every day (York, 1998).

2. Use puppets to illustrate cruelty to animals (person kicking a dog, not feeding hungry goats, whipping a horse, stepping on a bug). Let the children react, and give the puppet advice about how to be kind to animals. Ask the children how the animal might feel. Encourage the children to stand up for what they believe is right, and to tell the cruel puppet, "Stop hurting that animal." (York, 1998)

3. Use pictures of animals to help children identify stereotypes. Gather both realistic and not realistic pictures of animals, such as a cartoon bear wearing an Indian headdress or a chicken wearing an apron. Talk with children about what is real and what is not, and about how stereotypes make fun of people and hurt people's feelings (York, 1998).

4. When the British took over Palestine (before it was Israel), they brought with them cats to take care of the overpopulation of rats. Well, the cats got rid of the rats, for the most part, but now there is a large overpopulation of unwanted cats in Israel living in the streets. Talk with the children about what problems are associated with too many street cats (hungry cats, disease, cats getting into peoples' garbage, sad cats, etc). Brainstorm with the children how the Israeli people could take care of the street cats and fix the overpopulation problem, without being cruel to the cats. Visit a local animal shelter to see how street animals are taken care of in your country, and find out what the children can do to help.

Care for the Earth: Tikkun Olam

1. Make picking up litter a routine part of every trip outside or to the playground. By caring for their environment, children are making the world a better place for themselves and for other people.

2. People from all over the world help plant trees in Israel. Brainstorm and investigate why trees are so important to Israel. Find ways as a class to help plant trees in Israel.

3. Empower children to help reduce air pollution. Ask a parent or staff person to drive his/her car up to the school. Have the children stand at a safe distance and watch as the person starts the car. Have an adult hold a large paper coffee filter next to the exhaust pipe while the car is started. Show the children the exhaust residue on the filter. Talk about the pollution each car adds to the air, every time it is driven (York,

1998). Brainstorm ways children can help reduce car pollution (carpool, walk or ride a bike to a friend's house or to the park, take a bus or train). Team up with parents to form carpools and find other ways to reduce car usage. Not driving on Shabbat certainly helps solve this problem.

4. Empower children to make a difference in other people's lives. Flowers are beautiful and they help brighten people's spirits. Take a field trip and plant flowers at a nursing home or a school in a neighborhood where there are few flowers.

Care for People: Kavod, Hachnasat Orcheem, and Tzedakah

1. Model and teach respect and appreciation for the maintenance people in the school. Introduce the children to the janitor by name, be sure to greet him/her by name whenever you pass in the hall or a janitor comes into the room, say thank you when a maintenance person empties the garbage or helps clean up a spill. Help the children think about how their classroom gets so clean overnight.

2. Make it a regular practice to invite other classes to your room for snack or a story, and also to be invited as guests to other classrooms. Learn about ways to be a good guest (e.g., cleaning up when you are finished playing in someone else's room, saying thank you, bringing a gift or contribution). Likewise, study ways to be a good host (e.g., preparing the room or a special treat for the guests, sharing your toys and space with guests, saying thank you). Help the children be especially kind and helpful when the visitors are younger children, or grown-ups. Before and after a visit, talk about the benefits and responsibilities that go along with being a visitor or a host.

3. Collecting coins for *Tzedakah* every day or every week promotes a giving habit, and teaches children about this *mitzvah*. While collecting *Tzedakah*, talk with children about the kind of people they may be helping. How might those people be different from us? How might they be the same? What do you think the children we help like to play with? Why is it a *mitzvah* to give *Tzedakah*? How else can we help people in need each day?

4. When a new child will be joining the class, use a persona doll (a doll with a life story, used to introduce differences into the classroom, see Derman-Sparks, 1989), and brainstorm with the class about how to make the new person feel welcome. What might it feel like to be new in a school? new in town? How might the children make friends with the new person? What if the new child was in a wheelchair? Would he/she be able to get into the classroom? into the school building? What would he/she be able to do on the playground? How would the children help this new classmate get around and play? (York, 1998)

Klal Yisrael: Appreciating Our Differences

1. Incorporate holiday traditions from different Jewish cultures into every holiday celebration. On Chanukah, light an oil *chanukiah* and eat *sufganiot*. Examine different styles of *chanukiot* and talk about the different cultures from which they come. On Pesach, try the Afghani tradition of lightly beating others with green onions during the song *"Dayaynu."* Research holiday traditions of Jewish cultures from all over the word. For suggestions, see the bibliography at the end of this chapter, and/or search the Internet. Bringing in traditions from different cultures makes children aware that there are Jews all over the world, and although we are similar because we are one Jewish family, we all have different, authentic ways of celebrating.

2. Learn and use vocabulary from different Jewish cultures: Hebrew, Ladino, Yiddish.

3. Include in your classroom Jewish ritual objects (real objects or at least pictures) from different cultures. Show different *chanukiot*, *kipot*, Torahs,

dreidels (the Israeli dreidel has a *pay* instead of a *shin* — see chapter 13, "Chanukah," p. 192), and so on.

4. Present and validate role models of both men and women performing Jewish rituals. Allow boys to light candles, and girls to lead *Kiddush.* Allow girls to try on a *tallit,* encourage boys to bake *challah.* Even if these roles are not part of your community, let children know that "some Jews do this." When children ask, "Why do different Jews do different things?" tell them that ways of doing things are different in different countries. You can compare your community's ways of relating to God with the ways other Jews do it. If the children insist their way is best, assure them it is the best way *for them.*

TEACHABLE MOMENTS

We have seen how an anti-bias approach can be integrated successfully into the classroom through the use of diverse visuals and books that bust stereotypes, and by planning consciousness-raising activities. Yet, the most effective anti-bias learning, the moments which transform attitudes and inspire children to change their world, may come from "teachable moments." As any teacher knows, a teachable moment is that moment when a child discovers something, or asks a question, or does something that gives a teacher an opportunity to expand on wonder or turn an ordinary moment into an extraordinary experience. Such moments can sometimes be overlooked. But if we have grappled with anti-bias issues ourselves, and we are on the lookout for lurking biases and moments of potential justice, we can really hear children's questions and help them challenge their world when they encounter stereotypes or injustice.

Once, while teaching an after-school kindergarten class, I brought my class, consisting of just two boys that day, to play in a classroom while I helped some other teachers, all women, assemble a large loft in that room. One of the boys exclaimed, "You can't build a loft. That's man's work!" The other boy quickly agreed with his friend. We

teachers told the boys, "Oh yeah? You just watch." We proceeded to assemble the loft, and the boys broke down the boxes as we emptied them. When the loft was finished, we asked the boys, "Who built the loft?" "You did. But we helped." "Right, we all did it together. Building a loft isn't man's work. It's everyone's work." The boys did not become instant feminists, but they had witnessed at least one example of women doing what they had previously labeled as "man's work." Stereotypes were being challenged.

Teachable moments provide opportunities to look at the world through our children's eyes and help them see differences as beneficial, and to see themselves as agents of change. When preverbal children point to my mole, which is at the corner of my nose, I label it for them, I touch it, I let them touch it. Children learn that people have differences and it's okay to ask about them. When a child says to another child, with a negative tone, "Your skin is brown," we have a choice. We can say, "Don't say that, it's not nice," or we can say, "Yes, his skin is brown. Isn't it pretty? Let's look at our hands. Why do we all have different color skin?" We can reinforce fear of differences, or we can teach that every person is made *B'Tzelem Elohim,* that God intended each one of us to be different, and differences are good.

When a child says, "We don't light candles at my house for Shabbat," again we have a choice. We can tell the child, "All Jews light candles on Shabbat. Tell your mommy she should do it," or we can let the child know, "There are lots of ways to be Jewish. If you would like to light Shabbat candles at home, ask mom or dad if they will help you." We can teach tolerance or we can teach a child his family "does Jewish wrong."

Inviting intergenerational volunteers into your classroom is a consciousness-raising strategy that creates lots of opportunities for teachable moments. Every child may not be blessed with grandparents who live within visiting distance. Surrogate grandparents who visit the class on a regular basis give children exposure to this older age group, allowing children to gain the comfort to ask questions. Also, older Jewish adults bring to the classroom Jewish stories of celebrations and experiences to which the children's parents were not exposed. My parents grew up in New York, in non-observant families. My mom tells stories of her childhood holidays, which for her simply meant getting dressed up in new clothes, walking to synagogue with her grandparents and not necessarily going in for services. I can't wait for her to tell my children those stories. What questions will they ask as they hear about Jewish practices so different from their own? Their understanding of, and in turn their acceptance of, the larger Jewish world will be that much greater.

CONCLUSION

As our preschool children reach the age when they begin to notice differences, and begin to pick up on societal norms and biases, they should be surrounded by positive images of the diversity that exists in their world, both secular and Jewish. Not until I was 24 years old and had spent a year in Israel did I understand that Yiddish is not a universal Jewish language, that there is a substantial, non-Ashkenazic Jewish population which speaks Ladino or other localized dialects. What a loss that the world of my youth was so narrow, my Jewish experience so limited. Let us do better by the children we teach. Let us help them to benefit from the broad Jewish experiences, that they may be better equipped to love and understand their neighbor, to seek justice and pursue peace.

BIBLIOGRAPHY

GENERAL RESOURCES

Alvarado, Cecelia, et al. *In Our Own Way: How Anti-Bias Work Shapes Our Lives*. St. Paul, MN: Redleaf Press, 1999.

> Personal reflections of people who have worked in child care help others begin their own anti-bias journey.

Byrnes, Deborah A. "Addressing Race, Ethnicity and Culture in the Classroom." In *Common Bonds: Anti-Bias Teaching in a Diverse Society*, edited by Deborah A. Byrnes and Gary Kiger. 2d ed. Wheaton, MD: Association for Childhood Education International, 1996.

> Examines the growing diversity in schools in a constructive, empowering manner, identifies various forms of cultural diversity, and suggests ways to build inclusive classroom environments.

Derman-Sparks, Louise, and the ABC Task Force. *Anti-Bias Curriculum: Tools for Empowering Young Children*. Washington, DC: National Association for the Education of Young Children. 1989.

> The book that began a movement remains a classic to this day.

Hall, Nadia Saderman. *Creative Resources for the Anti-Bias Classroom*. Albany, NY: Delmar Publishers, 1999.

> Illustrates for teachers of infants through elementary children how to integrate anti-bias approach into all areas of curriculum planning.

Hohensee, Julie Bisson, and Louise Derman-Sparks. "Implementing an Anti-Bias Curriculum in Early Childhood Classrooms." *ERIC Digest*, 1992, EDO-PS-92-8. (http://ericeece.org/pubs/digest/)

> Outlines the steps needed to bring anti-bias education into the classroom. The Educational Resources Information Center (ERIC) is a national information system supported by the U.S. Department of Education that is designed to provide users with ready access to an extensive body of education-related literature. The ERIC Clearinghouse on Elementary and Early Childhood Education (ERIC/EECE) is one of 16 clearinghouses in the ERIC system.

McGovern, Margie. "Starting Small: Teaching Children Tolerance." Montgomery, AL: Southern Poverty Law Center, 1997.

> A 58-minute video that shows teachers how to create anti-bias environments. Available free with the book *Starting Small: Teaching Tolerance in Preschool and the Early Grades* (see the bibliography at the end of this volume, p. 375 for the address).

Payne, Lauren Murphy. *We Can Get Along: A Child's Book of Choices*. Minneapolis, MN: Free Spirit Publishing, 1997.

> Lessons that engage preschoolers regarding their feelings toward others and dealing with conflict. Includes a list of 25 appropriate ways to express anger and 50 words to describe feelings.

Segal, Maxine. *Anti-Bias Education in the Jewish Preschool*. Pasadena, CA: Pacific Oaks College, 1996. Master's Thesis.

> Explores appropriate models for anti-bias curriculum in a Jewish preschool. Contact Pacific Oaks College library, (800) 684-0500.

Teaching Tolerance Project. *Starting Small: Teaching Tolerance in Preschool and the Early Grades*. Montgomery, AL: Southern Poverty Law Center, 1997.

> An amazing book that helps teach fairness, respect, cooperation, and tolerance. Contains an extensive resource list for every aspect of anti-bias education. Available free with the video *Starting Small: Teaching Children Tolerance* (see the bibliography at the end of this volume, p. 375 for the address).

Whaley, Kimberlee, and Elizabeth Blue Swadner. "Multicultural Education in Infant and Toddler Settings." In *Childhood Education*, Summer 1990, pp. 238-240.

> A discussion of reasons multicultural education is important for children younger than three,

and how to go about implementing it in the infant/toddler classroom.

Whitney, Trisha. *Kids Like Us: Using Persona Dolls in the Classroom*. St. Paul, MN: Redleaf Press, 1999.

>A guide for teachers on using persona dolls to introduce topics such as emotions, social skills, bias or prejudice into the classroom.

Wolpert, Ellen. *Start Seeing Diversity: The Basic Guide To an Anti-Bias Curriculum*. St. Paul, MN: Redleaf Press, 1999.

>Helps teachers establish a framework to recognize emerging bias and strategies to respond effectively. Includes video and extensive guide.

York, Stacey. *Big as Life: The Everyday Inclusive Curriculum, Vols. 1 and 2*. St. Paul, MN: Redleaf Press, 1998.

>Through theme-based units, this book webs subject areas and integrates diversity, anti-racism and multicultural issues.

————. *Roots & Wings: Affirming Culture in Early Childhood Programs*. St. Paul, MN: Redleaf Press, 1991.

>A wonderful resource for those seeking to introduce anti-bias education in their classroom.

JEWISH RESOURCES
Adults

Abramovitz, Karen. *Hanukah: A Family Learning Kit*. Tel Aviv: Everyman's University, 1982. (Available from A.R.E. Publishing, Inc.)

>An extensive guide to Chanukah; includes a section on Chanukah through the Ages and around the World.

Goodman, Philip. *The Yom Kippur Anthology*. Philadelphia: Jewish Publication Society of America, 1971.

>Includes a section on "Yom Kippur in Many Lands." Goodman has authored six other such anthologies: *The Purim Anthology, The Hanukkah Anthology, The Passover Anthology, The Rosh Hashanah Anthology, The Sukkot and Simchat Torah Anthology*, and *The Shavuot Anthology*. Each includes a section about the holiday as it is celebrated in different countries.

Hessel, Carolyn Starman. *Our Story: The Jews of Sepharad: A Resource Guide*. New York: Coalition for the Advancement of Jewish Education, 1992.

>A compilation of resources about the Sephardic experience.

Children
Stories from Other Cultures

Roseman, Kenneth. *All in My Jewish Family*. New York: UAHC Press, 1984. (All ages)

>Lots of text, but also good pictures of Israeli children from different cultures.

Schur, Maxine Rose. *Day of Delight: A Jewish Sabbath in Ethiopia*. New York: Dial Books for Young Readers, 1994. (Ages 4-8)

>Depicts daily life in Ethiopia, including preparation for and celebration of the Sabbath.

Schwartz, Howard, and Barbara Rush. *The Sabbath Lion: A Jewish Folktale from Algeria*. New York: HarperCollins Publishers, 1992. (Ages 4-8)

>A beautiful story of a boy's faith and devotion to Shabbat.

Stories of Jews with Other Americans

Levine, Arthur A. *Pearl Moscowitz's Last Stand*. New York: Tambourine Books, 1993. (Ages 4-8)

>A terrific story of how Pearl Moscowitz teams up with her multicultural neighbors to save the trees on their street. Out of print, but worth looking for.

Polacco, Patricia. *Mrs. Katz and Tush*. New York: Dell Publishing, 1992. (Ages 3-8)

>Mrs. Katz befriends her African-American neighbors, sharing Passover with them.

————. *The Trees of the Dancing Goats*. New York: Simon & Schuster Books for Young Readers, 1996. (Ages 4-8)

>During a scarlet fever epidemic one winter, a Jewish family helps make Christmas special for their neighbors through a Chanukah miracle.

Rosen, Michael. *Elijah's Angel: A Story for Chanukah and Christmas*. San Diego: Harcourt Brace & Co., 1992. (Ages 5 and up)
A Jewish boy and an older African-American man share a friendship and an understanding of each other's traditions.

Wing, Natasha. *Jalapeño Bagels*. NY: Atheneum Books for Young Readers, 1996. (Ages 4-8)
For International Day at school, Pablo wants to bring something that reflects the cultures of both his Jewish father and his Mexican mother.

Jews with Disabilities

Gellman, Ellie. *Jeremy's Dreidel*. Rockville, MD: Kar-Ben Copies, 1992. (Ages 4-8)
Jeremy makes a Braille *dreidel* for his father, who is blind.

Goldin, Barbara Diamond. *Cakes and Miracles: A Purim Tale*. New York: Viking, 1991. (Ages 4-8)
The story of Hershel, a blind boy, who make beautiful Purim cookies from things he sees in his dreams.

Rosenfeld, Dina. *On the Ball*. Brooklyn, NY: HaChai Publications, 1998. (Ages 4-8)
The young boy who moves in next door can't possibly play ball — he's in a wheelchair! But Yossie and Laibel learn you can't judge a person by his or her appearance.

Chesed, Kavod, and Shalom

Bogot, Howard I. *Shalom, Salaam, Peace*. New York: CCAR Press, 1999. (All ages)
This unique and beautiful book is a poetic, evocative call for peace in the Middle East, and everywhere. The tri-lingual text (Arabic, English, and Hebrew) is accompanied by the full-color art of Norman Gorbaty. Has the makings of a modern classic.

Casely, Judith. *Apple Pie and Onions*. New York: Greenwillow Books, 1987. (Ages 4-8)
Embarrassed by her grandmother's use of Yiddish, a child listens to a story that helps her learn tolerance.

Harber, Frances. *The Brothers' Promise*. Morton Grove, IL : Albert Whitman, 1998. (Ages 4-8)
Yankel and Joseph are very different, even though they are brothers. Instead of growing apart, their mutual respect causes a miracle.

Prose, Francine. *You Never Know: A Legend of the Lamed-vavniks*. New York: Greenwillow Books, 1998. (Ages 4-8)
You never know who might be a *lamed-vavnik*, one of the 36 righteous peole on earth. Because of this, the people of Plotchnik learn to treat everyone with respect.

Cross-Cultural Similarities

Dooley, Nora. *Everybody Bakes Bread*. Minneapolis, MN: Carolrhoda Books, 1995. (Ages 4-9)
A young girl visits her neighbors and tastes bread from all over the world.

———. *Everybody Cooks Rice*. Minneapolis, MN: Carolrhoda Books, 1991. (Ages 4-8)
A child, sent to find a younger brother at dinnertime, is introduced to a variety of cultures through the different ways rice is prepared at the different households visited.

Evans, Lezlie. *Can You Count Ten Toes? Count To 10 in 10 Different Languages*. Boston, MA: Houghton Mifflin Co., 1999. (Ages 4-8)
Learn to count to ten in Spanish, French, Hebrew, and even Zulu!

Gershator, David and Phillis. *Bread Is for Eating*. New York: Holt, 1995. (Ages 4-8)
Mamita explains how bread is created in a song sung in both English and Spanish. The text is in English; song lyrics are in English and Spanish.

Morris, Ann. *Bread, Bread, Bread*. New York: Mulberry Books, 1993. (Ages 3-8)
Celebrates the many different kinds of bread and how it may be enjoyed.

INTRODUCTION TO PART II
THREE TREMENDOUS CONCEPTS

Judaism is a religion which centers around three tremendous ideas [concepts] — God, Torah and Israel" (Louis Jacobs, *The Book of Jewish Belief*)

God, Torah, and Israel are fundamental Jewish concepts. How we interpret these concepts may vary from person to person, but they form the foundation for Jewish life in general and life in the Jewish early childhood classroom as well.

This section contains three chapters designed to aid the Jewish early childhood educator in bringing God, Torah, and Israel into the classroom. Chapter 4, "God, Prayer, and Spirituality," explores the first of these — how to foster a child's relationship to God, using prayer and other modalities. Chapter 5, "Sharing Torah," reviews some existing Torah curricula for children, and goes beyond those to explore many different ways to bring Torah into any age early childhood classroom. Chapter 6, "Israel All Year," describes strategies for integrating the Land of Israel into the classroom all year.

The content in these chapters cannot be covered in a week or two. Each of these chapters represents an approach for shaping the rest of the curriculum in the Jewish early childhood classroom.

You may wonder, is it possible to run a classroom while always looking at the curriculum and thinking about God, Torah, and Israel? Yes, it is not only possible, it is essential. When these concepts form the framework from which all the rest of curriculum emerges, then your classroom will naturally be "Jewish every day." When God, Torah, and Israel are filters that color everything that takes place, then children gain a better sense of who they are, and are better prepared to go out into the world and feel pride as a Jew and competency as a human being.

Inviting God into your classroom, sharing Torah in a meaningful, consistent way, and making Israel a daily part of your classroom require a shift in how you approach your classroom. Each is a worthwhile, meaningful layer. However, don't try to add all of them at once! The task will seem too overwhelming, and as a result, no meaningful changes may occur. Instead, as you read through this section, think about which of these layers feels most natural to you right now, and start with it. As the year progresses, or as you are reflecting on your teaching next year, you can add still another layer to the one with which you have already become comfortable.

CHAPTER 4

GOD, PRAYER, AND SPIRITUALITY

Maxine Segal Handelman and Roberta Louis Goodman

God, prayer, and spirituality are subjects young children handle with ease. In fact, preschoolers come brimming with views, ideas, and experiences in regard to these subjects. Preschoolers are emotive, feeling human beings. They are filled with a sense of awe and wonder, as so many things are new to them. Preschoolers do not always distinguish between reality and fantasy. Talking to an imaginary play friend in front of others is natural for this age group. Miracles are a natural part of life. Hearing voices, seeing things that others do not, viewing events as miraculous (e.g., their views of how babies are born; belief in the tooth fairy) are commonplace for preschoolers.

God is person-like to this age group. Young children's images of God are very much affected by their everyday experiences. Their understanding of God is influenced and shaped by their relationships to authority figures, parents, and teachers alike. They are used to being commanded, to having someone set rules and regulations. They associate reward and punishment with following rules, because they love or care for the person who sets the expectations and limits.

In terms of prayer, young children are comfortable imitating behaviors of others and eager to touch, experience, and try out new things. Preschoolers enjoy performing new rituals, exploring symbols, and developing new competencies. As they are learning to verbalize things, it is just as natural for them to learn the word *"besameem"* as it is to learn the term "spice box." "Blessed are You, *Adonai*, God of the universe" is as foreign to them as *"Baruch Atah Adonai Elohaynu Melech HaOlam."* They enjoy repeating words over and over again until they master them.

Preschoolers are more open to dealing with God and prayer than most adults. Being adult means being rational, responsible, realistic, and in control of one's behavior. On the other hand, preschoolers show their mood changes openly. In a trusting environment, they freely share their views, feelings, and ideas. This makes them willing and able candidates to respond to God and to their spiritual selves.

Many questions arise when teachers strive to approach the topics of God and prayer and spirituality with their students. This chapter seeks to answer questions such as: How do I present God in my classroom and nurture spirituality? What difference does education make in understanding and relating to God, and in developing spirituality? What are the challenges to educators when dealing with God in the classroom? What is developmentally appropriate for the topics of God, prayer, and spirituality?

LITERATURE REVIEW

It is a given of Jewish thought that we cannot know exactly what God is. Dr. Saul Wachs, the Rosaline B. Feinstein Professor and Department Chair of Education at Gratz College in Philadelphia, notes that there are 105 names for God in Jewish tradition, driving home the point that, try as we might, it is impossible for us to pinpoint the essence of God (Wachs, 1998). From the Torah, the Talmud, the *Siddur*, and Jewish history, we have many images of God — parent, warrior, protector, creator, redeemer, partner — the list goes on and on. The 13 attributes of God (Exodus 34:6-7) —

gracious, compassionate, assuring love for a thousand generations, and granting pardon (to name a few) provide only a glimpse at the enormity of God. No wonder we ask twice a day, just as Moses and the Israelites asked after they left Egypt and crossed the Sea of Reeds, *"Mi Chamocha Ba-ayleem, Adonai?"* (Who is like You, O God, among the mighty?).

After Jacob, our biblical forefather, grappled all night with an unidentified being, he was given a special blessing. His name was changed to Yisrael, which means "one who wrestled with God." His descendants, the Jewish people, are called B'nai Yisrael — Children of Israel. We are "God-wrestlers" — a people that continues to wrestle with our concept of what God is, when God is, and how we might access and connect with the divine.

Our language is inadequate to describe God. We read of Moses and God speaking face to face, yet we know that God has no face, and no body. We argue about the terms "He" or "She" when referring to God, but we know that God has no gender. Love and anger are ascribed to God, yet we know that God does not feel emotions the way we feel emotions. We can speak of God only in metaphors. Professor Neil Gillman of the Jewish Theological Seminary finds four common elements that constitute a "core metaphor" that is almost always included in a Jewish image of God (Gillman, 1990, p. 4):

1. God is *Ehad*. Not only is God One, God is unique, alone.
2. God is sovereign. There is no power higher than God's.
3. God is limited, in that God has given us free will. Our acts can run counter to what God may expect.
4. God is personal. God is caring, and involved.

Wachs suggests two metaphors of God which are especially useful with young children (Wachs, 1998). Describing God as a "wise leader," a leader who arranged the world so that everything we need is here, fosters in children a sense of security. It encourages them to appreciate the gift of life

which they have been given, and to look for evidence of God's work in the world around them. Wachs also suggests the metaphor of God as "friend." Not just any friend, but that friend who never gives up on you. Thinking of God as a listener, as one who understands, can be extremely comforting to any child who might feel as if the people in his/her life are not listening.

Children are born with a sense of wonder about the world. Unless they are actively stifled, they take extreme pleasure in exploring, in asking questions, in discovering the "whys" of their world. Robert Coles, professor of psychiatry at Harvard Medical School, and author of the book *The Spiritual Life of Children*, writes, "Boys and girls are attuned to the heart of spirituality and have a natural ability to look inward in search of meaning and purpose . . . . Children pursue their questions while drawing pictures, stories, and poems, while indulging in the exploration of this wondrously enchanting planet" (Coles, 1996, p. 118). Coles further notes that all children need a spiritual life which is validated by their parents and other significant adults, including teachers. Even preschool children are aware of the gift of life, and are busy trying to understand it and figure out what they should do with it.

To this end, children ask lots of questions. Rabbi David Wolpe, author of *Teaching Your Children about God*, points out (1993) that very young children ask questions about God's beginnings: Was God born? What does God look like? Does God have a body? As children get older, they turn their focus more toward what God *does*. Does God speak to people? Is God still creating new things? Rabbi Daniel Gordis (1999) notes that when children ask about God, they are often not seeking information about God. Instead, children use God as one way to make sense of their world, a way to construct a world that makes sense, a world that is loving and not cruel.

Rabbi Harold Kushner warns adults to listen carefully when children ask questions, in order to know what the real question is. Kushner reminds us of Piaget's description of the functional orientation of the child's mind. When a child asks about what something is, he/she is really interested in knowing what it does, and how it is relevant to his/her life (1971). When children ask, "Where is God," Kushner suggests rephrasing the question. "Where is God" implies that God is a physical being, that God has a location. Even if we tell children that God is not a person, that God is everywhere, we may miss a great opportunity. Kushner recommends replacing the "where" question with "When is God?" This question suggests that God is not an object, but rather a relationship, a feeling, something that happens when the right elements are in place (when we light Shabbat candles, when we appreciate nature, and so on). Children tend to ask the most questions about God from the ages of four to 14. Adults can foster a sense of wonder, and initiate "God-talk," even with younger children. With the right nurturing, as pre-literal children get older, they can translate their wonders into questions.

FAITH DEVELOPMENT

Just as we can speak about developmentally appropriate behavior from a cognitive, physical, or social perspective, so, too, can we do so from a religious, meaning-making perspective. Dr. James Fowler gives us insight into how to describe and think about people at different stages, understand their faith struggles, and educate them. Fowler, a minister, teacher, and thinker created faith development theory based on his research of Jews, Christians, atheists, and others. His thinking reflects the influence of several developmental theorists including Jean Piaget, Eric Erikson, and Lawrence Kohlberg.

Faith development is about making meaning. "'Faith' or 'faithing'" is the process by which a person finds and makes meaning of life's significant questions, adheres to this meaning, and acts it out in his or her life span" (*A Test of Faith* by Roberta Louis Goodman, p. 1). The pursuit of

meaning is what distinguishes us as human beings. Faith is a common pursuit and quest of all individuals. Faith development theory provides a place for God and religious ways of being without mandating them.

While faith is universal to all human beings, the contents of people's faith differ widely. The contents of faith are affected by the families, community, religions, societies, cultures, and the like in which people are raised, as well as allegiances, loyalties, and commitments. Finally, education influences faith construction as well.

We are constantly in the process of making meaning out of life. We develop a story or stories about who we are, which helps us then frame what is meaningful in our lives. A person's faith is revealed and contained in such stories. This creation of a story is much like the portrait of a character in a novel or movie. People act out their stories in their day-to-day lives through the decisions they make, things they do or do not do, and their relationships to others.

Faith formation occurs in relation to others. It can be in relation to parents, synagogue, Jewish community, school, friends, or any group of people with whom one interacts. What Fowler calls "shared centers of value and power" mediate the relationship between the individual and others. These centers of value and power include: trust, fairness, financial gain, possessions, recognition, strength, beauty, integrity, humanism, holiness, and/or God.

A person's faith contains a worldview, a way of seeing, being, and acting. This worldview includes our values and ethics. Our sense of righteousness, justice, treatment of strangers, and the like are part of our worldview.

One's faith develops over the life span. Just as one's intellectual abilities, motor skills, and social behaviors change, so does one's faith. Views of God will not remain the same over one's lifetime. Fowler outlines one pre-stage and six stages of faith development. These stages are sequential and hierarchical, meaning that one goes through them in order. People do not skip around from one stage to another. The goal is not to go through all the stages necessarily — few people ever reach Fowler's Stage 6 — but rather to fill out each stage as completely as possible.

Faith can be nurtured, strengthened, and enhanced. Education in the fullest sense plays an important role in informing a person's faith development. The introduction of stories, rituals, prayers, vocabulary, and so much more can be part of the educational experiences that inform and form a child's faith.

The key for the early childhood educator is to make the pre-stage and Stage 1 life experiences as Jewishly rich as possible. The openness to new things, the mystery and majesty that children in these stages bring to their experiences and hence to Jewish rituals, symbols, stories, holidays, life cycle events, and celebrations is never fully recaptured again. Educators must both maximize the possibilities that these stages present, as well as encourage development into the next stages. Early childhood educators educate families as well as young children. We must remember that parents are not in the same stage as their children. While their children's enthusiasm is infectious, parents need to be nurtured at their own stage level. (For more about stages of faith for parents, see the chapter "Nurturing a Relationship to God and Spiritual Growth: A Developmental Approach" by Roberta Louis Goodman in *Teaching about God and Spirituality,* edited by Roberta Louis Goodman and Sherry H. Blumberg*).*

Following are highlights of the pre-stage and Stage 1 of faith, the stages that describe most preschoolers.

PRE-STAGE: UNDIFFERENTIATED FAITH OR PRIMAL FAITH

Fowler's pre-stage focuses on trust and mistrust. It is a pre-verbal stage; language is not well developed. From such personal and interpersonal acts as feeding, cleaning, dressing, and playing, the infant develops a sense of routine and ritual. This interaction between caretaker and infant is the basis for later images of God. Generally this pre-stage corresponds to children from birth to two years of age.

STAGE 1: INTUITIVE-PROJECTIVE FAITH

This stage emerges with the use of language and symbols with which to communicate, usually around the age of two. A Stage 1 person is self-centered; the world revolves around him or her. Individuals do not distinguish between their perspective and that of others. Self and others are the same.

At this stage, emotions are central and intense. A great sense of awe and mystery about the world prevails. This wonder underlies the view of God. The ability to think logically is not present, giving free reign to the imagination. Life has an episodic and mysterious quality to it. Rituals and stories create an alliance between the moral and the sacred. One obeys out of a desire to avoid punishment. Most children transition into Stage 2 about the time that preschool ends.

IMPLICATIONS OF THESE STAGES

The pre-stage and Stage 1 point to the importance of ritual, symbols, and stories to the preschooler's understanding of God and prayer. The use of one's imagination, pretending or playing, are natural things for preschoolers to do. Providing the preschooler with opportunities for making connections between their lives and Judaism through the use of moments of celebration, prayer experiences, symbols, rituals, stories, images, and the like will enrich the child's faith. Education creates memories. Having children construct their worldview through Jewish experiences at a young age creates a foundation and an orientation for the remainder of a child's life.

Making symbols and rituals developmentally appropriate even in the pre-stage is possible. Even young children pick up symbolic meanings of celebrations, symbols, and rituals. Some examples from Roberta Goodman's family reinforce this.

One night, when my husband and I were obviously going to go out and leave our daughter Shoshana behind with a babysitter, she brought her diaper bag over to the table near the coat closet where we usually put it before going out together. She was using a symbol to communicate her desire, putting in her vote for including her in our outing.

When Shoshana was less than a year old, my husband would have her hold and transport the different ritual objects — candlesticks, candles, *Kiddush* cups, *challah* plate — as he carried her to the Shabbat table in his arms. Together they would set and prepare the table for Shabbat.

On another night, when we were going out without Shoshana, and in the presence of a babysitter, she went over to the shelves where the Shabbat candlesticks were displayed. She made noises and signals to indicate that she wanted the Shabbat candlesticks. When these were taken down from the shelves and given to her, she went and put the candlesticks on the kitchen table. She was putting in her vote for all of us to dine together. Shabbat represented to her using the candlesticks and having the family together for a special meal.

Children at a pre-verbal stage assign significance and meaning to symbols. In many ways, the symbolic connections that Shoshana made with the candlesticks had to do with her weekly routine of helping her father set the Shabbat table. Not only were the symbols and rituals present at her Shabbat table, but she was connected to their symbolic meanings, as well.

Developmentally appropriate activities from the earliest stages can lead to a crescendo of connections and associations about symbols, rituals, and values. Again, an example about Shoshana:

When Shoshana was about one, we bought a *Tzedakah* box. Every Friday night, we added some *Tzedakah* to the box. At first, she watched us put in the coins. Early on she struggled with the fine motor skills needed to pick up

the coins and place them in the coin slot of the *Tzedakah* box. She smiled with pride when she could get a coin in, and, of course, we applauded and lauded her achievements. As she got older, around three, after placing the coins in the *Tzedakah* box, we would ask her, "Why do we give *Tzedakah*?" She would parrot back that *Tzedakah* was for "sad" people. At age four, she transferred her preschool classroom learning to our Shabbat dinner table. She expanded on her explanation of *Tzedakah*, adding that it is for poor and hungry people. One day when we were at the grocery store checkout, she asked me for coins to put in the "*Tzedakah* box" that was on the counter to help "sad people." She had made the connection from our home *Tzedakah* box used on Shabbat to a collection can in a grocery store.

Developing fine motor skills is clearly a task that the pre-verbal child is trying to master. Giving *Tzedakah* just before Shabbat is clearly a way of connecting and fostering child development with a Jewish task. The physical act lays a foundation and leads to a more complete understanding of a concept and value. Both the physical, and later the verbal, gave Shoshana an active role in the Shabbat celebration.

NURTURING SPIRITUAL CHILDREN

Marvell Ginsburg, Director Emeritus, Department of Early Childhood, Community Foundation of Jewish Education in Chicago, warns teachers that God may "come" into the classroom, whether or not teachers consciously put God in the curriculum. If children are free to explore and encouraged to wonder, then children will bring God in through their discoveries and with their questions. If teachers do not support exploration and wonder with warmth and respect, then God is likely to be conspicuously absent from the classroom.

In order to let God into the classroom, teachers must be at least somewhat comfortable talking and thinking about God. This is certainly not to say that teachers must know what (or when) God is. If that were the case, very few people would consider themselves qualified to teach about God. Wolpe (1993) assures us that when it comes to talking about God and making meaning of our lives, we can often give what we don't have. In fact, it is not our task as adults to transmit to children an exact copy of our faith and idea of God. Rather, it is our task to use our own faith — questions, ideas, and even doubts — to help children develop their own faith. It is our responsibility to help children develop their own ideas of God in a way that is valuable and true both to the traditions we hold and to what we know about the world.

To help children, we do need to have some sense of our own faith, or spirituality, or idea of God. Before we can really hear and deal with children's questions about God, we need to have asked our own questions about God, and have sought out some answers. We don't necessarily need to have *found* the answers, but we must be looking. Remember, Jews are God-wrestlers — doubt is part of the equation. Yet, Gordis (1999) warns us about sharing too many of our doubts with young children. In every aspect of life, it is our duty to assure children that they are living in a good, secure, safe world. The same guidelines apply to helping children think about God. Though we should never lie to children, it is not dishonest to help children grow up believing that God is loving and caring and treasures every human being, including them.

Never be afraid to tell a child, "I don't know." It's okay, in fact, it's important, for children to know that grown-ups don't have all the answers about God (or most anything else in life). Rather than make up an answer to a child's question, which will only cause the child to mistrust or to have to unlearn later, tell a child, "I don't know. What do you think?" Then *listen* to the child's answer, and ask questions to help the child expand on his/her own ideas of God.

Our job as teachers is to allow children the space and safety to explore God. There are many strategies to help children think about how the world works. The most valuable world explorations come when children learn that each person is created *B'Tzelem Elohim* — in the image of God. Being created in God's image means that every person has value, every person is deserving of respect and caring. When children know that they are created *B'Tzelem Elohim*, their own self worth is bolstered, and it is safer, and easier, to ask questions about God and the rest of their world.

HELPING CHILDREN THINK ABOUT GOD

There are countless ways to find evidence of God in a child's everyday world. Try watching the clouds for a few minutes, or wondering together over the miracle of a child's hands as you wash up for snack. It is possible to create opportunities to explore God, as well. Later in this chapter, you will find lists of God-activities for every aspect of the curriculum, but the following is an example of one of the best ways to help children think about God.

Shirley Newman teaches about "discovering God's secrets" (Wachs, 1998). She suggests having children collect leaves that, at first glance, seem to be exactly the same. As the children examine the leaves, they will discover that, indeed, no two leaves are identical. Then, show the children a sheet of postage stamps or stack of matching postcards. Upon examination, the children will discover that these person-made things are all identical. They have just discovered one of life's secrets. When people make things using machines, the objects all come out the same. When God makes things in nature, no two are the same. The question then becomes, "Why did God do that?"

The easiest, and also the hardest, way to help children explore their questions about God is to make "God-talk" a regular, normal part of the classroom. Gordis tells us that God-talk is *not* teaching our children anything specific. "Rather, God-talk is about making our children comfortable with the word 'God' as a part of their regular vocabulary" (1999, p. 60). If teachers refer to God in a comfortable, regular manner, then children will know it is safe for them to talk about God, and safe for them to explore their own understandings of God (e.g., Let's thank God before we eat our snack. Why do you think God made the animals talk differently from us? Did God build this table? How did God help build this table?).

Much of what makes our classrooms Jewish are Jewish rituals and our celebrations of Shabbat and holidays. Rabbi Daniel B. Syme encourages grown-ups to use these opportunities to help connect children to God (Syme, 1989). Rituals are a way to communicate not only with words, but with gestures and actions. Actions open the door to feelings. Rituals open the door to communication with God, because rituals give us an opportunity to feel spiritual (Wolpe, 1993). If only we take advantage of these opportunities. Over the course of the year, the Jewish holidays give us a chance to consider God in many different lights: Supreme Sovereign on Rosh HaShanah, Author on Simchat Torah, Miracle Maker on Chanukah, Rescuer on Pesach, Creator every Shabbat. This affords us many different ways to think about God with our children.

Watch Out for ...

Teaching about God, prayer, and spirituality is not always easy. As open as preschoolers are to these quests, certain behaviors can interfere or discourage them. Presented below are some things to watch out for in teaching about God, prayer, or spirituality.

1. Create moments for talking about or exploring God, prayer, or spirituality, but do not push too hard.

   For all their wondering about life, some children may not be responsive to your queries or teachable moments. Pick and choose when you will probe. Do not push too hard. As with all other subjects, let as many of the questions and concerns as possible emerge from the students' interests and questions. With this subject, it is often better to let the children answer their own questions than for you to respond immediately. Once they have responded, then you can act as their guide, gently introducing new ideas through stories, role playing, and sharing.

2. Remember there is always more than one right answer.

   Views about God and prayer are abundant and diverse within Jewish tradition. People tend to focus on the meanings or understandings that they find most important. As with stories that present multiple lessons about life, values, relating to God, and so forth, what you find important may not be where the students are focusing. Usually no one right answer exists. That many answers are within the boundaries of Jewish tradition broadly understood does not mean that all interpretations are acceptable. Children from mixed marriages or from non-Jewish families often raise ideas about God, prayer, and spirituality that are inimical to Judaism. A secular society can also spawn notions and concepts that run counter to Jewish values. Suggestions about how to handle these situations are presented in #5 below.

3. Watch for how much time the children talk versus the teacher talking.

   If children are to explore their understandings and relationships to God, then they must do the sharing. If children are having a hard time speaking up or articulating their views, give them something to respond to such as a story, prayer, song, experience, newspaper article, happening. The learning experiences that you help set up are your way of initiating a conversation.

4. Watch out for theological and ideological red flags.

   Education occurs in a setting with an institutional philosophy and approach. This applies to how you treat students, approach curriculum, and teach about God, prayer, and spirituality. Parents, administrators, or community members may react strongly to the use of certain terms or language that seem to reflect views not usually espoused by the institution. For example, a weekly note in a Conservative preschool contained a mention that the children learned that *HaShem* (The Name) is everywhere. In that setting, it would be expected that God would be referred to as God, not by the term *HaShem*. That precipitated phone calls to the teacher and principal. One of the congregation's Rabbis asked about this, too. It turned out that a parent had introduced a song from another school, but this information was not originally provided. Know your school philosophy. Be sensitive also to gender references about God, as these can provoke strong reactions in an egalitarian or feminist sensitive environment.

5. When Brian says Jesus is God . . .

First, and above all, it is most important to validate each child's experience. Although we are often caught off guard by children bringing Christianity into our Jewish school, we shouldn't be, especially if we've done our homework. Sometimes non-Jewish families enroll their children in a Jewish school because it's the best school in town, because it's one block away from their house, because their friends go there, or for other such reasons. Many children from interfaith families are in Jewish schools, and come from homes or extended families with both a Jewish and Christian presence. Children from Jewish, even observant, families are exposed to Christianity in the world around them, and may bring their questions to school.

If we've done our homework, we will know about the families from which our children come. So when Brian says, "Mommy said Jesus is God," you will know enough about his family to validate his experience and respond, "Lots of people think lots of different things

about God. In Mommy's church, they believe Jesus is God. In Daddy's synagogue and at school, we believe only God is God. It's okay for people to think different things about God, because nobody knows for sure." When Chloe says, "I want a Christmas tree like the one in the mall," you can say, "Christmas trees are for Christian families. Your family is Jewish, and your family has a *chanukiah*." (For more discussion on the topic, see Chapter 28, "Interfaith Families/Non-Jewish Children.")

Margie Zeskind and Sheila Silverberg, authors of *The S.A.G.A. Approach (Sensitive Alternatives for Guiding Affectively)*, created a set of guidelines for Jewish early childhood educators who deal with religious diversity (which is likely to be most of us). They advise teachers to be accepting of different religious practices, and to reserve judgment when dealing with children and families. They write,

Be careful to consider that children will act upon their curiosities based on their personal experiences. Allow for the expression of these curiosities in environments that will not inhibit them. Encourage the children in their quest for autonomy, by offering positive guidance in the control and management of impulsivity, without causing the loss of a sense of wonder (p. 131).

It is important to remember that, beyond all the labels and even though specifics can vary from child to child, each child has a sense of wonder to be fostered, and a personal relationship to God which teachers can nurture.

PARTNERSHIP WITH PARENTS

Parents are the teacher's partners in helping children think about God. In a synagogue early childhood program, it is likely that most will share similar though not identical beliefs about God. In a JCC or community program, the boundaries are generally less defined, as families come from a wider range of affiliations. In any case, it is essential for teachers to let parents know at the beginning of the year that God will be a welcome, frequent topic of conversation in the classroom. Teachers should assure parents that their main goal is to facilitate children's own explorations of God. Teachers should encourage parents to let them know if they have specific ways of talking about God at home, or if they have special rituals at home which help their children connect to God, such as saying the *Shema* at bedtime, or blessing the children on Shabbat. This communication and ongoing sharing with parents will help achieve several things. It will help ensure that what goes on in the classroom will support and reinforce what is going on at home, thus validating the child. It will help alleviate any parental fears that children will be taught that God is something in which the parents do not believe. Finally, it will encourage parents to examine their own ideas about God, and help them talk to and support their children better. (For more ideas, see the chapter "Helping Parents Become Jewish Spiritual Guides for Their Children" by Rabbi Julie Greenberg in *Teaching about God and Spirituality*, edited by Roberta Louis Goodman and Sherry H. Blumberg.) Clergy and other Jewish community leaders can also be the teachers' partners in helping children think about God. (For more on these invaluable resource people, see Chapter 25, "Clergy and Other Community Leaders," p. 306.)

GOD AND SPIRITUALITY CONCEPTS

A child's relationship to God will change greatly with age. Although most children do not start asking questions about God until around the age of four, there are many ways to infuse the classroom with "God concepts" from the earliest age. Following is a list of appropriate "God-concepts" for every age.

Infant To 24 Months
1. Wonder is a part of every day.

2. Blessings and God-talk are a part of every day.
3. Jewish ritual objects are a part of every day.
4. Rituals and routines, from the mundane to the sacred, are a part of every day.
5. Children's relationships with parents and caregivers provide a foundation for a relationship with God.
6. Just as Adam and Eve named the animals in the Torah, so, too, do children begin speaking and connecting to their world by naming things and people.
7. As children begin to speak, they issue commands in order to gain control over their world.

2 Years
1. Wonder is a part of every day.
2. Blessings and God-talk are a part of every day.
3. Jewish ritual objects are a part of every day.
4. Prayer and blessings are a way to talk to God.
5. We wonder about things in nature.
6. We can try to be *kadosh* (holy) like God.
7. When we treat other people with love and *chesed*, we are acting like God.
8. Children's relationships with parents and caregivers provide a foundation for a relationship with God.

3 Years
1. We can speak about our feelings of wonder and ask questions about God.
2. Blessings and God-talk are a part of every day.
3. We use Jewish ritual objects and Jewish rituals as opportunities to talk about God.
4. Prayer and blessings are a way to talk to God.
5. We wonder about things in nature.
6. We can try to be *kadosh* (holy) like God.
7. When we treat other people with love and *chesed*, we are acting like God.
8. Each and every person is created *B'Tzelem Elohim*, in the image of God.
9. We are thankful for God's gifts.
10. God created the world. On Shabbat, God rested, and so do we.

4 To 5 Years

1. We can speak about our feelings of wonder and ask questions about God.
2. Blessings and God-talk are a part of every day.
3. We use Jewish ritual objects and Jewish rituals as opportunities to talk about God.
4. Prayer and blessings are a way to talk to God.
5. We can talk to God with prayers that other people wrote, or prayers that we make up in our own hearts.
6. We try to be *kadosh* (holy) like God.
7. When we treat other people with love and *chesed*, we are being like God.
8. Each and every person is created *B'Tzelem Elohim*, in the image of God.
9. We treat every person with respect and compassion because each person is created *B'Tzelem Elohim*.
10. We are thankful for God's gifts.
11. Blessings are a way of saying thank you to God.
12. God can be felt in other people, in nature, in ourselves, etc.
13. God created the world. On Shabbat, God rested, and so do we.
14. We can learn about God from the Torah, the *Siddur*, and Jewish stories.
15. No one knows everything about God, so we need to keep asking questions.
16. We can explore our understandings of and relationship with God with grown-ups, such as parents, teachers, and Rabbis.
17. We are connected to other Jewish people because we are all connected to God.
18. God has many names.
19. Shabbat and holidays provide different experiences and images of God.

NAMES FOR GOD

The young child needs something concrete to help him/her learn. The subject of God presents a special challenge to this need for something tangible. While Judaism teaches many different ideas about God, there is general agreement that God has no human body or form. Thus, pictures or images of God are not to be made by Jews. When God is mentioned in anthropomorphic ways (e.g., God rescued the Jews from Egypt with "an outstretched arm"), this reference is taken as symbolic or metaphorical — not literally.

How does one meet the concrete needs of the young child when teaching about God? The names of God are a particularly fertile source to help address this concern. A name is something to which children can relate. Children know their own names well before they can even speak. Older children may know that their names have alternative meanings, (e.g., Ari is a lion or Sarah is a person from the Torah). They also often know that they were given their name to honor a relative, living or dead, thereby attaching additional associations and history to their names.

The Torah and *Siddur*, and other Jewish texts, both classical and modern, are filled with names for God. In addition to the more traditional sources, songs, stories, and blessings also contain names of God. These names are suggestive of how we understand and relate to God. For example, we call God *Melech* (King or Sovereign), *Aveenu* (our Father or Parent), and *Boray* (Creator). Although these names are meant to be understood on a metaphorical level, we can use these many names to help us think about God. We can ask questions such as: How do we act around a king or queen? What does a parent do? How is God like a parent? What types of feelings do parents have for their children? What types of feelings do children have for their parents? How does God create things? (See *Sacred Fragments* by Neil Gillman for further reading.) Young children can relate to these names for God when these are tied to their experiences or captivated by their imaginations. Stories about their lives and about the lives of others, real or fictional, can stimulate their gaining a deeper understanding of and relationship to God when connected to the various names for God.

RELATING TO GOD AND PRAYER

God is central to Jewish life. The covenantal relationship between God and the Jewish people as expressed through Torah laid the foundation for both a people and a God that were expected to act ethically, justly, and compassionately. Prayer is a way of acknowledging the importance of this relationship to God in our lives. Some of the issues surrounding God and prayer are described below.

RELATING TO GOD

Jewish tradition upholds a belief in one God. But monotheism does not mean that there is only one way to think of God or to relate to God. Abraham and Sarah, Isaac and Rebekah, Moses, King David, Elijah, and Maimonides each had differing views of God. On one end of the spectrum, Abraham communicated often with God. They challenged one another. Abraham even argued with God. On the other end of the spectrum, Maimonides believed that one could say with certainty only what God is not, but could not conceive of what God is. Although a fervently committed and scholarly Jew, for Maimonides, God's presence was much more complicated and remote than it was for Abraham.

Doubting and questioning are normal in understanding and relating to God. Abraham questioned God's sense of justice in wanting to destroy the righteous along with the wicked in Sodom and Gomorrah. Throughout the wilderness experience, the Israelites expressed doubt again and again that God's promises would be fulfilled.

God commands. The *mitzvah* system is based on two kinds of commandments: those between God and human beings, and those between one person and another. In a Hasidic tale, one person asks: "Which is more important: to love God or to love your neighbor?" The teacher answers, "To love your neighbor. By loving your neighbor, your show your love for God. The opposite is not always true." How we treat others points to our view of God.

In addition to being based on *mitzvot* (commandments), Jewish moral behavior is characterized by a system of *middot* (virtues), such as: a sense of being *kadosh* (holy) or imitating God (*B'tzelem Elohim*), doing the right thing (*Derech Eretz*), and caring for others (*Gemilut Chasadeem*). Much of our God-talk revolves around these *middot*, and because of this, our moral behavior implies an underlying spirituality. Both *mitzvot* and *middot* are important elements to underscore in the early childhood classroom. When the early childhood teacher expects students to internalize and act on *mitzvot* and *middot*, he/she is building an environment open to spirituality and God.

PRAYER

Prayer takes on many different forms. Prayer can arise spontaneously from the heart or occur at set times in fixed forms. Praying is our conscious reminder and expression of our connection to God. When we recite prayers, we bless, praise, thank, petition, or exalt God. The prayer service has a fixed order and a set of prayers that for all the variations in language, melody, and philosophy are remarkably similar for Jews around the world. Prayer can be one person's utterance, or an experience recited in unison by a *minyan* (prayer community). Prayer can be uttered in one's home, or in the synagogue, or when walking on the way. Prayers are often spoken whenever and wherever Jews assemble for a wedding, a funeral, during *tashlich* near running water, at a conference in a meeting center, or at a family gathering in a restaurant.

Aside from the daily, Shabbat, and holiday prayer services, many occasions throughout the day, weeks, months, and lifetime of a Jew are cause for a prayer. The basic function of eating is an opportunity to recite blessings before and after a meal or snack. *Birchot HaNeheneem* (blessings for enjoyment) contain blessings for all sorts of events that occur in nature and society, such as hearing a clap of thunder, smelling a fragrant spice, or seeing a scholar. Life cycle events, the holidays, and new experiences give rise to many *"Shehe-cheyanu"* moments that reveal our days as being filled with blessing and joy. There are also special prayers that are meant to comfort us when we experience sorrow and pain.

PRAYING WITH KAVANAH

Kavanah is the concept of praying with intention and fervor. It means paying attention to what we are doing and saying. Its opposite is *keva*, which refers to prayer as a routine or set part of our lives. In fact, both are needed to make prayer a spiritual experience.

Music, dance, and movement are ways of reaching a level of *kavanah* with young children. Music is an important aspect of praying. Often, music is used to enhance or heighten the prayer experience. Traditional liturgy, Torah and Haftarah chanting, and many *brachot* have *nusacheem* (melodies) associated with them. Psalm 150 is a reminder of the various instruments — cymbals, harp, timbrel, horn, and lute — that were used to praise God in the Temple in Jerusalem. Today, melodies of all styles are written as interpretations of the prayers. Music is used to enhance or heighten the prayer experience and to inspire the prayer participant. As much of this prayer music is sung in the synagogue as is played on cassettes and CD players in cars and homes.

Music is a way of capturing the attention, hearts, and minds of young children. Music provides the possibility of enhancing the prayer experience. Young children are familiar with music as a learning tool and a way of expressing their emotions. Early childhood classrooms are filled with songs that teach children about values and relationships, remind them of rules and behaviors, and challenge their minds and imaginations. The challenge is for the early childhood educator to use music, the various tunes, and instruments to enrich the experience of *kavanah*, of learning to pay attention to prayers and praying.

Children are constantly in motion. Coordination of all sorts is a challenge to them. They learn through the normal course of daily activity about the parameters of what their bodies can and cannot do. Many of their successes and accomplishments relate to acquiring these skills from walking to somersaulting, eating with utensils to writing letters with crayons, painting with their figures, and cutting with scissors. Dance and movement can be used to capture the energy of using the body and motion, increasing the ability of the young child to connect to prayers and praying. Many of the prayers come with their own "choreography." When we recite the phrase in the *Kedushah*, "Holy, holy, holy," we rise up on our toes toward the heavens. Our bodies naturally move with the *lulav* as we shake it in all directions, up, down, forward, backward, to the right, and to the left. It is not uncommon to find dancing in the aisles at services to set a mood, to accompany the Torah when it is taken out of the Ark, or to celebrate a special *simchah* (joyful occasion), such as a wedding blessing. Some educators use movement and dance as activities to learn more about the prayers, Torah, and our relationship to God (see the chapters "Encountering God in Dance" by JoAnne Tucker and "Encountering Spirituality through Movement: Incorporating Nonverbal Expression into Jewish Education" by Kate Mann in *Teaching about God and Spirituality*, edited by Roberta Louis Goodman and Sherry H. Blumberg).

PRAYER SERVICE

The daily, Shabbat, and holiday prayer services are models of the way Jews view the world. Many of the prayers reflect the central narratives in Jewish tradition: creation, revelation, and redemption. Other prayers give us a sense of how Jews have survived over the ages. Prayers mirror the relationship between the Jewish people and God. Prayer is an expression of our highest ideals and expectations. It is the expression of a longing for a better world. The language of prayer is one of addressing and speaking to You, God: Baruch *Atah* — we praise *You*.

The Torah service is a special part of many prayer services. It is a reenactment of the giving and receiving of the Torah at Mt. Sinai. Tradition says that we all stood at Sinai. The Torah service recreates that experience. We stand when we take the Torah, God's words, out of the *Aron Kodesh* (Ark). In many synagogues, one takes the Torah down from the *bimah* (pulpit) and brings it to the people standing, much as Moses took the tablets from the mountain down to the Israelites. We read the words from the Torah that God spoke to Moses. At the end, we raise the Torah up, show off the words, and declare that they were the words that Moses received from God. (For further information on the Torah service as it relates to the early childhood setting, see Chapter 5, "Sharing Torah.")

BLESSINGS FOR THE EVERYDAY

The Rabbis tell us that we should thank God at least 100 times a day. To this end, there are blessings for almost every aspect of our lives: when we eat, when we see a tree flowering for the first time, when we hear thunder, when we see a rainbow, when we wear a new garment for the first time, even when we experience an earthquake. Using daily blessings with children is a wonderful way to bring God-talk into the classroom, and to help children see how God is so much a part of their lives.

David Wolpe teaches about "normal mysticism" (1993). A "normal mystic," he says, is someone who constantly sees the closeness of God reflected in the world around him or her. Using blessings for daily events instead of just saying "Oh wow" helps us see the world as normal mystics. By blessing God for things in our world, we remind ourselves on a daily basis of God's presence in the world. The bibliography at the end of this chapter lists several beautifully illustrated collections of prayers and blessings that are appropriate for use with children on a daily basis.

Some of these blessings are listed below. Be aware that it is not necessary to use and teach all of them on a regular basis; pick one or two, such as "*Modeh Anee*" or the *Shema*, to integrate into your classroom every day. Others can be used at appropriate moments, such as during a lightning storm or when smelling flowers during a nature walk.

Traditionally recited in the morning upon waking:

מוֹדֶה אֲנִי לְפָנֶיךָ מֶלֶךְ חַי וְקַיָּם
שֶׁהֶחֱזַרְתָּ בִּי נִשְׁמָתִי בְּחֶמְלָה רַבָּה אֱמוּנָתֶךָ.

Modeh Anee L'fanecha, Melech Chai, V'kayam,
Sheh-hechezarta Bee Neeshmatee B'Chem'lah,
Rabah Emunatecha.

Thank you, God of everything, for the morning when I wake again to You.

Traditionally recited upon seeing natural phenomena, such as lightning, mountains, rivers, and even experiencing an earthquake:

בָּרוּךְ אַתָּה יְיָ אֱלֹהֵינוּ מֶלֶךְ הָעוֹלָם
עֹשֶׂה מַעֲשֵׂה בְרֵאשִׁית.

Baruch Atah Adonai Elohaynu Melech HaOlam
Oseh Ma'aseh V'raysheet.

We praise you, our God, Creator of the universe, Who made the wonders of creation.

Traditionally recited when seeing a rainbow, which, according to the story of Noah in the Torah, is a sign of God's promise never to destroy the world by flood again:

בָּרוּךְ אַתָּה יְיָ אֱלֹהֵינוּ מֶלֶךְ הָעוֹלָם
זוֹכֵר הַבְּרִית וְנֶאֱמָן בִּבְרִיתוֹ וְקַיָּם בְּמַאֲמָרוֹ.

Baruch Atah Adonai Elohaynu Melech HaOlam,
Zocher HaBreet V'Ne'eman Be'vreeto v'Kayam
b'Ma'amaro.

We praise you, our God, Creator of the universe, Who remembers the covenant and fulfills promises.

Traditionally recited when smelling flowers and herbs:

בָּרוּךְ אַתָּה יְיָ אֱלֹהֵינוּ מֶלֶךְ הָעוֹלָם
בּוֹרֵא עִשְׂבֵי בְשָׂמִים.

Baruch Atah Adonai Elohaynu Melech HaOlam Boray Ees-vay V'sameem.

We praise you, our God, Creator of the universe, Who creates fragrant flowers and herbs.

Traditionally recited upon seeing a Torah scholar or Rabbi:

בָּרוּךְ אַתָּה יְיָ אֱלֹהֵינוּ מֶלֶךְ הָעוֹלָם
שֶׁחָלַק מֵחָכְמָתוֹ לִירֵאָיו.

Baruch Atah Adonai Elohaynu Melech HaOlam Sheh-cha'lak Maychoch'ma'to Lee'ray'av.

We praise you, our God, Creator of the universe, Who has given knowledge to those who respect God.

Traditionally recited upon hearing good news:

בָּרוּךְ אַתָּה יְיָ אֱלֹהֵינוּ מֶלֶךְ הָעוֹלָם הַטּוֹב וְהַמֵּטִיב.

Baruch Atah Adonai Elohaynu Melech HaOlam, HaTov V'HaMayteev.

We praise you, our God, Creator of the universe, Who is good and the source of all goodness.

Traditionally recited when comfort is needed:

בָּרוּךְ אַתָּה יְיָ אֱלֹהֵינוּ מֶלֶךְ הָעוֹלָם
הַנּוֹתֵן לַיָּעֵף כֹּחַ.

Baruch Atah Adonai, Elohaynu Melech HaOlam, HaNo'tayn L'Ya'ayf Koach.

We praise you, our God, Creator of the universe, Who helps me when I am sad and tired.

The *Shema* is central to Jewish prayer, because it states a belief in one unique God. It is also our bedtime prayer.

שְׁמַע יִשְׂרָאֵל יְיָ אֱלֹהֵינוּ יְיָ אֶחָד.

Shema Yisrael Adonai Elohaynu Adonai Echad.

Listen, Children of Israel: *Adonai* is our God, *Adonai* is One.

Traditionally said for new experiences, joyous occasions and for tasting new fruits:

בָּרוּךְ אַתָּה יְיָ אֱלֹהֵינוּ מֶלֶךְ הָעוֹלָם
שֶׁהֶחֱיָנוּ וְקִיְּמָנוּ וְהִגִּיעָנוּ לַזְּמַן הַזֶּה.

Baruch Atah Adonai Elohaynu Melech HaOlam Shehecheyanu V'keeyamanu V'Higeeyanu LaZ'man HaZeh.

We praise you, our God, Creator of the universe, for giving us life, sustaining us, and helping us to reach this moment.

Of course, we say blessings when we eat. Traditionally said over bread at meals:

בָּרוּךְ אַתָּה יְיָ אֱלֹהֵינוּ מֶלֶךְ הָעוֹלָם
הַמּוֹצִיא לֶחֶם מִן הָאָרֶץ.

Baruch Atah Adonai Elohaynu Melech HaOlam HaMotzee Lechem Min HaAretz.

We praise you, our God, Creator of the universe, for making seeds grow in the ground so that we can make bread.

Traditionally said over baked goods other than bread:

בָּרוּךְ אַתָּה יְיָ אֱלֹהֵינוּ מֶלֶךְ הָעוֹלָם בּוֹרֵא מִינֵי מְזוֹנוֹת.

Baruch Atah Adonai Elohaynu Melech HaOlam Boray Minay M'zonot.

We praise you, our God, Creator of the universe, Who created all kinds of food.

Traditionally said over snacks and other kinds of food:

בָּרוּךְ אַתָּה יְיָ אֱלֹהֵינוּ מֶלֶךְ הָעוֹלָם שֶׁהַכֹּל נִהְיֶה בִּדְבָרוֹ.

Baruch Atah Adonai Elohaynu Melech HaOlam Sheh HaKol N'heeyeh Bid'varo.

We praise you, our God, Creator of the universe, Who made everything with a word.

Traditionally recited over fruit from trees:

בָּרוּךְ אַתָּה יְיָ אֱלֹהֵינוּ מֶלֶךְ הָעוֹלָם בּוֹרֵא פְּרִי הָעֵץ.

Baruch Atah Adonai Elohaynu Melech HaOlam Boray P'ree HaAytz.

We praise you, our God, Creator of the universe, Who created the fruit of the tree.

A very short version of the traditional blessing after meals:

בָּרוּךְ אַתָּה יְיָ הַזָּן אֶת-הַכֹּל

Baruch Atah Adonai, Chazan et HaKol.

We praise you, our God, Who provides our food.

BLESSINGS FOR THE HOLIDAYS

Shabbat and each of the holidays incorporate blessings that are specific to the rituals and celebrations connected to that holiday. You can find these blessings in each of the holiday chapters in Part III. The holidays provide wonderful opportunities to connect children to God. The blessings of each holiday are an awesome vehicle for achieving this. Rather than just saying the blessing for or with children, explore the concepts included in each blessing. Why would God command us to shake the *lulav* and *etrog*? How did God create the fruit of the vine? Why did God command us to eat *matzah* and not cheese crackers? Using the blessings of each holiday, you and your children can become normal mystics, and see God in everything around you.

INTEGRATING SPIRITUALITY AND GOD INTO THE EVERYDAY

ISSUES

Spirituality is a word that is widely used, but loosely defined. Spirituality has to do with a person's relationship to God and recognition of the sacred in life, often without reference to any formal religion. Spirituality is frequently viewed as a turning inward. Meditation, yoga, reciting a mantra, and other alternative forms of getting in touch with one's body and soul are often associated with the term. Spirituality appears to be an individualized, personalized, and idiosyncratic phenomenon.

While Hebrew lacks an authentic term for spirituality, *ruchaniyut* is the literal translation. Spirituality in a Jewish context has some important properties. Relating to God and being holy involve communal as well as individual expressions and experiences. Judaism requires no intermediary for relating to God, allowing for the individual to experience directly God's immanence or presence in the world. While such an individual or personal relationship is encouraged, Judaism balances the personal with the communal. Witnessing a ceremony such as a wedding or Bar/Bat Mitzvah, participating in a mourner's *minyan*, offering a *Mi Shebayrach* (prayer for healing), or attending a *Seder*, present themselves as opportunities for experiencing the sacred as a community. Finding a spiritual direction in Jewish life is as much a communal quest as it is a personal one. The recent creation of new rituals for events as wide-ranging as miscarriages and retirement, Rosh Chodesh for women's groups, and the proliferation of beautiful ritual objects is a sign that people are seeking spirituality in their lives. In addition, the experimentation and innovation going on in many congregations (e.g., the offering of special prayers or services for healing; dancing with the Torah; new rituals, such as welcoming all babies born during the year on Simchat Torah) are forging communal experiences that touch people deeply and promote a sense of personal spirituality.

Spirituality in a Jewish context balances that which is fixed and routine, *keva,* with that which is spontaneous and heartfelt, *kavanah.* These are in constant tension in terms of prayer. Tradition emphasizes the importance of the fixed and obligatory aspects of Jewish ritual and prayer, yet the mind and heart seek experiences that are passionate and meaningful.

INTEGRATING GOD AND SPIRITUALITY INTO THE CURRICULUM

God can be invited into the classroom through innumerable "teachable moments": saying a blessing upon the announcement of a new sibling, helping children grapple with their "God ques-

tion" of the moment. The subject of God can also be planned into the curriculum. Although a one or two-week unit of "God and Spirituality" would probably not do much in the way of allowing children to explore their ideas of God and increase their own spirituality, the following activities can be scattered throughout the curricular year.

LANGUAGE ARTS

1. Tell or read stories that include or teach about God. Torah stories, *midrashim*, folktales, and modern stories can be used to help explore different aspects of God.
2. After reading stories with God as a character, act out the story. Let several children have a chance to be God. Then ask, "How did it feel to be God?"
3. Take a prayer and analyze it. What does it mean? Make concrete connections for children between the prayer and the associated actions or feelings.
4. Say blessings before you eat a snack or meal.
5. Make a bulletin board of "God's Blessings." Include pictures of the children and their families, and/or let children bring in pictures of things that to them are God's blessings.
6. Let each child "become" a Torah. Make a Torah cover out of a pillowcase or paper bag. Help the children make the crown, breastplate, and *yad* to wear. Let each child choose his/her favorite story from the Torah to illustrate, and pin that on the "Torah cover." Have a different child wear the cover during story time each day.
7. Write letters to God.

SCIENCE

1. Examine ritual objects, and help children make connections between the objects and God.
2. Go on a nature walk. Take magnifying glasses with you. Smell. Touch. Experience nature.
3. Bring an animal into class. Watch the animal. Discuss what keeps it alive. Talk about our responsibilities to the animal and how caring for the animal makes us partners with God.

4. Demonstrate how people and God are partners in the world. Serve orange juice for a snack. Ask the children who made the orange juice. Let them know that God did not make the juice, but that God helped. People helped, too. Talk about how God helped the orange tree grow, but people picked the oranges, squeezed the juice, got the oranges to the store, etc. Give the children oranges cut into quarters, and let them squeeze out the juice. Say the appropriate blessing (. . . *Boray P'ree HaAytz*) before you drink the juice.

5. When children ask about where God is, or how we know God exists if we can't see God, take a glass of water and some sugar. Let the children taste the plain water. Put the sugar in the water and stir it until all the sugar dissolves. Can the children see the sugar? Let the children taste the sugar water. Can they tell the sugar is in the water, even though they can't see it? It is the same with God. We can find evidences of God in the world, even if we cannot see God.

6. When we look deeper, we find many unexpected things. Using magnifying glasses, examine a handful of soil to find the different phenomena present. The children might see tiny rocks, bits of leaves, bugs or parts of bugs, and some things they can't identify.

MATH

1. Learn the *Shema*. Study the number 1. Is the number 1 always unique? Why is God unique? What makes God special? What makes each person special?

2. With older children, examine some Jewish numbers: 1 God, 7 Days of Creation, 8 days of Chanukah, 40 days and nights of rain, 40 years in the desert, and so on. How are these numbers connected to God? How do numbers make us think of other things?

3. Make a series of feelie bags with a different number of Jewish objects in each bag. Let the children not only identify the objects, but count how many objects are in each bag. For younger children, use multiples of the same object in each bag; for older children, use different objects in each bag. Have children identify which objects God made and which objects people made.

4. Make a chart of the Jewish rituals that each child in the class does with his or her family, such as saying blessings over food, saying the bedtime *Shema*, eating Friday night dinner together, etc.

5. Sort play foods according to what blessing we say.

6. Count the number of times God is mentioned in various *brachot*.

ART

1. Let children finger paint to prayer melodies. How does the prayer make them feel? How does that influence their painting?

2. Learn the *Shema*. Make a collage about the number 1. Why is God one?

3. Make a mobile of the different types of foods that go with each food blessing. Let children cut out pictures of foods from magazines. Practice saying the different *brachot* together. At snack time, let children decide which is the appropriate blessing, depending on what is being served.

4. Read the story of creation. Let the children cut out pictures from a magazine and make a creation mural. Or make a creation book, using different media for each day.

5. Make a picture with seeds, as part of the ongoing cycle of creation.

6. Make a leaf collage.

7. Let children cut out pictures of God's creations: people, animals, plants, etc. Make a class collage, or let each child make his/her own picture. For individual pictures, cut up into puzzles (three to four pieces for two-year-olds; four to six pieces for threes, and six to ten pieces for four-year-olds), and store in Ziploc bags.

8. Make ritual objects out of scrap and recycled materials. Let the children know it is not the materials that make an object holy or sacred, but rather how we use them.

9. Make a collage out of God's names. Help the children find pictures that represent all the names of God they know.

MUSIC/MOVEMENT

1. Learn different melodies for prayers and use them.

2. Play tapes of *niggunim* and prayers during class or rest time.

3. Let children move and dance to the music of various prayers.

4. Sing the *Shema*. Compare singing the *Shema* with saying it, and compare singing it while covering the eyes, and with eyes uncovered.

5. Play an adaptation of *Red Light, Green Light*. Leader calls out various activities, and children move if they should do them, do not move if they should not do them. For example, the leader might call out: celebrate Shabbat, tell the truth, hit your brother, eat before saying a blessing. This game helps children think about the concept of being commanded.

6. Make a learning center that features Jewish and secular sounds. You might include, among other things, a *shofar, gragger,* a tape recording of Shabbat prayers, an alarm clock, a bell, a radio, a musical instrument. Let the children sort each of these into categories. Help the children think about what makes a sound Jewish.

7. Teach the children a prayer such as *"Sim Shalom"* or a song such as *"Hinay Mah Tov."* Talk about the meaning of the prayer or song, and have children develop movements to go with it. Put it all together and make a music video to show the parents.

CIRCLE TIME

1. Make show-and-tell a time to share Jewish symbols or ritual objects from home.

2. Have a tasting party to demonstrate the *brachah* for different foods. Eat apples, oranges, pears, and other tree fruits, and recite *". . . Boray P'ree HaAytz."* Eat *challah*, pita, and sandwiches and recite *"HaMotzi . . ."*

3. Show the children pictures of different kinds of people — from different cultures, of different abilities, with a wide age span. Ask the children how each of these people was created *B'Tzelem Elohim*.

4. After learning the story of Noah, make a large rainbow mural, and on it write each child's response to the question: "I promise to take care of the world by _____."

5. When children ask how to tell that God is there if we can't see God, pair each child with a friend. Tell the children to feel each other's hair, arm, toes, love. When children are not sure where to find the love so they can feel it, ask them if they know the love is there. We may not be able to touch God, but we know that God is there.

OUTDOORS/FIELD TRIPS

1. Take a nature walk. Look for evidences of creation. Look for evidences of day and night, wind and rain, the cycle of the seasons.

2. Visit a sanctuary. Allow lots of time for children to explore what makes them think of God, or "feel" God, in the sanctuary. Why do some people say that it's easier to talk to God in the sanctuary? Is that true?

3. Go on a "Thankful Scavenger Hunt." Either inside or outside the school, let the children search for things (and people) for which they are thankful. For younger children, teachers can make a list or take photos. Older children can draw pictures of the things they find, or look for one thing for every letter of the alphabet. Back in the classroom, teachers can help children find appropriate blessings for each of the things they found, or help the children write their own blessings.

4. Go on a *"Brachot* Treasure Hunt." Teach children the blessings over some things they might

find in and around the school (such as a scholar/Rabbi, *mezuzah*, food, Torah, etc.). Let the children go in search of the things for which they have learned a blessing, and say the blessing when they find it.

5. Go to the zoo to see God's creatures great and small. Talk about why God created so many different kinds of animals.

6. Be like God and help take care of other people. Visit a nursing home and sing songs, or help take care of a younger class.

7. Go to the supermarket. What did God create? What did people create? How are God and people partners?

Specifically for Infants

1. Play tapes with prayers and other Jewish music.
2. Kiss the *mezuzah* as you go through the door.
3. Sing the *Shema* to and with babies, especially when putting them down for nap.
4. Make sure God-talk is part of the regular vocabulary of the class as you talk to babies about their world.
5. Talk to babies about the wonderful things happening to them every day, and about all the ways they are growing.

Ideas for Teaching Families

1. Encourage families to create sacred space in their home. To create sacred space, put on the refrigerator or a bulletin board pictures from magazines or photographs of things that are reminiscent of God — e.g. sunset, child(ren)'s faces, favorite food, and so forth.

2. Encourage families to have ritual objects at home that are child safe and age appropriate that children can really play with. Provide families with suggestions of appropriate items and where to find them.

3. Give families the tools they need to use their evening ritual time as a time to tell stories about God and prayer. Sandy Sasso has written many beautiful stories about God.

4. Encourage families to get in tune with creation, both that of God's doing and that inspired by

God but created by human beings. For starters, families could gaze at the moon and the stars, go on nature walks, and center some dinner-time conversation about the most beautiful thing each family member saw that day.

5. Alert families to events at local synagogues and in the Jewish community geared toward young families, such as Tot Shabbat services or family retreats.

6. Recommended Reading: *Teaching Your Children About God* by David Wolpe, and *When Children Ask About God : A Guide for Parents Who Don't Always Have All the Answers* by Harold Kushner.

ENVIRONMENT

Environment contributes to a sense of the sacred, holy. Many ways exist to transform the classroom into a space that promotes a sense of *kedushah* (holiness) and spirituality, relating to God. Design interactive bulletin boards that focus on spiritual themes and occasions for blessings (e.g., announcements about new family members, special celebrations, and so forth). Other displays can portray miracles in our lives (e.g., new drug helps a family member get better, four generations come together to celebrate a Bat Mitzvah of a family member, or a family moves into a new home). Still other bulletin boards or displays can depict the majesty of creation (e.g., pictures of beautiful plants or animals, remains of plants or animals such as feathers or blossoms, and photographs of the sun and sky).

The classroom space can be transformed in other ways by creatively using the environment. One eighth grade teacher created sacred space in her classroom by bringing her home to the classroom. She set a table with a beautiful tablecloth and ritual objects that were important to her, such as Shabbat candlesticks, a *Kiddush* cup, a *challah* plate, and a *chanukiah*. The presence of these symbols and the stories that she told about them were daily reminders to her students of what was sacred in her life.

Schools have sacred spaces, too. Some programs are located in buildings with sanctuaries or chapels, museums or displays of ritual objects, or inspirational artwork. Opportunities to experience these special spaces can be used to create memorable moments, foster a feeling of comfort, and familiarize the young child with these places and the objects in them.

Schools can create other sacred spaces. As part of the Rosh Chodesh celebration at several preschools in the Chicago area, the children identify a space that they go to in recognition of each new Hebrew month. Some situate themselves under a certain tree on the grounds, others select the location because of the view around them, and some choose a bench or comfortable place to sit. Each month the children review the ways in which their lives have changed at home or in the classroom. They talk about a new animal or baby, a special project or concept, a birthday, or a holiday. They turn an ordinary space into a special, sacred space for their class. (For more information on this program, see Chapter 8 in this book, "Rosh Chodesh," p. 134, and the chapter "Rosh Chodesh: The Jewish Time Keeper" by Maxine Segal Handelman in *Teaching about God and Spirituality*, edited by Roberta Louis Goodman and Sherry H. Blumberg.)

Jewish early childhood educators can play a significant role in laying the foundations for children's relationships to God and their spiritual selves. As you embark on your search for God, you will be able to assist children as they set out on journeys of their own.

BIBLIOGRAPHY

ADULT

Coles, Robert. "The Spirit Within." *Parenting* X (10), December/January 1996, 116-118.
> Children have a natural sense of wonder and spirituality. It is up to the grown-ups around them to honor and support this by taking seriously children's spiritual lives.

———. *The Spiritual Life of Children.* Boston: Houghton Mifflin, 1990.
> A fascinating investigation of children from several religions and cultures, and their relationships to God and their spiritual selves.

Danan, Julie Hilton. *The Jewish Parents' Almanac.* Northvale, NJ: Jason Aronson Inc., 1993.
> A wonderful resource for parents interested in creating and maintaining a Jewish family.

Kushner, Harold. *When Children Ask about God: A Guide for Parents Who Don't Always Have All the Answers.* New York: Schocken Books, 1995.
> This book, which was originally published in 1971, was one of the first guides for Jewish parents on how to talk to their children about God. Kushner's advice is timeless.

Gillman, Neil. *Sacred Fragments: Recovering Theology for the Modern Jew.* Philadelphia: Jewish Publication Society, 1990.
> A thoughtful, informative review of leading ideas and issues in Jewish philosophy. National Jewish Book Award recipient.

Goodman, Roberta Louis, and Sherry H. Blumberg, eds. *Teaching about God and Spirituality.* Denver, CO: A.R.E. Publishing, Inc., forthcoming.
> A comprehensive anthology with chapters that present theory and practice on teaching about God and spirituality.

Gordis, Daniel. *Becoming a Jewish Parent: How to Explore Spirituality and Tradition with Your Children.* New York: Harmony Books, 1999.
> A guide for parents who want to introduce Judaism into their homes so that their children can grow up loving, understanding, and cherishing their heritage.

Leder, Steven Z. *The Extraordinary Nature of Ordinary Things.* West Orange, NJ: Behrman House, 1999.
> Through funny and sometimes poignant vignettes, Rabbi Leder connects everyday events to the teachings of Judaism.

Syme, Daniel B. "Talking To Kids about God." In *The Hadassah Magazine Jewish Parenting Book.* Edited by Roselyn Bell. New York: The Free Press, 1989.
> A collection of essays from the parenting column in issues of *Hadassah Magazine* from 1984 to 1989.

Wachs, Saul. "Talking To Little Children about God." *Jewish Education News* 19 (3), Fall 1998, pp. 35-36.
> We can encourage children to "do theology" — to think about God. As we do so, they are learning to make meaning of their experience through God-talk.

Wolpe, David J. *Teaching Your Children about God: A Modern Jewish Approach.* New York: Henry Holt and Company, 1993.
> A beautiful book, filled with *midrashim*; perfect for helping adults help children to discover God.

Zeskind, Margie, and Sheila Silverberg. *The S.A.G.A. Approach (Sensitive Alternatives for Guiding Affectively).* Miami, FL: Shemar Productions, 1996.
> Guidelines for educators in Jewish early childhood settings dealing with religious diversity.

CHILDREN

Bogot, Howard I., and Daniel B. Syme. *I Learn about God.* New York: UAHC Press, 1982. (Ages 3-5)
> This book approaches God through the eyes of a child sensitive to the wonders of nature and the miracle of growth.

Bogot, Howard I. *Becky and Benny Thank God.* New York: CCAR Press, 1996. (Ages infant-2)
> A "Pat-the-Bunny"-type book of all the things we are thankful to God for. (Board Book)

Brichto, Mira Pollak. *The God Around Us: A Child's Garden of Prayer.* rev. ed. New York: UAHC Press, 1999. (All ages)
> Blessings for the wondrous experiences of everyday life, over mountains, blooming trees, and different kinds of people, to list a few.

———. *The God Around Us, Volume II: Unending Wonder.* New York: UAHC Press, 2000. (All ages)
> More scenes of wonder and the blessings that accompany them.

Cone, Molly. *Hello, Hello, Are You There, God?* New York: UAHC Press, 1999. (Ages 3-7)
> A collection of stories that teach children what it means to be a part of the Jewish people, to cherish learning, and to love God.

Edwards, Michelle. *Blessed Are You.* New York: Lothrop, Lee & Shepard Books, 1993. (All ages)
> Traditional everyday Hebrew prayers.

Goodman, Roberta Louis. *A Test of Faith.* Los Angeles: Torah Aura Productions, Inc., 1985. (Ages 12-Adult)
> An instant lesson that introduces faith development.

Groner, Judye, and Madeline Wikler. *Thank You, God! A Jewish Child's Book of Prayers.* Rockville, MD: KarBen Copies, 1993. (All ages)
> A Jewish child's book of prayers.

Hample, Stuart, and Eric Marshall, eds. *Children's Letters To God: The New Collection.* New York: Workman Publishing, 1991. (Ages 2-adult)
> An insightful, often hysterically funny look at the questions children ask God.

Rich, Scharlotte. *Who Made the Wild Woods?* New York: Waterbrook Press, 1999. (Ages 4-8)
> As children follow animal characters on a romp through the woods, they discover that God made the woods and everything therein, including themselves.

Ruthen, Gerald C. *Daniel and the Silver Flute: An Old Hassidic Tale.* New York: United Synagogue Commission on Jewish Education, 1986. (Ages 3-7)
> Although he has trouble learning and participating in the synagogue services, Daniel discovers that his talent for playing the flute enables him to pray to God in his own way.

Sasso, Sandy Eisenberg. *God in Between.* Woodstock, VT: Jewish Lights Publishing, 1998. (Ages 5-10)
> When two people leave their lonely, confused town to find out if God really exists, they make an amazing discovery about where God can be found.

———. *In God's Name.* Woodstock, VT: Jewish Lights Publishing, 1994. (Ages 5-10)
> Everyone and everything in the world has a name. What is God's name?

———. *What Is God's Name?* Woodstock, VT: Jewish Lights Publishing, 1999. (Ages Infant-3)
> An abridged, board book version of Sasso's *In God's Name.* In this book, children will see and hear the many names people have for God. The first book of a new series called Early Childhood Spirituality. (Board Book)

Sose, Bonnie L. *Designed by God So I Must Be Special.* Winter Park, FL: Character Builders for Kids, 1988. (Ages 3-8)
> Details all of the ways God made each of us special.

Thompson, Marlena C., and Susan Van Dusen. *Let's Discover God: Teacher's Edition.* West Orange, NJ: Behrman House, 1998. (Ages 5-8)
> Simple poems, hands-on learning games, questions to ask, things to talk about, parent letters, and more, expose children to the beauty of God's world, and to basic prayers and blessings.

Wells, Rosemary. *Forest of Dreams.* New York: Dial Books for Young Readers, 1988. (Ages 2-8)
> Beautiful illustrations tell the story of all the things God made in us.

Wood, Douglas. *Old Turtle.* Duluth, MN: Pfeifer-Hamilton Publishers, 1992. (Ages 4+)
> In this beautifully illustrated book, the animals try to figure out what God is.

Children's Siddurim

Dvir, Azriel, and Mazal Mashat. *My Little Siddur: A Child's First Prayerbook*. New York: Adama Books, 1997. (Ages 3-7)

> Based on the Israeli version of *HaSiddur Sheli*, this *Siddur* from the Orthodox movement contains photographs of Israeli children and basic prayers for children.

Fine, Doreen, et al. *The Chief Rabbi's Children's Siddur*. West Hampstead, England: Jewish Continuity, 1995.

> Designed to bridge the gap between picture prayer books and a complete *Siddur*, this Orthodox *Siddur* from England contains Hebrew Text with translations and explanations, photographs and illustrations.

Isaacs, Ronald H., and Daniel Pressman. *Shir Chadash*. Hoboken, NJ: KTAV Publishng House, 1994. (Ages 6-12)

> A Sabbath and festival prayer book for youth and families, this *Siddur* uses gender neutral language and features original translations that are both fresh and spiritually enhancing. It is very suitable for *havurot* and family services.

Orkand, Robert; Joyce Orkand; and Howard I. Bogot. *Gates of Wonder: A Prayerbook for Very Young Children*. New York: Central Conference of American Rabbis, 1989. (Ages 2-5)

> A very simple book about prayer, God, and wonder. From the Reform Movement.

Pallay, Eva. *Sidduri*. New York: United Synagogue of Conservative Judaism, 1983.

> Lavishly illustrated book containing short lines of well-known prayers in large type, and original poems based on these quotations. Audiocassette also available.

Scharfstein, Sol, and Edythe Scharfstein. *My First Book of Prayers*. Hoboken, NJ: KTAV Publishing House, 1958. (Ages 5-9)

> This *Siddur* has great merit because the approach to prayer is positive, expressing appreciation and gratitude. Contains jingles and rhymes.

Silberman, Shoshana. *Siddur Shema Yisrael*. New York: United Synagogue of Conservative Judaism, 1996.

> A user-friendly *Siddur* for children ages eight through 13, junior congregations, and family services. Illustrated with two-color pages and gender free translations, it features discussion starters, stories, thoughts and questions. Also an excellent source book for teachers and families.

Walter, Roy A., and Kenneth D. Roseman. *Gates of Prayer for Young People*. New York: CCAR Press, 1997.

> A series of Shabbat and weekday services geared toward children in Grades 1 to 3 from the Reform movement.

CHAPTER 5

SHARING TORAH

Turn it and turn it; everything is contained in it.
(Pirke Avot 5:25)

The Torah is the greatest treasure of the Jewish people. By definition, the Torah consists of the Five Books of Moses: Genesis, Exodus, Numbers, Leviticus, and Deuteronomy. In its broadest definition, however, Torah encompasses the entire body of Jewish texts from the Hebrew Bible to later Rabbinical texts. Torah also is used as a generic term for Jewish studies of all kinds. Sharing the stories about Torah events and Torah people with young children promotes the development of Jewish identity. The Torah tells the story of the Jewish people's relationship with God, and enables children to meet God as an active force in their own story. Not only do children learn the history of their people and gain connection to holidays and the Jewish calendar through Torah, but they can become "Torah scholars," asking questions about the text and grappling with the answers in the same way that Jewish scholars have for countless generations. Jewish values that we strive to teach our children are woven through the Torah. When we share Torah stories, we give children yet another way to think about and deal with their own day-to-day life. A love for Jewish learning is one of the greatest things Jewish early childhood educators can give a child.

The concepts and values that come out of the Torah — *Tzedakah*, respect for all people, wonder for nature, hospitality, caring for others, and so on — are appropriate and relevant to all children, from the youngest of infants. Not all Torah stories are appropriate for every age child. While some stories are valuable to share with two and three-year-olds — Noah's Ark and Abraham and Sarah hosting guests, for example — ongoing study of Torah as the comprehensive story of the Jewish people is not developmentally appropriate for children below the age of four.

Presented below are strategies for sharing the Torah with very young children, age three and under, and for connecting children to the physical Torah and the rituals surrounding Torah. However, the bulk of this chapter is devoted to exploring different strategies for sharing Torah with four and five-year-olds, and with ways to integrate Torah stories and values into the classroom and curriculum.

A glossary and Hebrew vocabulary list may be found in figure 5 on the following page.

SHARING TORAH WITH VERY YOUNG CHILDREN

Since Torah is a treasure given to the Jewish people by God, when we see the Torah, we are filled with joy. This is a very important concept, which can be taught to very young children, even infants. When I am in synagogue on Shabbat morning, I watch the parents who bring their infants and toddlers to services with them. When the Torah is taken out of the *Aron Kodesh*, suddenly these parents are at attention. They hold their baby's hand so that the baby can touch the Torah as it passes by, and then they kiss their baby's hand. Parents of toddlers direct their children to the *Aron Kodesh* so they can see the Torah taken out, or they pick up their child so the child can touch the Torah as it passes. Young children clutch brightly colored stuffed Torahs and parade around just as grown-ups do with the actual Torah.

These wise parents are teaching their children to be excited about the Torah, to look forward to seeing it, and to be filled with the wonder of it, even though the infants and toddlers do not understand what's inside. In fact, once the hoopla of the marching and singing is over, and the Torah reading begins, oftentimes the young children are taken from the room or otherwise entertained with books or quiet toys. For very young children to sit quietly and listen to the reading or chanting of the Torah is developmentally inappropriate. But this does not diminish the possibility of instilling in them a love and excitement for the Torah.

It is also possible to foster this same love and excitement in the classroom setting. Begin by exposing the children to Torah. A few stuffed Torahs, store bought or homemade, should be permanent fixtures of every classroom. (These are not just for very young children; fours and fives should have stuffed Torahs, too, in addition to Torahs they can unroll and "read.") These stuffed Torahs should be a special part of the classroom. Children should be encouraged to hug their Torahs, kiss their Torahs, and treat their Torahs with a little more respect than the average stuffed toy. One daycare child I know always napped with the classroom stuffed Torah as his pillow.

If a sanctuary is available to use, young children, even infants, should be taken to visit the Torahs. If there is no sanctuary on site, arrange to take a field trip to a nearby synagogue where children would be welcomed and where they can "meet" the Torahs. With an air of great awe and excitement, open the *Aron Kodesh*, help children touch the Torahs, and marvel at the beautiful decorations the Torah wears. If the older preschool children (four and five-year-olds) study the Torah every week, perhaps the younger children could join them just for the dancing and singing when they take out the Torah. Even if no one else is present, teachers can take out a Torah (with permission) and dance and sing with infants and toddlers. Teach children to give the Torah a kiss, touching the Torah and then kissing their hand. Tell the children that inside the Torah are the best Jewish stories ever. Use the Hebrew names for the

	GLOSSARY AND HEBREW VOCABULARY	
אֲרוֹן הַקֹדֶשׁ	*Aron HaKodesh*	the Holy Ark
אַבְנֵט	*Avnayt* (wimpel)	the binder that holds the Torah together under the *k'tonet*
עֲצֵי חַיִּים	*Aytzay Chayim*	the wooden rollers, literally "tree of life;" also another name for the Torah itself
בִּימָה	*Bimah*	the "stage" where the pulpit and the *Aron Kodesh* are
חֹשֶׁן	*Choshen*	the breastplate or "shield" which hangs on the front of the Torah
כֶּתֶר	*Keter*	the crown that fits over both wooden rollers
כֻּתֹּנֶת	*K'tonet*	the fitted cloth cover
מְנוֹרָה	*Menorah*	the seven-branched symbol of Shabbat
נֵר תָּמִיד	*Ner Tamid*	the eternal light hanging above the *Aron Kodesh*
פָּרוֹכֶת	*Parochet*	the curtain in front of the *Aron Kodesh*
רִמּוֹנִים	*Rimmonim*	the bells on top of each wooden roller
יָד	*Yad*	literally, "hand"; the pointer, often with a tiny hand or finger at the end, used to read the Torah, because it is forbidden to touch the Torah with one's hands

Figure 5

Torah decorations and related synagogue items, so children can learn them, too.

With the permission or help of synagogue clergy, open a Torah so that two and three-year-olds can see the Hebrew writing inside. With close supervision, let children touch and hold the Torah decorations. Shake the *rimmonim* for infants so they can hear the bells. Twos and threes can hold the *yad* and pretend to read from the Torah. Encourage the children to feel the *k'tonet*, and talk about the beautiful clothes the Torah wears. When children come on to the *bimah*, remind them that it is a place where we respect the Torah, not a place to goof around and jump and play.

Looking, touching, and talking is just the beginning. Dancing and singing with the Torah will directly expose children to the joy the Jewish people everywhere feel about the Torah. If you have a small Torah, a homemade Torah, or even a stuffed Torah, a child or several children can hold the Torah while everyone else sings and marches behind them. Sing traditional songs such as "Torah Torah," or *"Aytz Chayim Hee"* as you march. You can adapt more difficult songs by replacing some of the Hebrew with English, while maintaining the meaning of the words. For example, the song *"V'ori-ta"* (Torah Aura) may be transformed into: I love the Torah, Torah, Torah, it teaches me to do the things I should. Torah Aura, Torah Aura, Halleluyah!" You can follow the same model and adapt other songs, such as *"Al Shloshah D'vareem"* or *"Aytz Chaim Hee."*

By familiarizing very young children with the Torah and its rituals, you pave the way for children to discover the wonders contained *inside* the Torah as they get older. When three-year-old children hear Torah stories, the stories should be specifically identified as stories that come from the Torah. These children can experiment writing a Torah as a *sofer* does, using black ink (thinned black paint) and big feathers. Spread Hebrew newspaper on the tables to show more of the Hebrew that is inside the Torah. This, too, is preparation for hearing Torah stories when they are four.

SHARING TORAH WITH FOUR AND FIVE-YEAR-OLDS

The goal of sharing Torah with young children is not just to introduce them to a wonderful source of Jewish literature. The Torah is the root of many concepts and values which are essential to the development of Jewish identity. These concepts and values include:

1. God created the entire world and everything in it.
2. We are partners with God in caring for the earth and all living things.
3. We are responsible for helping and caring for other people.
4. The Torah is the story of the Jewish people.
5. All Jewish people are one family.
6. People can learn and grow, even if they make mistakes.
7. God rested on Shabbat; therefore, we rest and celebrate Shabbat.
8. The Land of Israel is the Jewish home, and our special place.
9. Prayer is a way for us to talk to God, as individuals and as part of a group.

(Adapted from *First Steps in Learning Torah with Children* by Rivka Behar, Floreva Cohen, and Ruth Musnikow)

When sharing Torah with young children, we can integrate these concepts into their lives. Through the drama and beauty of Torah stories, children will begin to develop their own concepts of and connection to God. Values found in Torah stories begin to take on new meaning as their relevance to the children's lives becomes apparent. When children hear the story of Jacob and Esau making up after being apart for so many years, the value of carefully maintaining their own sibling relationships comes into clearer focus. Torah stories link children to the vastness of the Jewish experience, and connect them to the wider Jewish community — for Torah is our story.

TELLING TORAH STORIES

Before actually sharing a Torah story with the children, it is important to set the stage. Learning from the Torah is fun! The stories are dramatic and the characters are intriguing. We use our whole bodies to interact with the Torah. We sing with our mouths, march with our feet, kiss the Torah with our lips, see with our eyes, use our minds to think. Make sure all of these actions are part of the experience you create. Torah should be an important part of your daily activities. With the children, build a huge *Aron Kodesh* out of a refrigerator or oven box. The children can then become "Torahs," adding Torah covers made from pillowcases (cut out head and armholes). Early in the year, invite a scribe to demonstrate the art of writing a Torah. Supply children with a long scroll of butcher paper and large feathers for quill pens. They can write their own Torahs, and keep adding to them all year (after all, it takes a *sofer* a year to write a real Torah!).

Make Torah stories a regular part of the curriculum. Begin a weekly Torah study time right after Simchat Torah. In this way, children can begin their study when Jewish people everywhere are reading the Torah from the beginning once again. It is a good idea to establish a set time for Torah study. Cynthia Snyder, a teacher with whom I work, shares the Torah with her four-year-olds every Friday. Instead of practicing the Friday night rituals of lighting candles and blessing wine and *challah*, she and her co-teachers practice the Saturday morning rituals each week with the class. Reading from a homemade Torah with a copy of the weekly *parashah* (portion) attached along the length of the Torah scroll, they sing and march with the Torah each week.

For others, it is more feasible to establish Monday or Thursday as Torah study time. In generations past, Mondays and Thursdays were market days. All the merchants and farmers would gather on these days, and all the people would come to shop. The Rabbis decided that since everyone was already gathered together, Mondays and Thursdays would be good days to read from the Torah publicly. Even as markets became transformed, the tradition held, and Mondays and Thursdays remain Torah reading days in most synagogues. Although children may have little exposure to the Torah reading schedule in their synagogue, it is appropriate and valuable to get them in the habit of a Torah reading on an actual Torah reading day.

Share the Torah in the same special place each time. Use a special corner of the classroom, a different room, an actual sanctuary if it is available. Show the children the portion you are going to tell or read in a real Torah scroll, a homemade Torah scroll, or in a Chumash or Tanach with Hebrew or Hebrew and English together. If you can, read the first verse in Hebrew, and then translate. Keep your Torah in an *Aron Kodesh*. If there is no *Aron Kodesh* in the space you use, make a beautiful one. The children can help to decorate it, transforming a box into a ritual object. Make sure there is enough room in your designated space for the children to march with the Torah, and to be able to listen comfortably.

Be creative in your telling. Reading the Torah story from a prepared text is one option for exposing children to the *parashah*, but there are many other ways to be more creative and inviting. Study the story at hand, hone your storytelling skills, and give a dramatic telling. Ask the children questions as you tell the story, to get them to interact and think.

Puppets are a wonderful tool for telling biblical stories. I have one set of hand puppets that help me tell many different stories, wearing varied costumes or using different props (a kerchief over the "mother's" hair makes her a grandmother, a multicolored coat makes the boy puppet into Joseph). The set I bought is actually supposed to be a Hispanic family. I chose that set over the white puppet family because the characters in the Torah were Semitic people and they probably had darker skin.

The felt board is a great way to share Torah stories. The easiest way to make the stories is to use pictures from a graphics collection, such as "Davka Graphics Deluxe: Bible Times." Print in color, color the pictures yourself (or let children color them), laminate, and attach sticky-back hook velcro to the back. Keep each story in a Ziplock bag with a copy of the story. You can use these felt board materials time and again to tell the story to children. Children can then use them to retell the story. To drive home the point that these are not just any stories, that they are stories from the Torah, you can make a felt board shaped like an open Torah out of foam board. Cover the board with felt, and decorate the top of the rollers with glitter or sequins to look like *rimmonim*. Use the Torah felt board only for telling Torah stories.

There are many good books for children dealing with different stories from the Torah (see the bibliography at the end of this chapter). Although during your Torah study time, it is best to tell the story from a Torah or Chumash, related children's books are good for follow-up. When you read these storybooks, ask the children how this story is different from the story they heard read from the Torah earlier. The story in the storybook may include the author's or illustrator's interpretation. However, the use of such storybooks enables children to review the story on their own and with their friends.

Encourage children to act out the Torah stories they hear. The Torah is so full of rich characters and interesting plots. You can organize enactments at circle time. Give children the chance to "be" different characters, including God. You can ask such questions as: How did it feel to be Rebekah? Why did she do what she did? How did it feel to be God? Why do you think God said that? You can also place biblical props and costumes (long robes, sandals, stuffed animal sheep and camels, scarves, sheets to make tents, and so on) in the house corner or dramatic play area, thus encouraging and enabling children to recreate the stories on their own. As children experiment with "trying on" the Torah characters, they will better understand the characters, the stories, and themselves.

Do not teach the children anything they will have to unlearn later. This can be assured in several ways. Read the actual text yourself before you share it with children. Of course, you will not tell the story to children just the way you read it — many details are not appropriate or not relevant to children. We omit stories like Cain and Abel, and we gloss over some details, such as how Korach was punished. Still, if you know the story the way it was written, you can then transform it into an age appropriate version that the children will not have to unlearn later. There are several guides to help you decide what is appropriate to share with children. The Board of Jewish Education of Greater New York published a comprehensive curriculum entitled *First Steps in Learning Torah with Young Children* by Rivka Behar, Floreva Cohen, and Ruth Musnikow. In two volumes, the authors provide the text of Genesis and Exodus translated into child-friendly language. They outline the concepts to be extracted from the portion and list activities to extend the story. Another wonderful guide for sharing Torah with young children is *Torah Talk: An Early Childhood Teaching Guide* by Yona Chubara, Miriam P. Feinberg, and Rena Rotenberg. This book also provides the stories from Genesis in child-friendly language, and it offers questions about the text, themes, and activities in various modalities geared toward preschool children of different ages.

The following list may be used as a guide to the appropriate Torah stories to share with early childhood classes. You may decide that some stories on this list are not totally appropriate for your class, or that there are other stories you feel comfortable adding. That's fine. This is the list of stories with the exact verses that I've included in my Torah study with fours and kindergartners, and I've found it to be appropriate and engaging. One year, a child was very interested in Esau, who I had planned on treating as a very minor character. Due to his question, "What happened to Esau?" I added *Vayishlach* (Genesis 32), the story of the reunion between Jacob and Esau. One year, I told the children the story in Exodus 18 about how Jethro, Moses' father-in-law, instructs Moses to set up a judicial system. The story seemed to confuse the children more than enlighten them, so I have since deleted that story from my curriculum.

Beraysheet

- *Beraysheet (Genesis), part 1* – Seven days of creation (Genesis 1:1-2:3)
- *Beraysheet, part 2* – Adam and Eve (Genesis 2:4-3:24)
- *Noah* (Genesis 6:9-17)
- *Lech Lecha* – Abraham and Sarah journey to a new land (Genesis 11:26 - 12:9; 15:1-6; 17:1-17)
- *Vayera* – Abraham receives guests/a child is born (Genesis 18:1-15; 21:1-8)
- *Chayay Sarah* – Introducing Rebecca (a wife for Isaac) (Genesis 23:1-2; 24:1-67)
- *Toldot* – The adventures of Jacob and Esau (Genesis 25:19-34; 27:1-45)
- *Vayaytzeh, part 1* – Jacob's Journey (Genesis 28:10 - 29:14)
- *Vayaytzeh, part 2* – Jacob, Rachel, and Leah (Genesis 29:14 - 30:24)
- *Vayishlach* – Jacob meets Esau (Genesis 32:25-26; 33:1-11)
- *Vayayshev, part 1* – Rachel dies/Joseph is introduced (Genesis 35:16-20; 37:1-36)
- *Vayayshev, part 2* – Joseph in Egypt (Genesis 39:1-40:23)
- *Mikaytz, part 1* – Pharaoh's Dreams (Genesis 41:1-57)
- *Miketz, part 2* – Joseph's brothers (Genesis 42:1-36)
- *Mikaytz, part 3* – Joseph's brothers back in Egypt (Genesis 43:1-44:17)
- *Vayigash, part 1* – Joseph reveals himself (Genesis 44:18-45:28)
- *Vayigash, part 2* – Jacob comes to Egypt (Genesis 46:1-7, 27; 47:1-12)
- *Vayehi* – Blessing for 12 sons (Genesis 47:28-48:21; 49 — summary of blessings)

When we finish reading a book of the Torah, we pause to celebrate and congratulate ourselves, saying *"Chazak, chazak, v'nit-chazayk"* (May we go from strength to strength). Stand up and say this with the children after completing the portion *Vayehi*.

Shemot (Exodus)

- *Shemot*, part 1 – Introducing Moses (Exodus 1:8-22 - 2:1-10)
- *Shemot*, part 2 – The adventures of Moses (Exodus 2:11-25)
- *Shemot*, part 3 – The Burning Bush (Exodus 3:1-22; 4:1-5, 10-23)
- *Shemot/Vaera* – The plagues (Exodus 4:27-31; 5:1-14; 7:1-8:10)
- *Vaera/Bo* – More plagues (Exodus 8:11-10:29)
- *Bo*, part 2 – Last plague, holiday of Pesach (Exodus 11:1-3, 12:1-13:16)
- *Beshalach*, part 1 – The People of Israel leave Egypt (Exodus 13:17-15:21)
- *Beshalach*, part 2 – Complaining in the desert (Exodus 15:22-17:7)
- *Yitro*, part 1 – At Sinai (Exodus 19:1-25)
- *Yitro*, part 2 – The Ten Commandments (Exodus 20:1-18)
- Last Time – Fast forward to end of Torah

Keep Torah and midrash separate. There is a difference between Torah and *midrash* (stories about the Torah). In my view, it is appropriate to share *midrashim* with children — these represent some of our most wonderful stories. However, it is confusing to mix *midrashim* with Torah stories. Young children cannot distinguish between what is in Torah and what is interpretation or variation. It is unfair to teach children so that later they go looking in the Torah for the story of Abraham smashing the idols. They won't find it there — it's a *midrash*. It is therefore preferable to share *midrashim* with children at *other* story times. Let the children know that the Rabbis wrote the *midrash* to explain something in the Torah. Always invite the children to do the same. When they have learned some Torah, they should be encouraged to make up their own stories to explain parts of Torah stories that are missing or need further explanation.

Enable the children to become "Torah scholars." Encourage them to ask questions about the Torah stories, and then to create their own answers. Each week, after I've told the Torah story, the four-year-olds and kindergartners ask questions about the story they just heard. Their teachers write the questions down, and post the list in the classroom for the next week. In this way, parents can see the questions and talk with their children about them. Also, children can ask to hear their questions again (or read them themselves). Having the questions visible all week makes it possible, and more likely, that the teachers and children will engage in "Torah talk" during the week.

Children's questions will be very basic at the beginning of the year (e.g., How did God make the animals? How did God put the people on the ground?). The questions become more complex as the year progresses (e.g., Why did Moses just die on top of the mountain? Does anyone even know what God looks like?). Children may also ask questions about the story they heard the previous week. This is developmentally appropriate. It indicates that the children are still processing what they previously heard. Children also ask questions to demonstrate to teachers that they remember and have gained mastery over the previous material. In any case, teachers must walk a fine line between fielding children's questions about the story from the week before and encouraging them to ask questions about the new story they just heard.

With some help from teachers, children's questions can also become children's *midrashim*. It is not important if their *midrashim* make sense, or are contradicted by the Torah; it is just important that they are interacting with the text, and taking ownership. In this way, they are becoming "Torah scholars."

Don't feel tied to the weekly Torah reading cycle. The pace set in synagogue is not appropriate or relevant to children this young. Also, only the material in the first two books of the Torah, Genesis and Exodus, is interesting to them. So take

your time. Don't be afraid to take several weeks to study one story. Units on light and shadow, growing things, water, animals, insects, and the human body work right in with the story of Creation. Themes of water and flotation, animals, *Tikkun Olam* (repair of our world), colors, rainbows, and human relations go along with the story of Noah. Map work, family trees, hospitality, and the like are a good follow-up to the story of Abraham and his descendants. Webbing a story will help you to find all the themes embedded in the *parashah*. A web will reveal more than you could ever cover, but the technique evokes many ideas. (For more details on webbing, see Chapter 1, "Developmentally Appropriate Practice," p. 11.) Choose one or a few of these ideas that are pertinent to bring to your class. The Torah story of the week can be the backdrop for a myriad of other things going on in the class. And if you time it right, you can be studying Moses just in time for Pesach!

Involve parents in the process and in the learning. Parents are your partners in helping children develop a love of Torah. Parents can also become eager students themselves when you involve them in the Torah study program. A sample of an introductory letter to parents can be found below. Each week, send home the text of the portion you will be sharing with the children in the week to come, so that parents can share it with their children, and learn alongside them. Invite parents to join in the weekly Torah study time with their children. Ask parents to volunteer to help out during Torah study by reading or telling the story to the children, or by writing down the children's questions. When children ask good questions about the Torah portion, send home a note encouraging parents to explore some answers with their children.

A SAMPLE LETTER TO FAMILIES

Dear Families,

Immediately following Simchat Torah, the holiday when we end and begin reading the Torah again, we will begin our study of *Parashat*

HaShavua (literally, "the weekly Torah portion"). From 9:30-10:00 a.m. every Monday, both classes will join together with the Torah in our special "Torah spot."

Each week, we dance with the Torah and open it to the portion we are studying. We tell the children the story, staying as close to the text as possible, while keeping the story age appropriate. We do not always read the same portion being read in synagogue each week. Rather, over the course of the year, we make our way through Genesis and half of Exodus, ending up right around Pesach time with the account of the Hebrews leaving Egypt.

After the telling of the story, we march the Torah back to the *Aron Kodesh*. The children then have a chance to ask questions. The teachers record the questions, and you can read them in the classroom during the week. (The teachers need to read the portion each week before class, so they can engage the children in conversation about Torah and answer their questions.)

Each Friday, with your newsletter, you will receive the synopsis of the portion that we will cover the following Monday. Take time over the weekend to read the portion, and to talk about it with your child. In this way, you will be able to keep abreast of what your child is learning, and we can be partners in this endeavor. Your child will learn to love what he/she knows you value. [Include the following paragraph for the second year of the program and beyond.]

The kindergartners who were in the four-year-old class last year have studied *Parashat HaShavua* for a year already. So why repeat? Because even as grown-ups, we reread the Torah each year. Each year we hear the same stories. The stories never change, but *we* do. Each year we are in a different place, we've had new experiences, and we come to the Torah with new understanding. So much the more so is this true of our children. As five-year-olds, the children understand the world much differently from the way they did when they were four. We have taken steps to ensure that this Torah study is not an "Oh, we did that last year" experience for the children.

If you want to read more, Esta Cassway has written a wonderful version of the Torah entitled *The Five Books of Moses for Young People*. The Jewish Publication Society (JPS) has recently published a Hebrew/English edition of the Tanach (the Hebrew Bible) — a very good English translation. Everett Fox also wrote a very good English translation with some commentary called *The Five Books of Moses*.

If you have any questions or comments, please feel free to call. You are welcome to join us for *Parashat HaShavua* any time — please let us know when we can expect you.

L'Shanah Tovah Tikatayvu,

_____

(Teacher's Name)

CONCLUSION

Enjoy sharing Torah stories with your children! Feel free to learn with them, and don't be afraid to say "I don't know." And when children ask (and they will ask!), "Did that really happen?" it is always safe to say, "Well, I wasn't there, but that's what the Torah says. What do you think?" Pave the way to Torah for children and they will approach it eagerly.

BIBLIOGRAPHY

TEACHING TORAH

Behar, Rivka; Floreva Cohen; and Ruth Musnikow. *First Steps in Learning Torah with Young Children.* New York: Board of Jewish Education of Greater New York, 1993.

> Comprehensive curriculum for learning Genesis with four to six-year-olds. A companion curriculum for Exodus was published in 1995. For more information and an order form, consult the BJE web site: www.bjeny.org/early_childhood_education_depa.htm

Chubara, Yona; Miriam Feinberg; and Rena Rotenberg. *Torah Talk: An Early Childhood Teaching Guide.* Denver, CO: A.R.E. Publishing, 1989.

> Developmentally appropriate retellings of stories from Torah, along with activities in various modalities.

Feinberg, Miriam P., and Rena Rotenberg. *Lively Legends-Jewish Values: An Early Childhood Teaching Guide.* Denver, CO: A.R.E. Publishing, 1993.

> Age appropriate retellings of Jewish stories, legends, and *midrashim* which convey Jewish values, along with many activities.

Jacoby, Janine; Luisa Latham; and Leah Shecter. "Teaching Bible To the Young Child." *Jewish Education News*, Summer, 1997, pp. 32-33.

> An examination of the philosophical and pragmatic issues involved in creating a rationale and sample lessons for an early primary curriculum in Bible.

ENGLISH TRANSLATIONS OF THE TORAH

Tanakh: The Holy Scriptures. Philadelphia, PA: The Jewish Publication Society, 1999.

> An excellent Hebrew/English edition, this is one of the best English translations.

Fox, Everett. *The Five Books of Moses.* New York: Schocken Books, 1995.

> A very good English translation that is true to the rhythms and nuances of the Hebrew text, with some commentary.

Tanach: The Stone Edition. ArtScroll Series. New York: Mesorah Publications, 1998.

> Good English translation with Hebrew and commentaries.

TORAH TEXTBOOKS

Berman, Melanie, and Joel Lurie Grishaver. *My Weekly Sidra.* Los Angeles, CA: Torah Aura Productions, 1986. (Ages 6-7)

> While the activities may be too advanced for fours, the pictures are good for making felt board stories.

Grishaver, Joel Lurie. *A Child's Garden of Torah Read-Aloud Bible.* Los Angeles, CA: Torah Aura Productions, 1996. (Ages 3-6)

> A retelling of classic Torah stories. Part of The Gan Curriculum, which includes Torah lessons with stickers to help review the stories.

Rose, Shirley. *Let's Discover the Bible.* West Orange, NJ: Behrman House, 1992. (Ages 5-7)

> Sixteen story folders cover some of the most important stories from the Hebrew Bible. Set 1 covers creation through Joseph, and Set 2 covers Moses, Ruth and Naomi, King David, Jonah, and others.

Wise, Ira J., and Joel Lurie Grishaver. *I Can Learn Torah Volume 1: Stories from the Beginning.* Los Angeles, CA: Torah Aura Productions, 1992. (Ages 5-7)

> Creation through the Tower of Babel. Designed to involve parents in the learning process. Features an accompanying parent and teacher guide.

———. *I Can Learn Torah Volume 2: Stories of the First Jewish Family.* Los Angeles, CA: Torah Aura Productions, 1992. (Ages 5-7)

> The saga of Abraham and Sarah. Features an accompanying parent and teacher guide.

STORIES AND STORY COLLECTIONS

Araten, Harry. *Two by Two: Favorite Bible Stories.* Rockville, MD: Kar-Ben Copies, 1991. (Ages 2-6)
Presents popular stories from the Hebrew Bible in simple text and illustrations.

Cassway, Esta. *The Five Books of Moses for Young People.* Northvale, NJ: Jason Aronson Inc., 1992. (Ages 4-adult)
Retells the stories found in the first five books of the Hebrew Bible. Good for reading aloud.

Eisenberg, Ann. *Bible Heroes I Can Be.* Rockville, MD : Kar-Ben Copies, 1990. (Ages 2-6)
Introduces such biblical figures as Noah, Rebecca, and King David, and shows how their accomplishment and attributes can be emulated in modern times.

Gellman, Marc. *Does God Have a Big Toe? Stories about Stories in the Bible.* New York, NY: Harper & Row, 1989. (Ages 3-adult)
A collection of humorous *midrashim* derived from the Torah.

———. *God's Mailbox.* New York: Morrow Junior Books, 1996.
More humorous *midrashim* derived from stories in the Torah.

Goldin, Barbara Diamond. *A Child's Book of Midrash: 52 Jewish Stories from the Sages.* Northvale, NJ: Jason Aronson Inc, 1990. (Ages 4-10)
Presents stories of heroic individuals from the Talmud and Midrash.

Kolatch Alfred J., *Classic Bible Stories for Jewish Children.* Middle Village, NY: Jonathan David, 1994. (Ages 4-8)
Twenty-four stories about such familiar characters as Noah, Joseph, Moses, David and Goliath, Ruth and Naomi, and Daniel.

Nerlove, Miriam. *The Ten Commandments for Jewish Children.* Morton Grove, IL: Albert Whitman, 1999. (Ages 3-7)
Finally, a book that presents the Ten Commandments for older preschoolers.

Prenzlau, Sheryl. *The Jewish Children's Bible.* New York: Pitspopany Press, 1999. (Ages 3-adult)
This five-volume set includes all the major stories in the Torah. The simple, easy to read story line is ideal for young children. Each volume includes a faithful adaptation of the text and a section of *midrashim*. Also includes the books of Jonah, Esther, Ruth, and a children's *Haggadah*.

Ray, Eric. *Sofer: The Story of a Torah Scroll.* Los Angeles, CA: Torah Aura Productions, 1998. (Ages 4-8)
A Jewish scribe explains in detail how he shapes the Hebrew letters he uses in transcribing the Torah, and how he prepares the scrolls themselves.

Rosenfeld, Dina. *Kind Little Rivka.* Brooklyn, NY: HaChai Publishing, 1991. (Ages 3-8)
This inspiring story highlights Rivka's acts of kindness to others, including ten very thirsty camels.

———. *A Little Boy Named Avram.* Brooklyn, NY: HaChai, 1989. (Ages 3-8)
The famous *midrash* about how our forefather Avram, at the early age of three, discovered the existence of the one, true God.

Topek, Susan Remick. *Ten Good Rules.* Rockville, MD: Kar-Ben Copies, 1991. (Ages 2-6)
Introduces the Ten Commandments from a Jewish perspective. Certain commandments have been recast from negative to positive language for easier comprehension.

Zeldis, Yona. *God Sent a Rainbow and Other Bible Stories.* Philadelphia: Jewish Publication Society, 1997. (Ages 4-8)
Presents a series of stories, including God's creation of the world, Noah and the ark, the sacrifice of Isaac, Joseph and his brothers, and the giving of the Ten Commandments to Moses.

SPECIFIC BIBLE STORIES
Creation

Levin, Miriam. *In the Beginning*. Rockville, MD: Kar-Ben Copies, 1996. (Ages 3-8)

In this adaptation of the creation story, Adam awakes, surveys his room and the larger world, decides that all is good, and then proceeds to deal with his loneliness.

Waldman, Sarah. *Light: The First Seven Days*. San Diego, CA: Harcourt Brace Jovanovich, 1993. (Ages 3-6)

Gorgeous, contemporary graphics accompany a simple retelling of the story of creation by the artist's 13-year-old daughter.

Noah

Cousins, Lucy. *Noah's Ark*. Cambridge, MA: Candlewick Press, 1993. (Ages 2-7)

A simple retelling of the Bible story of Noah building an ark and saving two of each kind of animal from the great flood.

Figley, Marty. *Noah's Wife*. Grand Rapids, MI: W.B. Eerdmans Publishing Co., 1997. (Ages 4-8)

This retelling focuses on Noah's wife. The preparations for the flood disrupted her life, but she accepted these disruptions in trust and faith.

Geisert, Arthur. *After the Flood*. Boston, MA: Houghton Mifflin,1994. (Ages 4-8)

After surviving the flood, Noah and his family settle in a sheltered valley with the animals they have saved and begin the glorious experience of repopulating the earth.

———. *The Ark*. Boston, MA: Houghton Mifflin, 1988. (Ages 4-8)

Retells the familiar story, using etchings as illustrations, and vividly depicting life inside the ark.

Jonas, Ann. *Aardvarks, Disembark!* New York: Puffin Books, 1994. (Ages 4-8)

After the flood, Noah calls out of the ark a variety of little known animals, many of which are now endangered.

Lepon, Shoshana. *Noah and the Rainbow*. Brooklyn, NY: Judaica Press, 1993. (Ages 4-8)

An engaging retelling of the story of Noah and his family as they deal with problems of caring for the animals in the ark. The giraffes complain that the ceiling is too low, the penguins are too hot, and the llamas are too cold.

LeTord, Bijou. *Noah's Trees*. New York: HarperCollins, 1999. (Ages 3-7)

Through simple language, young children learn about Noah's love for trees and his faith in God.

Reid, Barbara. *Two by Two*. New York: Scholastic 1993. (Ages 3-8)

A simple retelling in verse about Noah, his family, and animals during 40 days and nights of rain. There is a different couplet for each number up to ten.

Rounds, Glen. *Washday on Noah's Ark*. New York: Holiday House, 1991. (Ages 4-8)

When the forty-first day on the ark dawns bright and clear, Mrs. Noah decides to do the wash. Having no rope long enough, she devises an ingenious clothesline.

Sasso, Sandy Eisenberg. *A Prayer for the Earth: The Story of Naamah, Noah's Wife*. Woodstock, VT: Jewish Lights Publishing, 1996. (Ages 4-9)

Noah's wife Naamah is called upon by God to gather the seeds of every type of plant on earth and to bring them safely onto the ark before the great flood.

Singer, Isaac Bashevis. *Why Noah Chose the Dove*. New York, Farrar, Straus and Giroux, 1987. (Ages 4-8)

With wonderful illustrations by Eric Carle, Singer tells this classic story from the point of view of the animals, all boasting about why Noah should take them on the ark.

Joseph

Lepon, Shoshona. *Joseph the Dreamer*. New York: Judaica Press, 1991. (Ages 4-8)

The story follows Joseph as he is sold into slavery, imprisoned in Egypt, and finally reunited with his brothers and father.

Moses

Cone, Molly. *Who Knows Ten? Children's Tales of the Ten Commandments*. rev. ed. New York: UAHC Press, 1998. (Ages 5-9)

Presents each of the Ten Commandments with stories illustrating their meanings.

Lepon, Shoshana. *The Ten Plagues of Egypt*. New York: Judaica Press, 1988. (Ages 4-8)

Recounts in verse how God sent ten terrible plagues to Egypt to persuade Pharaoh to let the Israelites return to Canaan.

CHAPTER 6

ISRAEL ALL YEAR

If I forget you, O Jerusalem,
Let my right hand wither,
Let my tongue stick to my palate if
I cease to think of you. (Psalms 137:5-6)

Our connection to and love for Israel is at the core of a Jewish identity. Our relationship with Israel connects us to other Jews all over the world. Israel is therefore an essential element of any Jewish early childhood program. We strive to instill in young children a feeling of belonging to Israel because Israel gives us so much: a sense of pride, a connection to our history, a gathering place for all Jews, and place to feel holy and close to God. While the concept of "country" is very difficult for young children, the concept of "home" is not. Israel is our Jewish home. We want children to love Israel, even if they don't understand just how far away it is.

To help children build a relationship with Israel, Israel needs to be an underlying theme not only during Tu B'Shevat and Yom HaAtzma'ut, but throughout the school year. Israel must be a part of the classroom every week. During the preschool years, our goal is to get every child to think of Israel as his/her Jewish Homeland. When a child leaves preschool, he/she should recognize the flag of Israel and the shape of Israel on a map. He/she should also be able to differentiate between Hebrew and English alphabets. Every child should know many words in Hebrew. The more Israel is personalized — with pen pals, stories of personal visits — the more concrete Israel will become.

What might we do to facilitate this? Have Hebrew and English food boxes in the house corner, Hebrew and English books on the bookshelf, and a map of Israel hanging in the class all the time. Teachers need to keep Israel constantly in mind. During a unit on winter, for example, you might say, "In Israel, it almost never snows." For more such ideas, see page 94.

There are many simple strategies, games, and props which will help bring Israel into your classroom. Integrating Israel will take some conscious thought on the part of every teacher, and some effort to become familiar with a basic Hebrew vocabulary. Many classes take an imaginary trip to Israel sometime during the year. *This trip can be meaningful to the children only if Israel is already a part of their every day classroom experience.* This chapter is designed to enable you to make Israel part of the culture in your classroom.

Teaching Israel requires knowledge. If you have never been to Israel, check out some picture books/ coffee table books on Israel from the library. *A Day in the Life of Israel* is a good first book. Browse through the pages, and try to imagine life in a country with so many different kinds of people, with cities and beautiful rolling hills, with desert and beaches no more than a few miles apart. Life in Israel is primitive and modern, hurried and holy, threatening and peaceful. Israelis know that there may be a terrorist with a bomb walking nearby along the *midrahov* (a combination of the words for "sidewalk" and "street"). Israelis, especially those in Jerusalem, also know that come Friday afternoon, everything will come to a halt, and the peace of Shabbat will settle over the city.

In the following pages, you will find some information about Israel, its peoples, and some of its geographical locales. *It is not important that children become experts in Israeli geography!* However, the names of some major cities, such as Tel Aviv and Jerusalem, should be familiar. This information is provided here to help teachers become a little more familiar with the layout of the Land.

Israel is a very small country, with an area about equal to the state of Massachusetts. It sits in the Middle East, bordered by Lebanon to the north, Syria and Jordan to the east, Egypt to the southwest, and the Mediterranean Sea to the west (see figure 6 on this page).

From her beginning, in 1948, Israel has had to fight for survival. Relations with her Arab neighbors have historically been quite antagonistic, although in recent decades, great strides have been made toward peace. In 1979, Israel and Egypt signed a peace agreement, and, in 1994, Israel signed a peace agreement with Jordan.

Even within her borders, Israel has struggled for peace. Decades later, the effort to bring into being a lasting peace between Israel and the Palestinians who live within her borders continues.

Israel has a population of close to six million people. About 80 percent are Jews, both native born and from some 70 countries around the world. Around 18 percent of the population are Arabs (mostly Muslim, but some Christian), and the rest are Druse and members of other small communities. Jews have been making *aliyah* (immigrating to Israel) in small numbers since the late 1800s, and by the hundreds of thousands since Israel became a state in 1948. In the decade of the 1990s, almost one million people emigrated to Israel. Of these, over 600,000 came from the former Soviet Union. Two major airlifts, Operation Moses in 1984 and Operation Solomon in 1991, brought over 30,000 Ethiopian Jews to Israel.

The official languages of Israel are Hebrew and Arabic, although on the streets, one can hear English, Russian, Yiddish (a combination of Hebrew and German, spoken by Jews from Eastern European countries), French, German, Amharic (Ethiopian), Ladino (a combination of Hebrew and Spanish), Farsi (spoken by Persian Jews), among other languages. Israel is both rural and

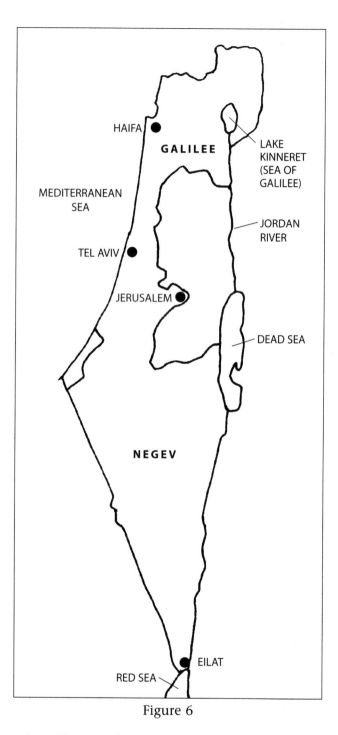

Figure 6

urban. There are large cities, small villages, farming communities called *kibbutzeem* (singular, *kibbutz*) and *moshaveem* (singular, *moshav*). Although it is impossible to provide information about every community in Israel within these pages, following you will find some information about some major cities, communities, and areas. For more resources, see the bibliography at the end of this chapter.

IMPORTANT CITIES AND SITES

JERUSALEM

Jerusalem is the capital of the State of Israel, and, along with Tel Aviv, is one of Israel's largest cities. It is also deemed the most holy city in Israel. Jerusalem is not holy just to Jews; it is sacred to Muslims and Christians as well. The city dates back over 3000 years to King David. *Bayt HaMikdash*, the first Holy Temple, was build by King Solomon, David's son, in Jerusalem around 960 B.C.E. (Before the Common Era). Solomon's Temple was destroyed in 586 B.C.E. by the Babylonians. The Second Temple was built around 520 B.C.E. (some say 420 B.C.E.), and was destroyed in 70 C.E. by the Romans. The only remaining part of the Second Temple is the Western Wall of the supporting walls (the walls that held up the mound of earth on which the Temple stood). This place, called the *Kotel* in Hebrew, is one of the holiest spots in the world for Jews. When visiting the *Kotel*, one is sure to see people praying, touching the huge stones, sometimes weeping. The cracks between the stones are jammed with tiny notes — prayers and petitions that people have written to God and brought there, believing that there they come close to God.

The Old City is walled, and portions of it date back to the time of King David. There are several gates into the Old City. The Old City is divided into quarters: Armenian, Christian, Muslim, and the Jewish quarter, which contains the *Kotel*. Archeological digs abound, revealing life in previous generations.

Surrounding the Old City is the New City. A bustling metropolis populated by every kind of Israeli, it is filled with shops and open markets called *shuks* (*Shuk Machaneh Yehudah* is the largest one), malls and movie theaters, colleges and the YMCA (pronounced *"yim-ka"* by Israelis), the King David Hotel and beautiful parks, many museums and the Knesset, Israel's seat of government. Egged (pronounced *eh-ged*) buses take people all over Jerusalem, from the ultra-Orthodox community of Me'ah Sha'arim down Jaffa Road, past the *midrachov* Ben Yehudah, through the German Colony, home to many Americans who have made *aliyah*, and out to the far-flung neighborhoods, almost suburbs, of Jerusalem.

TEL AVIV

Tel Aviv is the first modern Jewish city, founded in 1909 just north of the ancient port city of Jaffa. Except for the billboards which, of course, are in Hebrew, one is reminded of any major modern city. Nestled on the beaches of the Mediterranean Sea, Tel Aviv offers everything that any contemporary city boasts: large hotels, tall apartment buildings, industry, universities, a major airport, nightclubs, streets crammed with cars, buses, and cabs. Tel Aviv is Israel's commercial center. Its main street is a promenade along the beach which stretches all the way to ancient Jaffo some seven miles away. Yet, many streets in Tel Aviv are filled with trendy shops and sidewalk cafes. There is also an incredible fountain created by the artist Yaacov Agam on busy Dizengoff Street.

KIBBUTZ AND MOSHAV

A *kibbutz* is a communal agricultural settlement, in which all property, land, livestock, etc., is communally owned, and all the work and decisions are shared. The first *kibbutz*, Degania, was founded at the southern end of Lake Kinneret in 1909. Today, there are over 200 *kibbutzeem*, which house about 2% of Israel's population. The *kibbutz* takes care of all its members' needs — food, clothing, housing, education for the youngest children — and the members of the *kibbutz* all work together to run the *kibbutz*. Usually there is a *chadar ochel* (a dining room) where members can take their meals together, although individual apartments also have kitchens. Today, in addition to agricultural endeavors, most *kibbutzeem* also run a factory or high-tech industry. There exist religious and secular *kibbutzeem*, and also *kibbutzeem* established by the Reform and Conservative movements.

A *moshav* is a cooperative farming community. On a *moshav*, each family owns its own house and some land, but the *moshav* jointly owns land and farming equipment. The members of the *moshav* sometimes work the land together as well, dividing the expenses and profits. Beyond the work sphere, each family lives independently. About 3% of Israel's population lives on *moshaveem*.

Eilat

At the southern tip of Israel, bordering the Sinai Peninsula and the Gulf of Aqaba, is the beach resort town of Eilat. Eilat is home to a busy port, which dates back to the times of King Solomon. In Eilat, you can go scuba diving or snorkeling, and can see the beautiful coral reefs and many varieties of fish through a glass bottom boat. Vacationers can be found on the beach or sailing in the gulf almost all year. From the shores of Eilat, it is possible to see the Jordanian city of Aqaba, just across the bay. Since the peace agreement with Jordan in 1994, it is possible to cross the border into Jordan just outside of Eilat. To the north of Eilat is the wide expanse of the Negev Desert.

Negev Desert

The word Negev means "dry," and that's just what this huge desert is. It covers more than a third of *Eretz Yisrael*, the entire south of the country. A major challenge in creating the State of Israel has been to "make the desert bloom." That's just what has happened. Vast systems of irrigation pipelines installed by Israeli settlers over the past several decades have pushed the desert back, making it possible to grow crops and build cities

there. The largest city in the Negev is Beersheba. The rest of the Negev is dotted with small communities and *kibbutzeem*. Bedouin encampments can also be found scattered throughout the region. Bedouin are nomads who have lived in the Negev for generations. They reside in tents, and wander with their flocks of sheep and goats.

Bodies of Water

Israel contains many different bodies of water — seas, rivers, lakes. It is bordered on the west by the Mediterranean Sea, and has beaches and ports running along the coast.

Lake Kinneret, also known as the Sea of Galilee, is in the north of the country, in the area called the Galilee. A gorgeous fresh water lake, the Kinneret is the inspiration for songs and poems, and is the main water source for country.

The Jordan River runs from the Kinneret southward, and empties into the Dead Sea. In biblical times, Moses brought the Israelites from Egypt to the edge of the Jordan River, but he was not allowed to cross over with them into Israel. It was Joshua who brought them over the Jordan into the Land. Today, the Jordan River forms an eastern border of Israel.

The Dead Sea is the lowest spot on earth, almost 1300 feet below sea level. As previously mentioned, the Jordan River ends at the Dead Sea. The only way for the water to leave the Dead Sea is through evaporation, leaving minerals behind. In Hebrew the Dead Sea is called *Yam HaMelach* (Salt Sea). Today, salt and other minerals today are harvested from the Dead Sea and, in recent years, a few spas have sprung up in the area to enable people to take advantage of the mineral-rich mud. It is possible to float in the Dead Sea; in fact, it is practically impossible to submerge oneself. The water has a vile taste (should you be so unfortunate as to taste some) and burns the eyes as well as any cuts you may not have even realized you had before entering the water. Still, the water is good for the skin, and the floating experience is like none other.

GOALS AND CONCEPTS

At a World Zionist Organization Early Childhood Conference, Dr. Ruth Pinkenson-Feldman discussed thematic approaches to teaching about Torah and the land of Torah, Israel. She said that the child in the Diaspora is born into an Israel of the imagination. Unless (or until) children go to Israel, they can only imagine what it might be like (Zeskind, 1997). Thus, Jewish children need to be drawn into a relationship with Israel. Through the thematic study of concepts such as the geography of Israel, seasons, lifestyles, music, dance, people, foods, and holy sites, children can begin to construct social knowledge of our Jewish Homeland. Using books, stories, pictures, and any other strategies at their disposal, early childhood educators need to do everything in their power to help flesh out each child's imagination of Israel so that each child understands basic concepts about the country.

Based on this, here are concepts and goals for integrating Israel all year.

INFANTS TO 24 MONTHS
1. Blue and white are the colors of Israel.
2. I hear lots of Hebrew music.
3. There is a *Magen David* (Jewish star) on the Israeli flag.

2 YEARS
1. Blue and white are the colors of Israel.
2. I hear lots of Hebrew music.
3. The flag of Israel is blue and white, with a *Magen David* (Jewish star) in the middle.
4. I live in (name your town).
5. Other people live in other places.

3 YEARS
1. We live in the United States of America/Canada (Chicago/Toronto, etc.).
2. Other people live in other countries.
3. One of those other countries is Israel.
4. Israel is far away. We travel on an airplane to get there.

5. People who live in Israel are called "Israelis."
6. People who live in Israel speak Hebrew (and Arabic and English and many other languages).
7. I can say lots of words and sing songs in Hebrew.
8. Some children/teachers in our school are Israelis.
9. Israel is a Jewish country; many Jews live in Israel. Arabs also live in Israel. We call Israel the Jewish Homeland. Jews come from all over the world to live in Israel.
10. We care about Israel and feel connected to it. Israel is our Jewish home.
11. The flag of Israel is blue and white, with a *Magen David* (Jewish star) in the middle.

4 TO 5 YEARS
1. We live in the United States of America/Canada (Chicago/Toronto, etc.).
2. Other people live in other countries.
3. One of those other countries is Israel.
4. Israel is far away. We travel on an airplane to get there.
5. People who live in Israel are called "Israelis."
6. People who live in Israel speak Hebrew (and Arabic and English and many other languages).
7. I can say lots of words and sing songs in Hebrew.
8. Some children/teachers in our school are Israelis.
9. Israel is a Jewish country; many Jews live in Israel. Arabs also live in Israel. We call Israel the Jewish Homeland. Jews come from all over the world to live in Israel.
10. We care about Israel and feel connected to it. Israel is our Jewish home.
11. The flag of Israel is blue and white, with a *Magen David* (Jewish star) in the middle.
12. Israel is a very old place. Jews we read about in the Torah lived in Israel (or were trying to get to Israel). Israel is a part of many of our Jewish holidays.
13. Archaeologists dig to find out about people who lived in Israel long ago.

14. Israel is a new place. The modern State of Israel is younger than many of our grandparents.
15. In Israel there are mountains, deserts, oceans, rivers, lakes, cities, and trees which Jewish people from all around the world have helped to plant.
16. Seasons in Israel come at a different time of year from seasons where I live.
17. Israel is very small. I can recognize the shape of Israel on a map.
18. We pray for peace and no more wars in Israel. We pray that all the people in Israel can be friends.

ACTIVITIES

Integrating Israel into the culture of your classroom can be a natural process (rather than an added unit to cover). Following are ideas and activities that can be integrated all year long into your classroom and curriculum. (For more activities pertinent to this subject, see Chapter 17, "Yom HaAtzma'ut.")

LANGUAGE ARTS

1. Use Hebrew for greetings, body parts, please and thank you, and so on.
2. Older classes can form a pen pal relationship with a class in Israel. Children dictate letters and send with pictures. Contact your local Jewish Federation, the Jewish National Fund, the Israeli consulate, or friends and family in Israel to make pen pal connections.
3. Hang pictures and maps of Israel in the room all year. Be sure to include portrayals of the many different kinds of terrain found in Israel. Use photographs, calendar pictures, posters, and fine artwork.
4. Put Hebrew versions of familiar books (*Cat in the Hat, Good Night Moon*) in the book corner. Compare the same book in English and Hebrew. Read books on Israel during story time.

5. Use students' Hebrew names. (You may need to ask parents for these names. Do not give a child a Hebrew name.)
6. In the house corner, include Israeli scarves with the dress up clothes. Israeli foods (pita, empty food packages from Israel) can be in the kitchen.
7. Create a Hebrew activity center. Include Hebrew rubber stamps, stickers, Hebrew newspapers, magazines, Israel tourist booklets, etc.
8. In the writing center, create the opportunity for students to trace, copy, or rub the letters of the Hebrew alphabet. (Use colored glue to make the letters of the alphabet on index cards. Allow to dry. Students can place paper over these and rub.)
9. Create a matching game in which students match Hebrew letters (e.g., an *alef* to an *alef*).
10. Have students sort cards with Hebrew on them in one pile, and cards with English into another.
11. Sort newspaper fragments into an English pile and a Hebrew pile.
12. Use Hebrew words for objects in the room. If you already label your spaces in English, add Hebrew signs (see Appendix B, p. 359 for Hebrew labels for the classroom). If possible, refer to places in your room verbally in Hebrew as well.
13. If possible, serve snack using Hebrew words and sentences. (Ask a parent who speaks Hebrew to join you.)

SCIENCE

1. When talking about the daily weather, mention what the weather is like in Israel.
2. When celebrating holidays, talk about how children in Israel are celebrating the holiday.
3. Talk about the Dead Sea, and then do float/sink experiments. Gather various materials and let children test which ones float or sink in a water table or a bucket of water. Be sure to include guaranteed "floaters," such as corks, as well as guaranteed "sinkers," such as rocks,

and variable objects, such as sponges and bottle caps.

4. Plant a garden outside like those on *kibbutzim*.
5. Make a cow with a rubber glove udder and milk it.
6. Find Israel and your city on a map.
7. Make and taste Israeli foods from different cultural groups, such as bourekas (an Israeli Sephardic snack of phyllo dough with cheese or potato inside) or pita with falafel and hummus.
8. Place pieces of fruits (oranges, dates, figs, peaches, bananas, etc.) from Israel in small opaque containers; poke a hole to allow the smell to come through. Let student see other pieces of the fruits and match them up with the smells they get from the containers. Open the containers to check if they are right.
9. Dissect and compare the seeds of a fig with the seeds of an orange. You can also show what happens when you cut them horizontally or vertically.
10. Eat an Israeli breakfast — diced cucumber and tomato salad, yogurt, bread.
11. Compare an Israeli flag to your country's flag.
12. Sort pictures of Israel from pictures of your city or country.

MATH

1. Count in Hebrew.
2. When doing calendar, include the Hebrew months as well as the English months.
3. Make an Israeli flag sorting set, with flags of different sizes.
4. Compare and sort Israeli coins and those from your country.
5. Compare and sort Israeli stamps and those from your country.

ART

1. Make signs for your *shuk*.
2. Paint a desert scene mural, complete with camels. Put sand in the paint.
3. Make a backpack and a *kova* (hat) and go for a nature walk.
4. Cover the table with Hebrew newspaper during art projects. (Ask people who go to Israel to bring back Hebrew newspapers, or ask Israeli friends or children's family members who read Hebrew papers to bring them to class when they are done.)
5. Color or paint directly on Hebrew newspaper.
6. Make an orange print picture on an Israeli newspaper. Children roll a whole orange (or dip half an orange) in paint, then print with it on the paper.
7. Write students' names in Hebrew on their artwork.

MUSIC/MOVEMENT

1. Sing songs in Hebrew. Substitute Hebrew for some English in songs (e.g., such as "Old Goldenberg Had a Kibbutz, e-i-e-i-o" and "The Galgaleem on the Bus"). (For words to these songs, see Chapter 19, "Integrating Hebrew Every Day," p. 264.)
2. Play games such as *Shimon Omer (Simon Says)*.
3. Sing Hebrew songs, even when it is not Shabbat or a holiday.
4. Listen to Israeli "non-kid's" music such as on the recordings *Achinoam Nini Gil Dor* (NMC Music), *Both Sides of the Sea* by Noa (Mondo Melodies), and *First Collection* by David Broza (CBS Records).
5. Do some Israeli dancing. Teach simple dances such as *"Niggun Atik"* and *"Myeem,"* or make up dances (walking around in a circle, moving in and out of the center) to Hebrew/Israeli songs you like (see Chapter 22, "A Guide To Music in the Early Childhood Classroom, p. 285).
6. Play *Red Light-Green Light* using *kayn* (yes) and *lo* (no).
7. Listen to and sing *"Hatikvah."* Identify it as Israel's special song. Do the same with your country's national anthem. Compare the two anthems.
8. Sing the Hebrew songs listed in Chapter 14, "Tu B'Shevat," pp. 203-204, and Chapter 17, "Yom HaAtzma'ut," pp. 246-247.

CIRCLE TIME

1. Invite to class family members and friends who have visited Israel to talk about their trip and to share pictures and mementos. (Encourage them to bring and show objects.)
2. Show pictures of people in Israel. Talk about what the people are wearing, the climate, their activities, etc.
3. Watch an age appropriate video segment on Israel (e.g., *Rechov Sum Sum — Sesame Street*). Talk about life in Israel as compared to children's lives in your country.
4. Play *I'm Going To Israel and I'm Bringing a . . .* Encourage older children to pick something that starts with the same letter as their first name.

OUTDOORS/FIELD TRIPS

1. When you take a walk around the neighborhood, ask children questions to help them compare their city to those in Israel. Do you think houses look like this in Israel? Do you think you'd see this kind of dog in Israel? Do you think the trees look like this in Israel? Don't quiz for right answers, ask so as to help children wonder.
2. Take a trip to a farm or orchard and work together to harvest some fruit or vegetables. Compare this trip to living on a *kibbutz*.
3. Look at the flags hanging in your neighborhood. Can you find an Israeli flag?

SPECIFICALLY FOR INFANTS

1. Make a set of blue and white objects for babies to play with.
2. Hang an Israeli flag in your room all year. Talk to babies about the colors and shapes in the flag.
3. Play modern Israeli music and dance with babies.

IDEAS FOR TEACHING FAMILIES

1. With the children, make puzzles of the land of Israel. Send home for children to assemble with their families.

2. Encourage adults to shop with their children and each week or each month buy a different product from Israel (oranges, dates, and so on) for their dinner table.
3. Include current news of Israel in weekly or monthly newsletters.
4. Encourage family members to write notes to send to the children's Israeli pen pals.
5. Invite family members who have been to Israel (or who are from Israel) to come in and share their trip with the class.
6. Alert families to Israel-related events happening in the community: lectures, classes, Walk for Israel, and so on.
7. Recommended reading: *A Day in the Life of Israel,* edited by David Cohen, and *A Kid's Catalog of Israel* by Chaya Burstein.

INTEGRATING ISRAEL INTO SECULAR THEMES

The key to making Israel a part of your everyday classroom culture is always to keep Israel in the back of your mind. Below are some concept and activity ideas for integrating Israel into five typical early childhood themes: I'm Me — I'm Special, Community Helpers, Seasons, Senses, and Transportation. (The Hebrew vocabulary for each of these themes is in figure 7 on page 98.) With a little practice, you will be able to follow this model and integrate Israel into every unit you do.

I'M ME — I'M SPECIAL
Concepts

1. We live in America/Canada (Chicago/Toronto, etc.), but Israel is our special home. Israel is the Homeland for Jewish people. Israel is a special place for us to learn about and visit, because we are Jewish.
2. Many of us have a Hebrew name.
3. We can use our bodies to do Jewish things.

Activities

1. Read *Becky and Benny Thank God, A Sense of Shabbat, My Body Is Something Special,* and *I'm Growing* by Howard I. Bogot and Daniel B. Syme.
2. Use the children's Hebrew names, for attendance, on nametags and *kipot,* in general conversation. If the parents don't know the child's Hebrew name, that's okay. It's a good time for them to choose one.
3. Play *Shimon Omer (Simon Says)* and use Hebrew words for body parts.
4. Use the Hebrew words for family members.
5. Send your Israeli pen pals some pictures of class members. Ask them to send back some pictures of themselves.

COMMUNITY HELPERS
Concepts

1. In Israel, some very important community helpers are soldiers.
2. Everyone goes into the army for a few years after high school. Soldiers ride the bus and watch the streets to keep everyone safe.
3. Not only does Israel have grocery stores, but all year around there are outdoor markets. A market of this type is called a *shuk.*
4. On a *kibbutz,* everyone is a community helper. The cooks in the kitchen cook for everyone on the *kibbutz,* not just for their own family. The people who work in the laundry do laundry for everyone in huge machines. Others work in the chicken house or in the factory.

Activities

1. Find out what the parents of your pen pals do for a living. Until you get an answer, have the children guess. Be sure to keep a list of their guesses.
2. Set up a *shuk* in your classroom. Ask anyone who is going to Israel to bring back empty food boxes with Hebrew on them for your house corner.
3. Talk about how your classroom is like a *kibbutz,* with everyone helping each other.
4. Read *Chicken Man* by Michelle Edwards.

SEASONS
Concepts

1. Israel's climate is generally very warm.
2. It rarely snows. The winter is cold and rainy.
3. The summers are long and perfect.
4. The trees do not change colors in the fall.
5. Spring in Israel starts before spring in most of North America.

Activities

1. Watch *Shalom Sesame Sing around the Seasons* video.
2. Send fall leaves and photos of children playing outside to Israeli pen pals.
3. Ask Israeli pen pals what their weather is like.
4. Compare things that grow in Israel (palm trees, bananas, oranges, corn, carob trees) to things that grow in your area.
5. Have an "Israel window" (a window frame with views of Israel) and change the views according to the seasons in Israel.

SENSES
Concepts

1. Israeli children use their senses the same way we do.
2. There are different kinds of spices to smell, foods to taste, etc., in Israel (they also have many of the same foods and spices that we have).

Activities

1. Use Israeli spices and foods (oranges, zatar, hummus) for smelling jars and taste tests.
2. Make feelie bags with Jewish and Israeli objects.
3. Use Israeli music to play freeze dance, as background music or at nap time. In freeze dance, when the music stops, everyone freezes. Anyone who moves when the music is stopped must sit down until the next freeze.

TRANSPORTATION
Concepts

1. On the streets of Israel, there are lots of Egged and Dan buses.

HEBREW VOCABULARY

I'm Me — I'm Special

תִּינוֹק	baby	*tee-nok* (male); *teenoket* (female)
אָח	brother	*ach*
אַבָּא	father	*abba*
סַבְתָּא	grandma	*safta*
סַבָּא	grandpa	*saba*
אִמָּא	mother	*ee-ma*
אָחוֹת	sister	*a-chot*
רַגְלַים	feet	*rahg-la-yeem*
רֹאשׁ	head	*rosh*
בִּרְכַּים	knees	*beer-kai-yeem*
כְּתֵפַים	shoulders	*k'ta-fah-yeem*

Community Helpers

רוֹפֵא/רוֹפְא	doctor	*ro-feh/ro-fah*
קִבּוּץ	*kibbutz*	*kibbutz*
שׁוּק	market	*shuk*
מוֹרֶה/מוֹרָה	teacher	*moreh/morah*

Seasons

סְתָו	fall	*stav*
גֶּשֶׁם	rain	*geshem*
שֶׁלֶג	snow	*sheh-leg*
בֻּבַּת שֶׁלֶג	snowman	*boo-bat sheleg* (literally, "snow doll")
אָבִיב	spring	*a-veev*
קַיִץ	summer	*ka-yeetz*
שֶׁמֶשׁ	sun	*shemesh*
חֹרֶף	winter	*cho-rev*

Senses

אָזְנַים	ears	*oz-nai-yeem*
עֵינַים	eyes	*ay-nai-yeem*
אֶצְבָּעוֹת	fingers	*etz-ba-ot*
יָדַים	hands	*ya-dai-yeem*
פֶּה	mouth	*peh*
אַף	nose	*af*
לָשׁוֹן	tongue	*la-shone*

Transportation

מָטוֹס	airplane	*ma-tos*
אוֹטוֹבּוּס	bus	*auto-boos*
מְכוֹנִית	car	*m'-cho-neet*
סִירָה	boat	*oh-nee-yah*
רַכֶּבֶת	train	*ra-ke-vet*

Figure 7

2. Israel has its own airline called El Al.
3. In cities such as Tel Aviv and Jerusalem, there are lots of cars. People drive fast, so everyone has to be careful!
4. There are very few trains in Israel.
5. Israel has three ports: Haifa, Ashdod, and Eilat.
6. It takes about eight hours to drive from the top (Galilee) to the bottom (Eilat) of Israel.
7. Bedouin ride camels in the desert.

Activities

1. Sing the song *"Heenay Rakevet"* (there is a cute version on the tape *Aleph Bet Boogie* by Rabbi Joe Black), and move around the room like a train.
2. Make a bus from a large cardboard box and write "Egged" on the front.
3. When you sail boats, sail on the Mediterranean Sea into Haifa.
4. Make multi-ride tickets (*car-tees/car-tee-seem*) for children to ride the bus. (Punch a hole for each ride.)
5. Ask your Israeli pen pals to send you some old *carteeseem*.

SONGS TO INTEGRATE HEBREW

Note: For some songs that integrate Hebrew, see Chapter 17, "Yom HaAtzma'ut," pp. 246-248, and Chapter 19, "Integrating Hebrew Every Day," pp. 263-264.

BIBLIOGRAPHY

ADULT RESOURCES

Burstein, Chaya. *A Kid's Catalog of Israel*. rev. ed. Philadelphia, PA: Jewish Publication Society, 1998.
Everything a kid (or adult) needs to know about *Eretz Yisrael*.

Cohen, David, ed. *A Day in the Life of Israel*. San Francisco, CA: Collins Publishers, 1994.
Photographs by more than 60 of the world's best photojournalists, all taken on a single day, May 5, 1994.

Cohn, Jessica Plotnick, and Esther Cohen Hexter. *Teaching Israel To Young Children: A Touring Curriculum*. Materials from a CAJE Workshop 1994. Available from the CAJE Curriculum Bank, www.caje.org/learn/fs_pin.html, (800) CAJE-ERC.
Full of resources to help teach children about Israel.

Facts about Israel. State of Israel, Ministry of Foreign Affairs, 1999.
The web site supported by the State of Israel, www.israel.org, provides facts and information about every aspect of Israeli history, culture, and economy.

Gilbert, Martin. *Jerusalem in the Twentieth Century*. New York: J. Wiley & Sons, 1996.
The story of modern Jerusalem; covers every facet of the city's life.

Gonen, Amiram. *Israel: Yesterday and Today*. New York: Macmillan, 1998.
A photographic survey of the building of a nation.

Ullian, Robert. *Israel from $45 a Day: Frommer's*. 17th ed. New York: Simon & Schuster Macmillan Company, 1998.
This ultimate guide to low cost travel is also a terrific guide to everything about Israel.

Zeskind, Margie. *Teaching Israel in the Diaspora*. Miami: Central Agency for Jewish Education of Greater Miami, 1997. Available from the CAJE Curriculum Bank, www.caje.org/learn/fs_pin.html, (800) CAJE-ERC.

Curriculum inspired by attendance at a WZO Early Childhood Conference in Israel. A good look at early childhood education in Israel and how we can use that to teach Israel in the Diaspora.

CHILDREN'S BOOKS

Bogot, Howard I. *Becky and Benny Thank God*. New York: CCAR Press, 1996. (Ages infant-2)
A "Pat-the-Bunny"-type book of all the things for which we are thankful to God. (Board Book)

Bogot, Howard I., and Daniel B. Syme. *I'm Growing*. New York: UAHC Press, 1982. (Ages 2-5)
Children know they are growing when they learn new ways to understand and perform the important Jewish holiday activities depicted in this book.

———. *My Body Is Something Special*. New York: UAHC Press, 1981. (Ages 2-5)
An engaging picture book to teach children about holidays. Special activities are used to show how parts of the body can perform important Jewish tasks.

Carmi, Giora. *And Shira Imagined*. Philadelphia, PA: Jewish Publication Society, 1988. (Ages 3-8)
On a trip to Israel, a young girl uses her imagination as her parents describe Israel's cities. Out of print, but well worth the search.

Edwards, Michelle. *Chicken Man*. New York: Lothrop, Lee & Shepard Books, 1991. (Ages 4-8)
A silly story about life on a *kibbutz*.

Frankel, Max, and Judy Hoffman. *I Live in Israel*. New York: Behrman House, 1979.
Texbook geared to Grades 3-4 with simple information about several key cities and locales in Israel.

Grand, Samuel and Tamar Grand. *The Children of Israel*. New York: UAHC Press, 1972. (Ages 5-8)
Too much text to read, but good pictures.

Groner, Judye, and Madeline Wikler. *Israel Fun for Little Hands*. Rockville, MD: Kar-Ben Copies, 1995. (Ages 3-7)

Games, riddles, puzzles, and mazes introduce young children to Israel's famous sites.

Kendall, Jonathan. *My Name Is Rachamim*. New York: UAHC Press, 1987. (Ages 4-10)

When famine ravages the Gondar region of Ethiopia, Rachamim and his family journey to Israel via Operation Moses, the secret airlift that brought thousands of Ethiopian Jews home to Israel.

Kobre, Faige. *A Sense of Shabbat*. Los Angeles: Torah Aura Productions, 1989. (Ages 3-6)

Beautiful photos help describe the entire day of Shabbat through the senses.

Roberts, Bethany, and Patricia Hubbell. *Camel Caravan*. New York: Tambourine Books, 1996. (Ages 3-6)

Catch a wild ride with some camels who have had enough of hauling loads across the desert.

Segal, Sheila. *Joshua's Dream: A Journey To the Land of Israel*. New York: UAHC Press, 1985. (Ages 4-10)

Joshua learns about Zionism and the birth of the State of Israel.

Waldman, Neil. *The Two Brothers: A Legend of Jerusalem*. New York: Atheneum Books for Young Readers, 1997.

A story of why the site for the Temple in Jerusalem was chosen.

INTRODUCTION TO PART III
YOU SHALL CELEBRATE THESE DAYS

These are the set times of Adonai, the sacred occasions, which you shall celebrate each at its appointed time. (Leviticus 23:4)

Jewish life is choreographed by the Jewish calendar. Shabbat gives us pause each week; Rosh Chodesh marks the passing of each month; and scattered throughout the months are the Jewish holidays, each one with a story connecting us to our past, adding to the rhythm of Jewish life. Some of our holidays have a basis in Torah, such as Shabbat, Rosh Chodesh, Rosh HaShanah, Yom Kippur, Sukkot, Pesach, and Shavuot. Other holidays were developed later, such as Chanukah, Purim, and Yom HaAtzma'ut. Whatever their origin, each of the holidays has something to teach us about ourselves and about who we are as a Jewish People.

The Jewish holidays are full of concrete symbols, exciting rituals, and important values. Beginning with the observances outlined in the Torah and combining those with all the foods, ceremonies, and celebrations that have been added through the generations, the Jewish holidays are designed to make Jewish life attractive and captivating for all Jews, adults and children alike.

All together, the Jewish holidays comprise a framework around which much of Jewish life revolves. In Israel, people can always be heard to say, "I'll do it after the *chageem* (holidays)." No matter what day it is, it seems there are always more *chageem* right around the corner. Still, the Jewish holidays do not define the entirety of Jewish life. God, Torah, and Israel are important parts of each holiday, yet these concepts also have great significance of their own. The same is true

of Jewish values and *mitzvot*. Thus, it is important to remember that while teaching about and celebrating the Jewish holidays should be an integral part of the early childhood curriculum, the holidays represent only one of many meaningful aspects of Judaism.

So, celebrate the Jewish holidays with your children. Make each holiday as rich and exciting and creative as possible. Resist the urge to water down adult observances so as to make them "suitable" for children. Each holiday is already bursting with symbols, rituals, and celebrations in which children can participate. Then always go beyond the holidays as you strive to make your classroom a Jewish place all of the time.

Presented in the following 12 chapters are blueprints for celebrating the Jewish holidays in your classroom in developmentally appropriate ways, with strategies for integrating the concepts and values of the holidays into every aspect of your classroom, all year round.

Each holiday chapter contains the following:
- Overview – includes historical background of the holiday and contemporary practices
- Glossary – a listing of pertinent terms in English and Hebrew and their definitions
- Blessings (where applicable) – in English, Hebrew, and transliteration
- A diagram of a "web" – a beginning web of holiday concepts
- Concepts – important ideas to teach, divided into age groups: Infant to 24 months, 2 years, 3 years, and 4 to 5 years
- Activities – suggestions for activities in the areas of Language Arts, Math, Art, Music/Movement, Circle Time, Outdoors/Field Trips, Specifically for Infants, Ideas for Teaching Families

- Stories – a story or two that relates to the holiday
- Suggested newsletter article – already written article that can be sent home as is or adapted for your situation
- Recipes – easy recipes that children will enjoy making

- Bibliography – a useful listing of resources for adults and for children pertaining to the holiday

More general resources about holidays are listed in the comprehensive bibliography at the end of the book.

CHAPTER 7

SHABBAT

Remember the Sabbath day and keep it holy. Six days you shall labor and do all your work, but the seventh day is a Sabbath of Adonai your God; you shall not do any work. (Exodus 20:8-10)

More than Israel has kept the Sabbath, the Sabbath has kept Israel. (Ahad Ha'am)

OVERVIEW

Shabbat is the holiest day of the week. From sundown Friday night until an hour after sundown on Saturday night, Jews are blessed with a day of rest, a day of reflection and rejuvenation. The earliest mention of Shabbat is in Genesis 2, the account of creation. In six days, God created the entire world: light, darkness, day, night, plants, birds, and fish, animals, and human beings. By the seventh day, God finished the work of creating the world and rested. "And God blessed the seventh day and declared it holy, because on it God ceased from all the work of creation that God had done" (Genesis 2:3).

Most of us rush through the weekdays, packing as much as possible into each day and night. Shabbat is our reminder to slow down, to appreciate everything we have, and to give back to the world instead of taking from it. Shabbat itself is filled with rituals to guide our experience. Friday is ideally a time of preparation — to clean the house, prepare a special meal, wash our bodies, put on nicer clothes, and gather the family together. On Friday eve, we welcome in Shabbat. We think of Shabbat as a day that enters as a bride and departs as a queen. Just as we welcome the Sabbath Bride, we also welcome guests to our table for Shabbat. Hospitality, sharing Shabbat with others, is a *mitzvah*, and an integral part of the holiday.

For a glossary and Hebrew vocabulary list for Shabbat, see figure 8 on pp. 107 and 108.

EREV SHABBAT/FRIDAY NIGHT

As the sun sets on Friday night, we usher in Shabbat with the lighting of candles. Many families give *tzedakah* right before they light the candles, tying the act of providing for others directly to Shabbat. Lighting Shabbat candles presents us with a bit of a dilemma. Traditionally, we say a blessing and then do an act (e.g., bless bread, then eat it). But as soon as we say the blessing over the candles, Shabbat begins. Traditionally, no fire is kindled after Shabbat begins; hence, we could not light the candles. To solve this dilemma, we first light the candles, then cover our eyes, as if pretending the candles are not yet lit. Some wave their hands in a circle, three or more times, bringing in the warmth of the light to their eyes. We say the blessing, and then uncover our eyes, as if discovering the flames for the first time. Everyone kisses, hugs, and wishes each other *Shabbat Shalom* (a good Shabbat).

Some families go to synagogue on Friday night for Kabbalat Shabbat, the special service to welcome Shabbat. During the service, the prayer *"Lecha Dodi"* is sung. Everyone stands up, faces the synagogue door, and welcomes the Sabbath Bride. After the Kabbalat Shabbat service, the family goes home for Shabbat dinner.

At the dinner table at home, the song *"Shalom Alaychem"* (Peace be to you) is sung to welcome in Shabbat and the ministering angels. For a *midrash* about the two ministering angels who accompany each person home from synagogue on *erev* Shabbat, see p. 123 in this chapter.

Before proceeding to *Kiddush*, the blessing over the wine, various family members may bless each other. The husband (and children) may bless the wife with the reading of Proverb 31, *Ayshet Chayil* (A Woman of Valor), the wife may bless the husband with *Ashray HaEesh* (Happy is the man), and the parents may bless the children with the traditional blessings over a son/daughter. Family blessings give us an opportunity to appreciate the specialness and value of each member of the family — something we may not take enough time to consider during the week!

During the *Kiddush*, we bless the wine, but with this blessing we are also sanctifying the day, declaring it *kadosh* (holy), and praising God for giving us the special gift of Shabbat. Then it's time for *challah*, the special braided egg bread we eat on Shabbat. Some families insert a ritual hand washing with a special cup called a *klee* (tool) and say a blessing before they bless the *challah*. In order not to separate the hand washing from the *motzi* (blessing over the bread), there is no talking in between the two blessings (although sometimes a *niggun* — a wordless melody — is sung to help pass the time). *HaMotzi* is said over two *challot*, which reminds us of the double portion of manna gathered on Fridays by the generation in the Sinai desert, and everyone enjoys a piece of the *challah*. This first piece is sometimes sprinkled with salt to remind us of the offerings in the days of the Temple, and sometimes dipped in honey to honor newlyweds at the table.

Finally, the Shabbat meal is served. Traditionally, Shabbat dinner is the finest meal of the week. In poor Jewish communities, Shabbat was often the only time the family splurged and served meat and other delicacies. Today, the meal may consist of several courses and include traditional Jewish foods such as chicken soup, gefilte fish, and *kugel*. But even if the meal consists of pizza and Oreos for dessert, the important thing is that the family is taking time to sit together and enjoy the meal.

There are many *zemirot*, traditional songs, which may be sung before or after the meal. As we say or chant the *Birkat HaMazon*, blessing after the meal, we thank God for giving us the food which we have just enjoyed. Shabbat evening, after the table is cleared, presents the perfect opportunity to spend time together doing things that there is little time for during the rest of the week — singing songs, playing games, reading books, going for a walk, or actually talking with and listening to each other. Some families make a habit of attending later worship services at their synagogue on Friday evenings.

YOM SHABBAT/SATURDAY DAY

Shabbat begins Friday night, and it continues until after sundown Saturday night, when we can see three stars in the sky. Saturday morning, many families go to synagogue to pray, hear the Torah read, and be with the Jewish community. Shabbat lunch includes *Kiddush*, *challah*, and another opportunity to invite Shabbat guests to the table. The entire day is filled with opportunities to get together with friends, spend quality time together, nap, read, learn Torah, and recuperate from the rush of the week.

HAVDALAH

Inevitably, the sky begins to darken, and about 25 hours after we lit candles and welcomed in Shabbat, it is time to bid it good-bye. When three stars appear in the sky, about an hour after sunset, Shabbat is over. Havdalah is the ceremony with which we transition from Shabbat to the rest of the week. The word Havdalah means separation, and, indeed, it is our goal to separate Shabbat, a *kadosh* time, from the rest of the ordinary week. Just as we welcomed in Shabbat with candles and wine, so, too, we usher Shabbat out with a cup of wine, and a candle with two or more wicks. (If one does not have a special Havdalah candle, it is permissible to hold two candles together for Havdalah.) Instead of *challah*, however, we now bless and savor *besameem*, sweet spices, as we try to

GLOSSARY AND HEBREW VOCABULARY

אַבָּא	*Abba*	father
אֵשֶׁת חַיִל	*Ayshet Chayil*	literally, "A Woman of Valor," Proverbs 31:10-31, blessing said by the husband to the wife.
אַשְׁרֵי הָאִישׁ	*Ashray HaEesh*	literally, "Happy is the Man," Psalm 112, blessing said by the wife to the husband
בַּיִת	*Bayit*	house
	Benscher	Yiddish for prayer book; book of Shabbat blessings and songs, especially the *Birkat HaMazon*
בְּשָׂמִים	*Besameem*	sweet spices
בִּרְכַּת הַמָּזוֹן	*Birkat HaMazon*	blessing or grace said after meals
בְּרָכָה/בְּרָכֹת	*Brachah/Brachot*	literally, "blessing/blessings"
חַלָּה/חַלּוֹת	*Challah/Challot*	the special braided egg bread(s) that we eat on Shabbat
אִמָּא	*Eema*	mother
אֵלִיָּהוּ הַנָּבִיא	"*Eliyahu HaNavi*"	a song sung at Havdalah inviting Elijah the prophet to bring in a better world
עֶרֶב שַׁבָּת	*Erev* Shabbat	Shabbat eve, Friday night
הַמּוֹצִיא	HaMotzi	the blessing over *challah* and other bread
הַבְדָּלָה	Havdalah	the ceremony that separates Shabbat from the beginning of the new week
קַבָּלַת שַׁבָּת	Kabbalat Shabbat	Friday night synagogue service to welcome Shabbat
קָדוֹשׁ	*Kadosh*	holy
קִדּוּשׁ	*Kiddush*	the blessing said over wine, which makes the act "holy"
כִּפָּה	*Kipah*	head covering, *yarmelke*
כְּלִי	*Klee*	literally, "tool," specifically the two handled cup used for ritual washing before a meal
כּוֹס קִדּוּשׁ	*Kos Kiddush*	a special cup for the wine, often made of silver
לְכָה דוֹדִי	"*Lecha Dodi*"	a song sung during Kabbalat Shabbat to welcome Shabbat in the form of the Sabbath Bride
מְנוּחָה	*Menuchah*	rest
מִצְוָה	*Mitzvah*	literally, "commandment"
נֵר/נֵרוֹת	*Nayr/Nayrote*	candle/candles
נְטִילַת יָדַיִם	*Netilat Yadayeem*	washing of hands
נִגּוּן	*Niggun*	a wordless melody
פָּרָשַׁת הַשָּׁבוּעַ	*Parashat HaShavua*	weekly Torah portion
סַבָּא	*Sabba*	grandfather
סַבְתָּא	*Saftah*	grandmother
שַׁבָּת	Shabbat	the Jewish Sabbath, the seventh day of the week, begins Friday at sundown and ends Saturday after three stars appear
שַׁבָּת שָׁלוֹם	*Shabbat Shalom*	Hebrew greeting wishing someone a peaceful Shabbat
שָׁלוֹם עֲלֵיכֶם	"*Shalom Alaychem*"	literally, "Peace be to you," a song sung to welcome Shabbat
	Shabbos	Yiddish or Ashkenazic pronunciation of Shabbat

Figure 8

GLOSSARY AND HEBREW VOCABULARY		
שָׁבוּעַ טוֹב	"Shavua Tov"	a Havdalah song and greeting, as well as a wish for a good week
סִדוּר	Siddur	prayer book
תּוֹרָה	Torah	the five books of Moses
צְדָקָה	Tzedakah	literally, "justice," giving of oneself through charity or one's time
יוֹם שַׁבָּת	Yom Shabbat	the day of Shabbat; Saturday
יַיִן	Yayin	wine
זְמִירוֹת	Zemirot	traditional songs

Figure 8, Cont.

hold onto the sweetness of Shabbat even as we bid it good-bye. With blessings and songs (especially the singing of "Eliyahu HaNavi," beckoning Elijah to bring a better world for all, and "Shavua Tov" — A Good Week), families gather to let go of Shabbat and move into a brand new week.

SHABBAT BLESSINGS

Following are the blessings recited on Shabbat.

Candles:

בָּרוּךְ אַתָּה יְיָ אֱלֹהֵינוּ מֶלֶךְ הָעוֹלָם אֲשֶׁר קִדְּשָׁנוּ בְּמִצְוֹתָיו וְצִוָּנוּ לְהַדְלִיק נֵר שֶׁל שַׁבָּת.

Baruch Atah Adonai Elohaynu Melech HaOlam Asher Kid'shanu B'Mitzvotav V'Tzivanu Lihadleek Nayr Shel Shabbat.

We praise you, our God, Creator of the universe, Who has made us holy through Your mitzvot and commands us to kindle the Shabbat lights.

Blessing over Sons:

יְשִׂמְךָ אֱלֹהִים כְּאֶפְרַיִם וְכִמְנַשֶּׁה.

Y'simcha Elohim k'Efrayeem v'chiMenasheh.
May God make you like Ephraim and Menasseh.

Blessing over Daughters:

יְשִׂמֵךְ אֱלֹהִים כְּשָׂרָה רִבְקָה רָחֵל וְלֵאָה.

Y'simaych Elohim k'Sarah, Rivka, Rachel, v'Leah.

May God make you like Sarah, Rebecca, Rachel, and Leah.

Continue for Both Sons and Daughters:

יְבָרֶכְךָ יְיָ וְיִשְׁמְרֶךָ. יָאֵר יְיָ פָּנָיו אֵלֶיךָ וִיחֻנֶּךָּ. יִשָּׂא יְיָ פָּנָיו אֵלֶיךָ וְיָשֵׂם לְךָ שָׁלוֹם.

Y'vareche'cha Adonai V'yishm'recha. Ya'ayr Adonai Panav Aylecha Vichuneca. Yisa Adonai Panav Aylecha V'yasem L'cha Shalom.

May God bless you and watch over you. May God cause the Divine face to shine upon you and be gracious to you. May God lift up the Divine face toward you and give you peace.

Wine:
On erev Shabbat, Kiddush includes sections from the Torah which sanctify the day of Shabbat, as well as the wine. You can find the entire Kiddush in any Siddur or Benscher.

בָּרוּךְ אַתָּה יְיָ אֱלֹהֵינוּ מֶלֶךְ הָעוֹלָם בּוֹרֵא פְּרִי הַגָּפֶן.

Baruch Atah Adonai Elohaynu Melech HaOlam Boray P'ri HaGafen.

We praise You, our God, Creator of the universe, for creating the fruit of the vine.

Netilat Yadayeem (Handwashing):

בָּרוּךְ אַתָּה יְיָ אֱלֹהֵינוּ מֶלֶךְ הָעוֹלָם אֲשֶׁר קִדְּשָׁנוּ בְּמִצְוֹתָיו וְצִוָּנוּ עַל נְטִילַת יָדָיִם.

Baruch Atah Adonai Elohaynu Melech HaOlam Asher Kid'shanu B'Mitzvotav V'Tzivanu Al Netilat Yadayeem.

We praise you, our God, Creator of the universe, Who has made us holy through Your *mitzvot* and commands us to wash our hands.

HaMotzi:

בָּרוּךְ אַתָּה יְיָ אֱלֹהֵינוּ מֶלֶךְ הָעוֹלָם הַמּוֹצִיא לֶחֶם מִן הָאָרֶץ.

Baruch Atah Adonai Elohaynu Melech HaOlam HaMotzi Lechem Min HaAretz.

We praise You, our God, Creator of the universe, for bringing forth bread from the earth.

Very Short Version of Birkat HaMazon:
(Note: Longer version may be found in any *Benscher*.)

בָּרוּךְ אַתָּה יְיָ הַזָּן אֶת־הַכֹּל

Baruch Atah Adonai Chazan et HaKol.

We praise you God, the provider of food for all.

Havdalah Blessings:
(See p. 122 below.)

SHABBAT CONCEPTS

WEBBING THE CONCEPTS

Webbing the concepts of Shabbat (see Chapter 1, "Developmentally Appropriate Practice," p. 11 for more on webbing), can elicit ideas about what you want children to learn (and not just what you want them to make). This technique can also bring to mind connections to other things going on in your classroom. Figure 9 on p. 110 is the *beginning* of a web for Shabbat. You can extend the web with your co-teachers or your students, thus shaping the celebration of Shabbat to include the interests of everyone in your class. *You won't cover everything you web*, but you'll get a good idea of where you want to go.

(Note: Since we celebrate Shabbat all year, the concepts for the next age group may apply as children grow.)

Infant To 24 months
1. We celebrate Shabbat every week.
2. We light candles on Shabbat.
3. We drink wine (grape juice) on Shabbat.
4. We eat *challah* on Shabbat.

2 Years
1. We celebrate Shabbat every week.
2. Shabbat is a very special day.
3. I celebrate Shabbat with my family.
4. We light *nayrote* on Shabbat.
5. We don't blow out Shabbat *nayrote*.
6. We drink wine (grape juice) on Shabbat.
7. We put the wine/grape juice in a *kos Kiddush*.
8. We eat *challah* on Shabbat.
9. We cover the *challah* with a pretty *challah* cover.
10. We say lots of blessings on Shabbat.
11. We say *"Shabbat Shalom!"* to our friends and family.
12. Havdalah is the way we say good-bye to Shabbat.

3 Years

1. We celebrate Shabbat every week.
2. Shabbat is the last day of the week, the seventh day.
3. Shabbat is a very special, holy day.
4. I celebrate Shabbat with my family.
5. Shabbat is a day to rest and be with my family.
6. We rest because God rested on Shabbat when God created the world.
7. We give *tzedakah* before Shabbat begins to help other people.
8. We light *nayrote* on Shabbat.
9. We don't blow out Shabbat *nayrote*.
10. We wave our hands over the candles to bring the warmth in very close.
11. We drink wine (grape juice) on Shabbat.
12. We put the wine/grape juice in a *kos Kiddush*.
13. We eat *challah* on Shabbat.

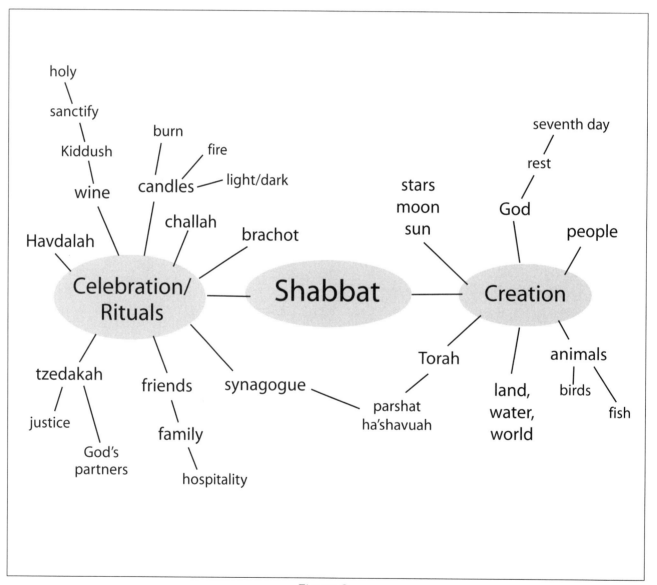

Figure 9

14. We cover the *challah* with a pretty *challah* cover, so that it is not jealous that it is last.
15. Each part of Shabbat has its own *brachah.*
16. We thank God for giving us such a special day.
17. We say *"Shabbat Shalom!"* to our friends and family to wish them a happy Shabbat.
18. Shabbat begins Friday night and ends Saturday night.
19. Havdalah is the way we say good-bye to Shabbat.

4 To 5 Years

1. We celebrate Shabbat every week.
2. Shabbat is the last day of the week, the seventh day.
3. Shabbat is a very special, holy day.
4. I celebrate Shabbat with my family.
5. Shabbat is a day to rest and be with my family.
6. God created the world in six days and rested on the seventh day. This is the story of creation. We find the story of creation at the beginning of the Torah.
7. God created the world, but I am God's partner in perfecting the world.
8. We rest because God rested on Shabbat after creating the world.
9. We give *tzedakah* before Shabbat to help other people.
10. To give *tzedakah* is to be righteous. We do our best to make this a righteous, just, fair world. I prepare for Shabbat by cleaning and helping others.
11. My family and my school prepare in special ways for Shabbat.
12. The whole country of Israel prepares in special ways for Shabbat.
13. We light *nayrote* to welcome in Shabbat.
14. We wave our hands over the candles to bring the warmth in very close.
15. We drink wine (grape juice) on Shabbat.
16. We put the wine/grape juice in a *kos Kiddush.*
17. We eat *challah* on Shabbat.
18. We cover the *challah* with a pretty *challah* cover so that it is not jealous that it is blessed last.

19. Each part of Shabbat has its own *brachah.*
20. When we say the *brachot* and take part in the rituals of Shabbat, we are thanking God for giving us such a special day.
21. *Brachot* make ordinary things *kadosh.*
22. We say *"Shabbat Shalom!"* to our friends and family to wish them a peaceful Shabbat.
23. On *Yom Shabbat*, we read from the Torah in the synagogue.
24. Shabbat begins Friday night and ends Saturday night.
25. Shabbat is over when we see three stars in the sky. Havdalah is the way we say good-bye to Shabbat.

ACTIVITIES

LANGUAGE ARTS

1. Make class books with Shabbat themes, or based on Shabbat songs, in which every child dictates and illustrates a page. Examples include using the song "What Do You Like about Shabbat?" or "I Took a Little Walk" (see *A Shabbat Primer*, edited by Lee Matansky). Class books can also focus on guests the children would like to invite for Shabbat, how the children get ready for Shabbat, or the children's favorite things to do on Shabbat.
2. Adapt popular books to reflect Shabbat themes. *Brown Bear, Brown Bear, What Do You See?* by Bill Martin could be *Shabbat, Shabbat, What Do You See? If You Give a Mouse a Cookie* by Laura Joffe Numeroff could *be If You Give a Mouse Some Challah.* Use some of the children's favorite books or favorite characters and put them in Shabbat settings.
3. Find pictures of families from various cultures around the world celebrating Shabbat. Bind these into book form and laminate. You can also incorporate into this book photos of the families of the children in the class celebrating Shabbat. Make this book part of the class library.

4. Pretend with the children to be different Shabbat objects, e.g., a *kipah*, candles melting, a *Kiddush* cup, wine, flour, yeast rising in a bowl, a *challah* cover, etc.

5. Make the children's favorite Shabbat stories into flannel boards so they can tell the story themselves. Photocopy the characters from the book, mount on tagboard, laminate, and put some hook velcro on the back.

6. Provide prop boxes to help children prepare for Shabbat. Butcher, bakery, synagogue, flower shop, grocery store, biblical settings, and *sofer's* workshop are all dramatic play opportunities which will let children develop their language skills in connection to Shabbat.

7. Make or buy board games, matching games, memory games, and dominoes with Shabbat symbols. Games for older children can be useful in introducing and reinforcing a wide range of Shabbat symbols. With younger children, use basic Shabbat symbols to reinforce color, sequencing, size, and number concepts.

8. When celebrating Havdalah, drip the candle onto a paper plate, and save the plate to drip onto each week. When the wax pile gets big enough, it can "tell stories." Put your hand on the wax pile, and tell the children it is telling you a story. Tell a Shabbat story or happening as if it happened to a child in the class (never reveal who the child is!). After a few weeks, let a child put his/her hand on the wax pile and "get" a story to tell the class.

SCIENCE

1. Bake *challah*.

2. Watch yeast rise. Measure the foam under different conditions (very hot water, cold water, warm water, in the refrigerator, on a warm windowsill, with sugar, with no sugar, after five minutes, after two hours, etc.). Growing the yeast in a clear measuring cup makes calculating growth easier.

3. Try different *challah* recipes and let the children have a taste test and vote on their favorite.

4. Provide small bins of flour for children to play with (you can put the flour bin in a larger sensory table).

5. Create a *challah* for children to braid. Stuff three brown panty hose legs with pillow stuffing. Tie the legs all together at one end, and tie each leg individually at the other end. To dye the strands darker brown, boil in a pot of strong tea or coffee until it is the color you desire (an hour or two). Add velcro squares at the ends to secure the braid.

6. Identify the five senses as they are used to accomplish various Shabbat activities (rolling *challah*, eating *challah*, lighting a candle, drinking wine, singing Shabbat songs, baking *challah*, smelling *besameem* at Havdalah, etc.).

7. Clean the pennies from the *Tzedakah* box by rubbing the pennies with salt and washing them in vinegar.

8. Experiment with candles. Time how long Shabbat, birthday, Chanukah, and Havdalah candles burn. Which ones drip?

9. Make Havdalah candles. Dip Chanukah candles or long thin birthday candles into very hot water until they are soft. Twist or braid the candles together.

10. Candles need oxygen to burn. Experiment by putting different sizes of glass jars over burning candles. What happens when the oxygen runs out?

11. Try the above experiment, but put the candle in a shallow pan of water. Watch the water rise in the jar as the oxygen runs out and the water moves to take its place.

12. Invite children to bring in *Kiddush* cups from home (or candlesticks or *challah* covers). Compare the objects. Let the children weigh them, measure the volume or the circumference, draw them, describe their own objects to their friends.

13. Use grape juice or grape colored water to explore volume concepts. Let children play with differently shaped containers that have the same volume. Let the children play with differently shaped/sized *Kiddush* cups.

14. Make grape juice. Put seedless grapes into a zip-lock bag and let the children smash the grapes. Compare the juice from different colored grapes. Say the blessing and drink the juice.

15. Dye white carnations by putting them in water with food coloring. Compare different colors and strengths of color with clear water. Demonstrate that the flower drinks the water through its stem the way we drink water through a straw.

16. Make a *besameem* "box" by sticking whole cloves into an orange. It still smells good even after the orange dries up. Do this with the *etrog*, too, after Sukkot (the *etrog* skin is thicker than an orange skin, but it's worth the effort).

17. Explore the concepts of creation. It is possible to expand a creation curriculum over several weeks or even an entire school year. The following ideas are culled from a workshop entitled "Integrating Science and Math into the Judaic Curriculum" by Tamar Andrews, from Westside JCC in Los Angeles (material used with permission of Tamar Andrews).

Day 1: Bringing Order from Chaos, Separation of Light and Dark, Day and Night

1. Give the children a plate with crackers and peanut butter. Let them instruct each other on how to make a mini-sandwich.
2. Give the children a large basket of toys (or buttons, etc.) and let them sort them.
3. Toss toys into a basket from all over the room.
4. Put colored water and oil into a bottle. Shake it and watch them separate.
5. Use a strong cow magnet to attract metal objects.
6. Sprinkle a layer of pepper on top of a bowl of water. Drip a drop of soap in the middle and watch the pepper move away.
7. Play with shadows. Outside, children can dance and watch their shadows dance. Tell them to tickle their friend's shadow without touching their friend. Inside, use flashlights in a darkened room to make shadows grow and shrink.

Day 2: Rain, Sky, Separation of Land and Water

1. Use tornado tubes to show water moving from one bottle to another.
2. Punch small holes on the bottom of a dish soap bottle and fill with water. When you lift the bottle top, the water comes out like rain. Pushing the top back down stops the rain.
3. Bring some rain sticks into the room.
4. Toss around whirly birds to experience wind.

Day 3: Dry Land and Plants

1. Bring in local plants.
2. Allow the children many different kinds of planting experiences.
3. Dig in sand.

Day 4: Sun, Moon, and Stars

1. Poke holes in black paper and paste on popsicle stick or the end of a toilet paper tube.
2. Make dot-to-dot pictures.
3. To test the sun's power, cover half of the cups in a muffin tray with aluminum foil. Put water and/or and apple slice in each cup. Put the tray on a sunny windowsill or outside in the sun. Let the children predict what will happen to the things in the cups with foil and those without.
4. Play with shadows. Children trace their shadows at different times of day while standing on the same spot. Have them look for their shadow at night.
5. Watch the moon wax or wane over several days (good to do in the winter).

Day 5: Fish and Birds

1. Take empty plastic strawberry baskets and fill with bits of string, paper, etc., and hang on trees for birds to take for nest building.

2. Make bird feeders.
3. Get some guppies for the class and watch them multiply.
4. Practice the Jewish value of *Tza'ar Ba'alay Chayim* (caring for animals).

Day 6: Animals and People

1. Hang a sheet from the ceiling (so children can walk behind it). Draw a nature scene (large tree, sun, sky, land) on the sheet. Make butterflies, birds, spiders, animals, people. Attach a magnet to each animal. Children can take another magnet, stand behind the sheet, and make the animals move and fly.
2. Focus on caterpillars: Children make a caterpillar, put in a decorated bag (the chrysalis), hang on tree on sheet. Some days later, before children come to school, replace caterpillars with butterflies. Magnets on these butterflies let them fly all over the sheet.
3. Do a unit covering every part of the human body.
4. Focus on the senses.
5. Study animal and people homes, animal tracks, what animals eat, animal and human babies. Share *midrash*im about how Adam named all the animals (see *Does God have a Big Toe?* by Marc Gellman and *The Naming* by Margaret Greaves).

Day 7: God Rests/Shabbat

(see other suggestions in this "Activities" section B)

MATH

1. Use Shabbat symbols to make a counting book.
2. Play Shabbat lotto or Shabbat Bingo.
3. Sort pictures of Shabbat objects into sets. Classify by size, shape, color, relationship, by number.
4. Count the money in the *Tzedakah* box. Sort by type of coin. An entire unit on money could follow.

5. Graph the kinds of coins in the *Tzedakah* box. Use concepts such as more, less, greatest, least, none, some, more, a lot.
6. Sequence pictures of getting ready for Shabbat.
7. Measure various candles, including different types of Havdalah candles.
8. Cut a *challah* into half, quarters, to reinforce the concept of fractions.
9. Pack grocery bags with items for Shabbat. Count the items. Compare the weight of different bags, using arms and a scale.
10. Play games such as *Five Big Challahs at the Bakery Shop.* Use five felt or plastic *challot.* Distribute one penny (real or pretend) to each of five children. Then children sing the following song:

    There were five big *challahs* in the bakery shop.
    The great big *challahs* — with the poppy seeds on top.
    Along came [insert child's name] with a penny to pay.
    He [she] bought one *challah* and he [she] walked away.
    (One child exchanges the penny for a *challah.*

    Continue singing: "There were four big *challahs* . . . ," etc.)
11. Make matching/counting cards with a *challah* on each card, and different numbers of raisins on each *challah.*

ART

Note: Over the course of a child's early childhood education, there is great value in providing opportunities for children to create usable Shabbat objects. Functional ritual objects transfer the experience and the learning to the family. Given this, it is important to remember that children learn best through process-oriented, child-centered art experiences. Included below are many strategies that are process-focused for creating functional Shabbat objects.

1. Make Shabbat place mats. Place mats set the tone for something special when used for

Shabbat snack or lunch. Laminate the finished mats, and be sure to wipe off after each use for longer life.

a. Cut Shabbat symbols out of tagboard. Let children pick and place some symbols on the mat, then spray with food colored water in spray bottles. For younger children, cut Jewish/Shabbat pictures from Judaica store catalogs (older children can choose and cut out their own pictures). Provide glitter, tissue paper squares, or other Shabbat shapes cut from construction paper, and let children create a collage place mat.

b. Provide the children with Jewish symbol stamps or Jewish symbol sponges to sponge paint. Use colors that connote Shabbat, including blue, white, silver, gold, and purple. For very young children, incorporate a photo of the child into the child's artwork.

c. Let children paint different size doilies and glue onto the place mat. Alternatively, children can paint a doily on the place mat, then remove the doily.

2. Make candlesticks.

a. Start with two empty, clean baby food jars with lids and two metal bottle caps. Children can decorate the outside of the jars with Jewish/Shabbat stickers, tissue paper squares, swatches of Hebrew newspaper, bits of aluminum foil, or pictures from a Judaica store catalog (basic collage materials). Use Mod-Podge for longer life. Older children can use paint markers. With a hot glue gun, the teacher can attach the bottle cap to the lid of the baby food jar.

b. Cut the top half off two-liter pop bottles. Tape the bottom so it is not sharp. Children can decorate with the basic collage items above or paint with glue mixed in. Put aluminum foil in between candle and plastic bottle.

c. Use modeling clay or homemade hardening clay. Children can shape the candle-sticks themselves or use cookie cutters to make shapes. Decorate with beads, large glitter and sequins (use Jewish glitter from the party store, too) and/or paint. Use Shabbat candles to make candle holes.

d. Provide a large assortment of plumbing, hardware, and recycled artifacts. Allow children to experiment with shape and design. This can be a several day project. Supervise the project closely to ensure that the candlesticks will be usable and safe.

e. Let the children decorate two mini-bagels with markers, paint, and/or glitter. Spray with shellac to preserve. Mount a metal bottle cap in the middle of each bagel with a hot glue gun.

3. Make *Kiddush* cups.

a. Begin with a plastic cup or wine cup. Decorate with basic collage items and cover with Mod-Podge.

b. Begin with a plastic cup. Provide modeling clay or homemade hardening clay. Display different *Kiddush* cups (pictures and actual cups) and let children create clay *Kiddush* cups to hold plastic cup. Decorate with beads and/or paint.

c. Let children decorate one plastic or Styrofoam cup as the base, using collage, markers, or paint. Glue another cup to the decorated cup — bottom to bottom — as the drinking cup.

4. Make *Challah* covers, Shabbat tablecloths, *kipot*.

a. Try tie-dying. First, tie fabric in knots or with rubberbands. (Use handkerchiefs for *challah* covers, inexpensive tablecloths for tablecloths, white cotton for *kipot*.) Then dip into liquid tempera paint made for tie-dying.

b. Paint children's hands and incorporate their handprints into a design.

c. Paint with sponges or cookie cutters in Jewish/Shabbat shapes.

d. Dribble paint in Shabbat colors.

e. Children use eyedroppers and water that is colored with food coloring.

f. Color with fabric crayons or make designs with paint markers.

5. Make *Tzedakah* boxes.

a. Great containers to use: baby wipe boxes, tins from General Foods International Coffee, gold Godiva chocolate boxes, checkbook boxes, coffee cans, yogurt containers, "Crystal Lite" cans, and so on. Allow children open-ended decorating freedom — basic collage materials, paint, pictures of coins, glitter, sequins. Provide strategies for incorporating the word "*Tzedakah*" in Hebrew and English into their design. For older children, use Hebrew letter stamps, pre-written on a sticker (provide models to copy).

6. Using film canisters, empty pill bottles, or small cloth bags, make containers children can use when bringing *Tzedakah* from home. Decorate with basic collage materials, paint, or stickers. Always include the word "*Tzedakah*."

7. Make a Shabbat book.
(Note: A Shabbat book is especially useful with younger children — twos and threes — to reinforce Shabbat symbols, and to foster transference of learning to home.

a. Allow older children to draw their own representations of Shabbat objects based on real objects or various pictures as models. Older children can decide what kinds of things to put in the book (symbols and experiences); with younger children, limit the number of pages, and provide written explanations and blessings on each page to foster family learning. Use one symbol per page. Provide an outline or cut-out shape of each symbol. The book may include some or all of the following pages:

b. Shabbat flowers – provide dried flower petals and pipe cleaners or string. Or use fingerprints to make flowers.

c. *Tzedakah* box – children decorate box shape with collage materials, paint, markers or crayons. Provide cut-out coin shapes to glue on, or glue a coin to the bottom of a film canister and use as a stamp with stamp pads.

d. Candles – Let children rub the candlestick shapes with wax candles and then paint with watercolors. Provide real wicks to glue on.

e. *Kiddush* cup – Children can make collages out of aluminum foil bits, and decorate with purple crayons.

f. *Challah* – Let children make collages using poppy seeds and many different kinds of brown materials (e.g., fabric, construction paper, pipe cleaners, yarn, felt, buttons).

g. Havdalah symbols – Braid pipe cleaners or string for the candle. Use real ground spices for the *besamim* and let the children choose which spices to use. For *Kiddush* cup, see above. Use gold stars or star stamps for the three stars we see at Havdalah.

8. Make Shabbat flowers and vases.

a. Let the children dye coffee filters using eye droppers and water colored with food coloring. When dry, attach to a popsicle stick or pipe cleaner.

b. Children decorate colored and foil cupcake liner with glitter, paint, markers. Poke a pipe cleaner through the middle.

c. Let the children decorate the outside of a tennis ball can with basic collage materials and the words "*Shabbat Shalom*."

9. Make *besameem* boxes.

a. Children decorate a film canister or other small container with a lid. Poke holes in the lid. Fill with spices.

b. Have children decorate an empty baby food jar. Fill with spices, and cover the top with a square of "smell-through" fabric or lace. Secure with a rubber band and a ribbon.

c. Older children can sew and decorate a mesh bag and fill with spices.

10. Give the children Shabbat colors and collage materials. Play Shabbat music and let them create freely.
11. Paint with Shabbat candles instead of paint-brushes.
12. Use Shabbat objects like the wicks of candles, flower petals, and poppy seeds to create Shabbat pictures.
13. Make murals. First, sing "I Took a Little Walk." On a warm day, roll out some butcher paper and put out plates with paint. Let children take off shoes and socks and walk through paint and across paper. (Warning: paint covered feet are slippery! Be sure to support the children for the first few steps.) Title the mural "I Took a Little Walk, A Long, Long Way from Home, I Saw [insert name of class] and I said *Shabbat Shalom.*"

MUSIC/MOVEMENT

(With musical contributions from Julie Jaslow Auerbach)

1. Sing *niggunim* (songs without words). These melodies may be found in various Jewish music books.
2. Sing *"Shabbat Niggun"* by Julie Jaslow Auerbach, an untraditional *niggun*, as it has simple words Auerbach (see Appendix A, p. 353 for music and lyrics). After the second verse, discuss what children will do to prepare for Shabbat. After the third verse, talk about what they will do over Shabbat that is restful.
3. Introduce movements that reflect the words in the song *"Shabbat Shabbat Shalom"* by Julie Jaslow Auerbach (see Appendix A, p. 354 for music and lyrics). As a variation, sing the song's verses and intersperse the Shabbat rituals.
4. Use the following adaptation by Julie Jaslow Auerbach of the song *"Hayom Yom Shishi,"* a popular Israeli children's Shabbat song.

Refrain: *Hayom yom shishi* (2x) [Today is Friday]
Machar Shabbat (2x) [Tomorrow is Shabbat]
Shabbat menuchah [Restful Shabbat]

Ask the children to tell you what they will do to get ready for Shabbat, and fill in the verses as follows:

Let's shine the candlesticks (2x)
Machar Shabbat (2x) [Tomorrow is Shabbat]
Shabbat menuchah [Restful Shabbat]

Other ideas:
We'll set the table . . .
Let's pour the wine . . .
We'll clean the house . . .

5. Sing the song "The Challah" by Julie Jaslow Auerbach while making a *challah* with the children (see Appendix A, p. 330). Use motions to pretend to be the *challah*.
6. Saying "goodbye" to Shabbat is as important as saying "hello." Since we do not have school on Saturday nights, consider beginning your Mondays with the Havdalah ritual and the song "Goodbye Sabbath Queen" by Julie Jaslow Auerbach (see Appendix A, p. 336 for music and lyrics).
7. Sing *"Bim Bam/Shabbat Shalom."* Use different movements, e.g., move arms side to side for the first part, clap after *"Shabbat Shalom – hey!"* And wave arms in the air for the third part.
8. Sing *"Mizmor Shir"* by Shlomo Carlebach. Use the names of children in the class — e.g., "and David is waiting to sing a song of Shabbat . . . "
9. Sing *"Shir Hamaalot"* by Craig Taubman. Use candle props or candles made of cardboard. The melody of the song lends itself to arm movements up and down.
10. Have the children add their own ingredients to "Stir the Soup" by Eve Lippman and Gladys Gewirtz. You can also sing this song while making chicken soup!
11. There are many recordings of Shabbat music, both children's tapes and adult music. Some of the best include: *The Seventh Day* by Fran Avni, *Because We Love Shabbat* by Leah Abrams, *Shabbat Shalom* by Cindy Paley, *Z'mirot Sing Along,* and *Z'mirot U'Lehibanot* from Z'mirot

Livnot. Play these tapes on the day you celebrate Shabbat in your classroom, and at other times, too.

12. Incorporate traditional songs such as *"Lecha Dodi," "Shalom Alaychem,"* and *"Adon Olam"* into your repertoire.

13. Use a variety of body movements to do Jewish/Shabbat activities. Kiss someone and say *"Shabbat Shalom."* Wave your hands over the candles. Carry a Torah. March behind the Torah. Sway to Shabbat music.

14. Improvise being a Shabbat object. Melt like a candle. Roll from a ball of dough to a dough snake. Pour like wine. Grow like a Shabbat flower. Dance like the Sabbath queen.

15. Name a Shabbat activity, and have the children touch the part of the body they do the activity with. (Examples: Eat *challah.* Smell *besameem.* March with the Torah. Read the *Siddur.* Listen to Shabbat songs. Sing Shabbat songs.)

SONG/MUSIC LIST
(Contributed by Julie Jaslow Auerbach)

The following listing includes the songs cited in this chapter, as well as songs from other sources that are related to Shabbat concepts. Each song and the book in which it is located is specified, along with the page number. (Please note: In this and other holiday chapters, there are many songs which are "preschool traditional," i.e., they have been around so long that no one knows the composer or the song's origin! Every effort has been made to find the source for all the songs listed.)

General
"Bim Bam/Shabbat Shalom" – The New Children's Songbook, p. 13
"Chiribim" – The New Children's Songbook, p. 13
"Hayom Yom Shishi" – The New Children's Songbook, p. 10
"I've Got That Shabbat Feeling" – adaptation of traditional camp song
"Mah Yafeh Hayom" – Manginot, p. 73
"Mizmor Shir" – The Shlomo Carlebach Anthology, p. 85

"My Favorite Day" – *Because We Love Shabbat,* p. 6
"Ose Shalom" – Israel in Song, p. 87
"Partners" – *Because We Love Shabbat,* p. 9
"Shabbat Is Here" – *Kooky Cookie Kids,* Paul Zim
"Shabbat Kodesh" – The New Children's Songbook, p. 14
"Shabbat Niggun" (see Music/Movement activity #2 above)
"Shabbat Shabbat Shalom" (see Music/Movement activity #3 above)
"Shabbat Shalom" – The New Children's Songbook, p. 10
"Sim Shalom" – Hasidic traditional
"What Do You Like about Shabbat? – Sing Yeladim, p. 18
"Yom Rishon" – The New Children's Songbook, p. 9 (see *Because We Love Shabbat,* p. 10, for activities)
"Yom Zeh L'Yisrael" – The New Children's Songbook, p. 12

Preparing for Shabbat
"Get Ready for Shabbat" – *Because We Love Shabbat,* p. 11
"Hayom Yom Shishi" – The New Children's Songbook, p. 10 (see Music/Movement activity #4 above)
"L'Cha Dodi" – Manginot, p. 77
"Let's Get Ready" (sung to the tune of *"Freres Jacques"*)
"Mother's Gone a' Marketing" – *Shabbat Song-Kit for Young Children,* p. 12, *Union Songster,* p. 122
"Our Sabbath Table" – *Sing for Fun Volume I,* p. 3
"Ready by Sundown" – *Because We Love Shabbat,* p. 14
"Shalom Aleichem" – Manginot, p. 77
"What Are You Wearing?" – *Learning Basic Skills through Music Volume I,* Hap Palmer

Candles
Blessing over the candles (see p. 108 of this chapter)
"Shir Hamaalot" – Craig Taubman Songbook, p. 22
"Two Little Candle Lights of Mine" (traditional preschool version; can also be sung to the tune of the folksong "This Little Light of Mine")

Wine

Blessing over the wine (see p. 108 of this chapter)
"Pouring Wine " – *Because We Love Shabbat*, p. 26

Challah

Blessing over *challah* (see p. 109 of this chapter)
"I Made a Little Challah" – *Shabbat Song-kit for Young Children*, p. 14; *Union Songster*, p. 124
"The Challah" (see Music/Movement activity #5 above)

Food

"Essen" – *Sing Yeladim*, p. 22
"Let's Get Ready" (sung to the tune of *"Freres Jacques"*)
"Moshe" – *Sing a Jewish Song*, "Miss Jackie"
"Put a Chicken in the Pot" – *Kooky Cookie Kids*, Paul Zim
"Shabbat Dinner" (sung to the tune of *"Alouette"*)
"Stir the Soup" – *Manginot*, p. 69
"The Chicken Ran Away" – *Kooky Cookie Kids*, Paul Zim

Dances

"Ani Noladti Lashalom"
"Od Lo Ahavti Dai" – *Israel Sings*, p. 15 (See Pesach Music/Movement activity #8, p. 229)
"Bim Bam Bom," – *Hebrew Songs for All Seasons Volume Two*, p. 14
"Uga, uga" – *The New Children's Songbook*, p. 60

Havdalah

Havdalah Blessings (see p. 122 of this chapter)
"Birchot Havdallah" – *Maginot*, p. 82
"Eliyahu" – *Manginot*, p. 150
"Eliahu HaNavi" – *Around Our Shabbat Table*, Margie Rosenthal and Ilene Safyan
"Goodbye Sabbath Queen" (see Music/Movement activity #6 above)
"Havdalah/Shalom Shabbat " – *Because We Love Shabbat*, p. 35
"Shalom Chaverim" – *The New Children's Songbook*, p. 41

"Shavua Tov" – *Havdalah Pajama Live*, Judy Caplan Ginsburgh
"Shavua Tov" – *Manginot*, p. 74
"Shavua Tov" – *Manginot*, p. 75

CIRCLE TIME

1. Play flannel board games with Shabbat symbols. Play *Memory* by having the children cover their eyes and remove one piece. Let the children "come to dinner" and set the Shabbat table by naming and choosing a flannel symbol to add to the board. Give clues about a specific Shabbat symbol ("I have poppy seeds." "I ride on a person's head.") The child who guesses correctly puts the flannel piece on the board.
2. Make a feelie bag with Shabbat symbols. Younger children can guess what they are touching. Older children can be given the task of feeling for a specific object.
3. Play *"Mee Anee?"* (Who Am I?) with Shabbat symbols. One child sits in a chair. The teacher or helper holds an object over the child's head so he/she can not see it. The other children call out clues until the child in the chair guesses the object.
4. Write Shabbat poems with the children. Show the children a Shabbat symbol, and let the children offer descriptive words. Together, mold the words into a poem.
5. Chart the children's favorite things to do on Shabbat.

OUTDOORS/FIELD TRIPS

1. Collect flowers and other things from nature to decorate the Shabbat table.
2. Bring Shabbat music outside to dance to.
3. Draw Shabbat symbols on the playground in chalk (several of each of three or four symbols) and play *Tag* or a ball game requiring children to run to specific symbols. All the children begin standing together. One child throws a ball in the air, and the rest of the children run to a Shabbat symbol. When the child catches

the ball, he/she calls out one of the Shabbat symbols. The children on the named symbol are "safe," but the other children must run to the named symbol without being tagged by the child who threw the ball. The first child tagged is the next ball thrower/symbol caller.

4. Celebrate Shabbat or Havdalah outside in nice weather.

5. Visit a sanctuary to see the Torahs and to become familiar with all of the elements of a sanctuary (*Aron HaKodesh, Ner Tamid, Siddurim,* stained glass windows, and so on). If possible, make a trip to the sanctuary part of your regular Shabbat celebration.

6. Take a trip to a bakery where *challah* is made.

7. Take a trip a winery or a candle store if you have one nearby.

8. Take a trip to do a *mitzvah* project. Bring flowers to a nursing home or deliver cans of food the children have collected to a food pantry.

SPECIFICALLY FOR INFANTS

1. Play and sing lots of Shabbat music.

2. Expose babies to Shabbat symbols — let them eat *challah* as soon as they are able.

3. With supervision, let babies handle clean, real *Kiddush* cups and candlesticks with supervision.

4. Light Shabbat candles in front of babies and sing the blessing. Let non-mobile babies watch the candles burn for several minutes from a safe distance. Watch with them and share their wonder.

5. Take pictures of the babies or their families doing Jewish/Shabbat activities (wearing a *kipah*, eating *challah*, watching the candles). Enlarge the picture (the least expensive way is to make an enlarged color copy at an office supply or copy store) and hang in the room at baby eye level. (This is actually a wonderful idea for any age classroom.)

IDEAS FOR TEACHING FAMILIES

1. Shabbat Bags (or Baskets) – There are many ways to do Shabbat bags, but the basic concept includes sending something home with each child (or with a different family in the class) each week that enables and encourages the family to celebrate Shabbat. The bag (or box) may contain all or some of the following: two candlesticks; a *Kiddush* cup; a *challah* cover; two candles; a little bottle of grape juice or wine, one or two *challot*; Shabbat dinner recipes; Shabbat blessings; the blessing over the children; Havdalah blessings; a letter from the class or school telling parents about the bag; a children's Shabbat book; a journal for families to record their Shabbat experiences through writing, drawings, and/or photos, and to review other families' experiences; a stuffed animal Shabbat guest; a *Tzedakah* box, Havdalah candle, *besameem* box. Families who are not in the habit of celebrating Shabbat are given easy access to the joy it can bring. For families who regularly celebrate Shabbat, the Shabbat Bag makes a wonderful home-school connection.

2. Invite family members to be Shabbat *eema* or *abba* (or *sabba* or *safta*). Invite them to share your Shabbat celebration and to bring a favorite story or treat to share.

3. Invite family members to come in and help cook or bake. Send home recipes of Shabbat foods you enjoy in class.

4. Inform families of any local synagogues that are welcoming to young families, especially synagogues with services designed specifically for very young children.

5. If you study Torah or *Parashat HaShavua* with the children, send home a synopsis of what has been learned each week.

6. Send home the Hebrew words and the Shabbat songs you learn, so families can reinforce and join along at home.

7. Recommended reading: *The Art of Jewish Living: The Shabbat Seder* by Ron Wolfson, and *The Shabbat Book: A Weekly Guide for the Whole Family* by Joyce Klein.

INTEGRATING SHABBAT INTO THE REST OF THE WEEK

1. Celebrate Havdalah when you get back to school after Shabbat.
2. Play Shabbat tapes interspersed with other music.
3. Prepare for Shabbat beforehand. Start making the *challah* dough on Thursday. Start cleaning the room on Thursday.
4. Early in the week, decide who your Shabbat guests will be.
5. Plant flower seeds for a future Shabbat.
6. Bake a special treat during the week and save it for Shabbat.
7. Decorate the Shabbat tablecloth or do other artwork during the week, and put it away until Shabbat.
8. Sing Shabbat songs during the week.
9. Keep Shabbat items (plastic *challah*, tablecloth, candlesticks, *Kiddush* cup, fake flowers) in the house corner all week long so children can "play Shabbat" whenever they want. Save a few props (*talitot*, certain books, or fancy dress up clothes) that only get put out on Fridays, to make the actual day of Shabbat extra special.
10. Keep some Shabbat books on the bookshelf available to children all week long.
11. When the days are shorter, watch the sunset. Tell the children, "If today was Friday, Shabbat would be starting." Look for three stars in the sky. Tell the children, "If this were Saturday night, Shabbat would be over."

SOME NOTES ON "MAKING SHABBAT"

BLESSINGS

1. Involve the children as much and as concretely as possible in saying the blessings. Select a child to lead each blessing. Set the Shabbat objects on the table where the children are, not at a separate table.

2. Tie the meaning of each blessing to the action as much as possible. Encourage the children to wave their hands around the candles, even if the candles are only in front of you. With younger children, pass out the juice immediately before you say the blessing, or as you say it. Do the same with the *challah*.

3. Make the moment as magical as possible. Learn to sing the blessings. Tell impromptu stories as you make Shabbat. (It's magic! The candles are magically lit when we say the blessing and cover our eyes. Why do we cover the *challah*?) Sing Shabbat songs at the table. Use things the children have created (e.g., Shabbat place mats, flowers and vases, tablecloth, *kipot*, *challah* cover) during your classroom celebration. If you have parents in the class, teach them the blessing over the children, and have parents bless the children after lighting candles. Make sure hugs and kisses are exchanged after the blessing.

CANDLES

Shabbat candles present early childhood educators with a dilemma. These candles are not birthday candles — we don't blow them out. One of our goals is to teach children this distinction. Yet, as early childhood educators, with classrooms full of active children, our number one job is to keep the children safe. It is sometimes risky to leave candles burning on a table with children nearby. One must carefully balance these two goals.

Light the candles, and move them to a *safe* location (a high shelf with nothing flammable nearby, a sturdy table or counter that children cannot reach). Say something like, "We may not move our candles at home, but our *nayrote* are going to watch us make the rest of Shabbat from up here." *Never* leave burning candles unattended. When the children leave the room or move on to the next activity, blow the candles out.

If there is no safe location for the candles, light the candles with the children, then take the candles off the table, turn your back to the children and blow the candles out. If children ask why you blew the candles out, simply explain you blew the candles out to keep the children safe. Never encourage the children to blow out the candles. It teaches them that we blow out Shabbat candles, even if you tell them every time, "We only blow out the candles in school."

CELEBRATING HAVDALAH

Havdalah separates Shabbat from the beginning of the new week. Since most early childhood educators are not with their students on Saturday night, Havdalah must be celebrated as a class some other time. The Rabbis say it is permissible to celebrate Havdalah as late as Tuesday. A good time to celebrate Havdalah with your class is Monday morning, or the morning you come back to school after the weekend. Havdalah is highly ritualized, and you can add your own ritual(s) to the ceremony. Find a regular time and place to celebrate Havdalah each week. Havdalah can be the perfect time for everyone to check in and recount what exciting things happened over the weekend. Singing the blessings to a tune such as *"Birchot Havdallah"* by Debbie Friedman (on her album *The World of Your Dreams*) makes Havdalah more special and engaging. Let the children pick one or two favorite songs that you will always sing with Havdalah.

1. Fill the *Kiddush* cup with grape juice.
2. Dim the lights in the room. Light the candle. (Have a plate ready to catch the drippings.)
3. Raise the *kos Kiddush* and say (or sing) the blessing over the juice:

בָּרוּךְ אַתָּה יְיָ אֱלֹהֵינוּ מֶלֶךְ הָעוֹלָם
בּוֹרֵא פְּרִי הַגָּפֶן.

Baruch Atah Adonai Elohaynu Melech HaOlam Boray P'ri HaGafen.

We praise You, our God, Creator of the universe, for creating the fruit of the vine. (Don't drink yet!)

4. Next, lift the *besameem* box and say (or sing) the blessing:

בָּרוּךְ אַתָּה יְיָ אֱלֹהֵינוּ מֶלֶךְ הָעוֹלָם
בּוֹרֵא מִינֵי בְשָׂמִים.

Baruch Atah Adonai Elohaynu Melech HaOlom Boray Meenay V'Sameem.

We praise you, our God, Creator of the universe, Who creates all kinds of spices.

5. Keep singing the *niggun* while you pass around the *besameem* and until everyone has had a chance to sniff the sweet scent.
6. Then hold the candle high and say (or sing) the blessing.

בָּרוּךְ אַתָּה יְיָ אֱלֹהֵינוּ מֶלֶךְ הָעוֹלָם
בּוֹרֵא מְאוֹרֵי הָאֵשׁ.

Baruch Atah Adonai Elohaynu Melech HaOlom Boray Mi'oray HaAysh.

We praise you, our God, Creator of the universe, Who creates the lights of the fire.

7. While the blessing is recited, all hold hands up toward the candle, palms up, and bend fingers to see the flame reflected in the fingernails.
8. One person (or everyone) takes a sip of wine, and then the candle is extinguished in the juice. Children are fascinated by this — where did the flame go?
9. Everyone wishes each other *shavua tov* (a good week). Sing some traditional Havdalah songs, such as *"Shavua Tov"* and *"Eliyahu HaNavi."* Other songs include a different version of *"Shavua Tov"* and *"Havdalah/Shalom Shabbat"* (see p. 119 for sources).

SOME STORIES FOR SHABBAT

THE SHABBAT ANGELS

(Adapted by Maxine Segal Handelman from *Shabbat* 119b)

There are many angels in this world who help God get everything done. Each angel has a special job. Two angels, Tov and Ra, are in charge of Shabbat *shalom*, Shabbat peace. On *erev* Shabbat, Tov and Ra follow Jews home from synagogue, peeking in the windows of every Jewish home. If the house is clean, the meal is prepared, and the family is gathered around the table, singing and welcoming Shabbat, then Tov blesses the house, saying, "May next Shabbat be just like this one." And Ra must agree by saying, "Amen." But if the house is a mess, if the children are fighting, and no one in the family is ready to welcome Shabbat, then Ra scolds the family and says, "May next Shabbat be just like this one." And Tov must agree by saying "Amen."

One day, Chaim Yonkel and his wife Esther had an argument. It was one of those little disagreements that gets bigger and bigger all by itself. The argument lasted all week, and as Shabbat approached, Chaim Yonkel was still angry, so he neglected to buy flowers for Esther for Shabbat. Esther was still so angry that she decided not to make Chaim Yonkel's favorite *kugel*, the *kugel* she had made every Shabbat for ten years. Esther and Chaim Yonkel were so busy being angry at each other that they forgot to check to see if the children had taken a bath or cleaned their rooms before Shabbat. The children were not used to seeing their parents argue. Seeing them this way made them scared, and the children started fighting with each other. When Shabbat arrived, the meal was not prepared, the table was not set, and everyone in the family was unhappy.

Tov and Ra followed Chaim Yonkel home from shul. For ten years, they had been following Chaim Yonkel home on Shabbat, and each week for ten years, Tov had blessed the shining happy family,

"May next Shabbat be just like this one." This week, Tov was about to give the usual blessing, when Ra stopped him and said, "Look!" Ra pointed in the window. Instead of seeing candles burning and happy faces singing, the two angels saw the youngest daughter pulling the hair of her older sister, toys strewn all over the living room, and angry sad faces on every member of the family. "It's my turn this week!" declared Ra. "May next Shabbat be just like this one." Tov bowed his head and said, "Amen."

On Shabbat afternoon, Chaim Yonkel and Esther had some time to sit down and talk. When they realized that they couldn't remember what they had been fighting about, they laughed and hugged each other. "I'm sorry I made you upset," said Esther. "I'm sorry I made *you* upset," said Chaim Yonkel. Chaim Yonkel and Esther gathered the children together and apologized to them for making their happy home such a sad place. By the end of Shabbat, everything was back to normal.

The week went by and everything was fine in the house. But as Shabbat approached, Ra's curse took effect. Chaim Yonkel became so busy at work that he forgot to buy flowers for Esther. Esther realized she didn't have all the ingredients for Chaim Yonkel's favorite *kugel*, but it was too late to go to the store and get what she needed before Shabbat. The children, having not cleaned their rooms the week before, found the mess had grown too large to finish cleaning before Shabbat.

When Tov and Ra followed Chaim Yonkel home from *shul* that night, Ra smiled triumphantly and said, "May next Shabbat be just like this one." And, sadly, Tov agreed and said, "Amen." Chaim Yonkel, Esther and the children were sad. What had happened to the *shalom* that had always filled their house on Shabbat?

When Shabbat was over, Chaim Yonkel, Esther, and the children went to see the Rabbi. "Two weeks ago, we were fighting," said Chaim Yonkel. "Our Shabbat was ruined," said Esther. "We stopped fighting, but this Shabbat wasn't any better," said the children. "We want our happy Shabbat back!" cried the whole family.

The Rabbi listened closely. "Hmm," he said. "It seems that Ra, the bad Shabbat angel, saw you fighting on Shabbat, and he cursed your home."

"Oh no!" cried Chaim Yonkel. "What can we do to get our happy Shabbat back?" asked Esther.

The Rabbi thought for a long moment. "It will not be easy. You will *each* have to do your part," he said, looking into the eyes of each member of the family. "You must begin to prepare for next Shabbat now, even though it is an entire week away. Begin shopping, baking, cleaning today. Do something toward Shabbat each day this week, so it is never out of your minds or far from your hearts. If each one of you does his or her part, you might be able to defeat Ra."

On the way home, Esther stopped by the market and bought all the ingredients for Chaim Yonkel's favorite *kugel*. When the children got home, they started cleaning their rooms. Every day that week, Chaim Yonkel brought Esther a few flowers. As Shabbat approached, the family increased their preparations. Esther baked a few new things she thought her family might like. Not only did the children clean their rooms, but each child went through his or her clothes and toys, and picked out a few things to give to children without enough clothes or toys. Chaim Yonkel made sure to leave work early, and he brought home the most beautiful bouquet of flowers he could find.

As the sun began to set, the family gathered together to light the Shabbat candles. The house was spotless, the meal was ready to serve, and each member of the family wore a big smile as they kissed and hugged and wished each other *Shabbat Shalom!* When Tov and Ra peeked in the window, they heard the voices of the family joined together in song, *"Shalom alaychem, malachay hasharayt . . . "* (Peace be to you, ministering angels . . .) Ra knew they were singing to him, telling him that they had defeated him. Tov smiled his kind, good smile, and said, "May next Shabbat be just like this one." Ra bowed his head and agreed, "Amen."

A SIMPLE RETELLING OF THE CREATION STORY (GENESIS 1:1-2:1)

In the beginning, God created the world. God created light.

God said, "This is good." That was the first day.

The next day, God made the sky and God made the water. God said, "This is good." That was the second day.

The next day, God made dry land. God covered the land with trees. God said, "This is good." That was the third day.

The next day, God made the sun to shine in the day and the moon and stars to shine at night. God said, "This is good." That was the fourth day.

The next day, God filled the waters with fish, the air with birds, and the land with insects. And God said, "This is good." That was the fifth day.

The next day, God made all kinds of animals, as well as the first man and woman. God said, "This is very good." That was the sixth day.

On the seventh day, God did not work at all. God rested. It was the first Shabbat.

WHY WE COVER THE CHALLAH

When we make Shabbat, the candles are always blessed first. The wine is always next. And the *challah* — the *challah* is always last. How would you feel if you were always last? That's right — sad, angry, jealous. Do you know how a sad, angry, jealous *challah* tastes? Not very good. In fact, a sad, angry, jealous *challah* tastes yucky! Salty! Hard! Blech! We don't want our *challah* to be sad and taste yucky. So we cover the *challah* so it doesn't know that it's last. Shhhh — don't tell. When we uncover the *challah*, the *challah* looks around and thinks to itself, "Ahhhh. I'm here. Now it's time for Shabbat to begin." And the *challah* feels happy. Do you know how a happy *challah* tastes? Yummy! Soft and sweet, crisp on the outside and just right inside. So in order to have yummy *challah* each week, we cover the *challah* so it never knows it's last. And don't you tell!

SHABBAT SPICE

(Adapted by Maxine Segal Handelman from *Shabbat* 119a)

Rabbi Joshua ben Hanania and Hadrian the Roman Emperor were friends. One day, just as Rabbi Joshua was sitting down to Shabbat dinner, he heard a knock at his door. He opened the door, and there was his friend Hadrian. Rabbi Joshua invited his friend to join him for dinner. As Hadrian ate, his eyes grew wide. Everything was so delicious! He asked for seconds and thirds. Hadrian had never tasted food so wonderful. When it was time to leave, Rabbi Joshua told his friend, "I'm so glad you enjoyed yourself. Feel free to come back any time."

Two days later, Emperor Hadrian was thinking about the delicious meal he had at Rabbi Joshua's house. That evening, when Rabbi Joshua was sitting down to dinner with his family, he heard a knock at his door. He opened the door, and there was his friend Emperor Hadrian. Rabbi Joshua invited his friend to join him for dinner. As Hadrian ate, he began to frown. The food was good, certainly, but nowhere nearly as good as it had been the other night. "My friend," began Hadrian. I don't mean to insult your food, but I must say that when I was here the other night, the food was much better. This food is missing something. A spice, perhaps? Something you've run out of? Something expensive, or from far away? Rabbi Joshua, I am the emperor. Whatever the missing spice is, no matter how far away or how expensive, I can get it for you!"

Rabbi Joshua smiled and shook his head. "Emperor Hadrian, my friend, there *is* something missing from this food. But it is not a spice you can buy, even for all the money in the world. The missing spice is Shabbat."

SUGGESTED NEWSLETTER ARTICLE

Note: At the beginning of the year, describe how Shabbat is celebrated in your class/school. Also, near the beginning of the year, describe your Shabbat-related goals for the children. Following is an example of what you might say.

On Fridays around 11:30, we gather the children together. We read a special Shabbat story, and sing some Shabbat songs. The children's favorites are *"Hinay Mah Tov"* and "I Made a Little Challah." We put the Shabbat tablecloth we made on the table, and all the children sit at the table. We put the candles, *kos Kiddush,* and *challah* on the table, and a different child each week helps to lead the blessings. Then we enjoy *challah,* juice, and a special Shabbat treat!

By the end of this year, our goal is for the four-year-olds to know the Shabbat blessings, and which blessing goes with which Jewish action. Our goal for the three-year-olds is to master a Shabbat Hebrew vocabulary, including the words *nayrote, kos Kiddush, Shabbat Shalom,* and *yayin.*

[Since Shabbat falls every week, you may want to make Shabbat happenings a part of each newsletter. An example follows.]

This week, David's father was our Shabbat guest. He brought the book *A Holiday for Noah* by Susan Topek, and the children really liked it. This week we learned a new song, "Penny in the Pushke." Ask your child to sing it for you! This month, our Shabbat *Tzedakah* project is collecting hats and gloves for the local homeless shelter. We studied the story of Abraham and Sarah welcoming guests. You can find the story in Genesis 18.

RECIPES

MAX'S SWEET CHALLAH

Note: You can make the dough on Thursday and let it rise overnight in the refrigerator if you like. This recipe yields two medium *challot*, or about eight mini-*challot*.

Ingredients
1 package yeast
1 C. very warm water
3 C. white flour (plus some extra)
1 C. whole wheat flour
¾ C. sugar (plus 2 tsp.)
1½ tsp. salt
3 eggs (plus 1 for topping)
½ C. oil or margarine, melted
poppy or sesame seeds

Directions
1. In a small bowl, mix yeast, 2 tsp. sugar and warm water. Set aside in a warm, draft-free place to rise. (The yeast is "working" if it begins to foam. If the yeast doesn't foam after a few minutes, try again.)
2. In a large bowl, mix white flour, whole wheat flour, sugar, and salt.
3. Add eggs, oil, and yeast. Mix well. Add more white flour as needed to keep the dough from getting too sticky.
4. Knead the dough on a well floured surface, until the dough bounces back when you poke your finger in.
5. Put the dough in a lightly oiled bowl, turning the dough so it is covered with oil. Cover the bowl with a towel and set it in a warm, draft free place to rise. (1-3 hours)
6. Punch the dough down. At this point, you can let the dough rise again overnight in the refrigerator, or again in a warm, draft free place for another 1-3 hours.
7. After the second rising (or in the morning), punch the dough down again.
8. Braid or shape.

9. Brush with beaten egg (mix sugar into the egg for a sweeter finish) and sprinkle with poppy or sesame seeds. Allow to rise for ½ hour.
10. Bake in preheated oven on a greased cookie sheet for 30-35 minutes at 350°.

DO-IT-YOURSELF CHALLAH

Note: This recipe yields three large *challot*, or about 12 mini-*challot*.

Ingredients
2 packages yeast
½ C. very warm water
1 tsp. sugar
5 eggs
¾ C. sugar
½ C. oil
1½ C. water
1 tsp. salt
10 C. flour
egg yolks
poppy seeds

Directions
1. Dissolve yeast in very warm water with 1 teaspoon of sugar. Let it set for 10 minutes. Yeast should begin to foam.
2. In a large bowl, beat eggs and sugar.
3. Add oil, water, and salt.
4. Mix yeast mixture into egg mixture.
5. Add one cup of flour at a time. Mix thoroughly until all the flour is incorporated.
6. Knead the dough on a floured surface. Add more flour if the dough is sticky. Knead until smooth.
7. Put the dough in a lightly oiled bowl, turning the dough so it is covered with oil. Cover the bowl with a towel and set in a warm, draft-free place to rise, until the dough doubles in size.
8. Punch the dough down.
9. Divide and braid or shape the dough.
10. Place on cookie sheets. Cover loosely with a towel. Let rise for about 1½ hours.

11. Combine egg yolks with some water. Brush the *challot* with egg yolk mixture and sprinkle with poppy seeds.
12. Preheat oven to 225°.
13. Place *challot* in oven, raise heat to 325°. Bake for 25-30 minutes.

The "God Piece"

It is traditional to break off a small piece of dough and burn it in the oven, as a token of thanks to God. This is called "taking *challah*," and it is where the name *"challah"* comes from. Children can each take a pinch of dough from their mini-*challah* to make a collective "God piece." Toss this in the oven while you bake the *challah*. Discard the piece after baking. Before tossing the piece in the oven, say this blessing:

בָּרוּךְ אַתָּה יְיָ אֱלֹהֵינוּ מֶלֶךְ הָעוֹלָם אֲשֶׁר קִדְּשָׁנוּ בְּמִצְוֹתָיו וְצִוָּנוּ לְהַפְרִישׁ חַלָּה.

Baruch Atah Adonai Elohaynu Melech HaOlam Asher Kid'shanu B'Mitzvotav V'Tzivanu L'Hafrish Challah.

We praise you, our God, Creator of the universe, Who has made us holy with Your *mitzvot* and commands us to separate *challah*.

NOODLE KUGEL

Ingredients
½ lb. medium noodles, cooked and drained
2-3 tbs. margarine
3 eggs, beaten
¼ C. brown sugar
1 tsp. cinnamon
½ tsp. vanilla
¼ C. crushed corn flakes
2 apples, peeled and grated (consider using raisins or pieces of pineapple or pears in addition to or instead or the apples)

Directions
1. Grease a 9" × 9" inch baking pan.

2. Sprinkle the bottom with about half the crushed corn flakes and cinnamon.
3. Add margarine to noodles and stir to melt.
4. Mix in the eggs along with the apples, brown sugar, cinnamon, and vanilla.
5. Pour the noodle mixture into the greased baking pan.
6. Sprinkle the rest of the crushed corn flakes and cinnamon over the top.
7. Bake at 375° for about 45 minutes. Do not overbake.

HAVDALAH CANDLE COOKIES

Ingredients
1 C. shortening (½ margarine, ½ Crisco)
1 C. sifted powdered sugar
1 egg
1½ tsp. almond extract
2½ C. flour
1 tsp. salt
blue food coloring

Directions
1. Mix first four ingredients, then sift and stir in the flour and salt.
2. Divide the dough in half and add a few drops of blue food coloring to one half.
3. Divide each half into small (golf ball size) balls. Each child uses two balls of one color and one ball of the other color.
4. Roll the balls into snakes, and braid the snakes together.
5. Bake on an ungreased cookie sheet at 375° for about 10 minutes (depending on how thick the braids are).

BIBLIOGRAPHY

ADULTS

Ganzfried, Solomon, comp. *Code of Jewish Law.* Hyman Goldin, trans. New York: Hebrew Publishing Co., 1963.

The Orthodox guide to *halachah* — Jewish Law.

Gersh, Harry. *When a Jew Celebrates.* West Orange, NJ: Behrman House, 1971.

Somewhat dated and text-booky, but good concise information.

Isaacs, Ronald H. *Every Person's Guide To Shabbat.* Northvale NJ: Jason Aronson Inc., 1998.

A complete guide to Shabbat rituals and liturgy.

———. *Sacred Seasons: A Sourcebook for the Jewish Holidays.* Northvale NJ: Jason Aronson Inc. 1997.

Provides biblical and Talmudic sources and stories for every Jewish holiday.

Klein, Joyce. *The Shabbat Book: A Weekly Guide for the Whole Family.* Israel: Scopus Films, 1994.

Stories, songs, and texts for each *parashah* provide good enrichments for the experience of Shabbat.

Matansky, Lee, ed. *A Shabbat Primer: An Integrated Curriculum on Shabbat for Use in the Early Childhood Classroom.* Chicago, IL: Pritzker Center for Jewish Education of the JCCs of Chicago, 1995, (847) 675-2200.

A comprehensive guide to Shabbat curriculum.

Palatnik, Lori. *Friday Night and Beyond: The Shabbat Experience Step by Step.* Northvale, NJ: Jason Aronson Inc., 1994.

A detailed exploration of Shabbat rituals. Includes recipes and tips for celebrating Shabbat while out of town.

Perelson, Ruth. *An Invitation To Shabbat.* New York: UAHC Press, 1997.

A beginners guide to weekly celebration from the Reform Movement. Comes with a CD of Shabbat blessings and music.

Wolfson, Ron. *The Art of Jewish Living: The Shabbat Seder.* New York: Federation of Jewish Men's Clubs and University of Judaism, 1985.

Wonderful resource for seeing how others have made Shabbat part of their lives.

CHILDREN
Infant To 2

Blue, Rose. *Good Yontif.* Brookfield, CT: Millbrook Press, 1997. (Ages 2-8)

A picture book about the Jewish year.

Eisenberg, Ann. *I Can Celebrate!* Rockville, MD: Kar-Ben Copies, 1988. (Ages infant-2)

Covers all the Jewish holidays. (Board Book)

Feder, Harriet. *What Can You Do with a Bagel?* Rockville, MD, Kar-Ben Copies, 1991. (Ages infant-2)

A comical look at what a toddler can do with a bagel. (Board Book)

Kress, Camille. *Tot Shabbat.* New York: UAHC Press, 1997. (Ages infant-2)

Beautifully illustrated story of a family celebrating a peaceful Shabbat evening. (Board Book)

Martin, Bill, Jr. *Brown Bear, Brown Bear, What Do You See?* New York: Henry Holt and Company, 1992. (Ages 2-4)

Gentle rhyming and gorgeous, tissue paper collage illustrations make this a classic picture book. On each page, a different animal nudges us to discover which creature will show up next.

Nerlove, Miriam. *Shabbat.* Morton Grove, IL: Albert Whitman and Company, 1998. (Ages 2-6)

A terrific introduction to Shabbat for very young children.

Rouss, Sylvia. *Fun with Jewish Holiday Rhymes.* New York: UAHC Press, 1992. (Ages 2-5)

Wonderful poems to sing and share all year.

Schanzer, Roz. *My First Jewish Word Book.* Rockville, MD: Kar-Ben Copies, 1992. (Ages 2-5)

Each major holiday comes to life in a two-page spread, which features detailed vignettes of families at home and at synagogue. Also introduces vocabulary basic to Jewish and everyday life.

Topek, Susan. *Shalom Shabbat: A Book for Havdalah*. Rockville, MD, Kar-Ben Copies, 1998. (Ages infant-2)

A sensory look at Havdalah, the ceremony that ends Shabbat. (Board Book)

Wikler, Madeline, and Judye Groner. *In the Synagogue*. Rockville, MD: Kar-Ben Copies, 1991. (Ages infant-2)

A look at all the symbols and ritual objects in the synagogue. (Board Book)

Zwerin, Raymond A., and Audrey Friedman Marcus. *Shabbat Can Be*. New York: UAHC Press, 1979. (Ages 2-4)

Explores all the things Shabbat can be.

3 Years

Drucker, Malka. *A Jewish Holiday*. San Diego, CA: Harcourt Brace and Company, 1996. (Ages 3-5)

An alphabet of holiday symbols.

Greaves, Margaret. *The Naming*. San Diego, Gulliver Books, 1992. (Ages 3-6)

A simple telling of how Adam named all the animals.

Kobre, Faige. *A Sense of Shabbat*. Los Angeles: Torah Aura Productions, 1989. (Ages 3-6)

Beautiful photos help describe the entire day of Shabbat through the senses.

Numeroff, Laura Joffe. *If You Give a Mouse a Cookie*. New York: Scholastic, 1985. (Ages 3-6)

"If you give a mouse a cookie, he's going to ask for a glass of milk. When you give him the milk, he'll probably ask you for a straw," and so on, in this delightful story about an energetic mouse and an accommodating little boy.

Rosenfeld, Dina. *The Very Best Place for a Penny*. New York: Merkos L'inyonei Chinuch, 1984. (Ages 3-5)

A delightful tale about *Tzedakah*.

Rouss, Sylvia. *Sammy Spider's First Shabbat*. Rockville, MD: Kar Ben Copies, Inc., 1997. (Ages 3-6)

Sammy learns about time as he learns about Shabbat.

Schweiger-Daniel, Itzak. *Hanna's Sabbath Dress*. New York: Simon & Schuster, 1996. (Ages 3-6)

When Hanna spoils her new Sabbath dress helping an old man, the moon comes to her rescue.

Swartz, Daniel. *Bim and Bom: A Shabbat Tale*. Rockville, MD: Kar Ben Copies, Inc., 1996. (Ages 3-6)

When Bim and her brother Bom see each other on Shabbat, they make it extra special for each other.

Topek, Susan. *A Holiday for Noah*. Rockville, MD: Kar Ben Copies, Inc., 1990. (Ages 3-6)

Noah's favorite holiday is Shabbat.

Waldman, Sarah. *Light: The First Seven Days*. San Diego, CA: Harcourt Brace Jovanovich, 1993. (Ages 3-6)

A beautiful book about creation.

4 To 5 Years

Herman, Charlotte. *How Yussel Caught the Gefilte Fish: A Shabbos Story*. New York: Dutton Children's Books, 1999. (Ages 4-8)

When he goes fishing with his father for the first time, a young boy hopes to catch the gefilte fish for his family's Shabbat dinner. Instead, he catches a carp, a trout, and a pike.

Levin, Miriam R. *In the Beginning*. Rockville, MD: Kar Ben Copies, Inc., 1996. (Ages 4-8)

A young boy's day mirrors the seven days of creation.

Schur, Maxine Rose. *Day of Delight: A Jewish Sabbath in Ethiopia*. New York: Dial Books for Young Readers, 1994. (Ages 4-6)

A beautiful introduction to the Ethiopian Jewish community.

Schwartz, Amy. *Mrs. Moskowitz and the Sabbath Candlesticks.* Philadelphia, PA: The Jewish Publication Society, 1983. (Ages 4-6)

When Mrs. Moskowitz moves to a new apartment, only her Sabbath candlesticks make it feel like home.

Schwartz, Howard. *The Sabbath Lion.* New York: HarperCollins, 1992. (Ages 4-6)

A Jewish folktale from Algeria.

CHAPTER 8

ROSH CHODESH

And on your joyous occasions — your fixed festivals and new moon days — you shall sound the trumpets over your burnt offerings and your sacrifices of well being. (Numbers 10:10)

OVERVIEW

The Jewish calendar is lunar and solar. The appearance and disappearance of the moon decides the beginning and end of each month. This lunar calendar is adjusted so that the holidays always fall in their proper season, as determined by the sun. Rosh Chodesh (Head of the Month) is the Jewish celebration of the New Moon and the corresponding start of a new Hebrew month. The day is signaled by the appearance of the first sliver of the new moon shining in the sky. Correctly sighting the new moon was crucial in ancient times. The date of every holiday was dependent on the date of the new moon. When the Jewish people all lived relatively near each other in the Land of Israel, a torch signal was passed from mountaintop to mountaintop at the first sighting of the new moon. Everyone's calendar was synchronized, and each holiday was celebrated on its proper day. When Jews moved away from the Land of Israel (during the Babylonian Exile), the system of torches broke down. In the Diaspora, Jews began to celebrate the holidays for two days instead of one to ensure that they would be celebrating on the correct day.

In ancient times, Rosh Chodesh was observed by refraining from work. In recent decades, Rosh Chodesh has become a holiday celebrated especially by women's groups gathering with song,

prayer, and storytelling to mark the new moon. The assignment of Rosh Chodesh as a women's holiday is attributed to a *midrash*. When Moses brought the Israelite people to Mt. Sinai, he left them waiting at the bottom of the mountain while he went up to the top to speak with God and receive the Torah. While Moses was away, the people panicked, thinking that he would never return, and that they would be deserted in the wilderness and left to die (Exodus 32). They demanded that Aaron, Moses' brother and right-hand man, build a golden calf for them to worship. According to the *midrash*, the women did not contribute to this panic, and indeed refused to give up their jewelry to the building of an idol. As a reward for the women's faith, God granted them the holiday of Rosh Chodesh, so that like the moon, women would be rejuvenated each month.

Why then is Rosh Chodesh an appropriate holiday to celebrate in Jewish preschools today? Rosh Chodesh is a calendar holiday — it marks the beginning of a new month. As we know, young children do not yet grasp time concepts as broad as "week," "month," or "year." While celebrating Rosh Chodesh, the name of the new Jewish month and the holidays coming up in that month can be mentioned, but these "facts" are not what the children will take away with them. The focus in the preschool is not on the Hebrew month, but rather on the cyclical nature of Jewish life. This concept can be stressed in very concrete ways, through the development of a connection to the moon, and by alerting children to the Jewish rhythm of the year. Because Rosh Chodesh happens every month, over time, the regularity and repetition of themes, songs, and prayers will help the children become aware of the moon as a Jewish symbol, and as a Jewish timepiece.

For a glossary and Hebrew vocabulary for Rosh Chodesh, see figure 10 below.

ROSH CHODESH BLESSING

The blessing for the new moon consists of an excerpt from the *Kiddush Levanah*, the Sanctification of the Moon. It is recited in its entirety while looking at the moon, about 72 hours after the new moon appears in the sky. This excerpt is recommended for use with children due to its brevity and the familiar beginning formula, which helps children relate to this blessing.

בָּרוּךְ אַתָּה יְיָ מְחַדֵּשׁ חֳדָשִׁים.

Baruch Atah Adonai, M'chadaysh Chodasheem.

Thank you God for renewing the months.

ROSH CHODESH CONCEPTS

WEBBING THE CONCEPTS

Chapter 1, "Developmentally Appropriate Practice," webbing the concepts of Rosh Chodesh (see p. 11 for more on webbing), can elicit ideas about what you want children more easily think about what you want children to learn (and not just what you want them to make). This technique can also bring to mind connections to other things going on in your classroom. Figure 11 on page 133 is the *beginning* of a web for Rosh Chodesh. You can extend the web with your co-teachers or your students, thus shaping the celebration of Rosh Chodesh to include the interests of everyone in your class. *You won't cover everything you web*, but you'll get a good idea of where you want to go.

Note: Because Rosh Chodesh is celebrated consistently over the course of the year, the concepts that your children grasp in Tishre can be expanded by the time you reach Sivan. Therefore, read all of the concepts to help guide you in the development of Rosh Chodesh over the whole year.

INFANT TO 24 MONTHS
1. I see the moon.
2. The moon changes shape.
3. I change as time goes by.

2 YEARS
1. I see the moon.
2. The moon changes shape every night.
3. Rosh Chodesh is the moon holiday.
4. I change and grow every month.

3 YEARS
1. I see the moon in the sky at night.
2. The moon changes shape every night.
3. The moon grows from a sliver to a full moon, and then shrinks until we can't see it at all.

GLOSSARY AND HEBREW VOCABULARY		
לָבָן	*Lavan*	white
לְבָנָה	*Levanah*	moon
מִדְרָשׁ	*Midrash*	Rabbinic story used to explain a piece of Torah text or to draw forth a moral or lesson.
רֹאשׁ חוֹדֶשׁ	Rosh Chodesh	literally "Head of the Month"; the Jewish celebration of the New Moon and the corresponding start of a new Hebrew month.
יָרֵחַ	*Yarayach*	moon

Figure 10

4. When we see the new crescent of the moon, we celebrate Rosh Chodesh.
5. We say a blessing over the new moon. Rosh Chodesh is the beginning of the new Jewish month.
6. I see how I grow and change every month.

4 TO 5 YEARS
1. I see the moon in the sky at night.
2. The moon changes shape every night.
3. The moon grows from a sliver to a full moon, and then shrinks until we can't see it at all.
4. This cycle of the moon happens over and over again.

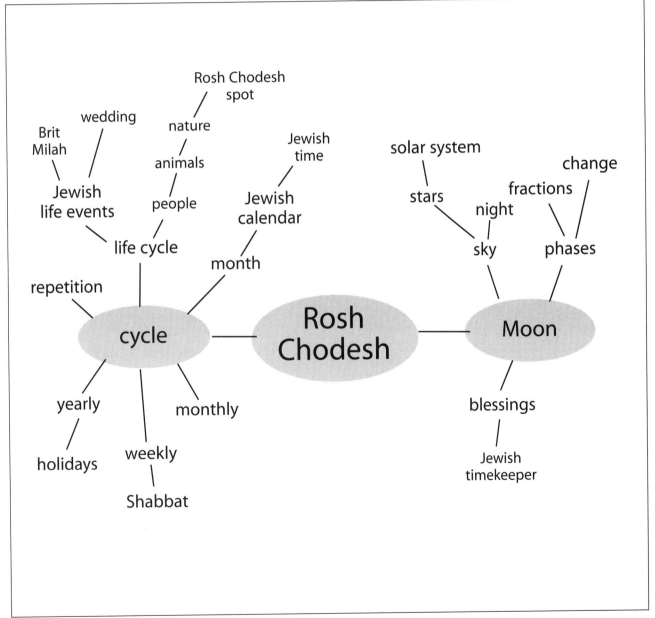

Figure 11

5. When we see the new crescent of the moon, we celebrate Rosh Chodesh.
6. We say a blessing over the new moon.
7. Rosh Chodesh is the beginning of the new Jewish month.
8. The moon is a Jewish timepiece.
9. I see how I grow and change every month.
10. I see how other things grow and change every month.

ACTIVITIES

LANGUAGE ARTS

1. Read lots of books and stories about the moon.
2. Allow children to make up their own moon stories.
3. There is a *midrash* about why the moon is a lesser light than the sun. This story provides an excellent way to relate the moon to God and put it in a Jewish framework. This *midrash* has been made into a children's book: *Why the Moon Only Glows* by Dina Rosenfeld.
4. Make lists of observations children make in the Rosh Chodesh spot (see Science activity #1, below). What changes do they notice? What do they predict will be different next month?
5. Older children can bring paper, writing utensils, and a clipboard out to the Rosh Chodesh spot, so they can document what they see for themselves.
6. Make a Rosh Chodesh book for each month. Include only Rosh Chodesh activities and observations, or include photos and other memoirs from the entire Hebrew month.

SCIENCE

1. The "Rosh Chodesh spot" provides a very concrete way to help children connect Rosh Chodesh to the cycle of Jewish life. At the beginning of the school year, each class chooses its own Rosh Chodesh spot: a tree, a hill, a garden. Each Rosh Chodesh, the class visits this spot, giving them over time a sense of ownership. A basic concept is that everything changes. Over a year, children will be able to observe one spot in nature die and be renewed. By tying this cycle of nature to Rosh Chodesh, itself a holiday of cycles, the children may come to relate nature to Judaism, and a groundwork may be established to further their understanding of the cyclical nature of Judaism.

2. Take photos of the children every Rosh Chodesh, especially of younger children. When the children see these pictures of themselves and their classmates gathered together in one place, they will be able to realize their own growth.
3. In the winter, when it gets dark earlier, go outside and look at the moon.
4. Make a model, or several models, of how the moon changes phases.
5. With older children, study how the moon shines and changes shape.
6. Don't forget to connect the moon with Jewish holidays. You'll always see the new moon crescent on Rosh HaShanah, because Rosh HaShanah is also "Rosh Chodesh" of Tishre. You'll always see the full moon through the *s'chach* of the *sukkah* on the first night of Sukkot, and when you open the door for Elijah on the night of the Pesach *Seder*.
7. Keep a Jewish calendar hanging in the classroom for easy reference.
8. Make or buy moon shaped cookies for a special treat on Rosh Chodesh.

MATH

1. Count how many days it takes the moon to go through its entire cycle.
2. Over the year, make a chart of which holidays fall in each Hebrew month.
3. Count how many nights the moon was visible in a given month.
4. Add the moon phase symbols to your regular calendar.
5. In addition to your regular calendar, mark off the days on a Hebrew calendar, too.

6. Sort and classify items collected in the Rosh Chodesh spot.
7. Make models of the moon in different phases for the children to sequence.
8. Use the moon to learn about fractions.

ART

1. Let the children draw pictures in and of the Rosh Chodesh spot.
2. Collect items from the Rosh Chodesh spot. Use these items to paint with, create collages and other pictures, texture pictures, etc.
3. Take rubbings of textures in the Rosh Chodesh spot.
4. Preview holidays coming up in the month with holiday-related artwork on Rosh Chodesh.
5. Make moons in different phases to hang around the room. Experiment with aluminum foil, papier mâché, painting with white paint on black paper.
6. Make a Rosh Chodesh "person" each month. Using a small paper plate for the face and a standard plain body shape attached with a brad, let the children decorate their Rosh Chodesh person with the name of the month, and symbols of the season and of the holidays in the month. Incorporate things found in the Rosh Chodesh spot.

MUSIC/MOVEMENT

(With musical contributions from Julie Jaslow Auerbach)

1. The monthly holiday of Rosh Chodesh offers us the opportunity to gaze into the nighttime sky to see not only the new moon, which is barely there, but all the stars as well. Sing songs about stars and the moon and the planets.
2. Play "The Planets" by Gustav Holst, and have the children move to the music. They can use scarves or other props, and maybe even costumes.
3. Have a family night at the school, go outside and sing "Twinkle Twinkle Little Star."
4. A great music and movement resource is *The Magic Forest* by Lynn W. Johnson. Pages 11 to

19 of that book form an entire section appropriate for Rosh Chodesh, including movement activities with scarves ("see How the Sky — An Introduction," p. 11), movement ideas for "Twinkle Twinkle Little Star," p. 12, and my personal favorite, "Sally Go 'Round the Stars," p. 15, a very pretty song.

5. Sing the song "I Love the Sun" in *It's Time for Music* by Mary Louise Reilly and Lynn Freeman Olson, p. 12, substituting the word "moon" for "sun." Use the book's suggested activities, which involve instruments, or use your arms, shaping the hands into a ball that can move across the sky.
6. Sing Jeremy Levin's adaptation, "Twinkle Twinkle Little Moon." With appropriate hand movements have the children curve their hands like a sign language "C" for the crescent moon.

Twinkle, twinkle little moon
I wonder if I'll see you soon
Up above the world so high
Like a crescent in the sky
Twinkle twinkle little moon
I wonder if I'll see you soon

7. Make up a special dance that you do only in your special Rosh Chodesh spot.
8. Preview holidays coming up in the month by singing holiday-related songs on Rosh Chodesh.
9. Have the children act out what it feels or looks like to be the moon, waxing and waning.
10. Sing or play these songs/recordings about the moon: *Or Zarua Latzadik* on *The Moishe Oysher Seder/Kol Nidre Night with Moishe Oysher/The Moishe Oysher Chanukah Party* (Leisure Time Music); "This Little Light of Mine" on *Chicken Soup for Little Souls: You're a Special Person* by various artists; and "Moon Shadow" on *Greatest Hits by Cat Stevens* (PDG/A&M); and the old favorites "Mr. Moon" and "I See the Moon."
11. Sing "The Jewish Calendar Song" by Julie Jaslow Auerbach (see Appendix A, p. 341 for

music and lyrics). March around the room as you sing.

CIRCLE TIME

1. Prayer is a vehicle for relating the moon to God and the Jewish framework. A lengthy Rosh Chodesh service may not be appropriate, but saying the brief Rosh Chodesh blessing on page 132 of this chapter allows children to understand that Rosh Chodesh is in the same category as "other things that have Jewish blessings."

2. When you say the Rosh Chodesh blessing, stand up and reach toward the moon.

3. Tell the children the name of the Hebrew month that is beginning, even if it's not developmentally appropriate for them to remember. Preview any holidays coming in the month. Use the moon to tell the children when the holiday will arrive (e.g., "When the moon is full, it will be time for Pesach").

4. Try this to explain Rosh Chodesh: Move your hands, palms together, in a big circle, representing the cycle of a whole year. On the first rotation, clap once. This illustrates the frequency of a Jewish holiday, which comes only once during the year. On the next rotation, clap your hands frequently as you move them around. This represents Shabbat, which comes every week. On the next rotation, clap your hands less frequently, only 12 times. This represents the frequency of Rosh Chodesh, which arrives monthly. Once you have shown the children this, make a game of it, letting the children play with the concept and use their own hands to demonstrate Jewish holidays through the year.

5. Have someone special visit every Rosh Chodesh (e.g., Frank Asch's *Moon Bear,* or an artsy crescent moon).

6. Create your own classroom rituals for Rosh Chodesh and repeat them every month.

OUTDOORS/FIELD TRIPS

1. Visit your Rosh Chodesh spot every month, no matter the weather. If it is terrible outside, visit very briefly.

2. Care for your Rosh Chodesh spot. Spend some time there when it's not Rosh Chodesh, planting flowers or picking up trash.

3. Go outside for moon sightings. Cheer when one of the children spots the moon.

4. If you can see the moon, give the children sidewalk chalk and encourage them to sketch the moon as it appears in the sky at that moment.

5. Take a trip to a planetarium to see the stars and the moon.

SPECIFICALLY FOR INFANTS

1. Take a photo of each baby every month on Rosh Chodesh. Mount the photos in a line at baby eye level. Look at these pictures often, and talk with babies about how they are growing.

2. Hang foil covered moons at different stages from the ceiling all over the room.

3. Expand babies' observation skills to include the sky. Point out the moon in the sky. Point out other things in the sky: clouds, the sun, birds, airplanes.

IDEAS FOR TEACHING FAMILIES

1. A parent bulletin board, or bulletin board and table, designated as a spot to inform about happenings and holidays in the school, is an ideal way to educate family members as they drop off and pick up their children. Busy parents need bold captions that will catch the eye with brief explanations that communicate. Topics such as "What Is Rosh Chodesh?" "Why Celebrate the Moon?" "How to Celebrate the Moon," and "Upcoming Holidays in Tishre" are appropriate and effective. Basic information about Rosh Chodesh can be repeated every month, or at least for the first several months of the school year.

Month Order	Month Name	Beginning Dates of Holidays
7	Tishre	1 – Rosh HaShanah 10 – Yom Kippur 15 – Sukkot 23 – Simchat Torah
8	Heshvan	No holidays (also known as *Mar Heshvan,* or "bitter Heshvan")
9	Kislev	25 – Chanukah
10	Tevet	No holidays, but Rosh Chodesh Tevet occurs on the seventh night of Chanukah
11	Shevat	15 – Tu B'Shevat
12	Adar (Adar I, or Adar Rishon, in a leap year)	14 – Purim (when it's not a leap year)
13	Adar II (Adar Shaynee in a leap year)	Added in leap years to ensure that the holidays remain in their proper season 14 – Purim (during a leap year)
1	Nisan	15 – Pesach
2	Iyar	5 – Yom HaAtzma'ut 18 – Lag B'Omer
3	Sivan	6 – Shavuot
4	Tammuz	No holidays
5	Av	9 – Tisha B'Av (a memorial to the destruction of the Temples in Jerusalem, along with other sad events in Jewish history)
6	Elul	No holidays, but this is the ideal time to start getting ready for Rosh HaShanah

Figure 12

2. Mention Rosh Chodesh in newsletters on a regular basis (see p. 138 below for a suggested article).

3. Invite family members into the classroom for the monthly Rosh Chodesh celebration and trip to the Rosh Chodesh spot.

4. Display Rosh Chodesh books in a spot where families can view or borrow them.

5. Send home a calendar grid (one month) with empty circles on each day. Encourage families to look at the moon each night and draw what they see, so they can chart the entire cycle of the moon.

6. After their children have been celebrating Rosh Chodesh for several months, invite families to the school one evening for an adult celebration of Rosh Chodesh. Include stories, song, prayer, study, and of course, food, in the celebration. This event will help parents understand why their children have become so taken with the moon, and will also enrich the lives of all family members.

7. Recommended reading: *Celebrating the New Moon: A Rosh Chodesh Anthology,* edited by Susan Berrin, and *Miriam's Well* by Penina Adelman.

THE HEBREW MONTHS AND THEIR HOLIDAYS

Above in figure 12 is a chart of the Jewish year that shows the months in order, the name of the month, and all of the holidays in each month.

There are four new years in the Hebrew calendar. Nisan is the first calendar month. Tishre is actually the seventh month, but it is also the month of Rosh HaShanah and the beginning of the school year, so it is listed first in the chart.

SUGGESTED NEWSLETTER ARTICLE

Rosh Chodesh means the "Head of the Month," or the beginning of the new Hebrew month. Rosh Chodesh is signaled by the first sliver of the new moon. Rosh Chodesh was traditionally a day of rest for women. At preschool, we will celebrate Rosh Chodesh each new month with prayer, stories, and songs. Each class will have its own Rosh Chodesh spot. They will visit this location each Rosh Chodesh, watching it change as the Jewish months pass. Be sure to point out the phases of the moon to your child. The cycle of the moon connects us to the cycle of Jewish life. With your child, you can watch the moon change and discover the wonder of this eternal Jewish timepiece.

NEWSLETTER ADDITIONS

Here are some examples of statements to include in your newsletter in order to connect Rosh Chodesh to holidays and to other things going on in your classroom.

- When it is Rosh Chodesh Nisan, we know that Pesach is only two weeks away!
- Rosh Chodesh _____ [insert month] is next _____ [insert day of week] night. On that night, look for the moon with your child after dark.
- Every month, the moon renews and recycles itself. We are learning to recycle materials in our class.
- One week after Rosh Chodesh, the moon looks like it is cut in half. At snack, we cut our cookies in half so they look like the moon. We can't wait for the full moon!

BIBLIOGRAPHY

ADULTS

Adelman, Penina. *Miriam's Well*. New York: Biblio Press, 1990.
    The original guide to women's celebration of Rosh Chodesh.

Agus, Arlene. "This Month Is for You: Observing Rosh Hodesh as a Women's Holiday." In *The Jewish Woman: New Perspectives*, edited by Elizabeth Koltun. New York: Schocken Books, 1986.
    Provides a historical overview of Rosh Chodesh and a look at modern celebrations.

Berrin, Susan, ed. *Celebrating the New Moon: A Rosh Chodesh Anthology*. Northvale, NJ: Jason Aronson Inc., 1996.
    Includes "Rosh Chodesh for Children: Learning about and Experiencing the Jewish Lunar Calendar" by Ellen Brosbe.

HERitage & HIStory: Visions for an Equal Future, A Sourcebook of Jewish Women's Issues. Jerusalem: World Union of Jewish Students, 1993. (Available from WUJS, 972 02 561 0133)
    Includes material for a wide range of Jewish women's programs, including poems and rituals for monthly Rosh Chodesh celebrations. For information on this book and a new version to be published in 2000, call WUJS, or e-mail them at wujs@netvision.net.il.

Solomon, Judith. *The Rosh Hodesh Table: Foods at the New Moon*. New York: Biblio Press, 1995.
    Recipes for every month's Rosh Chodesh celebration.

Umansky, Ellen, and Dianne Ashton, eds. *Four Centuries of Jewish Women's Spirituality*. Boston, MA: Beacon Press, 1992.
    A multiplicity of international voices reveal the many different spiritual paths that modern Jewish women have taken.

CHILDREN

Asch, Frank. *Happy Birthday Moon*. New York: Simon & Schuster, 1982. (Ages 2-5)

———. *Moonbear*. New York: Simon & Schuster, 1984. (Ages 2-5)

———. *Mooncake*. New York: Simon & Schuster, 1988. (Ages 2-5)

———. *Moondance*. New York: Simon & Schuster, 1993. (Ages 2-5)

———. *Moongame*. New York: Simon & Schuster, 1984. (Ages 2-5)
    Five delightful stories of Bear, his friend Little Bird, and the moon.

Asimov, Isaac. *The Moon*. Milwaukee, WI: G. Stevens Publisher, 1994. (Ages 4-8)
    Part of Isaac Asimov's new library of the universe; a scientific look at the moon.

———. *Why Does the Moon Change Shape?* Milwaukee, WI: G. Stevens Publisher, 1991. (Ages 4-8)
    Explains why the moon changes from crescent to full moon every 29 days.

Banks, Kate. *And If the Moon Could Talk*. New York: Farrar, Straus & Giroux, 1998. (Ages 4-8)
    A bedtime tale about what the moon would say if it could look down on the earth and tell us what it sees.

Carle, Eric. *Papa, Please Get the Moon for Me*. New York: Simon & Schuster, 1986. (3-8 yrs)
    Monica begs her father to bring her the moon. Shows the moon in different phases.

Fowler, Alan. *So That's How the Moon Changes Shape!* Chicago: Children's Press, 1991. (Ages 4-8)
    A simple explanation of the moon and why it changes shape throughout the month.

———. *When You Look Up at the Moon*. Chicago: Children's Press, 1994. (Ages 4-8)

Fowler, Susi G. *I'll See You When the Moon Is Full*. New York: Greenwillow Books, 1994. (4-8 yrs)
    A little boy's father is going away on a trip, but promises to return when "the moon is full."

Rosen, Sidney. *Where Does the Moon Go?* Minneapolis, MN: Carolrhoda Books, 1992. (Ages 4-8)

Follows the moon through its 29-day cycle around the earth and identifies its different phases.

Rosenfeld, Dina. *Why the Moon Only Glows.* New York: Hachai, 1992. (3-8 yrs)
Recounts the *midrash* about why the moon is smaller than the sun.

Russell, Ching Yeung. *Moon Festival.* Honesdale, PA: Boyds Mills Press, 1997. (Ages 4-8)
This story of children celebrating the traditional autumn moon festival is based on the author's memories of her childhood in China.

Schaefer, Carole Lexa. *Sometimes Moon.* New York: Crown Publishers, 1999. (Ages 4-8)
Delightful illustrations and magical text help children understand the phases of the moon.

Suen, Anastasia. *Man on the Moon.* New York: Viking Children's Books, 1997. (All ages)
Describes in illustrations and simple text the Apollo II mission to the moon.

Walker, Niki, and Bobbie Kalmen. *The Moon (Eye on the Universe).* New York: Crabtree Publishers, 1998.
Describes the characteristics and traces the history of our exploration of earth's nearest neighbor.

Whitcher, Susan. *Moonfall.* New York: Farrar, Straus and Giroux, 1993. (Ages 4-8)
The moon gets caught in Mrs. Schwartz's lilac bush, and Sylvie decides that the moon needs a good bubble bath.

CHAPTER 9

ROSH HASHANAH

In the seventh month, on the first day of the month, you shall observe complete rest, a sacred occasion commemorated with loud blasts. (Leviticus 23:24)

OVERVIEW

The Torah tells us to celebrate Rosh HaShanah with blasts of the *shofar*. Although the Torah refers to Rosh HaShanah as the Day of Remembrance (*Yom HaZikaron*) and the Day for Sounding the *Shofar* (*Yom Teruah*), the cause for celebration is unclear. By Talmudic times, the Rabbis had connected this first day of the seventh Hebrew month (Tishre) to the creation of the world and to the Jewish New Year (Rosh HaShanah translates as "Head of the Year"). There are actually four New Years in the Jewish calendar: Tishre 1 (Rosh HaShanah) — the anniversary of the creation of the world; Nisan 1 — the New Year for Kings and festivals (the first month of the calendar year); Shevat 15 (Tu B'Shevat) — the new year of the trees; and Elul 1 — the new year for tithes of plants and animals.

Rosh HaShanah is a one-day holiday. However, in traditional communities outside of Israel, a second day is observed. This is because Rosh HaShanah falls on the first day of the new month, which is determined by the new moon. In the days when the calendar was still based on the observation of witnesses, there was a risk that people in different parts of the world would start the month on a different day, and therefore might celebrate at different times. Two days of Rosh HaShanah gave everyone time to coordinate calendars.

The only ritual for Rosh HaShanah in the Torah is the blowing of the *shofar*. The *shofar* is a

horn taken from any kosher animal except a cow. The loud blasts serve to wake us up spiritually, to alert us to the challenges of reflecting on how we might become better persons. There are three *shofar* sounds (plus one variation on a theme):

Tekiah – one long blast _____

Shevarim – three short blasts ____ ____ ____

Teruah – nine staccato blasts – – – – – – – –

Tekiah Gedolah – one very long blast _____

The *mitzvah* (commandment) is to hear the *shofar* being blown, not to sound it ourselves. Even so, trying to blow the *shofar* is a fun, concrete way to welcome the new year.

Today, there are many more Rosh HaShanah customs. We dip apples in honey in order to symbolize the wish for a sweet new year. We make round *challot* instead of straight loaves. A round *challah* looks like a crown, which is most appropriate for this time of year when we think especially of God as royalty. Round foods such as apples and *challah* also further the concept of renewing ourselves for a whole new year, as the seasons cycle around again and again. On the afternoon of the first day of Rosh HaShanah, it is a custom to go to a body of water and empty pockets of crumbs and lint and — symbolically — of sins of the past year. This ceremony is called *Tashlich*.

Rosh HaShanah is especially a time when Jews gather in the synagogue to pray, read the Torah, listen to the *shofar*, and do some serious introspection. The days between Rosh HaShanah and Yom Kippur, the *Aseret Yamay Teshuvah* (Ten Days of Repentance), are devoted to self-reflection and seeking forgiveness.

Tradition tells us that on Rosh HaShanah, the Book of Life is opened, and God judges who will be written in it for the year ahead. For this reason, there are special greetings for this period of the year — *Shanah tovah* (A good year), *L'shanah tovah tikatayvu* (May you be inscribed for a good year in the Book of Life), or *L'shanah tovah u'metukah* (To a good and sweet new year).

For a glossary and Hebrew vocabulary for Rosh HaShanah, see figure 13 below on this page.

SPECIAL BLESSINGS FOR ROSH HASHANAH

We dip apples in honey for a sweet new year. This is the blessing we say over apples:

בָּרוּךְ אַתָּה יְיָ אֱלֹהֵינוּ מֶלֶךְ הָעוֹלָם
בּוֹרֵא פְּרִי הָעֵץ.

Baruch Atah Adonai Elohaynu Melech HaOlam Boray P'ri HaAytz.

We praise You, our God, Creator of the universe, Who created the fruit of the trees.

When we do (or taste) something we haven't done (or tasted) in a very long time, we thank God for bringing us to this special moment with this blessing:

בָּרוּךְ אַתָּה יְיָ אֱלֹהֵינוּ מֶלֶךְ הָעוֹלָם
שֶׁהֶחֱיָנוּ וְקִיְּמָנוּ וְהִגִּיעָנוּ לַזְּמַן הַזֶּה.

Baruch Atah Adonai, Elohaynu Melech HaOlam, Shehecheyanu, V'keeyamanu, V'Higeeyanu LaZman HaZeh.

We praise you, our God, Creator of the universe, for giving us life, sustaining us, and helping us to reach this moment.

ROSH HASHANAH CONCEPTS

WEBBING THE CONCEPTS

Webbing the concepts of Rosh HaShanah (see Chapter 1, "Developmentally Appropriate Practice," p. 11 for more on webbing), can elicit ideas about what you want children more easily think about what you want children to learn (and not just what you want them to make). This technique can also bring to mind connections to other things going on in your classroom. In figure 14 on the next page is the *beginning* of a web for Rosh HaShanah. You can extend the web with your co-teachers or your students, thus shaping the

GLOSSARY AND HEBREW VOCABULARY		
אָדֹם	*Adom*	red
עֲשֶׂרֶת יְמֵי תְּשׁוּבָה	*Aseret Yamay Teshuvah*	Ten Days of Repentance
דְּבַשׁ	*D'vash*	honey
מַחְזוֹר	*Machzor*	High Holy Day prayer book
רֹאשׁ הַשָּׁנָה	Rosh HaShanah	literally, Head of the Year; the Jewish New Year
שׁוֹפָר	*Shofar*	ram's horn, or the horn of any kosher animal except a cow
תַּפּוּחַ/תַּפּוּחִים	Tapooach/Tapoocheem	apple/apples
תַּשְׁלִיךְ	*Tashlich*	ceremony of symbolically throwing our sins into a body of water
תִּשְׁרֵי	Tishre	seventh month in the Hebrew calendar
טוֹבָה	*Tovah*	Good
יוֹם כִּפּוּר	*Yom Kippur*	Day of Atonement

Figure 13

celebration of Rosh HaShanah to include the interests of everyone in your class. *You won't cover everything you web,* but you'll get a good idea of where you want to go.

Infant To 24 Months
1. I hear and see and touch the *shofar*.

2. I eat apples and honey.
3. The Rosh HaShanah *challah* is round.

2 Years
1. On Rosh HaShanah, we eat apples.
2. We dip apples in honey.
3. The Rosh HaShanah *challah* is round.

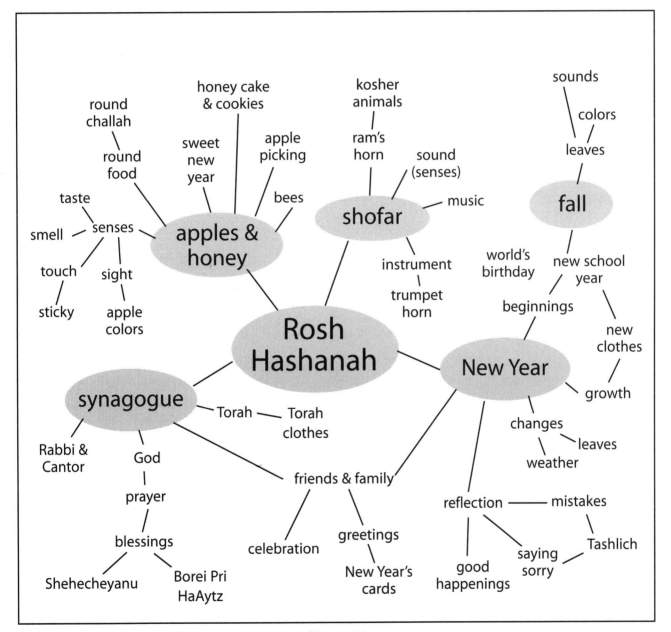

Figure 14

4. I go to synagogue with my family.
5. I see the Rabbi and *Hazzan* (Cantor).
6. I hear the sounds of the *shofar*. I can try to blow the *shofar*.
7. I see the Torah. The Torah wears a white mantle.
8. I say *"Shanah Tovah."*

3 Years

1. Rosh HaShanah is the Jewish New Year.
2. On Rosh HaShanah, we eat apples.
3. We dip apples in honey for a sweet new year.
4. Rosh HaShanah *challot* are round.
5. I go to synagogue with my family.
6. I see the Rabbi and *Hazzan* (Cantor).
7. On Rosh HaShanah, we pray to God. Prayer is a way we talk to God.
8. I hear the *shofar* blow. I can try to blow the *shofar*.
9. I see the Torah. The Torah wears a white mantle.
10. I say *"L'Shanah Tovah Tikatayvu."*
11. I try to be the best person I can be.

4 To 5 Years

1. Rosh HaShanah is the Jewish New Year.
2. Rosh HaShanah is the beginning of the Jewish year for Jews all over the world.
3. On Rosh HaShanah, we eat apples. We dip apples in honey for a sweet new year.
4. Rosh HaShanah *challot* are round.
5. I go to synagogue with my family.
6. I see the Rabbi and *Hazzan* (Cantor).
7. On Rosh HaShanah, we pray to God. Prayer is a way we talk to God.
8. We use a special prayer book called a *Machzor*.
9. I hear the *shofar*. I can try to blow the *shofar*.
10. I see the Torah. The Torah wears a white mantle.
11. I say *"L'Shanah Tovah Tikatayvu."*
12. I can see how I've grown.
13. I try to be the best person I can be. I think about how I can do better.
14. I can do *Tashlich* and say good-bye to my mistakes.

15. In Tel Aviv, people do *Tashlich* in the Mediterranean Sea.
16. On Rosh HaShanah, we try new foods, such as a pomegranate.

ACTIVITIES

LANGUAGE ARTS

1. There are many ways to make New Years cards: gluing things from nature, incorporating family pictures, collages with pictures cut from Jewish calendars and catalogs, apple stamping, etc. In any case, allow the children as much individuality as possible, and always make a trip to the mailbox part of the activity.
2. Write a class letter to your Israeli pen pals. Tell them how you are preparing for Rosh HaShanah (or how you celebrated it). The children can add illustrations.
3. Use old New Year's cards for collages, *Concentration*-type games, sorting (into pictures of *shofrot*, apples and honey, people, etc). Punch holes and make sewing cards. After the holidays, ask parents to bring in their old greeting cards so you can do this again next year.
4. Listen to the *shofar* calls. Let the children describe what the sounds make them think of, or how the sounds make them feel.
5. Write Rosh HaShanah prayers. Each child could dictate and illustrate his/her own prayers (which could then be combined into a book), or the entire class could write a prayer together.
6. Collect the children's wishes for the new year, and what they thank God for. Use this formula or something similar: Dear God, thank you [for my new baby brother. His toes are just perfect.] I hope [he learns to play soccer with me soon].

SCIENCE

1. We eat honey on Rosh HaShanah. Investigate bees and honey making.

2. We eat apples on Rosh HaShanah. Plant apple seeds. Tell the story of the "Apple Tree's Discovery," in *Chosen Tales* by Peninnah Schram and Rachayl Eckstein Davis, and cut the apple across the middle to find the star inside.
3. We blow the *shofar* on Rosh HaShanah. Experiment with blowing a *shofar*. If you can find several *shofarot*, compare them (by sight and sound).
4. Study the animals from which a *shofar* can be made (any kosher animal including ram, gazelle, antelope, goat, but not a cow because of the golden calf, not a deer, because it has antlers, not horns).
5. Ask parents to send in baby pictures of the children. Can the children identify each other?
6. Have the children compare cooked and raw apples.
7. Bake such things as *kugel* with apples (see recipe in Chapter 7, "Shabbat," p. 127), applesauce, honey cookies (see p. 150 below), etc.
8. Float apples in the water table. Use different colors and sizes of apples.
9. Put fall leaves in the sensory table.
10. Bring in new fruits, such as pomegranate or star fruit, for children to taste and explore. Say the *"Shehecheyanu"* blessing over the new fruits (see p. 142 of this chapter).

MATH

1. Count and classify apples.
2. Have children count (or use more sophisticated timing means) to see how long each person can blow the *shofar*.
3. How many leaves does a tree have in the summer? in the early fall? late fall? Read *The Fall of Freddie the Leaf* by Leo Buscaglia.
4. Chart the mistakes/mean things the members of the class have done. Chart the good things the members of the class have done. Make sure the good things side ends up longer than the bad things side!
5. Measure and weigh everyone in the class. Do this again at the end of the year to see how everyone has grown.

ART

1. Paint a huge *shofar* with chocolate pudding.
2. Make a round *challah* cover.
3. Cut apples different ways. Make prints with the various pieces.
4. Collect fall leaves and make collages with them.
6. Give the children various collage materials in yellow and black (pom-poms, pipe cleaners, fabric, construction paper) and various pictures of bees, and let them construct their own bees.
7. Make a class papier-mâché beehive.

MUSIC/MOVEMENT

(With musical contributions from Julie Jaslow Auerbach)

1. Sing songs about changes and growth. There have been many changes over the past year. Children who could barely walk last year are now running swiftly. Clothes that fit last year on children are now too small. Children are pedaling on tricycles.
2. Sing "Open Your Fingers" by Julie Jaslow Auerbach (see Appendix A, p. 349, for music and lyrics). Children as young as toddlers readily join in on this song. No introduction is really needed. If you use the tape, follow along with the children. What other kinds of changes can the children think of adding? Use instruments (e.g., shake the bells, now hold them still).
3. Sing songs of greetings, repeating over and over the names of the children in the class. Young children love to hear their names in a song, and through music we can teach and learn all of these names.
4. Sing songs about the *challah*, the apples and the honey while cooking and baking, or as an introduction to such activities. Visual aids are handy as a constant reminder of all of the symbols we treasure on this holiday.
5. Sound the *shofar* if you can or have someone who can do so visit the class. If someone can't be found, play a tape or CD with the sound of the *shofar* on it. (At the beginning of the song

"Happy Rosh HaShanah to You" by Julie Jaslow Auerbach on the tape "Seasoned with Song," a *shofar* is blown.) It is important for the children to hear this sound, as it is the music that signifies the new year. Because young children love to make their own music, try making your own *shofarot* (see activity #6.c. below). The actual notes for the calls can be found on p. 196 of *Songs of Childhood* by Judith Eisenstein and Frieda Prensky.

6. Move to the *shofar* calls. Movement reinforces sounds. It can also reinforce the concept of a New Year, an opening, a beginning, an awakening. The first call of the *shofar* is "*Tekiah*," a long stretched out sound. It tells us to wake up. The second call, "*Shevarim*," is three short blasts. It is a little more insistent and means "broken up." Like a persistent alarm, the third call of the *shofar*, at least nine short blasts, is "*Teruah*." "*Tekiah Gedolah*" is the final blast of the *shofar*. Long and lingering, it tells us that there is no getting around it. The New Year has arrived. Time to wake up our sleepy selves.

   a. Play the *shofar* calls on the piano, keyboard, or *chalil* (recorder), or use any other instrument on which you can play single notes.

   b. Show the children motions for the sounds:
   Tekiah – arms up/arms down
   Shevarim – arms up/shake your hands three times/arms down
   Teruah – arms up/arms down, repeated nine times
   Tekiah Gedolah – stretch arms really high and hold

   c. Make *shofarot* using toilet paper or paper towel rolls. Put a small piece of waxed paper over one of the openings and secure it with a rubber band. Have the children blow the *shofarot* as you say and/or play the calls.

   d. Choose one child to say the *shofar* calls as the others respond with their *shofarot* or with their arms.

   e. Ask the children to make up other ways to express the *shofar* calls.

   f. Use the notes of the *shofar* calls to compose a class song.

   g. Let the children play the notes of the *shofar* calls on the tone bells, xylophone, or metallophone.

   h. Use hand drums to tap out the rhythm of the *shofar* calls.

7. Sing "Happy Rosh HaShanah to You" by Julie Jaslow Auerbach (see Appendix A, pp. 338-339, for music and lyrics). This is a song for fives and sixes to sing, but don't teach all the verses at once. When they become more familiar with the song, they may want to add their own thoughts and make up verses. For younger children, try using a simple dance while playing the music. Circle to the right or left on the verses, and shake hands and dip apples on the refrain.

8. Sing the classic song "If I Knew You Were Coming" as adapted below by Julie Jaslow Auerbach. Rosh HaShanah is a time to visit friends and relatives. What do you do when you know you're going to visit someone? when you know someone is coming to visit you? Do you clap your hands? shout hooray? bake a cake? Here are the words:

   If I knew you were coming, I'd have baked a cake, baked a cake, baked a cake.
   If I knew you were coming I'd have baked a cake.
   How'd ya do? How'd ya do? How'd ya do?

   a. You can change the words of this classic song slightly and sing "If a New Year were coming . . . "

   b. Act out the song.

   c. Sing the song while baking.

9. Buzz like bees and fly around the room.

10. Play "Flight of the Bumblebee" by Nikolai Rimsky-Korsakov from *The Tale of Tsar Sultan Suite*, and let the children color or dance to the music.

11. Invite the children to pretend that they are a baby/a toddler/a child their own age/a teenager/a grown-up/an old person. Let the children move about the room "in character" for a few minutes until you move them on to the next age.
12. Put on some Rosh HaShanah music, and let the children dance using scarves as *talitot*.
13. Roll or do somersaults like a round *challah* or an apple.
14. Play *Red Light Green Light* with the *shofar* — *Tekiah* means the children can walk, *Shevarim* means the children can skip or hop, *Teruah* means the children can run, and *Tekiah Gedolah* means run back to base.

Song/Music List

(Contributed by Julie Jaslow Auerbach)

The following listing includes the songs in this chapter, as well as songs from other sources that are related to Rosh HaShanah concepts. Each song and the book in which it is located is specified, along with the page number. (Please note: In this and other holiday chapters, there are many songs which are "preschool traditional," i.e., they have been around so long that no one knows the composer or the song's origin. Every effort has been made to find the source for all the songs listed.)

Concepts
"Sing Along Song" – *Especially Wonderful Days*, p. 4

Changes
"B'Rosh Hashanah" – *Memeitiv Shiray Hachagim L'yeladim (From the Best of Children's Holiday Songs)*
"Brush Your Teeth" – *Kooky Cookie Kids*, Paul Zim
"Open/Shut Them" – preschool traditional
"Open Your Fingers" – Julie Jaslow Auerbach (see Music/Movement activity #2 above)

Growing
"Stretch Tall/Small" (see Tu B'Shevat Music/Movement Activity #7a)

"Happy *Rosh Hashanah* To You" – Julie Jaslow Auerbach (see Music/Movement activity #7 above)

Shofar
Shofar calls (see Music/Movement activities #5 and #6 above)
"A *Shofar* Is Too Hard to Blow" – *Union Songster*, p. 155
"The Shofar" – *Shalom Sings*, p. 5
"The Shofar Man" – *So We Sing*, p. 14
"The Sound of the *Shofar*" – *Shiru B'Mesheh Hashana (Sing through the Year*, Enid Lader)

Guests, Friends
"If I Knew You Were Coming" (see Music/Movement activity #8 above)
"I'm a Little Teapot" – preschool traditional
"People in Our Neighborhood" – *Sesame Street Songbook*, p. 43
"People in Our Synagogue" – *Shiron L'Gan*, p. 46
"Shalom Chaverim" – *The New Children's Songbook*, p. 41
"Uga, Uga" – *The New Children's Songbook*, p. 60

Greetings
"L'Shana Tova" – *Shirim Al Galgalim*, p. 10
"L'Shana Tova Tikateyvu" – *The New Children's Songbook*, p. 16
"L'Shana Tova To You" – *The Torah Connection*, p. 6

Apples
"Apple Tree" (Way up High . . .) – preschool traditional
"Tapuchim u'dvash" (Apples and Honey) – *The New Children's Songbook*, p. 16

Circle Time

1. Play *Fruit Basket Upset* using new fruits the children have tasted for Rosh HaShanah.
2. Pretend a ball is an apple or a round *challah*, and have the children roll it to one another (or, with younger children, back and forth to the teacher), and say (or sing) "I'm rolling the apple to [insert child's name] to say *L'Shanah*

Tovah Tikatayvu" [L'Shanah Tovah with younger children].

3. Name a Rosh HaShanah activity and have the children point to the part of their body they use to do the activity (blow the *shofar*, listen to the *shofar*, walk to synagogue, throw bread crumbs into water for *Tashlich*, pray to God, eat apples, dip apples in honey, etc.).

4. Reflect on last year and discuss the year which is just beginning. Make a chart of what the children liked best about last year, and what they are looking forward to doing now that they are in an older class. Pull this list out again toward the end of the year, and see how many things you have accomplished.

OUTDOORS/FIELD TRIPS

1. Collect fall leaves and other evidences of the changing season.

2. Take a walk around the neighborhood to see what's new.

3. Go apple picking.

4. Go on a *Tashlich* walk (for more details, see below on this page and the next).

5. Go to the local botanic gardens. Make this trip two or three times during the school year in different seasons, and compare the changes each time. Keep notes of the children's observations (or photos of each trip) so you can better review.

6. Compare how the *shofar* sounds inside the building and outside. Talk about what the neighbors might think when they hear the *shofar*.

7. Read the story about Winnie the Pooh and the honeybees ("In Which We Are Introduced To Winnie the Pooh and Some Bees" in *Winnie-the-Pooh* by A. A. Milne) while sitting under a tall tree. Let the children discuss what would happen if they were Pooh and wanted some honey up in this tree.

SPECIFICALLY FOR INFANTS

1. Let babies hold and touch (and even mouth) different kinds of *shofarot*.

2. Be sensitive to which babies might be scared by the loud sound of the *shofar* before blowing it for them. Play the sounds of the *shofar* on a tape for more sensitive babies.

3. Hold infants and fly them around, buzzing like a bee.

4. Let babies who can safely eat honey touch it and eat it from their fingers.

5. Make piles of fall leaves for babies to crawl in outside (supervised to prevent too much ingestion of leaves). Pick up leaves and let them fall gently on babies' heads.

IDEAS FOR TEACHING FAMILIES

1. Send home all the blessings families will need for Rosh HaShanah dinner.

2. Send home recipes (see p. 150 below).

3. Inform families of local synagogues that welcome families with young children.

4. Let families know about any community *Tashlich* outings.

5. Invite a parent or relative to come in and help bake honey cake.

6. Encourage parents to go through their children's old clothes together with their children. After reveling in how much their children have grown, they can donate the clothes to needy families. Or have a "gently used" children's clothing drive at your school.

7. Recommended reading: *Celebrate! The Complete Jewish Holidays Handbook* by Lesli Koppelman Ross, and *Beginning Anew*, edited by Gail Twersky Reimer and Judith A. Kates.

TASHLICH

The *Tashlich* ceremony takes place the afternoon of the first day of Rosh HaShanah. We throw bread crumbs from our pockets into a moving body of water, symbolizing casting away our sins of the past year. Traditionally, penitential prayers from Micah and Psalms are recited as the crumbs are thrown into the water. *Tashlich* is a perfect time for reflection (especially if you are sitting by a lake and the weather is nice).

Tashlich is a powerful, concrete ritual to do with preschoolers. Children from age three understand that they make mistakes. By throwing crumbs into water and saying (literally), "Good-bye mistakes, I'll try not to make them again," children can begin to take control of their actions, and begin the lifelong process of self-reflection.

A wonderful children's book on the topic of *Tashlich* is *A Rosh HaShanah Walk* by Carol Levin. In the classroom, *Tashlich* can be done in a number of ways, from (most complex but also most rewarding) digging a trench in the sandbox outside and running a hose from one end, creating a stream, to (simplest but still effective) filling a tub with water in the classroom. (You may want to avoid using the water table in the classroom in order to make this experience unique, and also to dissuade children from tossing bread crumbs into the water table all year round.) The *Tashlich* experience should include prior classroom discussions about mistakes, saying sorry to other people, trying to change behavior (and how hard that can be!) and how to make the new year a better one.

Putting bread in pockets, singing, saying good-bye to mistakes as the bread is tossed into the water, and saying something official sounding about letting mistakes go and making the new year a better year — all these are elements that make the *Tashlich* experience real and meaningful for the children.

STORIES TO TELL AND ACT OUT

Children learn best when they can experience something to the fullest extent possible. When they act out a story, they are able to identify, understand, and have lots of fun. Below are two suggestions for Rosh HaShanah stories that are especially appropriate for acting out.

1. "The Announcing Tool" in *Does God Have a Big Toe?* by Marc Gellman. This is the story of how the *shofar* came to be the instrument of choice for Rosh HaShanah.
2. "The Apple Tree's Discovery" by Peninnah Schram and Rachayl Eckstein Davis in *Chosen Tales*, edited by Peninnah Schram. This is the story of the apple tree's quest for stars on her branches.

SUGGESTED NEWSLETTER ARTICLE

It seems that we've just returned to school, and the Jewish holidays are upon us. Rosh HaShanah is the perfect holiday for the beginning of the school year. Celebrating the Jewish New Year gives us an excellent Jewish framework in which to study beginnings, to look at how much we've grown, and to reflect on where we've been and where we'll be going together this year.

On Rosh HaShanah, we go to synagogue and hear the *shofar* being sounded. The call of the *shofar* serves to wake us up, directs us to pay attention to the kind of person we are so as to become a better person in the year ahead. Although we do lots of grown-up, serious, prayerful things on Rosh HaShanah, don't neglect to share the fun, childlike aspects of the holiday with your child. Dip apple slices in honey, take a nature walk together and observe how the world is changing, look at baby pictures and let your child tell you how much he/she has changed!

Now is a good time to start a holiday photo album. Make a page for each holiday. Take a picture of your child and/or family at each holiday, and add it to the page — an easy way to see how much you've all grown from year to year! Teach your child about sharing good wishes for the New Year by letting him/her help make the cards. You can make something together on the computer, or photocopy your child's drawing to use as your card. And, of course, let your child drop all the cards in the mailbox!

As you apologize to all the people you may have hurt in the past year, don't forget to apologize to your child as well. *L'shanah tovah tikatayvu* — May you be inscribed for a good year in the book of life.

RECIPES

OLD FASHIONED HONEY CAKE (LEKACH)

Ingredients
1 C. honey
3 eggs
1 C. strong, hot black coffee
2 tsp. baking powder
1 C. oil
1 tsp. baking soda
3½ C. flour
¼ tsp. salt
1 tsp. cinnamon
1 tsp. nutmeg
½ tsp. cloves
¼ tsp. ginger
½ C. raisins or ¾ C. chopped walnuts (optional)

Directions
1. Preheat oven to 325°.
2. Line a 9" × 13" cake pan with wax paper. Grease the paper.
3. In a large mixing bowl, cream honey, oil, and sugar.
4. Add eggs one at a time, beating after each addition.
5. In a separate bowl, combine coffee, baking powder, baking soda; mixture will bubble.
6. In yet another bowl, combine flour with salt and spices. Add alternately with the coffee to the creamed honey mixture.
7. Dust nuts and/or raisins with flour and drop into the batter.
8. Pour the batter into the wax papered and greased pan. Bake for 1 hour.

APPLESAUCE

Ingredients
12 apples
brown sugar or honey to taste
cinnamon to taste
nutmeg to taste

Directions
1. Cut apples into quarters.
2. Put in a pot with a thin layer of water on bottom (so apples don't burn).
3. Add brown sugar or honey, cinnamon, nutmeg.
4. Cover and cook with very low flame. Stir frequently. Cook until apples are extremely soft and mushy.
5. Strain and enjoy.
(Thanks to Arlene Segal for this recipe.)

BIBLIOGRAPHY

ADULTS

Reimer, Gail Twersky, and Judith A. Kates. *Beginning Anew: A women's Companion To the High Holy Days*. New York: Touchstone, 1997.
> A collection of essays by modern female scholars on the Torah and Haftarah readings for Rosh HaShanah and Yom Kippur.

Ross, Lesli Koppelman. *Celebrate! The Complete Jewish Holidays Handbook*.
> Contains a wealth of information and resources for each of the Jewish holidays.

CHILDREN
Infant To 2 Years

Gellman, Ellie. *It's Rosh Hashanah*. Rockville, MD: Kar-Ben Copies, 1985. (Ages infant-2)
> Introduces the symbols of Rosh HaShanah. (Board Book)

Groner, Judye, and Madeline Wikler. *The Shofar Calls To Us*. Rockville, MD: Kar-Ben Copies, 1991. (Ages infant-2)
> Describes the sounds of the *shofar*. (Board Book)

3 Years

Epstein, Sylvia. *How the Rosh Hashanah Challah Became Round*. New York: Gefen, 1993. (Ages 3-6)
> Yossi trips down the stairs with the *challot*, and they roll down and become round.

Kimmelman, Leslie. *Sound the Shofar: A Story of Rosh Hashanah and Yom Kippur*. New York: HarperCollins, 1998. (Ages 3-7)
> Uncle Jack is practicing blowing the *shofar* every day in preparation for Rosh HaShanah.

Levin, Carol. *A Rosh Hashanah Walk*. MD: Kar-Ben Copies, 1987. (Ages 3-6)
> A group of children takes a Rosh HaShanah walk to do *Tashlich*.

Milne, A.A. *Winnie-the-Pooh*. New York: E.P. Dutton, 1926. (Ages 3-6)
> Classic stories of Christopher Robin and his bear, Winnie-the-Pooh.

Rouss, Sylvia. *Sammy Spider's First Rosh Hashanah*. Rockville, MD: Kar-Ben Copies, 1996. (Ages 3-6)
> Sammy celebrates the new year and learns about sizes.

Zalben, Jane Breskin. *Happy New Year, Beni*. New York: Henry Holt & Company, 1993. (Ages 3-6)
> Grandpa explains *Tashlich* and everyone enjoys Rosh HaShanah together.

4 To 5 Years

Goldin, Barbara Diamond. *The World's Birthday*. San Diego, Harcourt Brace & Jovanovich, 1990. (Ages 4-8)
> Daniel tries to figure out how to give the world a birthday party.

Hall, Zoe. *The Apple Pie Tree*. New York: Scholastic, 1996. (Ages 4-8)
> Describes an apple tree as it grows leaves, while a robin makes a nest in its branches. Includes a recipe for apple pie.

Polacco, Patricia. *The Bee Tree*. New York: Philomel Books, 1993. (Ages 4-8)
> A grandpa brings his granddaughter on a wild bee chase to teach her the value of reading.

Apples, Honey, Bees, and New Beginnings

Burckhardt, Ann L. *Apples*. Mankato, MN: Bridgestone Books, 1996. (Ages 3-5)
> Simple text introduces apples. Includes instructions for making an apple pomander.

Cole, Joanne. *Magic School Bus Inside a Beehive*. New York: Scholastic, 1996. (Ages 4-8)
> When the magic school bus turns into a beehive and the students turn into honeybees, a first-hand investigation of bees results.

Gibbons, Gail. *The Honey Makers*. New York: Morrow Junior Books, 1997. (Ages 4-8)
> Covers the physical structure of honeybees and how they live in colonies.

Kalman, Bobbie. *Hooray for Beekeeping!* New York: Crabtree Publishers, 1998. (Ages 4-8)

Introduces bees and beekeeping. Covers equipment and the making of honey.

Micucci, Charles. *The Life and Times of the Apple.* New York: Orchard Books, 1992. (Ages 4-8)

Presents a variety of facts about apples.

Patent, Dorothy H. *Apple Trees.* Minneapolis, MN: Lerner Publications, 1997. (Ages 4-8)

Describes the life cycle of an apple tree and how different varieties of apples are harvested.

Pluckrose, Henry. *Beginnings & Endings.* New York: Children's Press, 1996. (Ages 3-8)

Different beginnings and endings are explored through the use of photographs.

Schnieper, Claudia. *An Apple Tree through the Year.* Minneapolis, MN: Carolrhoda Books, 1987. (Ages 4-8)

Follows an apple tree through four seasons, detailing the yearly growth cycle.

Starosta, Paul. *The Bee: Friend of the Flowers.* Watertown, MA: Charlesbridge Publisher, 1992. (Ages 4-8)

Part of the animal close-up series, a scientific look at bees.

CHAPTER 10

YOM KIPPUR

The tenth day of this seventh month shall be a Day of Atonement, it shall be a holy day of gathering together, and you shall afflict your souls. (Leviticus 23:26-27)

Yom Kippur, the Day of Atonement, is the holiest day in the Jewish calendar. Yom Kippur is also called "the Sabbath of Sabbaths." In Israel, no one drives, and the streets are filled with people, most walking to synagogue. Yom Kippur is the culmination of the cycle of self-reflection and seeking forgiveness that began on the first day of Elul, a month before Rosh HaShanah. The ten days between Rosh HaShanah and Yom Kippur, the *Aseret Yamay Teshuvah* (Ten Days of Repentance), are days especially focused on self-reflection and seeking forgiveness. It is during these ten days that we make sure we have made peace with anyone we may have hurt in the previous year.

On Yom Kippur, Jewish adults fast. After a festival meal before sundown, adult Jews do not eat or drink again until after sunset the next day – some 25 hours later. There are many reasons given for the fast. By removing all distractions (such as eating) we are better able to focus on prayer. The long day is spent in synagogue praying and asking God for forgiveness. Children under the age of Bar/Bat Mitzvah do not fast. Still, young children are aware and curious that the adults in their lives are fasting. Even though children do not fast, they can recognize Yom Kippur as a time to take care of other's feelings and to improve their own actions toward other people.

In the synagogue, Yom Kippur begins with a prayer called *"Kol Nidray"* (All Vows). One of the readings for the day is the Book of Jonah. Yom Kippur ends with the Ne'ilah (closing) service, one final dramatic plea for God to hear our prayers. At the very end of the day, we hear one long final blast of the *shofar*.

Before Yom Kippur, people greet each other by saying *Tzom Kal* (Have an easy fast). During the ten days between Rosh HaShanah and Yom Kippur, tradition tells us that we have time to change. With *teshuvah* (turning), *tefilah* (prayer), and *tzedakah* (justice), we may be able to convince God to write our name in the Book of Life. Thus, during this time, the greeting is *"L'Shanah tovah tikatayvu v'tichataymu!"* (May you be written and sealed for a good year in the Book of Life). After Yom Kippur, until Sukkot, people greet each other with *"G'mar chatimah tovah"* (A good final sealing).

For a glossary and Hebrew vocabulary list for Yom Kippur, see figure 16 on page 155.

YOM KIPPUR CONCEPTS

WEBBING THE CONCEPTS

Webbing the concepts of Yom Kippur (see Chapter 1, "Developmentally Appropriate Practice," p. 11 for more on webbing), can elicit ideas about what you want children to think about and what you want children to learn (and not just what you want them to make). This technique can also bring to mind connections to other things going on in your classroom. Figure 15 on page 154 is the *beginning* of a web for Yom Kippur. You can extend the web with your co-teachers or your students, thus shaping the celebration of Yom Kippur to include the interests of everyone in your class. *You won't cover everything you web*, but you'll get a good idea of where you want to go.

INFANTS TO 24 MONTHS
1. I hear the *shofar*.
2. I eat apples and honey.
3. The *challah* is round.

2 YEARS
1. Yom Kippur is my Jewish holiday.
2. I help my family.

3. I go to synagogue. I see the Rabbi and Hazzan again.
4. I see the Torah again.
5. I hear the *shofar* again.

3 YEARS
1. Yom Kippur is a serious day.
2. Grown-ups are in synagogue most of the day.

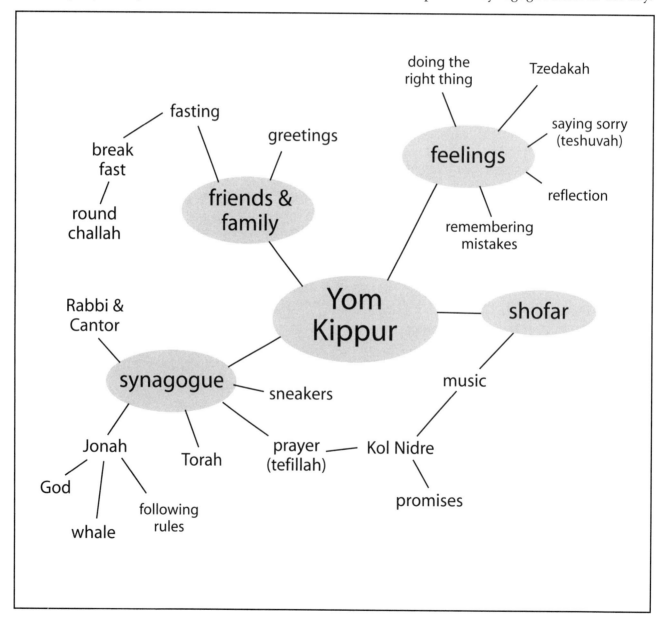

Figure 10

They read from a *Machzor*, a special prayer book.

3. On Yom Kippur, we pray to God. Prayer is a way we talk to God.
4. I say, "I'm sorry" if I hurt you.
5. I say, "I'll try to be friendlier and not hurt you."
6. I say to my family, *"Shanah Tovah"* and *"L'Shanah tovah tikatayvu v'tichataymu! "*
7. I hear the story of Jonah and the big fish.
8. I hear the *shofar* at the end of Yom Kippur.
9. I am thankful for the things I have.
10. It's not always easy to do the right thing.

4 TO 5 YEARS

1. Yom Kippur is a special, serious holiday.
2. Grown-ups are in synagogue most of the day. They read from a *Machzor*, a special prayer book
3. Grown-ups fast to help them think about how they have behaved over the last year.
4. On Yom Kippur, we pray to God. Prayer is a way we talk to God.
5. We hear the prayer *"Kol Nidray"* on the night of Yom Kippur. It is a serious prayer. We promise to do better, but ask God to forgive us if we still make mistakes.
6. Before Yom Kippur we say "I'm sorry" to our family and friends for anything we might have done to hurt them or make them sad.
7. We know we can help ourselves become better people.
8. It's not always easy to do the right thing.

9. I am thankful for the things I have.
10. I hear the story of Jonah and the big fish.
11. We hear the *shofar* at the end of Yom Kippur.
12. We wish everyone *"L'Shanah tovah tikatayvu v'tichataymu"* and *"G'mar chatimah tovah."*

ACTIVITIES

LANGUAGE ARTS

1. Make a class prayer book. Each child dictates and illustrates a prayer and signs his/her name. You'll have a great book for the book corner or to copy and send home.
2. Make a group feelings book. Let the children complete the sentence: Sometimes I feel happy [sad, angry, excited] when _____.
3. Let children list what they like about each of their classmates. Make a poster for each child.
4. Make a felt board of the story of Jonah. Present the story at circle time, and then leave the felt board out for the children to retell the story on their own.
5. Provide children with a *Siddur* and a *Machzor* and let them compare the two (make sure both books are from the same movement — Reform, Conservative, or Orthodox).
6. Interview the Rabbi or *Hazzan*. Before the interview, assess what the children think these professionals do. Conduct the interview in the Rabbi or *Hazzan's* office.

GLOSSARY AND HEBREW VOCABULARY		
עָצוּב	*Ah'tzoov*	sad
חֲבֵרִים	*Chavayreem*	friends
כָּל נִדְרֵי	*"Kol Nidray"*	literally, All Vows; the opening prayer of Yom Kippur
מִשְׁפָּחָה	*Mishpachah*	family
נְעִילָה	*Ne'ilah*	the closing service on Yom Kippur
שָׂמֵחַ	*Samayach*	happy
יוֹם כִּפּוּר	Yom Kippur	The Day of Atonement

Figure 16

SCIENCE

1. Use various items for reflection — mirrors, foil, water, eyes, etc.
2. Study whales and other large sea creatures.
3. Conduct sink and float experiments. (These expand on the Jonah and the whale theme.)
4. Continue the study of *shofar* and the animals which can contribute a horn to the cause.
5. Read "The Announcing Tool" in *Does God Have a Big Toe* by Marc Gellman, and investigate other possible announcing tools. Provide the children with pans and pot lids, buzzers, megaphones, and so on.

MATH

1. Chart the people to whom we have to say I'm sorry, and what we might say to them.
2. Collect pictures of people from catalogs and magazines. Graph the people according to feelings (happy, sad, mad, surprised, and so on).
3. Sequence photos of a person as he/she ages.

ART

1. Make a class whale/big fish.
2. Look and see a nicer me — use tin foil as a mirror and decorate a border.
3. Place *shofarot* and other holiday objects on blueprint paper (purchase from an art supply or photo store). Place in the sun for 5-10 minutes. The outlines of the objects remain on the paper.
4. When apple printing (or painting with apple pieces), make sure to cut the apples in different ways, and allow the children a choice.
5. Now is a good time of the year for each child to make a *Tzedakah* box (for ideas see Chapter 7, "Shabbat," p. 116).

MUSIC/MOVEMENT

(With musical contributions from Julie Jaslow Auerbach)

1. It is very difficult to convey the concepts of Yom Kippur to little ones. The best we can do is enable them to understand how important it is to be good people and good friends. Sing songs about feelings. Certainly, adapting "If You're Happy and You Know It" to include a range of emotions is a good activity to supplement the teaching of this holiday.

2. Sing *"G'mar Chatimah Tovah"* by Julie Jaslow Auerbach (See Appendix A, p. 335, for music and lyrics). God is anthropomorphic to young children, and the image of God writing our names in a great big book very vivid. While we may want to steer away from the more grown-up idea of who shall live and who shall die, young children can easily grasp thoughts about improving their behavior in order to have the coming year end happily.

   a. Introduce the refrain as the traditional greeting between Rosh HaShanah and Yom Kippur.
   b. Have the children repeat the words until you are comfortable that they know them.
   c. Sing a verse and ask them to join you on the refrain. I will often repeat the words several times, saying "Now what did you say?" and "Louder, please."
   d. Have the children add their own thoughts.
   e. Present this song using the brainstorming technique as an introduction (see Chapter 22, "A Guide To Music in the Early Childhood Classroom," p. 284, for an explanation of this technique). Ask the children what kinds of things they would like to do better in the coming year. This is hard for some children, and some assistance may be needed.

3. On the first evening of Yom Kippur, the highlight of the service is the singing of *"Kol Nidray."* In this prayer, we ask God to annul all the promises and vows that we will make under duress during the coming year. In this day and age, these vows might include to quit smoking, to drive more carefully, and so on. But, just in case we can't keep our vows, we declare our vows null and void, and we ask God's forgiveness in advance. Pretty powerful stuff!

Play a tape of *"Kol Nidray"* and discuss. Or, allow the children to color while listening. Is the music happy or sad? serious or playful? How does music communicate well without words? You could expand on this with "Peter and the Wolf" or music from the film *Fantasia*. Younger children might not be able to discuss the music, but they will still be enriched by hearing it.

4. Have a freeze dance to the sound of the *shofar*. (When the shofar stops playing, children freeze in place.)

5. Have children mirror each other or dance together to songs like *"Veahavta Le-rayeha Kamoha"* from *Especially Wonderful Days* by Steve Reuben. See *Creative Movement for a Song* by Joanne Tucker for more ideas.

6. Blindfold two to four children. Have them walk around inside the circle of children (standing and holding hands). When two of the blindfolded children bump into each other, they shake hands and say *"L'Shanah tovah tikatayvu v'techataymu!"* or *"G'mar chatimah tovah."*

7. Play cooperation games where everyone must help. For example, do a "group sit." Have everyone stand in a tight circle, with each person's right shoulder facing inside the circle. Everyone sits down into the lap behind him/her at the same time. Another group cooperation game is the "tangled circle." Standing in a circle, each person randomly grabs someone's left hand with his/her right hand. Everyone must work together to untangle the circle without letting go of hands.

Song/Music List
(Contributed by Julie Jaslow Auerbach)

The following listing includes the songs cited in this chapter, as well as songs from other sources that are related to Yom Kippur concepts. The album/songbook in which each is located is specified, along with the page number. (Please note: In this and other holiday chapters, there are many songs which are "preschool traditional," i.e., they have been around so long that no one knows the composer or the song's origin! Every effort has been made to find the source for all the songs listed.)

Feelings
"If You're Happy" (Sad/Angry) – preschool traditional
"No No No" – *My Toes Are Starting to Wiggle*, p. 182
"Let's Be Friends" – *The New Children's Songbook*, p. 17
"Slicha, Toda, B'vakasha" – *The New Children's Songbook*, p. 19
"G'mar Chatima Tova" – Julie Jaslow Auerbach (see Music/Movement activity #2 above)

Concepts
"Sing Along Song" – *Especially Wonderful Days*, p. 4
"Veahavta Le-rayeha Kamoha" – *Especially Wonderful Days*, p. 13

Circle Time
1. Talk about what things make each child feel better (e.g., I feel better when my mommy hugs me . . . when I eat ice cream . . . after I cry).
2. Invite the Rabbi or *Hazzan* to come talk to the children, read a story, or sing some songs with children.
3. Study the story of Jonah. Stop the story at various points (when Jonah decides to run away, when Jonah is on the ship, when Jonah is in the great fish's belly, at the end of the story), and let the children give Jonah advice.

Outdoors/Field Trips
1. Explore the synagogue or Jewish Community Center. Get to know the key people in the building.
2. Visit a sanctuary. Look at the Torah and all the elements of the synagogue. Sit in the seats and practice being quiet.
3. Continue to take walks to monitor weather changes.
4. Visit the spot where you performed *Tashlich* to see if the bread crumbs are still there.

SPECIFICALLY FOR INFANTS

1. Play the music of *"Kol Nidray"* for babies to listen to.
2. Make sure that babies meet the Rabbi, *Hazzan*, and other important people in the building.
3. Take babies outside. Talk to them about changes in the weather.
4. Show babies a round *challah* and a regular long *challah*. Let them touch and explore the way babies do — with their mouths!

IDEAS FOR TEACHING FAMILIES

1. Encourage parents to talk with their children about beginnings and changes. If they've started a holiday photo album, remind them to take a Yom Kippur picture. They may also look through family photo albums, noting the growth of all family members.
2. Depending on when the school year begins, Yom Kippur may be a great time for the teacher to connect with each family about how their child has transitioned into the new class.
3. Send home an adult translation of the Book of Jonah along with the developmentally appropriate version you use in your class. This is an opportunity to educate parents on how you approach Judaism in your class in a developmentally appropriate way.
4. Recommended reading: *Preparing Your Heart for the High Holy Days: A Guided Journal* by Kerry M. Olitzky and Rachel T. Sabath, and *The Five Megilloth and Jonah,* with introduction by H.L. Ginsberg.

SOME STORIES

THE STORY OF JONAH

Note: The Book of Jonah is the Haftarah read in synagogues on Yom Kippur. You can find it in any Machzor, Tanach (Hebrew Bible), or in *The Five Megilloth and Jonah,* with introductions by H.L. Ginsberg. Reading the adult version will help you grasp the story better and tell it to children with that much more understanding. This story teaches the overriding theme of the High Holy Days. We may do something wrong, but if we change our ways, God will forgive us. Following is an age appropriate version to share with the children.

God called to Jonah and told Jonah to go to the city of Nineveh. God said to Jonah, "The people of Nineveh are wicked and mean. Go to Nineveh and tell them to change their ways." But Jonah did not want to go to Nineveh. Instead, he decided to run away from God and go to Tarshish. Jonah got on a boat going to Tarshish.

This made God very angry. God sent a great wind over the sea. The boat tossed and turned in the water. All the sailors on the boat were very afraid of the great storm. They threw things overboard to make the ship lighter. They prayed for the storm to end. The people said, "Who made this storm happen?" Jonah said, "It is my fault. I ran away from God. Throw me overboard. Then you will be safe." But the sailors did not want to hurt Jonah. They rowed extra hard to reach the shore. But the storm became worse. The sailors prayed, "Please God, let us live!" Finally, they threw Jonah overboard, and the sea became calm.

God protected Jonah. God sent a huge fish to swallow Jonah. Jonah sat in the belly of the fish for three days, praying to God to forgive him. When God was sure that Jonah meant what he said, God told to fish to spit Jonah back onto the land. Once again, God told Jonah to go to Nineveh and tell the people to change their ways and stop being wicked. This time, Jonah listened to God. He went to Nineveh, and walked all over the town. He told the people that God wanted them to turn away from the wicked things they were doing. The people of Nineveh believed Jonah. They stopped doing wicked things, and they prayed to God to forgive them. God saw that they meant what they said, and God did not punish the people.

ANOTHER STORY

Daniel was always saying mean things about his friends. He didn't care if they weren't true. The children asked him to stop, but he laughed at them, and said that his stories weren't hurting anybody. Finally, the children went to the Rabbi to complain about Daniel's stories. The Rabbi called Daniel to come and see her. She said, "Daniel, your stories are hurting the children's feelings." Daniel said, "My stories are harmless. Besides, if someone is upset, I can just apologize to that person." Then the Rabbi told Daniel to fill a small bag with pebbles from a nearby field and bring it to her. Daniel thought, "That's easy!" and ran to collect the stones. When he returned to the Rabbi's office, she said, "Now I want you to put back each pebble exactly where you found it." "But that's impossible! I don't remember where I found each pebble!" cried Daniel. "So you see, Daniel," said the Rabbi, "just as you can't return all the pebbles, you can't find all the hurt that your stories cause people." From that time on, Daniel always kept a few pebbles in his pocket to remind him of the Rabbi's lesson, and he never told mean stories again.

SUGGESTED NEWSLETTER ARTICLE

G'mar Chatimah Tovah! May you be written in the Book of Life. Yom Kippur is a time when we stay in synagogue all day — a good chance to think about who and what we are. On *erev* Yom Kippur (also called *Kol Nidray* — the night when Yom Kippur begins), as you rush to eat before synagogue, remember that it is a *mitzvah* to have a big, joyous meal before the fast. Some explain that we are festive because we are hopeful that we will be written and sealed for a good year. We bless the children at the meal, give *Tzedakah*, and light the candles, which signals the beginning of the holiday. We recite *Kiddush*, and bless the food.

As you listen to the haunting somber tones of *"Kol Nidray,"* think about the promises we make to ourselves as well as to others

Remember, children before the age of Bar/Bat Mitzvah are not required to fast. Grade school children may be encourage to begin preparing for when they will fast by skipping one meal on Yom Kippur, or by eating only simple foods. Very young children are prohibited from fasting due to health concerns. Still, young children are curious. You can tell them why you are fasting. It is not reasonable to expect young children to spend the entire day at synagogue on Yom Kippur. But they will enjoy sitting with parents at the children's service and they will thrill at the experience of hearing the final, long blast of the *shofar* at the end of the day.

After we break the fast at the end of Yom Kippur, we make a dramatic shift to the joyous holiday of Sukkot. If you are building a *sukkah* at your home, talk to your child's teachers about having the class come to visit.

Tzom Kal — have an easy fast! *L'Shanah tovah tikatayvu v'tichataymu* — May you be written and sealed for a good year in the Book of Life.

BIBLIOGRAPHY

ADULTS

Ginsberg, H.L., ed. *The Five Megilloth and Jonah.*
Philadelphia: The Jewish Publication Society, 1994.
> A clear translation of the books of Esther, Ruth, Song of Songs, Lamentations, Ecclesiastes, and Jonah.

Olitzky, Kerry M., and Rachel T. Sabath. *Preparing Your Heart for the High Holy Days: A Guided Journal.*
Philadelphia, PA: Jewish Publication Society, 1996.
> A spiritual guide to preparing for Rosh HaShanah and Yom Kippur.

Reimer, Gail Twersky, and Judith A. Kates, eds. *Beginning Anew: A Women's Companion to the High Holy Days.* New York: Touchstone, 1997.
> A collection of essays by modern female scholars on the Torah and Haftorah readings for Rosh HaShanah and Yom Kippur.

CHILDREN
Infant To 2 Years
Fowler, Richard. *Honeybee's Busy Day.* San Diego, CA: Harcourt Brace, 1994. (Ages 2-6)
> Delightful story of a bee going about its business.

3 Years
Buehner, Caralyn. *I Did It, I'm Sorry.* New York: Dial Books for Young Readers, 1998. (Ages 3-8)
> Various animal characters encounter moral dilemmas involving such character traits as honesty, trustworthiness, and thoughtfulness.

Cohen, Floreva. *Sneakers To Shul.* New York: Board of Jewish Education, 1978. (Ages 3-6)
> Noah learns that on Yom Kippur, everyone wears sneakers to synagogue.

Packard, Mary. *Jonah and the Whale.* New York: Golden Books, 1996. (Ages 3-8)
> A simple retelling of the book of Jonah.

4 To 5 Years
Cohen, Barbara. *Yussel's Prayer: A Yom Kippur Story.* New York: Mulberry Paperback Book, 1981. (Ages 4-8)
> Yussel may not be allowed in synagogue, but it is his simple prayer that opens the Gates of Heaven.

Prose, Francine. *You Never Know: A Legend of the Lamed-Vavniks.* New York: Greenwillow Books, 1998. (Ages 4-8)
> Is Schmuel just a poor, stupid shoemaker, or is he one of the *lamed-vavniks*?

Rothenberg, Joan. *Yettele's Feathers.* New York: Hyperion Paperback for Children, 1995. (Ages 4-8)
> Yettele is spreading gossip. How will the Rabbi teach her to stop?

Siegel, Bruce. *The Magic of Kol Nidre.* Rockville, MD: Kar-Ben Copies, 1998. (Ages 4-8)
> An exploration of the prayer *"Kol Nidray."*

Whales
Kelsey, Elin. *Finding Out about Whales.* New York: Firefly Books, 1998. (Ages 8-12)
> Highlights fascinating new ways of looking at whales. Includes handsome photographs.

Kovacs, Deborah. *All about Whales!.* Bridgeport, CA: Third Story Books, 1994. (Ages 4-8)
> Features Sea World photography.

Holmes, Kevin. *Whales.* Mankato, MN: Bridgestone Books, 1998. (Ages 4-8)
> An introduction to whales, including their physical characteristics, habits, and relationships to humans.

Feelings
Avery, Charles E. *Everyone Has Feelings.* Seattle, WA, Open Hand Pub., 1992. (Ages 2-7)
> Photos of children displaying different emotions. In English and Spanish.

Crary, Elizabeth. *I Am Mad*. Seattle, WA, Parenting Press, 1992. (Ages 4-8)

In this book, a child's anger is recognized as a real and legitimate feeling. Part of the "Dealing with Feelings" series.

Krueger, David W. *What Is a Feeling?* Seattle, WA: Parenting Press, 1993. (Ages 4-8)

Presents situations which evoke feelings so as to help children put their feelings into words.

McHugh, Christopher. *Faces*. New York: Thomson Learning, 1993.

Examines how faces have been used as symbols and as illustrations of feelings around the world.

CHAPTER 11

SUKKOT

On the fifteenth day of this seventh month there shall be the Feast of Booths (Sukkot) to Adonai, *[to last] seven days. You shall live in booths seven days; all Israelites shall live in booths.* (Leviticus 23:34, 42)

OVERVIEW

After the somber day of Yom Kippur, we make a quick transition to the joyous celebrations of Sukkot. Translated as "booths" (one booth or hut is a *sukkah*), Sukkot occurs from Tishre 15 to 21. Sukkot is one of the three pilgrimage festivals of the Jewish year (along with Passover and Shavuot). During Temple times in Jerusalem, Jews from all over would make a pilgrimage there to bring harvest offerings to the Temple. Today, Sukkot still retains its agricultural element. It marks the time of the harvest before the oncoming winter. During the harvest, the workers lived in temporary huts in the fields. The *sukkot* we build now remind us of the farmers in ancient Israel, as well as the huts in which the Israelites dwelled as they wandered in the desert for 40 years after leaving Egypt.

Sukkot is a time of giving thanks to God for all our blessings. (The American Pilgrims took their cue from Sukkot when originating the holiday of Thanksgiving.) It is also a time of rejoicing. Another name for Sukkot is *Z'man Simchataynu,* literally "Season of our Rejoicing." Yom Kippur and Passover may be the most widely observed holidays by American Jews today, but in biblical times, Sukkot was the most important holiday. It was aptly known as *HeChag — The* Festival.

There are three *mitzvot* regarding Sukkot in the Torah: (1) living in the *sukkah;* (2) gathering together the *arbah minim* (the four species — *lulav hadasim, aravot,* and *etrog*); and (3) rejoicing during the holiday.

For a glossary and Hebrew vocabulary list for Sukkot, see figure 17 on page 164.

THE SUKKAH

The *sukkah* is built before the holiday begins — any time after Yom Kippur. The laws concerning the details of *sukkah* construction are extensive. The most strictly enforced aspect of the *sukkah* is the roof. The roof is made of *s'chach* (literally covering). The *s'chach* must be organic, specifically something that grew from the ground and is now detached from the ground. There should be enough *s'chach* to ensure more shade than sun, but not so much that you can't see the stars at night. The four walls (sometimes three) of the *sukkah* can be made out of anything, and must be assembled in a sturdy but temporary manner, so that an extremely strong wind can blow it over.

We are commanded to live in the *sukkah.* For the most part today, this means that we eat in the *sukkah.* The *sukkah* is a good place to hang out, study, and read. Some people sleep in the *sukkah.* The Rabbis are very clear that we are to *rejoice* in the *sukkah,* not suffer in it. If it is raining, or too cold, we are exempted from eating in the *sukkah.* Part of the joy of Sukkot is derived from the beauty of the holiday. To this end, we decorate the *sukkah,* in the most creative way possible.

Some Web sites where *sukkah* kits can be purchased are: www.sukkot.com – The Sukkah Project (klutz-proof *sukkah* kits at reasonable prices); The National Sukkah Outlet www.sukkahkits.com (wood, canvas, and prefab *sukkot*);

www.allthingsjewish.com (the Elaine Martin *sukkah* in several sizes and styles); Leiters Sukkah – www.leiterssukkah.com (manufacturers and distributors of prefabricated *sukkot* that include the patented Ease-lock system); The Sukkah Center – www.sukkah.com (sells all types of *sukkot* and accessories).

ARBA MINIM – LULAV AND ETROG

The Torah tells us to gather together the four species — *lulav* (palm branch), *hadaseem* (myrtle), *aravot* (willows), and *etrog* (citron) — and rejoice before God. To this end, we bind together the palm, myrtle, and willow branches into what is known collectively as the *lulav*, and shake the *lulav* with the *etrog* each morning in the *sukkah*. The *etrog* (which looks like a lemon, smells like a lemon, but is not a lemon) has a special tip called the *pitam*. We are very careful not to break the *pitam*. If it breaks, the *etrog* is no longer kosher and we can not use it in the *sukkah*. The directions for shaking the *lulav* are very specific (see the blessings section below). We shake the *lulav* in every direction to remind us that God is all around us.

The *arbah minim* are associated with parts of the body. The palm is straight and strong like a backbone. The myrtle leaves look like eyes. The willow leaves resemble a mouth. The *etrog* represents the heart. From this we learn that we can thank God with our whole body.

A *lulav* and *etrog* can be purchased from your synagogue or Jewish bookstore, or today one can be purchased on the Internet: Esrogim "C" Us at http://www.esrogim.com and Zaide Reuven's Esrog Farm at www.members.aol.com/zrsesrog.

Make sure that the stem on the *etrog* is unbroken. The *lulav* (palm branch) should be fresh and straight. The myrtle and willow should be green, fresh, and have the leaves intact.

USHPIZIN — GUESTS TO THE SUKKAH

Another custom associated with Sukkot is that of inviting symbolic guests — *Ushpizin* — to the *sukkah*. In addition to our friends and family who are, of course, invited to our *sukkah*, tradition

established a guest list to include Abraham, Isaac, Jacob, Joseph, Moses, Aaron, and David. Modern feminist tradition had added biblical women to the list. Customs vary, but one list includes Sarah, Rebecca, Rachel, Leah, Miriam, Abigail, and Esther.

BLESSINGS

On the first night of Sukkot, we light candles in the *sukkah*, and then we recite the *"Shehecheyanu"* blessing.

בָּרוּךְ אַתָּה יְיָ אֱלֹהֵינוּ מֶלֶךְ הָעוֹלָם
שֶׁהֶחֱיָנוּ וְקִיְּמָנוּ וְהִגִּיעָנוּ לַזְּמַן הַזֶּה.

Baruch Atah Adonai Elohaynu Melech HaOlam Shehecheyanu, V'keeyamanu V'Higeeyanu LaZ'man HaZeh.

We praise you, our God, Creator of the universe, for giving us life, sustaining us, and helping us to reach this moment.

At the beginning of the meal, the festival *Kiddush* is recited over wine.

בָּרוּךְ אַתָּה יְיָ אֱלֹהֵינוּ מֶלֶךְ הָעוֹלָם בּוֹרֵא פְּרִי הַגָּפֶן.

Baruch Atah Adonai Elohaynu Melech HaOlam Boray P'ri HaGafen.

We praise You, our God, Creator of the universe, for creating the fruit of the vine.

Then the blessing for sitting in a *sukkah* is recited:

בָּרוּךְ אַתָּה יְיָ אֱלֹהֵינוּ מֶלֶךְ הָעוֹלָם
אֲשֶׁר קִדְּשָׁנוּ בְּמִצְוֹתָיו וְצִוָּנוּ לֵישֵׁב בַּסֻּכָּה.

Baruch Atah Adonai Elohaynu Melech HaOlam Asher Kid'shanu B'Mitzvotav V'Tzivanu Layshayv BaSukkah.

We praise you, our God, Creator of the universe, Who has made us holy through Your *mitzvot* and commands us to dwell in the *sukkah*.

The *motzi* blessing is recited before the meal:

בָּרוּךְ אַתָּה יְיָ אֱלֹהֵינוּ מֶלֶךְ הָעוֹלָם
הַמּוֹצִיא לֶחֶם מִן הָאָרֶץ.

Baruch Atah Adonai, Elohaynu Melech HaOlam, HaMotzi Lechem Min HaAretz.

We praise You, our God, Creator of the universe, for bringing forth bread from the earth.

WAVING THE LULAV AND ETROG

To wave the *lulav* and *etrog*, hold the *lulav* in your right hand, and the *etrog* in your left. Both should touch each other. Always stand facing east toward Jerusalem. Recite the blessing:

בָּרוּךְ אַתָּה יְיָ אֱלֹהֵינוּ מֶלֶךְ הָעוֹלָם
אֲשֶׁר קִדְּשָׁנוּ בְּמִצְוֹתָיו וְצִוָּנוּ עַל נְטִילַת לוּלָב.

Baruch Atah Adonai Elohaynu Melech HaOlam Asher Kid'shanu B'Mitzvotav V'Tzivanu Al Netilat Lulav.

Praised are You, our God, Creator of the Universe, Who has made us holy through Your *mitzvot* and commands us to take hold of the *lulav*.

Shake the *lulav* in front of you (east), to the right (south), back behind you (west), to the left (north), above you (to heaven), and below you (to the earth), three times in each direction.

GLOSSARY AND HEBREW VOCABULARY		
אָדֹם	*Adom*	red
אַרְבַּע מִינִים	*Arba Mineem*	the four species – *lulav, hadaseem, aravot,* and *etrog*
חוּם	*Choom*	brown
אֶתְרוֹג	*Etrog*	Hebrew for "citron"; a lemon-like fruit shaken in the *sukkah* with the *lulav*
לוּלָב	*Lulav*	a palm branch tied together with willow branches and myrtle branches which is shaken with the *etrog* in the *sukkah*
פֵּרוֹת	*Payrot*	fruits
פִּיתָם	*Pitam*	the special stem on the *etrog,* which may not be broken
סְכָךְ	*S'chach*	Organic material that is used to form the roof of a *sukkah*
עָנָף	*Anaf*	a branch
סְתָו	*Stav*	autumn
סֻכָּה	*Sukkah*	a temporary dwelling, or hut (plural of *sukkah* is *sukkot*)
סֻכּוֹת	*Sukkot*	literally "booths," the Festival of Booths, marking the harvest
אוּשְׁפִּיזִין	*Ushpizin*	Jewish biblical ancestors ancestors invited into the *sukkah* as symbolic guests
צָהֹב	*Tzahov*	yellow
יָרֹק	*Yarok*	green
יְרָקוֹת	*Yerakot*	vegetables

Figure 17

SUKKOT CONCEPTS

WEBBING THE CONCEPTS

Webbing the concepts of Sukkot (see Chapter 1, "Developmentally Appropriate Practice," p. 11 for more on webbing), can elicit ideas about what you want children to think about and what you want children to learn (and not just what you want them to make). This technique can also bring to mind connections to other things going on in your classroom. Figure 18 below is the *beginning* of a web for Sukkot. You can extend the web with your co-teachers or your students, thus shaping the celebration of Sukkot to include the interests

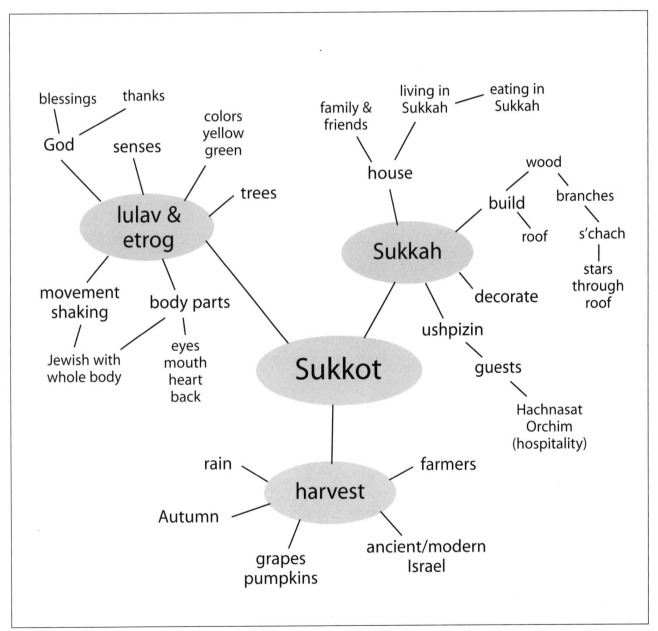

Figure 18

of everyone in your class. *You won't cover everything you web*, but you'll get a good idea of where you want to go.

INFANT TO 24 MONTHS

1. Sukkot is a fun, festive holiday.
2. I can smell and touch the *etrog* and the *lulav*.
3. I can decorate the *sukkah*.
4. I can go in the *sukkah* and look through the roof.

2 YEARS

1. Sukkot is my holiday and it's fun.
2. I can smell and touch and hold the *etrog*. You have to be very gentle with the *etrog*.
3. I can touch and shake the *lulav*. The *lulav* is made from three different kinds of plants.
4. I can decorate the *sukkah*.
5. I can eat in the *sukkah*. Some people sleep in the *sukkah*.
6. I say blessings in the *sukkah*.

3 YEARS

1. Sukkot is my holiday and it's fun.
2. I can smell and touch and hold the *etrog*. You have to be very gentle with the *etrog*.
3. An *etrog* is different from a lemon.
4. I can touch and shake the *lulav*. The *lulav* is made from three different kinds of plants. The parts of the *lulav* remind us of parts of our bodies.
5. I can decorate the *sukkah*.
6. I can eat in the *sukkah*. Some people sleep in the *sukkah*.
7. I say blessings in the *sukkah*.
8. Jewish farmers used to live in a *sukkah* during harvest time.
9. On Sukkot, we give thanks to God for good food, for family, and for everything we have.

4 TO 5 YEARS

1. Sukkot is my Jewish holiday. It's a time to rejoice.

2. I can smell and touch and hold the *etrog*. You have to be very gentle with the *etrog*. Don't break the *pitam!*
3. An *etrog* is different from a lemon. An *etrog* grows on a tree.
4. I can touch and shake the *lulav*. The *lulav* is made from three different kinds of plants. The parts of the *lulav* remind us of parts of our bodies.
5. I can learn the names of the parts of the *lulav*.
6. In Israel, people start building their *sukkah* as soon as Yom Kippur is over.
7. I can decorate the *sukkah*. Making the *sukkah* beautiful is part of the holiday.
8. I can eat in the *sukkah*. Some people sleep in the *sukkah*.
10. I say blessings in the *sukkah* when I spend time there and when I shake the *lulav* and *etrog*.
11. Jewish farmers used to live in a *sukkah* when it was harvest time.
12. The roof of a *sukkah* is made of *s'chach*. We can see the stars through the *s'chach*. The *sukkah* is made so that it is a temporary building.
13. On Sukkot, we give thanks to God for good food, for family, and for everything we have.
14. The American holiday of Thanksgiving is based on Sukkot.

ACTIVITIES

LANGUAGE ARTS

1. Invite some *Ushpizin* — symbolic guests to the *sukkah*. Traditionally these are biblical characters, but feel free to expand on the list. What if Pete Seeger's monster Abiyoyo (see bibliography of this chapter) came to visit in the *sukkah*? What if Cat in the Hat came? or Arthur? or the school director? Let the children dictate and illustrate a book about *Ushpizin* in their *sukkah*.
2. After taking trip(s) to the *sukkot* of families in the class, the children can make illustrations and dictate descriptions of what they saw.

Combine into one book the children's drawings with photos you take of the trip. Hospitality (sharing meals in friends' *sukkot*) is also a big part of Sukkot, so invite grandparents or other special relatives to come in for a snack in the *sukkah*. Remember to sing in the *sukkah* and have lots of fun! Older children can write or design the invitations themselves.

3. Make a flannel board of the children's favorite Sukkot stories *(Tamar's Sukkah* by Ellie Gellman works well and, for older children, so does *The House on the Roof* by David Adler)*. Photocopy some pictures from the story, mount them on poster board, laminate, and affix hook velcro on the back. Keep the pieces in a bag with the flannel board so children can retell the story themselves.

4. Make felt pieces for a flannel board of several people and of a *sukkah* (several brown pieces for the walls, several green pieces for the *s'chach*, fruits for decorations). Let the children make up their own stories using the felt pieces and the board.

5. Older children can compose letters to the traditional *Ushpizin*, inviting them to the *sukkah*, based on what they know about each person, for example, "Dear Abraham, Please come visit our *sukkah* because you were the first Jew." "Dear Esther, We know Purim is really your holiday, but please come to our *sukkah* anyway." "Dear Moses, Will you bring the Ten Commandments with you to our *sukkah*?" "Dear Rachel, We don't know very much about you. We have a girl named Rachel in our class. Will you come to our *sukkah* and tell us your story?"

6. Make up Sukkot poems, based on the likeness of the *etrog* and *lulav* to parts of the body. Ask the children: "If the myrtle leaves look like eyes, what might they see? The willow leaves look like mouths — what might they say? Why is the *lulav* straight like our spine?" Record their answers and transform them into poems.

7. For what are the children thankful? Let the children dictate and illustrate prayers of thanksgiving.

SCIENCE

1. Make birdfeeders or other animal food things to hang in the *sukkah*. Watch and see what kind of animals come to be guests in your *sukkah*.

2. *S'chach* can be made of many different kinds of things (evergreen boughs, corn stalks, bamboo). Compare some of these by smell, texture, appearance, durability, etc.

3. Explore how farmers harvest their crops. What machines do they use now? How did farmers harvest long ago?

4. We can see the stars through the *s'chach*. Study constellations, make stars to hang in your room, and make star viewers. Do this by covering one end of a paper towel roll with black paper. Let the children make constellations with a pin.

5. Explore Sukkot via each of the senses. We smell the *etrog* and the *s'chach*, we hear the shaking of the *lulav*, we touch the bumpy *etrog* and the pointy palm branch, we see the beauty of the *sukkah* when we decorate it, we taste our snack in the *sukkah*.

6. Make stone soup. Invite each child to bring a vegetable and make the soup together.

7. Bring pumpkins and gourds into the class. Roast pumpkin seeds, bake pumpkin cookies, cut up some gourds and let others dry out to make rattles.

8. After Sukkot, stick whole cloves in your *etrog* to make a *besameem* holder for Havdalah.

9. Soak a pinecone in water. The pinecone will close up to protect its seeds. Watch it open again as it dries out.

MATH

1. Count the sides of all the different *sukkot* you come across.

2. Make a graph of how many meals or snacks each child eats in a *sukkah* during Sukkot.

3. Collect many different gourds. Let children sort, classify, and sequence by size.

4. Weigh a few gourds. Let them dry in your class for several months. When they have dried out

enough to rattle when shaken, weigh them again.

5. Weigh a pumpkin. Take out the seeds. Weigh the seeds. Weigh the empty pumpkin. How does it compare? (Do seeds + empty pumpkin = uncut pumpkin?)

6. Provide the children with many kinds of seeds: pumpkin, gourd, apple, grape, lemon (they look like *etrog* seeds). Let the children sort, classify, sequence, and predict what kind of things will grow from the seeds. Eventually, you can plant the seeds.

ART

1. Build a real *sukkah* at your school. Ask parents to help build one from boards, or purchase a pre-fabricated *sukkah* to use each year (see "Suggested Newsletter Article" on p. 171 below for helpful resources).

2. Decorate the *sukkah*! Some ideas include stringing food, such as popcorn or berries. String up natural stuff, such as flowers, pinecones, or cornstalks. Make paper chains and hang children's pictures of fruits from the chain. Let your imagination go wild.

3. Let the children decorate a *sukkah* picture. Cut the inside to make a flap to lift. Tape a picture of the child or his/her family under the flap, so the child is "in" the *sukkah*.

4. Give the children *sukkah* parts (either cut from paper and other fancy materials, or gathered sticks and leaves) and let them experiment with their own *sukkah* designs. Older children can cut their own parts.

5. Use old New Year's cards (ask parents to bring them in) to make any kind of decorations for the *sukkah* and for the room.

6. Make weathergrams. These are of Japanese origin, and they work perfectly in a *sukkah*. They are made of biodegradable paper (brown paper grocery bags work well, cut into 3' by 12' strips), and then decorated with short poems and bits of multicolored tissue paper. When these are hung outdoors, they are mellowed by nature. Fold down a flap on one end;

punch a hole through the flap. Tie a string through the hole. Write the child's dictated poem or thoughts about Sukkot on the weathergram. Illustrate and decorate with tissue paper squares. Hang outside in the *sukkah*. (From *Jewish Parent Page*, UAHC Department of Education, vol. II, no. 3)

7. Build and decorate a *sukkah* in your classroom. Use your loft, a corner of your room, or a refrigerator box. Take photos of the building process, and then let the children use the photos for a sequencing game. Incorporate stars the children make into or above the roof, so the children can be sure to "see the stars through the *s'chach*."

8. Paint gourds to hang around the room or in the *sukkah*.

9. Provide lots of green materials (pipe cleaners, fabric, paint or popsicle sticks and green paint, construction paper, and so on) and let children create their own *lulav* to wave.

10. Create papier-mâché *etrogim*.

11. Paint with different kinds of gourds. Laminate the end results and create special Sukkot place mats to be used only when eating in the *sukkah*.

12. Play with Sukkot/autumn colors: yellow, green, brown, orange, purple.

13. Paint with pinecones and acorns.

MUSIC/MOVEMENT

(With musical contributions by Julie Jaslow Auerbach)

Sukkot

1. Listen to sounds — the wind, the rain, the rustle of the *s'chach* in the *sukkah*, the sounds of the *sukkah* being built. Use the song "Fall" by Julie Jaslow Auerbach to act out a fall scene (see Appendix A, p. 333 for music and lyrics), and also "Falling" (see Appendix A, p. 334).

2. Sing songs about fruits and vegetables. Adapt other songs to include fruits and vegetables.

3. Sing about the *Shalosh Regalim* (literally "three feet"). It was on these holidays — *Sukkot*, *Pesach*, and *Shavuot* — that the ancient

Israelites would bring their agricultural offerings to the Temple in Jerusalem. Use the song *"Al Shalosh Regalim"* by Julie Jaslow Auerbach (See Appendix A, page 328 for music and lyrics).

4. If you were going to Jerusalem to celebrate the holiday of Sukkot, what would you need to bring? This is the question that can start a very serious round of brainstorming in advance of singing this song. Children should be guided with such questions as: What do you need to build a *sukkah*? If you're staying overnight what will you need? Will you bring anything you've grown in your garden?

   a. Younger children can be encouraged to march to this song, as it has a very good marching beat.

   b. Older children can imagine what it might be like to march to Jerusalem, and even pretend to be doing so.

   c. Pre-readers can be encouraged to think of things they would take to Jerusalem using the alphabet or alphabet sounds: Can you think of something we would pack that begins with the letter "a"? Or: Let's think of something to pack that begins with a "b" sound.

5. Sing "Build Me a Sukkah" by Julie Jaslow Auerbach (See Appendix A, p. 329 for music and lyrics). This song provides a great opportunity to leave out words and let the children fill in the blanks with rhyming words. Nursery rhymes and cartoon characters can be brought to the *sukkah* and rhymed. You can present the song as if you now and then forget the words.

6. Bring in a *lulav* and *etrog* and show the children how we shake them. Play the song "The Lulav" by Julie Jaslow Auerbach on the "Seasoned with Song" tape and move along with the music (see Appendix A, p. 343 for music and lyrics). Or, sing the words to the class. Some practice shakes might be in order. Both the Sephardic and Ashkenazic versions of the

order for the shaking of the *lulav* are included. You can use the real thing, have each child make their own *lulav* and shake with it, or even have each child "become" a *lulav!*

7. Sing *"Mechi Kapayim,"* a traditional Israeli clapping game. Here are the words:

   Mechi mechi kapayim (clap clap your palms)
   Naysah Yerushalayim (we're going to Jerusalem)
   Achat shtayim shalosh (1-2-3)
   Yadayim al harosh (hands on the head)

8. Sing *"Hag Sameach"* from *The New Children's Songbook,* edited by Velvel Pasternak. Use different motions for each of the phrases; i.e., *Chag Sameach* – clap hands; la la — wave arms; *shiru shiru* — pat knees.

9. Sing *"Hallelu/Hallelujah"* or *"Hallelu/Hallelu."* Alternate standing and sitting for the different phrases. These songs can be found on a collection of Israeli children's dances. The best source: the *shlicheem* who come to our camps each summer!

10. Have the children pantomime building a *sukkah.* Some children might be the builders, others might be the components of the *sukkah.*

11. Play a Sukkot song such as "My Sukkah" from *Growin' Volume II* by Kol B'seder, "Build a Sukkah" from Rabbi Joe Black's *Aleph Bet Boogie,* or "This Is What We Need to Build a Sukkah" by Debbie Friedman on *Songs for Jewish Holidays.* Act out the building going on in the song. Pretend to be greeting each other in the finished *sukkah,* with handshakes, hugs, and *"Chag Samayach."*

12. Play classical music or Israeli folk songs and let the children pretend to be in the fields harvesting.

13. Shake like a *lulav.* Wave like a willow tree. Stand like a palm tree.

14. During nap or rest time, let the children take turns resting in the classroom *sukkah.*

Shemini Atzeret

Note: On Shemini Atzeret, the eighth or additional day after Sukkot, we add the prayer for rain to the synagogue liturgy. In ancient times, this prayer was added at this time so as to give the people who had come to Jerusalem for Sukkot a chance to get home before the rains came. Shemini Atzeret provides a good opportunity to "play" with rain concepts with young children.

1. On Shemini Atzeret, we switch from praying for dew to praying for rain in the Land of Israel. Listen to the rain and raindrops, make rain sounds on the Orff instruments and other percussion instruments — and even with voices and bodies.

2. Sing songs about rain, such as "Pitter Patter" by Julie Jaslow Auerbach (see Appendix A, p. 350 for music and lyrics). Try this song with different instruments — or even create a rain dance!

   a. Start out with one finger tapping lightly on the palms of hands for the "pitter patter."
   b. Use two fingers are "splitter splatter."
   c. Clap hands for "splishing splashing."
   d. Make a whole storm with feet and hands while singing "thunder lightning."

3. Sing songs that rhyme parts of the body (because rain can fall all over us), or as in the song "Raindrops" by Julie Jaslow Auerbach (see Appendix A, p. 352 for music and lyrics), rain falls on different body parts. Let children insert their own rhymes. Leave out words as you lead the song, or ask the children to lead the song.

4. "Myeem" is the perfect dance for this holiday, but its steps are too complex for preschoolers. Turn the dance into a story about looking for water. Have children circle one way to look for water, then circle the other way. They walk in to the center of the circle and clap hands, for they have found the "water." Walk back to the circle and make a "small sprinkler" by crossing one foot over the other. Then make a bigger "sprinkler" by crossing feet and waving arms in the air.

5. Use Orff instruments as an ostinato bass for the song "Rain" from *It's Time for Music*.

SONG/MUSIC LIST

(Contributed by Julie Jaslow Auerbach)

The following listing includes the songs cited in this chapter, as well as songs from other sources that are related to Sukkot concepts. Each song and the book in which each is located is specified, along with the page number. (Please note: In this and other holiday chapters, there are many songs which are "preschool traditional," i.e., they have been around so long that no one knows the composer or the song's origin! Every effort has been made to find the source for all the songs listed.)

Fall/Leaves

"Autumn Leaves Are Falling Down" (to the tune of "London Bridge")
"Fall" – Julie Jaslow Auerbach (see Music/Movement activity #1 above)
"Falling Leaves" – Julie Jaslow Auerbach (See Music/Movement activity #1 above)
"Bim Bam Bom" – Hebrew Songs for All Seasons Volume Two, p. 14

Harvest

"Apple Tree" – preschool traditional
"I Love the Harvest" – unpublished manuscript by Doug Lipman
"Old MacDonald" (with vegetables and fruits)
"Rainbow" – *Hand in Hand*, Bev Bos
"Thanks a Lot" – *The Second Raffi Songbook*, p. 19
"Thank You, God" – *Doug Cotler Songbook*, p. 71
"We Thank Thee" – *So We Sing*, p. 62

Going to Jerusalem

"Al Shalosh Regalim" – Julie Jaslow Auerbach (see Music/Movement activity #3 above)
"Mechi Mechi Kapayim" (see Music/Movement activity #7 above)

Sukkah

Blessings recited in the *sukkah* (see pp. 163-164 above)

"Build Me a Sukkah" – Julie Jaslow Auerbach (see Music/Movement activity #5 above)
"I'm Building Me a Sukkah" – *Songs of Childhood*, p. 204
"Patish Masmer" – *The New Children's Songbook*, p. 20
"Shlomit Bona Sukkah" – *Hebrew Songs for All Seasons Volume Two*, p. 56
"This Is What We Need to Build a Sukkah" – *Shiron L'Gan*, p. 23
"To the Sukkah" – *So We Sing*, p. 18
"V'samachta B'chagecha" – *Favorite Songs of Israel*, p. 114

Guests
"Uga, Uga" – *The New Children's Songbook*, p. 60
"Lemonade" – Julie Jaslow Auerbach (see Lag B'Omer Music/Movement activity #2 in Chapter 16, "Pesach, with Lag B'Omer," p. 236)
"If I Knew You Were Coming" (see Rosh HaShanah Music/Movement activity #8, p. 146)
"Sukkati" – *Memeitiv Shiray Hachagim L'yeladim – The Best of Children's Holiday Songs*

Lulav and Etrog
Blessings recited when waving the *lulav* and the *etrog* (see p. 164 above)
"Lulav" – *Kol Bamidbar*, Sam Glaser
"The Lulav" – Julie Jaslow Auerbach (see Music/Movement activity #6 above)
"The Lulav Is Tall" – *First Steps*, p. 16

Celebrating
"Chag Sameach" – *The New Children's Songbook*, p. 33 (see Music/Movement activity #8 above)
"Hallelu/Hallelujah" – (see Music/Movement activity #9 above)
"Hallelu/Hallelu" – (see Music/Movement activity #9 above)

Rain
"Pitter Patter" – Julie Jaslow Auerbach (see Movement/Music activity #2 under Shemini Atzeret, p. 170).

"Myeem" – see Movement/Music activity #4 under Shemini Atzeret, p. 170.
"Raindrops" (snowflakes) – Julie Jaslow Auerbach (see Music/Movement activity #3 under Shemini Atzeret, p. 170)
"Rain" – *It's Time for Music*, p. 22 (see Music/Movement activity #5 under Shemini Atzeret, p. 170)

CIRCLE TIME
1. Play "I'm going to the *sukkah* and I'm bringing ____." Older children can use the first letter of their name to think of something to bring.
2. Play the above game with a flannelboard set.
3. Name a Sukkot activity. Have the children point to the part of their bodies they do the action with (shake a *lulav*, walk to the *sukkah*, smell the *etrog*).
4. Make a *sukkah* train. Sing "We're going to the *sukkah*, the *sukkah*, the *sukkah*, we're going to the *sukkah*, please come too" (to the tune of "Following the Leader" or some other appropriate song). One child starts in the middle of the circle, then calls another child's name at the end of the refrain. The second child joins the first in the middle, train-fashion. Sing the song again, and the second child invites someone to join them on the *sukkah* train. Continue until everyone is on the train.

OUTDOORS/FIELD TRIPS
1. Visit the *sukkah* of a child in your class. Bring the *lulav* and *etrog* (if they don't have one), and plan to have a snack in their *sukkah*. If there is more than one *sukkah* in the area, do some "*sukkah* hopping" so the children can make comparisons.
2. If you have a *sukkah* at your school, use it! Eat snack, have circle time, read books, live in your *sukkah* as much as you can.
3. Visit *sukkot* in other classrooms.
4. Take a walk around the neighborhood to observe the continued progress of autumn. Do you spy any neighborhood *sukkot*?

5. Collect nature materials to use in the building of mini-*sukkot*.

SPECIFICALLY FOR INFANTS

1. Take babies to the *sukkah*. Talk to them about what they are seeing. Hold them up to touch the *s'chach*.
2. Shake the *lulav* for infants. Do this many times, both inside the classroom and in the *sukkah*.
3. Dance with babies to Sukkot songs.
4. Make the entire room feel like a *sukkah*. Drape green crepe paper from the ceiling, cover the walls with colorful sheets, fall leaves and pictures of harvest fruits (pumpkins, corn, grapes).
5. String colorful construction paper chains across the room. Let the babies watch you make the chains and play with the chains in progress before you hang them up.

IDEAS FOR TEACHING FAMILIES

1. Send home all the blessings for Sukkot.
2. Send home recipes for Sukkot (see below).
3. Involve families by going to visit the *sukkot* of the children in the class. Invite parents to come along on the visits.
4. Invite families to share snack and some *lulav* shaking in the school's *sukkah*.
5. Point families to the resources they need to have a *sukkah* at home and acquire the *lulav* and *etrog* (see pp. 162-163 above).
6. Invite parents or other relatives to come in and help make soup or roast pumpkin seeds.
7. Recommended reading: *The First Jewish Catalog* by Richard Siegel, Michael Strassfeld, and Sharon Strassfeld, and *The How To Handbook for Jewish Living* by Kerry M. Olitzky and Ronald H. Isaacs.

SUGGESTED NEWSLETTER ARTICLE

Sukkot is Tishre 15 to 21, which falls on [insert date] this year. Sukkot is considered the most joyous time of the year. It is the third pilgrimage festival (after Pesach and Shavuot). We celebrate the harvest and the fulfillment of God's promise to bring us to Israel after years of wandering.

You can bring the joy of the holiday to your own home through the *mitzvah* of constructing a *sukkah*. When you build a *sukkah*, a temporary booth, you recreate for your family the experience of living in the fields as farmers did in biblical times. Inviting guests, eating in the *sukkah*, studying under the branches, even sleeping inside the walls of the *sukkah* will bring your family much joy and excitement. Your synagogue, local Jewish bookstore, or even the Internet (www.esrogim.com or www.sukkah.com) can help you find a pre-fabricated *sukkah* to buy. Or, check out books such as *The First Jewish Catalog*, ed. by Richard Siegel, Michael Strassfeld, and Sharon Strassfeld, and *The How To Handbook for Jewish Living* by Kerry M. Olitzky and Ronald H. Isaacs for guidelines on how to build a *sukkah* from scratch. If you choose not to build one at your home, you can bring your child to the *sukkah* at school. Make some decorations at home to add to the beauty of the *sukkah*, and bring a snack to enjoy together in the *sukkah*.

RECIPES

JACOB'S CREAMY PUMPKIN SOUP
Note: This is a dairy recipe. To make it parve, substitute margarine for the butter, and rice or soy milk for the milk.

Ingredients
1 small butternut squash or baking pumpkin (approximately 1 lb.)
2 tbs. honey
1 tbs. butter
3 small onions, minced
5 C. milk
½ tsp. ginger
1 tsp. rosemary

1½ tsp. ground coriander
salt, pepper, and honey to taste

Directions
1. Cut squash/pumpkin in half. Remove seeds.
2. Squeeze honey on squash/pumpkin meat. Roast in preheated oven at 350° until tender (approximately 1½ hours). Cool and spoon out flesh from skin.
3. Put butter in the soup pot. Add minced onions. Cook over low heat until butter is melted. Add spices and continue sautéing until onions are translucent.
4. Add squash/pumpkin and milk. Raise heat to medium until the soup lightly boils.
5. Reduce heat to low and add salt, pepper, and more honey to taste. Simmer for 10 minutes. Let soup cool.
6. Puree soup in a blender. Soup will be thick and rich. Reheat before serving.

VEGETABLE SOUP

Note: Have children each bring some vegetables for the soup, or buy all the ingredients and have children help cut the vegetables.

Ingredients may include any or all of the following:
Tomatoes
Carrots
Celery
Sweet potatoes
Onions
Peas
Zucchini
Beans
Parsley
Peppers
Corn
Potatoes
Bouillon cubes

Directions
1. In a large pot, add chopped veggies, bouillon cubes, herbs and seasonings to water. Use 2 cups of chopped veggies for every 3 cups of water.
2. Bring all ingredients to boil, then simmer until veggies are tender. Season to taste.

PUMPKIN BARS

Ingredients
2 C. flour
1½ C sugar
2 tsp. baking powder
2 tsp. cinnamon
1 tsp. baking soda
¼ tsp. salt
¼ tsp. ground cloves
4 eggs, beaten
1 16 oz. can of pumpkin
1 C. oil

Directions
1. Preheat oven to 350°.
2. Combine flour, sugar, baking powder, cinnamon, baking soda, salt, and cloves.
3. Stir in eggs, pumpkin, and oil until thoroughly combined.
4. Spread batter into an ungreased 15" by 10" by 1" inch baking pan.
5. Bake at 350° for 25 to 30 minutes or until a toothpick inserted in the middle comes out clean.
(Makes 48 bars)

BIBLIOGRAPHY

ADULTS

Abrams, Judith. *Sukkot: A Family Seder*. Rockville, MD: Kar-Ben Copies, 1993.

A Sukkot celebration; includes blessings and "Four Questions" that explain the history and customs of the holiday.

Olitzky, Kerry M., and Ronald H. Isaacs. *The How To Handbook for Jewish Living*. Hoboken, NJ: KTAV Publishing House, 1993.

Detailed directions for many of the rituals and experiences of Jewish life.

Siegel, Richard; Michael Strassfeld; and Sharon Strassfeld. *The First Jewish Catalog*. Philadelphia, PA: The Jewish Publication Society, 1973.

Now a classic, this is a useful guide to many aspects of Jewish life.

CHILDREN

Infant To 2 Years

Gellman, Ellie. *Tamar's Sukkah*. Rockville, MD: Kar-Ben Copies, 1999. (Ages infant-2)

A new version of this favorite story about how Tamar and her older friends build a *sukkah*. (Board Book)

Wikler, Madeline, and Judyth Groner. *Let's Build a Sukkah*. Rockville, MD: Kar-Ben Copies, 1986. (Ages infant-2)

A simple story about building a *sukkah*. (Board Book)

3 Years

Lepon, Shoshana. *Hillel Builds a House*. Rockville, MD: Kar-Ben Copies, 1993. (3-7 years)

Hillel loves to build houses, and discovers that Sukkot is the perfect holiday for him.

Zalben, Jane Breskin. *Leo & Blossom's Sukkah*. New York: Henry Holt and Company, 1990. (3-6 years)

Leo and Blossom celebrate Sukkot by building a *sukkah*.

4 To 5 Years

Adler, David. *The House on the Roof*. Rockville, MD: Kar-Ben Copies, 1976. (Ages 4-7)

Grandpa's mean landlady doesn't like the "shack" he's built on her roof, but can Grandpa convince the judge to let him keep it?

Brown, Marc Tolon. *Arthur's Birthday*. Boston, MA: Joy Street Books, 1989. (Ages 4-8)

Arthur and a classmate are having birthday parties on the same day. How can Arthur make sure that the children come to *his* party?

David, Aubrey. *Bone Button Borscht*. Toronto: Kids Can Press, 1995. (Ages 4-9)

A Jewish version of the stone soup story.

Goldin, Barbara Diamond. *Night Lights*. San Diego, CA: Harcourt Brace, 1995. (Ages 4-8)

A boy struggles to overcome his fear of the dark so he can sleep in the *sukkah*.

Lebovics, Aydel. *The Wind and the Sukkah*. New York: Merkos L'inyonei Chinuch, 1982. (Ages 4-8)

The wind provides Mr. Levi with the materials he needs to build a *sukkah*.

McGovern, Ann. *Stone Soup*. New York: Scholastic, 1986. (Ages 3-8)

A good telling of this classic tale.

Polacco, Patricia. *Tikvah Means Hope*. New York: Bantam Doubleday Dell Books, 1994. (4-8 years)

No one can find Tikvah the cat during the fire until they look in the *sukkah*.

Seeger, Pete. *Abiyoyo*. New York: Scholastic, 1986.

Delightful story of how the monster Abiyoyo is defeated with a song. A tape is also available from the same publisher.

Houses and Building

Barton, Byron. *Building a House*.: New York: Mulberry Books, 1990. (Ages 2-5)

Brilliant yet simple words and pictures illustrate each step of how a house is built.

Dorros, Arthur. *This Is My House*. New York: Scholastic, 1992. (Ages 4-8)

A description of houses of children all over the world.

Kalman, Bobby. *Homes around the World*. New York: Crabtree Publishing Company, 1994. (Ages 3-8)
Homes from all over the world are explored through uncaptioned photographs and simple text.

Steele, Philip. *Houses through the Ages*. Mahwah, NJ: Troll Association, 1994. (Ages 4-8)
Describes a succession of human habitations in Western Europe from the caves of Stone Age hunters to modern apartment houses.

Autumn

Fowler, Allan. *How Do You Know It's Fall?* Chicago, IL: Children's Press, 1992. (Ages 4-8)
Presents many signs of fall, including geese flying and squirrels hiding acorns.

Maestro, Betsy. *Why Do Leaves Change Color?* New York: Harper Collins, 1996. (Ages 4-8)
Explains how leaves change color and then separate from the tree as the tree prepares for winter.

Saunders-Smith, Gail. *Animals in the Fall*. Mankato, MN: Pebble Books, 1998. (Ages 4-8)
Simple text and photos present behavior changes of animals as winter approaches.

———. *Autumn Leaves*. Mankato, MN: Pebble Books, 1998. (Ages 4-8)
Simple text and photos present the different types of leaves found in the Northern hemisphere.

Schweninger, Ann. *Autumn Days*. New York: Puffin, 1993. (Ages 3-7)
Explores the months of and activities related to the fall. Includes easy to do projects.

Harvest, Fruits, and Vegetables

Anderson, Joan. *The American Family Farm: A Photo Essay*. New York: Harcourt Brace, 1997. (Ages 4-8)
A pictorial essay on the American family farm that focuses on the daily lives of three families.

Burckhardt, Ann L. *Pumpkins*. Mankato, MN: Bridgestone Books, 1996. (Ages 3-7)
Simple text introduces pumpkins. Includes instructions for making a pumpkin tamborine.

Chandler, Clare. *Harvest Celebrations (Festivals)*. Brookfield, CT: Millbrook Press, 1998. (Ages 4-8)
Using easy, concise text, this book covers religions and countries from around the world.

Ehlert, Lois. *Growing Vegetable Soup*. New York: Harcourt Brace, 1990. (Ages 3-7)
A father and child grow vegetables and then make them into a soup.

McMillan, Bruce. *Growing Colors*. New York: Mulberry Books, 1994.
Photos of different vegetables illustrate the colors of nature.

Rockwell, Ann. *Apples and Pumpkins*. New York: Aladdin Books, 1994. (Ages 2-5)
In simple language, a girl tells of her family's journey to a farm to pick apples and pumpkins.

CHAPTER 12

SIMCHAT TORAH

On three things the world depends: on Torah, on prayer, and on deeds of loving-kindness. (Pirke Avot 1:2.)

The holiday of Sukkot ends with Shemini Atzeret, which marks the addition of the prayer for rain into the seasonal cycle of liturgy in the synagogue. Right on the heels of Shemini Atzeret comes the dancing and festivities of Simchat Torah. On Simchat Torah, we celebrate the cycle of the Torah reading. We read the very last passages of the Torah, and then roll back to the very beginning, and begin to read the Torah all over again. By ending and beginning at the same time, we acknowledge, with great ceremony, that Jewish learning never ends. The Torah is comprised of the first five books of the Hebrew Bible — the Five Books of Moses. Contained within these books are stories, laws, history, covenants — essentially, the foundation of the Jewish People. No wonder we celebrate this incredible document!

On *erev* Simchat Torah (the night when Simchat Torah begins), Jewish people gather in the synagogue. All of the Torah scrolls are taken out, and they are danced around the synagogue as people sing and dance along. There are seven *hakafot* (processions), during which most everyone gets a chance to carry a Torah. Children also wave flags, sometimes topped with an apple. After these *hakafot*, passages from near the end of the Torah are read. Traditionally, this is the only time when the Torah is read at night.

In the morning, there are more *hakafot*, with more singing and dancing. Then the very end of the Torah is read, and immediately, the very beginning of the Torah is read. Custom maintains that on Simchat Torah everyone receive an *aliyah*, an opportunity to bless the Torah. Even children are invited to receive this honor, in a special *aliyah* called *Kol HaNa'areem*.

For a glossary and Hebrew vocabulary list on Simchat Torah, see figure 19 on page 177.

BLESSING FOR SIMCHAT TORAH

When we finish a book of the Torah, especially the last book, the congregation rises, and we chant:

חֲזַק חֲזַק וְנִתְחַזֵּק!

Chazak, chazak, v'nit-chazayk!

May we go from strength to strength!

SIMCHAT TORAH CONCEPTS

WEBBING THE CONCEPTS

Webbing the concepts of Simchat Torah (see Chapter 1, "Developmentally Appropriate Practice," p. 11 for more on webbing), can elicit ideas about what you want children to think about and what you want children to learn (and not just what you want them to make). This technique can also bring to mind connections to other things going on in your classroom. Figure 20 on page 178 is the *beginning* of a web for Simchat Torah. You can extend the web with your co-teachers or your students, thus shaping the celebration of Simchat Torah to include the interests of everyone in your class. *You won't cover everything you web*, but you'll get a good idea of where you want to go.

INFANTS TO 24 MONTHS
1. I see the Torah.
2. I dance with the Torah.
3. I wave a flag.

2 YEARS
1. I see and touch the Torah.
2. I dance and sing with the Torah.
3. I make a flag to wave on Simchat Torah.
4. I can kiss the Torah.
5. Simchat Torah is a happy holiday.

3 Years
1. I see and touch and hold the Torah.
2. I dance and sing with the Torah.
3. I make a flag to wave on Simchat Torah.
4. I march in the *hakafah*.
5. I can kiss the Torah.
6. Simchat Torah is a happy holiday.
7. The Torah tells us Jewish stories.
8. The Torah is written in Hebrew.

9. The Torah wears special clothes, including a *yad*, a breastplate, and *rimmonim*.
10. In the synagogue, we finish and begin reading the Torah on Simchat Torah.

4 TO 5 YEARS
1. I see and touch and hold the Torah.
2. I dance and sing with the Torah.
3. I make a flag to wave on Simchat Torah.
4. I march in the *hakafah*.
5. I can kiss the Torah.
6. Simchat Torah is a happy holiday.
7. The Torah tells the story of the Jewish people.
8. I hear the stories in the Torah.
9. I can ask questions about stories in the Torah.
10. The Torah is written in Hebrew.
11. The Torah wears special clothes, including a *yad*, a breastplate, and *rimmonim*.
12. A person called a *sofer* writes the Torah.
13. In the synagogue, we finish and begin reading the Torah on Simchat Torah, and then begin it again.

GLOSSARY AND HEBREW VOCABULARY		
עֲלִיָה	*Aliyah*	honor of being called to bless the Torah
אֲרוֹן הַקֹדֶשׁ	*Aron HaKodesh*	the Holy Ark
בְּרֵאשִׁית	*Beraysheet*	Genesis, the first book of the Torah; also, the first Torah portion
דֶּגֶל	*Degel*	flag
הַקָּפָה/הַקָּפוֹת	*Hakafah/Hakafot*	procession/processions
כָּל הַנְעָרִים	*Kol HaNa'areem*	special *aliyah* on Simchat Torah in which children are called to bless the Torah
מָגֵן-דָּוִד	*Magen David*	star of David
פְּרָשַׁת הַשָּׁבוּעַ	*Parashat HaShavua*	weekly Torah portion
רִמּוֹנִים	*Rimmoneem*	Torah bells
שִׂמְחַת תּוֹרָה	Simchat Torah	literally, "Rejoicing in the Torah"; holiday which marks the end and the beginning of the reading of the Torah
סוֹפֵר	*Sofer*	Torah scribe
תּוֹרָה	Torah	the first five books of the Hebrew Bible; the Five Books of Moses
יָד	*Yad*	pointer

Figure 19

SIMCHAT TORAH ACTIVITIES

Because Simchat Torah comes on the heels of Sukkot, it is difficult to prepare for the holiday beforehand. Rather, Simchat Torah is a perfect point for *beginning* a Torah unit. Younger children can use Simchat Torah to begin learning about the physical aspects of a Torah. Older children can begin a weekly Torah study program (*Parashat HaShavua*) with *Beraysheet*, the first portion in the Torah, which we read on Simchat Torah. This way, the study of Torah is not bound to the holiday of Simchat Torah, and can continue as the interest

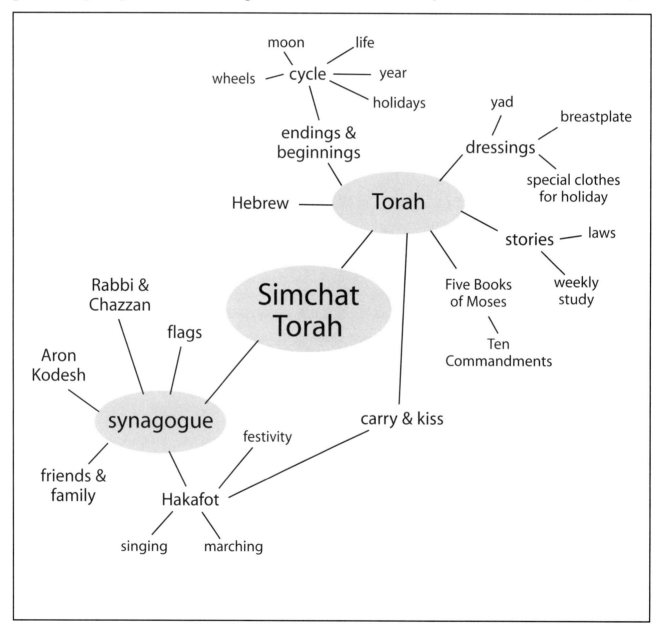

Figure 20

of the class dictates. (See Chapter 5 "Sharing Torah," for more ideas.)

LANGUAGE ARTS

1. Practice writing like a *sofer*, with feather quill pens.
2. Put sheets of a Hebrew newspaper on the table during art projects so the children become more familiar with Hebrew print.
3. Make a class Torah. It can contain solely the story of creation, selected portions from the entire Torah, or a collage of class rules and stories. Let the children illustrate some of their favorite Torah stories in the Torah.
4. Visit a sanctuary. Take out a Torah (or ask the Rabbi or *Hazzan* to help you) and open it so the children can see the writing. Talk about the Torah's "clothes." Let the children have turns using the *yad* and pretending to read from the Torah. Read a few passages (or ask someone to do this). Compare all the Torah scrolls in the *Aron Kodesh*.
5. Take a picture of each child "reading" Torah. Using the picture, let the child dictate what they read from the Torah.
6. Create a writing center (*sofer's* studio) with Hebrew newspaper, Hebrew letter stamps, Hebrew letter stencils, feathers, and bottles of black ink (thin black tempera paint), parchment-like paper.
7. Why was the Torah written on a scroll, not in a book? Experiment with creating scrolls and books. Allow the children to experiment with different kinds of rollers, ways to tie a scroll, and ways to bind a book.
8. Examine the last letter *(lamed)* and the first letter *(bet)* of the Torah. Let children play with the *layv* (heart) concept (see *midrash* on p. 181 below). Cut out *lameds, bets*, and heart shapes and let the children make a collage of these symbols and other Torah symbols.

SCIENCE

1. Experiment writing with different kinds of instruments.

2. Invite a *sofer* to come and teach about how a Torah is written.
3. Play matching games with flags from different countries.
4. Bake a *challah* in the shape of a Torah.
5. Study different cycles, both literal ones (wheels on a bike or baby carriages, Ferris wheels, turnstile at the store) and figurative ones (life of an animal or person, the year, the moon, reading the Torah).
6. Examine the writing in the Torah with a magnifying glass.

MATH

1. Compare the weight and size of several different Torahs.
2. Play with "Torah numbers": one *yad*, two *rimmonim*, five books of Moses, seven *Hakafot*, Ten Commandments. Make a counting book.
3. Make a set of Torahs rolled to different places in the reading cycle. Allow children to sequence the Torahs.
4. Count the Torahs in the *Aron Kodesh*.

ART

1. There are many ways to make a flag. Use old New Year's cards or Jewish art gallery catalogs for collage. Provide different Jewish symbols which older children can trace, cut and glue, and which younger children can choose and glue on. Incorporate the words Israel (יִשְׂרָאֵל) — the last word in the Torah, and *Beresheet* (בְּרֵאשִׁית) — the first word in the Torah — into the flag.
2. Build an *Aron Kodesh* in your classroom. Use a small box in which to put child-made Torahs, or use a stove or refrigerator box to allow the children to be the Torahs.
3. Cut head and arm holes out of pillowcases to be child-size Torah covers. Decorate with fabric paint or markers. Provide Jewish shapes such as a *Magen David*, Ten Commandments, or a crown to trace, and pictures of Torah covers to inspire.

4. Paint with feathers instead of paint brushes.

5. Make individual Torahs. Use popsicle sticks and narrow paper, or cardboard rods from wire hangers and larger paper. Younger children can decorate with Hebrew letter stamps; older children can fill their Torah with the story of creation, or lots of their favorite Torah stories.

6. Study the Torah dressings — *k'tonet, rimmonim, yad*, breastplate (pictures or the real thing), and give the children lots of different kinds of materials (including bells). Let the children create their own dressings for their Torahs. Allow lots of time or several days for this project.

MUSIC/MOVEMENT

(With musical contributions from Julie Jaslow Auerbach)

1. Use Jewish folk songs and march around the classroom with flags and small Torah scrolls. The children can create both during art time. Any collection of Jewish folk songs and Israeli dances is good for this.

2. Sing "*Dundai*." The words are "*Eretz Yisrael b'li Torah, hi k'guf b'li neshama.*" (The people of Israel without the Torah are like a body without a soul.) There is an ostinato bass (a recurring up and down refrain) that repeats the words "*Dundai*" over and over. Little ones can do this as you sing the words.

3. Sing "Marching in the Synagogue" by Julie Jaslow Auerbach (See Appendix A, pp. 346-347 for music and lyrics), a happy, catchy tune that allows the preschool child to add his or her own name to the Simchat Torah march. You may need to explain, however, what the word "meek" means!

4. Substitute the names of the children in your class for Abraham in "Abraham Danced on Simchat Torah." Abraham certainly wasn't the only one dancing!

5. March in a *hakafah* with child-made flags.

6. Dance with Torahs. Use child-made Torahs, stuffed Torahs, or mini-Torahs. Put on music and really dance up a storm.

7. Practice kissing the Torah. Stand in a circle and pass the Torah person to person. As each person hands off the Torah, he/she can kiss it.

8. Play Simchat Torah music such as "The Torah" on *Growin' Vol. II*, by Jeff Klepper, "To Be a Torah" from *Aleph Bet Boogie* by Rabbi Joe Black, or "When We March on Simchat Torah" from *Songs for Jewish Holidays* by Debbie Friedman. Have each child pretend to hold a Torah, and during the song, act out lifting the Torah, kissing the Torah, dancing fast or slow, or spin with the Torah.

9. Dance with beginnings and ends in mind. Start slow, speed up in the middle, and end slow.

10. Have each child put on a pillowcase Torah cover and dance to Simchat Torah music as if he/she was a Torah.

SONG/MUSIC LIST

(Contributed by Julie Jaslow Auerbach)

The following listing includes the songs cited in this chapter, as well as songs from other sources that are related to Simchat Torah concepts. Each song and the book in which it is located is specified, along with the page number. (Please note: In this and other holiday chapters there are many songs which are "preschool traditional", i.e., they have been around so long that no one knows the composer or the song's origin! Every effort has been made to find the source for all the songs listed.)

Hakafot, Torah

"*Dundai*" – *The Songs We Sing*, p. 358 (see Music/ Movement activity #2 above)

"Marching in the Synagogue" – Julie Jaslow Auerbach (see Music/Movement activity #3 above)

"Parade of the Torah" – from trope

"Round and Round" – Gladys Gewirtz (preschool traditional)

"*Torah Tziva Lanu Moshe*" (Little Torah) – *Union Songster*, p. 26

"*Tora Tora*" – *The New Children's Songbook*, p. 38

"*Toralee*" – *Shiron L'Gan*, p. 24

Celebrating

"Abraham Danced on Simchat Torah" – *Songs of Childhood*, p. 217 (see Music/Movement activity #4 above)
"Agil V'esmah" – *The New Children's Songbook*, p. 21
"Hag Sameach" – *The New Children's Songbook*, p. 33 (use instruments, dance)
"Shiru Li" – *Come Sing with Me, p. 41*

CIRCLE TIME

1. Invite the Rabbi or *Hazzan* in to tell the children about the Torah.
2. Create enough hearts of tag board so there is enough for half per child. Write *layv* (לֵב) on each heart, and cut each heart differently, so that there is a *lamed* or *vet* on each piece. Pass out the heart halves and let the children find their *layv* match.
3. Have children act out a life cycle, from infant to old person. Do the same with a plant life cycle.
4. Lead the children through the cycle of the Jewish holidays, by giving each child a symbol or picture from a holiday. Let the children assemble into groups according to holiday. The teacher then calls on each holiday group to sing a song or recount a memory from that holiday.

OUTDOORS/FIELD TRIPS

1. Make two sets of child-size Torah dressings. Have a relay race during which children run to the "*Aron Kodesh,*" put on the Torah clothes, run around a flag, take the Torah clothes off, and run back to tag the next child.
2. March in a *hakafah* with flags and/or Torahs. March to the sanctuary, other classrooms, through the school, outside the school.
3. Visit a Jewish store to see books and Torah objects.

SPECIFICALLY FOR INFANTS

1. Carry babies and join another class for a *hakafah*.

2. Carry the babies and dance to Simchat Torah music.
3. Show the babies real Torahs. Let them touch the soft covers.
4. Take the babies to the sanctuary, spread out a blanket on the *bimah*, and let the babies play for a while. Talk to them about where they are.

IDEAS FOR TEACHING FAMILIES

1. Recommend Jewish children's favorite Jewish books to families. Arrange for children to borrow books from school.
2. If you have a weekly *Parashat HaShavua* program, send home a weekly synopsis of what you study, so families can answer children's questions and stimulate more questions. Occasionally, invite families to join in.
3. Inform families about synagogues that welcome families with young children.
4. Recommended reading for adults: *The Five Books of Moses* by Everett Fox, and *Seasons of Our Joy: A Modern Guide To Jewish Holidays* by Arthur Waskow.

A MIDRASH

The last word in the Torah, in the book of Deuteronomy, is *Yisrael* (יִשְׂרָאֵל). The first word of the Torah, in the book of Genesis, is *Beresheet* (בְּרֵאשִׁית). If you take the last letter of the Torah, *lamed* (ל) and the first letter of the Torah, *bet* (ב), it spells *layv* (לֵב) in Hebrew. *Layv* means "heart." The *midrash* tells us that the Torah is the *layv* — the heart — of the Jewish people.

SUGGESTED NEWSLETTER ARTICLE

Simchat Torah celebrates the cycle of the Torah reading. We finish the Torah and begin again with "In the beginning . . . " all in one fell swoop, to emphasize the continuity of Jewish learning. The

Torah is the foundation, the heart, of the Jewish people. Simchat Torah translates as "Rejoicing in the Torah," and this is exactly what we do. Simchat Torah is a wonderful time to bring even the youngest children to synagogue. Just make sure to put your dancing shoes on! On Simchat Torah we take out all the Torah scrolls and dance and sing — seven whirling, happy, musical *hakafot* (processions) around the synagogue.

On Simchat Torah, we begin the reading of Torah with *Beraysheet*, the first portion in the Torah. It's a perfect time to begin Jewish study with your child. Invest in Jewish books for children (your child's teacher can recommend some favorites) and integrate them into your bedtime rituals. When children see Jewish books in their homes — children's books as well as adult books, scholarly books and coffee table books of Jewish art and Israel-related themes — then children know that Jewish learning is important in their family.

BIBLIOGRAPHY

ADULTS

Chubara, Yona; Miriam P. Feinberg; and Rena Rotenberg. *Torah Talk: An Early Childhood Teaching Guide*. Denver, CO, A.R.E. Publishing, Inc., 1989.
> An unsurpassed guide to teaching Torah creatively.

Fox, Everett. *The Five Books of Moses*. New York: Schocken Books, 1995.
> A very clear, modern English translation, with commentary, that is true to the rhythms, nuances, and stylistic devices in the original.

Waskow, Arthur. *Seasons of Our Joy: A Modern Guide To Jewish Holidays*. Boston, MA: Beacon Press, 1990.
> A wonderful blend of information and innovation that will help readers find both traditional and new meaning in Jewish holidays.

CHILDREN

Infant To 2 Years

Cousins, Lucy. *Noah's Ark*. Cambridge, MA: Candlewick Press, 1993. (Ages infant-2)
> A simple telling of the story of Noah with bright attractive illustrations. (Board Book)

Eisenberg, Ann. *Bible Heroes I Can Be*. Rockville, MD; Kar-Ben Copies, 1990. (Ages 2-6)
> Introduces various biblical characters so that children can identify with them.

3 Years

Ray, Eric. *Sofer: The Story of a Torah Scroll*. Los Angeles: Torah Aura Productions, 1998. (Ages 3-8)
> Describes how a Torah scroll is created.

4 To 5 Years

Hollender, Betty. *Bible Stories for Little Children*, Volumes 1-4. New York: UAHC Press, 1988. (Ages 3-8)
> Bible tales to read aloud.

Lepon, Shoshana. *Joseph the Dreamer*. New York: Judaica Press, 1991. (Ages 4-8)
> The story of Joseph and his brothers told using simple rhyming text and bold, bright illustrations.

————. *Noah and the Rainbow*. New York: The Judaica Press, 1993. (Ages 4-8)
> Rhyming text is easy to read, and the illustrations are bold and bright.

Rael, Elsa. *When Zayde Danced on Eldridge Street*. New York: Simon & Schuster, 1997. (Ages 5-8)
> During the celebration of Simchat Torah, eight-year-old Zeesie sees a different side of her stern grandfather.

Singer, Isaac Bashevis. *Why Noah Chose the Dove*. New York: Farrar, Straus and Giroux, 1973. (Ages 4-8)
> The Noah story through the viewpoint of the animals, beautifully illustrated by Eric Carle.

Spier, Peter. *Noah's Ark*. Garden City, NY: Doubleday, 1977. (Ages 4-8)
> An almost wordless telling of the story of Noah. A Caldecott award winner.

Zeldis, Yona. *God Sent a Rainbow and Other Bible Stories*. Philadelphia, PA: Jewish Publication Society, 1997. (Ages 4-8)
> Popular Bible stories retold alongside beautiful folk art.

CHAPTER 13

CHANUKAH

The Jews celebrated joyfully for eight days as on the Feast of Booths (Sukkot). By public edict and decree, they prescribed that the whole Jewish nation should celebrate these days every year. (II Maccabees, 10:6, 8)

OVERVIEW

Chanukah is the only major Jewish holiday rooted firmly in history, but not mentioned in the Hebrew Bible. Chanukah (literally, "dedication") is celebrated for eight days beginning on the twenty-fifth day of Kislev — corresponding to November/December. We learn the history of Chanukah from I Maccabees and II Maccabees, written in the second century B.C.E., which are found in the Apocrypha (writings excluded from the Tanach — the Hebrew Bible). An historian named Josephus, who wrote toward the end of the first century C.E., about 200 years later, also wrote about the events of Chanukah. The Rabbis wrote about Chanukah in the Gemara (late Rabbinic material which, along with the Mishnah, is part of the Talmud), in the fourth or fifth century C.E., but their version differs sharply from earlier tellings.

The Books of Maccabees and the writings of Josephus detail the struggle between Antiochus, the Greek Ruler of Syria, and the Maccabees — Jews dedicated to God and to the preservation of Jewish life and institutions. In 168 B.C.E., Antiochus decreed that all of the peoples under his rule must Hellenize, that is, adopt the culture of the Greeks. Because Israel was at that time under Greek rule, this meant that all Jewish practices, such as circumcision and the public celebration of the Festi-

vals were outlawed. Some Jews willingly exchanged Judaism for the excesses of Greek culture; others resisted Hellenism and were killed by Antiochus's army.

The soldiers of Antiochus eventually came to the town of Modin, in Israel, and set up an altar in the city square. They commanded the Jews to sacrifice a pig on the altar, to demonstrate their loyalty to Antiochus and to the Greek god Zeus. Mattathias, the elder priest of Modin, became so enraged when he saw a fellow Jew about to follow the command that he killed him. Mattathias and his five sons retreated to the hills with their supporters, and commenced a guerrilla war against the Greeks. Mattathias turned the leadership over to his son, Judah the Maccabee (literally, "hammer"). Using superb strategy, quick maneuvers, and with a supreme faith in God, Judah and the Maccabees defeated the Greek army. While they were fighting, they had missed the eight-day holiday of Sukkot. When they defeated the Greeks, they cleaned and sanctified the Temple in Jerusalem, and declared a better-late-than-never celebration of Sukkot.

The Rabbis, writing in the Gemara some 500 years later, barely mention the battle between the Maccabees (later known as Hasmoneans) and the Greeks. Instead, the Rabbis focus on the sanctification and rededication of the Temple. The Rabbis tell how when the Hasmoneans entered the defiled Temple, they found only one small cruse of oil which had not been desecrated. The oil was enough to last only one day. It was required that the Eternal Light in the Temple be kindled each day, but it would take a while to make more holy oil. "A miracle occurred, and [the little bit of oil] lasted for eight days. The next year they ordained these days a holiday with songs and praises" (*Shabbat* 21b). Perhaps the Rabbis did not want to encourage the celebration of a military battle. They may have wanted to stress the role of God over the strength of people. They may have played down the victory of the Maccabees because the victory lasted less than a hundred years. Or, they may not have wanted the Jewish people, who at that time were living under Roman rule, to be inspired to revolt by a "few over the many" story. In any case, the miracle of the oil story has persevered to the present day, and many modern versions simply combine the story of the battle with the miracle of the oil.

Chanukah is celebrated by lighting the *chanukiah* each night of the holiday, by playing *dreidel*, and by eating foods cooked in oil, such as *latkes* and *sufganiot*. In America, Chanukah has become a big gift giving time as well, due to its proximity to Christmas. In Israel, without the competition of Christmas, gifts are not a part of the holiday celebration. Over the centuries, children have been given a few coins, or *gelt*, with which to play *dreidel*. Today, we give and use chocolate *gelt* coins.

For a glossary and Hebrew vocabulary on Chanukah, see figure 21 below.

GLOSSARY AND HEBREW VOCABULARY			
		Antiochus IV	Greek ruler of Syria
		Apocrypha	"hidden" — ancient writings that were excluded from the Tanach
חֲנֻכָּה		Chanukah	Festival of Lights, literally "dedication"
חֲנֻכִּיָּה		*Chanukiah*	eight-branch *menorah* plus *shamash* used on Chanukah
דְּרֵיידְל		*Dreidel*	four sided spinning top with a Hebrew letter (*nun, gimel, hay, and shin*) written on each side. The letters stand for the sentence *Nays Gadol Hayah Sham* (A Great Miracle Happened There).
		Gemara	Rabbinic material which, along with the Mishnah, comprises the Talmud
		Hasmoneans	leaders of the Jewish people after the war against the Hellenists
		Hellenize	to force others to adopt the culture and religion of the Greeks
		Judah Maccabee	hero of the Chanukah story
		Latkes	potato pancakes
		Maccabees	name given to the heroes of the Chanukah story
מְנוֹרָה		*Menorah*	seven-branch candelabra in the synagogue
		Modin	city in Israel where Judah Maccabee and his family lived
נֵר/נֵרוֹת		*Nayr/Nayrot*	candle/candles
סְבִיבוֹן		*Sevivon*	*dreidel*
שַׁמָּשׁ		*Shamash*	helper candle
סֻפְגָּנִיּוֹת		*Sufganiot*	jelly donuts fried in oil (a favorite especially in Israel)

Figure 21

CHANUKAH CANDLE LIGHTING BLESSINGS

We can light the Chanukah candles any time after dark. The *mitzvah* (commandment) of lighting candles is called *pirsum ha'nays*, to publicize the miracle (of the victory and of the oil). To this end, the *chanukiah* is traditionally placed in a window facing onto the street, except in times when this would put the family in danger. The Rabbis maintained it was best to light very soon after dark, while people were still walking in the street. Now that more people drive than walk, it may be preferable to light the candles when the whole family can be home together. We add one candle for each night of Chanukah and light them with the *shamash* (helper candle). We place the candles into the *chanukiah* from right to left. We light the candles with the *shamash* starting on the left — the most recently added candle — and let the candles burn all the way down. In the half hour or so that the candles are burning, the Rabbis tell us to refrain from work. This is a good time to play *dreidel*, sing songs, eat *latkes*, or spend some quality time with our friends and family.

We say all three blessings when we light the *chanukiah* on the first night of Chanukah (we add the *Shehecheyanu* because we haven't celebrated this holiday for a year). We say only the first two blessings on the other seven nights.

בָּרוּךְ אַתָּה יְיָ אֱלֹהֵינוּ מֶלֶךְ הָעוֹלָם
אֲשֶׁר קִדְּשָׁנוּ בְּמִצְוֹתָיו וְצִוָּנוּ לְהַדְלִיק נֵר שֶׁל חֲנֻכָּה.

Baruch Atah Adonai Elohaynu Melech HaOlam Asher Kid'shanu B'Mitzvotav V'Tzivanu L'Hadlik Ner Shel Chanukah.

We praise you, our God, Creator of the universe, Who has made us holy through Your *mitzvot*, and has commanded us to light the Chanukah lights.

בָּרוּךְ אַתָּה יְיָ אֱלֹהֵינוּ מֶלֶךְ הָעוֹלָם
שֶׁעָשָׂה נִסִּים לַאֲבוֹתֵינוּ בַּיָּמִים הָהֵם בַּזְּמַן הַזֶּה.

Baruch Atah Adonai Elohaynu Melech HaOlam She'asah Nissim La'Avotaynu Ba-Yamim HaHaym BaZ'man HaZeh.

We praise you, our God, Creator of the universe, Who made miracles for our ancestors in their days at this time of the year.

בָּרוּךְ אַתָּה יְיָ אֱלֹהֵינוּ מֶלֶךְ הָעוֹלָם
שֶׁהֶחֱיָנוּ וְקִיְּמָנוּ וְהִגִּיעָנוּ לַזְּמַן הַזֶּה.

Baruch Atah Adonai Elohaynu Melech HaOlam Shehecheyanu, V'keeyamanu, V'Higeeyanu LaZ'man HaZeh.

We praise you, our God, Creator of the universe, for giving us life, sustaining us, and helping us to reach this moment.

CHANUKAH CONCEPTS

WEBBING THE CONCEPTS

Webbing the concepts of Chanukah (see Chapter 1, "Developmentally Appropriate Practice," p. 11 for more on webbing), can elicit ideas about what you want children to think about and what you want children to learn (and not just what you want them to make). This technique can also bring to mind connections to other things going on in your classroom. Figure 22 on the next page is the *beginning* of a web for Chanukah. You can extend the web with your co-teachers or your students, thus shaping the celebration of Chanukah to include the interests of everyone in your class. *You won't cover everything you web*, but you'll get a good idea of where you want to go.

INFANT TO 24 MONTHS

1. I see the candles burn.
2. We light another candle on the *chanukiah* each day.
3. I eat *latkes* and *sufganiot*.
4. I see the *dreidel* spin. (Be sure the *dreidel* is big enough that children can't choke on it.)

2 YEARS

1. I see the candles burn.
2. I can see, touch, and smell different Jewish candles (Chanukah, Shabbat, Havdalah)
3. We light another candle on the *chanukiah* each day.
4. I can count the candles in the *chanukiah*.

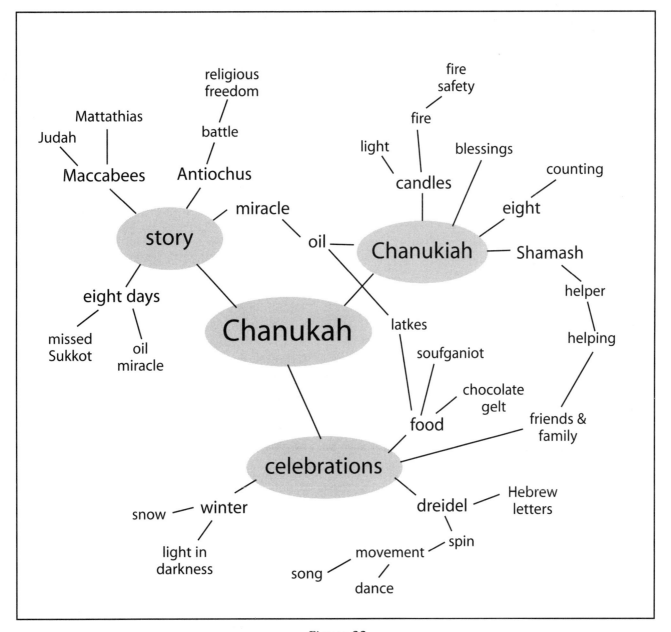

Figure 22

5. I eat *latkes* and *sufganiot*.
6. I see the *dreidel* spin. I can try to spin the *dreidel*.
7. I can hear the story of the brave Maccabees.
8. I can celebrate Chanukah with my family.

3 YEARS

1. I see the candles burn.
2. I see, touch, and smell different Jewish candles (Chanukah, Shabbat, Havdalah)
3. I compare how different Jewish candles burn.
4. We light another candle on the *chanukiah* each day. We add one candle for each night of Chanukah.
5. I can count the candles in the *chanukiah*.
6. I use the *shamash* to light the other candles.
7. I eat *latkes* and *sufganiot*. I can help make these yummy treats.
8. I spin the *dreidel* and play the *dreidel* game (with adult help).
9. I hear the story of the brave Maccabees.
10. I can see how people in Israel celebrate Chanukah.
11. I celebrate Chanukah with my family and friends.

4 TO 5 YEARS

1. I see the candles burn.
2. I see, touch, and smell different Jewish candles (Chanukah, Shabbat, Havdalah)
3. I can compare how different Jewish candles burn.
4. We light another candle on the *chanukiah* each day. We add one candle for each night of Chanukah.
5. I count the candles in the *chanukiah*.
6. I use the *shamash* to light the other candles.
7. I eat *latkes* and *sufganiot*. I can help make these yummy treats.
8. I spin the *dreidel* and play the *dreidel* game.
9. I hear the story of the brave Maccabees. I can act like a Maccabee.
10. The Maccabees fought for the freedom to be Jewish.
11. I can talk about miracles.

12. I can see how people in Israel celebrate Chanukah.
13. I celebrate Chanukah with my family and friends.

CHANUKAH ACTIVITIES

LANGUAGE ARTS

1. Act out the story of the Maccabees.
2. Let children watch some Chanukah candles burn. Have them describe what they see. Using their words, write a poem (or poems) about light/candles/Chanukah.
3. Compare an American/Diaspora *dreidel* to an Israeli *dreidel*. Find the letter that is different. Talk about the reasons for this (see page 192 below). Let the children practice writing the Hebrew letters found on a *dreidel*. This is a great time to have Hebrew newspapers on the table.
4. Let the children dictate their favorite *latke* recipe and illustrate it. Make a book!
5. Invite another class for a Chanukah feast and a story swap.
6. On the job chart, consider naming the helper child the *shamash*.
7. Read *Hershel and the Hanukkah Goblins* by Eric Kimmel. Discuss: What would happen if Hershel met the Nightmare? Read *There's a Nightmare in My Closet* by Mercer Mayer. Discuss: What if the boy in Mayer's story met the Hanukkah Goblins? if the Goblins met the Nightmare?
8. Read *Like a Maccabee* by Raymond A. Zwerin and Audrey Friedman Marcus. Discuss: How can you be "like a Maccabee"?

SCIENCE

1. Compare Jewish lights (Shabbat candles, Chanukah candles, Havdalah candle, the moon, *Ner Tamid* in the synagogue). See which burn the longest, the biggest, the brightest. Compare Jewish lights to "secular" lights (light bulb, birthday candles, the sun, flashlights).

2. Is it snowing yet? Can you make a *chanukiah* out of snow? Why do so many winter holidays focus on light?

3. Put snow in the sensory table to play with. Keep refilling it for several days. After a day or two, add food coloring to the snow. Watch it melt.

4. Focus on fire safety.

5. Experiment with oil. Make olive oil by squishing some olives. How many olives would it take to make a whole bottle of olive oil? Make an oil and water shaker bottle (add Chanukah shape glitter from a party store and blue food coloring to the water).

6. Light a regular *chanukiah* and an oil *chanukiah* in your class (or school). Buy floating wicks from a Jewish bookstore, and use nine glasses (one slightly larger than the others for the *shamash*). Fill each glass ¾ full with water (add food coloring if you choose). Add a thin layer of oil (any kind — vegetable oil works fine) to the glass, then put in the floating wick. Use a long match or a candle to light. Fill one more glass each day (just as you add one more candle for each day of Chanukah). Experiment using different amounts or types of oil.

7. Make *latkes* (see recipes, p. 194 and 195). Make *sufganiot* (see recipes, p. 194 and 195). Use the five senses before and after cooking. Make a connection between the frying oil and the oil in the Temple.

MATH

1. Compare a *menorah* and a *chanukiah*. Talk about why one has seven branches, the other nine.

2. Discuss: If there are eight days of Chanukah, why does the *chanukiah* have nine branches?

3. Take pictures of the same *chanukiah* with candle(s) on each night of Chanukah. Let children sequence the pictures.

4. Provide children with an entire box of Chanukah candles. Let them sort by color, make designs, make patterns, and otherwise explore.

5. Why are there 44 candles in a box of Chanukah candles? Let children explore ways to find out the answer to this question.

6. Blow out some candles at different points in burning. Let the children sequence the remaining parts of the candles by size.

7. Time an activity by a burning a Chanukah candle (takes about one half hour).

8. Chart the children's favorite Chanukah food. Chart which toppings the children like on their *latkes*.

ART

(Note: Remember to focus on process not product!)

1. Cut out a Chanukah shape and use the outline for a frame. Let children drip food coloring on a paper towel. Staple the paper towel to the frame. Hang in the window, or laminate for a drip tray.

2. Hands can be traced for *chanukiot*.

3. For younger children, provide cut-outs of very basic shapes with which to make a *chanukiah* or a *dreidel*. (Remember, children's pictures of *chanukiot* don't always need to have the perfect number of branches.)

4. Dip plastic *dreidels* in paint, and spin on paper. Paint in other ways with *dreidels*, candles, Chanukah cookie cutters, etc.

5. Paint on the foil from Chanukah *gelt*.

6. Provide children with all sorts of materials with which they can create their own *chanukiah* (decorative or functional). Also provide lots of pictures (from art books and catalogs) so they can get different ideas for their own *chanukiah*.

7. Provide children with a variety of brown and gold materials with which to make *latkes*. Draw a mural size frying pan and let the children decorate with paint, markers, and/or bits of aluminum foil. Glue on the children's *latkes*.

MUSIC/MOVEMENT

(With musical contributions from Julie Jaslow Auerbach)

1. Make up new verses to "I Have a Little Dreidel." Of what else might a fantasy *dreidel* be made? (Thanks to Doug Cotler for this idea.)

2. Act out melting like a candle. Flicker like a flame.
3. Act out being Maccabees cleaning the Temple after defeating the Syrians.
4. Have a freeze dance to Chanukah music. (When the music stops, everyone freezes in place.)
5. Practice "Stop, Drop, and Roll" for fire safety.
6. Choose songs for your little ones in the same way as we used to choose food in a Chinese restaurant: one from column A (story), one from column B *(dreidel),* one from column C (*chanukiah,* light) and one from column D (food, *latkes)* to reflect the abundance of good Chanukah songs which are available to us in the twenty-first century. Blessings are a must, as may be the beginnings of the song *"Maoz Tsur."* How we blend the tradition with the newer melodies is key throughout all your musical endeavors with these children.
7. Use Orff instruments, which are available in most schools these days. The song "Chanukah" by Julie Jaslow Auerbach makes use of them to create an ostinato bass line (See Appendix A, p. 331 for music and lyrics). Should the xylophones or metallophones not be available, use wood blocks and other rhythm instruments. Since there are three parts to the song, a different instrument can be used for each section.
8. Use other instruments at this time of year, such as the triangle or finger cymbals, as an auditory metaphor on light.
9. Sing "Peel Potatoes" by Leah Abrams. Act out the recipe her song provides or sing it while making the actual *latkes* in class.
10. Spin like a *dreidel* while singing the classic song *"Sov Sov Sov"* by Gladys Gewirtz.
11. Play *Hide and Seek* with a partner using the song "I Am a Sivivon" by Leah Abrams.
12. Count the candles with your fingers while singing "The Chanukiah" by Fran Avni. Another effective technique is to divide the children into two groups and have one sing the first part of the song (the question), and the other group sing the second part of the song (the answer).
13. Sing *"Ner Li,"* and have children pretend to be candles that shine. Or, use candle props that children can move up and down with the song. Other candle songs can be choreographed in a similar fashion.
14. Have the children pick a favorite color to "be" while singing "Pink Blue Orange Red Yellow" by Leah Abrams When a child's color is mentioned in the first verse, the child stands up. When mentioned in the second verse, the child shines using his/her hands, then melts back to his/her seat in verse 3. Additionally, children can sort colored candles with this song.
15. Sing "The Maccabees" from *So We Sing,* and have the children give the answer "The Maccabees" after each question. This is an especially effective way to use this song with very young children.
16. Act out the story of the Maccabees using songs such as "Maccabee March" from *Chanukah Music Box,* and "The Marching Maccabee" by Julie Jaslow Auerbach (see Appendix A, p. 348 for music and lyrics).
17. Sing the song *"Sivivon Sov Sov Sov."* Divide the group into parts corresponding to the song. You can also use instruments with this song, for example, all the bells play on *"sov sov sov,"* all the wood blocks play on *"sivivon,"* etc.

SONG/MUSIC LIST
(Contributed by Julie Jaslow Auerbach)

The following listing includes the songs in this chapter, as well as songs from other sources that are related to Chanukah concepts. Each song and the book in which it is located is specified, along with the page number. (Please note: In this and other holiday chapters, there are many songs which are "preschool traditional," i.e., they have been around so long that no one knows the composer or the song's origin! Every effort has been made to find the source for all the songs listed.)

Latkes

"The Latke Song" – *Miracles and Wonders*, p. 19
"One Little, Two Little, Three Little Latkes" (to the tune of "One Little, Two Little, Three Little Indians")
"Peel Potatoes" – *Apples on Holidays and Other Days*, p. 13 (see Music/Movement activity #9 above)

Dreidel

"I Am a Sevivon" – Israeli preschool traditional, free translation by Leah Abrams (see Music/Movement activity #11 above)
"I Have a Little Dreidel" –*The New Children's Songbook*, p. 24 (see Music/Movement activity #1 above)
"I'm a little Dreidel" (to the tune of "I'm a little Teapot")
"Nun Gimmel Hey Shin" – *Shiron L'Gan*, p. 26
"Sivivon Sov Sov Sov" – *Manginot*, p. 117 (see Music/Movement activity #17 above)
"Sov Sov Sov" – *Chanukah Music Box* (see Music/Movement activity #10 above)

Candles

"Banu Choshech Legaresh" – Classic Israeli Chanukah song found on Israeli Chanukah tapes
"Chanukiyah Li Yesh" – *Memeitiv Shiray Hachagim L'yeladim* (*From the Best of Children's Holiday Songs*)
"In the Window" – *Union Songster*, p. 268
"Light a Candle for Hanukkah" – *Shirim Al Galgalim*, p. 14
"Light the Menorah" – *Miracles and Wonders*, p. 16
"Ner Li" – *The New Children's Songbook*, p. 22 (see Music/Movement activity #13 above)
"On This Night"– preschool traditional
"Pink, Blue, Orange, Red, Yellow" – *Apples on Holidays and Other Days*, p. 11 (see Music/Movement activity #14 above)
"Twinkle, Twinkle Chanukah Light" – *Union Songster*, p. 266
"The Chanukiyah" – *Holiday Songbook for Kids*, p. 13 (see Music/Movement activity #12 above)

Chanukah Story

"Maoz Tsur" – *Manginot*, p. 112
"Maccabee March" – *Chanukah Music Box* (see Music/Movement activity #16 above)
"The Maccabees" – *So We Sing*, p. 28 (see Music/Movement activity #15 above)
"The Marching Maccabee" – Julie Jaslow Auerbach (see Music/Movement activity #16 above)

CIRCLE TIME

1. Instead of *Hot Potato*, play *Hot Latke*.
2. Split the class into groups of three or four, provide pennies or M & Ms or buttons, and play organized games of *dreidel*.
3. Play *Chanukah Basket Upset (Fruit Basket Upset)* using the names and symbols associated with Chanukah (Maccabees, Syrians, elephants, *dreidels*, candles).
4. In a darkened room, light a candle in the middle of the circle. Sit quietly in the dark for a few moments. Talk about how the light in the darkness feels. Ask: "How would you feel if there was no candle light at all?"

OUTDOORS/FIELD TRIPS

1. Play in the snow (if there is any), or in the changing weather. Compare the weather now to the weather during Sukkot.
2. Outside, put candle-shaped bases (cut from construction paper and laminated, perhaps), two to three in each color, all over the playground. All the children must run to the appropriate candle when that color is called. If the caller tags a child before he/she makes it to the candle/base, the tagged child joins the caller as a Chanukah goblin, and tries to tag more children.
3. Visit a nursing home or a children's hospital. Sing Chanukah songs, and bring pictures the children have made to give to the people there.
4. Visit a candle store, a synagogue gift shop, or a Judaica store to look at all the different kinds of candles. Check out all the different *chanukiot* while you're there, too.

SPECIFICALLY FOR INFANTS

1. Let babies watch a *chanukiah* burning for as long as it is safe.
2. Acquire large *dreidels* so babies can explore (chew on) them.
3. Play Chanukah music and dance with babies.
4. Bring in snow for babies to touch.
5. String blue streamers around the room and cover the walls with pictures of *dreidels* and *chanukiot*.
6. Take photos of the babies mouthing *dreidels* or watching Chanukah candles burn, and enlarge the pictures (at a copy or office supply store). Hang the pictures all over the room.

IDEAS FOR TEACHING FAMILIES

1. Send home all the blessings families will need to light Chanukah candles.
2. Send home the rules of *dreidel* so families can play at home.
3. Invite a parent or relative to come in and help make *latkes* or *sufganiot*. Send home the recipes of everything you make in class.
4. Alert families to social service/*Tzedakah* opportunities they can do together, so children can have the opportunity of giving on Chanukah.
5. Have a Chanukah party in your class or school. Let the children show off what they've learned about Chanukah. Light an oil *chanukiah*. Invite every family to bring and light their own *chanukiah*. See how many *dreidels* you can get spinning at the same time. (The Kaplan JCC in Skokie, Illinois spun 297 at one time in 1998!)
6. Recommended reading: *I Maccabees* and *II Maccabees: Translation and Commentary* by Jonathan Goldstein, and *The Art of Jewish Living: Hanukkah* by Ron Wolfson. For good Chanukah stories, *see The Power of Light: Eight Stories for Hanukkah* by Isaac Bashevis Singer.
7. Many interfaith families struggle especially at this time of year. For them, you can recommend books such as *If I'm Jewish and You're Christian, What Are the Kids? A Parenting Guide for Interfaith Families* by Andrea King, and *Mixed Blessings: Overcoming the Stumbling Blocks in an Interfaith Marriage* by Paul Cowen with Rachel Cowen.

THE GAME OF DREIDEL

The *dreidel* is a four-sided spinning top with a Hebrew letter on each side. In Hebrew it's called a *sivivon*. Tradition suggests that when Antiochus forbade Jewish celebration, many Jews continued to gather in secret. They would bring along small tops. If Antiochus' soldiers approached them, they would busy themselves with the tops as if they had just gathered to play the game. The letters were added later, to commemorate the events of Chanukah. The letters *nun, gimel, hay, and shin* stand for the sentence *Nes Gadol Hayah Sham* (A Great Miracle Happened There).

Israeli *dreidels* do not commemorate the miracle that happened *there (Sham)*, but rather the miracle that happened *here (Poh)*. On Israeli *dreidels*, therefore, the *shin* is replaced with a *pay*.

THE RULES OF THE GAME

Each player starts with 10 or 15 pennies (or peanuts, or M & Ms, or pebbles, etc.). Each player puts one of these items in the center (the pot). Players take turns spinning the *dreidel*. The player's action on that turn is determined by which letter is face up when the *dreidel* falls:

נ *(Nun)* stands for "nothing." Player does nothing.
ג *(Gimel)* stands for "get all." Player takes everything in the pot. Each player then adds one more item to the middle to replenish the pot.
ה *(Hay)* stands for "half." Player takes half of what is in the pot.
ש/פ *(Shin* or *pay)* stands for "put one in." Player puts one item into the pot.
If a player runs out of (or eats) all his/her items, that player is out of the game.

THE CHANUKAH STORY (SIMPLE VERSION)

A very long time ago, the King of Syria, Antiochus, took charge of Israel. He wanted everyone to be like him, so he told the Jewish people that they could no longer do Jewish things. No more studying Torah, no more celebrating Shabbat, no more praying to God. Antiochus and his army came in and ruined the Jewish Temple in Jerusalem. This made Judah Maccabee and his family and friends very angry. They fought back against mean Antiochus and his army. It took a long time, but with some clever moves and help from God, Judah Maccabee's little army defeated Antiochus' large army. Judah and the Maccabees went straight away to the Temple to start cleaning it up. When it was all clean, they wanted to light the *Ner Tamid* to rededicate the Temple. They could only find one small bottle of holy oil, enough to last one day. It would take many days to make more holy oil. They poured the little bottle of oil into the *Ner Tamid,* and a miracle happened! The oil burned for eight days, which was enough time to make more oil and keep the light burning. They decided to celebrate the miracle that had happened every year, so they declared a holiday — Chanukah!

THE DECEMBER DILEMMA

The proximity of Chanukah and Christmas causes many American Jewish adults to agonize — what to do about Christmas?

For interfaith families, this time of the year causes the most confusion. You need to be aware of which children in your class come from interfaith families, and how they handle the holidays (do they celebrate Chanukah and Christmas in their home? Did one parent convert, but they still celebrate Christmas at Grandma's?). If you understand how the holidays are approached at home, you can do your best to support each child in your classroom. As teachers, we are caught in a difficult place. A major goal of Jewish early childhood education is to instill Jewish identity, to teach Jewish holidays and values. But we also must be careful to validate every child. Rather than telling a child, "We don't talk about Christmas here," it is crucial to acknowledge the whole reality of the child. (Jonah: "My Grandparents have a Christmas tree!" Teacher: "Jonah's grandma and grandpa are Christian. Jonah, tell us about the Christmas tree at their house. Did you help decorate it?")

Even Jewish parents struggle at this time of the year, worrying when their child expresses interest in participating in Christmas rituals. The children in your class will see around them all the evidences of Christmas: the lights, ads on TV, Santa in the mall. This is part of their lives. As teachers in Jewish schools, it is our job to reinforce the joys of being Jewish, of celebrating Chanukah, Shabbat, and all the other holidays. Christmas is a beautiful holiday. But it is someone else's holiday. Just as children learn that every birthday party does not celebrate their own birthday, children can learn to respect Christmas as someone else's holiday, while reveling in all the joys that comprise being Jewish. In the classroom, this may mean allowing the children to talk about their Christmas observations, while always framing the discussion in the context of "someone else's party." A useful strategy for parents may be to allow their child to help a Christian friend celebrate, and to invite the Christian friend to join in some Chanukah celebrations. ("You may help Megan decorate her Christmas tree. Let's invite Megan and her family to light the *chanukiah* and share some *latkes* with us.")

(For more about working with interfaith families, see Chapter 28, "Interfaith Families/Non-Jewish Children," p. 316.)

SUGGESTED NEWSLETTER ARTICLE

Note: With Chanukah, there is so much for families to think about. You may choose to use all or parts of this newsletter material, depending on the needs of your class or school.

When Judah and his brothers defeated the Syrian Army and declared that "the whole Jewish nation should celebrate these days every year" (II Maccabees, 10:8), they probably couldn't imagine the hoopla that North American Jews make today over the holiday of Chanukah. The Maccabees fought a guerilla war against Hellenism for the right to live as Jews. Their small, untrained army managed to run the Syrian army out of town (a miracle in its own right) and then came back to Jerusalem to clean up the Temple. While fighting, they missed the celebration of Sukkot. In catching up on the delayed Sukkot celebrations, Chanukah also became an eight-day holiday. They celebrated with feasts, songs of praise to God, the playing of harps, prayer, and the lighting of lamps. We learn this from the first and second books of Maccabees, written less than 50 years after the events commemorated by Chanukah. The story we all recall from childhood of the miracle of the oil lasting for eight days appears in the Talmud, written at least 500 years after the events.

In Israel today, people concern themselves with *pirsum ha-nes* (publicizing the miracle) of Chanukah. Candles burning in *chanukiot* can be seen burning in windows and in glass boxes outside of the front doors of houses. Families get together to eat *sufganiot* (jelly donuts fried in oil) which take the place of *latkes* there as the traditional Chanukah food. Gift giving is not a widely practiced tradition at all.

We might take a hint from our Israeli cousins. Chanukah is a minor holiday in the Jewish calendar. It is a time to publicize the miracle. Rather than a fancy present, why not give your children the gift of your time. Light candles with them, play

dreidel, take them to a Chanukah party or to a Jewish storytelling hour.

Let's avoid the competition and confusion of this season. Let's not teach our Jewish children that it's great to be Jewish because the *chanukiah* can sparkle brighter than a Christmas tree. Judaism is filled with beautiful experiences and holidays. Jewish parents can share apples and honey with their children on Rosh HaShanah, build a *sukkah* with them on Sukkot, dress in costumes on Purim, crunch *matzah* and hunt for the *afikoman* on Passover, and best of all, light candles and eat sweet *challah* together every week on Shabbat. Parents who share these joys of being Jewish with their children all year will have no problem explaining that Christmas is not our holiday, and that Chanukah is not the be-all and end-all of being Jewish. So relax. Spend time together this Chanukah. Light the candles, and play *dreidel* while they burn. And don't forget to plant trees together when Tu B'Shevat rolls around!

RECIPES

POTATO LATKES

Ingredients
4 potatoes, peeled
1 tbs. Lemon juice
3 tbs. Flour
freshly ground pepper to taste
1 large onion, grated
4 eggs
1 tsp. salt
oil for frying

Directions
1. Let children peel and cut potatoes into large chunks.
2. Finish the grating process in a food processor. Process the onions as well.
3. Immediately transfer the grated potatoes to a large bowl.
4. Children can add the onion, lemon juice, eggs, flour, salt, and pepper. Let children mix well.

5. In a large heavy skillet or, better yet, frying pan, heat ⅛ inch oil.
6. With a tablespoon, spoon the batter onto the hot oil and flatten the *latkes* with the back of the spoon.
7. Fry for 3 to 5 minutes per side, turning only once, until golden brown.
8. Drain on paper towels and serve immediately, with applesauce or sour cream.

SUFGANIOT

Note: These round donuts were a favorite Chanukah treat in Turkey, Greece, Morocco, and other eastern Sephardic countries where potatoes were not common. Today, they are *the* Chanukah treat in Israel.

Ingredients
1½ C. flour
1 package yeast
½ C. very warm water
1 egg
¼ tsp. salt
¼ C. sugar, plus 2 teaspoons
½ tbs. Oil
oil for frying
powdered sugar

Directions
1. Measure the flour into a large bowl and set aside.
2. Put ¼ cup warm water in a small bowl with the yeast and 2 tsp. sugar. Mix until the yeast dissolves.
3. Add the egg, salt, sugar and ½ tbs. oil. Mix well.
4. Pour the yeast mixture into the flour and mix.
5. Add the remaining ¼ cup of warm water and mix well. The dough will be sticky.
6. Cover the bowl with a towel. Let it rise in a warm, draft-free place for one hour.
7. In a large heavy skillet or, better yet, frying pan, heat 3 inches of oil to about 375°.
8. Dip the tablespoon into the oil, then put about a tablespoon of dough into the oil. Be careful not to drop the dough in to avoid splashing the oil.
9. The *sufganiot* will puff up and float in the oil. Cook a few at a time. Turn them with a slotted spoon until they are golden brown all over.
10. Drain on a paper towel. Dust with powdered sugar and serve warm.

(Makes 20 *sufganiot*.)

BIBLIOGRAPHY

ADULTS

Frishman, Elyse D., ed. *These Lights are Holy: Haneirot Halalu: A Home Celebration of Chanukah* New York: CCAR Press, 1989.

> The first complete compendium of liturgy and reading for home use at Chanukah.

Goldstein, Jonathan. *I Maccabees And II Maccabees: Translation and Commentary.* Anchor Bible Series.

> Complete translations with commentaries of these two books of the Apocrypha.

Singer, Isaac Bashevis. *The Power of Light: Eight Stories for Hanukkah.*

> Eight tales — one for each night of Chanukah — tell of a world full of miracles, in which love triumphs and faith prevails.

Wolfson, Ron. *The Art of Jewish Living: Hanukkah.* New York: Woodstock, VT: Jewish Lights Publishing, 1996.

> Discusses the origin of the holiday, reasons for Chanukah candles, and customs, and provides everything from recipes to family activities.

CHILDREN
Infants To 2 years

DePaola, Tomie. *My First Chanukah.* New York: G.P. Putnam's Sons, 1989.

> May be out of print, but worth looking for. (Board Book)

Kress, Camille. *Let There Be Lights!* New York: UAHC Press, 1997.

> Beautiful illustrations and simple text make this book a delight. (Board Book)

Sagasti, Miriam, illus. *Hanukkah Oh Hanukkah.* Rockville, MD: Kar-Ben Copies, 1995.

> The traditional song set to pictures. Includes the music to the song. (Board Book)

Shostak, Myra. *Rainbow Candles.* Rockville, MD: Kar-Ben Copies, 1986.

> The traditional folk song in pictures. Includes the music to the song. (Board Book)

3 Years

Backman, Aidel. *One Night, One Hanukkah Night.* Philadelphia: Jewish Publication Society, 1990. (Ages 3-7)

> Illustrations depict the homes past and present when the silver *chanukiah* has been lit.

Feder, Harriet. *Judah Who Always Said No!* Rockville, MD: Kar-Ben Copies, 1990. (Ages 3-8)

> Judah the Maccabee stood up to the Syrian soldiers.

Holland, Cheri. *Maccabee Jamboree: A Hanukkah Countdown.* Rockville, MD: Kar-Ben Copies, 1998. (Ages 3-5)

> Count down with Chanukah symbols and events.

Jaffe, Nina. *In the Month of Kislev.* New York: Viking, 1992. (Ages 3-8)

> When Mendle and Rivka's daughters are accused of stealing the scent of the rich man's *latkes*, what will the Rabbi do?

Kimmel, Eric. *The Chanukah Guest.* New York: Holiday House, 1988. (Ages 3-6)

> Bubbe Brayna thinks the Rabbi has come to her house for Chanukah, but really her guest is someone quit different — a bear!

Kimmelman, Leslie. *Hanukkah Lights, Hanukkah Nights.* Harper Collins Publishers, 1992. (Ages 3-5)

> The extended family celebrated Chanukah.

Nerlove, Miriam. *Hanukkah.* Morton Grove, IL: A. Whitman, 1989. (Ages 3-6)

> Rhyming text and illustrations follow a little boy and his family as they prepare for Chanukah.

Rouss, Sylvia. *Sammy Spider's First Chanukah.* Rockville, MD: Kar-Ben Copies, 1993. (Ages 3-6)

> Sammy learns about Chanukah and his colors.

Topek, Susan Remick. *A Turn for Noah.* Rockville, MD: Kar-Ben Copies, 1992. (Ages 3-6)

> Noah struggles to learn to spin a *dreidel.*

Zalben, Jane Breskin. *Beni's First Chanukah.* New York: Henry Holt & Company, 1988. (Ages 3-6)

Beni celebrates the first Chanukah he is old enough to remember.

———. *Papa's Latkes*. New York: Henry Holt and Company, 1994. (Ages 3-6)

When Mama decides not to make *latkes*, Papa declares a *latke* contest.

4 To 5 Years

Adler, David. *Malke's Secret Recipe*. Rockville, MD: Kar-Ben Copies, 1989. (Ages 4-8)

Berel tries to steal Malke's *latke* recipe, with very funny results. That recipe is included. This book is out of print, but worth looking for.

Drucker, Malka. *Grandma's Latkes*. San Diego, CA: Voyager Books, 1992. (Ages 4-8)

Molly's grandmother teaches her the story of Chanukah as they make *latkes* together.

Gellman, Ellie. *Jeremy's Dreidel*. Rockville, MD: Kar-Ben Copies, 1992. (Ages 5-10)

Jeremy creates a *dreidel* with which even his father, who is blind, can play.

Greene, Jacqueline Dembar. *Nathan's Hanukkah Bargain*. Rockville, MD: Kar-Ben Copies, 1986. (Ages 4-9)

Nathan's grandfather teaches him the art of bargaining when they go shopping for a *chanukiah* for Nathan. This book is out of print,

but worth looking for.

Hirsh, Marilyn. *Potato Pancakes All Around*. Philadelphia, PA: The Jewish Publication Society, 1982. (Ages 4-8)

A wandering peddler teaches the villages how to make *latkes* from a crust of bread (similar to *Stone Soup*).

Kimmel, Eric. *Hershel and the Hanukkah Goblins*. New York: Holiday House, 1985. (Ages 4-8)

Hershel must rid the synagogue of goblins so the town can celebrate Chanukah again.

———. *The Magic Dreidles*. New York: Holiday House, 1996. (Ages 4-8)

When an old lady swindles him out of his magic *dreidels*, Jacob tries to get them back in time for his family celebration.

Mayer, Mercer. *There's a Nightmare In My Closet*. New York: Dial Books for Young Readers, 1968.

A boy defends himself against the nightmare in his closet. What if the Nightmare met Hershel's Chanukah goblins?

Zwerin, Raymond A., and Audrey Friedman Marcus. *Like a Maccabee*. New York: UAHC Press, 1991. (Ages 4-9)

Children can be brave like a Maccabee. Good values lessons.

CHAPTER 14

TU B'SHEVAT

There are four New Year days [including] the first of Shevat, the New Year for Trees — according to the followers of Shammai. Those who follow Hillel say (and we abide to this ruling): it is on the fifteenth of Shevat." (Rosh HaShanah 1:1)

OVERVIEW

Hillel and Shammai, sages in Israel in the first century C.E., almost always disagreed when it came to Jewish law. Hillel's rulings usually prevailed. With regard to Tu B'Shevat (literally, "the fifteenth day of Shevat"), Hillel based his ruling on the life cycle of the trees themselves. In Israel, most of the rain falls in the winter, before the Hebrew month of Shevat. On the fifteenth day of Shevat, the almond trees begin drawing nourishment from their sap, and are just beginning to bloom. The new fruit is beginning to form, signaling the beginning of spring and a new year, or birthday, for the trees. According to tradition, Tu B'Shevat holds the same meaning for trees as Rosh HaShanah does for human beings, a day of judgment. On Tu B'Shevat, God decides how bountiful the fruits of the trees will be in the year to come. Thus, another name for Tu B'Shevat is Rosh HaShanah L'Ilanot, or Rosh Hashanah of the Trees.

After the exile of the Jews from Israel, Tu B'Shevat became very important in reinforcing Jewish ties to *Eretz Yisrael*. One very concrete way we do this is by eating fruits associated with the land of Israel. Based loosely on Deuteronomy 8:8, this list includes grapes, oranges, figs, dates, carobs, pomegranates, almonds, and olives. In Israel today, planting trees is a major part of this holiday.

School children turn out in droves to plant trees all over Israel. In parts of North America, where the winter weather may make a planting holiday seem oddly timed, we can send money through the Jewish National Fund for someone to plant a tree in our stead. Contact the JNF at 42 East 69th Street, New York, NY 10021, (800) 542-TREE. The JNF is also a good source of posters and curriculum materials for your classroom.

For a glossary and Hebrew vocabulary list on Tu B'Shevat, see Figure 23 on page 199.

TU B'SHEVAT SEDER

The Kabbalists created a formal vehicle for eating fruits of Israel on Tu B'Shevat. The ceremony, modeled after the Passover *Seder*, combines eating fruits and drinking wine with blessings and stories of trees and Israel. Specifically, at the Tu B'Shevat *Seder*, we eat from three categories of fruits or nuts:

1. Fruits with a hard outer shell or peel that cannot be eaten — these include orange, tangerine, kiwi, coconut, almond, pomegranate, banana, and mango
2. Fruits with an edible outside, but an inedible pit or seeds — these include olives, dates, cherries, avocados, apricots, plums, and peaches
3. Fruits which are edible inside and out — these include grapes, raisins, figs, rasberries, cranberries, apples, pears, strawberries, and carob

There are many good resources for planning your own Tu B'Shevat *Seder*. These include *A Seder for Tu B'Shevat* by Harlene Winnick Appelman and Jane Sherwin Shapiro (designed for use with children), and *Seder for Tu B'Shevat: The Festival of the Trees* by Adam Fisher (geared to use with adults, but contains much material which can guide and add to a *Seder* for children).

BAL TASHCHEET AND TIKKUN OLAM

There are two *mitzvot* and Jewish values which are intimately connected to Tu B'Shevat. *Bal Tashcheet* means "do not destroy." *Tikkun Olam* means "repair of the world." The Torah gives us strict instructions with regard to *Bal Tashcheet* and trees. When we go to war, we are instructed not to destroy fruit trees, because they provide food for people. We are also told not to cut down trees, for a tree can not move or defend itself as a person can. On Tu B'Shevat, we redouble our efforts to help take care of the earth. Now it is a good time to renew emphasis on recycling, caring for the animals and for the materials in our classrooms.

SHABBAT SHIRAH

Close to Tu B'Shevat comes a special Shabbat called Shabbat Shirah, literally "Shabbat of Song/Praise." On this Shabbat, we read the Torah portion *Beshalach*, which includes the song of praise which the Jewish people sang to God when they crossed the Sea of Reeds to freedom. A custom of feeding the birds comes from a *midrash* about the portion as well. Moses instructed the people to gather a double portion of manna on Fridays, because no manna would fall on Shabbat. A few people with a grudge against Moses spread out some manna on Shabbat, to make the people think Moses had lied to them. But the birds came and ate the manna, foiling the plot (*Sefer Ha-Ta-amim, Mechilta 27*). Today we feed the birds on Shabbat Shirah to reward them for their good deed.

GLOSSARY AND HEBREW VOCABULARY		
עֵץ	*Aytz*	tree
בַּל תַּשְׁחִית	*Bal Tashcheet*	literally, "do not destroy."
אֶרֶץ יִשְׂרָאֵל	*Eretz Yisrael*	the Land of Israel
גֶּשֶׁם	*Geshem*	rain
	Hillel and Shammai	first century Sages of the Mishnah in Israel
	Jewish National Fund	organization which owns land and has planted millions of trees in Israel; all the land the JNF buys belongs to all the Jewish people.
	Kabbalists	teachers and students of Jewish mysticism
מָן	Manna	bread-like stuff which God sent to feed the Israelites in the desert
פֵּרוֹת	*Payrot*	fruits
רִמּוֹן	*Rimmon*	pomegranate
רֹאשׁ הַשָּׁנָה לָאִלָנוֹת	Rosh HaShanah L'Ilanot	another name for Tu B'Shevat; literally, "Rosh HaShanah of the Trees."
שַׁבָּת שִׁירָה	Shabbat Shirah	literally, "Shabbat of Song/Praise."
שֶׁלֶג	*Sheleg*	snow
שֶׁמֶשׁ	*Shemesh*	sun
שְׁקֵדִים	*Shkaydeem*	almonds
תָּמָר/תְּמָרִים	*Tamar/tamareem*	date/dates
תִּקּוּן עוֹלָם	*Tikkun Olam*	literally, "repair of the world"
ט״ו בִּשְׁבָט	Tu B'Shevat	literally, "the fifteenth day of Shevat," the New Year, or birthday of the trees
יָרֹק	*Yarok*	green

Figure 23

BLESSINGS FOR TU B'SHEVAT

Before eating fruit from a tree:

בָּרוּךְ אַתָּה יְיָ אֱלֹהֵינוּ מֶלֶךְ הָעוֹלָם
בּוֹרֵא פְּרִי הָעֵץ.

Baruch Atah Adonai Elohaynu Melech HaOlam Boray P'ri HaAytz.

We praise You, our God, Creator of the universe, for creating the fruit of the trees.

Before drinking wine or grape juice:

בָּרוּךְ אַתָּה יְיָ אֱלֹהֵינוּ מֶלֶךְ הָעוֹלָם
בּוֹרֵא פְּרִי הַגָּפֶן.

Baruch Atah Adonai Elohaynu Melech HaOlam Boray P'ri HaGafen.

We praise You, our God, Creator of the universe, for creating the fruit of the vine.

For the first time one sees a tree in bloom each spring:

בָּרוּךְ אַתָּה יְיָ אֱלֹהֵינוּ מֶלֶךְ הָעוֹלָם
שֶׁלֹּא חִסַּר בְּעוֹלָמוֹ דָּבָר וּבָרָא בּוֹ בְּרִיּוֹת טוֹבוֹת
וְאִילָנוֹת טוֹבִים לְהַנּוֹת בָּהֶם בְּנֵי אָדָם.

Baruch Atah Adonai, Elohaynu Melech HaOlam She'lo Hisar B'olamo Davar Uvarah Vo Briyot Tovot V'Ilanot Toveem L'Hanot BaHem B'nai Adam.

We praise You, our God, Creator of the universe, You left nothing lacking in Your world, and created in it goodly creatures and beautiful trees to delight people's hearts.

When eating a new fruit, or one you haven't tasted in a year, be sure to say the *"Shehecheyanu"* blessing (see Chapter 13, "Chanukah," p. 186).

TU B'SHEVAT CONCEPTS

WEBBING THE CONCEPTS

Webbing the concepts of Tu B'Shevat (see Chapter 1, "Developmentally Appropriate Practices," p. 11 for more on webbing), can elicit ideas about what you want children to think about and what you want children to learn (and not just what you want them to make). This technique can also bring to mind connections to other things going on in your classroom. Figure 24 on the following page is the *beginning* of a web for Tu B'Shevat. You can extend the web with your co-teachers or your students, thus shaping the celebration of Tu B'Shevat to include the interests of everyone in your class. *You won't cover everything you web*, but you'll get a good idea of where you want to go.

INFANT TO 24 MONTHS
1. I see trees.
2. I plant seeds.
3. I sing about trees and planting.

2 YEARS
1. I see different kinds of trees.
2. I compare/contrast different seeds, leaves, bark, etc.
3. I plant seeds and watch them grow.
4. I sing about trees and planting.
5. I pretend to grow like a seed.
6. I taste new fruits and nuts from Israel.

3 YEARS
1. Tu B'Shevat is the birthday/New Year of the trees.
2. I see and learn about different trees.
3. Trees help people, and people help to care for trees.

4. I compare/contrast different seeds, leaves, bark, etc.
5. I plant seeds and watch them grow.
6. I sing about trees and planting.
7. I pretend to grow like a seed.
8. I taste new fruits and nuts from Israel. I can participate in a Tu B'Shevat *Seder*.
9. Tu B'Shevat is the beginning of spring in Israel.
10. Children in Israel plant trees on Tu B'Shevat. I can send money to plant a tree in Israel.
11. I am a partner with God. It is my job to help care for the earth by planting, recycling, not littering, and caring for animals.

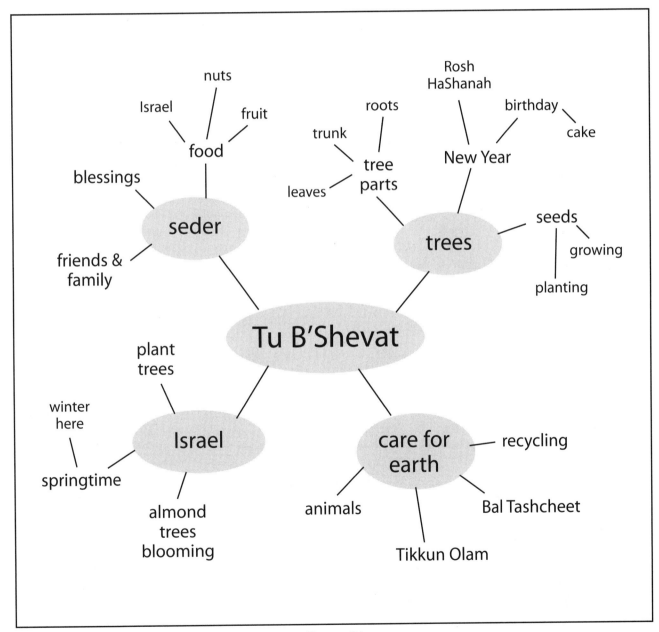

Figure 24

4 TO 5 YEARS

1. Tu B'Shevat is the birthday/New Year of the trees.
2. I see and learn about different trees.
3. Trees help people, and people help to care for trees.
4. I compare/contrast different seeds, leaves, bark, etc.
5. I plant seeds and watch them grow.
6. I sing about trees and planting.
7. I pretend to grow like a seed. I can act out stories about trees.
8. I taste new fruits and nuts from Israel. I can participate in a Tu B'Shevat *Seder*.
9. Tu B'Shevat is the beginning of spring in Israel.
10. Children in Israel plant trees on Tu B'Shevat.
11. Planting trees is a way to do *Tzedakah*. I can send money to plant a tree in Israel.
12. I am a partner with God. It is my job to help care for the earth by planting, recycling, not littering, caring for animals, and so on.
13. On Tu B'Shevat especially, we observe the *mitzvah* of *Bal Tashcheet* (Do not destroy).

ACTIVITIES

LANGUAGE ARTS

1. Create a corner of the room "shaded by trees" for the children to play under.
2. Act out "Honi and the Carob Tree," or other tree-related stories.
3. Explore how trees help people, and how people help trees.
4. Help children plan a birthday party for their favorite tree.
5. Place nuts, twigs, wood items, etc., in a bag. Have children reach into this "secret bag" and describe what they feel.
6. Write to your Israeli pen pals and ask them how they celebrate Tu B'Shevat. Send them photos of class members playing in the snow.
7. The next time someone goes to Israel and plants a tree, ask them to take photographs of

the entire planting process. Mount and laminate the pictures for children to sequence or use to tell a story.
8. Have a recycling drive in your class. Encourage children to use both sides of sheets of paper. Enlist children to brainstorm strategies of how to color and create without wasting paper.

SCIENCE

Note: This holiday was made for scientific exploration!

1. Plant seeds. One method is to place lima and other beans on a wet paper towel in a Ziploc bag (tape some bags to the window and some to the wall in the closet and compare later). Another is to plant fruit seeds which children bring in (soak the seeds overnight for quicker germination, be sure to label and date the seed containers, and don't neglect to use date seeds and carob seeds).
2. Fill up the sensory table with dirt and stir in seeds and water. Sunflower seeds, beans, and corn grow fast, as does grass seed. Encourage the children to check the progress of the seeds every day. Planting at the end of the week makes the wait seem shorter.
3. Plant parsley which the children can use at their *Sedareem* on Passover.
4. Put plant cuttings in water until they grow roots, then plant these new plants
5. Put a dried corn cob in a pan of shallow water. Cut carrot tops and put in water. Soak potatoes in a jar. Be sure to have children make predictions about when things will grow!
6. Study the parts of trees.
7. Soak celery or a white carnation in food coloring and water.
8. Weigh nuts, acorns, pine cones, and so on.
9. Make bird feeders. Some suggestions: spread peanut butter and birdseed on pine cones, cut milk cartons and fill them, string cereal.
10. Discuss: Why do we plant in the dead of winter? Be sure to talk about the fact that spring is beginning in Israel, almond trees are

blooming there, and that is why we celebrate Tu B'Shevat when we do.

11. Have a Tu B'Shevat *Seder*. Taste Israeli fruits and nuts: oranges, almonds, figs, dates, raisins, olives, grapes, pomegranates, and carob. Encourage the children to try new things. Describe how all these things taste. Feel each thing, test how hard/soft it is. Listen to the crunching sounds. Sort into sets.

12. Make a large outline of Israel. Have the children "fill Israel" with trees made out of clay, twigs, green thumbprints, and sponge painting. This could take several days, depending on the size of your map and how you put in the trees. Children can count how many trees they "planted" in Israel. Older children can learn about the Negev desert, and decide where *not* to plant trees.

13. Use some of your *Tzedakah* money to plant a tree in Israel.

MATH

1. Make a chart of things in the room which come from trees/don't come from trees.

2. How old are individual trees? Let the children hypothesize.

3. Provide the children with different kinds of nuts that grow on trees. Let the children sort, classify, and sequence the nuts.

4. Let the children sequence pictures of the growth of a tree.

ART

1. Paint with twigs, pine needles, pine cones, leaves, etc.

2. Make a large winter mural that can be displayed in the classroom for a while. As the season changes to spring, remove the winter scenes, paint green over the snow, and add spring items to the mural.

3. Make trees out of sandpaper.

4. Make bark, seed, and leaf rubbings.

5. Make handmade paper. For good directions, see *Ecoart! Earth-Friendly Art and Craft Experi-*

ences for 3- To 9-Year Olds by Laurie Carlson, p. 18. Add such things as grass or flower petals for a neat effect.

6. Iron leaves and other natural items with some crayon chips between two pieces of wax paper.

7. Remember, if you provide lots of Tu B'Shevat experiences, the children should be able to express their feelings through any art medium. If you provide the paper, twigs, pipe cleaners, green and yellow peas, glue, string, and so on, the children's creations will demonstrate what they have learned about Tu B'Shevat.

MUSIC/MOVEMENT

(With musical contributions from Julie Jaslow Auerbach)

1. Pretend to grow like a seed. Act out planting a tree in Israel.

2. Split the class in half — one half are seeds and the other half are farmers. To classical music, have the children curl up like seeds on the floor. The "farmers" dance around the seeds, pretending to plant and tend to the seeds. Then the "seeds" begin to grow, until they grow into tall trees, and everyone dances together.

3. Dance to Tu B'Shevat songs, such as "Tu B'Shevat Song" by Debbie Friedman on *Songs for Jewish Holidays*, and "The Planting Song" from *Growin' Vol. II* by Kol B'seder.

4. Have the children act out getting dressed in the springtime and getting dressed in the winter. For younger children, provide the clothing props.

5. Connect with all kinds of Israeli music and themes, Israeli dances, Israeli culture. Introduce Israeli dances. (See Chapter 22, "A Guide To Jewish Music in the Early Childhood Classroom," p. 285 for guidance on how to choreograph your own dances to Israeli music.)

6. Sing songs on planting themes and pioneering.

7. Sing *"Zum Gali Gali,"* an Israeli folk song "must-do." Use hands to slide on the *"zum"* and roll on the *"gali gali."* (I first saw this technique used by the musical duo known as Gemini.)

8. Sing *"Achshav"* (which can be introduced again at Yom HaAtzma'ut). Use flags as well as the dance described here. Here are the words:

   Achshav, Achshav, b'Eretz Yisrael (2x)
   Hey!
   Tumba, Tumba, Tumba, b'Eretz Yisrael (2x)

   Introduce the song first. Tell the children that this is a song the early pioneers of Israel might have sung as they were planting and working on the land. The words mean simply, "Now, now, the land of Israel." (The word *"tumba"* has no meaning.) When the children are comfortable with the words, you can vary the way you sing it by getting quieter and quieter on the first part and louder and louder after the "Hey!" Finally, introduce the dance. Children take partners and hold hands. The first part of the dance is the "Mexican Hat Dance," with legs going in and then out. In the second part, the dancers swing each other with linked arms or just walk around in a circle.

9. Sing *"Mah Mezeg Ha'avir?"* by Julie Jaslow Auerbach, because weather is also a Tu B'Shevat theme (see Appendix A, pp. 344-345 for music and lyrics). It is a difficult concept for the young child to understand that it is spring in Israel at Tu B'Shevat, when most parts of North America still have some cold and snow. This song is a weather song that can be used with a weather chart each morning. The words mean "What's the weather today?"

10. Sing *"Eretz Yisrael"* by Julie Jaslow Auerbach, a simple song with a simple refrain that tells the story of the building of the Land of Israel. You can also act out the verses. (See Appendix A, p. 332 for music and lyrics.)

11. In the dead of winter, movement activities are an important part of the preschool teacher's repertoire! Here are some ideas for two songs that connect with Tu B'Shevat:

   a. "Stretch Tall/Small"

      I'm stretching very tall, and now I'm very small [stretch on tip toes, crouch]
      Now tall, now small [3-4 times, faster and slower] [stretch and crouch]
      Now I'm a little ball [or "I'm not there at all"] [curl up]

   b. *"Atzey Zeytim Omdim"* (Olive Trees are Standing)

      Atzey zeytim omdim (4x) [tap thighs 2x, arms up 2x then down and begin again]
      La, la la la la la… etc. [wave arms gently in air]
      La la la la… etc. [wave arms more quickly as the music gets faster]

      I like to have the children pretend to be olive trees. When their hands drop, the ripe olives drop.

12. Act out a poem, such as the following by Julie Jaslow Auerbach:

   Spring Is a-Comin'!

   Spring is a-comin'
   Can you see the trees?
   Spring is a-comin'
   Can you feel the breeze?
   Let's wake up the flowers
   The birds and the grass
   Get up everyone
   Winter's over at last!

13. Sing *"Mi Yivneh HaGalil,"* an old Israeli folk song. Use instruments to denote the different parts of the song. Create a simple dance.

14. Sing *"David Melech Yisrael."* Would you believe this is also a song about trees? Tap your knees twice (prepare the ground), clap your hands twice (put in the seeds), cross your hands twice one way and then the other (smooth the

ground), pound your fists twice one way and then twice the other (pound in the seeds), left hand on right elbow, right hand on left elbow (up come the trees!).

SONG/MUSIC LIST

(Contributed by Julie Jaslow Auerbach)

The following listing includes the songs in this chapter, as well as songs from other sources that are related to Tu B'Shevat concepts. Each song and the book in which it is located is specified, along with the page number. (Please note: In this and other holiday chapters, there are many songs which are "preschool traditional," i.e., they have been around so long that no one knows the composer or the song's origin! Every effort has been made to find the source for all the songs listed.)

Growing

"Planting Season's Here" – *Sing and Celebrate*, p. 18
"Stretch Tall, Small" (see Music/Movement activity #11.a. above)
"Shibolet Basadeh" – *Favorite Songs of Israel*, p. 122

Trees

"Apple Tree" – preschool traditional
"Atzey Zeytim Omdim" – *The Songs We Sing*, p. 142 (see Music/Movement activity #11.b. above)
"David Melech Yisrael" – *The New Children's Songbook*, p. 11 (see Music/Movement activity #14)
"Let's Go Plant Today" – *Manginot*, p. 119
"Plant a Tree for Tu B'Shevat" – *Shirim Al Galgalim*, p. 18
"Tu B'Shevat" – *Especially Wonderful Days*, p. 10
"Tzaddik Katamar Yifrach" – *Israel in Song*, p. 54

A Tree's Needs

"I Love the Sun" – *It's Time For Music*, p. 12
"Mayim" – dance

Weather

"Mah Mezeg Ha'avir" – Julie Jaslow Auerbach (see Music/Movement activity #9 above)
"Pitter Patter" – Julie Jaslow Auerbach (see Appendix A, p. 350 for the music and words)

"Rain" – *It's Time for Music*, p. 22
"Raindrops" – Julie Jaslow Auerbach (see Appendix A, p. 352 for the music and words)

Israel

"Achshav" – *The New Children's Songbook*, p. 61 (see Music/Movement activity #8 above)
"David Melech Yisrael" – *The New Children's Songbook*, p. 11 (see Music/Movement activity #14 above)
"Eretz Zavat Chalav" – *Manginot*, p. 258
"Eretz Yisrael" – Julie Jaslow Auerbach (see Music/Movement activity #10 above)
"Kee Tavou el Haaretz" – *The Songs We Sing*, p. 147
"Mi Yivneh Hagalil" – *The Songs We Sing*, p. 353 (see Music/Movement activity #13 above)
"Zum Gali Gali" – *Manginot*, p. 171 (See Music/Movement activity #7 for an activity on this folk song)

Spring's Coming

"Spring Is a-Comin'" – Julie Jaslow Auerbach (see Music/Movement activity #12 above)

CIRCLE TIME

1. Make a flannelboard of all the parts of a tree.
2. To see this tree "grow," have children assemble the tree piece by piece. Later, make the flannel set available for free time exploration.
3. Play *If I Were a Seed, I'd Grow into a ____.* Encourage the children to be wildly creative. Make a book of the children's answers.
4. Talk about how the children would like to go to Israel, if they could — by boat or plane? What would they take? What would they need if they were going to plant trees in Israel?
5. Play "*Chalutzeem, Chalutzeem, Where's Your Tree?* instead of *Doggie, Doggie, Where's Your Bone?* Use a leaf for the "bone."

OUTDOORS/FIELD TRIPS

1. Take the outside temperature in the shade and in the sun. Compare results for several days.

2. Hug a tree. Can you find a one-kid tree? A three-kid tree? How many kids does it take to hug the biggest tree you can find?
3. Walk through the neighborhood to see the different kinds of trees. Which trees still have leaves? What are the characteristics of nature in your neighborhood at this season?
4. Search for animal tracks in the snow. Can you tell which belong to big animals? little animals? Was the animal running? walking?

SPECIFICALLY FOR INFANTS
1. Bring branches and leaves into the classroom for babies to explore in a supervised fashion.
2. Plant seeds in the room, and show the babies when they start to grow. Start to teach babies the appreciation of growing things.
3. Dance with babies to Tu B'Shevat music.
4. Act out growing from a seed into a tall tree with babies.

IDEAS FOR TEACHING FAMILIES
1. Send home blessings for Tu B'Shevat.
2. Provide families with materials or information so that they can plant a tree in Israel through the JNF.
3. Ask families to send in seeds from fruits they eat to plant in class.
4. Inform families of community Tu B'Shevat *Sedarim* they can attend at local synagogues or JCCs.
5. Invite family members in to help set up and participate in your classroom Tu B'Shevat *Seder*.
6. Recommended reading: *A Seder for Tu B'Shevat* by Harlene Winnick Appelman and Jane Sherwin Shapiro, *Seder for Tu B'Shevat: The Festival of the Trees* by Adam Fisher, and *Ecology & the Jewish Spirit*, edited by Ellen Bernstein.

A   STORY

THE TREES' MEETING
By Judy Aronson (printed with permission of the author)

At the same time that Moses was on top of Mt. Sinai receiving the Torah from God, there was another meeting going on in the world. No one seemed to notice it because everyone was waiting for Moses to bring down God's Law. But the trees of the world were all deeply concerned about the stone tablets Moses was carving with the laws of God. The trees were talking with each other, trying to decide what to do.

Are you wondering how the trees all talked with each other? Well, it was quite easy. The winds would gently blow through their branches, and their leaves would rustle and whisper. The wind carried their whispering from tree to tree, all over the world. Perhaps you've heard trees talking this way? With the help of the wind, at least a million trees could be talking their special language at the same time. Because trees are rooted in their places, they are quite patient, and excellent listeners. Try talking to a tree someday. You can be sure it will not turn its back on you, answer a ringing telephone, or change the channel on the TV just as you are getting to the best part of what you are trying to say.

In any event, the trees' meeting had to do with how the message of the Torah would be spread to people everywhere. The stone tablets Moses had carved were simply not portable. They might last a long time, but they were too heavy to carry around everywhere. At that time, books had not been invented yet. The closest thing was a scroll made of parchment. Scrolls are nice, but they can be very long. How could a person carry around a scroll that contained all of God's laws?

The trees gave this problem a lot of thought, and came up with a clever solution. You could roll the scroll on a wooden pole! Putting a wooden pole at each end of the scroll was even better. Then when you wanted to read it, you could just unroll it to the right section. Using two poles, you could roll it in either direction without any trouble at all.

The trees were quite pleased with their solution. There were two trees that were very good friends: the bramble tree through which God spoke to Moses, and the stately cedar of Lebanon that would be used in the building of the Temple in Jerusalem. These two trees placed a second problem before their friends. What kind of trees should have the honor of giving their branches to make rollers for the Torah? It was such a special job. Each tree hoped to be chosen, but no tree wanted to hurt another's feelings by claiming the honor and leaving someone else out. After much rustling of leaves, the trees decided to take turns. They would let the carpenters decide what kind of wood they liked each time they made rollers for God's holy Torah.

As Moses came down from the mountain, God heard the whispering of the beautiful trees that grew all over the world. God thought, "Trees are so useful. They provide shade when it is hot, and firewood when it is cold. They have delicious fruit and nuts growing on them. They have beautiful flowers as well. Forests encourage the rain to fall. Green leaves allow all of My other creatures to breathe, since they cleanse the air of pollution." God loved the trees, and was curious about their concerns.

The trees whispered to God about all they had thought and agreed upon. God liked the plan to store the Torah on scrolls of parchment. God thought about the rollers and told the trees that they would be called *aytzeem*, or *trees*, in their honor. The trees were proud that they had helped God in the work of creating the Torah. But God was not finished.

God said, "Trees, you are such good friends to each other. Tall or short, colorful or drab, fruit-bearing or not, you have respect for each and every tree. This is an important lesson for all my creations. You are placed here in this world to respect each other, not to think that one of you is better than the other because of your size or appearance. Therefore, I am going to give you a holiday all your own. It will be called Tu B'Shevat, the New Year of the Trees. It will take place each year on the fifteenth day of the month of Shevat. Jewish people all over the world will plant trees in Israel

and in other countries as well. They will have wonderful feasts and eat different kinds of fruits and nuts. Then they will remember that every tree is an important creation, and they will become My partners in preserving the world from generation to generation."

The trees were grateful to God and whispered together, "Bless us, *Adonai,* with sun and rain. Keep us tall and strong, and help us always to be friends to each other and to all your creations."

SUGGESTED NEWSLETTER ARTICLE

The holiday of Tu B'Shevat, the New Year of the Trees, is right around the corner. Tu B'Shevat dates back to the Talmud. The Rabbis considered the new year of trees as beginning when the new fruit begins to form. Although winter is still upon us here, spring has already begun in Israel. On the fifteenth day of the Hebrew month of Shevat, this year on _____ [insert date], children all over Israel plant trees. In most of North America, it's still a little too cold for outdoor planting, so we are planting seeds inside instead. Planting a tree in Israel through the Jewish National Fund is a wonderful way to honor someone or pay tribute to someone's memory. A tradition on Tu B'Shevat is to taste new fruits, especially fruits native to Israel, such as almonds, figs, carob, and dates. Some people have a Tu B'Shevat *Seder*, tasting fruits and drinking wine in different shades to represent each season. Check your synagogue or local JCC for a Tu B'Shevat *Seder*, or to make your own, see *A Seder for Tu B'Shevat* by Harlene Winnick Appelman and Jane Sherwin Shapiro.

Tu B'Shevat is a reminder to us that it is our responsibility to care for the earth. Brainstorm with your child ways you can recycle and save energy in your home. Plant seeds at home — nothing grows faster (and is more rewarding to a child with limited ability to delay gratification) than birdseed on top of a sponge in a pan of water. You can also plant parsley now and use it at your Passover *Seder*.

RECIPE

ISRAELI DATE CAKE

Ingredients

½ C. boiling water
1 lb. chopped dates
2 C. chopped pecans or walnuts
1 C. sugar
2 tbs. butter
2 eggs
3½ C. flour
2 tsp. baking soda
½ C. carob powder or cocoa (optional)
2 tsp. vanilla
dash of cinnamon

Directions

1. In a large mixing bowl, pour boiling water over chopped dates.
2. Add nuts, sugar, and butter.
3. Beat eggs slightly and add to other ingredients.
4. In a separate bowl, mix flour, baking soda, and carob powder or cocoa.
5. Add to wet mixture.
6. Add vanilla and cinnamon and mix well.
7. Bake in a lightly greased 9" × 13" pan at 350° for about one hour – do not overcook. Allow to cool before serving. Dust with powdered sugar.

BIBLIOGRAPHY

ADULTS

Appelman, Harlene, and Jane Shapiro. *A Seder for Tu B'Shevat*. Rockville, MD: Kar-Ben Copies, 1984.
A Tu B'Shevat *Seder* for younger children.

Bernstein, Ellen, ed. *Ecology & the Jewish Spirit: Where Nature & the Sacred Meet*. Woodstock, VT: Jewish Lights Publishing, 1998.
Respected experts from all walks of Jewish life explore Judaism's ecological message.

Carlson, Laurie. *Ecoart! Earth-Friendly Art and Craft Experiences for 3- To 9-Year-Olds*. Charlotte, VT: Williamson Publishing, 1992.
Arts and crafts projects that benefit the environment. Includes a recipe for making paper.

Elon, Ari; Naomi Mara Hyman; and Arthur Waskow, eds. *Trees, Earth, and Torah: A Tu B'Shevat Anthology*. Philadelphia, PA: Jewish Publication Society, 1999.
A comprehensive collection of Jewish resources for observing Tu B'Shevat.

Fisher, Adam. *Seder Tu B'Shevat: The Festival of the Trees*. New York: CCAR Press, 1989.
Provides a wealth of information for organizing a Tu B'Shevat *Seder*.

CHILDREN
Infant To 2 Years

Barrett, Mary B. *Leaf Baby*. San Diego, CA: Red Wagon Books, 1998. (Ages 2-5)
Simple story of a child raking fall leaves.

Iverson, Diane. *I Celebrate Nature*. Nevada City, CA: Dawn Publications, 1995. (Ages 2-7)
Beautiful full-color illustrations and a simple rhyming story line portray a group of children discovering the joys of nature in a variety of settings and seasons.

MacLean, Moira. *In the Woods*. New York: Todtri Productions, Ltd., 1999. (Ages infant-2)
Beautiful illustrations of a young child in the woods. (Board Book)

Schimmel, Schim. *Dear Children of the Earth: A Letter from Home*. Minoqua, WI: North Wood Press, 1994. (All ages)
Discusses our responsibility to protect the earth. Spectacular illustrations.

3 Years

Ehlert, Lois. *Red Leaf, Yellow Leaf*. San Diego, CA: Harcourt Brace & Jovanovich, 1991. (Ages 3-7)
A child describes the growth of a maple tree from seed to sapling.

Mallett, David. *Inch by Inch: The Garden Song*. New York: Harper Trophy, 1997. (Ages 3-6)
An illustration of the popular song.

Ross, Betty Ann. *Dates As Sweet As Honey*. New York: Board of Jewish Education of Greater New York, 1982. (Ages 3-6)
A wonderful story of Israel and Jews coming to the *Bayt Mikdash* to bring, among other things, dates as sweet as honey.

Udry, Janice May. *A Tree Is Nice*. New York: HarperCollins, 1988. (3-8)
A classic, simple tale of trees. A Caldecott Award winner.

Zalben, Jane Breskin. *Pearl Plants a Tree*. New York: Simon & Schuster, 1995. (Ages 3-6)
Pearl celebrates Tu B'Shevat by planting a tree like the one her grandfather planted when he came to America.

4 To 5 Years

Cherry, Lynne. *The Great Kapok Tree: A Tale of the Amazon Rain Forest*. San Diego, CA: Harcourt Brace & Company, 1990. (Ages 4-8)
A wonderful story about the interdependence of species in the rain forest.

Gershater, Phillis. *Honi's Circle of Trees*. Philadelphia, PA: Jewish Publication Society, 1994. (Ages 4-6)
The classic story of Honi and the carob tree.

Romanova, Natalia. *Once There Was a Tree*. New York: Dial Books, 1985. (Ages 4-8)
> A Russian story about the web of life.

Sasso, Sandy Eisenberg. *A Prayer for the Earth: The Story of Naamah, Noah's Wife*. Woodstock, VT: Jewish Lights Publishing, 1996. (Ages 4-9)
> Noah may have saved the animals from the flood, but Naamah saved the plants.

Segal, Sheila. *Joshua's Dream: A Journey To the Land of Israel*. New York: UAHC Press, 1992. (Ages 4-10)
> Joshua loves to hear the story of his aunt who helped Israel become a country. He dreams of the day when he will go to Israel and plant a tree.

Van Allsburg, Chris. *Just a Dream*. Boston, MA: Houghton Mifflin, 1990. (Ages 4-8)
> The story of what will happen in the future if we are not environmentally aware.

Waldman, Neil. *The Never-Ending Greenness*. New York: Morrow Junior Books, 1997. (Ages 4-8)
> When a young boy comes to live in Israel after WWII, he begins planting and caring for trees, a practice that spreads across the entire country.

More Books about Trees

Bunting, Eve. *Someday a Tree*. New York: Clarion Books, 1996. (Ages 4-8)
> Alice and her parents try to save an oak tree that has been poisoned by chemicals. Alice's sadness is alleviated when she plants the acorns she has been collecting from the tree.

Canizares, Susan. *Look at This Tree*. New York: Scholastic, 1998. (Ages 4-8)
> A science emergent reader that looks at the components of trees.

Dorros, Arthur. *A Tree Is Growing*. New York: Scholastic, 1997. (Ages 4-8)
> Tells about the structure of trees, how they grow, and their uses.

Gile, John. *The First Forest*. Rockford, IL: John Gile Communications, 1989. (Ages 4-8)
> A modern fable of how greed enters the first, perfect forest and spoils the trees' beauty and grace.

Lauber, Patricia. *Be a Friend To Trees*. New York: Harper Collins, 1994.
> Discusses the importance of trees as sources of food, oxygen, and other essential things.

Wiggers, Ray. *Picture Guide To Tree Leaves*. New York: Franklin Watts, 1991. (Ages 8-12)
> Demonstrates through photos how different kinds of trees can be identified. While geared to older children, the book is useful for the photos.

CHAPTER 15

PURIM

Mordecai charged the people to observe the fourteenth and fifteenth days of Adar every year . . . They were to observe them as days of feasting and merrymaking, and for the exchange of gifts of food and alms to the poor. (Esther 9:20-22)

OVERVIEW

The fourteenth day of the Hebrew month of Adar (sometime in February/March) is the joyous, no-holds-barred holiday of Purim. In walled cities, the celebration is continued through the fifteenth of Adar, because Shushan, where the story takes place, was a walled city. Purim celebrates the miraculous escape of the Jews from annihilation some 2,400 years ago in Persia. The story of Purim is found in *Megillat Esther*, the Book of Esther, in the Hebrew Bible. There is a brief synopsis below, as well as two versions for children, but you will be able to teach your children most effectively if you've read the "whole *megillah*" yourself. You can find the Book of Esther in any Tanach (Hebrew Bible), or in *The Five Megilloth and Jonah* with introduction by H.L. Ginsberg.

The story of Esther is a twisting, turning tale of suspense and drama. The book opens to King Ahasuerus and the banishment of his queen, Vashti. This leaves the king with a problem — he needs a queen. He establishes a contest through which he discovers and falls in love with Esther. Raised by her Uncle Mordecai, Esther follows his directions and does not reveal to the king that she is a Jew. Haman, the king's top advisor, wants every person to bow down to him to demonstrate his power, but Mordecai, on account of being a

Jew, refuses. Haman is angered, and draws lots (*purim*) to choose a date on which to destroy all the Jews. Mordecai turns to Esther to use her position to avert disaster, and she bravely foils Haman's plan and saves the Jewish people.

There are four *mitzvot* of Purim:

1. *Mishloach Manot* (also called *Shalach Manot*) – Sending gifts to friends

   Mordecai tells us to celebrate Purim by sending baskets of food and drink to our friends. "Therefore, the Jews . . . observe the fourteenth day of the month of Adar with joy, feasting and festival, and the exchange of gifts of food with one another" (Esther 9:19). The word for gifts, *manot*, is plural, so we send two gifts to at least two friends. You can use a bag, box, or basket — the only requirement is that you use at least two different kinds of food. Typically, *Mishloach Manot* include *hamantaschen*, candy, nuts, fruit, and juice or wine. But you can get as creative as you want. Children make great deliverers of *Mishloach Manot*.

2. *Matanot L'Evyoneem* – Sending gifts to the Poor

   Tzedakah is an important part of every Jewish holiday and life cycle moment, and Purim is no exception. We share and care during Purim by providing gifts of money to the poor and needy, to at least two people. "Mordecai recorded all these matters and sent letters to the Jews in all the provinces . . . enjoining them to observe the fourteenth and fifteenth days of Adar . . . making them days of feasting and merrymaking for the exchange of gifts of food and alms to the poor" (Esther 9:20-22).

3. Listening to the *Megillah*

We retell the story of Purim every year. "Therefore because all the words of this letter . . . the Jews ordained, and took upon them and upon their seed . . . that they would keep these two days according to the writing thereof, and according to the appointed time thereof, every year, and that these days should be remembered and kept throughout every generation, every family, every providence, and every city" (Esther 9:26-28). Just as with the *shofar* on Rosh HaShanah, the *mitzvah* is to *hear* the *megillah*, not necessarily to read it oneself. Custom holds that when we hear the name of Haman, we blot out his name with noisemakers, shouting, and stamping of feet.

4. Participating in a Purim feast

"And on the fourteenth day they rested, and made it a day of feasting and gladness" (Esther 9:17). Purim is a time for gathering with friends, recalling our triumph over yet another enemy, and, of course, eating. We nosh on *hamantaschen*, wine, and other yummy treats.

For a glossary and Hebrew vocabulary list for Purim, see figure 25 below on this page.

BLESSINGS FOR PURIM

Before we read the *Megillah*, we say three blessings. The first is for the reading of the *Megillah*:

בָּרוּךְ אַתָּה יְיָ אֱלֹהֵינוּ מֶלֶךְ הָעוֹלָם
אֲשֶׁר קִדְּשָׁנוּ בְּמִצְוֹתָיו וְצִוָּנוּ עַל מִקְרָא מְגִלָה.

Baruch Atah Adonai Elohaynu Melech HaOlam Asher Kid'shanu B'Mitzvotav V'Tzivanu Al Mikra Megillah.

We praise you, our God, Creator of the universe, Who makes us holy through Your *mitzvot*, and commands us to read the *Megillah*.

The second blessing is to give thanks to God for all the times the Jews have been saved from wicked enemies. (Recognize this one from Chanukah?)

GLOSSARY AND HEBREW VOCABULARY

אֶסְתֵּר	Esther	became queen after Vashti, and saved the Jewish people.
הָמָן	Haman	the king's vizier, who plotted against the Jews.
הָמָן-טַאשֶׁן	*Hamantaschen*	triangle-shaped cookie wih filling inside, modeled after the triangle hat Haman purportedly wore
הַמֶּלֶךְ אֲחַשְׁוֵרוֹשׁ	King Ahasuerus	somewhat foolish king of Persia
מַסֵּכוֹת	*Masaychot*	masks
מַתָּנוֹת לְאֶבְיוֹנִים	*Matanot l'Evyoneem*	giving gifts of *Tzedakah* (charity) to the poor
מְגִילָה	*Megillah*	scroll
מְגִילַת אֶסְתֵּר	*Megillat Esther*	the Book of Esther
מִשְׁלֹחַ מָנוֹת	*Mishloach Manot*	sending gifts to friends
מָרְדְּכַי	Mordecai	Jewish man in Shushan, Esther's uncle/cousin
פּוּר/פּוּרִים	*Pur/Purim*	lot/lots
רַעֲשָׁן	*Ra'ashan*	*gragger* (noisemaker)
שׁוּשַׁן	Shushan	walled city in Persia where the story of Purim takes place
תנ"ך	Tanach	Hebrew Bible, includes the Torah, Prophets, and Writings
וַשְׁתִּי	Vashti	the king's first wife, banished for not appearing at his party

Figure 25

בָּרוּךְ אַתָּה יְיָ אֱלֹהֵינוּ מֶלֶךְ הָעוֹלָם
שֶׁעָשָׂה נִסִּים לַאֲבוֹתֵינוּ בַּיָּמִים הָהֵם בַּזְּמַן הַזֶּה.

*Baruch Atah Adonai Elohaynu Melech HaOlam
She'asah Nissim L'Avotaynu BaYameem HaHaym
BaZ'man HaZeh.*

We praise you, our God, Creator of the universe,
Who made miracles for our ancestors in their days
at this time of the year.

The third blessing is the *"Shehecheyanu"* (see
Chapter 13, "Chanukah," p. 186), celebrating that
we have reached this time of year once again.

PURIM CONCEPTS

WEBBING THE CONCEPTS

Webbing the concepts of Purim (see Chapter
1, "Developmentally Appopriate Practice," p. 11
for more on webbing), can elicit ideas about what
you want children to think about and what you
want children to learn (and not just what you
want them to make). This technique can also bring
to mind connections to other things going on in
your classroom. Figure 26 on the following page
is the *beginning* of a web for Purim. You can extend
the web with your co-teachers or your students,
thus shaping the celebration of Purim to include
the interests of everyone in your class. *You won't
cover everything you web*, but you'll get a good idea
of where you want to go.

INFANTS TO 2
1. Purim is a fun holiday.
2. On Purim we dress up.
3. We hear the story of Esther.
4. We shake a *gragger*.
5. We taste *hamantaschen*.

2 YEARS
1. Purim is a fun holiday.
2. On Purim we dress up. We can make masks
   and costumes.
3. We hear the story of Purim in different ways.
4. We shake a *gragger*. We make a *gragger*. In
   Hebrew, a *gragger* is called a *ra'ashan*.
5. We taste and make *hamantaschen*.
6. We sing Purim songs.

3 YEARS
1. Purim is a fun holiday.
2. On Purim we dress up. We can make masks
   and costumes.
3. We hear the story of Purim in many different
   ways (through books, puppets, felt board, etc.).
4. We act out the Purim story.
5. We meet Esther, Mordecai, Haman, and King
   Ahasuerus.
6. We can be like Mordecai and Esther. Esther
   and Mordecai were very brave. They acted on
   what they believed in, and saved the Jewish
   people. We have the right to be different.
7. We shake the *gragger* to drown out Haman's
   name. In Hebrew, a *gragger* is called a *ra'ashan*.
8. We make a *gragger*. We experiment with different kinds of sounds.
9. We taste and make *hamantaschen*.
10. We make *Shalach Manot* baskets for our friends
    or family. We give *Tzedakah* on Purim.
11. The story of Purim is written in the *Megillat
    Esther*.
12. We listen to the *Megillah* at school and in
    synagogue. We can make a *megillah*.

4 TO 5 YEARS
1. Purim is a fun holiday. We dress up. We can
   make masks and costumes.
2. We hear the story of Purim in many different
   ways (through books, puppets, felt board, etc.).
3. We act out the Purim story.
4. We meet Vashti, Esther, Mordecai, Haman,
   and King Ahasuerus.

5. We can be like Mordecai and Esther. Esther and Mordecai were very brave. They acted on what they believed in, and saved the Jewish people. We have the right to be different. One person can make a big difference.

6. We have a responsibility to care for each other and help each other.

7. We shake the *gragger* to drown out Haman's name. In Hebrew, a *gragger* is called a *ra'ashan*.

8. We experiment with different kinds of sounds.

9. In Israel, people parade in their costumes through the streets.

10. We taste and make *hamantaschen*.

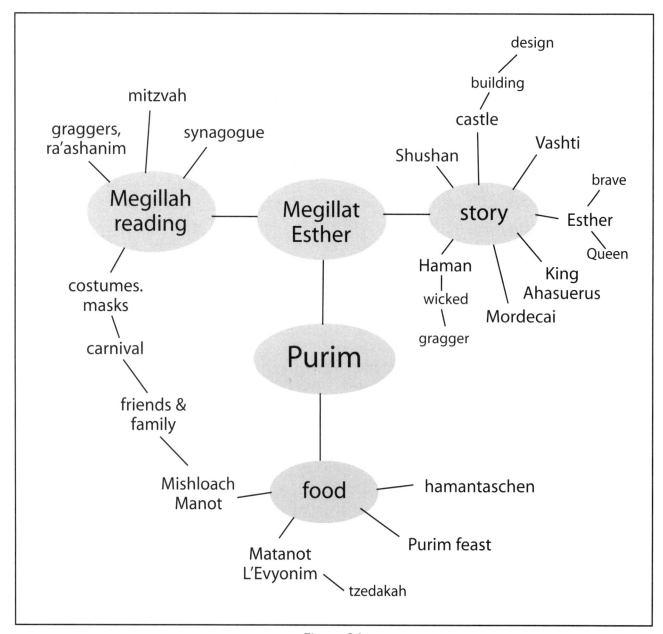

Figure 26

11. We make *Shalach Manot* baskets for our friends or family. We give *Tzedakah* on Purim.
12. The story of Purim is written in the *Megillat Esther*.
13. We listen to *Megillat Esther* at school and in synagogue. We can make a *megillah*.

ACTIVITIES

LANGUAGE ARTS

1. Tell the story of Purim using lots of different media. Act out the story of Purim! Provide dress up clothes, puppets, felt board characters, etc., so children can retell the story in their own play.
2. Make a *megillah*. Have every child contribute to a class *megillah*, and/or let every child draw their favorite scene and dictate the story for his/her own *megillah*.
3. Discuss the feelings of each of the characters with the class. Make feeling puppets, or a "So-and-so feels _____ when _____" book. Include Vashti, at least with older children. Vashti was a strong character, who stood up for herself and said no when someone asked her to do something that didn't feel right. This is what we are trying to teach our children to do.
4. "Piggyback" Purim symbols onto popular stories. Substitute the "*hamantaschen* man" for the gingerbread man, and have the whole cast of Purim characters chasing after him.
5. Substitute a *hamantaschen* in the oven for a turnip in the ground, from the story *The Enormous Turnip* by Kathy Parkinson, and you've got a brand new story for Purim. Try using Hebrew for the characters: *sabba* (grandpa), *safta* (grandma), *yaldah* (girl), *yeled* (boy), *kelev* (dog), *chatool* (cat), *achbar* (mouse).
6. Examine a *Megillat Esther*. Compare it to a Torah.

SCIENCE

1. Experiment with sound. Make *graggers* using different fillings and different containers.

2. Fill milk bottles with different levels of water and compare the sound when tapped.
3. Build all sorts of castles using many different materials (blocks, different shaped boxes, film canisters, murals). Talk about how Shushan was a walled city, and how Jerusalem is still a walled city today. Build Shushan in part of your room.
4. Bake *hamantaschen* and fill with different kinds of fillings. Experiment with making a triangle-shaped cookie out of a circle.

MATH

1. Make cards with pictures of *hamantaschen* with different colored fillings, in different sizes. Let children sort, classify, make patterns.
2. Encourage children to draw a design or blue-print for a castle, and then build it.
3. Chart who the children's favorite Purim characters are.
4. Make *purim*, lots, with different numbers on them. Let the children pretend to be Haman and pick a *pur* out of a bag/box. What date would they choose for Purim?

ART

1. Let the children use many different materials to make their own masks. Provide pictures and real examples of different kinds of masks to give children ideas.
2. Children can design their own costumes. Provide pictures of different kinds of costumes and different artistic representations of the Purim characters.
3. Give the children a very large selection of supplies with which to make *ra'ashaneem* (*graggers*). Again, supply pictures and examples of actual *ra'ashaneem* to give the children ideas. Providing limited supplies or a finished, teacher-made example of how their *ra'ashan* should look will stifle the children's creativity. *Do* help ensure that the finished *ra'ashan* will not leak its innards when shaken!
4. Make the baskets for sending *Shalach Manot* as beautiful as you can.

5. Help children design fancy, fun cards for their *Shalach Manot* baskets.

6. Turn a corner of your room into the castle in Shushan. Let the children design, build, and decorate it.

MUSIC/MOVEMENT

(With musical contributions from Julie Jaslow Auerbach)

1. Sing funny songs (e.g., "Pop Goes the Weasel"), as such songs — and the drama — are the key elements in the music for this holiday. Just as we do for Chanukah, we need to cover the story, the food, and the characters in song and movement.

2. Sing "Purim's a Time" by Julie Jaslow Auerbach (see Appendix A, page 351 for music and lyrics). After each Purim character is mentioned in this song, there is a place for an action and words. The song can be done as a dance, with the chorus a la "Ring around the Rosie," and with children standing still for the verses.

3. Sing "Haman's on His Horse," an adaptation by Julie Jaslow Auerbach of a Halloween song. Children tap their knees in a lap chant accompanying the words, getting faster or slower as the music dictates.

Haman's on his horse, riding very slow
Oh-oh, oh-oh, where's he gonna go?

Haman's on his horse, riding into town
Oh-oh, oh-oh, he's the worst around!

Haman's on his horse, riding very fast
Oh-oh, oh-oh, Purim's here at last!

(More verses can be made up by the children!)

4. Sing *"Chag Purim,"* a classic Purim song, accompanying the song with musical instruments.
   a. Use different instruments for different words
   b. Have all instruments play only on the *"Chag Purim"* refrain
   c. Use any combination of the above.

5. Sing "Oy Oy Uncle Mordechai" by Fran Avni. The children will enjoy putting their hands on their cheeks and moving their heads back and forth in woeful expression as they sing "Oy Oy . . . " in the refrain.

6. Using a suitcase as the "trunk" and props, sing "All Aboard for Shushan" from *Sing For Fun Volume I* by Ray M. Cook. At each verse you can pull out something else from the trunk. This is also a good song to use in a Purim parade.

7. Play fun Purim music and have a parade in costume.

8. Fill the dress-up corner with wild, wacky, fun clothes in which to dress up for Purim.

9. Play happy music and dance happy with songs like "Purim's a Time" on *Seasoned with Song* by Julie Jaslow Auerbach. Play sad music and dance sad with Purim songs like "Sad People" on the recording *Latkes and Hamentashen* by Fran Avni.

10. Listen to a tape of the chanting of *Megillat Esther* (Chadish Media CS 133). Let the children color while listening.

11. Sing Purim songs while the children are dressed up like different Purim characters.

SONG/MUSIC LIST

(Contributed by Julie Jaslow Auerbach)

The following listing includes the songs in this chapter, as well as songs from other sources that are related to Purim concepts. Each song and the book in which it is located is specified, along with the page number. (Please note: In this and other holiday chapters, there are many songs which are "preschool traditional," i.e., they have been around so long that no one knows the composer or the song's origin! Every effort has been made to find the source for all the songs listed.)

Costumes, Players

"All Aboard for Shushan" – *Sing for Fun Volume I*, p. 12 (See Music/Movement activity #6 above on this page)

"Haman's on His Horse" (see Music/Movement Activity #3 on p. 216)

"Lakova Sheli" – *The New Children's Songbook*, p. 29

"My Hat It Has Three Corners" – folk song

"Oy Oy Uncle Mordechai" – *Latkes and Hamentashen*, p. 21 (see Music/Movement activity #5 on p. 216)

"Purim's a Time" – Julie Jaslow Auerbach (see Music/Movement activity #2 on p. 216)

"Purim Masqueraders" – *The New Children's Songbook*, p. 30

"The Purim Ball" – *Shirim Al Galgalim*, p. 23

"When You Hear the Name" (to the tune of "If You're Happy")

"Wicked Wicked Man" – *The New Children's Songbook*, p. 32

Celebrating

"Ani Purim" – *Union Songster*, p. 281

"Chag Purim" – *The New Children's Songbook*, p. 28 (see Music/Movement Activity #4 on p. 216)

    Movements: clap, stamp

    Instruments

    Beanbag toss

    Marching

"Shoshanat Yaakov" – *The Songs We Sing*, p. 171

"Utsu Etsa V'tufar" – *The Songs We Sing*, p. 168

Surprises, Miracles

"Jack in the Box" – preschool traditional

"Humpty Dumpty" – nursery rhyme

"Pop Goes the Weasel" – traditional folk song

"Utsu Etsa V'tufar" – *The Songs We Sing*, p. 168

"Leitzan Katan" – *The New Children's Songbook*, p. 62

Concepts

"Al Ha-neeseem" – *Especially Wonderful Days*, p. 11

CIRCLE TIME

1. Play *Hot Hamantaschen* instead of *Hot Potato*.
2. Play *Gossip in Esther's Court* (an adaptation of *Telephone*).
3. Give each child a stick mask with a happy face on one side and a sad face on the other, with just the eyes cut out (either teacher-made or child-made). Present a series of feelings situations, and have the children "wear" how they would feel in that situation. Use some obvious situations (e.g., "Mom just bought me and my friends ice cream." "My dog ran away from home.") and some not so obvious situations (e.g., "I am going grocery shopping with my Dad after school." "We are moving to a bigger house so I will have my own bedroom.") This is a good activity for working on perspective as well as feelings, because children must put on the face that reflects what they are feeling facing *away* from themselves.
4. Once all the children have become familiar with the Purim characters, have one child act out a Purim character. The other children guess who it is. With younger children, make props available.

OUTDOORS/FIELD TRIPS

1. Take a trip to a nursing home or hospital to deliver *Mishloach Manot*. Sing some songs or act out the Purim story.
2. Take a trip to a music store to investigate musical instruments.
3. Take a walk outside. Are there any evidences of spring yet?
4. If it is possible, build a temporary wall and make the entire playground into Shushan.

SPECIFICALLY FOR INFANTS

1. Put on Purim music and dance with babies.
2. Let babies taste *hamantaschen* if they are old enough.
3. Be careful with masks around babies. Very young children are often scared of clowns and people they can't recognize.
4. Provide some funky hats and costumes, and show babies their dressed up selves in a mirror. Use sensitive skin face makeup to give babies a red clown nose, and look in the mirror and share their reaction.

IDEAS FOR TEACHING FAMILIES

1. Send home the recipe for *hamantaschen* so families can bake at home.

2. Invite family members in to help bake *hamantaschen* in your class.

3. Inform families of *Megillah* readings and carnivals at local JCCs and synagogues that welcome families with young children.

4. Send home the Purim story, both the full account (the Book of Esther) and the version you tell in your class.

5. In addition to having children make and exchange *Mishloach Manot* in class, send home directions and explanations so families can make and deliver their own *Mishloach Manot*.

6. Explain the *mitzvah* of *Matanot l'Evyoneem* to families. Have a school-wide food drive, and encourage every family to participate.

7. Recommended reading: *The Purim Anthology* by Phillip Goodman, and *The Tanach: Stone Edition*, which contains the Book of Esther.

GAMES

Purim is a time for frivolity, carnivals, and games. Here are a few suggestions for games.

1. *Hit the Hamantaschen:* Draw a *hamantaschen* with velcro at the center. Let the children throw velcro "Poppy seeds" at the *hamantaschen* to fill it. Or, play *Pin the Filling on the Hamantaschen* or *Pin the Crown on Esther/Vashti/Ahasuerus*.

2. *Gossip in Esther's Court:* The basic game of *Telephone*, but with Purim words or phrases.

3. *Hide the Gragger:* The basic "hot and cold" game, but hide a *gragger*. Have the children sing a Purim song softly for cold, and loudly for hot.

4. *Mee Anee? (Who Am I?):* Seat a child facing the rest of the children. Hold a Purim item or character over the child's head so he/she cannot see it. The other children must give clues about the item until the seated child guesses the item.

THE PURIM STORY

FOR VERY YOUNG CHILDREN

A long, long time ago, in a town called Shushan, there lived a king named Ahasuerus. The king had a queen. Her name was Esther. King Ahasuerus had a helper named Haman. Haman was mean. He wanted everyone to bow down to him, to show how powerful he was. Queen Esther had an uncle named Mordecai. Mordecai told Haman, "I won't bow down to you! Jewish people bow down only to God." This made Haman very angry. He decided to punish all of the Jewish people in Shushan.

Mordecai found out about Haman's mean plan, and he went to tell Esther. "You're the only one who can save the Jewish people," Mordecai said to Esther. Esther was afraid to go and talk to the king — what if he got angry at her for bothering him? But Esther knew this was very important, so she gathered up all her courage and went to talk to the king about Haman's mean plan. The king wasn't angry! He was happy to help Esther because he loved her! King Ahasuerus told Haman that it wasn't okay to hurt the Jewish people. The king got rid of Haman, and he never bothered the Jewish people again. Everyone was so happy that they declared a holiday — Purim!

FOR OLDER CHILDREN

A long time ago, in a town called Shushan, lived a king named Ahasuerus. The King had a queen named Vashti. One time, the King had a big party. He wanted to show off his beautiful wife. He called her to come and dance for his guests. But Vashti refused to show up. She told King Ahasuerus, "I will not come dance for your friends." King Ahasuerus was angry (and a little embarrassed). He said, "Well, then you can't be the queen anymore." And he sent Vashti far away from Shushan.

Now the King had a problem. He needed a queen. He held a contest and invited all the young women in Shushan to come and try out to be the queen. A Jewish woman named Esther lived in Shushan with her Uncle Mordecai. Mordecai told Esther, "You should go and try to be the queen." Esther wasn't so sure it would be a good idea, but Uncle Mordecai convinced her at least to try. Mordecai also told Esther not to tell the King she was Jewish. So Esther went and waited with all the other women at the palace.

Each woman got a turn to go before the King. Some of the women put on lots of makeup and fancy clothes. When it was her turn, Esther went before the King. She wore no makeup and had on a plain dress. But King Ahasuerus could see that Esther was wise and kind and beautiful, and he immediately fell in love with her. He asked her to marry him and become the queen, and she said yes. She remembered Uncle Mordecai's advice, and she didn't tell the King she was Jewish.

King Ahasuerus had a helper, his top assistant, named Haman. Haman ordered that everyone bow down to him, to show how important he was. But Mordecai refused to bow down. Mordecai told Haman, "I won't bow down to you! Jewish people only bow down to God." This made Haman very angry. He decided to punish all of the Jewish people in Shushan. He cast lots (*purim*) to pick the day he would punish the Jews. When Haman had his plan, he went to King Ahasuerus and he told him some lies. "King Ahasuerus," he said, "did you know that there are people in your kingdom who don't like you? The Jewish people don't follow your rules, and they say mean things about you." Haman was telling lies, but the King believed him. "What should we do?" asked the King. "I've got a plan to punish them," said Haman. "Do whatever you see fit," said the King.

Mordecai found out about Haman's terrible plan. Mordecai went to Esther and told her that she must go see the King and stop Haman. Esther told Mordecai that there was a law that you could go to see the King only if you had been invited, and the King had not invited her. "Esther!" said Mordecai, "you are the only one who can save the

Jewish people. If Haman punishes all the Jews, you won't be safe either." Esther was very frightened, but she knew Mordecai was right. She gathered up her courage and went to the King's door. When King Ahasuerus saw that it was Esther at his door, he wasn't angry at all. He was glad to see Esther, because he loved her. He invited her to come in and talk with him.

"Esther," said King Ahasuerus, "tell me what you want. You can have anything, even half of my kingdom." "I do not want half of your kingdom," said Esther. "I want you to stop Haman's plan to punish the Jews." "But Haman told me the Jewish people don't follow my rules and say bad things about me," said the King. "I am Jewish," said Esther. "Haman told you lies about the Jewish people. If Haman punishes the Jews, he will have to punish me, too." The King became angry. "He told me lies? Then Haman is the one who must be punished! I will punish him the way he wanted to punish the Jews! Don't worry Esther, I won't let anything happen to you or your people."

Haman was punished, and he never bothered the Jews again. Mordecai became advisor to the king. Esther and Mordecai and the Jewish people were so happy that they decided to celebrate with parties and by sending gifts to each other and to poor people. They wrote down the whole story and we read it every year in *Megillat Esther* on the holiday of Purim!

SUGGESTED NEWSLETTER ARTICLE

Be Happy! It's Adar! _____ [insert this year's date for Rosh Chodesh Adar] corresponds to the first day of the Hebrew month of Adar, which means that Purim is right around the corner. We read *Megillat Esther* on the night of _____ [insert date of reading]. Purim continues on _____ [insert date]. Purim is the perfect children's holiday. At school, your children will soon be involved in dressing up in costumes, baking *hamantaschen*, acting out the story of Esther and Mordecai, and drowning out the name of evil Haman. Through the story of Purim, which we read in *Megillat Esther* (the Scroll of Esther), we learn of courage, faith, and the value of the Jewish people. At home, you can ask your child to tell you the story of Esther and Mordecai. Check the local synagogues for times of Purim carnivals, where you and your child can share the fun of Purim together. You can read the whole *Megillah* in any version of the Tanach (Hebrew Bible), or check out *The Purim Anthology* by Phillip Goodman for everything you might want to know about Purim. Some good children's books include *A Costume for Noah* by Susan Remick Topek, *Esther* by Miriam Chaikin, and *Goldie's Purim* by Jane Breskin Zalben. Have a happy Purim!

RECIPE

HAMANTASCHEN

Ingredients
3 C. flour
1 C. sugar
2½ tsp. baking powder
2 eggs
1 C. margarine
4 tbs. orange juice

Directions
1. In a bowl, sift together the flour, sugar, and baking powder.
2. Mix eggs, margarine, and juice in food processor.
3. Add flour mixture and continue to mix.
4. Knead dough briefly.
5. Shape dough into a disk and wrap in plastic wrap. Flatten disk slightly so there is no air inside plastic wrap. Refrigerate for a few hours or overnight.
6. On a well floured surface, roll out dough and cut into 2½" circles (a cup or mug works well for this).
7. Fill with about a teaspoon of filling (suggestions below) and fold into a triangle.
8. Squeeze corners securely.
9. Bake in a 350° oven for 20-30 minutes, or until nicely browned.

Potential Fillings
Pie filling – poppy seed, prune, almond, apple, cherry, etc.
Jelly/jam – strawberry, apricot, orange, etc.
Chocolate chips
Carob chips
Chocolate spread from Israel
Peanut butter (best with the chocolate spread — makes Reese's *hamantaschen!*)
Fruit cut into small chunks — apples, bananas, strawberries, etc.
Any combination of the above. Take a chance!

BIBLIOGRAPHY

ADULTS

Goodman, Phillip. *The Purim Anthology*. Philadelphia, PA: Jewish Publication Society, 1988.
    Provides a wide range of information about Purim, including stories from around the world, music, and recipes.

Tanach: The Stone Edition. ArtScroll Series. New York: Mesorah Publications, 1998.
    Contains the entire Hebrew Bible, including the Book of Esther.

CHILDREN
Infant To 2 Years

Groner, Judye, and Madeline Wikler. *The Purim Parade*. Rockville, MD: Kar-Ben Copies, 1986. (Ages infant-2)
    Introduces each of the Purim characters. (Board Book)

Kress, Camille. *Purim!* New York: UAHC Press, 1998. (Ages infant-2)
    Beautiful illustrations and the feelings of Purim. (Board Book)

Nerlove, Miriam. *Purim*. Morton Grove, IL: Albert Whitman & Company, 1992. (Ages 2-5)
    Simple retelling of the Purim story.

3 Years

Feder, Harriet. *It Happened in Shushan*. Rockville, MD: Kar-Ben Copies, 1988. (Ages 3-7)
    A different retelling of the Purim story in rebus form.

Goldin, Barbara Diamond. *Cakes and Miracles: A Purim Tale*. New York: Puffin Books, 1991. (Ages 3-8)
    Hershel may be blind, but he can still create amazing Purim cookies.

Parkinson, Kathy. *The Enormous Turnip*. Morton Grove, IL: Albert Whitman, 1986. (ages 3-7)
    One of Grandfather's turnips grows to such an enormous size that the whole family, including the dog and cat, must work together to pull it out.

Rouss, Sylvia. *Sammy Spider's First Purim*. Rockville, MD: Kar-Ben Copies, 1999. (Ages 3-6)
    Sammy wants to spin the *gragger,* but his mother reminds him that spiders don't spin *graggers,* they spin webs.

Topek, Susan Remick. *A Costume for Noah: A Purim Story*. Rockville, MD: Kar-Ben Copies, 1995. (Ages 3-7)
    Noah's classmates are busy making costumes for Purim, but Noah is preoccupied with the imminent arrival of a new baby.

4 To 5 Years

Cohen, Barbara. *Here Come the Purim Players*. New York: UAHC Press, 1984. (Ages 4-8)
    The Purim Players come to Prague to tell the Purim story.

Schotter, Roni. *Purim Play*. Boston, MA: Little, Brown & Company, 1998. (Ages 4-8)
    Frannie is upset that her older neighbor is going to be in the Purim play.

Sidon, Efrayim. *The Animated Megillah: A Purim Adventure*. New York: Jonathan David Publishers, 1987. (Ages 4+)
    A translation of the *Megillah* with dramatic illustrations.

Wolkstein, Dianne. *Esther's Story*. New York: William Morrow, 1996. (Ages 4-8)
    The Purim story told in diary form from the point of view of Esther.

Masks

Earl, Amanda. *Masks*. New York: Thomson Learning, 1995. (Ages 8-12)
    Describes how masks are used by different cultures. Although it is targeted at older children, the book is useful for the pictures.

Mack, John. *Masks and the Art of Expression*. New York: Harry N. Abrams, 1994. (All ages)

One hundred and fifty amazing visuals of masks from archaic cultures to modern-day festivals.

The Metropolitan Museum of Art: Masks. New York: DK Ink, 1997. (Ages 8-12)
   Spectacular masks from the collection of the Metropolitan Museum of Art. Although geared to older children, the book is useful because of the pictures.

Schaefer, Lola. *Masks.* Mankato, MN: Pebble Books, 1998. (Ages 2-7)
   Beautiful photographs and easy to read text.

CHAPTER 16

PESACH, WITH LAG B'OMER

This day shall be to you one of remembrance: you shall celebrate it as a festival to God throughout the ages . . . Seven days you shall eat unleavened bread. (Exodus 12:14-15)

OVERVIEW

Pesach (Passover), which begins on the fifteenth day of the Hebrew month of Nisan, celebrates the Exodus of the Israelite people from Egypt. Pesach continues for seven days, through Nisan 21, although many communities in the Diaspora (outside of Israel) add an eighth day. In the English calendar, Passover can fall anytime from late March to late April. Whereas Tu B'Shevat signals the dawning of springtime, Pesach, also called *Chag HaAviv* (The Spring Festival), comes while spring is in full bloom. The Jewish calendar is organized in such a way that the holidays always occur in their appointed seasons. Spring is a time of new life and rebirth, and these themes are prevalent in the story and symbols of Pesach.

The account of the Passover is found in the Torah, Exodus 1-15. The Hebrew name, Pesach, comes from the offering *(pesach)* which God asks the Jewish people to make before they leave Egypt. The English name, Passover, comes from the tenth plague, in which the angel of death *passed over* the homes of the Jews, which, according to God's instructions, were marked with blood. The holiday has several other names. *Z'man Chayrutaynu* (Time of Our Liberation) reminds us that the central theme of Pesach is liberation and freedom. *Chag HaMatzot* (Festival of Unleavened Bread) high-lights a most important symbol of Pesach. As the

Jews prepared to leave Egypt, God instructed them in preparations for the first *Seder*: "They shall eat the meat that same night; they shall eat it roasted over the fire, with unleavened bread and with bitter herbs" (Exodus 12:8). We read later (Exodus 12:34) that the Jews left Egypt in such a hurry they had no time for their bread to rise. This unleavened bread is our *matzah*. It can tell the entire story of Pesach. *Matzah* is called "*lechem onee*," literally poor man's bread, or the bread of affliction, because it reminds us of the poverty and anguish of our life in Egypt. But it is also the bread of liberation, created as we burst forth from slavery in Egypt to become free people, ready to take on the laws in the Torah and form a partnership with God.

Telling the story of Pesach is the highest goal of the holiday. We are told in the *Haggadah* that even if we were all people of wisdom, understanding, experience, and knowledge of the Torah, it would still be an obligation upon us to tell about the Exodus from Egypt. Only on this holiday are we commanded to tell the story. Every year we do all we can to relive the Exodus from Egypt. This is the crucial event that marks the beginning of the Jewish people. It is referred to repeatedly in Jewish liturgy and throughout the Torah and other Jewish texts. For this reason, on Pesach, we imagine that we ourselves were liberated from Egypt. In order to help us relive the experience of leaving Egypt, there are three *mitzvot* concerning Pesach: to tell the story, to eat *matzah*, and to refrain from eating or owning *chametz* (anything containing yeast or leavening).

The vehicle for telling the Pesach story is the *Seder*, which occurs on the first night (or the first two nights in the Diaspora). *Seder* means "order," and indeed, there is a specific order to the *Seder*, to ensure that we tell the whole story. The *Seder* is guided by the *Haggadah*, the book which contains the liturgy of the *Seder*. The word *Haggadah* comes from the Hebrew root "to tell." Today, there exist a myriad of *Haggadot* from which to choose, with commentaries from various viewpoints and interests, including *Haggadot* designed especially for children or families, as well as feminist *Haggadot*. The *Seder* is steeped in rituals. Asking questions, dipping and tasting different foods including *matzah* and *maror* (bitter herbs), study and song, all designed to draw every member of the family into the story of the Exodus from Egypt.

Pesach is especially important as a family holiday. The entire family is called upon to help prepare for the holiday as well as to celebrate. The rituals of *Bidikat Chametz* and *Biur Chametz* help fulfill the *mitzvah* of not owning *chametz* during the holiday. More than any other holiday, Pesach is the time when American Jews gather together to celebrate with friends and family. Pesach places supreme importance on conveying the story and meaning of Pesach to the next generation. The Rabbis have always known that the future of the Jewish people lies with our children.

For a glossary and Hebrew vocabulary list on Pesach, see figure 27 below on this page.

GLOSSARY AND HEBREW VOCABULARY		
אֲפִיקוֹמָן	*Afikoman*	hidden *matzah*
אָבִיב	*Aviv*	spring
בְּדִיקַת חָמֵץ	Bidikat Chametz	literally, the search for *chamaytz*, a ritual performed the night before the day of the first *Seder*
בִּעוּר חָמֵץ	*Biur Chamaytz*	literally, burning the *chamaytz*, the morning of the day of the first *Seder*
חַג הָאָבִיב	*Chag HaAviv*	literally, The Spring Festival
חָמֵץ	*Chamaytz*	bread stuff, or anything leavened
חֲרוֹסֶת	*Charoset*	apple, nuts, and wine mixture that reminds us of bricks and mortar of slavery
אֵלִיָּהוּ הַנָבִיא	*Eliyahu HaNavi*	Elijah the Prophet
הַגָּדָה	*Haggadah*	from the Hebrew word "to tell," the book which contains the story and liturgy of the *Seder*
כַּרְפַּס	*Karpas*	greens on the *Seder* table
מַה נִשְׁתַּנָה	*Mah Nishtanah*	the Four Questions; literally, "What is different?"
מַצָה	*Matzah*	literally, unleavened bread
מָרוֹר	*Maror*	literally, bitter herbs (often horseradish is used at the *Seder*)
מִצְרַיִם	*Mitzrayim*	Egypt
עוֹמֶר	*Omer*	measurement
פֶּסַח	Pesach	also called Passover; celebrates the Exodus of the Israelite people from Egypt
סֵדֶר	*Seder*	literally, order; the home service/meal at which we retell the Pesach story
זְמַן חֵרוּתֵנוּ	*Z'man Chayrutaynu*	literally, Time of Our Liberation

Figure 27

PESACH CONCEPTS

WEBBING THE CONCEPTS

Webbing the concepts of Passover (see Chapter 1, "Developmentally Appropriate Practice," p. 11 for more on webbing), can elicit ideas about what you want children to think about and what you want children to learn (and not just what you want them to make). This technique can also bring to mind connections to other things going on in your classroom. Figure 28 below is the *beginning* of a web for Passover. You can extend the web with your co-teachers or your students, thus shaping the celebration of

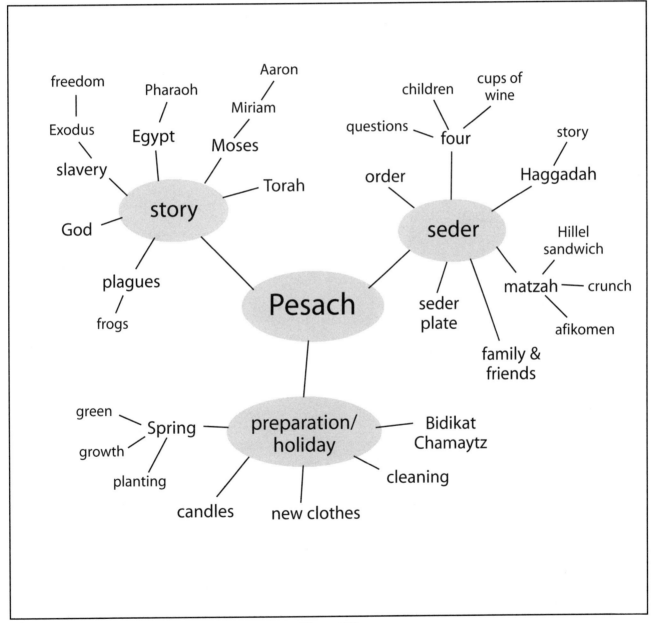

Figure 28

Passover to include the interests of everyone in your class. *You won't cover everything you web*, but you'll get a good idea of where you want to go.

INFANT TO 24 MONTHS
1. Pesach is a holiday to be with family.
2. We taste *matzah* and *charoset*.
3. We have a special dinner called a *Seder*.
4. We hear the story of Moses and the Jewish people in Egypt.
5. We sing songs about Pesach.
6. I look for the *afikoman*.

2 YEARS
1. Pesach is a holiday to be with family.
2. We taste new foods like *matzah* and *charoset*.
3. We have a special dinner called a *Seder*.
4. We read a book called a *Haggadah*.
5. We tell the story of Moses and the Jewish people in Egypt.
6. We sing songs about Pesach.
7. I help look for the *afikoman*.

3 YEARS
1. Pesach is a holiday to be with family.
2. We invite guests to our *Seder*.
3. Pesach tells us that spring has arrived.
4. *Seder* means "order." At the *Seder*, we read the *Haggadah*, which helps keep order.
5. We tell the story of Moses and the Jewish people in Egypt.
6. The Jewish people were slaves to Pharaoh in Egypt.
7. With God's help, Moses led the Jewish people to freedom
8. We taste things at the *Seder* to help us remember the story.
9. *Matzah* reminds us of the people leaving Egypt in a hurry.
10. *Charoset* reminds us of the mortar they used to build Pharaoh's cities.
11. I search for the *afikoman* after the *Seder* meal.
12. We can help our families clean and get ready for Pesach.

13. Before Pesach, we search for *chamaytz* in our house and classroom (*Bidikat Chamaytz*).
14. We hear stories about *Eliyahu HaNavi* — Elijah the Prophet.
15. Pesach is a time to ask lots of questions!

4 TO 5 YEARS
1. Pesach is a holiday to be with family. We invite guests to our *Seder*.
2. Pesach tells us that spring has arrived.
3. "*Seder*" means "order." At the *Seder*, we read the *Haggadah*, which helps keep order.
4. We tell the story of Moses and the Jewish people in Egypt.
5. The Jewish people were slaves to Pharaoh in Egypt.
6. With God's help, Moses led the Jewish people to freedom.
7. We taste things at the *Seder* to help us remember the story of Moses.
8. *Matzah* reminds us of the people leaving Egypt in a hurry.
9. *Charoset* reminds us of the mortar they used to build Pharaoh's cities.
10. *Maror* reminds us of the bitterness of slavery.
11. Jewish people all over the world make *charoset* in lots of different ways.
12. We are thankful to be free. There are other people in the world who are not free.
13. We can help our families clean and get ready for Pesach.
14. Before Pesach, we search for *chamaytz* in our house and classroom (*Bidikat Chamaytz*).
15. We burn the *chametz* to show we are doing our best to get ready for Pesach (*Biur Chamaytz*).
16. We search for the *afikoman* after the *Seder* meal.
17. We hear stories about *Eliyahu HaNavi* (Elijah the Prophet).
18. Pesach is a time to ask lots of questions! I can ask my own questions, and also some of The Four Questions (*Mah Nishtanah*).

ACTIVITIES

LANGUAGE

1. *Seder* means "order." Give children lots of opportunities to put the Pesach story in order, with pictures, puppets, acting out. Provide costumes and props.

2. Teach and sing the Four Questions (especially with four-year-olds). Provide ample ways for children to connect meaning with the words — pictures, puppets, tasting and smelling and dipping while singing, reclining on a pillow for the last question.

3. Pesach is the time for questions! Encourage children to ask questions. Write their questions down (even those of the youngest children).

4. Make Pesach question books with the children's questions, and send the questions home for families to find the answers together.

5. Share various Elijah (*Eliyahu HaNavi*) stories (see the bibliography of this chapter).

6. Provide props for children to act out being different characters in the Pesach story: Moses, Miriam, Aaron, God, Pharaoh, a slave.

SCIENCE

1. Prepare for Pesach well in advance. To help older children understand *matzah* fully, be sure to explore bread and yeast with them before Pesach. Watch yeast rise. Mixing the water and yeast in a measuring cup allows the children to see and measure the growth of the yeast. Bake *challah*, paying close attention to the role of the yeast. Then bake *matzah* (see recipe on p. 235), and let the children taste and discuss the differences.

2. Make *charoset* (see recipe on p. 235).

3. Let children compare raw *maror* (horseradish root) and prepared horseradish (white and dark red). Smell each one, warn the children that it is very spicy, but they can taste it if they want to.

4. Pesach is *Chag HaAviv* — the spring holiday. Help the children investigate all the evidences of spring as you prepare for Pesach: new buds on the trees, bugs and animals appearing, changes in the soil, in the weather, in their clothing.

5. Instead of the Hillel sandwich, let children create funny sandwiches of their own.

6. Formulate theories about who drinks from Elijah's cup at the *Seder*. Remind the children that if the *Seder* is on a clear night, they will be able to see the full moon when they open the door for Elijah.

7. Investigate the basic elements of Pesach. Explore sand. Compare wet and dry sand. Make bricks of sand. Make bricks of mud and bake them in a low oven for several hours. Compare with a real brick. Find many ways to build cities with blocks. Imagine what it would be like to build Pharaoh's palace. Act it out.

8. Conduct experiments with salt.

9. Compare things that taste salty, bitter, sweet.

10. Conduct a *Bidikat Chamaytz* search in your classroom (see below for a full description). Then burn the *chamaytz*. Use a coffee can outside, or dig a pit in the sandbox outside. Line the hole with aluminum foil and burn the *chamaytz* — paper bags, feathers, candle, and all. Make sure the children stand far enough back so everyone feels safe. This is a very dramatic way to get children ready for Pesach, and let them feel they helped prepare their classroom. Best for threes and up!

MATH

1. Count the *Omer*. Especially in classes that already do "math their way," start the second day of Pesach (or immediately upon return from Pesach break). Be sure to prep the children for this before Pesach. Count the 49 days between Pesach and Shavuot (see p. 231 below for more information).

2. Make a counting book using Pesach symbols (one *Seder* plate, two candles, three *matzot*, four cups of wine, five pyramids, six frogs, etc.)

3. Make *matzah* and time it. Can you complete the whole process in 18 minutes?

4. Play with the fours: four cups of wine, four children, Four Questions.
5. Make pictures of the process of making *matzah* for the children to sequence.

ART

1. Children will want to contribute to their family *Seder* tables with handiwork of their own. There are many ritual objects to make for Pesach — *Haggadah*, Elijah's cup, *Seder* plate, *matzah* cover, *afikoman* bag, etc. Allow children as much freedom of design as possible, by providing lots of materials and different pictures of the real thing, rather than an example of the finished project. Coordinate with your whole school so children do not make the same things every year.
2. Make puppets of the Pesach characters (Moses, Miriam, Pharaoh, slaves, the people leaving Egypt). Make sure the children take these home in time to use at their own *Sedarim*.
3. Decorate pillows to recline on at the *Seder*. Start with white pillowcases or cloth to sew up and stuff later. Use fabric paint, sponges in the shape of Jewish ritual objects or cookie cutters (no *challah* shape!), hand prints or markers.
4. Corrugated cardboard makes great *matzah*.
5. Paint with sand (for the desert) or salt. This is an excellent sensory activity.

MUSIC/MOVEMENT

(With musical contributions from Julie Jaslow Auerbach)

1. Sing "Soon It's Gonna Be Pesach" by Julie Jaslow Auerbach (see Appendix A, p. 357 for music and lyrics). If desired, children can dance through the cleaning and other preparations for the holiday to this song or other Passover melodies. Please be sensitive to the fact that not all Jewish families follow the traditions of cleaning thoroughly before the holiday. Clean your classroom as this song is played in the background. Ask the children what they do in their homes to get ready for the holiday and the *Sedarim*, and then include their words in an additional verse.

2. Reconstruct the Pesach story using the song "Goshen" by Julie Jaslow Auerbach (see Appendix A, p. 337 for music and lyrics). Have the children help you insert the words for this story of the Israelites and their lives in Goshen. Acting out the verses also will be fun for them.
3. Sing the following version of *"Mah Nishtanah"* as adapted by Julie Jaslow Auerbach. It encapsulates the essence of both the young child and the Pesach tradition of questioning. The questions of a young child are key to the Pesach *Seder*, but to many children and parents the Hebrew language is still very remote.

Mah nishtanah halaila hazeh
Mikol halaylot, mikol halaylot
Oh why is this night so different tonight
Why do we eat only *matzah* tonight
Oh why oh tell me why —
Oh why oh tell me why.

4. Begin singing *"Dayaynu"* by first telling the children to tap their knees. Ask them if they can hear the Israelites marching out of Egypt. Then introduce the following chant:

One two three four
Here we go out the door
One two three four
We won't be in Egypt any more!
Ilu hotzi hotzianu . . ., etc.
Da-da-yaynu [clap hands]

Note: You can also use this chant as a bridge to Yom HaAtzma'ut:
One two three four
Boy are my feet sore
One two three four
Look there's Israel, that's for sure!

5. Pesach is one of the three Pilgrimage Festivals we call *Shalosh Regaleem*. Sing *"Al Shalosh Regaleem"* by Julie Auerbach (see Appendix A, p. 328 for music and lyrics). Use this song for Sukkot and Shavuot as well (see Sukkot, Music/Movement activity #3).

6. It is traditional to use a feather, a wooden spoon and a candle to look for stray *chametz* during the *Bedikat Chamaytz* rituals the night before the first *Seder*. Sing songs about feathers (see below under Song/Music List).

7. Sing "*Avadim Hayinu*" as an echo song. It makes it much easier for young children — and much more fun!

8. Dance with props. Use ribbons with "*Od Lo Ahavti Dai*" and feathers with "*HaTzipporim*."

9. Act out being a slave.

10. Act out crossing the Sea of Reeds to freedom. Songs such as "Song of Freedom" on *Bible People Songs* by Jeff Klepper and Jeff Salkin, and "Hurry Up" by Fran Avni on *Mostly Matzah* help this dramatic play along.

11. Play Debbie Friedman's "Miriam's Song" on the album *Debbie Friedman At Carnegie Hall*. With instruments, encourage the children to dance as if they've just crossed the Sea of Reeds to freedom.

Song/Music List
(Contributed by Julie Jaslow Auerbach)

The following listing includes the songs in this chapter, as well as songs from other sources that are related to Pesach concepts. Each song and the book in which each is located is specified, along with the page number. (Please note: In this and other holiday chapters, there are many songs which are "preschool traditional," i.e., they have been around so long that no one knows the composer or the song's origin! Every effort has been made to find the source for all the songs listed.)

Cleaning/Feathers
"Put Your Feather in the Air" (to the tune of "Put Your Finger in the Air")
"Soon It's Gonna Be Pesach" – Julie Jaslow Auerbach (see Music/Movement activity #1 above)
"Tickeley" – *Songs to Sing with Babies*, p. 52 (see Music/Movement activity #6 above)
"Waltzing Cat" – *Leroy Anderson Favorites*

Exodus Story
"Bang Bang Bang" – preschool traditional
"Oh Listen" – preschool traditional
"March Out of Egypt" – *Shalom Sings*, p. 29
"Israeli March Medley" – *The Barry Sisters in Israel*
"Dayaynu" – Pesach traditional (see Music/Movement activity #4 above)
"Hag Sameach" – *The New Children's Songbook*, p. 33 (see Sukkot, Music/Movement activity #7)
"Goshen" – Julie Jaslow Auerbach (see Music/Movement activity #2)
"Frog Song" (2 versions: "One morning, Pharaoh awoke . . ." in *The New Children's Songbook*, p. 34, and "God punished Pharaoh . . ." in *So We Sing*, p. 38)
"Pass Over the Water for Passover" – *Shirim Al Galgalim*, p. 28
"Al Shalosh Regalim" – Julie Jaslow Auerbach (see Sukkot Music/Movement activity #3 on p. 168)

Concepts
"Pesah Is Here Today" – *Especially Wonderful Days*, p. 14

Four Questions/Seder
"Avadim Hayinu" – *Manginot*, p. 157 (see Music/Movement activity #7 above)
"Dayenu" – *Manginot*, p. 140, and chant (see Music/Movement activity #4)
"Echad Mee Yodea" – *Manginot*, p. 160
"Here We Go" – *So We Sing*, p. 38
"Kadesh Urechatz" – *The New Children's Songbook*, p. 34
"Lashanah Haba-a" – *Israel in Song*, p. 47
"Mah Nishtanah" – *Manginot*, p. 154, adapted by Julie Jaslow Auerbach (see Music/Movement activity #3 above)

Food
"Bake a Matzah" – *Union Songster*, p. 224
"Chop Chop Chop" – *So We Sing*, p. 40

Spring
"HaTzipporim" – (see Music/Movement activity #8 above)

"How Do We Know It's Spring? – preschool traditional

"Od Lo Ahavti Dai" – *Israel Sings*, p. 15 (see Music/Movement activity #8 above)

"Simcha Raba" – *The New Children's Songbook*, p. 33

CIRCLE TIME

1. Ask the children what they remember about Pesach last year. Write down their answers. Then ask what they hope will happen this year. Write this down, too. After Pesach, check to see if the things they anticipated actually happened.
2. Play *Moses, Moses, Where's Your Afikoman?* instead *of Doggie, Doggie, Where's Your Bone?*
3. Chart who is having guests for *Seder*, and who is being a guest at someone else's *Seder*. Let the children discuss if they are going somewhere, and how they are getting there.
4. Name a Pesach activity, and have the children point to the part of their body they use for the action (crunch *matzah*, look for the *afikoman*, smell the *maror*, dip the *karpas*, ask the Four Questions).

OUTDOORS/FIELD TRIPS

1. Take a walk around the neighborhood to look for evidences of spring.
2. Collect evidences of spring to use in artwork or to decorate the *Seder* table.
3. Visit a *matzah* factory to see *matzah* being made.
4. Visit a bakery to see *challah* being made (to compare it to *matzah*).
5. If it's not too early, plant outside. Or, plant inside (sunflowers, corn) and scout out the future outdoor planting spot.

SPECIFICALLY FOR INFANTS

1. Let babies play with *matzah*, crunch it up, taste it (if they're old enough).
2. Dance with babies to Pesach music, both kid's music and adult, *Seder* music.
3. Let babies smell *maror* and watch their noses crinkle. *Do not* let babies taste *maror*!

4. Take babies outside, and point out to them evidences of spring.
5. Take babies to be guests at an older class's *Seder* until their attention span runs out.

IDEAS FOR TEACHING FAMILIES

1. Inform families of local synagogues that host *Sedarim* designed for young families.
2. Serve as a hospitality clearing house: find out which families are willing to host other families, and which families need a place to go for *Seder*, and help them get together.
3. Invite family members to join your class *Seder*.
4. Coordinate with a local Jewish bookstore so that families can buy *Haggadot* designed for children and young families directly through the school.
5. Send home the *Haggadah* that the children use in class, so parents can use it at home, too, and teach their family.
6. Organize families to help with *Ma'ot Chiteem* or the local Pesach relief effort for needy families.
7. If "Kosher for Pesach" food items are difficult to find in your area, help organize an import of *matzah* and other Pesach foods from the nearest source.
8. Recommended reading: *A Different Night* by Noam Zion and David Dishon, and *1001 Questions and Answers on Pesach* by Jeffrey M. Cohen.

BIDIKAT CHAMAYTZ/BIUR CHAMAYTZ

Chamaytz is any food with leavening. We don't eat such things during Pesach. In order to prepare ourselves fully for the holiday, we search for *chamaytz*. A largely symbolic search, *Bidikat Chamaytz* is done after nightfall on the evening before the first *Seder*, after all of the real, heavy-duty cleaning has been completed. You will need a feather, a wooden spoon, a candle, and a paper bag. To set the stage, hide ten pieces of bread around the house. All the lights are turned off, and the search is conducted with a candle, scooping the bread into the paper bag using the feather and wooden spoon (make sure to find all ten pieces). Before beginning the search, say the blessing:

בָּרוּךְ אַתָּה יְיָ אֱלֹהֵינוּ מֶלֶךְ הָעוֹלָם אֲשֶׁר קִדְּשָׁנוּ בְּמִצְוֹתָיו וְצִוָּנוּ עַל בִּעוּר חָמֵץ.

Baruch Atah Adonai, Elohaynu Melech HaOlam Asher Kid'shanu B'Mitzvotav V'Tzivanu Al Biur Chamaytz.

We praise you, our God, Creator of the universe, Who has made us holy through Your *mitzvot*, and has commanded us about the removal of *chametz.*

After the search, the *chamaytz* is wrapped up and put away until the next morning. The following declaration is made. It is very important that the person saying the declaration understand what he/she is saying. The original declaration was written in Aramaic, a cognate of Hebrew. Here it is in English:

Any *chamaytz* that is in my possession, which I did not see and remove, and which I do not know about, shall be as if it does not exist and shall become ownerless, like the dust of the earth.

When searching for *chamaytz* with children, make sure to translate the declaration into language that they can understand, too. You can say something along the lines of:

I have done my best to find and get rid of all the *chamaytz* in my house/classroom. If there is still some *chamaytz* that I didn't find, it's okay, because I did my best.

The next morning, right after breakfast, it is time for *Biur Chamaytz,* burning the *chamaytz* you found and set aside the night before. You can even add the crumbs from breakfast to the bag. Place the bag with the bread, feather, spoon, and candle in a coffee can or foil-lined pit in the sandbox. Make sure everyone can see from a safe distance. After the burning, recite this declaration:

Any Chametz that is in my possession, whether I did or did not recognize it, whether I did or did not see it, whether I did or did not remove it, shall be as if it does not exist and shall become ownerless, like the dust of the earth.

THE SEDER

The *Seder* is a wonderful opportunity to join together with another class or to invite families in to share the excitement, for community building; it is a fabulous learning opportunity. A *Seder* requires lots of advance preparation. There are songs and blessings to learn, questions to ask and seek answers to, foods to buy and prepare, and rituals to become familiar with. Although it is beyond the scope of this book to provide all the information necessary to make a *Seder*, a list of *Haggadot* for adults and for children may be found in the bibliography at the end of this chapter.

Although it is certainly possible to conduct a *Seder* simply working from a children's *Haggadah,* the teacher who takes some time to study an adult *Haggadah* will be able to teach his/her children from the heart, with more confidence, comfort, and enjoyment.

SEFIRAT HAOMER/ COUNTING THE OMER

An *Omer* is a measurement. The period of Counting the *Omer* is 49 days, or seven weeks between Pesach and Shavuot (literally "weeks"). The second day of Pesach is the first day of the *Omer*. Shavuot is the day after the *Omer* (the fiftieth day). In ancient Israel farmers would bring barley in bundles to the Temple at Pesach. The period of the *Omer* is a sad time, with no weddings or happy celebrations, because the students of Rabbi Akiva suffered at the hands of the Romans and died from a plague during this time. The one respite was the thirty-third day of the *Omer*, Lag B'Omer (see below, p. 236 for more information).

You can count the *Omer* in any number of ways. Some ideas include: (1) make a seven-week chart with spaces to write numbers or affix pictures of bundles of barley or real barley; (2) number the pages of a large pad of paper 1 to 49, and rip off a page each day; or (3) have children tape straws to a poster in groups of five (looks like a bundle of barley). Remember to alert children to the *Sefirat HaOmer* before Pesach begins, so that when you return to school after the *Sedarim*, you can fill in the first few days and keep going from there.

THE PESACH STORY

Here are three versions of the Pesach story for various age levels, beginning with the youngest. These versions have been written with close attention to the accuracy of the text and God. Remember that God is a major factor in the Pesach story. To tell the children that Moses decided to save the Jewish people on his own belies the biblical account. The Pesach story in our Torah (Exodus 1:1-15:22) is rich and colorful. Take just 15 minutes to read the whole story for yourself in a favorite version of the Torah. (*The Five Books of Moses*, translated and edited by Everett Fox, and *The Torah: The Five Books of Moses*, published by the Jewish Publication Society are both good translations.) Then you can decide how true these versions are to the text, and you can make your own retellings of the story exactly age appropriate *and* accurate, so your children do not need to unlearn the story later.

FOR CHILDREN AGES INFANT TO 2

Long ago, many Jewish people lived in a land called Egypt, where it is very hot. They had to work very hard for the king, the Pharaoh. He wanted them to build cities in which to store food. The Jews had to work without rest, because they were slaves of the Pharaoh.

God saw how unhappy the Jewish people were. God called to a Jewish man named Moses, and told him to go to Pharaoh and tell him to let the Jewish people go. Moses told Pharaoh to let the Jewish people go, but Pharaoh said "No!" God sent terrible things called plagues to change Pharaoh's mind, but each time Pharaoh said "No!"

Ten times Moses asked Pharaoh to let the Jewish people go, and each time Pharaoh said "No!" Finally, Pharaoh was so tired of the terrible things happening that he let the Jewish people go free. Moses told the people to pack quickly, so quickly that their bread had no time to rise. The people baked *matzah* instead.

Now the Jewish people were free, free from slavery and hard work, free to go to the land of Israel. They sang songs of thanks to God. We remember what happened to the Jewish people a long time ago and we celebrate the holiday of Pesach. We have a *Seder*, eat *matzah*, sing songs, and say "thank you" to God.

FOR CHILDREN AGES 2 TO 4

A long time ago in the land of Egypt, there was a king, called Pharaoh. He was very mean to the Jewish people. He forced them to build storage buildings for his cities in Egypt. The Jewish people had to work all day long. They didn't have time to eat breakfast, lunch, or dinner. They hardly had any time to sleep. They could not spend time with their families and friends — all they did make bricks out of mud and straw and build day after day.

Finally, the Jewish people said, "We're really tired. We can't stand this anymore." God heard the people's cry. God went to a brave Jewish man named Moses and said, "Moses, go tell Pharaoh to let the Jewish people go free." Moses said, "Are you sure you want me? I don't speak very well." God said, "Yes, I want you to do it." So Moses went to Pharaoh and said, "Let the Jewish people leave Egypt." Pharaoh said "No!" God sent a terrible thing called a plague, to change Pharaoh's mind. When Pharaoh woke up, all his water had turned into blood — YUCK! Pharaoh called Moses and told him the Jewish people could leave Egypt. The blood turned back to water, and Pharaoh changed his mind — the Jewish people had to stay and be slaves. God then sent another plague — when Pharaoh woke up, there were frogs everywhere. Pharaoh told Moses all the Jews could leave. But when the frogs went away, Pharaoh changed his mind again! Eight more times, God sent a plague and Pharaoh said the Jewish people could go free, but each time he changed his mind. Finally, the plagues were too terrible, and Pharaoh told the Jewish people to get out.

Moses called his people together and told them to pack their bags — it was time to leave Egypt. "Hurry," he said, "before Pharaoh changes his mind again!" The people packed so quickly that they did not have time to let their bread dough rise. They baked it and it came out flat — *matzah*! The Jewish people left Egypt as quickly as they could. When they were safe on the other side of the Sea of Reeds, they sang songs of thanksgiving to God, and they danced and were very happy to be free at last.

To remember the time when the Jewish people left Egypt and became free, we get together with our friends and families every year to celebrate. We have a *Seder*, tell the Pesach story, and sing songs. We read the *Haggadah* and eat special foods, such as *matzah* and *charoset* and *maror*. We are happy to be free to live the way we want to, and not be slaves anymore.

FOR CHILDREN AGES 4 TO 6

Remember Joseph and his multicolored coat? Remember how his whole family came to live in Egypt? While Joseph was alive, the Jewish people got along very well with the Egyptian king, called Pharaoh. Many years after Joseph died, there came a mean Pharaoh who never knew Joseph. He was afraid of the Jewish people — there were so many of them! He decided to make them slaves. He made them work very hard all the time. The Jewish people made bricks and built storage buildings and cities for Pharaoh. They were not free to do what they wanted; they could only do what Pharaoh wanted them to do. As the work got harder and harder, the Jewish people became very unhappy. They cried out to God to help them.

God heard the cries of the Jewish people and decided to help. God picked a Jewish man named Moses to help. One day Moses saw a fire in a bush, but the bush wasn't burning up. God spoke to Moses from the fire in the bush and said, "Moses! Go tell Pharaoh to let My people go!" Moses said, "Are you sure you want me? I'm too scared to do it. And I'm not a very good speaker." God said, "Yes, I want you to do it." So Moses went to Pharaoh and said, "Let the Jewish people leave Egypt." Pharaoh said "No!" God sent a terrible thing called a plague, to change Pharaoh's mind. When Pharaoh woke up, all his water had turned into blood — YUCK! Pharaoh called Moses and told him the Jewish people could leave Egypt. The blood turned back into water, and Pharaoh changed his mind — the Jewish people had to stay and be slaves. God sent another plague — when Pharaoh woke up, there were frogs everywhere. Pharaoh told Moses all the Jews could leave. But when the frogs went away, Pharaoh changed his mind again! Eight more times, God sent plagues and Pharaoh said the Jewish people could go free, but each time he changed his mind. Finally, the plagues were too terrible, and Pharaoh told the Jewish people to get out.

Moses called the Jewish people and told them to pack their bags — it was time to leave Egypt. "Hurry, before Pharaoh changes his mind again!" The people packed so quickly that they did not have time to let their bread dough rise. They baked it, and it came out flat — *matzah*! The Jewish people left Egypt as quickly as they could, walking as fast as they could go. God led the Jewish people with a big cloud. Soon, Pharaoh changed his mind again! He and his men set out in chariots to bring the Jews back to Egypt. The Jewish people had just arrived at the edge of the Sea of Reeds when they saw Pharaoh and his men behind them. They were very frightened and called to Moses, "What are we going to do?" Moses called to God for help. God said, "Lift up your staff [walking stick] and hold your arm over the sea, and the water will split." So Moses did, and the water split, and the Jewish people crossed the sea, walking on dry land between the walls of water. God moved the big cloud behind the people so that Pharaoh and his men would not be able to see the Jewish people crossing the sea.

[Note: This following bit is somewhat violent, and so a *midrash* is included in the first of the three paragraphs. If you chose, you can delete this whole part of the story, until the children ask, "What happened to Pharaoh and his men?"]

Pharaoh and his men followed the Jewish people into the sea. When the last Jewish person had reached the other side safely, the waters came together. Pharaoh and his men drowned in the water. When the angels saw that Pharaoh and the Egyptians were drowning, and that the Jewish people were free, they began to cheer. God stopped them and asked, "Why are you cheering? All people are my creations, and over there my creations are drowning."

When they were safe and free on the other side of the Sea of Reeds, the Jewish people sang songs of thanksgiving to God, and they danced and were very happy to be free at last.

To remember the time when Jewish people left Egypt and became free, we get together with our friends and families every year to celebrate. We have a *Seder*, tell the Pesach story, and sing songs. We read the *Haggadah* and eat special foods, such as *matzah* and *charoset* and *maror*. We are happy to be free to live the way we want to, and not be slaves anymore.

SUGGESTED NEWSLETTER ARTICLES

PESACH

Among American Jews, Pesach is the most celebrated of all Jewish holidays. Why is that? Pesach presents us with the opportunity to get together with family and friends. We can look at any *Haggadah* and know pretty much what to do and how to go about doing it. And of course, Pesach is centered around that favorite Jewish pastime — eating! But if we look deeper at the meaning behind Pesach, we discover it is most appropriate that Pesach is so well celebrated. Indeed, without Pesach, there would be no Jews. On Pesach, we celebrate the Exodus of the Israelite people from slavery in Egypt to the freedom to serve God and be Jewish. On Pesach, we retell the story of how Moses led the people out of Egypt, a story which is referred to countless times in Jewish liturgy and other texts. Pesach marks the birth of the Jewish people. So it is very fitting that on Pesach we gather together with friends and family and celebrate our right to do so.

At school, the children have been busy preparing, cleaning, baking, experimenting, searching their rooms for the last traces of *chamaytz* , transforming their space from a non-Pesach place to a Pesach place. Pesach is all about preparation and transformation. If you have never "changed over" your house for Pesach, consider trying it. Start small. Do an extra thorough spring cleaning this year. Next year, consider using only food that is kosher for Pesach. After all the work, it is an incredible feeling to sit back, look around your transformed kitchen, and know that you are a part of what has kept the Jewish people alive for over 3000 years.

COUNTING THE OMER

Beginning on the second day of Pesach, we will be counting the *Omer* every day in class. The *Omer* is the seven-week period between Pesach and Shavuot. It is a sad time — traditionally, we don't have weddings or get haircuts during this period. Remember to ask your child what day of the *Omer* it is every day after school during this time.

RECIPES

MATZAH

Note: Be sure to make these *matzot* before Pesach, for pre-Pesach consumption (*matzah* made from regular flour is not kosher for Pesach). A great book to read before making *matzah* is *The Mouse in the Matzah Factory* by Francine Medoff. Use a kitchen timer to see if you can complete the process in 18 minutes. This recipe is enough for eight mini-*matzot*.

Ingredients
2 C. flour
¾ C. water
pinch of salt (optional)

Directions
1. Mix flour and water (and salt). Add more flour if dough is sticky.
2. Divide into small balls. On a well floured surface, roll out dough as thin as possible.
3. With a fork, poke holes in dough to prevent bubbles.
4. Bake on a greased cookie sheet at 550° for approximately ten minutes or until lightly browned.

MATZAH GRANOLA

Note: This is a very large recipe, enough to feed a whole class.

Ingredients
1 lb. brown sugar (approximately 2 C.)
1 stick margarine
1 C. water
2 lbs. *matzah farfel*
1 lb. raisins
½ lb. walnuts
½ lb. sliced almonds
½ lb. pecans
½ lb. chocolate chips

Directions
1. Boil and set aside brown sugar, margarine, and water.
2. Mix *matzah farfel* with the rest of the ingredients.
3. Combine boiled sugar mixture with dry mixture and mix well.
4. Spread mixed over two greased cookie sheets in a thin layer.
5. Bake at 350° for 15 minutes. Mix once or twice while baking. Cool, store in a sealed container, and enjoy!

CHAROSET

Note: There are many different *charoset* recipes from Jewish cultures all over the world. This is the most basic American (Ashkenazic) recipe.

Ingredients
4 apples
½ C. shelled walnuts
1 tbs. cinnamon
2 tbs. brown sugar
½ C. sweet wine or grape juice

Directions
1. Core and chop apples.
2. Add the rest of the ingredients. Mix well. Store in a covered container in the refrigerator.
3. *Charoset* is often better after a day or two.

LAG B'OMER

Lag B'Omer is the thirty-third day of the Counting of the *Omer*. The name comes from the fact that every Hebrew letter has a numerical value. The letter *lamed* (ל) equals 30, and the letter *gimel* (ג) equals 3. *Lamed* and *gimel* together (לג) are read as *"lag."* Thus Lag B'Omer literally means the thirty-third day of the Counting of the *Omer*.

Historically, Lag B'Omer is the one bright day in the entire *Omer* period. The *Omer* marks a period of mourning for the students of Rabbi Akiva, who died of a plague during that time. Others say it was not a plague, but the Romans getting the upper hand in battle against the Jews during the Bar Kochba revolt in 132-135 C.E. In any case, Lag B'Omer marks the day on which the plague is said to have lifted or the tables turned in the revolt, and so we celebrate with picnics, bonfires, and bows and arrows. Some authorities end the mourning of the *Omer* (and the restrictions on weddings, haircuts, and concerts) on Lag B'Omer; others return to the mourning period after Lag B'Omer.

Lag B'Omer is a perfect day to have a picnic lunch with the children, and to play games outside, such as relays and circle running games (*Duck Duck Goose*, etc.).

ACTIVITIES

1. Share stories of Akiva and Shimon Bar Yochai (see the bibliography of this chapter for some resources).
2. Build a "bonfire" in your classroom with branches collected from outside; yellow, orange, and red cellophane; and a flashlight in the middle. Pretend to roast marshmallows while you sit around your bonfire and share songs and stories.
3. Have a picnic outside.
4. Play games outside, such as relays and running circle games (e.g., *Duck Duck Goose*).
5. Build kites out of paper, sticks, and string. Decorate brightly.
6. Fly real kites outside.
7. Find all the sets of three you can (in honor of the thirty-third day of the *Omer*). When the children line up to go somewhere, line up in trios instead of in pairs.
8. Traditionally, children play with bows and arrows to remember Akiva's students, who pretended to be hunting when they went to study. If you are uncomfortable with these in your classroom, practice throwing bean bags at a target.
9. Traditionally, the *Omer* is a time to study *Pirke Avot* (Ethics of the Fathers). A good resource for teaching *Pirke Avot* to preschoolers is *Pirke Avot Early Childhood Curriculum* by Ruth Pinkenson Feldman.

Music/Movement
(Contributed by Julie Jaslow Auerbach)

1. Sing every picnic song you've ever known, as well as songs about bugs! I like using the "Peanut Butter and Jelly" chant, as well as "I'm a Little Tea Pot."
2. Sing "Lemonade" by Julie Jaslow Auerbach (see Appendix A, p. 342 for music and lyrics). You can accompany this song with movements (squeezing, pouring, etc.). You can make lemonade as you sing it. A picture chart can also be brought in as a prop. And, of course, why not use instruments as sound effects?
3. Sing "A Special Way of Saying Thanks" by Julie Jaslow Auerbach (see Appendix A, p. 358 for music and lyrics). Because the children are now going outside more at this season of year, this is a good time to introduce this song which summarizes the *brachot* for many different things. You can add more to the body of the song for others of God's miracles.
4. Sing "Creepy Crawlies" (lyrics below by Julie Jaslow Auerbach) to the tune of *"Freres Jacques."* The rhymes in this song can be adapted in numerous ways, even to include bugs crawling on body parts with the appropriate rhyme!

Creepy crawlies (2x)
Bugs bugs bugs (2x)
Crawling up the walls
Or flying down the halls are
Bugs bugs bugs.

Creepy crawlies (2x)
Bugs bugs bugs (2x)
Crawling up the trees
Or flying in the breeze are
Bugs bugs bugs.

Song/Music List

(Contributed by Julie Jaslow Auerbach)

The following listing includes the songs in this chapter, as well as songs from other sources that are related to Lag B'Omer. Each song and the book in which it is located is specified, along with the page number. (Please note: In this and other holiday chapters, there are many songs which are "preschool traditional," i.e., they have been around so long that no one knows the composer or the song's origin! Every effort has been made to find the source for all the songs listed.)

Picnic

"Goin' on a Picnic" – *The Raffi Singable Songbook*, p. 30
"I'm a Little Teapot" – preschool traditional
"Lemonade" – Julie Jaslow Auerbach (see Lag B'Omer Music/Movement activity #2 above)
"Old MacDonald Had a Picnic" (to the tune of "Old MacDonald Had a Farm")
"Pat-a-cake" – traditional nursery rhyme
"Peanut Butter" – *Elephant Jam*, p. 47
"Row, Row, Row Your Boat" – traditional folk song

"Sailboat" – traditional folk song
"The Bear Went over the Mountain" – traditional folk song
"Uga, Uga" – *The New Children's Songbook*, p. 60

Bugs

"Arabella Miller" – *Elephant Jam*, p. 45
"Baby Bumblebee" – *It's Time for Music*, p. 16
"Creepy Crawlies" – see Lag B'Omer Music/Movement activity #4 above
"Eensy Weensy Spider" – preschool traditional
"Little Peter Rabbit" – *Elephant Jam*, p. 55

Traveling

"Wheels on the Bus" – preschool traditional
"Bim, Bam, Bom" – *Hebrew Songs for All Seasons Volume Two*, p. 14
"Marching To Pretoria" – traditional folk song

God's Wonders

"A Special Way of Saying Thanks" – Julie Jaslow Auerbach (see Music/Movement activity #3 above)

SUGGESTED NEWSLETTER ARTICLE; LAG B'OMER

The thirty-third day of the *Omer* is called Lag B'Omer, and it falls on _____ [insert date] this year. Lag B'Omer is the day when the restrictions of the *Omer* period are relaxed. Many people get married or get their hair cut on Lag B'Omer. We will be celebrating in our class by having a picnic outside for snack/lunch. For more information about Lag B'Omer, see *The Jewish Holidays: A Guide & Commentary* by Michael Strassfeld.

BIBLIOGRAPHY

ADULTS

Cohen, Jeffrey M. *1001 Questions and Answers on Pesach*. Northvale, NJ: Jason Aronson Inc, 1996.
> A comprehensive volume that provides information on every aspect of Pesach.

Nadich, Judah. *Rabbi Akiba and His Contemporaries*. Northvale, NJ: Jason Aronson Inc., 1997.
> The history of and stories about over 15 Rabbis from the time of Akiba, including Akiba himself.

Rush, Barbara, and Cherie Karo Schwartz. *The Kids' Catalog of Passover*. Philadelphia, PA: Jewish Publication Society, 2000. (Ages 8-adult)
> A delightful collection of Passover material from around the world, including stories, recipes, and community projects for kids.

Tabs, Judy, and Barbara Steinberg. *Matzah Meals: A Passover Cookbook for Kids*. Rockville, MD: Kar-Ben Copies, 1985.
> Contains over 70 kid-tested recipes for Passover meals, plus a *Seder* menu and the Passover story.

ADULT HAGGADOT

Levitt, Joy, and Michael Strassfeld. *A Night of Questions: A Passover Haggadah*. Elkins Park, PA: The Reconstructionist Press, 2000.
> A gender sensitive Reconstructionist *Haggadah*. Features questions from the Four Children throughout the evening, and provides many options for readings and commentaries, as well as creative rituals and activities.

Stern, Chaim, ed. *Gates of Freedom: A Passover Haggadah*. West Orange, NJ: Behrman House, 1998.
> A Reform *Haggadah* with an introduction by Rabbi Eugene Borowitz. Includes commentaries, poems, and songs.

Rabinowitz, Rachel Anne, ed. *The Feast of Freedom*. New York: United Synagogue Book Service, 1982.
> A Conservative *Haggadah* with illuminating commentaries and beautiful artwork by Israeli artist Dan Reisinger.

Scherman, Nosson, and Avie Gold. *The Family Haggadah*. Brooklyn, NY: Mesorah Publications, 1988.
> An Orthodox *Haggadah* that combines economy, accuracy, and the famed ArtScroll elegance.

Zion, Noam, and David Dishon. *A Different Night*. Jerusalem: The Shalom Hartman Institute, 1997.
> An incredible resource to help make the *Seder* exciting and different every year.

STORY COLLECTIONS ABOUT ELIJAH THE PROPHET

Jaffe, Nina. *The Mysterious Visitor: Stories of the Prophet Elijah*. New York: Scholastic, 1997.
> Eight classic Elijah tales, adapted by Jaffe for telling to young audiences.

Pearl, Sydelle. *Elijah's Tears: Stories for the Jewish Holidays*. New York: Henry Holt and Company, 1996.
> Five Elijah stories designed to connect with the holidays of Passover, Sukkot, Chanukah, and Yom Kippur.

Schram, Penninah. *Tales of Elijah the Prophet*. Northvale, NJ: Jason Aronson Inc, 1997.
> Thirty-six tales of Elijah the prophet, retold by a master storyteller.

CHILDREN
Children's Haggadot

Bogot, Howard, and Robert Orkand. *A Children's Haggadah*. New York: CCAR Press, 1994. (Ages 3-adult)
> Simple and clear.

Gindi, Elie M. *Family Haggadah: A Seder for All Generations*. West Orange, NJ: Behrman House, 1999. (Ages 3-adult)

Combines family-friendly text and magnificent reproductions from many different illuminated *Haggadot.*

Groner, Judith, and Madeline Wikler. *My Very Own Haggadah.* Rockville, MD: Kar-Ben copies, 1983.
> A *Haggadah* for the youngest children. Contains pictures to color, songs and activities.

Musleah, Rahel. *Why on This Night? A Passover Haggadah for Family Celebration.* New York: Simon & Schuster, 2000.
> An excellent *Haggadah* for families with young children. The bright illustrations suggest folk art.

Silberman, Shoshana. *A Family Haggadah.* Rockville, MD: Kar-Ben Copies, 1987.
> A Haggadah designed for families with young children, with just the right amount of text and commentary. Prayers and songs are transliterated.

Wark, Mary Ann Barrow. *We Tell It To Our Children: The Story of Passover: A Haggadah for Seders with Young Children.* St. Paul, MN: Mt. Zion Hebrew Congregation Rabbi's Publication Fun and Mensch Makers Press, 1988.
> A participatory *Haggadah* that features puppets, ideal for families with small children or for Religious School. Includes nine puppets (Moses, Miriam, Pharaoh, Taskmaster, Slave, etc.) to cut out.

Infant To 2 Years

Groner, Judye, and Madeline Wikler. *Where Is the Afikomen?* Rockville, MD: Kar-Ben Copies, 1989. (Ages infant-2)
> A toddler treasure hunt to find the *afikoman.* (Board Book)

Kress, Camille. *A Tree Trunk Seder.* New York: UAHC Press, 2000. (Ages infant-2)
> Join the squirrel family as they celebrate with *matzah,* a *Haggadah,* a *Seder,* and laughter and song. The beautiful illustrations of the author are sure to make this book a delightful addition to Passover.

Nerlove, Miriam. *Passover.* Morton Grove, IL: Albert Whitman & Company, 1989. (Ages 2-5)
> Simple telling of the Pesach story.

Wikler, Madeline. *Let's Have a Seder.* Rockville, MD: Kar-Ben Copies, 1997. (Ages infant-2)
> A very first *Seder* service in rhyme. (Board Book)

Wikler, Madeline, and Judye Groner. *I Have Four Questions.* Rockville, MD: Kar-Ben Copies, 1988. (Ages infant-2)
> A colorful retelling of the classic questions asked by the youngest child at the *Seder.* (Board Book)

3 Years

Bogot, Howard, and Mary Bogot. *Seder with the Animals.* New York: CCAR Press, 1995. (Ages 3-8)
> Beautiful illustrations involve animals and the senses in learning about the *Seder.*

Hildebrand, Ziporah. *This Is Our Seder.* New York: Holiday House, 1999. (Ages 3-7)
> Simple story of a family's celebration of Passover. The symbols, food, and traditions are depicted in colorful, humorous illustrations.

Medoff, Francine. *The Mouse in the Matzah Factory.* Rockville, MD: Kar-Ben Copies, 1983. (Ages 3-8)
> A mouse follows the process of *matzah* making from wheat harvest to the store.

Miller, Deborah Uchill. *Only Nine Chairs: A Tall Tale for Passover.* Rockville, MD: Kar-Ben Copies, 1982. (Ages 3-8)
> What to do if there are 19 guests at the *Seder,* but only nine chairs. In ryhme.

Rouss, Sylvia. *Sammy Spider's First Passover.* Rockville, MD: Kar-Ben Copies, 1995. (Ages 3-6)
> Sammy wants to help find the *afikoman,* but his mother tells him to spin a web instead.

Topek, Susan Remick. *A Taste for Noah.* Rockville, MD: Kar-Ben Copies, 1993. (Ages 3-7)

Though he tastes it reluctantly, Noah loves *charoset.*

Zalman, Jane Breskin. *Happy Passover, Rosie.* New York: Henry Holt & Company, 1990. (Ages 3-6)
Rosie celebrates Pesach with her family.

Zusman, Evelyn. *The Passover Parrot.* Rockville, MD: Kar-Ben Copies, 1983. (Ages 3-8)
The pet parrot can sing the Four Questions better than Leba.

4 To 5 Years

Cohen, Barbara. *The Carp in the Bathtub.* Rockville, MD: Kar-Ben Copies, 1972. (Ages 4-10)
Leah and Harry try to save Joe the fish from becoming gefilte fish.

Fishman, Cathy. *On Passover.* New York: Atheneum Books for Young Readers, 1997. (Ages 4-8)
A little girl learns about Pesach as she helps her family prepare.

Goldin, Barbara Diamond. *The Magician's Visit.* New York: Viking, 1993. (Ages 4-8)
A poor couple is rewarded for their hospitality by a mysterious magician.

Heymsfeld, Carla. *The Matzah Ball Fairy.* New York: UAHC Press, 1996. (Ages 4-8)
The Matzah Ball Fairy's magic adds lots of lift to the *Seder.*

Lepon, Shoshana. *Ten Plagues of Egypt.* New York: The Judaica Press, 1988. (Ages 4-8)
The plagues, with dramatic and bold illustrations.

Manushkin, Fran. *The Matzah the Papa Brought Home.* New York: Scholastic, 1995. (Ages 4-8)
A Passover story in the style of *This Is the House That Jack Built.*

Polacco, Patricia. *Mrs. Katz and Tush.* New York: Picture Yearling, 1994. (Ages 4-8)
Mrs. Katz and Darnell grow a friendship around a cat named Tush, and learn how their own histories are similar.

Poskanzer, Susan Cornell. *What Can It Be? Riddles About Passover.* Englewood Cliffs, NJ: Silver Press, 1991. (Ages 4-6)
Riddles about Passover to test and delight.

Schilder, Rosalind. *Dayenu — Or How Uncle Murray Saved the Seder.* Rockville, MD: Kar-Ben Copies, 1988. (Ages 4-9)
Aunt Helen tries to skip some of the steps for *Seder,* but Uncle Murray saves the day.

Schwartz, Lynne. *The Four Questions.* New York: Penguin Group, 1989. (Ages 4-6)
The Four Questions accompanied by unusual and delightful illustrations.

Silverman, Erica. *Gittel's Hands.* Mahwah, NJ: Bridgewater Books, 1996. (Ages 4-6)
What Gittel can make with her hands surprises everyone.

CHAPTER 17

YOM HAATZMA'UT

"If you will it, it is no dream." (Theodor Herzl, Der Judenstaat [The Jewish State], 1896)

For this reason we are gathered here today . . . and by virtue of the . . . historical rights vested in us . . . we hereby proclaim the establishment of a state in the Land of Israel, to be known as the State of Israel. (David Ben-Gurion, the Declaration of Independence, 1948)

OVERVIEW

We have barely emptied our shelves of *matzah* and it is time to celebrate the birth of our Jewish country, Israel. On the fifth day of the Hebrew month of Iyar in 5708 (May 14, 1948), Israel's first Prime Minister, David Ben-Gurion, proclaimed the creation of the new state. Yom HaAtzma'ut, Israeli Independence Day, was declared a holiday the next year. Each year in Israel, Yom HaAtzma'ut is celebrated with parades and sirens and large celebrations. When Americans celebrate the Fourth of July (American Independence Day), most feel quite distant from the men and women who fought for independence from England and created the country. However, almost every Israeli has a family member, or family members, who fought in wars, and perhaps died, so as to make Israel a reality and keep her safe. The national anthem, *"HaTikvah,"* gives voice to how long we have hoped for and dreamed of our own state.

Israel is a small country, about the size of New Jersey. Within her borders, the land is the model of variety. There are mountains and deserts; beaches with water in which to swim; the Dead Sea which is thick with salt and minerals; busy cities and small, isolated towns; as well as *kibbutzeem,* where people live and work all together. The people of Israel are as varied as the land. Jews make up the majority of the population. Jews come to live in Israel from all over the world: Eastern Europe, Yemen, Morocco, Iran, Iraq, U.S.A., Russia, Ethiopia — the list goes on to include over 70 countries. When a Jew moves to Israel, he/she doesn't just immigrate. We say that the person has made *"aliyah,"* literally *"to go up."* Although it is the Jewish Homeland, Israel is home to more than just Jews. Arabs, Muslims, Druse, Christians, and Bedouin, among others, also call the country of Israel home. (For more detailed information on Israel, see Chapter 6, "Israel All Year.")

For the youngest children, a celebration of Yom HaAtzma'ut will consist of the following: Hebrew music, playing with the colors blue and white and with more concrete Israeli symbols (a seven-branched *menorah*, clothes, animals such as camels), and perhaps a birthday party with a blue and white cake and a big stuffed Israel in the birthday chair. Older children can learn more in depth about Israel, and can even take a pretend trip to Israel, complete with passports and tickets and a *falafel* lunch. Perhaps they can "go to visit" their pen pals?

You can make Israel a part of your room all year. Play Hebrew and Israeli music regularly. Hang pictures and maps of Israel in the room through-out the year. Invite family members and friends who have been to Israel to talk about their trip and share pictures and momentos. Add Israeli scarves to the dress up clothes; keep Israeli foods (pita, empty food packages from Israel) in the kitchen corner. Occasionally cover the tables with Hebrew newspapers during art projects. When making a calendar, include the Hebrew months as well as the English months. When talking about the daily weather, mention what the weather is like in Israel. When celebrating holidays, talk about how children in Israel are celebrating the holiday. Sing Hebrew songs, even when it is not Shabbat or a holiday. Use Hebrew for "please" and "thank you," body parts, and so on. (See Chapter 6, "Israel All Year" for more suggestions and activities.)

It is tempting to celebrate Yom HaAtzma'ut by loading all of the children on a pretend airplane and "flying" off to Israel for a day or two or three. This can be a wonderful idea, especially if the children have been forming a connection to Israel all year. However, we must be careful not to create a "tourist curriculum," as it is called in *Anti-Bias Curriculum: Tools for Empowering Young Children* by Louise Derman-Sparks and the ABC Task Force, NAECY, 1989. In other words, if we talk about

Israel for a week, then strap the kids into a "plane," fly to Israel, visit one or two places, and head back home, we risk giving the children a very stereotypical, exotic view of Israel. This is not a good way to build the foundation for a relationship we hope will grow throughout the children's entire lives.

There are other effective ways of establishing a meaningful relationship with Israel: making Israel part of the daily or weekly culture of the class, explaining how Israeli children celebrate the holidays, discussing what the weather is like in Israel throughout the year, arranging for pen pal relationships, showing photographs from a classmate's or teacher's visit to Israel, etc. If you are doing all these things, then a fantasy trip to Israel can be a fun and concrete way to continue and build on the already established relationship with the Jewish Homeland.

To research a fantasy trip to Israel, reflect on your own trip (if you're lucky enough to have been

GLOSSARY AND HEBREW VOCABULARY

עֲלִיָּה	Aliyah	literally, "going up"; to move to Israel
עַצְמָאוּת	Atzma'ut	independence
מָטוֹס	Matos	airplane
דֶּגֶל	Degel	flag
הַתִּקְוָה	"HaTikvah"	The national anthem of Israel; literally, "The Hope"
יִשְׂרָאֵל	Israel	the Jewish Homeland; a state in the Middle East
כָּחֹל	Kachol	blue
קִבּוּץ	Kibbutz	collective farm
כּוֹתֶל	Kotel	the Western Wall
כּוֹבַע	Kova	hat
לָבָן	Lavan	white
מִזְרָח	Mizrach	East
שָׁלוֹם	Shalom	peace, hello, goodbye
שֶׁקֶל	Shekel	Israeli currency
שׁוּק	Shuk	market
יִשְׂרָאֵל	Yisrael	Hebrew for Israel
יוֹם	Yom	day
יוֹם הָעַצְמָאוּת	Yom HaAtzma'ut	Israeli Independence Day, the fifth of Iyar
יוֹם הֻלֶּדֶת שָׂמֵחַ	Yom Huledet Sameach	Happy Birthday

Figure 29

to Israel), and consult religious school textbooks about Israel. See especially *Our Jerusalem* by Yaffa Ganz, *I Live in Israel* by Max Frankel and Judy Hoffman, and *A Young Person's History of Israel* by David Bamberger.

Israel is our Jewish Homeland. The concept of "country" is in itself a difficult one for our children to grasp. Trying to give them a sense of commitment, a sense of connection, and a sense of pride in Israel, a place most of our students have never seen, is even more difficult.

If we can give our children the foundation for a strong, caring bond with Israel, we will have done both our children and the Jewish people a great service. How good it is to go right from Passover to Yom HaAtzma'ut! Our people struggled to gain their freedom from Egypt. They triumphed and set out for Israel. Now we celebrate the existence of our Jewish homeland. To understand Yom HaAtzma'ut in this light gives a person, even a four-year-old, a tremendous sense of history and belonging and pride.

For a glossary and Hebrew vocabulary list, see figure 29 on the previous page.

CONCEPTS

WEBBING THE CONCEPTS

Webbing the concepts of Yom HaAtzma'ut (see Chapter 1, "Developmentally Appropriate Practice," p. 11 for more on webbing), can elicit ideas about what you want children to think about and what you want children to learn (and not just what you want them to make). This technique can also bring to mind connections to other things going on in your classroom. Figure 30 on the following page is the *beginning* of a web for Yom HaAtzma'ut. You can extend the web with your co-teachers or your students, thus shaping the celebration of Yom HaAtzma'ut to include the interests of everyone in your class. *You won't cover everything you web*, but you'll get a good idea of where you want to go.

INFANT TO 24 MONTHS
1. Israel is the Jewish home.
2. People in Israel speak Hebrew.
3. I can say some words and sing songs in Hebrew.
4. I can help Israel celebrate its birthday.
5. I can explore the symbols of Israel, such as the blue and white colors of the flag and the seven-branched *menorah*.

2 YEARS
1. Israel is the Jewish home.
2. People in Israel speak Hebrew.
3. I can say some words and sing songs in Hebrew.
4. I can help Israel celebrate its birthday.
5. I can explore symbols of Israel, such as the blue and white colors of the flag and the seven-branched *menorah*.
6. Children in Israel like to play just like me.
7. Israel is far away. We travel on an airplane to get there.
8. Yom HaAtzma'ut is Israel's birthday.

3 YEARS
1. Israel is the Jewish home. Israel is also my home.
2. People in Israel speak Hebrew.
3. I can say some words and sing songs in Hebrew.
4. Yom HaAtzma'ut is Israel's birthday.
5. I can help Israel celebrate its birthday.
6. I can explore symbols of Israel, such as the blue and white flag and the seven-branched *menorah*.
7. Children in Israel like to play just as I do.
8. Israel is far away. We travel on an airplane to get there.
9. Israel is over 50 years old.
10. People in Israel celebrate Yom HaAtzma'ut with dancing and singing and parties.
11. Jewish soldiers fought hard to make Israel a country. We are proud of them when we celebrate Yom HaAtzma'ut.

12. We pray for peace and no more wars in Israel. We pray that all the people in Israel can be friends.

13. In Israel there are mountains, deserts, oceans, rivers and lakes, and cities. There are many trees which Jewish people from all around the world have helped to plant.

4 TO 5 YEARS

1. Israel is the Jewish home. Israel is also my home.
2. People in Israel speak Hebrew.
3. I can say some words and sing songs in Hebrew.
4. Yom HaAtzma'ut is Israel's birthday. Yom HaAtzma'ut means Independence Day.

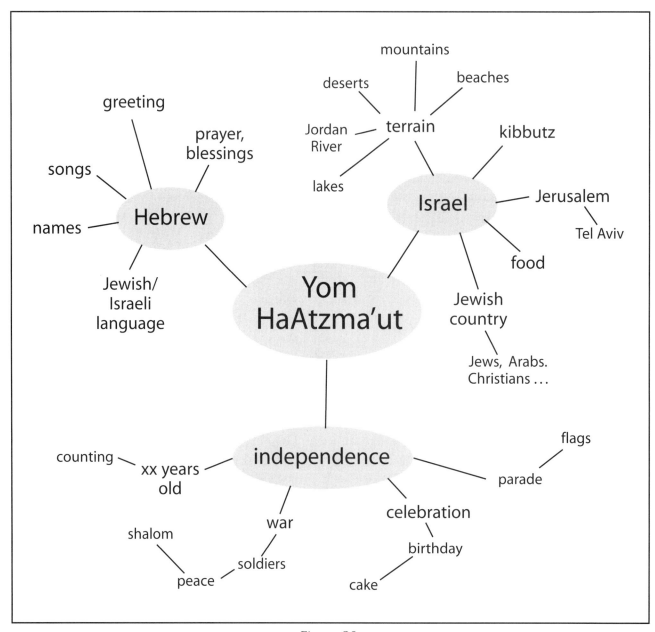

Figure 30

5. Israel is over 50 years old.
6. I can help Israel celebrate its birthday.
7. People in Israel celebrate Yom HaAtzma'ut with dancing and singing and parties.
8. I can sing *"HaTikvah,"* the Israeli national anthem.
9. I can explore symbols of Israel, such as the blue and white flag and the seven-branched *menorah*.
10. Children in Israel like to play just like me.
11. Israel is far away. We travel on an airplane to get there.
12. Jewish soldiers fought hard to make Israel a country. We are proud of them when we celebrate Yom HaAtzma'ut.
13. We pray for peace and no more wars in Israel. We pray that all the people in Israel can be friends.
14. In Israel there are mountains, deserts, oceans, rivers and lakes, and cities. There are many trees which Jewish people from all around the world have helped to plant.
15. Seasons are different in Israel.
16. I can find Israel on a map. Israel is very small.
17. Jews come from all over the world to live in Israel.
18. Many of the places we read about in the Torah are in Israel.
19. The Land of Israel is a very old place. Archaeologists dig to find out about people who lived in the Land of Israel long ago.
20. The Land of Israel is a very old place, but the State of Israel is a young place.
21. I can send and receive pictures and letters from my Israeli pen pals.

ACTIVITIES

LANGUAGE ARTS

1. Build a *Kotel* in your room or school. Write prayers to place in the cracks between the "stones."
2. Talk about what it means to fight for your country. Write letters to soldiers in the Israeli army.
3. Make your room into an Israeli *shuk* (market). Make buses to drive around in, and write *"Egged"* (the name of the main Israeli bus company) on the sides. Make Israeli money to spend at the *shuk*.
4. Make a Hebrew writing center with Hebrew letter stamps, stencils, *alef bet* charts, and Hebrew newspapers.
5. Make letter magnets in Hebrew and English available all the time.
6. Read *And Shira Imagined* by Giora Carmi. Let the children verbalize what Shira imagined on the pages that have no words.
7. Compare the Israeli celebration of Yom HaAtzma'ut to the American celebration of Fourth of July (or the celebration of Canada Day).

SCIENCE

1. Turn your sand box/table into an archeological dig. Hide items for the children to find.
2. Bake a cake for Israel's birthday. Bake milk and honey cookies.
3. Play with the colors blue and white. Finger paint, make a collage with blue and white objects, have blue pudding with whipped cream for snack.
4. Put camels and people and tents into your sand table.
5. Cover the blocks so they look like Jerusalem stone, and let the kids build Jerusalem or the *Kotel*. Or build a big *Kotel* with all the hollow blocks.
6. Taste some Israeli fruits.
7. Make orange juice. Talk about Jaffa oranges.
8. Freeze grapes and eat them frozen.

MATH

1. Count out Israel's age. Make footprints, one for each of Israel's years, and let Israel's "history" trail through the halls of your school.

2. Count the candles you put on Israel's birthday cake.

3. In two jars, put birthday candles. One jar with the number of candles for America's age, the other jar with candles equaling Israel's age. Let children compare and discuss.

4. Supply photos and drawing of different kinds of terrain in Israel — mountains, lakes, rivers, the Old City of Jerusalem, fields of crops — for children to sort and seriate (arrange in a series – e.g., smallest to largest, lightest to darkest, etc.).

ART

1. Examine a *tallit* and the Israeli flag. Let the children know that the stripes on the flag come from the *tallit*, because Israel is a Jewish country. Give the children all sorts of different materials with which to make an Israeli flag. (Don't worry if the stripes aren't straight!)

2. Paint a desert scene mural, complete with camels. Put sand in the paint.

3. Make a big birthday card for Israel.

4. Make a big stuffed paper Israel, which can then sit in the birthday chair at the party.

5. Make cards to send to your Israeli pen pals to wish them Yom HaAtzma'ut *Sameach* (Happy Independence Day).

6. After reading *Joshua's Dream*, give the children lots of different kinds of collage/art materials, and on a large mural, allow them to "Make the Desert Bloom." Label each child's contribution and hang where everyone can see. Be sure to use sand as one of the materials.

7. Jews all over the world pray in the direction of Jerusalem, to the east. In Hebrew, "east" is מִזְרָח *(mizrach)*. So as to know which direction is east, many Jews hang a *mizrach* picture on their east wall. Such a *mizrach* frequently pictures Jerusalem or the *Kotel*. Make a class *mizrach* using images cut from Jewish New Years cards or a catalog from a Jewish gallery, or cut and glue construction paper to look like the *Kotel*. Be sure to include the word *"mizrach"* in Hebrew and/or English. Hang your *mizrach* on an east wall of the classroom.

MUSIC/MOVEMENT

(With musical contributions from Julie Jaslow Auerbach)

1. Reintroduce the Israeli songs and dances presented at Tu B'Shevat.

2. Use Israeli flags as props for the song *"Achshav"* that was introduced at Tu B'Shevat. Instruments and the dance can also be used (see Tu B'Shevat Music/Movement activity #8).

3. Sing "Shtuyot (Let's All Take a Trip!)" by Julie Jaslow Auerbach (see Appendix A, p. 356 for music and lyrics). Use this song as an opportunity to teach some basic Hebrew expressions. I learned the ones in this song from the Israeli *shlicheem* for our JCC camps. Teach the children the refrain first, then the Hebrew vocabulary. After they are comfortable with the song, children can act out the situations.

4. Listen to *"HaTikvah,"* the Israeli national anthem. Have children draw pictures of what they think Israel looks like. Here are the words:

Kol od b'layvav p'nimah
Nefesh y'hudi homiyah
Ul'fa'atay mizrach kadimah
Ayin l'tzion tzofiah.
Od lo avdah tikvataynu
Hatikva bat sh'note alpayim
Lihyot am chofshi b'artzaynu
Eretz tzion v'Yerushalayim.

As long as in the depths of the heart
The Jewish soul still yearns
And towards the East,
The eye continues to seek Zion.
We have not yet lost our hope,
The hope of two thousand years
To be a free nation in our homeland
The land of Zion and Jerusalem.

5. Sing *"Heenay Rakevet."* Form a train as you sing and go around the room.

Heenay rakevet	Here comes a train
He mistovevet	That goes around
Al galgaleem (3X)	On wheels (3X)
Woo Woo	Woo woo

6. Sing (*"Yom Huledet Sameach"*) (Happy Birthday to You) to Israel in Hebrew. Here are the words:

Yom huledet sameach (4X)

7. Play games such as *Shimon Omer (Simon Says)*.

8. Act out walking through different parts of Israel: climbing a hill, climbing Masada, swimming in Lake Kinneret, floating in the Dead Sea, kissing the *Kotel*, plowing a field on a *kibbutz*.

9. Sing songs in Hebrew. Substitute Hebrew words in songs such as "The Eensy Weensy *Akavish* [spider]" and "Head Shoulder Knees and Toes." Here are the words to these two songs:

The eensy weensy *akaveesh*
Climbed up the *myeem* spout
Down came the *geshem* and washed the *akaveesh* out.
Out came the *shemesh* and dried up all the *geshem*
And the eensy weensy *akaveesh*
Climbed up the spout again.

Rosh, kitafayeem, berkayeem, raglayeem (2X)
Aynayeem, oznayeem, peh, v'af
Rosh, kitafayeem, berkayeem, raglayeem

Note: For other such songs, see Chapter 17, "Yom HaAtzma'ut," p. 264.

10. Sing "Hebrew Counting Song" by Julie Jaslow Auerbach (see Appendix A, p. 340).

SONG/MUSIC LIST
(Contributed by Julie Jaslow Auerbach)

The following listing includes the songs in this chapter, as well as songs from other sources that are related to Yom Haatzma'ut concepts. Each song and the book in which it is located is specified, along with the page number. (Please note: In this and other holiday chapters, there are many songs which are "preschool traditional," i.e., they have been around so long that no one knows the composer or the song's origin! Every effort has been made to find the source for all the songs listed.)

Birthday
"Am Yisrael Chai" – *The New Children's Songbook*, p. 40
"Happy Birthday" – traditional (see Music/Movement activity #6 above)
"Sing & Shout Hooray" – *Sing and Celebrate*, p. 40
"Happy Birthday for Yom Ha'Atzmaut" – *Shirim Al Galgalim*, p. 30
"Yom Huledet" – *The New Children's Songbook*, p. 51

Celebrate
"Chag Sameach" – *The New Children's Songbook*, p. 33 (see Sukkot, Music/Movement activity #7, p. 169)
"If You're Happy" – preschool traditional
With cake: *"Uga, Uga"* – *The New Children's Songbook*, p. 60
With dancing: *"Achshav"* – *The New Children's Songbook*, p. 61 (see Music/Movement activity #2 above)
With flags: *"Degel Tov"* – *The New Children's Songbook*, p. 21
With parade and instruments: "Israeli March Medley" – *The Barry Sisters in Israel*
"Am Yisrael Chai" – *The New Children's Songbook*, p. 40
"The Hebrew Counting Song" – Julie Jaslow Auerbach (see Music/Movement activity #10 above)

Hebrew
"Af Peh Ozen" – *Manginot*, p. 25
"Alef Bet" – *Manginot*, p. 46
"The Jewish Calendar Song" – Julie Jaslow Auerbach

"Ma Mezeg Ha'avir" – Julie Jaslow Auerbach (see Tu B'Shevat Music/Movement activity #9 on p. 204)

"Shalom Ema" – *Sing a Jewish Song*, "Miss Jackie"

"Shtuyot (Let's All Take a Trip)" – Julie Jaslow Auerbach (see Music/Movement activity #3 above)

"Slicha, Toda, B'vakasha" – *The New Children's Songbook*, p. 19

Israel

"Achshav" – *The New Children's Songbook*, p. 61 (see Music/Movement activity #2 above)

"Am Yisrael Chai" – *The New Children's Songbook*, p. 40

"David Melech Yisrael" – *The New Children's Songbook*, p. 11 (see Tu B'Shevat Music/Movement activity #14, p. 204)

"Degel Tov" – *The New Children's Songbook*, p. 21

"Eretz Zavat Chalav" – *Manginot*, p. 258

"Kachol V'lavan" – *Israel in Song*, p. 31

"Mi Yivneh Hagalil" – *Songs We Sing*, p. 353 (see Tu B'Shevat Music/Movement activity #13, p. 204)

"Shtuyot (Let's All Take a Trip)" – Julie Jaslow Auerbach (see Music/Movement activity #3 above)

"Ufaratza" – *Manginot*, p. 257

CIRCLE TIME

1. Play *Israel's on the Phone*. Hold a phone, and hand a phone to a child. Tell the children that you are calling from Israel and you can only speak Hebrew, although you understand English. Pretend to call the child with the phone. Begin with the child's name and say, *"Shalom."* Continue the conversation using only Hebrew. The child can respond in English or Hebrew. Use lots of facial expressions and hand movements to help convey meaning. Keep the conversation short and simple. End each conversation with, *"L'hitraot.* Bye." Have the child pass the phone on to the next child.

2. Make a chart of the children's definitions of peace/*shalom.*

OUTDOORS/FIELD TRIPS

1. Take a walk to look at flags flying. Compare and discuss sizes, heights, designs. Take pictures of the flags you see so you can continue the discussion back in class.

2. Take a walk to compare your local terrain to Israel's. Are you in a big city like Tel Aviv? Do you have hills like Jerusalem? fields of crops as on a *kibbutz*?

3. On the playground, draw a large circle made up of little Israeli flags. Have snack or lunch inside the circle of flags.

SPECIFICALLY FOR INFANTS

1. Visit another class and share their birthday celebration until babies' attention spans run out.

IDEAS FOR TEACHING FAMILIES

1. Alert families to community celebrations or a local Walk for Israel in which they can participate as a family.

2. Invite family members in to help "fly" your class to Israel.

3. Invite in Hebrew speaking family members to teach the children some Hebrew words or songs. Teach other families the words the children learn through newsletters or by posting lists.

4. Invite in family members who have made a trip to Israel to share pictures and stories of their trip.

5. If the children have been corresponding with Israeli pen pals, inform parents about the pen pals and share with them the letters you receive.

6. Recommended reading: *Israel* by Fabio Bourbon, and *Kids Love Israel/Israel Loves Kids* by Barbara Sofer.

SUGGESTED NEWSLETTER ARTICLE

Yom HaAtzma'ut, Israeli Independence Day, is the fifth of Iyar, which corresponds this year to _____ [insert secular date]. Yom HaAtzma'ut is a wonderful time to share with your child how special Israel, our very own Jewish country, is to us. You can celebrate with your child by participating in community celebrations. In school, the children will be getting ready to celebrate Israel's birthday. They may play with the colors blue and white, learn some Hebrew, make an Israeli flag, or learn about animal life in the desert. They may even take a pretend trip to Israel.

Many of the older classes have been writing back and forth to pen pals in Israel this year. This pen pal relationship helps our children understand children in Israel (and see how similar they are). Our children have enjoyed sending and receiving letters, photos, and drawings, and their connection to Israel has really been strengthened.

Over 50 years ago, the dream of the Jewish people became a reality. We are proud to plant in our children the seeds of pride, love, and belonging to Israel, our Jewish Homeland. Enjoy celebrating with your child!

RECIPES

HONEY COOKIES

Ingredients
3 eggs
½ C. sugar
½ C. oil
8 oz. honey
3½ C. flour
1 tsp. baking soda

Directions
1. In a large mixer, beat eggs, sugar, oil, and honey together until well blended, about 5 to 7 minutes.
2. Gradually sift in flour and baking soda.
3. Refrigerate overnight.
4. Preheat over to 350°.
5. Flour hands well. Make one-inch balls of dough. Place on floured cookie sheets and flatten balls.
6. Bake for 12 to 15 minutes until golden brown. Remove from cookie sheet to cool.

(Makes 5 dozen cookies)

ISRAELI SALAD

Ingredients
2 large tomatoes
2 cucumbers
1 large onion
4 tbs. finely chopped parsley
juice of ½ lemon
¼ C. extra virgin olive oil
salt and pepper to taste
chopped fresh mint, optional

Directions
1. Dice tomatoes, cucumbers, and onion into very small pieces.
2. Squeeze lemon juice over diced vegetables.
3. Add parsley, olive oil, and salt, pepper and/or mint. Toss well.

BIBLIOGRAPHY

Note: For more books appropriate for Yom HaAtzma'ut, see Chapter 6, "Israel All Year."

ADULTS

Bamberger, David. *A Young Person's History of Israel.* 2d ed. West Orange, NJ: Behrman House, 1995.
> A textbook designed for Grades 5-7 that traces the story of the Jewish people and their Homeland from biblical to modern times.

Bourbon, Fabio. *Israel.* New York: Smithmark Publishers, 1994.
> A beautiful pictorial view of Israel's land, cultures, and peoples.

Cohen, David. *Jerusalem: In the Shadow of Heaven.* San Francisco, CA: Collins, 1996.
> Photographic journal of the city of Jerusalem.

Ganz, Yaffa. *Our Jerusalem.* West Orange, NJ: Behrman House, 1977.
> A set of eight four-page folders which present a tour of Jerusalem through the eyes of a young child.

Paris, Alan. *Jerusalem 3000: Kids Discover the City of Gold.* New York: Pitspopany Press, 1995.
> The history of Jerusalem as revealed by archeological research.

Sofer, Barbara. *Kids Love Israel/Israel Loves Kids.* Rockville, MD: Kar-Ben Copies, 1996.
> A terrific guide to Israel for anyone traveling with kids.

CHIDREN

Note: For more children's books appropriate for Yom HaAtzma'ut, see Chapter 6, "Israel All Year."

3 Years

Carmi, Giora. *And Shira Imagined.* Philadelphia, PA: Jewish Publication Society, 1988. (Ages 3-8)
> On a trip to Israel, a young girl imagines as her parents describe Israel's cities. Out of print, but worth looking for.

Roberts, Behany, and Patricia Hubbell. *Camel Caravan.* New York: William Morrow, 1996. (Ages 3-6)
> Catch a wild ride with some camels that have had enough of hauling loads across the desert.

4 To 5 Years

Edwards, Michelle. *Chicken Man.* New York: Mulberry Paperback Books, 1991. (Ages 4-8)
> A silly story about life on a *kibbutz.*

Grand, Samuel and, Tamar Grand. *The Children of Israel.* New York: UAHC Press, 1972. (Ages 5-8)
> Too much text for preschoolers, but good for pictures of Israeli children.

Nover, Elizabeth Z. *My Land of Israel.* West Orange, NJ: Behrman House, 1987.
> Activity pages which lead children on an imaginary trip to Israel.

Roseman, Kenneth. *All in My Jewish Family.* New York: UAHC Press, 1984. (Ages 5-8)
> Good for photos of the Jewish children in familiar and exotic communities.

Note: To find familiar books, such as *Cat in the Hat* by Dr. Seuss, *Goodnight Moon* by Margaret Wise Brown, and *Where the Wild Things Are* by Maurice Sendak in Hebrew, contact Multilingual Books, 12-5 East Pike St., Seattle, WA 98122, (800) 218-2757, fax: (206) 328-7447, www.esl.net/mbt/hebrew.html.

CHAPTER 18

SHAVUOT

You shall count off seven weeks; start to count the seven weeks when the sickle is first put to the standing grain. Then you shall observe the Feast of Weeks for Adonai *your God, offering your freewill contribution according as* Adonai *your God has blessed you.* (Deuteronomy 16:9-10)

OVERVIEW

The passage above the Torah spells out the origin of the holiday of Shavuot (Feast of Weeks). Shavuot occurs on the sixth of Sivan, the fiftieth day after the first day of Passover (we count seven weeks in between the two holidays). Originally, the holiday of Shavuot celebrated the end of the grain harvest. Shavuot is one of the three pilgrimage festivals (along with Passover and Sukkot). In bibilical times, the Jews celebrated Shavuot by bringing offerings from the harvest to the Temple in Jerusalem *(Chag HaKatzir)*. They also celebrated the beginning of a new agricultural season by bringing the first fruits to the Temple as well *(Chag HaBikureem)*.

When the Temple was destroyed in 70 C.E., the nature of Shavuot began to change. The holiday became associated with the giving of the Ten Commandments at Mt. Sinai, which occurred in Sivan (the same Hebrew month in which Shavuot takes place).

Today we celebrate Shavuot by decorating the synagogue with greens to remember the first fruits which the Jewish farmers brought to the Temple, and by staying up all night to study *(Tikkun Layl Shavuot)*. It is traditional to read the Book of Ruth, because the story takes place around harvest time, and because the story traces lineage from Ruth to King David who, according to legend, was born and died on Shavuot.

We also eat dairy foods, such as blintzes and cheesecake. One reason for this is because the words of Torah are like milk and honey. Another reason for eating dairy, according to folklore, is that after receiving the Ten Commandments at Sinai, the Jewish people were too tired to cook. They trudged back to their tents and feasted on milk and cheese and other easy to fix foods. Some say that two blintzes remind us of the two tablets of the law. Many synagogues hold Confirmation on Shavuot, tying together the end of the school year, the giving of the Torah to the Jewish people, and the expression of commitment of young people to their Jewish faith.

For a glossary and Hebrew vocabulary list, see figure 31 on the following page.

SHAVUOT CONCEPTS

WEBBING THE CONCEPTS

Webbing the concepts of Shavuot (see Chapter 1, "Developmentally Appropriate Practice," p. 11 for more on webbing), can elicit ideas about what you want children to think about and what you want children to learn (and not just what you want them to make). This technique can also bring to mind connections to other things going on in your classroom. Figure 32 on page 253 is the *beginning* of a web for Shavuot. You can extend the web with your co-teachers or your students, thus shaping the celebration of Shavuot to include the interests of everyone in your class. *You won't cover everything you web*, but you'll get a good idea of where you want to go.

Note: By Shavuot, most of the twos have turned three, and so on, so you may want to read through all the concepts to decide which ones are appropriate for your children.

INFANT TO 2 YEARS

1. Shavuot is our Jewish holiday.
2. Shavuot is a spring holiday.
3. We decorate our room with flowers and greens for Shavuot.

3 YEARS

1. Shavuot is our Jewish holiday.
2. Shavuot is a spring holiday.
3. We decorate our room and the synagogue with flowers and greens for Shavuot.
4. Shavuot ends the cycle that begins with Passover.
5. Shavuot marks the time of the barley harvest.
6. We bring *bikureem* and other foods to help people who don't have enough food to eat.

7. Shavuot marks the time when Moses received the Ten Commandments from God at Mt. Sinai.
8. The Ten Commandments are ten especially important rules in the Torah.
9. We eat dairy foods, such as blintzes and cheesecake, because the words of Torah are like milk and honey.
10. On Shavuot, we hear the story of Ruth from the Bible; the story takes place at harvest time.

4 TO 5 YEARS

1. Shavuot is a Jewish holiday in the spring.
2. We decorate our room and the synagogue with flowers and greens for Shavuot.
3. Shavuot is the fiftieth day after Passover. It comes after we finish counting the 49 days of the *Omer*.
4. Shavuot ends the cycle that begins with Passover.
5. Shavuot marks the time of the barley and wheat harvest.
6. We bring *bikureem* and other foods to help people who don't have enough food to eat.

G L O S S A R Y A N D H E B R E W V O C A B U L A R Y		
בִּכּוּרִים	*Bikureem*	first fruit of the harvest
חַג הַבִּכּוּרִים	*Chag HaBikureem*	Holiday of the First Fruits
חַג הַקָּצִיר	*Chag HaKatzir*	Holiday of the Harvest
חֶסֶד	*Chesed*	loving-kindness
עוֹמֶר	*Omer*	a measure of grain, which the Jewish people brought to the Temple as a thanksgiving offering; we count the period of the *Omer (Sifirat HaOmer)* from the second day of Passover until Shavuot (49 days, or seven weeks).
שָׁבוּעוֹת	Shavuot	Feast of Weeks, celebrated seven weeks after Passover
	Ten Commandments	the ten very significant laws in the Torah, given to the Jewish people at Mt. Sinai
תִּקּוּן לֵיל שָׁבוּעוֹת	*Tikkun Layl Shavuot*	all night study sesion on the night of Shavuot
תּוֹרָה	Torah	the Five Books of Moses; the first five books of the Hebrew Bible
זְמַן מַתָּן תּוֹרָתֵנוּ	*Z'man Matan Torataynu*	Time of the giving of the Torah

Figure 31

7. Shavuot also marks the time when Moses received the Ten Commandments from God at Mt. Sinai.
8. The Ten Commandments are ten especially important rules in the Torah.
9. We eat dairy foods such as blintzes and cheesecake because the words of Torah are like milk and honey.
10. We hear the story of Ruth because it takes place at harvest time.
11. From Ruth, Naomi, and Boaz we learn about loyalty, helping others, kindness (*chesed*), and *Tzedakah.*
12. In Israel, summer is beginning. Many *kibbutzeem* have a parade and march with their

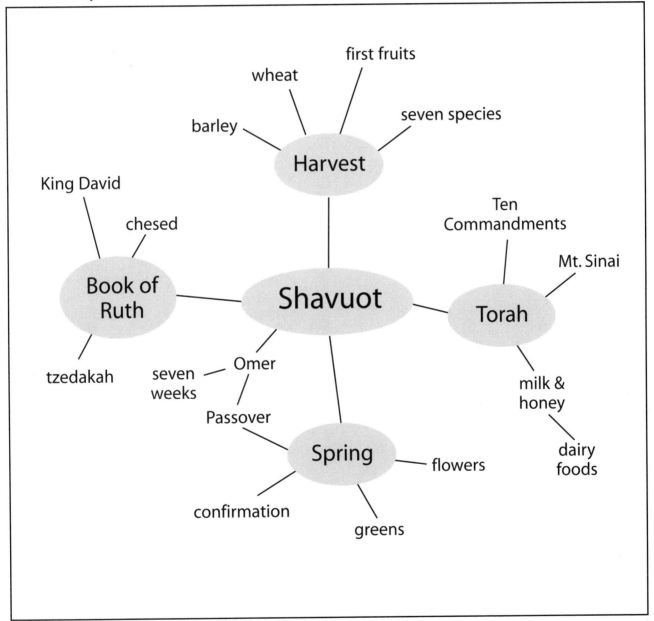

Figure 32

own first fruits. Afterward, they have a party with milk and honey biscuits.

ACTIVITIES

LANGUAGE ARTS

1. Tell the story of Ruth. It is also a good story to act out.
2. Make a felt board of the characters in the story of Ruth so the children can retell it on their own.
3. Tell the story of Moses and the Israelite people at Mt. Sinai. This is also a very good story to act out, to make a felt board about, or to make illustrations for.
4. Set up a sheet tent in the room and let the children experience life in a tent. What it was like to come out of Egypt and through the desert to Mt. Sinai? What signs of spring did the Jewish people see in the desert?
5. Read some of *The 11th Commandment* by The Children of America, and let your children dictate and illustrate their own eleventh commandment.
6. Read *Ten Good Rules,* and make up Ten Commandments for the class.
7. Take out the Torah and show it to the children. Let them use the *yad* and pretend they are reading.
8. Cover the table with Hebrew newspaper

SCIENCE

1. Bake blintzes (see recipe below on p. 258).
2. Have a tasting of the seven species (wheat, barley, grapes, figs, pomegranates, olives, and dates).
3. Make butter (see recipe below on p. 258).
4. Make bird feeders – it is a *mitzvah* to care for animals.
5. Play *I See Something That Makes It Spring.* Develops observation skills and can be played indoors or out (indoors, look for lighter coats or umbrellas).
6. Grow butterflies. You can order the Butterfly Garden kit from J.L. Hammett Co., (800) 333-4600, www.hammett.com, or from Childcraft, (800) 631-5652.

MATH

1. If you weighed/measured your children at the beginning of the year, now is a good time to take their measurements again to see how much they've grown.
2. Provide a collection of different kinds of hard-shelled nuts and baskets (egg cartons are good, too). Allow children to sort and pattern any way they choose.
3. Consider these Shavuot numbers: 7 species, 7 weeks from Pesach, 10 commandments, 49 days from Pesach.
4. Play the game *Get Moses To the Top of Mt. Sinai.* On a large piece of paper, draw a large mountain with the Ten Commandments at the top. Make a little Moses, stick him at the bottom of the mountain with tape or velcro (with velcro steps going up the mountain). Let the children move him up in steps through any one of a variety of means: as they answer Shavuot questions, as they do acts of *chesed,* as they taste one of the seven species.

ART

1. Make flowers to decorate the room and school.
2. Make a Torah (either individual or one big class one).
3. Decorate Ten Commandment tablets.
4. Make a spring mural.
5. Create a large Mt. Sinai mural (perhaps with Moses holding the Ten Commandments at the top). Let the children take off their shoes and make footprints on the mountain — so that they, too, can be "standing at Sinai."
6. Make a harvest fruit basket. Use the top of an egg carton and make a handle with pipe cleaners. Older children can draw, cut, and paste their own fruit. Younger children can glue on pre-cut fruits or magazine pictures.

MUSIC/MOVEMENT

(With musical contributions from Julie Jaslow Auerbach)

1. Shavuot is one of the three Pilgrimage Festivals we call the Shalosh Regalim. Reprise *"Al Shalosh Regalim"* (see Sukkot, Music/Movement activity #3). Music and lyrics are on p. 328 of Appendix A.

2. Sing songs about summer and warmer weather.

3. Sing counting songs that help us remember that there are Ten Commandments.

4. Sing "Hebrew Counting Song" by Julie Jaslow Auerbach (see Appendix A, p. 340 for music and lyrics). You can use it to count things beyond the fingers and toes of the verses.

5. Act out harvesting a field. Divide the class into reapers, gatherers, pickers. Let children watch each other and then work together.

6. Play and sing a song such as "Shavuot" by Steve Reuben. Act out gathering the harvest and bringing it to the Temple.

7. Play classical music and dance the harvest.

8. Have the children pretend to be a flower. Let them grow from a seed into a tall blossom. Have some children be flower pickers, and pick flowers and arrange beautiful bouquets. Use colorful scarves as props. Dance to *"Od Lo Ahavti Dai."*

9. Pretend to climb Mt. Sinai. Carry the Ten Commandments down. Be careful — they're heavy!

SONG/MUSIC LIST

(Contributed by Julie Jaslow Auerbach)

The following listing includes the songs in this chapter, as well as songs from other sources that are related to Shavuot concepts. Each song and the book in which it is located is specified, along with the page number. (Please note: In this and other holiday chapters, there are many songs which are "preschool traditional," i.e., they have been around so long that no one knows the composer or the song's origin! Every effort has been made to find the source for all the songs listed.)

Ten Commandments

"1&2&3 Commandments" (to the tune of "Ten Little Indians")

"Torah Tziva Lanu Moshe" – *Union Songster*, p. 26

"V'taher Libeynu" – *Union Songster*, p. 42

"The Hebrew Counting Song" – Julie Jaslow Auerbach (see Music Activity #4 above)

Feelings

"No No No" – *My Toes Are Starting to Wiggle*, p. 182

"If You're Happy" – preschool traditional

"Come On and Join into the Game" – folk song

Going to Jerusalem

"Mechi Mechi Kapayim" (see Sukkot, Music/Movement activity #6)

"Israeli March Medley" – *The Barry Sisters In Israel*

"Al Shalosh Regalim" – Julie Jaslow Auerbach (see Sukkot, Music/Movement activity #3)

"Ki Mitzion Tetzeh Torah" – *Chag Sameyach*, p. 18

First Fruits

"Saleynu" – *Songs We Sing*, p. 212

"Chag Shavuot" – *The New Children's Songbook*, p. 37

"Shibolet Basadeh" – *Songs We Sing*, p. 122

"Od Lo Ahavti Dai" – (see Pesach, Music/Movement activity #8)

Celebrating

"Hag Sameach" – *The New Children's Songbook*, p. 33

"Shavuot" – *Especially Wonderful Days*, p. 15

"Shiru Li" – *Come Sing with Me*, p. 41

"Yism'chu Hashamayim" – *Israel in Song*, p.42

Summer

"Rainbow" – *Hand In Hand*, Bev Bos

"Creepy Crawlies" (see Lag B'Omer, Music/Movement activity #4, p. 236)

"Arabella Miller" – *Elephant Jam*, p. 47

"HaTzipporim" – (see Pesach, Music/Movement activity #8, p. 229)

"I Love the Sun" – *It's Time For Music*, p. 12

"Open Your Fingers" – Julie Jaslow Auerbach (see Rosh HaShanah, Music/Movement activity #2, p. 149)
"Ad Or Haboker" – Israel Sings

CIRCLE TIME

1. Play *I'm Going To Jerusalem and I'm Bringing _____*. Let the children name a fruit or food they especially like, or encourage them to use the first letter of their name to guide their choice.
2. Make a chart of the acts of *Chesed* in the story of Ruth. Make another chart of the acts of *Chesed* the children performed.
3. Name an action, and let the children decide on the commandments to which it applies. Here are some examples:
   Listening to your mom – "Honor your mother and father"
   Lighting Shabbat candles – "Keep Shabbat"
   Saying blessings before snack – "I am *Adonai* your God"
   Sharing – "You shall not steal"
   Be happy with what you have – "You shall not covet"

OUTDOORS/FIELD TRIPS

1. Go on a walk, and pretend you are walking to Jerusalem to bring your *bikurim*. Is it a long way? Are the baskets of fruit heavy to carry, or did you bring a donkey to carry everything?
2. Gather flowers and other beautiful greenery to decorate the classroom and synagogue.
3. Go on a walk through the neighborhood to look for evidences of summer. Is it coming? How does the neighborhood look now in comparison with how it looked at Chanukah or Tu B'Shevat?
4. Go on a field trip to a farm and do some actual harvesting.
5. Visit a sanctuary. Look for the shape of the Ten Commandments.

SPECIFICALLY FOR INFANTS

1. Decorate the room with flowers and greenery.
2. Take the babies outside, and talk about the changing weather.
3. Make cookies for babies to eat in the shape of the Ten Commandments.
4. Take the babies to a sanctuary and tell them about what they see.

IDEAS FOR TEACHING FAMILIES

1. Share the story of Ruth with families. Send home a copy of the story (see below on this page), and/or invite them to come and see their children act it out.
2. Inform families of local opportunities at synagogues or the JCC to attend a *Tikkun Layl Shavuot*.
3. Invite parents or relatives in to help make blintzes or butter.
4. Send children home with a *Chesed* book. Encourage parents to record their children's acts of *Chesed* in the book together with their children.
5. Organize a food drive in the school. Encourage families to help their children pick out food to bring to class to donate to those in need.
6. Recommended reading: *The Jewish Parents' Almanac* by Julie Hilton Danan, and *Reading Ruth* edited by Judith A. Kates and Gail Twersky Reimer.

STORIES

RUTH AND NAOMI

(Adapted by Marvell Ginsburg and used with permission; revised by Maxine Segal Handelman)

A very long time ago, a woman named Naomi, and her daughters-in-law, Ruth and Orpah, were living in a far away land called Moab. One day, Naomi said to them, "I want to return to my own country, to the town of Bethlehem in Judah. You stay here in your land of Moab, with your people. You are young and can be happy here. I want to live the rest of my days in my own homeland. I am old and poor and have nothing to offer you."

Orpah kissed Naomi good-bye and returned to Moab. But Ruth loved Naomi very much. She cried and begged her not to say such a thing. "Oh Naomi," cried Ruth. "I love you. Do not ask me to leave you or to stay here. Where you go I will go. Your people will be my people. Your God will be my God."

Naomi saw that Ruth really meant what she said. She agreed that they would go together to Naomi's home in Bethlehem. They arrived in Bethlehem when the barley was ripe. Farmers were reaping their barley from the fields. Ruth and Naomi had no money. Ruth had a good idea. She said to Naomi, "It is a rule that the reapers leave whatever barley they forget or drop in the fields for poor people to take for their food. I will go to the fields and get some barley for us." Naomi said, "That's a wonderful idea, Ruth."

Ruth went to the fields. She worked very hard. She gathered the barley the reapers left. One day, Boaz, the owner of the field, noticed Ruth. When he found out that she was Naomi's daughter-in-law, he exclaimed, "Why, Naomi is my relative! I have heard how devoted and kind Ruth has been to Naomi. Let Ruth gather all that she needs in my fields."

Ruth was able to gather more than enough barley to feed herself and Naomi. Ruth worked in Boaz's fields through the barley harvest. Ruth showed Boaz how kind she was. Boaz loved Ruth, and Ruth loved Boaz. Ruth told Boaz she would marry him. Soon they were married, and they had a baby boy named Oved.

So Ruth, Boaz, Oved, and Naomi all lived happily for a very long time.

When Oved grew up, he had a son named Jesse. When Jesse grew up, he had a son named David. David grew up to become one of the most famous Jewish kings in Israel. There are many stories about King David in the Bible. There are also many beautiful poems in the Bible called psalms, that were written by King David. Some say that King David was born and died on Shavuot.

As you get older and study more Torah, you will be able to read the Book of Ruth by yourself. You will learn all the stories about King David and the beautiful psalms he wrote.

On Shavuot, we read the Book of Ruth. We like to hear about such a kind, loving person. We are happy to know that she became the great-grandmother of King David.

ANOTHER STORY

Shmuel the beggar was walking past a rich man's house on Shavuot when he smelled the mouthwatering scent of frying blintzes. He rushed the rest of the way home.

"Rivka," he called to his wife. "Make us some blintzes! For once let's enjoy Shavuot like the rich people do."

"But Shmuel, to make blintzes we need cheese and eggs. We don't have any cheese or eggs." said Rivka.

"So leave out the cheese and eggs."

"We also need a little sugar and butter." Rivka continued.

"Stop worrying about the details, " Shmuel said impatiently. "Just make some blintzes!"

Rivka shrugged. She mixed flour, water, and oil. She fried the batter and served it to Shmuel. He took one bite and jumped up from the table. "Yuck!" he cried. "Blintzes taste terrible. How can rich people eat this stuff?"

SUGGESTED NEWSLETTER COPY

As Spring turns to summer, the Jewish calendar reminds us to think about harvest and Torah. The holiday of Shavuot always falls on the sixth of Sivan. This year, this occurs on _____ [insert date]. Shavuot celebrates the grain harvest and the giving of the Torah at Mt. Sinai. On Shavuot we read the Book of Ruth, a wonderful story of *Chesed* (loving-kindness), and of the genealogy of King David. We decorate the synagogue with greens and flowers, stay up the night of Shavuot to study (*Tikkun Layl Shavuot*), and we eat dairy foods, such as blintzes and cheesecake, because the words of Torah are like milk and honey.

Shavuot is a wonderful opportunity to take your child to synagogue to see and hear the Torah. See if your synagogue has a *Tikkun Layl Shavuot*, or create your own *Tikkun Layl Shavuot* at home with your children. Let everyone stay up a little late, and tell the story of Ruth, or the story of Moses receiving the Torah at Mt. Sinai. Let your child ask lots of questions, and figure out the answers together. (To help you find answers, check out books such as *The Jewish Parent's Almanac* by Julie Hilton Danan.) You might also have a cheesecake tasting party with friends. *Chag Sameach!*

RECIPES

Note: To prepare blintzes in advance: Make the thin pancakes in advance according to the recipe below. Wrap them in a tea towel to prevent drying out.

BLINTZES

Ingredients
1 C. white flour
¼ tsp. salt
2 eggs
1½ C. milk
1 tbs. oil
oil for frying

Directions
1. Mix the flour and salt together. Add the eggs, milk, and oil. Beat with a whisk until smooth.
2. Lightly oil a shallow pan and heat oil.
3. Pour in just enough batter to thinly coat the bottom of the pan. When brown, flip the blintz out onto a plate. Repeat until the batter is used up.
4. Children put a spoonful of jam in the center of the each pancake, then fold.
5. Put the blintzes in a buttered dish, dot with butter, and bake until brown at 375° for 30 minutes.
(Serves 8-10)

BUTTER

Supplies
Baby food jars with lids
Large plastic containers with screw-on lids
Spoon
Clean marbles

Ingredients
Whipping cream
Salt

Directions
1. Pour whipping cream into plastic containers. Add a few marbles. Screw lids on tightly! Children take turns shaking the container.
2. When cream begins to thicken, add a little salt.
3. When the butter begins to form, alert the children to the presence of two things in the container (butter and skim milk). Pour off the skim milk.
4. Each child may take home a sample of butter in a baby food jar.

BIBLIOGRAPHY

ADULTS

Danan, Julie Hilton. *The Jewish Parents' Almanac.* Northvale, NJ: Jason Aronson Inc., 1997.

A wonderful guide for parents (and teachers) on how to create a Jewish life for children.

Kates, Judith A., and Gail Twersky Reimer, eds. *Reading Ruth: Contemporary Women Reclaim a Sacred Story.* New York: Touchstone, 1997.

A fabulous collection of both traditional and unorthodox readings of the Book of Ruth by contemporary female scholars.

CHILDREN
Ten Commandments

The Children of America. *The 11th Commandment.* Woodstock, VT: Jewish Lights Publishing, 1996. (Ages 3-8)

Children's ideas of what the eleventh commandment should be.

Cone, Molly. *Who Knows Ten? Children's Tales of the Ten Commandments.* New York: UAHC Press, 1998. (Ages 5-10)

Stories to illustrate each of the Ten Commandments.

Nerlove, Miriam. *The Ten Commandments for Jewish Children.* Morton Grove, IL: Albert Whitman, 1999. (Ages 3-7)

Finally, a book which presents the Ten Commandments for older preschoolers.

Topek, Susan Remick. *Ten Good Rules.* Rockville, MD: Kar-Ben Copies, 1991. (Ages 2-6)

The Ten Commandments in simple, appropriate language.

Wheat and Harvest

Bial, Raymond. *Corn Belt Harvest.* Boston, MA: Houghton Mifflin, 1991. (Ages 8-12)

Text and photos describe the United States corn belt region and its harvest season. While targeted to an older age group, the book is nonetheless useful for the photos.

Fowler, Allan. *The Wheat We Eat.* Danbury, CT: Children's Press, 1999. (Ages 4-8)

Follows wheat from the field to the table in an easy to read format. A Rookie Read-about Science book.

Johnson, Sylvia. *Wheat.* Minneapolis, MN: Lerner Publications, Co., 1990. (Ages 4-8)

Explains the cycle of wheat from planting to harvest, and how wheat feeds people all over the world.

Landau, Elaine. *Wheat (True Book).* Danbury, CT: Children's Press, 1999. (Ages 4-8)

An introduction to wheat, with up close and personal photographs and accompanying basic facts.

INTRODUCTION TO PART IV
THE REST IS COMMENTARY — NOW GO AND STUDY

A prankster once came to Shammai and said, "Can you teach me the whole Torah while I stand on one foot?" Shammai was so outraged at the preposterous request that he chased the man away. The man then came to Hillel and proposed the same challenge, "Can you teach me the whole Torah while I stand on one foot?" Hillel told the man, "The whole of Torah is this: what is hateful to you, do not do to others. All the rest is commentary. Now go and study." The man was so impressed with Hillel's remarks that he converted to Judaism and studied with his whole heart the rest of his life. (*Shabbat* 31a)

This part of the book contains ten short chapters that cover some of the "commentary" of Jewish early childhood education. Chapter 19 will help you integrate Hebrew into your classroom every day. Chapter 20 contains a detailed *mezuzah* curriculum, including goals and activities for each age group. In Chapter 21, there is a guide to making storytelling an integral part of your classroom, while Chapter 22 features a useful guide music in the early childhood classroom by Julie Jaslow Auerbach. Julie has also provided a comprehensive list of music resources and a thorough discography, which may be found in the bibliography at the end of this book, pp. 367-371. The Jewish holidays were covered in Part III; in this section, Chapter 23 focuses on some secular holidays and how to integrate them into the Jewish classroom (or, for some of these offers reasons for not doing so). Some important Jewish life cycle moments — birth and death — are the focus of Chapter 24. The importance of involving clergy and other significant people in your school, and how to do it, is addressed in Chapter 25. Although the needs of infants and toddlers have been addressed in other parts of the book, here Chapter 26 addresses the special needs and most successful approaches to working with infants and toddlers within a Jewish framework. The special needs and concerns of non-Jewish teachers and interfaith families are addressed in Chapters 27 and 28 respectively. A guide to keeping kosher at school is the theme of Chapter 29. Finally, ways to ensure that the summer, too, is a Jewish time are explored in Chapter 30.

No one book can provide all the information you will ever need to master the craft of teaching the very young, but this book does provide most of the tools and resources you will need to start you on the right path toward that goal. The essence is here. Now go and study.

CHAPTER 19

INTEGRATING HEBREW EVERY DAY

Hebrew is the language of the Jewish people. The Torah is written in Hebrew, and Hebrew is one of the official languages of the Land of Israel. Hebrew is the language of Jewish prayer. We cannot teach our children what it means to be Jewish without making Hebrew an integral part of what we teach and how we teach. Hebrew must be integrated into the physical environment of the school, and into the daily activities and rituals which take place within the classroom. This book provides a model for doing so. Hebrew vocabulary and strategies are woven throughout almost every chapter. The chapters on Israel and the holiday of Yom HaAtzma'ut, especially, are laden with Hebrew vocabulary and activities, and, wherever possible, Hebrew terms have been used.

Studies have long demonstrated the overall cognitive and academic benefits for students immersed in a second language program (Ofek, 1997, p. 1). Recent brain research has shown that repeated exposure to a multitude of phonemes (the sounds of the human language) at a very young age can help form dedicated connections in the brain's auditory cortex (program notes from *Baby Einstein* video). Young children can learn a second language with much greater ease than older children or adults. Exposing children to Hebrew consistently, or even immersing children in Hebrew in their preschool years will lay a strong foundation for Hebrew as part of their entire lives.

There are several programs designed to help teachers teach Hebrew in the early childhood classroom. These include *"Aleh,"* a Hebrew curriculum program from the BJE of Greater New York, which comes with puppets, props, and teaching suggestions; *"Yofi Lilmod Ivrit"* (Hebrew Is Fun), a Hebrew

reading readiness program for six and seven-year-olds; and *"Tal Sela"* and *"Tal Am"* from the BJE of Montreal. Additionally, the Melton Reseach Center for Jewish education, in close cooperation with the William Davidson Graduate School of Jewish Education at the Jewish Theological Seminary, is currently working on the creation of Hebrew language immersion preschools to give children an early start on Hebrew language acquisition at an age at which learning a second language is easiest. Currently, two nursery schools deliver content in a semi-immersion model, meaning half a day of conducting all activities in Hebrew. Finally, Bina Guerrieri, at the Bureau of Jewish Education in San Francisco, has been working with a program called "Total Physical Response" (TPR), in which children act out the Hebrew they hear. To obtain information on these programs, see addresses in the bibliography of this chapter.

In order to make Hebrew a regular feature in the classroom, teachers must have some knowledge of Hebrew. Certainly, a teacher does not need to read or write Hebrew fluently to integrate it into the classroom, but a basic vocabulary is a good start. The Community Foundation for Jewish Education in Chicago began an Adult Hebrew Ulpan program in 1998. This program was specifically designed for early childhood teachers to enable those with minimal Hebrew skills to integrate Hebrew into their classrooms. The 22 teachers who went through the program studied modern Hebrew and techniques for integrating the language into their classrooms. Check to see if your community has a similar program, or find a teacher and a group of colleagues and start your own Hebrew Ulpan.

HEBREW TOOLS

Following are some tools that are helpful for integrating Hebrew into the classroom. These include a chart of the Hebrew alphabet, music/movement activities, and a list of Hebrew vocabulary words. A list of words in Hebrew, English, and transliteration for classroom labels may be found in Appendix B, p. 359.

THE ALEF BET — THE HEBREW ALPHABET

Hebrew is written from right to left. The vowels are lines and dots which are written below, beside, or above the letters.

There are 22 letters in the Hebrew alphabet, including two that are silent letters. Five Hebrew letters take a different form at the end of a word. Figure 34 on this page will guide you through the *alef bet*.

HEBREW VOCABULARY LISTS

While all the Hebrew vocabulary you might want to use in a classroom cannot be listed in this book, the list in figure 35, pp. 264-266 will be helpful.

As you add Hebrew vocabulary words to your classroom and to the themes you study, teach the parents, too, through signs in the classroom and/or newletters. Through these, parents will learn to understand the Hebrew words their children say, and they will be able reinforce the learning at home.

MUSIC/MOVEMENT ACTIVITIES

(With musical contributions from Julie Jaslow Auerbach)

Note: For more related Music/Movement activities, see Chapter 17, "Yom HaAtzma'ut," p. 246.

1. Sing the "Alef Bet Song" by Debbie Friedman (*Manginot*, p. 46). At Temple Emanu El in Cleveland, Rabbi Daniel Roberts has three preschool teachers hold up the letters one at a time. He points to each letter as the children sing the song.

2. Sing songs about parts of the body substituting Hebrew words.
3. Sing songs about colors using Hebrew words for colors.
4. Shape your body like a Hebrew letter (see figure 34 below).
5. The popular camp song *"Ivrit Daber Ivrit"* (literally, "Hebrew, Speak Hebrew"), can be cleverly used to teach Hebrew words and their

Sounds Like ...	Name of Hebrew Letter	Hebrew Letter
Silent	Alef	א
B V	Bet Vet	בּ ב
G	Gimmel	ג
D	Daled	ד
H	Hay	ה
V	Vav	ו
Z	Zayin	ז
Ch (not like the "ch" in chalk; make this sound in back of your throat)	Chet	ח
T	Tet	ט
Y	Yud	י
K Ch	Kaf Chaf	כ כ
L	Lamed	ל
M	Mem	מ
N	Nun	נ
A	Samech	ס
Silent	Ayin	ע
P F	Pey Fey	פ פ
The "zz" in the in the middle of the word "pizza"	Tzadee	צ
K	Koof	ק
R	Raysh	ר
Sh Sin	Shin Sin	שׁ שׂ
T	Tav	ת

Figure 34

Hebrew equivalents. Have children put one hand under the elbow of the opposite arms as they sing a Hebrew word. Then switch to arms and hands and sing the English equivalent. Repeat several times. Here are the words:

Ivrit, ivrit, ivrit daber ivrit (2x)

6. Sing the following songs:

Old Goldenberg Had a Kibbutz
(Sing to the tune of "Old Macdonald Had a Farm")

Old Goldenberg had a *kibbutz*, e-i-e-i-o
And on his *kibbutz* he had a *parah* (cow), e-i-e-i-o
With a moo moo here, and a moo moo there,
here a moo, there a moo,
everywhere a moo moo
Old Goldenberg had a *parah*, e-i-e-i-o.

For other verses:
soos (horse)
oaf (chicken)
tayeesh (goat)

The Galgaleem on the Bus
(Sing to the tune of "The Wheels on the Bus")

The *galgaleem* [wheels] on the bus go round and round,
Round and round,
Round and round
The *galgaleem* on the bus go round and round
All through Tel Aviv.

For other verses:

delet (door)   *abba* (father)
chalone (window)   *yeladeem* (children)
kessef (money)   *tinokeem* (babies)
eema (mother)

HEBREW VOCABULARY		
Members of the Family		
מִשְׁפָּחָה	family	*mish-pa-chah*
סַבָּא	grandfather	*sab-ba*
סַבְתָּא	grandmother	*sav-ta*
אַבָּא	father	*ah-bah*
אִמָּא	mother	*ee-mah*
אָח	brother	*ach*
אָחוֹת	sister	*ah-chot*
תִּינוֹק	baby	*tee-nok*
דּוֹדָה	aunt	*doe-dah*
דּוֹד	uncle	*dode*
Parts of the Body		
רֹאשׁ	head	*rosh*
עֵינַיִם	eyes	*ay-na-yeem*
אָזְנַיִם	ears	*ahz-na-yeem*
אַף	nose	*af*
סַנְטֵר	chin	*sahn-tayr*
שִׁנַּיִם	teeth	*shee-na-yeem*
יָדַיִם	hands	*ya-da-yeem*
כְּתֵפַיִם	shoulders	*k'ti-fa-yeem*
בִּרְכַּיִם	knees	*beer-ka-yeem*
רַגְלַיִם	feet	*rahg-la-yeem*
גַב	back	*gav*
בֶּטֶן	stomach	*beh-ten*
פֶּה	mouth	*peh*

Figure 35

HEBREW VOCABULARY

Numbers

אַחַת	1	*ah-chat*
שְׁתַּיִם	2	*shta-yim*
שָׁלֹשׁ	3	*sha-losh*
אַרְבַּע	4	*ar-ba*
חָמֵשׁ	5	*cha-maysh*
שֵׁשׁ	6	*shaysh*
שֶׁבַע	7	*sheh-vah*
שְׁמוֹנֶה	8	*shmo-neh*
תֵּשַׁע	9	*tay-shah*
עֶשֶׂר	10	*eh-ser*
אַחַת-עֶשְׂרֵה	11	*ah-chaht es-ray*
שְׁתֵּים-עֶשְׂרֵה	12	*shtaym es-ray*
שְׁלוֹשׁ-עֶשְׂרֵה	13	*shlosh es-ray*
אַרְבַּע-עֶשְׂרֵה	14	*ar-ba es-ray*
חֲמֵשׁ-עֶשְׂרֵה	15	*cha-maysh es-ray*
שֵׁשׁ-עֶשְׂרֵה	16	*shaysh es-ray*
שְׁבַע-עֶשְׂרֵה	17	*shvah es-ray*
שְׁמוֹנֶה-עֶשְׂרֵה	18	*shmo-neh es-ray*
תְּשַׁע-עֶשְׂרֵה	19	*t'shah es-ray*
עֶשְׂרִים	20	*es-reem*

Clothing

נַעֲלַיִם	shoes	*na-a-lah-yeem*
גַּרְבַּיִם	socks	*gar-bah-yeem*
שִׂמְלָה	dress	*seem-lah*
מִכְנָסַיִם	pants	*meech-na-sah-yeem*
חֻלְצָה	shirt	*chool-tzah*
גּוּפִיָּה	undershirt	*goo-fee-yah*
כּוֹבַע	hat	*ko-va*

Animals

כֶּלֶב	dog	*keh-lev*
חָתוּל	cat	*cha-tool*
צִפּוֹר	bird	*tzee-poor*
פִּיל	elephant	*peel*
דֹּב	bear	*dov*
סוּס	horse	*soos*
קוֹף	monkey	*kof*
נָחָשׁ	snake	*na-chash*
שָׁפָן	rabbit	*sha-fan*
תַּיִשׁ	goat	*ta-yish*

Foods

בָּנָנָה	banana	*ba-na-nah*
דַּיסָה	oatmeal	*dye-sah*
בֵּיצָה	egg	*bay-tzah*
תַּפּוּחַ	apple	*ta-poo-ach*
תַּפּוּז	orange	*ta-pooz*
חָלָב	milk	*cha-lav*

Figure 35, cont.

HEBREW VOCABULARY

Foods (continued)

עוּגָה	cake	oo-gah
עוּגִיּוֹת	cookies	oo-gee-yote
לֶחֶם	bread	leh-chem
מִיץ	juice	meetz

Colors

כָּתֹם	orange	katom
יָרֹק	green	yah-roke
כָּחֹל	blue	ka-chol
אָדֹם	red	ah-dome
לָבָן	white	la-vahn
שָׁחֹר	black	sha-chor
חוּם	brown	choom
סָגֹל	purple	segol

Holidays

שַׁבָּת	Shabbat	
רֹאשׁ חוֹדֶשׁ	Rosh Chodesh	
רֹאשׁ הַשָּׁנָה	Rosh HaShanah	
יוֹם הַכִּפּוּרִים	Yom Kippur	
סֻכּוֹת	Sukkot	
שִׂמְחַת תּוֹרָה	Simchat Torah	
חֲנֻכָּה	Chanukah	
ט׳׳ו בִּשְׁבָט	Tu B'Shevat	
פּוּרִים	Purim	
יוֹם הָעַצְמָאוּת	Yom HaAtzma'ut	
פֶּסַח	Passover/Pesach	
שָׁבוּעוֹת	Shavuot	

Miscellaneous

יֶלֶד	boy	ye-led
יַלְדָּה	girl	yal-dah
מוֹרָה	teacher (fem.)	mo-rah
מוֹרֶה	teacher (masc.)	mo-reh
דֶּגֶל	flag	deh-gel
שָׁעוֹן	clock	sha-on
שֶׁלֶג	snow	sheh-leg
רוּחַ	wind	roo-ach
עֵץ	tree	aytz
עָלֶה	leaf	ah-leh
שָׁמַיִם	sky	sha-ma-yim

Useful Phrases

מַה שְׁלוֹמֵךְ	How are you? (fem.)	Mah shlo-maych?
מַה שְׁלוֹמְךָ	How are you? (masc.)	Mah shlom-cha?
טוֹב, תּוֹדָה	Fine, thanks	Tov, to-dah
טוֹב מְאֹד	very good	tov m'ode
שָׁלוֹם	hello/goodbye	sha-lom
בֹּקֶר טוֹב	Good morning	Boker tov
לְהִתְרָאוֹת	Be seeing you	L'hit-ra-ote
אֲנִי פֹּה	I am here	Ani po

Figure 35, cont.

HEBREW VOCABULARY		
Useful Phrases (continued)		
אֵיפֹה	where	*ay-fo*
לָמָּה	why	*lah-mah*
תּוֹדָה רַבָּה	Thank you very much	*Todah rabah*
בְּבַקָּשָׁה	Please/you're welcome	*Be-va-ka-shah*
סְלִיחָה	Excuse me	*Slee-chah*

Figure 35, cont.

CONCLUSION

Hebrew is an integral part of being Jewish. When Hebrew is a natural component of the early childhood classroom, the children — who have the ability to learn languages with great ease — readily integrate Hebrew into their own Jewish identities. When they "meet" Hebrew on a regular basis, it becomes standard, commonplace, familiar. I was once asked by a child, "How do you say 'Shabbat' in Hebrew?" To her, "Shabbat" was as comfortable a term as "Tuesday" or "bicycle."

With a little dedication, any teacher can make Hebrew an active part of the classroom. This can be done by making the environment rich with Hebrew through labels (see Appendix B, p. 359), by incorporating songs and games that use Hebrew on a regular basis, by adopting a few favorite phrases and using them in various situations (e.g., saying *"Boker Tov"* as the children arrive, *"z'man linakote"* at clean-up time, *"Shalom"* at the end of the day). The tools in this chapter will help you welcome Hebrew into the classroom. Chapter 6, "Israel All Year," and Chapter 17, "Yom HaAtzmau't," also contain ideas and resources for bringing Hebrew into the classroom.

B'chatz'lachah (with success) as you embark on your Hebrew journey!

BIBLIOGRAPHY

ADULTS

Bredekamp, Sue, and Carol Copple, eds. *Developmentally Appropriate Practice in Early Childhood Programs. Revised Edition.* Washington DC: National Association for the Education of Young Children, 1997.

> The most up-to-date guide to developmentally appropriate practice.

Ofek, Adina. "Learning the Hebrew Language in Early Childhood." *Melton Gleanings*, Autumn 1997, p. 1. (Published by Melton Reseach Center for Jewish Education and available at www.jtsa.edu/melton/gleaning/v2i1/learnheb.html)

> A description of the motivations for and the process involved in the Melton Research Center's initiative to create model Hebrew immersion programs in early childhood settings.

CHILDREN

(For more related books for children, see Chapter 17, "Yom HaAtzma'ut.")

Baby Einstein. Available in media stores, or contact Baby Einstein Company, 10840 Bobcat Terrace, Littleton, CO 80124; (800) 793-1454; Fax: (303) 706-9864.

> This video is for babies to use with or without parents. Research has shown that infants distinguish and assimilate the sounds of all languages, but that this ability begins to fade with age. Thus, the audio component of *Baby Einstein* exposes infants to a multitude of phonemes in a fun, baby-friendly way.

Blitz, Shmuel. *The Aleph Bet Word Book.* Brooklyn, NY: Mesorah Publications, Ltd., 1995. (Ages 3-8)

> Part of the ArtScroll Youth Series, this is a pictorial Hebrew-English dictionary for children.

Genet, Barbara. *Ta-poo-ach Means Apple.* Denver: A.R.E. Publishing, Inc., 1985. (Ages 3-8)

> Through Hebrew names for 29 objects, this attractively illustrated hardback book introduces Hebrew letters and words. Includes transliteration, and translation.

ADDRESSES FOR HEBREW PROGRAMS

"Aleh" and *"Yofi Lilmod Ivrit"*
Board of Jewish Education of Greater New York
426 West 58th St.
New York, NY 10019
(212) 245-8200
Fax: (212) 247-1957
www.bjeny.org

"Tal Sela" and *"Tal Am"*
Board of Jewish Education of UJA Federation of Greater Toronto
4600 Bathurst St., Suite 232
Willowdale, Ontario M2R 3V3
Canada
(416) 633-7770

Melton Research Center for Jewish Education
Jewish Theological Seminary
3080 Broadway
New York, NY 10027
(212) 678-8031
www.jtsa.edu/melton

Bureau of Jewish Education of San Francisco
639 14th Avenue
San Francisco, CA 94118
(415) 751-6983
Fax: (415) 668-1816
www.bjesf.org

CHAPTER 20

A MEZUZAH CURRICULUM

A *mezuzah* should be the first thing a person, child, or adult, sees when he/she enters a Jewish school or classroom. For an entire year, the classroom will be home to a group of children and teachers, and the symbol of a Jewish home is a *mezuzah*, hung proudly on the doorpost.

The word *mezuzah* means "doorpost," and actually refers to the *klaf*, or parchment, which is inside the case. A *sofer* (scribe) writes the first two paragraphs of the *Shema* in Hebrew on the parchment scroll (Deuteronomy 6:4-9 and 11:13-21). The *Shema* includes the words, "And you shall write them [all of the commandments] on the doorposts of your house and upon our gates." When we see the *mezuzah* upon entering a room in a Jewish house, we are reminded of our relationship to God and the Torah. As a sign of respect, some people kiss the *mezuzah* (by touching it and then touching fingers to lips) as they pass by.

The *mezuzah* case can be made of any material, and can take any shape. Often, the letter "shin" or the Hebrew word "*Shaddai*" appears on the case. "*Shaddai*" means breast, or figuratively, mountain. "*Ayl Shaddai*" (God of the mountain) was one of God's names. "*Shaddai*" is also seen as an acronym referring to God, meaning "protector of the doors of Israel" (*Shomer Dalatot Yisrael*).

Traditionally, the *mezuzah* is hung on the right-hand doorpost leading into a home or room. It is hung about head level (in the top third of the doorway) with its top inclined at an angle into the room. Although a *mezuzah* traditionally hangs at a specific height and in a certain place, we must consider that, *l'shaym chinuch*, in the name of education, we bend certain rules. A *mezuzah* is much more relevant to a child if the child can reach it to look at it and kiss it. When you affix a *mezuzah*, you are dedicating your home or classroom as a sacred Jewish space.

If your school or classroom has no *mezuzah*, the beginning of the year is a wonderful time to learn about *mezuzot* and to go about acquiring one for your door. If you do have a *mezuzah*, studying *mezuzot* will reinforce the children's relationship to the *mezuzah* they pass on their doorway every day. Following is an entire *mezuzah* curriculum unit for ages infant to 4 years. *Mezuzot* frequently mark the beginning of a new Jewish home, so a *mezuzah* unit fits in well with the beginning of the school year, when children are settling in to a new classroom. The fall holidays may take precedence as the beginning of the year curriculum, but once things settle down, studying *mezuzot* and creating one for the room will help children take ownership of their school and classroom.

Begin by webbing the concept of *mezuzah* (see figure 19 on page 270 for the beginning of a *mezuzah* web). Many of the concepts can be addressed differently with different age levels, and can serve as foundations for the entire year. The *Shema* can be sung on a regular basis, and discussions about God throughout the year can trace their roots back to the *mezuzah*. The habit of kissing the *mezuzah* starts with a good role model.

CONCEPTS

Figure 36 on the following page is the beginning of a web for the topic of *mezuzah*. It is followed by a list of concepts that are appropriate for each age level. The list contains both concrete and conceptual ways for children to connect with the topic at hand.

INFANT TO 24 MONTHS
1. I recognize the *mezuzah.*
2. I hear the *Shema* sung.
3. I can kiss the *mezuzah.*

2 YEARS
1. I recognize the *mezuzah.*

2. I hear the *Shema* sung.
3. The *Shema* tells us there is one God.
4. I can kiss the *mezuzah.*
5. I can make a *mezuzah* case.

3 YEARS
1. I recognize the *mezuzah.*

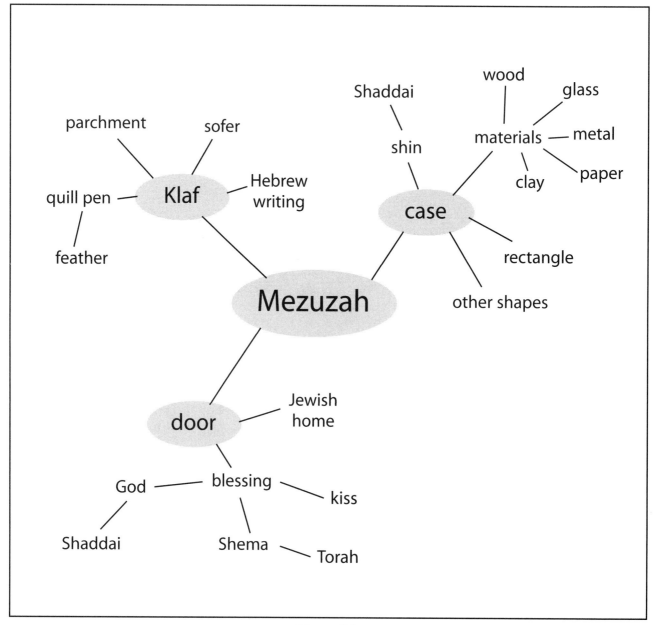

Figure 36

2. I hear the *Shema* sung.
3. I can sing the *Shema*.
4. The *Shema* tells us there is one God.
5. I can kiss the *mezuzah* when I go through the doorway.
6. I can make a *mezuzah* case.
7. The *mezuzah* shows this is a Jewish room.

4 To 5 Years

1. I see and touch the *mezuzah*.
2. I hear and sing the *Shema*.
3. The *Shema* tells us there is one God.
4. The *Shema* prayer is from the Torah. I can also find it in the *Siddur*.
5. Prayer is how we talk to God.
6. I kiss the *mezuzah* when I pass it to show respect.
7. I can make a *mezuzah* case.
8. The *mezuzah* shows this is a Jewish room.

Before diving into a *mezuzah* unit, there are some practical matters to consider. A kosher *mezuzah klaf* contains text from the Torah, as well as the name of God. A *mezuzah* is a ritual object, not a toy. At the same time, making a *mezuzah* and writing a *klaf* are valuable experiences for a child.

There are several options for making the study of *mezuzot* concrete and valuable, and at the same time creating a *mezuzah* for the doorpost that is both developmentally appropriate and religiously respectful and in keeping with the philosophy of the school. Some of these options include:

1. Hang a *mezuzah* with a kosher *klaf* at the traditional height. Hang an additional, child-made *mezuzah*, with a photocopied or child-made *klaf*, at an appropriate height for the children in the class.
2. Hang one *mezuzah*, either child-made or store bought, with a kosher *klaf*, at an appropriate height for the children in the class. If using a store bought *mezuzah* case, consider using one designed for children, and letting the children choose from a few designs. Be sure the *mezuzah*

is affixed well enough so that even with lots of small hands offering kisses, the *mezuzah* is not in danger of falling off.

On the classroom doors of children too young to walk, the *mezuzah* should be hung at adult shoulder height, at the level babies are carried. On the doorposts of adult rooms (offices, kitchen, etc.), hang the *mezuzah* at the traditional height. Rooms like bathrooms and storerooms do not require a *mezuzah*.

ACTIVITIES

LANGUAGE ARTS

1. Talk about the *mezuzah* while walking through the doorway.
2. Allow children to write like a *sofer* with quill feathers and thin black ink.
3. Talk about what the *Shema* means, and Jewish prayers as a way to talk to God.
4. Find the *Shema* in the Torah (Deuteronomy 6:4) and in the *Siddur*.
5. Look at the *shin* on the *mezuzah* case. Talk about *Shaddai* and why that is a good name for God.
6. Encourage the children to write their own *klaf*. Provide examples of the word *Shema* in Hebrew and English for children to work from.
7. Cover the table with Hebrew newspaper to expose children to Hebrew writing.

SCIENCE

1. Examine many different *mezuzot*.
2. Weigh and measure different *mezuzot*.
3. Compare the different kinds of materials used to make *mezuzot*.
4. Compare real parchment to paper.
5. Let children feel *mezuzot* with their eyes closed and describe them.
6. Experiment writing a *klaf* with different kinds of feathers. Make the ink different consistencies (tempera paint with different amounts of water).

7. With a basic sugar cookie recipe and lots of different kinds of decorations, let children make *mezuzah* cookies.

MATH

1. Compare the shapes and sizes of different *mezuzot*.
2. Provide the children with several different and similar *mezuzot*. Allow them to classify and sort by shape, material, size, etc.
3. Compare a *mezuzah* to other objects — a knife, *challah*, book, etc. Is it larger, smaller, thicker?
4. Measure the doorway of the classroom using a *mezuzah* as the measuring stick. How many *mezuzot* would fit from the floor to the top of the doorway? Try this using different *mezuzot*.
5. Chart how many *mezuzot* the children can find on their doorposts at home.

ART

1. Make a *mezuzah*. Any materials will do, as long as it can hold a *klaf* and be affixed to a doorway. Some optimal materials might include:
   - Match box with tongue depressor
   - Clay. Let the children style freely, or mold over a fat crayon.
   - The cardboard tube from a dry cleaner hanger, cut into 3" pieces and mounted on tag board or a tongue depressor
   - Clear tube from a flower stem (from a florist)
   - Seashell with an adequate opening
   - Paper towel tube, cut in half or thirds
   - Older children can coat pieces of wrapping paper, Hebrew newspaper, and cut-out magazine and newspaper pictures with glue and layer over a fat crayon or one-inch roll of wax paper. Apply several layers and allow to dry. Gently rub with fine sandpaper in some spots to reveal different layers. Paint with Mod-Podge.

   Let the children decorate their *mezuzot* with a wide option of materials and methods. Provide pictures or real examples of different

mezuzot to stimulate the children's creativity. When you send the *mezuzah* home, be sure to include a child-made *klaf* or photocopy of the *Shema* (see Music/Movement activity #2 below. Let families know that if they hang the *mezuzah* at home, they should acquire a kosher *klaf*, and provide suggestions as to where to acquire one.

2. Make a *mezuzah* for the classroom door. Let all the children help who want to.
3. Encourage the children to make *mezuzot* for the house corner, or houses they build in the block corner.
4. Provide older children with clip boards, paper, and drawing materials, and let them sketch the *mezuzot* they find around the building.
5. Paint on onion skin or parchment paper with feathers.

MUSIC/MOVEMENT

1. Let the children make a *shin* with their bodies.
2. Sing the *Shema*.

שְׁמַע יִשְׂרָאֵל יְיָ אֱלֹהֵינוּ יְיָ אֶחָד.

Shema Yisrael Adonai Elohaynu Adonai Echad.

Hear O Israel, *Adonai* is our God, *Adonai* is one.

3. Let the children make up interpretive dances to the *Shema*.
4. Learn to sign the *Shema* using American Sign, or make up your own movements to the words.
5. Practice kissing the *mezuzah*. To kiss the *mezuzah*, touch your fingertips to the *mezuzah*, then kiss your fingertips.
6. Hold up children so they can kiss adult height *mezuzot*.
7. Search the room for other things that make it a Jewish classroom.
8. Sing the song *"Mezzuzah"* from *"Especially Jewish Symbols"* by Jeff Klepper, p. 13.

CIRCLE TIME

1. Allow the children to talk about God.
2. Talk about the reasons for having a *mezuzah*.
3. Display several different *mezuzot*. Have the children cover their eyes and remove one. Let the children guess which one is missing by describing it.
4. Read a familiar children's book in Hebrew.
5. Using shapes instead of fruits, play *Fruit Basket Upset*. Arrange the children on chairs in a circle. Assign each child a shape, using four or five different shapes (so there are several children assigned the same shape). One child stands in the middle of the circle and calls out a shape. All the children assigned to that shape must get up and find a new chair. The child who was in the middle also takes a chair, leaving a new child without a chair. This child now calls a shape, and those children run for a new chair. The child in the middle may also call "Fruit basket upset," or in this version, "Shape explosion," at which point all the children get up and find a new chair.

OUTDOORS/FIELD TRIPS

1. Take a trip through the school and building to find all the *mezuzot* you can.
2. Visit the homes of nearby school families to see their *mezuzot*.
3. Visit the gift shop or local Jewish art gallery to see the *mezuzot*.
4. Visit a *sofer*, or invite a *sofer* to come to the school. Learn about how a *sofer* writes a *mezuzah klaf* and a Torah.
5. Walk around the outside of the school. How can you tell this is a Jewish place?

SPECIFICALLY FOR INFANTS

1. Talk about the *mezuzah* while walking through the doorway.
2. Point out the *mezuzah* in the classroom and on the door to the synagogue.
3. Model kissing the *mezuzah* with fingertips.
4. Hold children so they can touch the *mezuzah*.

5. Sing the *Shema* prayer, not just when looking at the *mezuzah*, but at random times as well. It's a very soothing tune for sleepy babies.

IDEAS FOR TEACHING FAMILIES

1. Invite families to *Chanukat HaGan*. Be sure to provide lots of information beforehand about *mezuzot* and why you have chosen to study them.
2. Provide examples of kosher and non-kosher *klafeem* (plural of *klaf*) so adults can see the differences.
3. Inform families of places they can buy *mezuzah* cases and kosher *klafeem*.
4. Invite artistic family members in to help the class make *mezuzot*.
5. Recommended Reading: *The Jewish Home: A Guide for Jewish Living* by Daniel B. Syme, and *The How To Handbook for Jewish Living* by Kerry M. Olitzky and Ronald H. Isaacs.

CHANUKAT HAGAN

The logical culmination of a *mezuzah* unit is a *Chanukat HaGan* (Dedication of the Preschool) ceremony. The ceremony can be as simple or as elaborate as you choose, with families or without, the whole school together or each class on its own. You might sing the *Shema* or other songs the children make up about their *mezuzah*.

"Piggyback" *mezuzah* songs on familiar tunes. Here's a sample, to the tune of "I Have a Little Dreidel":

I have my own *mezuzah*
I hung it by the door
I kiss it when I pass it
On my way to the store
Now listen my *mezuzah*
You mustn't go away
I know this room is Jewish
When I see you each day!

The blessing you say when you affix the *mezuzah* to the doorpost is:

בָּרוּךְ אַתָּה יְיָ אֱלֹהֵינוּ מֶלֶךְ הָעוֹלָם
אֲשֶׁר קִדְּשָׁנוּ בְּמִצְוֹתָיו וְצִוָּנוּ לִקְבּוֹעַ מְזוּזָה.

Baruch Atah Adonai Elohaynu Melech HaOlam
Asher Kid'shanu B'Mitzvotav V'Tzivanu Likboa
Mezuzah.

We praise you, our God, Creator of the universe,
Who has made us holy through Your *mitzvot*, and
commands us to affix the *mezuzah*.

You don't need to say the blessing for each
individual *mezuzah* you put up, just one blessing
for the entire *Chanukat HaGan*. You might also
want to say the "*Shehecheyanu*" blessing, especially
if this is the first time you are putting up a
mezuzah on this doorpost.

בָּרוּךְ אַתָּה יְיָ אֱלֹהֵינוּ מֶלֶךְ הָעוֹלָם
שֶׁהֶחֱיָנוּ וְקִיְּמָנוּ וְהִגִּיעָנוּ לַזְּמַן הַזֶּה.

Baruch Atah Adonai Elohaynu Melech HaOlam
Shehecheyanu, V'keeyamanu V'Higeeyanu
LaZ'man HaZeh.

We praise you, our God, Creator of the universe,
for giving us life, sustaining us, and helping us
to reach this moment.

After you attach the *mezuzah* to your doorway,
model kissing the *mezuzah*. Be sure everyone has
a chance to walk through the doorway and give
the *mezuzah* a kiss.

SUGGESTIONS FOR A NEWSLETTER OR CHANUKAT HAGAN INVITATION

We are delighted at how much the children
and families consider our school a home away
from home. Judaism is full of rituals to mark life
in a Jewish home. The symbol of a Jewish home
is a *mezuzah*, hung proudly on the doorpost. The
word *mezuzah* means "doorpost," and actually
refers to the *klaf*, or parchment, which is inside
the case. A *sofer* (scribe) writes the first two paragraphs of the *Shema* in Hebrew on the parchment
scroll (Deuteronomy 6:4-9 and 11:13-21). When
we see the *mezuzah* upon entering a room in a
Jewish house, we are reminded of our relationship
to God and the Torah. Some people kiss the
mezuzah as they pass by, as a sign of respect. When
you affix a *mezuzah*, you dedicate your home as
a sacred Jewish space.

The children have been busy studying *mezuzot*
and creating *mezuzot* of their own. Each class has
created a beautiful *mezuzah* for their doorway. We
are ready to dedicate our classrooms by hanging
our own *mezuzot*. We invite all our families to join
us at [insert day, date, time] for *Chanukat HaGan*
(Dedication of the Preschool). It will be a powerful
experience. The children are participating in marking their classrooms as Jewish spaces. We hope that
families will be able to join us as we hang our
mezuzot and celebrate this significant moment.

TO SEND HOME WITH A CHILD-MADE MEZUZAH

Shalom! Your child is bringing home a
mezuzah, which he/she has worked very hard to
make. In class, we learned all about the *mezuzah*
hanging on the classroom doorpost. It will therefore be especially meaningful to your child if you
affix the *mezuzah* he/she made on a doorpost at
home. Inside it, you may even find a *klaf* (scroll)
which your child wrote him/herself with a feather
"quill pen," just like a real *sofer* (scribe). The
mezuzah can be affixed to a doorpost with mount-
ing tape. If you would like to add a kosher *klaf* (or
replace your child's *klaf*), you can purchase one
at any Jewish bookstore. The *klaf* contains the
Shema prayer, which includes the words, "And you
shall write them [the commandments] upon the
doorposts of your house and upon your gates."

The ceremony for affixing a *mezuzah* is found in *The Jewish Home: A Guide for Jewish Living* by Daniel B. Syme (Reform), or *The How To Handbook for Jewish Living* by Kerry M. Olitzky and Ronald H. Isaacs (Traditional). We hope this *mezuzah* brings beauty to your home for years to come.

CONCLUSION

The *mezuzah* is just one important Jewish symbol that lends itself to an entire unit of study. This chapter can serve as a model as you plan ways to focus your curriculum on other symbols, ritual objects, and other related topics. These might include the *Magen David* (Jewish Star), *tallit* and *kipah* (and perhaps *tefillin*), or such topics as Jewish artists or Klezmer music. The trick is always to web your topic to find the concepts that are most interesting, and the related concepts as well. Once you have explored all the concepts and elements of your desired topic, you can brainstorm and search existing curricula and activity sources to find language arts, math, science, art and music activities to integrate the topic into your whole classroom. A unit on *mezuzah* is a valuable way to begin the year, and it will set the stage for other similar explorations.

BIBLIOGRAPHY

ADULTS

Olitzky, Kerry M., and Ronald H. Isaacs. *The How To Handbook for Jewish Living.* Hoboken, NJ: KTAV Publishing House, 1993.

This fact-filled manual contains the basic things that a Jew needs to know to live a Jewish life.

Syme, Daniel B. *The Jewish Home: A Guide for Jewish Living.* New York: UAHC Press, 1989.

A clear, concise, and beautifully written guide to Jewish family life from a Reform perspective.

Teutsch, Betsy Platkin, and Ellen Frankel. *Encyclopedia of Jewish Symbols.* Northvale, NJ: Jason Aronson Inc., 1992.

Defines 266 Jewish symbols, including ceremonial objects and images, personalities, places, concepts, motifs, and events.

CHILDREN

Jacobs, Chana. *Take Care of Me.* New York: HaChai Publications, 1989. (Ages 3-6)

When Moishy the *mezuzah* becomes sick, will the Fine family get him to a *sofer* in time?

Kitman, Caarol, and Ann Hurwitz. *One Mezuzah: A Jewish Counting Book.* NJ: Rossel Books, 1984. (Ages 2-8)

A counting book of Jewish objects.

Leiberman, Sarah. *A Trip to Mezuzahland.* New York: Mercaz, 1988. (Ages 3-8)

Children sail on their magic boats to visit a *sofer* and watch him write a *mezuzah*.

Ray, Eric. *Sofer: The Story of a Torah Scroll.* Los Angeles, CA: Torah Aura Productions, 1986. (Ages 4-8)

Describes in simple language and pictures how a *sofer* writes *mezuzot, tefillin,* and the *Sefer Torah*.

Syme, Deborah Shayne. *The Jewish Home Detectives.* New York: UAHC Press, 1982. (Ages 3-7)

Two children search their home for Jewish objects.

CHAPTER 21

THE ART OF STORYTELLING

There is magic in being able to tell a good story. And there are many joys, too — seeing children looking at you in wonder, watching an audience become tense as the plot thickens, noticing that even the babies have stopped crying and are hanging on your every word. Telling stories to preschool children doesn't require an advanced degree, a fancy business card, or even a finely honed talent. All it takes is a little wonder, a desire to delight, and a bit of confidence. Oh, yes, and perhaps a little practice.

We all tell stories all the time. "What did you do this weekend," your friend asks. "Oh," you reply, "let me tell you what happened." There — you're telling a story. You haven't practiced, you haven't fretted over the telling, and yet the story of your brother's cat escaping into a tree for 17 hours delights and entertains your listener. Children are similarly entranced and engaged by stories, although they may be a slightly harder audience.

READING BOOKS TO CHILDREN

Reading books to children is one important form of storytelling for the early childhood teacher. I recommend choosing only those books that you yourself enjoy. There are two reasons for this. The first is that when you enjoy a book, you won't mind so much when children ask you to read it again and again, which, of course, they will do. The second reason is that if you really like a book, you can approach it with wonder and make playful additions as you read it. For example, you

might add funny voices, or ask the children questions about the story, or talk about what is going on in the illustrations. Or, you might change some of the details of the story, in which case the children will stop you and demand that you tell it the "right" way. Each of these things is important when sharing a book with children.

Among the methods of reading stories to children is the group story time. This works best with older children. Gather the children into a group or circle, making sure each child is comfortable and can see well. Sit on a chair or on the ground, and hold the book next to you or (if you're really talented) in front of you, so that all the children can see the pictures. Try to make eye contact with the children as you read, and make sure to show the pictures all around so that each time you turn the page, children don't have to call out, "I didn't see the picture!"

While a group story time can be very effective, I prefer the spontaneous reading time. Plop down on the floor with some of your favorite books and at least one kid. With the child and the book in your lap or on the floor next to you, start reading. Pretty soon you'll have two kids in your lap, one or two on each side, and maybe one or two hanging over your shoulders. Be flexible about adjusting the position of the kids and the book to make sure everyone can see. Start a pile of requested books that children bring you as they join the group. With younger children, don't feel that you need to finish a book, or even read the pages in order. Some two-year-olds like to go backwards through books. Some one-year-olds like only the full color pages of *Good Night Moon*. Be fair about who gets to turn the pages. Feel free to ignore the words in the book, and just make all the animal sounds on each page. Point at the pictures and allow babies to do the same.

Spontaneous reading is an important supplement to group story time for older children. A good story told to one or two children allows deep, life affirming conversations to emerge. Spontaneous reading is like bedtime reading by a parent to a child. Both involve that crucial element that stories are meant to provide — human contact.

TELLING STORIES

WHICH VERSION?

The wonderful thing about telling a story is that you don't have to tell it exactly the same way each time. In fact, you don't even have to tell it exactly the same way it was written. How many times have you said, "Oh, I heard that story, but it was a Jewish grandmother instead of a butcher's wife." That's because stories are fluid; they change a little each time because the storyteller is always an element of the story. The relationship between the storyteller and the story changes each time it's told. Even my most favorite stories, those that I tell over and over, come out differently each time I tell them, depending on my mood and the needs of my listeners.

Every human culture has a creation story. For the Greeks, it all began with Zeus, in ancient Sumer it was Inanna, and for us, it was Adam and Eve. We all need to explain our beginnings, and in each case, the stories are similar. It's the details that are different. Many cultures also share similar folk tales. For example, there is in almost every culture a version of "Sleeping Beauty," "Little Red Riding Hood," and "Cinderella." In some cases, different versions of the same story exist in the same culture. One example is the classic tale of the overcrowded house.

HOW TO TELL A STORY

In recent years, three authors have written a version of that same Jewish tale of the overcrowded

house: *Could Anything Be Worse* by Marilyn Hirch, *It Could Always Be Worse* by Margot Zemach, and *Terrible, Terrible!* by Robin Bernstein. This is clear evidence that when telling such a story (and it's a great story to tell), you don't have to worry about the details. They're not important. What *is* important? The problem of the overcrowded house.

There is a man (or maybe in your version, it's a woman). He or she lives in a house that's small and crowded. What's it crowded with? It's up to you. You the storyteller are in charge. So maybe it's crowded with a noisy spouse making supper, a few fighting kids — you decide how many — and a baby. It's always good to have a baby because the crying is good for audience participation. So the man or the woman . . . what did you name her? Rachel? Rachel goes to the Rabbi to seek some help. The Rabbi (male or female, you decide) tells Rachel to bring some animals into her house. Which animals? Again, you decide. But do pick some animals that make good noises for your listeners to contribute. One day at a time, one animal at a time, the Rabbi instructs Rachel to fill up her house with livestock until the house is crowded and noisy and smelly, and your "listeners" are mooing and crowing and baa-ing and crying and everyone (except Rachel) is having a great time. Then (of course, just in time for Shabbat or the holiday or Rachel's birthday), the wise Rabbi tells Rachel to return all those animals to their proper homes. Rachel runs home to clear out her house. She throws open the windows and enlists the entire family to help clean the house. Finally, surrounded by all the same sounds that existed at the beginning of the story, Rachel experiences the most wonderful peace she's ever known.

A few important things just happened. You told a story and took ownership of the heart of the story, and you let the details happen. Also, you enabled your listeners to become part of the story. Yet, even as you invite listeners to become a part, be sure you maintain control of the story. At the beginning of the telling, establish a hand signal or key word that alerts listeners that it is their turn to participate. Remember that sometimes involving the listeners is not possible, or even desirable. In a story that depends on timing and mystique, there might be little or no room for audience participation. The story of the overcrowded house, however, has built-in roles for listeners: the making of animal and baby noises at appropriate points in the story. The potential for audience involvement is one of the reasons this is a great story to tell.

Even when you tell a story with no built-in roles for listeners, it's still possible, and often beneficial, to pause during the telling and ask, "What do you think happened next?" or "Who do you think was at the door?" Questions such as these will engage your listeners, wake up kids who may be drifting, and empower children to think. Sometimes, you'll get questions or contributions without soliciting them. When that happens, acknowledge the comment or briefly answer the question, and return to your telling with as little fuss as possible.

TELLING STORIES WITH PROPS

Not everyone can read a story a few times, find the heart of the story, then feel free enough to let the details fall into place and just tell the story. The use of visuals and props can be a great help to every storyteller; they can also help the audience pay closer attention to a story.

Different kinds of puppets may be the best aid of this sort, because you can maintain maximum eye contact with your listeners as you use them. Hand puppets, homemade from socks or store-bought, stick puppets, finger puppets, marionettes if you are really talented, etc., can all help you tell a story. You may want to practice a little with puppets in front of a mirror, just to get an idea of how high to hold them, which ways to turn them, and how much to move your mouth when speaking for a puppet.

Felt board characters and props are other useful tools. You can cut and create figures and backgrounds using felt. Or, you can mount pictures from a book or magazine on cardboard, laminate them, and attach Velcro to the back. Allow children to retell the story with the felt board props after they have heard you tell it. Pay close attention to the children's versions of the story. This will give you clues as to how well you told the story, and about which parts of the story were most meaningful to the children.

YOUR OWN STORIES/MAKING UP STORIES

Some of the best stories I have told have been made up on the spot, on demand. Once during a parent and child "Tot Shabbat" class, we had just finished baking *challah*, and I hadn't planned on telling a story. Then Brandon, about two at the time, pointed to the shelf and demanded, "Puppets." I took down the puppets, and suddenly I was telling a story. My story revolved around several of the animal puppets in the box. Smelling something delicious, these animals came to find the source. When they got to our classroom and discovered the *challah*, the animals were afraid the children wouldn't share, but (and here I named each child in the class) all the children did indeed share their *challah*, and everyone had a wonderful Shabbat. Instant stories may not turn out perfectly, but they are almost always a lot of fun. And children are always eager to help supply an ending.

Children also love stories about their teacher. As soon as they are old enough to ask, they will ask for stories about when you were little, what you did over the weekend, and tales about your pets. When you share these stories with the children in your class, you will be sharing even more than Jewish values and history and culture and morals. You will be sharing yourself.

CONCLUSION

I have always loved to tell stories. When I was still new at it, but had already discovered the intoxicating joy of telling a really good story, I told one to a group of about 40 three and four-year-olds. I used my whole body, but no props and no book. When I was finished, I received one of the best compliments I have gotten to this day, when a three-year-old immediately piped up from the first row, "Read it again!"

BIBLIOGRAPHY

ADULTS

Bettelheim, Bruno. *The Uses of Enchantment: The Meaning and Importance of Fairy Tales*. New York: Vintage Books, 1989.

> The great child psychologist gives us a moving revelation of the enormous and irreplaceable value of fairy tales — how they educate, support, and liberate the emotions of children.

Cooper, Patsy. *When Stories Come To School: Telling, Writing, and Performing Stories in the Early Childhood Classroom*. New York: Teachers & Writers Collaborative, 1993.

> Combines early childhood theory with storytelling and writing techniques.

Gillard, Marni. *Storyteller, Storyteacher: Discovering the Power of Storytelling for Teaching and Living*. York, ME: Stenhouse Publishers, 1996.

> A committed teacher, storyteller, and listener presents a highly readable how-to book about involving both adults and students in storytelling. Gillard shows why storytelling can be so satisfying and enlarging for tellers young and old as she discusses the meaning of anecdote, "Just talk," personal tales, and age-old stories that tell aspects of one's own inner journey.

Greene, Ellin, and Augusta Baker. *Storytelling: Art and Technique*. New Providence, NJ: R.R. Bowker, 1996.

> Discusses approaches to learning stories and interactions between storyteller and audience and other storytelling skills.

Maguire, Jack. *The Power of Personal Storytellling: Spinning Tales to Connect with Others*. New York: J.P. Tarcher, 1998.

> A professional storyteller explains how to mine your memories to communicate more effectively, enhance personal and professional relationships, and understand yourself better so that you can better understand others.

Mellon, Nancy. *The Art of Storytelling*. Rockport, MA: Element, 1998.

> The author outlines the essential energies of every good story and teaches how to use visualization and imagination to evoke them. Each chapter focuses on different aspects of the stories.

Sawyer, Ruth. *The Way of the Storyteller*. New York: Penguin USA, 1998.

> First published in 1942, this classic work is unique in its blend of literary history, criticism, analysis, personal anecdote, and how-to instructions. Sawyer examines storytelling as a folk art and a still-living art, tracing its evolution from the earliest narrative impulses that developed as stories were written down.

Schram, Penninah. "Storytelling: Role and Technique." In *The New Jewish Teachers Handbook*. Denver: A.R.E. Publishing, Inc., 1994.

> After a brief explanation of what storytelling is and why it is valuable, noted storyteller Schram describes how to prepare oneself to tell stories, how to select stories, how to prepare the telling, and how to tell a story.

CHILDREN

Brown, Margaret Wise. *Good Night Moon*. New York: Harper & Row, 1947.

> Good night room, good night moon, good night cow jumping over the moon. This calm rhyme and repetition has entranced generations of children.

Hirsh, Marilyn. *Could Anything Be Worse?* New York: Holiday House, 1974.

> A classic retelling of the Yiddish tale of the overcrowded house.

Zemach, Margot. *It Could Always Be Worse*. New York: Farrar, Straus and Giroux, 1976.

> Another classic retelling of the Yiddish tale of the overcrowded house.

Bernstein, Robin. *Terrible, Terrible!* Rockville, MD: Kar-Ben Copies, 1998.

A modern retelling of the Yiddish tale of the overcrowded house.

STORY COLLECTIONS

Frankel, Ellen. *The Classic Tales: 4000 Years of Jewish Lore.* Northvale, NJ: Jason Aronson Inc., 1989.

A thick volume packed with the stories of our tradition.

Gellman, Marc. *Does God Have a Big Toe?* New York: Harper Collins, 1989.

Stories about stories in the Torah.

Jaffe, Nina. *The Univited Guest and Other Jewish Holiday Tales.* New York: Scholastic, 1993.

Wonderful original stories for each holiday.

Jaffe, Nina. *The Mysterious Visitor: Stories of the Prophet Elijah.* New York: Scholastic, 1997.

Favorite tales of the Prophet Elijah, perfect for telling.

Kimmel, Eric. *Days of Awe: Stories for Rosh Hashanah and Yom Kippur.* New York: Viking, 1991.

A small volume of powerful stories.

Pearl, Sydelle. *Elijah's Tears: Stories for the Jewish Holidays.* New York: Henry Holt and Company, 1996.

Original stories featuring Elijah, and even his sister, Eliora.

Schram, Peninnah, ed. *Chosen Tales: Stories Told by Jewish Storytellers.* Northvale NJ: Jason Aronson Inc., 1995.

A collection of stories told by Jewish story-tellers from all over the world.

Schwartz, Howard, and Babara Rush. *The Diamond Tree: Jewish Tales from around the World.* New York: Harper Collins, 1991.

Mystical and magical tales for telling.

Schram, Peninnah. *Jewish Stories One Generation Tells Another.* Northvale, NJ: Jason Aronson Inc., 1993.

A fabulous collection of classic Jewish stories retoled by a master storyteller.

Simon, Solomon. *The Wise Men of Helm and their Merry Tales.* New York: Behrman House, 1973.

Light joyful tales of Chelm. Best for older children. Look for other Chelm books, too.

CHAPTER 22

A GUIDE TO MUSIC IN THE EARLY CHILDHOOD CLASSROOM

Julie Jaslow Auerbach

You're sitting on the floor in front of a class of 15 children under the age of five. You have 20 minutes to teach them a few songs for Rosh HaShanah. What do you do? What songs will you choose? How many? What should come first? what second? The answers to these questions can be found in this chapter as you explore different facets of the teaching of music to young children.

Music is a key part of the early childhood curriculum. How many of us as young children learned to remember the ABC's through the song? Young children can often be heard singing familiar songs, for they enjoy repetition, and even making up their own melodies. They have fun experimenting with sounds. Music is an integral form of expression to them, as well as an integral form of self-directed lessons.

This chapter will guide you through a brief course in music for the early childhood classroom. It will also provide an overview of the different schools of thought and some creative and educationally sound suggestions for use of movement, dance, and instruments.

GETTING STARTED

Start with a song that tells the children, "It's music time. Let's enjoy some songs together." The song you choose to signify music time also has another purpose. It puts you, the teacher, in gear. It's a warm-up song, a signal that tells one and all that what will follow will be pleasant, fun, and enjoyable for all. No athlete would think of beginning a game without a warm-up; in like manner, a warm-up is essential when beginning a new

activity in the preschool. Pick a song you enjoy and are comfortable with — a good "Hello" song, such as *Heyvaynu Shalom Aleychem*" or "If You're Happy and You Know It." When you have found a song that works for you and suits your students, use it at the beginning of every music session.

Many preschoolers fall apart at transitions. Therefore, transition songs that move the young child from one activity to another, such as "Put Your Finger on the Wall" (to the tune of "Put Your Finger in the Air") are important tools for early childhood teachers. You'll find that children respond more readily to the music of such a song than to your request to stop what they are doing. The tenuous attachments they have made in the classroom are tested as they must switch gears to focus on a new activity. By thoughtfully *and musically* calling attention to and reiterating the procedures and activities to come, we help these children to become more adept at managing transitions from one activity to another or from one location to another.

You will also want to find a song that signals the end of the music session. For several years, I used "If You're Happy and You Know It." ("*Shalom Chavereem*" has the right words and sentiments, but the version most of us know can be a difficult melody for young, developing voices because of its vocal range.) Together, the children and I clapped hands, nodded our heads, and reviewed key concepts from the lesson. For example, on Rosh HaShanah, if we were happy, we "blew" our *shofar*, "dipped" an apple in the honey, and then waved good-bye. Another year, I chose "I've Got That Happy Feeling," an old camp song. We put the happy feeling in our heads, our voices, our hands, and our feet. When the happy feeling was "all over us," I told the children that I hoped that they would keep their happy feelings until the next music time.

ORGANIZING THE MATERIAL

What songs will you use the first week? the second week? Should you build up from September to some culmination at the end of the school year? Or, should you organize the material with several small culminations? To what kinds of songs do young children relate?

I've always looked to the "givens" for my guidelines when organizing materials. For instance, it is a given that school starts in September, generally close to the High Holy Days. It is a given that we will end the school year in May or June, generally close to Shavuot. The Jewish calendar thus provides a useful road map for early childhood educators and music specialists to follow, especially if we are aware of the values and other Jewish concepts that go along with it.

One year, I tried to move away from my emphasis on the Jewish calendar as a natural organizer. I tried to teach "music for music's sake," beginning with an emphasis on beat and the integral parts of music. I found that both the teachers and I were very dissatisfied with teaching music in this manner in a Jewish setting. The organizing principle was missing. We learned that it is essential to ground all the music we introduce in what is already going on in the classroom.

The tendency to think of a Jewish preschool music curriculum either as holiday-based or as music for music's sake leaves great gaps. Jewish life is not comprised of holidays alone, and music can be an integral tool in all preschool learning experiences. Sensory experiences and hands-on activities set the groundwork for future development. Emphasis and reemphasis in various modalities and media reinforce the lessons. A Jewish child will live by the calendar and these values all his or her life. The impressions made on children in these early childhood years, and the songs they will learn to reinforce these values and concepts, will enrich that lifetime.

Watch for secular units that can be enhanced Jewishly. For example, community helpers are certainly policemen/women and doctors, but they are also Rabbis and Cantors. Colors can be presented in English — and Hebrew! The more you reinforce what is learned in the classroom through different modalities, the more easily the child will synthesize the material.

Finally, when organizing your music program, it is important to keep it simple. Too much information too soon will confuse young children. Choose songs with a narrow melody range and a simple rhythm. Too often, we judge a song by adult standards and not by the standards of a young child. For young children, songs need to be easy and uncomplicated. If the movement in a song is what's important to teach, teach it first without the words. If it's the words that are important, teach them first and reinforce by adding a movement later as a special variation.

OUTLINE FOR A SHORT MUSIC SESSION

As you read through this chapter, many insights about music for young children will be presented. A preschool teacher will want to use music throughout the day; a preschool music specialist will have his/her special time. No matter what your role, you will find this basic outline useful for any 15-20 minute music session:
1. Opening song
2. Lap chant (see the section "Beat and Rhythm," (see p. 286 below)
3. 2-3 curricular-related songs (holidays, values, concepts)
4. Concluding song

GUIDELINES FOR TEACHING MUSIC

SCHOOLS OF THOUGHT

There are many schools of thought regarding the teaching of music to young children, and many methods and terms you may encounter. The three most often mentioned methods are Dalcroze-Eurythmics, Kodaly (pronounced Ko-dai), and Orff Schulwerk.

Dalcroze-Eurythmics, named for the nineteenth century Swiss, Emile Jacques Dalcroze, stresses physical movement and the development of awareness of music through physical movement, with an emphasis on learning to listen in order to move to the music.

According to the Kodaly method, named for the late nineteenth century Zoltan Kodaly, a Hungarian, a child's music education begins when the child starts to make his/her own music, i.e., his/her own sounds. The child's voice is thus most important. Music is taught as a language through folk songs and games.

Orff Schulwerk, named for the early twentieth century German, Carl Orff, makes use of specially designed percussion instruments that are easy for little ones to play. Examples are the metallophone and the xylophone. The pentatonic scale is employed. In that scale, the fourth and seventh tones are omitted from the diatonic scale we generally use; for example, in the key of C major, F and B would be omitted. Every combination of notes in this scale sounds okay. Without dissonant sounds, the child immediately feels success. Orff followers maintain that the most natural line for musical development in the young child is speech, then rhythm, and, finally, song.

Each of these schools of thought is important. Just as there are different kinds of learners in the classroom, so, too, are there children who will relate to music in different ways. Making use of each of these methods will enable you to reach every child and to help each feel successful.

SETTING THE STAGE

There are two ways to approach the teaching of a song. The first is the "jump in and start" method. You begin by singing the song. This works well for your catch-all variety songs such as "I've Got That Happy Feeling." Ella Jenkins' "Clap Clap Clap Your Hands," or when you need to get the attention of the class quickly. In most cases, however, taking that little extra time to set the stage or to explain the song will better enable the child to understand the song's meaning and its connection to the rest of what you may be teaching.

The following form of brainstorming is an example of one technique to use when setting the stage for learning a song.

Teacher: What do you do when you're feeling happy?

Sarah: I smile.

Matt: I laugh.

Teacher: Do you do anything with your hands?

Lisa: Oh — I clap them.

Brian: I raise my hands in the air.

Teacher: How about your feet? Do you do anything special with them when you're happy?

Matt: I jump up and down.

Lisa: I dance.

Teacher: And your head? What is it doing?

Sarah: I shake my head like this.

Brian: I nod my head.

This class is now ready to learn "If You're Happy and You Know It." When preparing children to learn a song through this brainstorming method, we are also teaching them a useful technique for the future.

THE SCRIPT

Once you've set the stage by explaining the meaning of the song or by brainstorming, you will need to give the "players" the "script."

Sing the song once or twice through. Then divide it up into small parts. Have the children repeat the words after you. Try it rhythmically without music as a poem. Then add the music. Next you might drop a word at the end of a line and let them fill it in, a very successful technique, as it makes the children feel very successful very quickly!

1. Teacher sings song once or twice through.
2. Teacher speaks one line at a time; children echo.

3. Teacher sings one line at a time; children echo.

4. Teacher sings two lines at a time; children echo.

5. Teacher and children sing together.

6. Teacher sings with children, but omits words here and there.

7. Add motions, instruments, or a simple dance. (These suggestions are more fully explained in the sections which follow.)

Other useful techniques to add to your script, especially when presenting a song a second or third time around, are:

1. Addition – add an introductory lap chant (see "Beat and Rhythm" p. 286 below) or musical overture (see Chapter 16, "Pesach," Music/ Movement activity #4, the *Dayaynu* chant).

2. Variation – have children create their own verses (see Chapter 7, "Shabbat," Music/Movement activity #3 on adapting the song *"Hayom Yom Shishi"*).

3. Adaptation – translate some of the Hebrew words in a song to give greater meaning for the children (see Chapter 16, "Pesach, with Lag B'Omer," Music/ Movement activity #4 under Pesach, p. 228, which translates the song *"Mah Nishtanah"*).

4. Improvisation – use basic movements to construct a choreography for a song or more sophisticated dance (see "Dance and Improvisation" below).

ADDING MOTIONS

Some songs have wonderful motions that accompany them (e.g., the song "My Hat It Has Three Corners"). Sometimes we can develop our own motions to go along with songs. In this context, Phyllis Weikart, High Scope Movement and Dance Consultant, suggests that there are three parts to the presentation of movement:

1. Separate – Separate your words from your actions. Don't describe while you are doing. Show the movement first without words, then have the children imitate. The goal is to have the children perform the movement success-fully. Once the movement is understood, then the words can be successfully introduced.

2. Simplify – Present one movement at a time. Pause, then repeat it. Give the children time to repeat the first movement before adding the second one. Then put the two movements together and do them in sequence. Pause, and repeat them a second time. Pause, then repeat the two. Finally, give each movement a word that children will recognize as a command.

3. Facilitate – When the children have done the movement and heard the words, review the entire sequence. What comes first? second? etc. Young children learn by doing. When they actively participate in the learning process, they are more successful learners.

DANCE AND IMPROVISATION

It is not necessary to be a skilled dancer to get little ones up and dancing. Simple movements that are appropriate for young children will help them to be successful. Don't be afraid to use Israeli dance tapes. You can make up your own easy steps to such dances as *"Myeem"* and *"Tzaddik Katamar Yifrach,"* two traditional Israeli dances.

Improvisational dances also work well with young children. Here are some suggested movements:

Hands and arms:	Tapping body parts
	Clapping hands
	Waving
	Shaking our hands
Feet:	Walking
	Stomping
	Running
	Jumping
	Marching
	Tip-toeing
	Turning
	Jogging
	Swaying:
	With arms overhead
	With arms side to side

With arms by knees
Moving in and out of the
center of the circle
Walking in a circle
Sliding in a circle
Sliding side-to-side
Partners

Contrasts: Scrunch/stretch
Walk/run or jog
Tip-toe/march or stomp
Sway/freeze
Skip/hop or jump

Don't get caught up in concepts of left and right with young children. This is not as important at first as the enjoyment of the music and movement. Simply count between musical phrases and adjust movements accordingly.

BEAT AND RHYTHM

Young children are explorers. They want to touch, taste, and experiment with everything. Because they learn by doing, they need lots of manipulatives with which to work. Similarly, during music time, we need to give them the time and opportunity to manipulate and play with music. This can be done through the use of sounds, movements, and instruments.

In order for young children to make intelligible music, they need to master some degree of self-control and at least one basic musical concept — beat. Beat is the integral heart of each song. It directs us to move our voices or instruments quickly or slowly. Rhythm, on the other hand, reflects the song's uniqueness within the beat structure. Of the two concepts, rhythm is the easier of the two for the young child to master.

One of a number of simple beat songs called "lap chants" should be repeated during each music session. The following song, "Beat Is Steady," is a favorite of mine. It was written by Phyllis Weikart and goes to the tune of *"Freres Jacques."*

Beat is steady, beat is steady
Feel the beat, feel the beat

Keep the beat so steady, keep the beat so steady
Feel the beat, feel the beat.

As with all basic lap chants, start out beating the knees, and then move to the heads. ("Can you feel the beat in your heads?" I ask as I prepare the children to move their hands to another part of their bodies.)

Here is a useful lap chant to recite that has no melody:

Tap, tap, tap your knees,
Tap your knees if you please.
Now let's tap our head,
Our head, our head,
Is it made of lead
Our head, our head?

Can you tap your cheeks,
Your cheeks, your cheeks?
Are there any leaks
In your cheeks, your cheeks?

Shoulders . . . feel like boulders
Chin . . . fat or thin
Eyes . . . oh my, oh my
Hair . . . if you care
Etc.

Conclude by returning to the knees. Returning to the song's starting point gives the children a sense of completion.

Once the children are comfortable with the basic beat song, you can try a variation. Make one child the leader and let him/her introduce a new lap chant. As the weeks go by, the children will spontaneously begin to initiate lap tapping as they listen to a piece of music with a strong beat. I've even successfully used a lap chant with a statement and echo response as an introduction to a concept or as conversation on a topic:

Teacher: Fall days, cool days
What will you do?
I'll go to school.
How about you?

Child: Fall days, cool days
         What will you do?
         I'll rake the leaves
         How about you?

INSTRUMENTS

In addition to the Orff instruments mentioned above (see p. 284), there are many wonderful rhythm instruments available. Young children enjoy making music with them all. However, it is important to introduce the instruments one at a time, providing ample opportunity for the children to explore and experiment with the instrument and the sounds it is capable of making. Let the children sort the properties of several different kinds of instruments. (If, however, you want children to react to the music, it is better to give each of them the same instrument.)

There are, of course, numerous ways in which instruments can be used in the early childhood classroom, including accompanying a song you've already taught, accompanying a tape or CD, or even as part of a story or play. Try telling a story and punctuating it with instruments, or have the instruments speak instead of the characters. This is especially good with something like "Goldilocks and the Three Bears," which features a little voice, a medium voice, and a big voice. Build on the children's love of games by playing musical games with them — leave out words for them to fill in, have them act out the songs. Let your imagination and love of music and children dictate your lesson plans.

CONCLUSION

This chapter has presented the basics for a successful music program. You'll use a terrific opening song and an equally terrific closing song. In between these, you'll sing a basic beat song or chant relevant to your lesson. Choose two to three songs related to your curriculum, one or two of which is new and one of which you may have introduced at the previous session. Review this latter song by singing it through with the children. Then try a variation on it, such as using additional movements or instruments or perhaps improvising a dance. Or, if the children seem to need a little more time to get ready to learn something new, present the newer song after reviewing the older song.

Remember to hook your song selection to what's already going on in the classroom. Make up a story that moves from song to song if you want to bind the lesson together. Use props, gimmicks, and visuals. One year, for example, I introduced each holiday using "What Do You Like about Shabbat?" by Miss Jackie. I changed "Shabbat" to the particular holiday the children were studying, and drew each of the symbols or ritual objects appropriate to the holiday out of a big red straw bag as we sang the song. The objects in the bag served to introduce the holiday, and also to review previously studied holidays as well. You can also preview upcoming holidays with four-year-olds using this technique.

When young children are comfortable with our expectations for them, and when they understand the material we are presenting to them in a simple manner, they are in the best position to sing a song. When they feel successful, they will be eager to learn and to do more music activities with you. It requires two essentials: patience to set the stage slowly for learning and the use of an appropriate script. These will enable you to share those feelings of success as you watch the children spontaneously engage in or initiate musical activities.

Use the songs and musical activities that appear in this chapter and throughout this book, and, most important, rely on your own creativity. Listen to and watch your students well, for they are the best guides of all. (For a complete listing of music resources and a discography, see the bibliography at the end of this volume, pp. 367-371.

CHAPTER 23

APPROACHES TO SECULAR HOLIDAYS

In a Jewish early childhood classroom, we spend a great deal of time learning about and celebrating Jewish holidays. However, there are often disagreements about if, and how secular or North American holidays should be observed or noted. Some of these holidays are relevant and appropriate for our Jewish classrooms; others are not. It is important to give serious consideration to the background and meaning of each secular holiday before introducing it in your classroom.

In this chapter, the first such holiday to be discussed is Thanksgiving. It is perhaps the most pertinent to the Jewish early childhood classroom. Other holidays/occasions included in this chapter are: Halloween, New Year's Eve, Columbus Day and Presidents' Day, Victoria Day, Martin Luther King Day, Valentine's Day, Memorial Day/Remembrance Day, and the Fourth of July/Canada Day.

THANKSGIVING

It is highly likely that for Thanksgiving each of the children in your class will be gathering with friends or relatives to take in some turkey. Thanksgiving is therefore a very relevant unit of study in your classroom. The traditions inherent in the holiday include gathering together with family, eating lots of food, and taking time to appreciate what we have, all elements of many Jewish holidays.

STEREOTYPES AND MYTHS

Be careful to make Thanksgiving part of your classroom without reinforcing stereotypes and myths. The popular story of how the Pilgrims and Indians became great friends is a myth (Kessel,

1983; Barth, 1975). As the Pilgrims and other Europeans came to America, they took over the ancient homes of the Native Americans, taking their land by force and killing them either with guns or with diseases against which the Native Americans had no natural defenses. It is true that there may have been some cooperation between the passengers of the Mayflower and some Native Americans who were not killed by smallpox. Perhaps there was even a feast, based on the Massasoit Thanksgiving feast called the "Green Corn Dance." But the great Pilgrim feast we emulate almost certainly bore very little resemblance to our modern day celebration. The facts surrounding the story may not be true, but there are still good reasons to teach this story. (Historians certainly debate the historical truth of the Purim story, yet that has never kept us from teaching about Esther and Uncle Mordecai.)

There are, however, other reasons not to teach this story. Popular culture around Thanksgiving time is filled with images of half-naked Native Americans wearing feather headdresses, smiling happy Pilgrims, and cartoon animals dressed like Pilgrims or Native Americans. These images are stereotypes, and they are negative. Animals do not wear aprons and Pilgrim bonnets. Native Americans do not go around all the time in feathers, carrying bow and arrows. Native Americans do not still live in teepees, nor did all Native Americans ever live in teepees. Young children can not distinguish between history and the present. When we embellish the Thanksgiving story with these aspects, we are reinforcing these stereotypes.

To make your Thanksgiving study free from stereotypes and bias, it is necessary to seek out the books which share your values. Choose books that focus on more modern family celebrations, and not on Pilgrims. But, wait, now that you're not making feather headbands and setting up a teepee in your room, how *do* you approach Thanksgiving?

YOUNGER CHILDREN

For younger children, the essence of Thanksgiving can be conveyed through concrete symbols, such as the turkey and pumpkins. While these can be part of your focus, they should not predominate over important Jewish values. Put the emphasis on family, *Tzedakah*, God, and blessings. One popular belief is that the Pilgrims modeled their Thanksgiving on the biblical holiday of Sukkot, another harvest holiday with a focus on God and giving thanks. Following that example, use Thanksgiving as a time to recall the things we were thankful for at Sukkot, and reflect on the things we are thankful for now, as the weather gets colder and nothing is growing outside.

Thanksgiving is not just a time to think about what we are thankful for. Go beyond making turkeys with feathers, and find out what each child is thankful for. You might hang up a long "I am thankful for" list for parents to enjoy. On Yom Kippur, we are told that we have not truly done *teshuvah* (repentance) until we actually apologize to those people we have offended. We can empower our young children to make the same connections on Thanksgiving. Instead of simply writing down what children are thankful for as part of an art project or class book, help children write notes to the people who deserve their thanks, and actually send the notes (Darvick, 1999). Thanking the people in our lives for the wonderful things they have done for us paves the way to thanking God for all the wonderful things God has done and created for us.

Once you've found ways to thank the people who should be thanked, go one step further, and find ways to give back. Make *Tzedakah* an active part of your Thanksgiving celebration. Collect canned goods, assemble sandwiches for a home-less shelter or soup kitchen, draw pictures and bring them to children who are in the hospital over the holiday. Encourage and enable acts of *Chesed*, such as making something special for the school secretary or maintenance person. Make the *mitzvah* of *Hachnasat Orcheem*, hospitality, part of your Thanksgiving preparations by inviting another class to feast with you.

Of course, as with Jewish holidays, family is an important part of Thanksgiving as well. Thanksgiving is a good time to focus on each child's family and the different shapes a family can take. Each family has different traditions for each holiday, and these should be included in your classroom study as well.

OLDER CHILDREN

Thanksgiving can be expanded to include a very exciting area of investigation for four and five-year-olds. At Thanksgiving, we traditionally tell the story of how the Pilgrims came to be here in America. But how many Jewish families were actually on the Mayflower? Engaging in a study of "Coming To America" (or, as a teacher I worked with dubbed it, "I Never Met a Pilgrim"), sets children and families off on a meaningful journey. The children really relate to this approach to Thanksgiving because it involves stories about their family, and also values their families' experiences. In some way, at some time, someone in each of the children's families *came* to America. Some of the children may be first generation Americans. Many parents or grandparents experienced immigration to America. Children can learn about the whole world in a way that relates to them and their friends.

A few weeks before Thanksgiving, invite families to send to class with their child the story of how they (or their forebears) came to North America. To get the best results, you may want to send home a specific questionnaire, with questions such as: From what country does your family originate? Who in your family came to this country? How did they travel (boat, plane, train)? Why did they come? What special things did they bring? Encourage parents to talk with their children about the answers to the questionnaire. Solicit pictures, items brought over from "the old country," recipes that have been passed down from generation to generation, and ask parents or grandparents to come in and tell first-hand immigration stories.

In class, study the Jewish immigration experience. Make a chart of the different types of transportation used by each family to get to America. Transform the house corner with suitcases, long skirts, shawls, and other "old country" articles of clothing, doctor kits, and Ellis Island signs. Build the Statue of Liberty out of boxes. Post a world map with pushpins marking all the countries or cities of origin, and mark your town prominently. Make family trees that include the people who immigrated in each family. Talk about what the children would pack if they were moving to a new, faraway place. Read the book *The Keeping Quilt* by Patricia Polacco, and make a class quilt. Other excellent children's books about immigration experiences, Jewish and otherwise, are *How Many Days To America?* by Eve Bunting, and *Watch the Stars Come Out* by Riki Levinson. (See the bibliography for this chapter for more suggestions.)

Through a unit such as "Coming To America" or "I Never Met a Pilgrim," Jewish preschoolers will learn about their own families, and be able to share their own history with their friends. And, as they sit down to Thanksgiving dinner, every family that has had the opportunity to explore these stories of theirs will have a deeper sense of just why we are so thankful to be American.

When studying Thanksgiving, tell children that Jews are supposed to say 100 *brachot* a day. Use this holiday, which has its roots in Sukkot, as an opportunity to sing and reinforce appropriate blessings. Also sing "A Special Way of Saying Thanks" by Julie Jaslow Auerbach (see Appendix B, p. 358).

Clearly, Thanksgiving is an American holiday that can have deep meaning for young Jewish children and a great significance in the Jewish early childhood classroom.

HALLOWEEN

Halloween has its roots in pagan and Christian cultures and the holiday is devoid of Jewish values. For this reason, it is one of the most problematic American holidays for Jewish early childhood educators. Still, all children become totally obsessed with the rituals of costumes and candy collection.

A brief history of Halloween may help clarify why Halloween has no place in the Jewish classroom. The word "Halloween" comes from All Hallows Eve, which was created by Pope Boniface IV in the seventh century to honor saints and martyrs. However, the origins of the holiday itself can be traced back to the fifth century B.C.E. to a holiday called Samhain, the Celtic New Year, which fell on October 31, the last day of the Celtic year. On Samhain, the curtain dividing the realms of the living and the dead was believed to be at its thinnest. This allowed spirits to spend this night visiting the world of the living and possibly finding bodies to possess. Celtic tradition involved dressing up in costume (mostly by adults) to avoid being recognized by the spirits.

By 43 B.C.E., when the Romans had conquered much of the Celt's territory, Samhain began to resemble some Roman holidays, including one honoring Pomona, the goddess of fruit and trees. This is very likely the reason for the modern tradition of bobbing for apples. Centuries later, the medieval Christian authorities adapted the holiday to be the church sanctioned holiday of All Hallows Day. In 1000 C.E., the church declared November 2 to be All Souls Day to honor the dead. In parts of Europe, poor people would go door to door on this day, begging for pastries and in return promising to pray for the dead. Hence the tradition of trick-or-treat. Later, European immigrants brought Halloween to America, and it enjoyed moderate popularity. In 1846, Irish immigrants, fleeing the Irish potato famine, greatly popularized the holiday. Jack-o'-lanterns find their origin in Irish legends about a man named Jack, whose soul could not get into hell or heaven when he died. So he carved a lantern out of a turnip and wanders about at night (Chambers, 1997). The turnip was later replaced by the pumpkin, but the tradition remains. By the 1920s and 30s, Halloween had become a staple of American culture.

These origins of Halloween illustrate why Halloween is antithetical to Judaism. With the exception of the dybbuk, we don't find in Judaism spirits roaming free over the earth, or possession of living people by spirits. Judaism teaches us to give *Tzedakah*, without being asked, and does not encourage begging from door to door. Saints, martyrs, and goddesses are strangers to the Jewish culture. There is nothing Jewish children can take or learn from Halloween.

So, you might argue, nobody's trick-or-treating nowadays to honor the dead, and we aren't dressing up to hide from Celtic spirits anymore. What's the harm in dressing up a little and eating a little candy? There probably is no harm, but there's no benefit either. Why spend precious classroom time on Halloween when there are so many beneficial, more interesting things you could be exploring with your children?

Of course, this doesn't address the biggest dilemma. In most schools, even if the decision has already been made not to teach Halloween, children will bring in Halloween anyway. They are eager to talk about what costume they are going to wear, how much candy they collected, how they carved their jack-o'-lantern. It is important to validate children's experiences, but the question is, how do we do that without enduring an entire unit of Halloween?

First of all, allow children to talk about their Halloween experiences. You can even build on their experiences to form appropriate units in your classroom. Costumes are important things to explore. Children benefit from "trying on"

different roles. We know this because we watch them play dress-up all year long. With the help of different costumes, children can investigate feeling scared, grown-up, glamorous, powerful, silly, and on and on. Masks can help children talk about feelings, and try to see the world through different eyes. There can be great creativity in making masks or costumes, using media ranging from brown paper bags to papier mâché.

Another way to solve this "October dilemma" is to take a Halloween symbol and use it in your classroom without connecting it to Halloween. Pumpkins, even without a face, are an incredible early childhood tool. Open up a great big pumpkin in your class. Let all the children feel the slimy, gooey insides. Take out the seeds. Wash them, count them, make art with them, or better yet, roast them! Save some seeds to plant in your classroom. You could have a pumpkin vine growing in your room in the middle of the winter! Cut up the pumpkin and make pumpkin pie or pumpkin soup or pumpkin cookies or pumpkin bread with the meat. It might just be preferable to buy canned pumpkin. This could prevent everyone from getting sick after all the children have handled the pumpkin inside and out. Once you cut up the pumpkin, use the skin as canvas for painting. Use the children's Halloween experiences, but expand on them outside the context of Halloween.

Once you've made the decision not to have a Halloween costume parade in school, how do you explain this to children? You could remind them that we dress up in school on Purim, but that's four or five months away, and they may not remember Purim from last year. It is helpful to explain to children that Halloween is not a Jewish holiday, so we don't celebrate it at school. You might also tell children that costumes are for *after* school. Be sure to enlist the parents' help in reinforcing this message.

Halloween is assuredly not an appropriate holiday for the Jewish early childhood classroom. Yet, it is possible to validate children and to use their Halloween experiences to other ends while maintaining a Halloween-free school.

NEW YEAR'S EVE

There are very few reasons to celebrate New Year's Eve in the Jewish early childhood classroom. It is unlikely that children will be staying up until midnight to watch the ball drop in Times Square. At best, young children have a limited understanding of calendar. For children younger than four, the calendar, and thus New Year's Eve, holds no relevance. Older children, for whom "calendar" may be a regular, daily feature, can connect more to the new year and the new month.

There is one Jewish connection that is important to include if you study New Year's Eve with older children. Four and five-year-olds can draw similarities and differences between the secular New Year and the Jewish New Year, Rosh HaShanah. The Hebrew calendar is based on the moon; the secular calendar on the sun. On Rosh HaShanah, we think about the kind of person we are, and we talk with God about how to become a better person. On the secular New Year, many people make resolutions, which are "deals" with themselves, to do better in the year to come. Rosh HaShanah comes with traditions, such as the *shofar*, and apples dipped in honey. The secular New Year brings with it party horns, hats, noise, and glitzy parties. If you do celebrate the secular New Year in your classroom, be sure to compare it to the Jewish New Year. By doing so, you help children see how Jewish values are a part of every aspect of their lives.

COLUMBUS DAY AND PRESIDENT'S DAY

Christopher Columbus, George Washington, and Abraham Lincoln are historical figures. Their lives, accomplishments, and contributions are embedded in a history which is far beyond the understanding of young children. Further, the lessons of these men are not significant in the lives of young children. Leave the study of these holidays to elementary school.

VICTORIA DAY (CANADA)

Queen Victoria became the Queen of England in 1837, and she ruled for over 60 years until her death in 1901. Her birthday was May 24, and so Victoria Day is celebrated in Canada on the first Monday thereafter. Like the American presidents, Queen Victoria is an historical figure, with little relevance to the life of the average Jewish Canadian preschooler. Enjoy the barbecues and the beginning of summer, but leave the studies of Queen Victoria until children are older.

MARTIN LUTHER KING DAY

The study of Martin Luther King, Jr., in relation to Martin Luther King Day, is probably outside the scope of what is understandable and relevant to young Jewish children. However, Martin Luther King, Jr. stood for values which are very appropriate to the Jewish classroom: equality, justice, and working to make sure this world is fair for everyone. These are lessons which should be a part of every day in the Jewish early childhood classroom. We need not limit the study of these values to one unit on Martin Luther King Day.

VALENTINE'S DAY

More correctly, the name of this holiday is St. Valentine's Day. The holiday is named for St. Valentine of Rome, who died on February 14, 269 C.E. He was killed for helping Christian martyrs. In 469 C.E., the Christian Church established the day of his death as a day to honor him. Saint Valentine was associated with lovers, because he was accused of performing marriages during wartime and interfering with war recruitment. He also was said to have fallen in love with his jailer's daughter while he was incarcerated, sending her passionate love letters and curing her of blindness. The modern holiday of Valentine's Day grew out of an integration of the fertility festival of Lupercalia into the Christian calendar, adding Greek and Roman symbols, such as Cupid, hearts, daisies, and violets to the holiday (O'Keeffe, 1999; Bulla, 1999).

In modern American culture, Valentine's Day has lost some of its overt Christian and pagan connections. You might argue that it is simply a day to demonstrate your love and friendship to other people. These qualities are without a doubt valuable elements for our classrooms. But, again, why limit teaching about them to one day? Find creative ways to make friendship and love part of every day. The ritual of exchanging Valentines with everyone in the class has no place in the Jewish early childhood classroom.

MEMORIAL DAY (U.S.)/ REMEMBRANCE DAY (CANADA)

Memorial Day in the United States and Remembrance Day in Canada are set aside to remember those who have died protecting the country during a war. For a majority of citizens, however, these holidays have become simply a day for picnics and skipping work. Especially for young Jewish children, who may not know anyone who has ever served in the military, Memorial Day and Remembrance Day hold no particular meaning. However, these days have some interesting connections to Yom HaZikaron, the Israel Memorial Day.

In Israel, it is difficult to find a family who has not lost someone — a son, brother, father, husband, uncle, grandfather — in a war or military encounter. On Yom HaZikaron, which is the day before Yom HaAtzma'ut (Independence Day), sirens go off across the entire country. As the sirens blare, the entire country comes to a halt, as every person comes to attention. Cars and buses stop in the street. People get out of their cars and stand by them; people on buses stand up near their seat. People come out of shops and schools and offices and stand silently for a few minutes while the siren sounds. (This is similar to the two minutes of silence observed on Remembrance Day in Canada.) Each Israeli is remembering a loved one, friend, or family member who died fighting to protect Israel. For Israelis, Yom HaZikaron is fully relevant.

In preparation for Memorial Day or Remembrance Day, compare the holiday to Yom HaZikaron. Assess what children know about wars that have been fought by their country. Collect stories of family members, if any, who fought for their country. Describe the personal connection of Yom HaZikaron to Israelis, and how they observe with a siren. Solicit ideas from the children for a class ritual in observance of Memorial Day or Remembrance Day. You might sound a siren, salute the flag, parade in the school with the flag, or write letters and send pictures to a local veterans hospital.

FOURTH OF JULY (U.S.)/ CANADA DAY (CANADA)

The Fourth of July, the American Independence Day, and Canada Day, the anniversary of the union of Upper and Lower Canada, New Brunswick, and Nova Scotia, have particular meaning for young Jewish children when compared to the celebrations for Yom HaAtzma'ut, Israel Independence Day. Both Americans and Israelis tried to win their independence through the use of words. And, when words didn't work, these countries won their independence, their freedom, by fighting for it. Today, we celebrate America's birthday and Canada's unification in the same way we celebrated Israel's birthday, a few months before. Americans celebrate with American colors: red, white and blue. Canadians celebrate with Canadian colors: red and white. Israelis celebrate with Israel's colors: blue and white. These are the colors on each country's flag. Americans celebrate with parades and fireworks. Canadians celebrate with concerts and fireworks. Israelis celebrate with bonfires, picnics, and hikes around the country.

CONCLUSION

So many of our secular holidays are rooted in ancient superstition, folklore, or in other religions. Others are tied directly to historical figures or events. While it is always appropriate, even important, to validate a child's attitude toward celebra-

tion of such holidays or observances, with few exceptions they are outside the purview of the Jewish preschool curriculum. At the very most, the teacher may explore with the children significant core values exemplified by these holidays — love, honesty, faith, courage, trust, etc. — and tie those values to Jewish holidays and observances which also celebrate them. At the very least, it is preferable simply to skip over the observance or connection of the school to most of the secular holidays.

BIBLIOGRAPHY

ADULTS

Barth, Edna. *Turkeys, Pilgrims, and Indian Corn: The Story of the Thanksgiving Symbols*. New York: Clarion Books, 1975.

> Traces the history of this American harvest festival and the development of its symbols and legends.

Bulla, Clyde Robert. *The Story of Valentine's Day*. New York: HarperCollins Publishers, 1999.

> A book packed with historical facts and customs about Valentine's Day.

Chambers, Catherine. *All Saints, All Souls and Halloween*. Austin, TX: Steck-Vaughn Company, 1997.

> Examines the traditions and celebrations occurring around the world on Halloween, All Saint's Day, and All Soul's Day.

Darvick, Debra B. "Completing a Circle of Gratitude." In *Chicago Jewish News*, November 19-25, 1999, p. 17.

> Darvick examines the Jewish tradition to discover how we can more fully give thanks at the Thanksgiving season.

Kessel, Joyce K. *Squanto and the First Thanksgiving*. Minneapolis: Carolrhoda Books, 1983.

> Describes the role Squanto played in the survival of the Pilgrims.

O'Keeffe, Christine. *Christine O'Keeffe's Valentine's History*. 1999.

> The author's web site is filled with information about Valentine's Day, including history, recipes, and customs: www.geocities.com/Athens/Parthenon/1502/valen.html

CHILDREN

Bunting, Eve. *How Many Days To America? A Thanksgiving Story*. New York: Clarion Books, 1990. (Ages 4-8)

> After the police come, the family is forced to flee their Caribbean island and set sail for America in a small fishing boat. Other refugees crowd the boat, and the voyage is a long one. But when the family arrives, they discover it's a special day in more ways than one.

Harvey, Brett. *Immigrant Girl: Becky of Eldridge Street*. New York: Holiday House, 1987. (Ages 4-8)

> Becky, whose family has emigrated from Russia to avoid being persecuted as Jews, finds growing up in New York City in 1910 a vivid and exciting experience.

Herrold, Maggie Rugg. *A Very Important Day*. New York: William Morrow & Co., 1995. (Ages 4-8)

> On a snowy day in New York City, people of different ethnic origins travel by foot, subway, train, or ferry to the place where they will become U.S. citizens.

Joosse, Barbara. *The Morning Chair*. New York: Clarion Books, 1995. (Ages 4-8)

> Bram and his family leave their small village in the Netherlands to build a new life amid the hustle and bustle of New York City.

Levine, Arthur. *All the Lights in the Night*. New York: Tambourine, 1991. (Ages 4-8)

> Moses and Benjamin begin their escape from Russia to Palestine at Chanukah time. They light their battered old lamp, tell the story of Chanukah, and hope for a miracle.

Levinson, Riki. *I Go with My Family To Grandma's*. New York: Dutton, 1992. (Ages 4-8)

> Immigration experiences involving five cousins from various lands.

———. *Watch the Stars Come Out*. New York: Puffin, 1995. (Ages 4-8)

> A young girl's experiences on the ship coming to America.

Macklin, Mikki. *My Name Is Not Gussie*. Boston, MA: Houghton Mifflin Co., 1999. (Ages 4-8)

> A series of beguiling stories about the Jewish immigrant experience as seen through the eyes of a young and curious child.

Maestro, Betsy. *Coming To America: Story of Immigration*. New York: Scholastic, 1996. (Ages 4-8)

Told in warm prose with child-friendly watercolor illustrations, this history of immigration to the United States offers young readers a perspective on the heritage that all Americans share.

Perry, Roslyn Bresnick. *Leaving for America.* New York: Children's Book Press, 1992. (Ages 4-8)
A funny, tender, and true portrayal of life in a Russian Jewish community in the 1920s. The narrator is a seven-year-old girl who is leaving with her mother to start a new life in America.

Polacco, Patricia. *The Keeping Quilt.* New York: Simon & Schuster, 1994. (Ages 4-8)
A homemade quilt ties together the lives of four generations of an immigrant Jewish family. It remains a symbol of their enduring love and faith.

Pomeranc, Marion. *The Hand-Me-Down Horse.* Morton Grove, IL: Albert Whitman & Co., 1996. (Ages 4-8)
David and his family have fled from the Nazis and are waiting to go to America. One day, an old rocking horse appears at the door, a gift from a child who has already left for the new land. Astride the hand-me-down horse, David and his friend Martha dream of America. When the time comes for David to leave, he gives the horse to just the right person.

———. *The American Wei.* Morton Grove, IL: Albert Whitman & Co., 1998. (Ages 4-8)
Wei Fong and his parents have immigrated to America from China, and are about to attend the ceremony during which they swear allegiance to their new country. Wei is almost as nervous about losing a wobbly tooth as he is about becoming a citizen.

Pryor, Bonnie. *The Dream Jar.* New York: William Morrow & Company, 1996. (Ages 4-8)
Valentina's family has come from Russia with a wonderful dream — to own a store. Valentina discovers how to help her family's dream come true.

Rael, Elsa Okron. *What Zeesie Saw on Delancy Street.* New York: Simon & Schuster, 1996. (Ages 4-8)
In 1930s New York, Zeesie goes to her first "package party," a feast where funds are raised for immigrants in the Jewish community. There she learns a valuable lesson in sharing.

Rosenberg, Liz. *Grandmother and Her Runaway Shadow.* San Diego, CA: Harcourt Brace, 1996. (Ages 4-8)
A young girl tells the story of her courageous grandmother, who left her home and family in Russia to travel to the New World.

Ross, Lillian. *Bubba Leah and Her Paper Children.* Philadelphia: Jewish Publication Society, 1991. (Ages 4-8)
Bubba Leah's fervent wish to see her children in faraway America is realized when she receives a special letter in the mail.

Say, Allen. *Grandfather's Journey.* Boston, MA: Houghton Mifflin, 1993. (Ages 4-8)
In this tale of immigration and acculturation, both the narrator and his grandfather long to return to Japan. But when they do, they feel anonymous and confused.

Tarbescu, Edith. *Annushka's Voyage.* New York: Clarion Books, 1998. (Ages 4-8)
Follows the journey of two young Jewish sisters at the turn of the century as they travel from their small village in Russia to join their papa in America.

Yorinks, Arthur. *Oh Brother.* New York: Farrar, Straus and Giroux, 1989. (Ages 4-8)
Two orphan English brothers in New York learn that life can be harsh and bitter. But fate, in the guise of a kindly tailor, intervenes, and love and hope triumph over tragedy.

Ziefert, Harriet. *When I First Came To This Land.* New York: Putnam Publishing Group, 1998. (Ages 4-6)
America holds a world of promise for a poor young man who arrives with nothing but a

strong back, a loving heart, and a sense of humor.

Books on Related Subjects

Levine, Ellen. *If Your Name Was Changed at Ellis Island.* New York: Scholastic, 1994. (All ages)
   This history of Ellis Island and immigration discusses why people came to America, what Ellis Island looked like then, and other related issues.

Penner, Lucille. *Statue of Liberty.* New York: Random House, 1995. (Ages 4-8)
   The construction, history, and symbolism of the Statue of Liberty in a brightly illustrated, entertaining book for beginning readers. Part of the "Step into Reading" series.

Quiri, Patricia. *Ellis Island: A True Book.* New York: Children's Press, 1998. (Ages 4-8)
   A straight up, factual look at the experience of coming through Ellis Island.

———. *Statue of Liberty.* New York: Children's Press, 1998. (Ages 4-8)
   Recounts how the Statue of Liberty was planned, built dedicated, repaired over the years, and then restored in the 1980s. Part of the True Book Series.

CHAPTER 24

LIFE CYCLES: BIRTH AND DEATH

Every major milestone can be marked in some Jewish way, if only by saying the *"Shehecheyanu"* blessing. There are elaborate Jewish rituals to mark the birth of a baby, to herald a child's coming of age (Bar or Bat Mitzvah), and to accompany marriage, divorce, and death, among other life cycle events.

In this chapter you will find information about the Jewish rituals and customs surrounding birth and death, the Jewish life cycle events most relevant for the early childhood classroom. Certainly, other life cycle events can play a role in the lives of young children — when an older sibling or cousin becomes a Bar or Bat Mitzvah, when parents divorce, or a beloved teacher or relative gets married. But the arrival of new siblings is a frequent occurrence and a key event in the lives of children under five, and children are curious about the rituals that surround new brothers and sisters. Death, the other key life cycle, is sadly not a stranger to the early childhood classroom. It is not uncommon for a young child to experience the death of a grandparent or pet, or less frequently, a parent or teacher. Jewish early childhood teachers must know how to deal with both birth and death in their classrooms.

BIRTH

PREGNANCY

Many Jewish customs abound about pregnancy. Most are based on superstitions rooted in eastern European folklore (e.g., the evil eye). These customs derived from the view that nothing is for certain until it has happened. In other words, we don't celebrate until there is something tangible to celebrate. For this reason, many Jewish couples will not announce their pregnancy to their friends and family until they have safely reached the twelfth week of pregnancy. Rather than saying a hearty *"Mazal tov,"* it is customary to say to a parent-to-be or excited relative upon hearing of a pregnancy, *"B'Sha'ah Tovah,"* literally, in a good hour, or more loosely, "Everything should happen in its proper time."

For these same reasons, many prospective Jewish mothers-to-be discourage baby showers. Gifts are sent only after the baby is born. Along these same lines, many Jewish couples will actually buy nothing for their expected baby before the birth. Everything may be ordered, and the father or other relative will pick up the new clothes and furniture immediately after the mother gives birth. Many Jewish couples will not announce their choice of names before the baby is born, and others will not reveal the baby's name until the *Brit Milah* or naming ceremony. This custom is based on the Talmudic belief that the baby is not fully viable until the eighth day (Weber, 1990).

MAZAL TOV! IT'S A BOY!

When a Jewish baby boy is born, assuming he is healthy, he will have a *Brit Milah* when he is eight days old. Before this, in traditional communities, the new family will host a *Shalom Zahor* on the first *erev* Shabbat following the birth. This is an informal opportunity for the community to rally around the new parents and get a peek at the infant.

The main event, however, is the *Brit Milah*. This ceremony is also referred to as a *Bris* or *Brit*

Milah. The word *"brit"* means covenant; *"milah"* means circumcision. This ritual comes directly from the Torah. God said to Abraham, "Such shall be the covenant between Me and you and your offspring to follow which you shall keep: every male among you shall be circumcised. You shall circumcise the flesh of your foreskin, and that shall be the sign of the covenant between Me and you" (Genesis 17:10-11). Through *Brit Milah*, we confirm the covenant between the Jewish people and God. *Brit Milah* is so important that it remains one of the most significant Jewish connections made even by otherwise assimilated Jews in North America.

The *Brit Milah* is held on the eighth day because this is what the Torah dictates. Isaac, the son of Abraham, was circumcised on the eighth day, and in two places in the Torah we read, "And throughout the generations, every male among you shall be circumcised at the age of eight days" (Genesis 17:12 and Leviticus 12:3). The *Brit Milah* is performed by a *mohel*, a ritual circumciser. The *mohel* is sometimes a Rabbi and sometimes a Jewish doctor with special training. Traditionally, the new father is obligated to perform the *Milah,* but nowadays, he usually hires a *mohel* to take over this responsibility.

At the *Brit Milah*, the baby is brought in and set for a moment on a *Keesay shel Eliyahu* (a special chair set aside for Elijah the Prophet). Then the *mohel* will say the appropriate blessings and cut the foreskin off of the baby's penis. The baby is given wine as an anesthetic, but needless to say, the moment is highly emotional for the entire family. After the *milah* is performed, the parents will often explain how they chose their son's name and after whom he was named. Then everyone is invited to stay for the *se'udat mitzvah* — the festive meal. (For more sources on *Brit Milah*, see the bibliography at the end of this chapter.)

MAZAL TOV! IT'S A GIRL!

Jewish ritual is not nearly as prescribed for baby girls as for boys. Traditionally, in generations past, the father was called to bless the Torah in the week following the birth. This was the only Askenazic ritual connected to the birth of a girl. The father said the *"Mi Shebayrach"* blessing (the blessing for healing and well-being), and in it stated the name of his daughter (Diamant, 1993). Sephardic Jews have more customs connected to the birth of a baby girl (see *The New Jewish Baby Book* by Anita Diamant for more information about Sephardic customs).

Today, there are many new welcoming ceremonies for newborn Jewish girls. These ceremonies are called variously: *Brit Bat* (covenant of a daughter); *Simchat Bat* (rejoicing on account of a daughter); *Hachnasat Bat L'Brit* (welcoming a daughter to the covenant, a Reform ceremony); *Brit Banot Yisrael* (covenant for the daughters of Israel, a Reconstructionist ceremony, as described in *A Ceremonies Sampler: New Rites, Celebrations and Observances of Jewish Women* by Elizabeth Resnick Levine, p. 25); and *Zeved Bat* (celebration of the gift of a daughter, a Sephardic tradition, as found in *The New Jewish Baby Book,* p. 131). In any case, these ceremonies are largely open to the creative desires and energies of the new parents. Most *Brit Bat* ceremonies include at the minimum blessings for the new baby and explanations of her name.

The timing of a *Brit Bat* is up to the new parents. Some parents hold a *Brit Bat* on the eighth day, while others do it at a more convenient time, usually some weeks or months after the daughter has arrived. The ceremony can be performed at the synagogue on Shabbat during a worship service. It can be performed at home by anyone: a Rabbi, a friend, or the parents themselves. Roles can be written in for older siblings and other relatives. This is still a Jewish occasion, so there is usually a *se'udah simchah* (a festive Oneg Shabbat or a meal) afterward.

ROLE OF THE TEACHER

The community is always invited to the *Shalom Zahor* (if there is one) and to the *Brit Milah,* but formal invitations are never issued. Rather, the time and place are announced, but the family is not held to the formality of inviting specific people. The same is usually true for a *Brit Bat*. It is considered a *mitzvah* to attend a *Brit Milah* or *Brit Bat*, so if you can go, go. There is no need to bring a gift, but prepare to eat well afterward! You can wish everyone at the *Brit Milah* or *Brit Bat* a hearty *mazal tov*. Be sure to pay some extra attention to the sibling who is in your class. Parents and relatives tend to be concentrating on the infant, so your presence can serve to help older siblings feel remembered and involved.

IN THE CLASSROOM

The classroom is the perfect place to celebrate a child who is now an older sibling. All the children in the class can help make a *Mazal Tov* poster for the child and his/her family, announcing the birth and the name of the new baby. This also serves to inform other families in the school. Give the new older sibling lots of opportunities to talk about the new baby and any rituals surrounding the arrival. The more you know about the ceremonies in which the family is engaged for the new baby, the more you will be able to understand, support, and validate the older sibling in your class. Encourage the child to bring in pictures or videos to show off the new baby. The new baby can be welcomed at a show-and-tell as soon as the mom is ready and willing.

Remember that there are many changes going on in the child's home, the least of which is that he/she may be getting less attention. Be on the lookout for changes in behavior, and be ready to provide lots of extra attention in class after the arrival of a new baby.

If several children in the class are in the process of becoming big siblings, a unit on babies may be appropriate. Include many opportunities to care for baby dolls, visits to younger classes to help out, invitations to pregnant moms and new babies to come and talk to the class, and discussions with children about what they are looking forward to being able to do with their new siblings. Read

books such as *Welcoming Babies* by Margy Burns Knight, and *A Baby Sister for Frances* by Russell Hoban. (See the bibliography in this chapter for other titles.) Seek out creative, supportive ways to make this Jewish life cycle event a part of your classroom.

DEATH

While in Judaism, death is considered an integral part of life, losing a loved one is never easy to deal with. So Jewish law and custom attempt to put some order to the confusion of grief. The overall goal of Jewish mourning practices is to surround the mourners with a supportive community.

When a Jewish person dies, he/she is buried as soon as possible. This forces those left behind to face reality quickly, and enables mourners to begin the mourning process. The most immediate members of the deceased person's family are the mourners (*onayn/onaneem* in Hebrew). Traditionally, upon hearing the news of a death, a mourner will tear his/her clothes. Today, more often, mourners wear pinned to their clothing a piece of black ribbon which has been torn or cut.

A Jewish funeral may take place in a funeral parlor, in a synagogue, or at graveside. This decision is usually up to the wishes of the family. The body of the deceased may be present in a coffin, traditionally a plain pine box, and the coffin is never open. The service consists of some psalms and prayers, including *"Ayl Malay Rachamim"* (God, full of compassion). A Rabbi or family member(s), or both, will deliver a eulogy. Pallbearers, usually members of the family or close friends, will carry the coffin. The interment service is concluded at the graveside. According to Rabbi Earl Grollman (1990), a noted authority on children and death, children should be given the option to attend the funeral. Their feelings of confusion and fear will be lessened if they know what is going on. This funeral is a chance to honor and remember the person who has died, and children should be included in this process if they choose to be.

After the burial, the mourners and others return to the *shivah* house, where a meal has been prepared for the mourners. *Shivah* means seven, and it connotes the first week-long period of mourning. During this time, mourners do not work or engage in other normal daily activities. Meals are prepared for them by friends and family, and visitors come by each day to comfort them and join in the *minyan*, the thrice-daily service conducted in the *shivah* house, during which the *Kaddish*, the prayer in praise of God, is recited in memory of the dead.

After the *shivah* period, the period of *shlosheem* continues. *Shlosheem* means 30, and this is the month-long period in which the intense mourning is lessened, but life has not yet returned to normal. Mourners return to work and other daily activities, but festive occasions, such as parties or live music, are avoided. Some men do not shave during *shlosheem* and, traditionally, men and women do not cut their hair. The mourning period ends after *shlosheem*, except for mourning a parent, in which case it continues for 11 months.

TEACHER'S ROLE

If a family member or a staff member or child dies, you may want to go to the funeral or to the *shivah* house. It is a *mitzvah* to comfort the mourner, so go if it is at all possible. At the funeral, you may have a chance to greet the mourners. You need not say anything special — your presence is the important thing.

Ron Wolfson provides clear guidelines (1996) for making a *shivah* call. When you arrive at the house, just walk in. There is no need to ring the bell, the door should be open. This saves the mourners the need to answer the door frequently. Find the mourners as soon as possible after you get to the house. Again, there is no need to say anything special; a hug or a handshake will serve to communicate your support. Follow the mourner's lead. If he/she wants to talk about the deceased, join in. Do not dominate the mourner's time. There are others waiting to offer their

support, too. There will probably be lots of food at the *shivah* house, but remember, the food is there mostly for the mourners. If you are invited to eat, go ahead, but in moderation. If you bring food, just put it in the kitchen. Someone there will take care of it. If you are at the *shivah* house during the *minyan*, participate in the service to the best of your ability. Finally, don't stay too long — an hour is plenty. Being a mourner during *shivah* is difficult and tiring, so show your support and leave.

If you have a special relationship with the children at a *shivah* house, be sure to spend some time with them. Don't be surprised if children do not want to talk about or do anything related to the grief you think they must be feeling. The feelings associated with the death can be very overwhelming for children, and they may need to deal with them by playing or talking about unrelated things.

IN THE CLASSROOM

When talking with children in the classroom about death, above all it is important not to lie to children or use metaphorical language. Children interpret euphemisms for death, such "sleeping" or "gone away," in a literal fashion, and such terms can be very scary for them. Define death for children in simple, honest terms, such as, "When someone dies, the body stops working" (Roth, 1998). Very young children believe in magic. Talk with them about what is real and what is pretend (e.g., the things they see on television). Work with children to develop a true understanding of "dead." One of the most important things a teacher can do is to help children understand that death is not a taboo subject, and that they can explore their fears about death with understanding adults.

Don't wait for a death to occur before talking about death in your classroom. Read books such as *The Fall of Freddie the Leaf* by Leo F. Buscaglia, and talk about how things in nature die as the seasons change. Read stories in which characters die, such as *Mrs. Katz and Tush* by Patricia Polacco, and let the children talk about what it means to die, and how it feels when someone we love dies. If you discuss death in the classroom before anyone is truly grieving, it will be easier to deal with death when it becomes a real issue.

For children, the death of a pet may be as significant as the death of a person. Be sure to validate and support feelings when children report such a death. When a classroom pet dies, use the opportunity to talk about death with the class as a whole. This is also a good time to explore the elements of a Jewish funeral. Bury the pet, and allow any child who wishes to do so to share a fond memory or otherwise memorialize the pet. Be sure to allow plenty of time for sharing feelings of grief over the next few days and weeks, as every child deals with grief and processes death differently.

When a child experiences a death in the family, or if the school experiences the death of a teacher, teachers need to provide many ways to process the death. Allow children to deal with the death in their time and manner. Some children may not be able to talk about it at all at first; others may constantly ask questions and want to share stories of the deceased for days or weeks. Be prepared to give extra love, understanding, and attention to children experiencing grief.

Be creative in finding ways to remember people or pets who have died. Write books about the wonderful characteristics and accomplishments of the person. Build a block structure in memory of the deceased. Collect pictures of the person who

has died, and let children share their memories. Engage in some of the activities the person liked to do. Plant a garden in his or her memory. Whatever you do, you are demonstrating to children that it is safe to talk about loved ones who have died, and important to keep their memories alive.

CONCLUSION

Throughout your teaching years, the children in preschool classes will experience nearly every life cycle event. Some will welcome new siblings into their home and thus be personally involved in witnessing the naming or *Brit Milah* ceremony. Some will experience the death of a pet or of a family member, and they will look to their teacher and their school setting for understanding, comfort, and a safe haven during turbulent times. Some will be tossed hither and yon as parents and household split apart. They may then observe the dating and remarriage of one or both parents, followed by having to deal with step-parents and step-siblings and sharing rooms and sharing parent time, and moving from one place to another week after week. The early Jewish childhood educator has the opportunity to provide support and a sense of stability to students in transition, as well as the responsibility to "be there" for children who struggle to cope with change and to gain mastery over new feelings and emotions. Their needs are great; so, too, can be your rewards.

BIBLIOGRAPHY

ADULTS

General

David, Jo, and Daniel B. Syme. *The Book of Jewish Life*. New York: UAHC Press, 1998.

In this textbook for intermediate grades, each chapter relates a stage or milestone of life, its traditional practices, and its modern observance.

Isaacs, Ronald H. *Rites of Passage: A Guide To the Jewish Life Cycle*. Hoboken, NJ: KTAV Publishing House, 1992.

Covers the more traditional life cycle ceremonies, such as *Brit Milah*, *Pidyon HaBen*, and Bar and Bat Mitzvah. Also introduces some new life cycle rituals and ceremonies, such as *Simchat Bat* and a Jewish adoption ceremony.

Levine, Elizabeth Resnick, ed. *A Ceremonies Sampler: New Rites, Celebrations and Observances of Jewish Women*. San Diego, CA: Woman's Institute for Continuing Jewish Education, 1991.

A unique collection of new ceremonies created to recognize significant events in a Jewish woman's life.

Orenstein, Debra, ed. *Lifecycles, V. 1: Jewish Women on Life Passages & Personal Milestones*. Woodstock, VT: Jewish Lights Publishing, 1998.

The first comprehensive work on Jewish life cycles that fully includes women's perspectives.

Birth

Barth, Lewis M., ed. *Berit Mila in the Reform Context*. Los Angeles, CA: Berit Mila Board of Reform Judaism, 1990.

A textbook intended for doctors and other licensed practitioners who are interested in becoming certified as Reform *mohelim*. Provides an enormous amount of information about *Brit Milah*.

Diamant, Anita. *The New Jewish Baby Book: Names, Ceremonies & Customs: A Guide for Today's Families*. Woodstock, VT: Jewish Lights Publishing, 1994.

A superb guide to Jewish customs and rituals for welcoming a new child into the world.

Lieberman, Dale. *Witness To the Covenant of Circumcision: Bris Milah*. Northvale, NJ: Jason Aronson Inc., 1997.

This volume of photographs reveals the significance of *Brit Milah* for its celebrants.

Weber, Douglas, and Jessica Brodsky Weber. *The Jewish Baby Handbook: A Guide for Expectant Parents*. West Orange, NJ: Behrman House, 1997.

A little book which guides expectant parents through the pleasant unknowns of Jewish law and custom with just the right combination of information and warm feeling.

Death

Cutter, William, editorial committee chair. *The Jewish Mourner's Handbook*. West Orange, NJ: Behrman House, 1996.

This little book blends consolation and information about Jewish rituals of death and mourning.

Grollman, Earl A. *Talking about Death: A Dialogue between Parent and Child*. 3d ed. Boston, MA: Beacon Press, 1991.

This book is a compassionate guide for adults and children to read together, featuring a read-along story, answers to questions children ask about death, and a comprehensive list of resources and organizations that can help.

Lamm, Maurice. *The Jewish Way in Death and Mourning*. New York: Jonathan David, 1972.

A thorough and complete guide to Jewish mourning practices.

Roth, Tammie. "Mrs. Seidenberg Died, and That Means She's Not Ever Coming Back." In *Ganenet*, vol.1(2), 1998. (Community Foundation for Jewish Education, Chicago)

Article that examines the death of a preschool teacher and how the school coped.

Wolfson, Ron. *A Time to Mourn, A Time to Comfort*. Woodstock, VT: Jewish Lights Publishing, 1996.

A sensitive guide to Jewish traditions for death and mourning.

CHILDREN
Birth

Alexander, Martha G. *When the New Baby Comes I'm Moving Out.* New York: Dial Books for Young Readers, 1992. (Ages 4-8)

Oliver is going to be a big brother, and doesn't like the idea one bit.

Brown, Marc Tolon. *Arthur's New Baby Book: A Lift-the-Flap Guide to Being a Great Big Brother or Sister.* New York: Random House, 1999. (Ages 1-3)

Arthur was bored at first when his sister D.W. was born. Then they started having fun. Through reminiscing about playing *Peekaboo*, spitting up, and learning the alphabet and nursery rhymes, Arthur is able to help D.W. get used to the idea of another brand new baby in the house.

Clifton, Lucille. *Everett Anderson's Nine Month Long.* New York: Henry Holt and Company, 1987. (Ages 4-8)

Another fine addition to the Everett Anderson series, this book welcomes a new baby to share the family's love.

Cole, Joanna. *The New Baby at Your House.* New York: Morrow Junior Books, 1999. (Ages 2-6)

This revised edition of a much-loved classic prepares children for the ups and downs of having a new baby in the house. Features over 40 vivid, full-color photographs.

———. *I'm a Big Brother.* New York: William Morrow & Company, 1997. (Ages 3-7)

———. *I'm a Big Sister.* New York: William Morrow & Company, 1997. (Ages 3-7)

Each of these two books, written in the first person, tells what babies like, why they cry, what they are too little to do yet, what the big brother or sister can do now, and how much parents love their older child. They are identical, except for the words "sister" and "brother."

Hoban, Russell. *A Baby Sister for Frances.* New York: HarperCollins Publishers, 1993. (4-8 years)

When things change around the house after her baby sister is born, Frances decides to run away — but not too far.

Knight, Margy Burns. *Welcoming Babies.* Gardiner, ME: Tilbury House Publishers, 1994. (Ages 4-10)

The varied and diverse ways that cultures around the world celebrate new life.

Lewis, Deborah Shaw. *When You Were a Baby.* Atlanta, GA: Peachtree Publishers, 1995. (Ages 3-adult)

This simple book allows parents to explore and explain the birth and life of their child within the context of their own family.

Silverman, Judy. *Rosie and the Mole: The Story of a Bris.* New York: Pitspopany Press, 1999. (Ages 6-9)

When Rosie hears that the *mohel* is coming, she thinks a mole from the zoo is coming to do the *Bris*. A charming story for older siblings.

Stein, Sara. *Oh, Baby!* New York: Walker & Co., 1995. (Ages 1-5)

The perfect picture book for baby-loving toddlers and soon-to-be big brothers and sisters. Through irresistible photographs of real babies and toddlers, see how babies grow and develop — from first cry to first steps.

Wilkowski, Susan. *Baby's Bris.* Rockville, MD: Kar-Ben Copies, 1999. (Ages 4-8)

Chronicles the first eight day's of Baby's life, as seen through the eyes of his big sister.

Death

Buscaglia, Leo F. *The Fall of Freddie the Leaf: A Story of Life for All Ages.* New York: Holt, Rinehart & Winston, 1982. (Ages 4-8)

As Freddie experiences the changing seasons along with his companion leaves, he learns about the delicate balance between life and death.

Lanton, Sandy. *Daddy's Chair.* Rockville, MD: Kar-Ben Copies, 1991. (Ages 5-10)

When Michael's father dies, his family sits *shivah*, observing the Jewish week of mourning, and remembers the good things about him.

Mellonie, Bryan, and Robert Ingpen. *Lifetimes: A Beautiful Way to Explain Death To Children*. Toronto: Bantam Books, 1983. (Ages 3-8)
Explains death to children by talking about the lifetimes of plants, animals, and people.

Techner, David, and Judith Hirt-Manheimer. *A Candle for Grandpa: A Guide To the Jewish Funeral for Children and Parents*. New York: UAHC Press, 1993. (Ages 5-8)

A young boy describes the events surrounding the death of his grandfather, including his and his family's feelings of grief and the Jewish funeral service in which they participate. Also includes answers to frequently asked questions regarding death and funerals.

Zalben, Jane Breskin. *Pearl's Marigolds for Grandpa*. New York: Simon & Schuster Books for Young Readers, 1997. (Ages 3-8)
A young girl copes with the death of her grandfather by remembering all the things she loved about him. Includes information about funeral customs of various religions.

CHAPTER 25

CLERGY AND OTHER IMPORTANT PEOPLE

There are important resources in your community just waiting to be tapped! Whether your Jewish early childhood school is part of a synagogue, a Jewish Community Center, a day school, renting space in a church, or housed in retail space in a mall, there are adults who should be part of your program. Rabbis, Cantors, JCC Center Directors, and building administrators have an amazing amount to give to the young children in your program. It's your job to let these individuals know how much they are needed, and to show them how to become a part of your school.

Personal talents aside, professionals such as Rabbis, Cantors, Center Directors, and building administrators play an important role in making connections for young children. Jewish professionals can represent the wider Jewish world to children — if they take the time to become part of children's lives. When children form relationships with such people, they expand the realm of adults they can trust, and do so in a Jewish context. As they get to know adults who are deeply involved in Jewish life, children come to understand that being Jewish is not just for children, and it's not just something that happens at their home or in their classroom. There are grown-ups out there who make being Jewish part of their work life, too. By example, children learn that being Jewish is a serious, grown-up, fun thing to do.

Jewish professionals help children to become enthusiastic about being Jewish. Once a relationship has been formed, children become excited when they see their Rabbi in the hall, when the Center Director joins them for snack, when the Cantor sings songs with them on Shabbat, when the building administrator takes them on a tour of the building's kitchen. This excitement and familiarity spills over to help forge a connection between the child, and the child's family, and the host organization of the early childhood program. For example, the child does not just go to school at Gan Yeladim Preschool. He/she goes to the JCC! Or, after being in the four-year-old room at Gan Beth El, children become thrilled to go to Religious School at Beth El Synagogue, where they can continue to see their friend the Rabbi. These connections are crucial in drawing families into Jewish organizations, and Jewish professionals are invaluable resources for making this happen.

Early childhood teachers and Directors are important links between the children they serve and Jewish professionals. Some Jewish professionals may not yet have the skills to grab and hold the attention of three-year-olds. They may not know the best ways to get to know children. They may need guidance about how to speak to children, what to talk about, how long to talk, how to listen, and what exactly to do with children. For these reasons or others, the Jewish professionals most closely connected to your school may be reluctant to begin a relationship with your children. As an early childhood professional who recognizes the importance of such links, it is your job to establish relationships, to help maintain them, and to be a model for Jewish professionals in terms of how to act with preschoolers.

INVITING JEWISH PROFESSIONALS INTO YOUR PROGRAM

It may be easiest to start small, especially if the Jewish professionals are reluctant to enter the early childhood wing of the building, or claim to be "too busy" to become involved in the early childhood center. Point out to these individuals just how important their involvement is, both in terms of the benefits it will bring the children, and the potential value it could hold in bringing families into their organization. From your own experience, you can tell them how much joy they in turn will receive from spending just a small amount of time each week with young children.

If the Jewish professionals are already willing to work with your children, you're one step ahead. Ask the Rabbi and *Hazzan* (or Center Director) to put it in his/her calendar to stop by each classroom on Fridays, just to wish the children *"Shabbat Shalom."* These visits provide a wonderful opportunity to sing "The Rabbi" and "The Cantor" by Jeff Klepper and Susan Nanus in *Especially Jewish Symbols,* pp. 9 and 10, as well as "The People in My Synagogue" by Julie Jaslow Auerbach and Nancy Rubin in *Shiron L'Gan,* p. 46. Other verses may be added for other staff in the synagogue or Center.

The classes could take turns inviting the Cantor or building administrator to join them for snack, with a child-made, hand delivered invitation. Find times for the children to take a field trip to the Rabbi's office. Ask the Rabbi to meet you there, so he/she can tell you all about the many books that line the shelves. Make sure it's okay to do so, and then poke your head into the building administrator's office every time you pass by, just to say hello. Stress to your Jewish professionals the importance of getting to know the children's names.

As the children become more comfortable with the Jewish professionals, work to find more ways to integrate these people into your program. Might the Cantor sing with the children as they get ready for Shabbat each week? Would the Rabbi come in to tell a Jewish story each week or so, during Circle Time, or in preparation for Shabbat? I had the honor and pleasure of working one year with Rabbi Herbert Weinberg, who served our congregation during his sabbatical year. He would join the children's Shabbat celebration every other week to tell a story. Not only did he develop into an excellent storyteller by the end of the year, but the children loved him and could not get enough of him. They stopped by his office, where they were greeted warmly, they hugged him when they saw him in the hall, and they wrote and drew beautiful, heart warming cards at the end of the year when his year with us was over.

Do any of the Jewish professionals play the guitar, or accordion, or piano? How often can you convince them to share some music with your children? Even committing to spend one half hour a week during free play can add greatly to the program. As a Jewish professional gets to know children in this informal way, especially during free play, which is the time children are learning the most, children will have the opportunity to ask questions about his/her life and Jewish role. When the Center Director visits a class and offers to read a story to the children, that strengthens the bond between the children and that person, and also between the Jewish professional and the teachers.

Jewish professionals can play a strong role around holiday time as well. Can the building administrator blow the *shofar*? Would the Center Director like to share his/her collection of *graggers* with the children? Seek out these talents and recruit them for the early childhood center. The more time your Jewish professionals spend with your children, the richer the connections will be, and the more the children, families, professionals, and institutions will benefit.

If you have no Jewish professionals on site beyond your early childhood Director (who should already be an integral part of every classroom), investigate "borrowing" a Jewish professional on a regular basis. Try to find a Rabbi or Cantor from a neighborhood synagogue without its own early childhood program who might be willing to donate a few hours a month to your school. When recruiting someone to become part of the life of your school, stress the importance of connecting the children to the greater Jewish world. Emphasize the significance of a regular relationship, the personal joy the professional will feel when spending time with such adorable children, and the value to the families in the program as well.

CONCLUSION

Jewish professionals can also play a very important role in the ongoing Jewish education of early childhood teachers and Directors. They can teach classes for early childhood educators, or make available to them classes that are going on in the organization and in the community. Jewish professionals can also make their resources — books and other connections — available to early childhood educators. Most importantly, they can make themselves available to early childhood educators as resources and as support. In this way, they enrich the Jewish knowledge base of early childhood educators, and thus enrich the lives of the children in these programs. Of course, it will most likely be up to early childhood educators themselves to reach out to Jewish professionals and ask for this relationship. Don't be afraid to take this step. It will be highly rewarding to both sides.

CHAPTER 26

INFANTS AND TODDLERS

Infants and toddlers *absorb* culture and religion as opposed to learning them directly. They are busy figuring out what the world means and how it relates to them in broad, general terms. It should therefore be obvious why we should send our youngest children to Jewish day care and other Jewish early childhood programs instead of to other high quality programs.

Children in a high quality, rich Jewish environment can soak up the flavor of Judaism every day through songs, foods, blessings, pictures on the wall, and rituals such as lighting candles and eating *challah*. Such an atmosphere can be a factor in the development of a strong Jewish identity.

This chapter presents ways to create a Jewish environment which will help very young children begin to form the foundation of their Jewish identity. Tips for teaching the families of infants and toddlers are also included.

ABOUT INFANTS

Infants are engaged in the task of discovering their world. They are attempting to distinguish others from themselves, to form trusting relationships, and to gain physical mastery over their own bodies and the world around them. Recent research on brain development teaches us that the young child's brain is developing at an incredible rate in the first few months and years of life (Shore, 1997). This has significant implications for the stimulation we provide them. The things in their environment that are most familiar are the things that become most cherished and trusted.

Exposure to Judaism in a loving, warm, natural, fun way is key. Infant care involves a great deal of basic care: feeding, diapering, soothing, and putting down to sleep. All of these care moments can be accompanied by a song, and in fact may go more smoothly with some musical accompaniment. Making this song a Jewish song adds Jewish feeling to the environment in a natural, enjoyable way. A holiday song, Jewish lullaby, Hebrew or Yiddish tune does the trick quite nicely.

Beyond basic care, infants also need the right amount of stimulation, in the form of simple games, songs, books, and toys. In order to create a Jewish atmosphere and make Judaism a natural part of the baby's world, a good percentage of toys and books should be Jewish in nature. There are many good, attractive Jewish board books (see the bibliographies of the holiday chapters, and also of Chapter 2, "Jewish Every Day," pp. 33-34 for some good suggestions). By reading Jewish board books with infants, a *shofar* can become as familiar as a puppy. When filling an infant's environment with soft toys, stock up on stuffed Torahs, plush *dreidels*, and soft *alefbet* blocks, in addition to all the other Jewish hugables that are available.

Introduce infants to real Jewish rituals and objects. Let them hear and handle a real *shofar*. Bless and light Shabbat candles and wave your hands over them each week so they can see and hear this important ritual. In a room full of babies who don't yet crawl or walk, you can leave the candles on a table where the infants can watch them. When babies start to move, blow the candles out or move them to a high, very safe location. Give babies *challah* each week as soon as they are old enough to eat it. Make removing the *challah* cover and the blessing important acts. Bring babies into the *sukkah*. Obtain large plastic *dreidels* that are safe for infants to chew on. Freeze mini-bagels for older infants to teeth on. Light a Havdalah candle with infants each week just long enough to sing *"Eliahu HaNavi"* (see *Manginot,* p. 150, or the cassette tape *Around Our Shabbat Table* by Margie Rosenthal and Ilene Safyan).

Making Jewish experiences warm, loving, inviting, and real helps babies gain high levels of comfort and confidence in Jewish surroundings. A richly Jewish environment in an infant classroom or program will have an impact on the development of strong Jewish identities.

TODDLERS

Toddlers are, of course, more active than infants. They move about their environment and actively investigate every aspect of their world. Fill the toddlers' environment with opportunities for Jewish discovery. Be creative in incorporating Jewish symbols and visuals into all areas of the environment. For example, attach Jewish shapes in different colors onto chairs and under tables with Contact paper. Use such shapes to make a mobile to hang over the changing area, and alternate it with every new holiday. Hang Jewish shapes from the ceiling. Tape Jewish stars or Torahs to the bottom of a favorite set of nesting cups.

Jewish music and books become even more important, as toddlers can now participate more. They can repeat and request stories and songs. Sing simple Hebrew songs that repeat, such as *"David Melech"* or *"Heenay Mah Tov"* (see Chapter 2, "Jewish Every Day," page 31 for the words and translations of these songs). Choose Jewish books and share them frequently with toddlers. Hebrew vocabulary, and Yiddish, too, if used on a regular basis, will become a natural part of a toddler's experience. A toddler can find his *beten* and *tush* as easily as his tummy and his bottom. A toddler greeted with a happy *"Boker tov!"* upon waking from nap will gain comfort with Hebrew vocabulary without even realizing he/she is learning something extraordinary.

Teachers of toddlers need to model a love and excitement for Judaism. Their enthusiasm will be contagious. These young children look up to the adults in their environment. They copy the behavior of the adults around them and react based on the reactions of the adults. When toddlers see adults light Shabbat candles with awe and excitement, they, too, become excited. If adults choose Jewish books and music, toddlers will, too.

Teachers of toddlers can also work to integrate Jewish values into the classroom. Encourage each child to be a *mensch* as he/she plays with or near other children. When children display kindness toward each other, praise them for showing *Chesed*. Toddlers love to put small objects into larger containers. Capitalize on this, and get these little ones into the *Tzedakah* habit. Every week, as part of your Shabbat celebration, sing "Penny in the Pushka" on the album *Help Us Bake a Challah* by Elayne Robinson Grossman and Daniel T. Grossman (Creative Enterprises), and allow children to put coins into a coffee can or other such container. Let them feel the container getting heavier each week.

Toddlers in an environment rich with Jewish symbols and values become comfortable and enamored with their Jewish selves, and are well on their way to being extremely well grounded in their Jewish identity.

DON'T FORGET THE FAMILIES

The greatest beneficiaries of Jewish day care and early childhood programs for infants and toddlers are the families. Through an infant or toddler enrolled in full day care or mom-and-tot classes, parents become connected to a Jewish institution, be it a synagogue or JCC. Jewish learning and rituals, such as lighting Shabbat candles or hearing the *shofar* sounded on Rosh HaShanah, may be new experiences for a family. Through the child's school, or even through an infant class, the possibilities for leading a Jewish life can be explored in a non-threatening, relevant, child and family-centered way.

Teachers of infants and toddlers must remember that the family is also their student. Be sure to send home educational information about Jewish holidays and other Jewish happenings at the school. Invite family members to celebrate Shabbat with the class, even though the children are not at an age when they can "perform." Alert parents to relevant Jewish family events at the host institution and in the community. Establish a lending library that addresses the concerns of Jewish families. Be creative in seeking out new ways to involve and educate families.

As a child grows and continues in the Jewish school, the family will continue to grow and learn right along with the child. Over several years in a warm, loving, exciting Jewish environment, the child gains a strong Jewish identity and love for Judaism. When this is the case, two major goals are fulfilled. Not only is the child on his/her way to becoming an invested, knowledgeable Jew, but the family becomes involved in living Jewishly.

CONCLUSION

The identity formation and education of children begins before they are able to speak. The early childhood educator can by his/her enthusiasm for Jewish culture and ritual play an important role in transmitting knowledge, while also setting the stage for later Jewish learning. As this is true for infants and toddlers, it is also true for their families. The Jewish early childhood educator can be a gate keeper for families which are looking for an entry into Jewish observance and into the Jewish community.

BIBLIOGRAPHY

Bransford, John D.; Ann L. Brown; and Rodney R. Cocking, eds. *How People Learn: Brain, Mind, Experience, and School.* Washington, DC: National Academy Press, 1999.

> A contemporary account of principles of learning based on recent research.

Brierley, John. *Give Me a Child Until He Is Seven: Brain Studies and Early Childhood Education.* London: Falmer Press, 1994.

> A thorough study of the effects of brain research on early childhood education.

Goldberg, Sally. *Parent Involvement Begins at Birth: Collaboration between Parents and Teachers of Children in the Early Years.* Boston: Allyn and Bacon, 1997.

> Intended for the early childhood caregiver and administrator, here is a three-part strategy for a parent involvement program that provides a population of students ready to learn and achieve as soon as they begin school.

Hast, Fran, and Ann Hollyfield. *Infant and Toddler Experiences.* St. Paul, MN: Redleaf Press, 1999.

> Organized by the "three Cs" — curiosity, connection, and coordination. Experiences for infants and toddlers are described simply, complete with necessary materials and procedures.

Lally, J. Ron, et al. eds. *Caring for Infants and Toddlers in Groups: Developmentally Appropriate Practice.* Washington, DC: Zero To Three, 1995.

> This book provides assistance in meeting the needs of each individual child, recognizing early developmental stages, achieving necessary health and safety standards, creating good relationships, developing training and mentoring programs, providing continuity of care, and being sensitive to cultural and linguistic needs.

Shore, Rima. *Rethinking the Brain: New Insights into Early Development.* New York: Families and Work Institute, 1997.

> An outstanding, thorough, and highly accessible review of new research on the development of children ages 0-5. Along with Carnegie Corporation's Starting Points report issued in 1994, this book was the source of inspiration for the recent explosion of interest in young children's healthy development.

Snow, Charles W. *Infant Development.* 2d ed. Upper Saddle River, NJ: Prentice Hall, 1998.

> This text covers infant development from an interdisciplinary perspective from conception though the first years of life. A balanced coverage of theory, research, and practical application, as well as a strong emphasis on the interrelationships between various developmental domains and the importance of the "whole" infant.

CHAPTER 27

NON-JEWISH TEACHERS

A great deal of early childhood education is atmosphere. To a degree, what makes a Jewish school Jewish is not the formal curriculum, but the level of *Yiddishkeit* that is present. Like any good *Yiddish* phrase, the word defies translation, and its meaning can only be approximated. *Yiddishkeit* connotes a Jewish feeling, a sense of Jewishness, the smell of a Jewish grandma's kitchen. It's the way a teacher will automatically exclaim "*Mazel tov!*" when Shoshanah announces she is a big sister, or the way Jacob is asked to sit on his *tush* at circle time. It doesn't require a lot of Jewish knowledge to infuse a classroom with *Yiddishkeit*; rather, it takes an almost unconscious familiarity with Jewish ways of being. Without that familiarity, it requires a very concerted effort to create a Jewish atmosphere.

Yiddishkeit, along with a steady supply of Jewish teachers, was once a staple of the Jewish early childhood classroom. But gone are the days when teaching was one of the only professions open to women, when oftentimes mothers would come to teach in the nursery school when their youngest child graduated to first grade. Today, these women have many options open to them, and while some mothers certainly do come to teach in the early childhood classroom, bringing *Yiddishkeit* with them, the numbers are far fewer than in generations past.

Certainly, mothers of former students are not the only source of *Yiddishkeit*. Many different kinds of teachers bring different kinds of Jewish feeling into the classroom. But the loss of these mothers as source of teachers, in addition to other factors, has led in recent years to a severe shortage of teachers for Jewish early childhood programs.

The Jewish Early Childhood Association (JECA) of the Board of Jewish Education of Greater New York has become so concerned with the lack of teachers, it has formed a task force to investigate the problem (Fisher, 1999). Directors must search for teachers wherever they can be found. More and more, non-Jewish teachers are being hired for teaching positions in Jewish schools.

NON-JEWISH TEACHERS

A non-Jewish teacher can be a real asset in a Jewish school. Such a person provides diversity on the staff, enabling the entire staff to learn from him/her. Such a person comes in with different viewpoints, which can cause other staff members to think through their own opinions and can help to put a new spin on old ideas. And that person can act as a connection to non-Jewish children who may be in the program.

Furthermore, a non-Jewish teacher is often an eager learner. Recognizing that he/she is now being required to teach Judaism, this teacher will ideally ask lots of questions and seek out opportunities to learn more about Judaism and the Jewish holidays. These teachers sometimes possess no less Jewish knowledge than some of their Jewish counterparts. Jewish teachers with weak backgrounds can often learn from their non-Jewish colleagues and become motivated learners themselves.

Difficulties sometimes arise when the staff of a Jewish early childhood school includes several non-Jewish members on its teaching staff. The sense of *Yiddishkeit* in these situations is no longer automatic. In order to cultivate a Jewish feeling in the school, the entire staff will need to work together. To maintain *Yiddishkeit* requires an awareness of the Jewish atmosphere that already exists, and an acknowledgement of the need to maintain a strong Jewish feeling in the school. *Yiddishkeit* is important because, just like the unspoken curriculum on the walls of each classroom, *Yiddishkeit* teaches and informs the overall Jewish early childhood experience. Every effort should be made to emulate the Jewish environment of the home. This can be done by including Jewish books in the book corner, placing potholders or oven mitts with Jewish stars on them in the house corner, using vocabularies peppered with Yiddish or Hebrew phrases, singing Yiddish lullabies at naptime, and integrating Jewish values into all aspects of the curriculum.

While this may not come naturally to every Jewish teacher, it is even less likely to come naturally to non-Jewish teachers. Still, to a large degree, *Yiddishkeit* can be a learned skill. A committed Director, teachers willing to learn, and some mentors are required to help teachers without a native Jewish background to bring *Yiddishkeit* to their classrooms.

YIDDISHKEIT MENTOR

A *"Yiddishkeit* mentor" can be another teacher, a Director, a parent volunteer, a volunteer *bubbe* or *zayde* (grandmother or grandfather), who is willing to take non-Jewish teachers, and teachers with weak Jewish backgrounds, under his or her wing for some ongoing exposure to *Yiddishkeit*. Such a person is not expected to impart Jewish learning, per se, although this is also important and will be addressed below. A *Yiddishkeit* mentor might invite the "mentoree" over for a Shabbat or holiday meal. Together, they might watch *Fiddler on the Roof*, while the mentor provides a running commentary. Or they might watch *Schindler's List, Crossing Delancy, The Frisco Kid,* or *A Life Apart: Hasidism in America,* followed by discussion. They could see a

play with a Jewish theme, or share some Jewish music. The mentor can teach some Yiddish phrases, such as *tush* (rear end), *shayna punim* (cute face), etc.

A *Yiddishkeit* mentor can help give a non-Jewish teacher a feeling for Jewish culture, which the teacher can then transfer to the classroom atmosphere. But this mentoring is only a beginning. A non-Jewish teacher must be willing to study and learn. There is a list of beginning books and resources on Judaism in the bibliography at the end of this book. Reading, asking questions, observing other teachers' classrooms, and taking Basic Judaism classes and similar courses at local synagogues or JCCs are some ways a non-Jewish teacher can gain some of the Jewish knowledge needed to teach Judaism to young children.

Once a non-Jewish teacher has begun to learn about Judaism, a Director, *Yiddishkeit* mentor, or other teachers can be instrumental in helping him/her implement and integrate Jewish aspects into the classroom. Teaching and transmitting a culture that is not one's own is a challenging task. Besides enriching his/her own Jewish knowledge, the non-Jewish teacher should be encouraged to use methods that create a Jewish atmosphere, such as Jewish music and Jewish visuals to help integrate Judaism into the classroom. Inviting a Jewish grandmother or grandfather to volunteer regularly in the classroom can also help supplement the Jewish atmosphere in the classroom.

THE HONEST APPROACH

While it is certainly the job of a non-Jewish teacher in a Jewish school to create a Jewish atmosphere and to teach and transmit Jewish culture and religion, such a teacher should never lie about who he/she is. Young children are very much caught up in the process of figuring out who they are. One of the ways they do this is by comparing what they know about themselves to what they know about others.

As children come to understand that they celebrate or observe certain things, they seek to find out who around them celebrates the same thing. One standard question that comes from four-year-olds in almost any Jewish preschool around December goes like this: "I celebrate Chanukah. Do you?" Because of more and more intermarried families with multiple observances, another uncommon question is: "I only celebrate Chanukah. What do you do at your house?" (See Chapter 28, "Interfaith Families/Non-Jewish Children" for related information.) Children not only ask other children these questions, they ask their teachers, too.

Non-Jewish teachers should always be honest when children ask them questions about their own practices or celebrations. It is perfectly appropriate to tell children, "No, I don't celebrate Chanukah in my home, but I like to light the candles at school." With any response a non-Jewish teacher gives, he/she must always be honest, expose children to non-Jewish people and practices in a positive way, and validate the child's Jewish identity and practices.

CONCLUSION

For non-Jewish teachers to be an asset in a Jewish school, they must be willing to learn about Jewish culture and religion. Opportunities are plentiful, and the rewards are great. Any teacher can become a better teacher by increasing the level of their Jewish knowledge. And not only that, they can enrich their encounters with the Jewish community at large and their understanding of the Jewish way of life. If you are a non-Jewish teacher in a Jewish school, or a Jewish teacher whose Jewish education is but a distant memory, there is much you can learn from a mentor, as well as from your Director and the other teachers on your staff.

BIBLIOGRAPHY

Fisher, Fern. "The Field of Early Childhood Education." In *First School Years* 49, Fall 1999. (Published by Jewish Early Childhood Association of the Board of Jewish Education of Greater New York.

CHAPTER 28

INTERFAITH FAMILIES/NON-JEWISH CHILDREN

Whatever the philosophical orientation of the school, every early childhood program attempts to foster in the children a Jewish identity and love for Judaism. When the goals and philosophy of the school are in exact alignment with the home practices of the child's family, everything that happens at school naturally validates the child's home life.

In many Jewish early childhood programs today, the population of children is far from homogeneous. This is especially true in a community program that attracts families from many different Jewish affiliations. Estimates are that some 50% of marriages taking place in the U.S. are intermarriages (somewhat less in Canada and England). Thus, it is obvious that there are many children from interfaith families enrolled in Jewish early childhood programs. In some of these programs, non-Jewish families have also chosen to enroll their children. Clearly, our task is far more complex today than in previous times. Sensitivity to these issues on the part of teachers and Directors is essential if we are to ensure a positive and enriching experience for every child and family.

families should be welcomed and clearly informed about the Jewish philosophies of the school and the Jewish activities in which their child will take part on a daily basis.

Having a non-Jewish child in a Jewish program can be a wonderful experience for both the family and the school. The non-Jewish family will learn about what it means to be Jewish, enabling them to be tolerant, understanding, and supportive of Jews and Jewish observance. Being exposed to Jewish rituals opens the door for the family to explore their own rituals with their child, and to expand their child's appreciation for differences. The school is called upon to heighten its sensitivities and to validate each child while still maintaining a Jewish framework. The Jewish children in the program are able to make friends with those who have different beliefs and practices, thus expanding their appreciation for differences.

If the enrollment procedure and the orientation process are handled appropriately, with prior disclosure and ongoing support and feedback, a non-Jewish family can enrich the lives of the Jewish children in the program as well as their own.

NON-JEWISH FAMILIES

There are many reasons why non-Jewish families enroll their children in Jewish programs. They may choose a Jewish school because it is the most convenient location, because it provides the highest quality education in their locale, because all their friends send their children to that school, or for some other similar reason. If it is your school's policy to accept non-Jewish children, these

INTERFAITH FAMILIES

The issues surrounding the presence of interfaith families in a Jewish early childhood program are many and complex. A child from an interfaith family may be enrolled in a Jewish program because a united decision has been made to raise the child as a Jew. It may be that the Jewish parent was allowed to choose the preschool, but later, when the child gets older, that same child may go to Religious School at the non-Jewish parent's church. It is possible that no decision has been made regarding the religion of the family, but the Jewish preschool program just happens to be the most convenient. In some cases, one parent may have converted to Judaism. This, then, is not considered an interfaith marriage, but because the extended family on one side is not Jewish, the child will be exposed to many non-Jewish practices and observances. Also, the Jew by Choice will not have childhood memories of Jewish celebrations, and may want or need both support and learning opportunities.

To make matters more complicated, the school does not always have all of the pertinent information. Rarely does a family walk into the Director's office and say, "Hi, he's Jewish and I'm Lutheran. I go to church every Sunday and we are planning to raise our child with both religions. We have enrolled our child in your school because her paternal grandparents are members of this synagogue and they're paying for our child to be here." It is often up to the school to gather the details that are necessary to provide a supportive experience for the child and the family.

GETTING MORE INFORMATION

As with non-Jewish families, before enrollment all interfaith families should be apprised of the Jewish philosophies of the school and of the Jewish activities in which their child will take part. One can hope that during that discussion, a family would volunteer information about the practices or affiliations of their family. But this is not always the case. What is more, it may be uncomfortable or even illegal, depending on state laws, to ask a family outright about their religious make-up, especially if it has any connection to enrollment. Still, to support the family and to provide the most developmentally appropriate education for each child, it is in the school's best interest (and the best interest of each family) to have at least a general sense of the religious home life of each child.

Intake forms are one way to obtain such useful information. In addition to general information about a child upon enrollment, such as toileting habits and names of pets or siblings, the forms can also ask for a child's Hebrew name, synagogue membership, and a general description of Jewish practices observed at home. While none of these questions requires a mandatory answer, they can provide the school with some insight into the child, and may encourage the parents to share any exceptional circumstances.

The winter holiday season will often provide ample opportunities to discuss religious practices at home. As Chanukah approaches, and the world around gears up for Christmas, children suddenly become "celebration detectives," shaping their own identities by comparing them to the identities of their friends and teachers. They will ask such questions as: "Do you celebrate Chanukah? We got Christmas presents from Grandma." "I'm Jewish, what are you?" Teachers might take this opportunity to learn more about their families. Try conversation openers such as: "Sarah mentioned she went to decorate a Christmas tree at her Aunt Melissa's house. Can you tell me more about this? Or: "I know you are very involved in your church and that Seth's mother is a member of this synagogue, but Seth hasn't mentioned any preparations for Christmas at home. Can you help me to understand what his holidays are like at home?" Remember, all this information seeking is solely for the purpose of serving children and families better.

TEACHER'S ROLE IN SCHOOL

The most important thing to remember is to validate each child's experience. We do this by providing information and by allowing children to expand their understanding of their own lives. We invalidate the child's experience when we tell a child, "That's nice that you went to church with

Mommy, but we don't talk about church at school. We only talk about going to synagogue." Zeskind and Silverberg (1996) provide many examples of children in a Jewish early childhood program as they grapple with non-Jewish experiences. These researchers also point out appropriate and inappropriate responses. Their advice is to "accept the fact that children from interfaith families will be exposed to diverse religious life cycle practices. Consider the child's stage of development and listen attentively to what the child is sharing. Respond by acknowledging both the experience and the statements made. Answer questions carefully based on the child's level of understanding" (p. 27).

CONCLUSION

It is up to us as teachers and Directors to try to understand the kind of identity the family is striving to provide for the child. In this way, the school and family can find the best ways to support the child. By helping children understand the interfaith experiences they have had, and acknowledging these experiences as a valid and important part of the child and his/her family, we can reinforce and extend a child's Jewish identity and self-concept.

BIBLIOGRAPHY

ADULTS

Diamant, Anita. *Choosing a Jewish Life*. New York: Schocken Books, 1997.
> A handbook for people converting to Judaism and for their family and friends.

King, Andrea. *If I'm Jewish and You're Christian, What Are the Kids? A Parenting Guide for Interfaith Families*. New York: UAHC Press, 1993.
> Assists interfaith families in choosing a religious identity for their children.

Levin, Sunie. *Mingled Roots: A Guide for Jewish Grandparents of Interfaith Grandchildren*. Washington, DC: B'nai B'rith Women, 1992.
> Helps Jewish grandparents with the challenges of dealing with interfaith relationships.

Magida, Arthur J., ed. *How to Be a Perfect Stranger: A Guide To Etiquette in Other People's Religious Ceremonies*. Woodstock, VT: Jewish Lights Publishing, 1996.
> A guide to rituals and celebrations of America's largest faiths for interested guests.

Petsonk, Judy, and Jim Remsen. *The Intermarriage Handbook: A Guide for Jews & Christians*. New York: Quill, 1991.
> A practical self-help book.

Zeskind, Margie, and Sheila Silverberg. *The S.A.G.A. Approach (Sensitive Alternatives for Guiding Affectively)*. Miami, FL: SheMar Productions, 1996.
> Guidelines for educators in Jewish early childhood settings as they deal with religious diversity.

CHILDREN

Gertz, Susan Enid. *Hanukkah and Christmas at My House*. Middleton, OH: Willow & Laurel Press, 1991. (Ages 4-8)
> A story about a family with a Jewish mother and a Catholic father. Includes factual information about each holiday. Good for children of interfaith families.

Portnoy, Mindy Avra. *Mommy Never Went To Hebrew School*. Rockville, MD: Kar-Ben Copies, 1989. (Ages 3-8)
> A mother explains her conversion to her six-year-old son.

Wing, Natasha. *Jalapeño Bagels*. New York: Atheneum Books for Young Readers, 1996. (Ages 5-8)
> For International Day at school, Pablo wants to bring something that reflects the cultures of both his parents — his Jewish father and his Mexican mother.

CHAPTER 29

KEEPING KOSHER AT SCHOOL

Kashrut is a central feature of Jewish life. Not all Jews adhere to the laws of *kashrut*. Even among those who do keep kosher, there are many variations of what this actually means in practice. Even for Jews who do not maintain a kosher home, *kashrut* may still have some influence over their personal choice of foods, and may come into play when they consider the food to be served at Jewish events or meals with other Jews. In any case, for most Jews, kosher is a relationship. We Jews are a people highly connected to food and the rituals of food, and our relationships to food and Judaism change and evolve as we do.

KOSHER? WHAT'S THAT?

The basic laws of *kashrut* are derived from the Torah, which specifies which animals we may and may not eat (Leviticus 11:1-43). The mammals we are allowed to eat must have split hooves and chew their cud. This includes cows, sheep, goats, and deer; it does not include camels, horses, and pigs. Domestic fowl are permitted, wild birds and birds of prey are *treif* (not kosher). This means that chicken, turkey, tame ducks, geese, and pigeons are okay for dinner. Eagles, vultures, hawks, and ostriches are off limits. The fish we are allowed to eat must have fins and scales. This includes tuna, white fish, salmon, and perch, among others; it excludes shellfish, such as lobster, oysters, shrimp, and crabs. Insects with wings are not allowed. Walking insects, such as crickets and grasshoppers, are fine for a snack. All amphibians (frogs, alligators, lizards) are excluded from the kosher Jewish diet.

There is also a separation between milk and meat. Three times the Torah states, "You shall not boil a kid in its mother's milk" (Exodus 23:19, 34:26, and Deuteronomy 14:21). This, according to Siegel (1973), illustrates concern for the cruelty involved in combining the milk (the life giving element of an animal) with its flesh (the death element). Over time, this simple separation has been expanded to prohibit the mixing of milk and meat in any way. More on this below.

The Torah gives us these two basic parameters, and a few others, such as not eating the blood of an animal, because the life is in the blood (Leviticus 17:11). So how do we get from "You shall not boil a kid in its mother's milk" to separate sets of dishes for milk and meat? Over the past 2000 years, Rabbis have interpreted the words of the Torah, and determined how to eat Jewishly. They outlined exactly how to kill an animal in the most painless way, because keeping kosher means having mercy on animals even as we prepare to eat them. The Rabbis have tried to figure out just how separate milk and meat have to be. There is general agreement that milk products and meat products cannot be used in the same recipe, nor can they be served at the same meal. This means using vegetable stock instead of chicken stock if you want to serve the soup with an entrée of lasagna, and it means no ice cream after a meat dinner.

Just to make sure that no one makes a mistake, the Rabbis "put a fence around the Torah." Many materials, such as china, plastic, and ceramics, are absorbent. To avoid the mixing of milk and meat on the dishes themselves, strictly observant Jews have at least two sets of dishes (and silverware) —

one for milk meals and one for meat meals. I say at "least," because often there's one milk set for everyday use, one milk set for company, one meat set for everyday use, one meat set for entertaining, and we haven't even begun to talk about Pesach! Then there's the waiting period between eating meat and milk. Some communities wait six hours between a meat meal and eating dairy, some three, some only one. Ask a Rabbi if you need some guidance in this area.

There are a few reasons why there are so many variations in how people keep kosher. First of all, Rabbis don't always agree. Also, modern Rabbis have had to figure out what it means to keep kosher with a dishwasher, microwave oven, and grocery stores full of prepared foods. A good guideline is to find a Rabbi you respect, and abide by his or her decisions.

Secondly, there are many ways to be Jewish in our world today. Reform Jews do not hold *halachah* (the major body of Jewish law, including the laws of *kashrut*) binding, yet many Reform Jews do keep kosher. Other Reform Jews have derived their own ways to make eating a Jewish activity. Many Jews who do not keep strictly kosher may still separate milk and meat, or avoid pork and shellfish, in order to make eating a Jewish experience. Some Jews choose to keep a strictly kosher home, but they will eat out in non-kosher restaurants. Some Jews eat out, but only dairy, not meat. The Orthodox, Conservative, Reconstructionist, and Reform movements each have something to say about how to eat Jewishly, and within each movement, each person might make his/her own decisions.

IS THIS KOSHER?

The Torah tells us which animals are permitted as food, but an animal or fowl has to be slaughtered by a *shochet* (a kosher butcher) in a certain way, in order to be considered kosher. According to Genesis 1:29, all fruits and vegetables, at least before they've been processed in any way, are completely kosher. What about prepared foods? Foods in the grocery store that are kosher — meaning that all the ingredients are kosher and the food has been prepared in specific, kosher ways, including no mixing of milk and meat — are marked with a special symbol called a *hechsher*. Lest you think there is just one symbol to let you know if a product is kosher, remember that Jews are a diverse group. There are over 70 kosher symbols, each signifying the approval of a group of Rabbis. Check with a Rabbi or on the Internet for local symbols (see www.kosherquest.org, or www.kosher.co.il for lists). Since it is not possible to trademark a single letter, a "K" on a package does not necessarily mean there is a reputable Rabbi or group of Rabbis supervising that product. Many products with a "K" *are* strictly kosher. But, to be sure, check with a Rabbi.

KASHRUT AND YOUR SCHOOL

Jewish early childhood centers across North America are sponsored by Orthodox, Conservative, Reform, and Reconstructionist synagogues. There are also Jewish preschool and daycare centers sponsored by JCCs and other community organizations. Each of these institutions has a different philosophy and approach to keeping kosher. It is not possible here to outline one way of keeping kosher that would be suitable for every school. Therefore, this chapter provides guidelines and suggestions for maintaining a kosher environment. Naturally, there will be communities that will assert, "That's not strict enough." For others, the guidelines in the following pages will be too strict. The goal here is to provide the tools; each teacher or each school must decide how to use these tools.

With infants and toddlers, it's important to remember that breast milk is considered *parve*, that is, neither milk nor meat. You can serve a child a bottle of breast milk and a hamburger, if you so choose. As long as it's come up, what exactly is *parve*? A food is *parve* if it contains neither milk products nor meat products. Unprepared fruits and vegetables are *parve*, vegetable oil is *parve*, some margarines are *parve* (but many contain whey, and are therefore dairy), juice is *parve*, so is fish. *Parve* foods can be served with a hamburger or a cheese sandwich; they are neutral.

With older children, you have to be more careful about making sure the sippy cup has juice in it, not milk, if meat is being served. In full day care situations, be aware of how long a wait between meat and milk your school requires. Since the body digests meat more slowly than it does dairy products, most Rabbis require a longer wait after eating meat before eating dairy. If you serve a meat lunch, it is usually safest to have a snack that is *parve* in the afternoon.

Many schools invite children to bring their own lunches. In most cases, requiring dairy lunches only (e.g., peanut butter and jelly, tuna fish, pasta, meatless pizza, and the like) solves the problem of mixing milk and meat. Other schools have "meat" days and "milk" days, although that can get a bit confusing.

DISHES

Many schools use paper plates and plastic ware to reduce clean up and avoid *kashrut* mix-ups. This works well, but one still must be careful with serving and baking utensils. Mixing bowls, measuring cups and spoons, mixing and serving spoons, and so on, should be clearly marked for either meat or dairy. Traditionally, dairy things are marked with blue, and meat things are marked with red. I don't know who chose these colors, but it's a tradition, not a law. If green and yellow work better for you, go for it. Just make sure everyone in the school agrees on one system. *Parve* brownies can be baked in a meat pan or a dairy pan; just make sure you use all meat or all dairy utensils.

A note about glass. Glass is a very hard material; it does not absorb food. Glass is therefore considered *parve* — it can be used for both meat and dairy. Still, some people don't consider Pyrex

the same as glass, so they don't consider Pyrex *parve*. Again, check with your Rabbi.

Washing dishes continues the process of keeping kosher. Some people have two sinks, one for dairy and one for meat. Some people use washtubs in the sink, one for dairy and one for meat. Some people use sink racks or liners. You get the idea. Even when the food is mostly gone and dishes are being washed, the separation remains. Many people use different drying racks for meat and dairy dishes as well. Whatever your school policy is, be sure to follow it carefully.

FOOD FOR TEACHERS

We've covered food for children, but what about food for grown-ups? Each school will have a different policy about what food teachers can bring into the school, and even where they can eat it. Whatever the requirements might be, follow the school's kosher policy carefully, even if you yourself don't keep kosher at home. When each person makes an effort to maintain the same level of *kashrut* at school, everyone can feel comfortable eating and being together.

The same courtesy applies to bringing in food to share with other teachers. If there are teachers who keep strictly kosher and your home is not kosher, bring in store-bought, kosher goods, not home baked items, to share. Then everyone will be able to share and feel part of the group.

CONCLUSION

Keeping kosher at school is really not difficult. Kosher is a habit, and once you're in the habit, it's a piece of cake (kosher cake, that is!). If you have more questions, consult the resources in the bibliography below. The Internet is a wonderful resource as well. Some sites are listed below, but if you plug in "kosher" into your favorite search engine, you'll find more information than you could ever read and absorb.

BIBLIOGRAPHY

ADULTS

Greenberg, Blu. *How to Run a Traditional Jewish Household*. Northvale, NJ: Jason Aronson Inc., 1989.
> A modern, comprehensive, traditional guide to making an observant Jewish home.

Siegel, Richard; Michael Strassfeld; and Sharon Strassfeld. *The First Jewish Catalog*. Philadelphia: The Jewish Publication Society, 1973.
> An extraordinary guide to many aspects of Jewish life and observance, including *kashrut.*

Welfeld, Irving. *Why Kosher? An Anthology of Answers*. Northvale, NJ: Jason Aronson Inc., 1996.
> Reflections on the question "Why keep kosher?" from many sources throughout Jewish history.

WEB SITES

American-Asian Kashrus Services: www.kashrus.org

The All Kosher Index of the United Kashrut Authority: www.kosher.co.il

Kosher Quest: www.kosherquest.org

Orthodox Union: www.ou.org

JEWISH COOKBOOKS

Kinderlehrer, Jane. *Cooking Kosher the New Way: Fast, Lite & Natural*. New York: Jonathan David Publishers, Inc., 1995.
> Traditional Jewish recipes revised to be lighter and more nutritious.

Nathan, Joan. *Jewish Cooking in America*. New York: Alfred A. Knopf, 1994.
> A splendid feast of over 300 kosher recipes, old and new, along with stories from Sephardic and Ashkenazic Jews.

———. *The Children's Jewish Holiday Kitchen*. New York: Schocken Books, 1995.
> Seventy ways to have fun with kids and make family celebrations special.

Spice and Spirit: The Complete Kosher Jewish Cookbook. A Kosher Living Classic. Brooklyn, NY: Lubavitch Women's Cookbook Publications, 1990.
> A treasure-house of kosher dishes presented against the backdrop of the rich tapestry of Jewish life.

Zeidler, Judy. *Master Chefs Cook Kosher*. San Francisco: Chronicle Books, 1998.
> Recipes from the television show "Judy's Kitchen Now," all kosher to the letter.

CHILDREN

Carle, Eric. *Pancakes, Pancakes!* Saxonville, MA : Picture Book Studio, 1992. (Ages 3-8)
> By cutting and grinding the wheat for flour, Jack starts from scratch to help make his breakfast pancake.

Davis, Aubrey. *Bone Button Borscht*. Toronto: KidsCan Press, Inc., 1995. (Ages 4-8)
> A Jewish version of the folktale "Stone Soup."

Forest, Heather. *Stone Soup*. Little Rock, AR: August House LittleFolk, 1997. (Ages 4-8)
> Two hungry travelers use a stone as a soup starter and demonstrate the benefits of sharing. Includes a recipe for soup.

French, Vivian. *Oliver's Vegetables*. New York: Orchard Books, 1995. (Ages 3-7)
> While visiting his grandfather, who has a wonderful garden, Oliver learns to eat vegetables other than potatoes.

Hoban, Russell. *Bread and Jam for Frances*. New York: HarperCollins, 1993. (Ages 3-8)
> Frances decides she likes to eat only bread and jam at every meal until — to her surprise — her parents grant her wish.

Miller, Deborah Uchill, and Karen Ostrove. *Fins and Scales: A Kosher Tale*. Rockville, MD: Kar-Ben Copies, 1991. (Ages 4-8)
> The Jewish dietary laws of keeping kosher are explained in humorous rhyme.

CHAPTER 30

SUMMERTIME, AND THE LIVING IS JEWISH

For many Jewish early childhood programs, summertime represents a change of pace. New children may enter the program, there may be staff changes, children may move up to the next older group, and the program may be restructured to resemble more closely summer camp, with smaller groups, an increased emphasis on outdoor physical and water play, and an overall more relaxed feeling. It is important, amidst all these changes, not to forget to maintain a focus on the Jewish elements of your school.

The summer, which is lacking in major Jewish holidays, save Tishah B'Av, Shabbat, and Rosh Chodesh, is a wonderful time to focus on Jewish culture. The idea is to make the atmosphere of summer feel Jewish and to take advantage of the outdoors as a Jewish place. Many of the suggestions in Chapter 2, "Jewish Every Day," are applicable in the summer as well. Following is a list of suggestions tailored especially to the summer.

1. Make sure that some of the books on the children's bookshelf are Jewish/Hebrew books. Likewise, make sure that some of the stories which teachers choose to read or tell are Jewish stories. Focus especially on books of Jewish folktales, and stories that highlight Jewish values. See the bibliography of this chapter for some good summer reading suggestions.

2. Choose Jewish stories for the children to act out. Some good ones are *Hannah's Sabbath Dress* by Izhak Schweiger-Dmi'el, *It Could Always Be Worse: A Yiddish Folk Tale* by Margot Zemach, and "The Apple Tree's Discovery" by Penninah Schram and Rachayl Eckstein Davis.

3. Sing Jewish/Hebrew songs in addition to secular songs. Holiday songs children have learned

or will learn during the school year are appropriate, as they provide a wonderful review/preview.

4. Substitute Hebrew words in familiar songs, such as "The Eensy Weensy Akavish" and "Old Goldenberg Had a Farm" (see Chapter 19, "Integrating Hebrew Every Day," p. 264).

5. Use Jewish shapes/cookie cutters for play dough and sponge painting. Use symbols from many different holidays. Take Jewish shapes outside to paint sidewalks and walls with water or washable paints.

6. Play games outside, substituting Hebrew words and Jewish concepts in games the children know. For example, play *Shimon Omer* instead of *Simon Says*; *Ohr Adom/Ohr Yarok* instead of *Red Light/Green Light*; *Latke Latke Hamantaschen* instead of *Duck Duck Goose*; *Kelev, Kelev, Where's Your Bone?* instead of *Doggie, Doggie, Where's Your Bone?*; and *Chatool V'Achbar* for *Cat and Mouse*. For older children, use concepts such as *Gemilut Chasadeem* (deeds of loving-kindness) for games during which you do something nice for someone, or *Klal Yisrael* (the Jews are one people) for games during which everyone has to work together to win.

7. Make sure there are always Jewish objects and costumes in the house corner. Extend dramatic play outside with a tent and props for playing Torah characters, along with camels and pyramids for the sandbox.

8. Whether you eat a snack indoors or outside, be sure to say a blessing first.

9. Celebrate Shabbat outside. It is worth *shlepping* the table with the candles, etc., to the playground or a lawn. Even if the whole group

celebrates Shabbat together inside, you can do a private pre-Shabbat with your children outside. Better yet, meet with the whole school outside to celebrate Shabbat. Form a circle outside, and sing some Shabbat songs. Dance some Israeli folk dances in the grass. See how long the candles will stay lit before the wind blows them out. Share your *challah* crumbs with the birds.

10. Start each week by celebrating Havdalah outside.

11. Use flowers or grasses picked by the children for the Havdalah spices. Dandelions work well. The blessing is over "spices," so it is traditional to have at least two spices.

12. Watch the moon. Celebrate Rosh Chodesh with the children. Pick a special spot and eat crescent shape cookies there. (See Chapter 8, "Rosh Chodesh," for more ideas of how to celebrate it.)

13. Take a nature walk and notice new life. How is God a part of the world outside? Talk about how it is a Jewish responsibility, indeed, an important Jewish value, to help take care of the earth. It's called *Tikkun Olam*.

14. Use things collected from nature to decorate Jewish objects. Press leaves, sticks, and flowers into clay for candlesticks. Mod-Podge leaves, grass, flowers, or twigs onto cups to make *Kiddush* cups or onto boxes to make *Tzedakah* boxes.

15. Make *challah* every week. You can make the dough on Thursdays and bake it on Fridays.

16. Collect *Tzedakah* every week. Have a special *Tzedakah* project for the summer. Set a goal, and have a field trip at the end of the summer to deliver your *Tzedakah* collection to the predetermined recipient, or to go shopping for the *Tzedakah* items you decided on, and then deliver those.

17. Compare your summer camp experiences to places, things, or events in Israel. Talk about what children in Israel do in the summer. Compare a camp garden to a garden that

might grow on a *kibbutz*. Pretend the sprinklers are the waterfalls at Ein Gedi.

18. Practice the *mitzvah* of *Tza'ar Ba'alay Chayim* (care for animals) by making bird feeders and keeping them stocked. Keep an eye out for new animal life in your area, and provide assistance to local animals by supplying food or shelter, or just by staying at a safe distance to observe.

19. Sing picnic songs and songs about bugs. (See Chapter "Pesach, with Lag B'Omer," p. 236-237, for specific songs and movement activities.)

20. A favorite old camp song is called "Swimming." It goes like this:

Swimming, swimming [make swimming movements with your arms]
In the swimming pool [draw a circle with fingers]
When days are hot [mop brow]
When days are cold [hug body as if shivering]
In the swimming pool [draw a circle with fingers]
Breaststroke, sidestroke [two hands together then push forward; two hands together, then one goes up while other goes down]
Fancy diving, too [put hands together to dive, or hold nose with fingers]
Oh, don't you wish
Therre was nothing else to do!

CONCLUSION

The most important thing in any summer early childhood program is always to encourage children to relate to each other in Jewish ways. Especially in the summertime, when children may be getting used to new classmates or new classrooms, it is important to take extra time to create a cohesive community. Teach Jewish values, such as being a *mensch*, having respect (*Kavod*) for other people, caring for the environment (*Tikkun Olam*), having compassion for animals (*Tza'ar Ba'alay Chayim*), and caring for other people (*Gemilut Chasadeem*) to bring children together and create stable relationships. There are many *mitzvot* and *middot* (Jewish virtues) with which children and their

teachers can be involved even as they play and enjoy the summer.

BIBLIOGRAPHY

CHILDREN

Aroner, Miriam. *Kingdom of Singing Birds.* Rockville, MD: KarBen Copies, 1993. (Ages 4-8)
When his collection of rare and exotic birds refuse to sing, the king calls wise Rabbi Zusya for help.

Podwal, Mark. *Golem: A Giant Made of Mud.* New York: Greenwillow Books, 1995. (Ages 4-8)
A wonderful retelling of the classic folktale of the clay man who aids the Jews of Prague.

Rosenfeld, Dina. *The Very Best Book.* Brooklyn, NY: Hachai Publishers, 1997. (Ages 2-5)
Familiar items that a child sees every day are used for various *mitzvot*.

Schram, Peninnah, and Rachayl Eckstein Davis. "The Apple Tree's Discovery." In *Chosen Tales*, edited by Peninnah Schram. Northvale, NJ: Jason Aronson Inc., 1995. (Ages 3-adult)
The story of the star hidden inside the apple in a perfect version for telling.

Schweiger-Dmi'el, Izhak. *Hanna's Sabbath Dress.* New York: Simon & Schuster Books for Young Readers, 1996. (Ages 4-7)
When Hanna helps an old man and her new Sabbath dress gets dirty, she is afraid her mother will be angry.

Shulevitz, Uri. *The Secret Room.* New York: Farrar, Straus and Giroux, 1993. (Ages 4-8)
Wisdom triumphs over greed, as the king's clever treasurer clears his name after being accused of stealing.

Wood, Douglas. *Making the World.* New York: Simon & Schuster Books for Young Readers, 1998. (Ages 3-7)
Reveals the secret of how our unfinished world is being made complete by everyone who lives in it, including the reader.

Zemach, Margot. *It Could Always Be Worse: A Yiddish Folk Tale.* New York: Farrar, Straus & Giroux, 1990.
When he could no longer stand his overcrowded and noisy home, a poor man goes to the Rabbi for advice. The advice has an amazing result.

APPENDIX A

Sheet Music

Al Shalosh Regalim

Julie Jaslow Auerbach
Copyright © 1984 by Julie Jaslow Auerbach

Use this song for the three Pilgrimage Festivals of Sukkot, Pesach, and Shavuot.

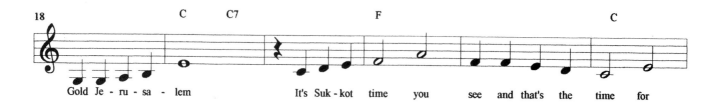

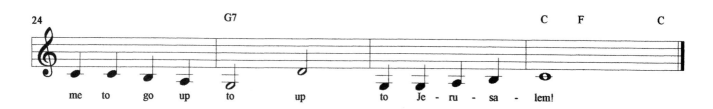

Build Me a Sukkah

Julie Jaslow Auerbach
Copyright (c) 1988 by Julie Jaslow Auerbach

Children can write verses/fill in the blanks, e.g. Build it with a hammer and saw and nails. Put in some lights, but no gray … (whales)

The Challah

Julie Jaslow Auerbach
Copyright © 1987 by Julie Jaslow Auerbach

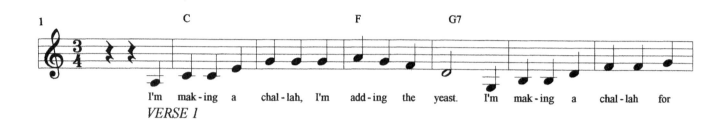

I'm mak-ing a chal-lah, I'm add-ing the yeast. I'm mak-ing a chal-lah for

VERSE 1

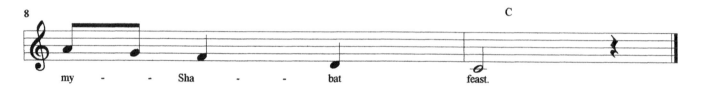

my - - Sha - - bat feast.

Verse 2: *
I'm making a *challah* with flour and eggs.
I'm making a *challah*, I'll watch as it bakes.

Verse 3:
I braid it and twist it (Add twisting motions) and tuck in the ends.
I braid it and twist it, it has so many bends.

Verse 4:
I watch as it rises (slowly rise) so slowly at first.
I watch as it rises, I hope it doesn't burst.

Verse 5: *
Up to the top (rise higher and higher) of the oven it grows.
Up to the top, where it stops – oh, no one knows!

Verse 6:
My *challah*, my *challah*, you're so good to eat.
My *challah*, my *challah*, so warm and fresh and sweet.

* May be omitted for a shorter song.

Chanukah

Julie Jaslow Auerbach
Copyright © 1988 by Julie Jaslow Auerbach

Line 1: Xylophone Line 2: Tamborine or Bells Line 3: Maracas

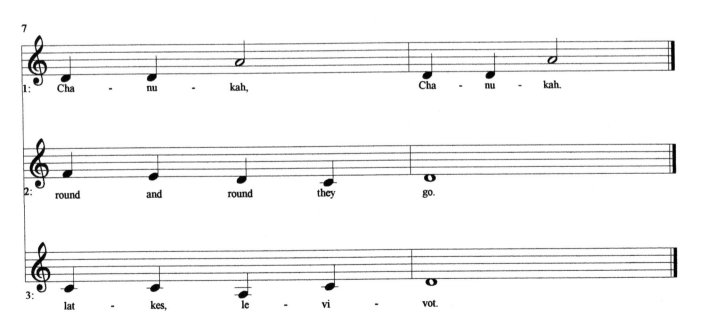

Eretz Yisrael

Julie Jaslow Auerbach
Copyright © 1984 by Julie Jaslow Auerbach

Sing in a lively fashion.

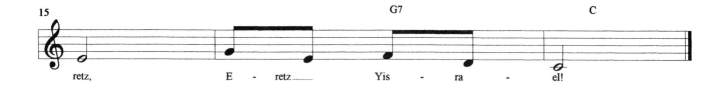

Verse 2:
Drain the swamps for farmland.
A Kibbutz will make it grand.
Drain the swamps for farmland.
A Kibbutz will make it grand.
The Huleh Valley won't be pale.
Eretz, Eretz Yisrael.

Verse 3:
Jews will come from far and wide
To visit and reside.
Jews will come from far and wide
To visit and reside.
Eretz, Eretz Yisrael.
Eretz, the dream is now so real!

Fall

Julie Jaslow Auerbach and Nathaniel Auerbach
Copyright © 1987 by Julie Jaslow Auerbach

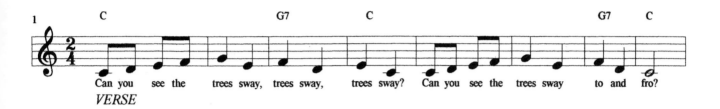

VERSE
Can you see the trees sway, trees sway, trees sway? Can you see the trees sway to and fro?

REFRAIN
That's be-cause it's wind-y wind-y, wind-y. That's be-cause it's wind-y all day long.

Other verses: leaves fall, leaves blow, etc.

Falling

Julie Jaslow Auerbach
Copyright © 1987 by Julie Jaslow Auerbach

G'mar Chatima Tova

Julie Jaslow Auerbach
Copyright © 1999 by Julie Jaslow Auerbach

Other verses: I'll try to be a friend to everyone … listen to my mom and dad … kids make up verses … end as below

Goodbye Sabbath Queen

Julie Jaslow Auerbach
Copyright © 1987 by Julie Jaslow Auerbach

It's time to say good - bye a - gain to our Sab - bath Queen. It's

time to say good - bye a - gain to our Sab - bath Queen. Sha - vu - a tov, Sha -

vu - a tov, good - bye, good - bye, good - bye. Sha - vu - a tov, Sha - vu - a tov, good -

bye, good - bye, good - bye.

Goshen

Julie Jaslow Auerbach
Copyright © 1988 by Julie Jaslow Auerbach

Make up verses as you go along to tell the Pesach story.

The Jews were slaves in Go-shen. The Jews were slaves in Go-shen The

Jews were slaves in Go - shen. Gosh oh gosh oh Go-shen!

Happy Rosh HaShanah To You

Julie Jaslow Auerbach
Copyright © 1984 by Julie Jaslow Auerbach

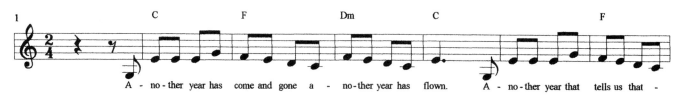

A - no-ther year has come and gone a - no-ther year has flown. A - no-ther year that tells us that -

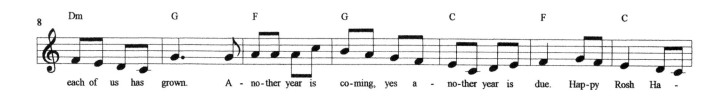

each of us has grown. A - no-ther year is co-ming, yes a - no-ther year is due. Hap-py Rosh Ha -

Sha - nah to you.____ Let's take the ap-ple and let's (CLAP) dip it so, in hon-ey stick-y and so sweet,

____ and say "Sha - nah To - vah u - (CLAP) m' - tu - kah" as friends and re - la - tives we greet.

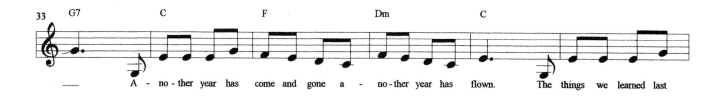

____ A - no-ther year has come and gone a - no-ther year has flown. The things we learned last

year at school have now be - come well known. A - no-ther year is co - ming filled with things both old and

new. Hap-py Rosh Ha - Sha - nah to you._____ Hap-py Rosh Ha - Sha - nah to you._____

Hebrew Counting Song

(Achat Shtayim)

Julie Jaslow Auerbach
Copyright © 1994 by Julie Jaslow Auerbach

A - chat shta - yim sha - losh ar - bah, cha -
Refrain

mesh shesh she - va she - mo - na te - sha e - -

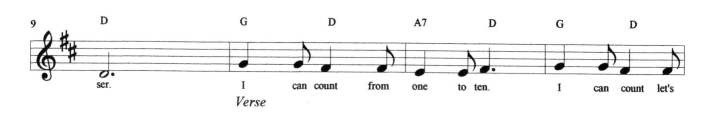

ser. I can count from one to ten. I can count let's
Verse

do it a - - again!

Verse 2:
Eser etsbaot bayadayim, eser etsbaot baraglayim!

The Jewish Calendar Song

Julie Jaslow Auerbach
Copyright © 1984 by Julie Jaslow Auerbach

Tish-rei starts the year with Rosh Ha-Sha-nah, Yom Kip-pur. - De-co-rate your suk-kah and then

march on Sim-chat To-rah. Chesh-van Kis-lev it's turned cold and time to spin our drei-dls.

Here comes Spring it's Te-vet She-vat A - dar and brave Queen Es-ther.

Verse 2:
Pesach comes, the flowers bloom.
It's Nissan, Iyar, Sivan.
When it's hot
It must be Tammuz, Av and Elul.
It's so nice to celebrate
Our holidays so festive.
And our year will start again
With Tishrei, Cheshvan, Kislev.

Lemonade

Julie Jaslow Auerbach
Copyright © 1989 by Julie Jaslow Auerbach

Try making lemonade while singing this song!

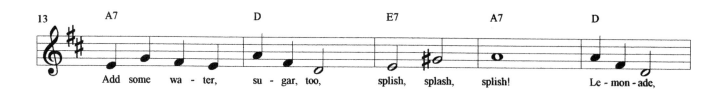

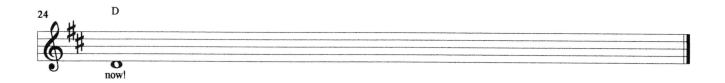

The Lulav

Julie Jaslow Auerbach
Copyright © 1987 by Julie Jaslow Auerbach

Shake me, Shake me, I'm the lu-lav, Shake me, Shake me, up and down. Shake me, shake me,

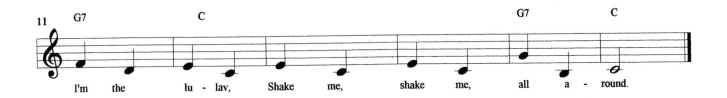

I'm the lu - lav, Shake me, shake me, all a - round.

Mah Mezeg Ha'avir?

(What is the Weather?)

Julie Jaslow Auerbach
Copyright © 1988 by Julie Jaslow Auerbach

* Children answer with "ken" or "lo".

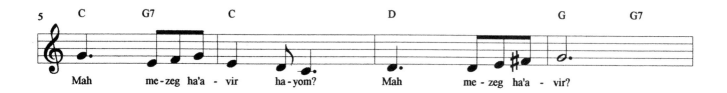

21

F · C · G7 · C · F · C · G7 · C

Ge-shem yo-red?* Kar - ba-chutz?* Cham - ba-chutz?* me-zeg a - vir.

Is it raining? *Is it cold outside?* *Is it hot outside?*

Marching in the Synagogue

Julie Jaslow Auerbach
Copyright © 1994 by Julie Jaslow Auerbach

You can add other relatives, too!

Grand-ma has one too. We're mar-ching in the syn-a-gogue, it's me and ev'-ry Jew. We

read V'-zot Ha-b'-ra-cha and then read B'-re-shit. We start at the end and then be-gin a-

gain! We're mar-ching in the syn-a-gogue, we're mar-ching one by one. We're

mar-ching in the syn-a-gogue, we're ha-ving so much fun. And now I have a To-rah and we're

dan-cing cheek to cheek. Now here is one for you and you can dance too, don't be meek!

The Marching Maccabee

Julie Jaslow Auerbach
Copyright © 1988 by Julie Jaslow Auerbach

Instead of marching, the Maccabees can be clapping, walking, tapping, tip-toeing, etc.

Open Your Fingers

Julie Jaslow Auerbach
Copyright © 1987 by Julie Jaslow Auerbach

O - pen your fin - gers, now - close them tight. O - pen your fin - gers, now -

close them tight. O - pen your fin - gers, now - close them - tight And

clap your hands - with - all your might.

Other verses: use mouths ... smack, eyes ... blink, arms ... hug yourselves, fingers ... wave hello

Pitter Patter
(Raindrops)

Julie Jaslow Auerbach
Copyright © 1987 by Julie Jaslow Auerbach

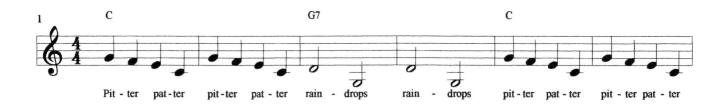

Verse 2: Splitter, Splatter.
Verse 3: Splishing, Splashing
Verse 4: Thunder, lightning.

Purim's a Time

Julie Jaslow Auerbach
Copyright © 1987 by Julie Jaslow Auerbach

Pur - im's a time when we dress up and play dress up and play

dress up and play Pur - im's a time when we dress up and play Oh hap - py hol - i -

day! Ha - man is mean Es - ther's the Queen
(Make a mean face.) *(Put a crown on your head.)*

Mor - de - chai he's the brav - est we've seen! And oh my gosh,
(Make a muscle.) *(Put your hands on your face.)*

there's King A - chash Ha - man's plan he did squash.
(He needs a crown, too.) *(Squash with your foot.)*

Raindrops

(Snowflakes)

Julie Jaslow Auerbach
Copyright © 1999 by Julie Jaslow Auerbach

Tell children you've forgotten some of the words and omit capitalized words. Make up other body-part rhymes.

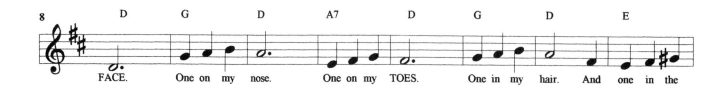

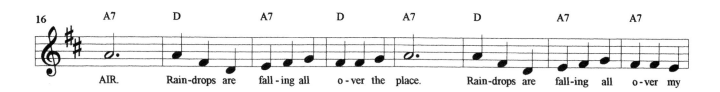

Shabbat Niggun

Julie Jaslow Auerbach
Copyright © 1992 by Julie Jaslow Auerbach

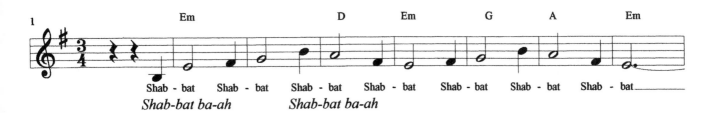

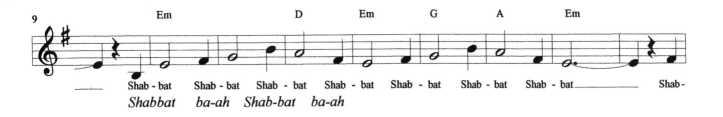

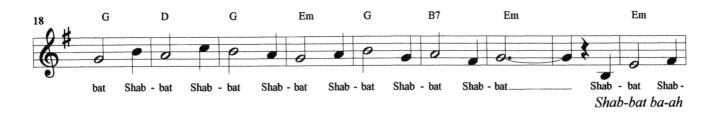

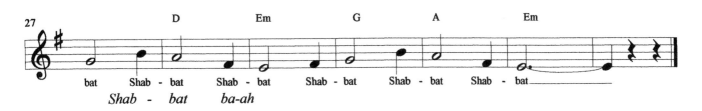

Verses 3 and 4: Shabbat menuchah, Shabbat Shalom.

Shabbat, Shabbat Shalom

Julie Jaslow Auerbach
Copyright © 1985 by Julie Jaslow Auerbach

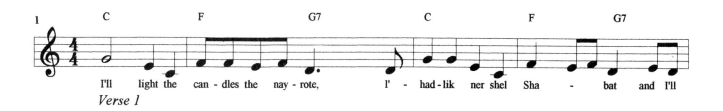

I'll light the can-dles the nay-rote, l'-had-lik ner shel Sha-bat and I'll

Verse 1

watch them shine on my whole fam-i-ly, Sha-bat, Sha-bat Sha-lom. -

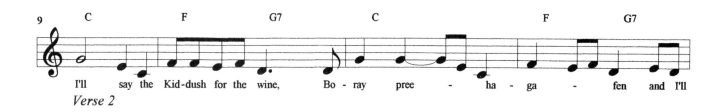

I'll say the Kid-dush for the wine, Bo-ray pree - ha-ga - fen and I'll

Verse 2

share the kos with my whole fam-i-ly, Sha-bat, Sha-bat Sha-lom. -

I'll taste the chal-lah it's the best, Ha-mo-tzi le-chem min ha-a - retz. And I'll

Verse 3

eat the meal with the whole fam - i - ly, Sha - bat, Sha - bat Sha - lom. -

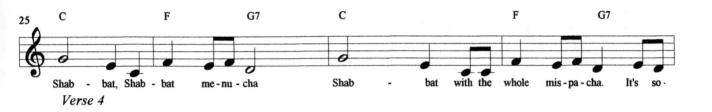

Shab - bat, Shab - bat me - nu - cha   Shab - bat with the whole mis - pa - cha. It's so

Verse 4

nice to be to - geth - er Jew - ish - ly, Sha - bat, Sha - bat Sha - lom. -

Shtuyot (Let's All Take a Trip!)

Julie Jaslow Auerbach
Copyright © 1985 by Julie Jaslow Auerbach

This song is dedicated to all the shlichim who come from Israel to our summer camps each year.

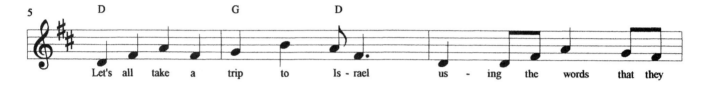

Verse 2:
Rega's what you yell when you rush for the bus.
Kama zeh, how much does it cost?

Verse 3:
Before you eat a meal say *B'tay avon*.
What all of a sudden, *ma pitom*!

Verse 4:
Betach is of course, *beseder* okay,
For nonsense it's *shtuyot* that you say!

Soon It's Gonna Be Pesach

Julie Jaslow Auerbach
Copyright © 1987 by Julie Jaslow Auerbach

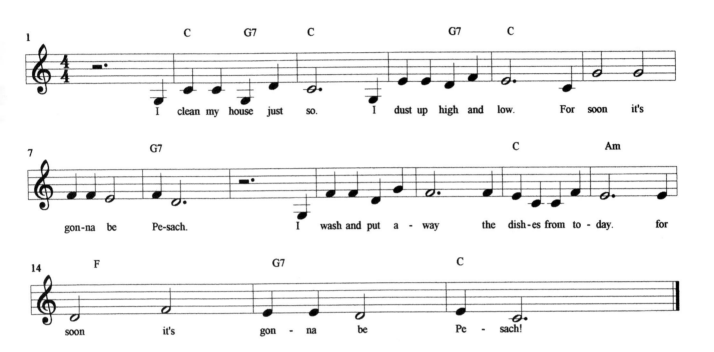

Verse 2:
Let's clean and wipe around.
A bread crumb I have found,
For soon it's gonna be *Pesach*.
Let's polish and let's scrub,
And wash around the tub,
For soon it's gonna be *Pesach*.

Verse 3:
Some curtains new and bright,
A tablecloth that's white,
For soon it's gonna be *Pesach*,
A new time now is here,
The Springtime of the year,
And soon it's gonna be *Pesach*.

Verse 4:
We'll need four cups of wine,
Charoset chopped so fine,
And *matza* just for *Pesach*.
Egg, lamb bone and *maror*,
And greens to dip for sure,
Let's celebrate – it's *Pesach*!

A Special Way of Saying Thanks

Julie Jaslow Auerbach
Copyright © 1989 by Julie Jaslow Auerbach

Verse 2:
For the crackers that we eat at snack
There are special words we say:
Say *boray minay mizonot*
Crackers taste so good today.

Verse 3:
For the *challah* on *Shabbat* we eat
There are special words we say:
Say *hamotzi lechem min ha'aretz*
For the bread we share today.

Verse 4:
For the apple or the pear we eat
There are special words we say:
We will say *boray pree ha-aytz*
For the fruit from trees today.

Verse 5:
When we smell a rose or fragrant tree
There are special words we say:
Say *boray atzay besameem*
The world smells so good today.

Verse 6:
For the seasons and our holidays
There are special words we say:
Say *Shehechiyanu* everyone
For life's special every day.

APPENDIX B

Hebrew Labels for the Classroom

A print-rich environment stimulates the development of language and literacy skills (Bredekamp, 1997, see p. 18 for citation). Labels in the classroom on chairs, doors, scissors, and so on, create such an environment. Labeling objects and areas in Hebrew as well as English brings the written Hebrew language into the classroom in a meaningful way.

These labels will help you to expose children to written Hebrew language on a daily basis. Having the words in transliteration as well enables anyone to use the Hebrew names for things in the room. Note that the labels on the following pages are much smaller than actual classroom labels should be. Photocopy and enlarge these to a size that is easy to see from across the room. Not all of these labels are appropriate for every classroom. A good guideline is to use these labels for whatever you would normally label in English.

loft

עֲלִיַּת גַּג

aliyat gahg

large motor toys

צַעֲצוּעוֹת לְמוֹטוֹרִיקָה גַּסָה

tza'a-tzu'ote l'mo-to-ri-ca gah-sah

slide

מַגְלֵשָׁה

magleyshah

toy box

קוּפְסַת צַעֲצוּעַ

kuf-sat tza-ah-tzu-ah

stairs

מַדְרֵגוֹת

ma-dray-gote

blocks

קוּבִּיּוֹת

ku-bi-yote

small motor toys

צַעֲצוּעוֹת לְמוֹטוֹרִיקָה עָדִינָה

tza'a-tzu'ote l'mo-to-ri-ca ah-dee-nah

books

סְפָרִים

s'fah-reem

reading corner

פִּנַת הַסֵּפֶר

pee-nat ha-sefer

door

דֶּלֶת

delet

tunnel

מִנְהָרָה

min-hah-rah

playground

חָצֵר

cha-tzayr

eating area

פִּנַת אוֹכֶל

pee-nat oh-chel

bathroom

שֵׁירוּתִים

shay-ru-teem

refrigerator

מְקָרֵר

m'-ka-rare

sink

כִּיוֹר

kee-yor

eating utensils

צַלָחוֹת וְסַכּוּ"ם

tz'la-chote v'sa-kum

shelf

מַדָף

madaf

gate

שַׁעַר

sha'ar

felt board

לוּחַ פְּלַנֶל

loo-ach fla-nel

sleeping area

אֵיזוֹר שֵׁינָה

ay-zor shay-nah

rocking chair

כִּסֵא נַדְנֵדָה

kee-say nad-nay-dah

garbage can

פַּח אַשְׁפָּה

pach ahsh-pah

closet/cabinet

אָרוֹן

ah-rone

storeroom

מַחְסָן

mach-san

children's bins

קוּפְסַת יְלָדִים

kuf-sat ye-la-deem

chair

כִּסֵּא

kee-say

table

שֻׁלְחָן

shul-chan

window

חַלּוֹן

cha-lone

clock

שָׁעוֹן

sha-ohn

telephone

טֶלֶפוֹן

te-le-fone

bird's nest

כַּן צִיּוּר

kan tzeeyoor

dolls

בֻּבּוֹת

boo-bote

doll house

בֵּית בֻּבּוֹת

bayt boo-bote

wall

קִיר

keer

scissors

מִסְפָּרַיִם

mis-pah-rah-yeem

mirror

מַרְאֶה

mar-eh

flag

דֶּגֶל

deh-gel

cars

מְכוֹנִיוֹת

m'cho-nee-ote

airplane/jet

מָטוֹס

mattos

train

רַכֶּבֶת

rak-keh-vet

oven

תַנוּר

ta-noor

truck

מַשָׂאִית

ma-sa-eet

crayons/markers

צְבָעִים

tz'va-eem

sand table

שׁוּלְחָן חוֹל

shul-chan chol

water table

שׁוּלְחָן מַיִם

shul-chan my-yeem

puzzles

פָּזְלִים

pa-za-leem

BIBLIOGRAPHY

GENERAL JEWISH RESOURCES
History
Ben-Sasson, H. H. *A History of the Jewish People.* Cambridge, MA: Harvard University Press, 1985.
> The sum total of Jewish experiences and achievements through the ages, both in the Land of Israel and the Diaspora.

Mendes-Flohr, Paul, and Jehuda Reinharz, eds. *The Jew in the Modern World: A Documentary History.* New York: Oxford University Press, 1995.
> Contains documents which illustrate modern Jewish history from the 1600s on.

Pasachoff, Naomi, and Robert J. Littman. *Jewish History in 100 Nutshells.* Northvale, NJ: Jason Aronson Inc., 1995.
> One hundred of the most important events in Jewish history for the reader on the go.

Sachar, Howard M. A *History of the Jews in America.* New York: Vintage Books, 1993.
> A history of the Jews in America from the earliest days of settlement to recent tensions in Israel. Sachar discusses the impact of America on Jewish culture, the contributions that Jews have made, the conflicts, noted Jewish Americans, and more.

Trepp, Leo. *A History of the Jewish Experience: Eternal Faith, Eternal People.* rev. ed. West Orange, NJ: Behrman House, Inc., 1996.
> A classic, one volume introduction to Judaism that is appropriate for the scholar, the student, and the general reader.

Beliefs and Practices
David, Jo, and Daniel B. Syme. *The Book of the Jewish Life.* New York: UAHC Press, 1998.
> The first text on the Jewish life we actually live today, according to feedback from leaders of the liberal Jewish community.

Dosick, Wayne. *Living Judaism: The Complete Guide to Jewish Belief, Tradition and Practice.* New York: HarperSanFrancisco, 1995.
> A thorough and all encompassing guide.

Ganzfried, Solomon. *Code of Jewish Law: Kitzur Shulhan Arukh,* translated by Hyman E. Goldin. New York: Hebrew Publishing Company, 1963.
> *The Orthodox guide to halachah — Jewish Law.*

Grishaver, Joel Lurie. *40 Things You Can Do to Save the Jewish People.* Los Angeles, CA: Torah Aura Productions, 1993.
> A creative, dynamic look at Jewish parenting, and, by extrapolation, Jewish teaching practices.

Holtz, Barry, ed. *Back to the Sources: Reading the Classic Jewish Texts.* New York: Summit Books, 1984.
> A guide to the great books of the Jewish tradition and an explanation of how to read them.

Jacobs, Louis. *The Book of Jewish Belief.* West Orange, NJ: Behrman House, 1984.
> Everything students in Grades 9 through adult should know about Jewish faith and values.

———. *The Book of Jewish Practice.* West Orange, NJ: Behrman House, 1996.
> A comprehensive and practical guide to Jewish beliefs in action. Companion volume to *The Book of Jewish Belief.*

Klein, Isaac. *A Guide to Jewish Religious Practice.* Philadelphia: Jewish Publishing Society, 1979.

The Conservative guide to Jewish law and practice.

Kushner, Harold. *To Life! A Celebration of Jewish Being and Thinking*. Boston, MA: Warner Books Inc., 1993.

A concise portrait of Jewish values and beliefs.

Olitzky, Kerry M., and Ronald H. Isaacs. *The How To Handbook for Jewish Living*. Hoboken NJ: KTAV Publishing House, 1993.

———. *The Second How To Handbook for Jewish Living*. Hoboken NJ: KTAV Publishing House, 1996.

These two volumes are filled with the facts that every Jew needs to know to live a Jewish life.

Ornstein, Debra, and Jane Rachel Litman. *Lifecycles 2: Jewish Women on Biblical Themes in Contemporary Life*. Woodstock, VT: Jewish Lights Publishing, 1997.

An exploration of the life themes found in the Torah and in women's lives.

Prager, Dennis, and Joseph Telushkin. *Nine Questions People Ask about Judaism*. New York: Simon & Schuster, Inc., 1981.

Explores Judaism as a rational, moral alternative to contemporary society.

Siegel, Richard; Michael Strassfeld; and Sharon Strassfeld, compilers. & eds. *The First Jewish Catalog*. Philadelphia, PA: Jewish Publication Society, 1973.

Strassfeld, Sharon, and Michael Strassfeld, compilers & eds. *The Second Jewish Catalog: Sources and Resources*. Philadelphia, PA: Jewish Publication Society, 1976.

———. *The Third Jewish Catalog: Creating Community*. Philadelphia, PA: Jewish Publication Society, 1980.

Each of the three volumes in this series contains a wealth of information on subjects such as holidays, Jewish calendar, life cycle events, and more.

Syme, Daniel B. *The Jewish Home: A Guide for Jewish Living*. New York: UAHC Press, 1989.

Explains the "why" of major Jewish rituals from a Reform perspective, from the birth of a child to the Jewish wedding, Bar and Bat Mitzvah, Jewish divorce, Confirmation, and the holidays. Ideal introduction to Jewish family living.

Telushkin, Joseph. *Biblical Literacy*. New York: William Morrow and Company, Inc., 1997.

Short, but useful entries of the "most important people, events, and ideas of the Hebrew Bible."

———. *Jewish Literacy*. New York: William Morrow and Company, Inc., 1991.

Concise and informative entries on the most important things to know about the Jewish religion, the Jewish people and their history.

———. *Jewish Wisdom*. New York: William Morrow and Company, Inc., 1994.

A collection of stories from the Bible and Talmud, along with the insights of Jewish commentators and writers, both classic and contemporary.

Trepp, Leo. *The Complete Book of Jewish Observance: A Practical Manual for the Modern Jew*. New York: Summit Books, 1996.

An excellent overview of the celebrations of the year and the celebrations of life.

Washofsky, Mark. *A Guide to Jewish Living and Practice*. New York: UAHC Press, 1999.

The definitive guide for Reform Jewish practice, and a complete source for those who wish to incorporate Jewish practice into their everyday lives.

JEWISH EARLY CHILDHOOD EDUCATION
Curriculum Guides

Machon L'Morim: B'reshit Curriculum Guides. Baltimore, MD: Center for Jewish Education, 1998.

A professional development program for Jewish Early Childhood Educators designed to facilitate the integration of Jewish concepts and values into everyday secular themes. For more information, contact Program Director,

Machon L'Morim: B'reshit, Center for Jewish Education, 5800 Park Heights Avenue, Baltimore, MD 21215, 410-578-6948, Fax: 410-466-1727.

Musnikow, Ruth. *First Steps: Learning and Living for Young Jewish Children*. New York: Board of Jewish Education of Greater New York, 1980.

A curriculum for young children ages three through eight that follows the Jewish calendar, with sections devoted to holidays and special events. Includes practical suggestions for integrating Jewish living with the developmental and cognitive needs of young children.

Regosin, Ina, and Naomi Towvim, eds. *Milk and Honey: Five Units Integrating Jewish and General Curricula in the Early Childhood Setting*. Boston: The Early Childhood Institute, Board of Jewish Education of Greater Boston, 1990.

Each of these five curricula units helps teachers of young children to integrate Jewish values with general curriculum areas such as music, math, science, art, language arts and dramatic play. Units include: Reading Plus — Children's Books with Jewish Themes and Values (Ages 3-5); Noah and the Flood (Age 3); Noah's Ark (Ages 4-5); The Mishkan — Building Community from Biblical Bases (Ages 3-5); and Familiar Games the Jewish Way (Ages 3-5).

Silverberg, Sheila, and Margie Zeskind. *Webbing Out with the Jewish Holidays: Connecting the Holidays, Israel, Jewish Values and the Torah To Our Young Children*. Miami, FL: Helene & A.B. Wiener Early Childhood Department, Central Agency for Jewish Education, 1999.

A compilation of original poems, webs, concepts, and curriculum ideas with additional selected recipes and curriculum projects taken from sources on the reference list. Wonderful examples of webs for each holiday.

HOLIDAYS
General Adult References

Einstein, Stephen J., and Lydia Kukoff. *Every Person's Guide to Judaism*. New York: UAHC Press, 1989.

Examines the hows and whys of Jewish holidays and life cycle events in a straightforward manner.

Goodman, Robert. *Teaching Jewish Holidays: History, Values, Activities*. Denver, CO: A.R.E. Publishing, Inc., 1997.

Complete historical overview of each holiday, vocabulary lists, dozens of activities, and comprehensive resource list.

Strassfeld, Michael. *The Jewish Holidays: A Guide & Commentary*. New York: Harper & Row, 1985.

A well written, comprehensive exploration of all the Jewish holidays, excluding Shabbat. The discussion of each holiday, both major and minor, provide an extensive explanation of the practices involved in observance of that holiday and the religious principles and philosophy behind each tradition.

Waskow, Arthur. *Seasons of Our Joy: A Celebration of Modern Jewish Renewal*. Boston, MA: Beacon Press, 1990.

A lively guide that provides the origin, history, and seasonal significance of the holidays, bringing fresh insights to each festival.

Weber, Vicki L., ed. *The Rhythm of Jewish Time: An Introduction to Holidays and Life-Cycle Events*. West Orange, NJ: Behrman House, 1999.

A comprehensive walk through the Jewish calendar and life cycle, with photos, to help families bring Jewish traditions into their homes.

General Children's References

Adler, David A. *The Kid's Catalog of Jewish Holidays*. Philadelphia: Jewish Publication Society, 1996.

A cornucopia of riches celebrating the Jewish holidays, this easy to use introduction to each of the Jewish holidays gathers together a rare blend of stories, poems, recipes, songs, crafts, puzzles, cartoons, and more.

Burstein, Chaya. *The Jewish Kids Catalog.* Philadelphia: Jewish Publication Society, 1993.
Everything a kid wants to know about being Jewish. It's a fun-filled, illustrated look at holidays and customs, as well as at key people and events in Jewish history, origins of Jewish names, and much more.

ARTS AND CRAFTS

Brinn, Ruth E. *Jewish Holiday Crafts for Little Hands.* Rockville, MD: Kar-Ben Copies, Inc., 1993.
Wonderful craft ideas for each Jewish holiday, accompanied by a brief description and vocabulary list for each holiday.

Kops, Simon. *Fast, Clean, and Cheap: Or Everything the Jewish Teacher and Parent Needs to Know about Art.* Los Angeles, CA: Torah Aura Productions, 1989.
Included are magic tricks, art projects, ways to reconsider even the simple task of drawing with crayons, and an important list of suppliers.

Magnus, Joann, with Howard I. Bogot. *An Artist You Don't Have to Be! A Jewish Arts and Crafts Book.* New York: UAHC Press, 1990.
This book contains "recipes" for Jewish arts and crafts related to such topics as Bible, family, Hebrew, history, Israel, holidays, Shabbat, values, and synagogue.

Sharon, Ruth. *Arts and Crafts the Year Round.* New York: United Synagogue Book Service, 1971.
Crafts for every holiday and Jewish symbol. Many are geared to school age children, but can be adapted for preschool.

Sher, Nina Streisand, and Margaret Feldman. *100+ Jewish Art Projects for Children.* Denver CO: A.R.E. Publishing, Inc., 1996.

Contains over 100 easy to do art projects in the areas of holidays, symbols/ritual objects, Bible, Israel, and more.

ARTS AND CRAFTS SUPPLIES
Chai Kids
21346 St. Andrews Blvd. PMB 218
Boca Raton, FL 33433
(888) CHAI-KID
Fax: (561) 362-0206
www.chaikids.com
Great Jewish crafts and toys.

Dreidelmaker Crafts Kits & Projects
P.O. Box 1904
Frederick, MD 21702
Phone/Fax: (301) 695-4375
Kits to make permanent, usable, and attractive wood *dreidels,* as well as other items, such as *graggers, Kiddush* cups, spice boxes, candlesticks, *mezuzot,* wood shapes ready to paint, etc.

Judaic Art Kits
170 Edgemore Road
Rochester, NY 14618
(800) 862-3449
Fax: (716) 442-1695
www.artkitsetc.com
Kits for making *tallitot, challah* covers, *mezuzot, matzah* bags, and more. Ideal for family programs.

Just for the Mitzvah
625 N. E. Terrace
North Miami Beach, FL 33162
(888) 4-THE-MIT
Fax: (305)653-7496
www.jewishcrafts.com
Judaic arts and crafts for holidays and *mitzvot* every day. Great for family programs.

S & S Worldwide
P.O. Box 513
Colchester, CT 06415
(800) 243-9232
Fax: (800) 566-6678
www.snswwide.com

Arts and crafts supplies, special catalog for Judaic projects.

MUSIC/MOVEMENT RESOURCES

(Compiled by Julie Jaslow Auerbach)

Note: The following is a very comprehensive list of written musical resources for teachers in Jewish early childhood programs. Every effort has been made to determine which of these resources is currently in print. Entries marked with "o.p." are "out of print," but they are generally available in synagogue or central agency libraries. The list was compiled with the help of teachers in the Jewish Education Center of Cleveland's Fall 1999 Movin' and Groovin' class, with additional input from Kim Lausin, preschool teacher, and Rachel Gonsenhauser, Early Childhood Coordinator, at Solomon Schechter Day School, Cleveland, Ohio.

Abrams, Leah. *Because We Love Shabbat.* Cedarhurst, NY: Tara Publications, 1987.

———. *Apples and Other Holidays.* Cedarhurst, NY: Tara Publications, 1989.

Avni, Fran. *Holiday Songbook for Kids.* Cedarhurst, NY: Tara Publications, 1990.

———. *Z'man LaShir Songbook.* Denver, CO: A.R.E. Publishing, Inc.

Bagdade, Gail, et. al., eds. *Apples and Honey & Grape Juice Too! Songs for the Jewish Preschool Sung to Old Familiar Tunes.* Chicago: Board of Jewish Education of Metropolitan Chicago, 1988.

A collection of "piggyback" songs — Jewish theme words to familiar tunes such as "Row Your Boat" and "Old McDonald Had a Farm." Available from the BJE of Chicago at 847-634-0363.

Beall, Pamela Conn, and Susan Hagen Nipp. *Wee Sing.* Los Angeles, CA: Price/Stern/Sloan, 1981.

———. *Wee Sing around the Campfire.* Los Angeles, CA: Price/Stern/Sloan, 1983.

———. *Wee Sing and Play.* Los Angeles, CA: Price/Stern/Sloan, 1983.

———. *Wee Sing Nursery Rhymes and Lullabyes.* Los Angeles, CA: Price/Stern/Sloan, 1985.

Black, Rabbi Joe. *The Rabbi Joe Black Songbook.* Lanitunes. Distributed by A.R.E. Publishing, Inc.

Carlebach, Shlomo. *The Shlomo Carlebach Anthology.* Cedarhurst, NY: Tara Publications, 1992.

Cotler, Doug. *Doug Cotler Songbook.* Woodland Hills, CA: Wail and Blubber Music, 1992.

Cook, Ray M. *Sing for Fun, Volume I.* New York: Union of American Hebrew Congregations, 1955, o.p.

———. *Sing for Fun, Volume II.* New York: Union of American Hebrew Congregations, 1957, o.p.

Coopersmith, Harry. *More of the Songs We Sing.* New York: The United Synagogue Commission on Jewish Education, 1975.

———. *The New Jewish Songbook.* New York: Behrman House, Inc., 1965.

———. *The Songs We Sing.* New York: The United Synagogue Commission on Jewish Education, 1950, o.p.

Ebstein, Roz. *Shabbat Song-Kit for Young Children.* Chicago, IL: Board of Jewish Education of Metropolitan Chicago, n.d.

Eisenstein, Judith Kaplan. *The Gateway to Jewish Song.* New York: Behrman House Inc., 1939, o.p.

Eisenstein, Judith, and Frieda Prensky. *Songs of Childhood.* New York: The United Synagogue Commission on Jewish Education, 1955, o.p.

Etkin, Ruth. *The Singing Calendar.* Cedarhurst, NY: Tara Publications, 1992.

Feingold, Ida Rose ("Skipper"). *The Torah Connection.* Kansas City, MO: Ida Rose Feingold, 1985.

Friedman, Debbie. *Miracles and Wonders.* San Diego, CA: Sounds Write Productions, Inc., 1992. Distributed by A.R.E. Publishing, Inc.

———. *Shirim Al Galgalim*. San Diego, CA: Sounds Write Productions, Inc., 1995.

Glaser, Sam. *Kol Bamidbar*. Los Angeles, CA: Glaser Musicworks, 1999. Distributed by A.R.E. Publishing, Inc.

Glazer, Tom. *Music for Ones and Twos*. Garden City, NY: Doubleday and Company, 1983.

Grossman, Elayne Robinson, and Daniel T. Grossman. *Help Us Bake a Challah*. Cedarhurst, NY: Tara Publications, 1991.

Hebrew Songs for All Seasons Volume Two. Toledo, OH: Toledo Bureau of Jewish Education, 1979.

Janowski, Max. *Chag Sameyach*. Chicago, IL: A Friends of Jewish Music Publication, 1964.

Klepper, Jeff, and Susan Nanus. *Especially Jewish Symbols*. Denver, CO: A.R.E. Publishing, Inc., 1977.

Kol B'seder. *Songs for Growing*. Denver, CO: A.R.E. Publishing, Inc., 1992.

Levy, Sara C., and Beatrice L. Deutsch. *So We Sing*. New York: Bloch Publishing Company, Inc., 1950.

Lipman, Doug. *Folksongs for Teachers and Parents*. Doug Lipman, n.d.

Livnot U'Lehibanot. *The Z'mirot Songbook Z'mirot Livnot*. Owings Mills, MD: Tara Publications, n.d.

Marquis, Margaret Hurley. *Rhythms Rhymes & Songs*. Hicksville, NY: M. Hohner, Inc., 1965.

"Miss Jackie. *My Toes Are Starting to Wiggle*. Overland Park, KS: "Miss Jackie" Music Company, 1989.

———. *Sing Yeladim*. Overland Park, KS: "Miss Jackie" Music Co., 1978.

———. *Songs to Sing with Babies*. Overland Park, KS: "Miss Jackie" Music Company, 1983.

Music for Children Volume 1 Orff Schulwerk. New York: Schott Music Corp., 1982.

Neumann, Richard. *Israel Sings*. Cedarhurst, NY: Tara Publications, n.d.

Palmer, Hap. *Hap Palmer Songbook*. Freeport, NY: Educational Activities, n.d.

Pasternak, Velvel, ed. *Favorite Songs of Israel*. Cedarhurst, NY: Tara Publications, 1985.

———. *Jewish Holidays in Song*. Cedarhurst, NY: Tara Publications, 1997 (This book has just about every traditional song you might need!)

———. *The New Children's Songbook*. Cedarhurst, NY: Tara Publications, 1981.

Rabinowitz, Nili. *18 Chai Songs for Children*. Cedarhurst, NY: Tara Publications, 1988.

Raffi. *The Raffi Singable Songbook*. New York: Crown Publishers, 1980.

———. *The Second Raffi Songbook*. New York: Crown Publishers, Inc., 1986.

Raposo, Joe, and Jeffrey Moss. *The Sesame Street Songbook*. New York: Children's Television Workshop, Inc., 1971.

Reader's Digest Children's Songbook. Pleasantville, NY: Reader's Digest Association, Inc., 1985.

Reilly, Mary Louise, and Lynn Freeman Olson. *It's Time for Music*. Van Nuys, CA: Alfred Publishing Co., Inc., 1985.

Reuben, Steve. *Especially Wonderful Days*. Denver, CO: A.R.E. Publishing, Inc., 1976.

Richards, Stephen, ed. *Manginot*. New York: Transcontinental Music Publications and New Jewish Music Press, 1992.

Rivkin, Nacha, and Ella Shurim. *Come Sing with Me*. Cedarhurst, NY: Tara Publications, 1984.

Serling, Elaine. *Sing and Celebrate*. Farmington Hills, MI: Danza Publications, 1987.

Sharon, Lois & Bram. *Elephant Jam*. Whitby, Ontario, Canada: Pachyderm Music, McGraw-Hill Ryerson Limited, 1980, o.p.

Shiron L'Gan. New York: Transcontinental Music Publications and New Jewish Music Press, 1993.

Shiron L'Yeladim. New York: Transcontinental Music Publications and New Jewish Music Press, 1993.

Taubman, Craig. *The Craig Taubman Songbook*. Sherman Oaks, CA: Sweet Louise Productions, n.d.

Tucker, JoAnne. *Creative Movement for a Song: Activities for Young Children.* Denver, CO: A.R.E. Publishing, Inc., 1993.

Union Songster. New York: Central Conference of American Rabbis, 1960, o.p.

Weikart, Phyllis. *Movement Plus Rhymes, Songs and Singing Games.* Ypsilanti, MI: High/Scope Press, 1988.

DISCOGRAPHY
(Compiled by Julie Jaslow Auerbach)

Note: Unlike books, tapes and CDs are not uniformly documented. Some are produced by specific companies, while others are produced by the artist. Every effort has been made to document these materials accurately.

Abrams, Leah. *Because We Love Shabbat.* Leah Abrams. (LA360)

———. *Apples on Holidays and Other Days.* Leah Abrams. (LA370)

Auerbach, Julie Jaslow. *Seasoned with Song.* Julie Auerbach. Distributed by A.R.E. Publishing, Inc.

Anderson, Leroy. *Leroy Anderson Favorites.* RCA Victor.

Avni, Fran. *Israel Song Favorites – Volume 1 and 2.* Fran Avni Productions. Distributed by A.R.E. Publishing, Inc.

———. *Mostly Matza.* Lemonstone Records. Distributed by A.R.E. Publishing, Inc.

———. *Latkes and Hamentashen.* Lemonstone Records. Distributed by A.R.E. Publishing, Inc.

———. *The Seventh Day.* Lemonstone Records. Distributed by A.R.E. Publishing, Inc.

———. *Z'man LaShir.* Published and distributed by A.R.E. Publishing, Inc.

Barry Sisters. *Barry Sisters in Israel.* Roulette Records, 1963.

Bartels, Joanie. *Morning Magic.* Discovery Music.

———. *Sillytime Magic.* Discovery Music.

Behrman House. *Home Start* Series. Behrman House, o.p.

———. *Let's Celebrate* Series. Behrman House.

Black, Rabbi Joe. *Aleph Bet Boogie.* Lanitunes. Distributed by A.R.E. Publishing, Inc.

———. *Everybody's Got a Little Music.* Lanitunes. Distributed by A.R.E. Publishing, Inc.

Bos, Bev. *Hand in Hand.* Turn the Page Press.

Broza, David. *First Collection.* (CBS Records)

Budin, Noah. *Hallelujah Land* (ARK001)

Celebrate with Us: Chanukah. Jewish Family Productions. Distributed by A.R.E. Publishing, Inc.

Celebrate with Us: Passover. Jewish Family Productions. Distributed by A.R.E. Publishing, Inc.

Celebrate with Us: Shabbat. Jewish Family Productions. Distributed by A.R.E. Publishing, Inc.

Chanukah Music Box. Kinor Records.

Chanukah Singalong for Kids. Provident.

Chapin, Tom. *Moonboat.* Columbia.

Cohen, Myrna. *Lullabies & Quiet Time.* Distributed by Sounds Write Productions, Inc.

Come and Play (Bo-u Nesachayk). Acum.

Cotler, Doug. *It's So Amazing!* (Spigot 152) Distributed by A.R.E. Publishing, Inc.

Friedman, Debbie. *Miracles and Wonders.* Sounds Write Productions, Inc. Distributed by A.R.E. Publishing, Inc.

———. *Shanah Tovah — A Good Year.* Sounds Write Productions, Inc. Distributed by A.R.E. Publishing, Inc.

———. *Shirim Al Galgalim.* Sounds Write Publications. Distributed by A.R.E. Publishing, Inc.

Gemini. *Good Mischief Songs and Dances for Children.* Gemini Records.

———. *Pulling Together.* Gemini Records.

———. *Swingin!* Gemini Records.

Glaser, Sam. *Kol Bamidbar.* Glaser Musicworks.

Greg & Steve. *On the Move.* Youngheart Records.

Grossman, Elayne Robinson, and Daniel T. Grossman. *Help Us Bake a Challah.* Creative Enterprises.

Helzner, Robin. *I Live in the City.* RAH Productions.

Klepper, Jeff, and Susan Nanus. *Especially Jewish Symbols: Sing Along Songs for the Primary Grades.* Published and distributed by A.R.E. Publishing, Inc. (Songbook also available)

Klepper, Jeff, and Jeff Salkin. *Bible People Songs.* Published and distributed by A.R.E. Publishing, Inc. (Songbook also available)

Kol B'seder. *Growin'. Volumes I and II.* Kol B'seder. Distributed by A.R.E. Publishing, Inc.

———. *The Bridge.* Kol B'seder. Distributed by A.R.E. Publishing, Inc.

———. *In Every Generation.* Kol B'seder. Distributed by A.R.E. Publishing, Inc.

———. *Shalom Rav.* Kol B'seder. Distributed by A.R.E. Publishing, Inc.

———. *Sparks of Torah.* Kol B'seder. Distributed by A.R.E. Publishing, Inc.

Lader, Enid. *B'Mesheh Hashana (Sing through the Year).* Haren Productions.

Livnot U'Lehibanot. Z'mirot Livnot. Owings Mills, MD: Tara Publications, n.d.

Memeitiv Shiray Hachagim L'yeladim (From the Best of Children's Holiday Songs). Hataklit Ltd. Distributed by Isradisc.

"Miss Jackie." *Hello Rhythm.* "Miss Jackie" Music.

———. *Sing a Jewish Song.* "Miss Jackie" Music.

Paley, Cindy. *Shabbat Shalom.* Cindy Paley.

Palmer, Hap. *Getting to Know Myself.* Educational Activities, Inc., Activity Records.

———. *Learning Basic Skills through Music, Volume I.* Educational Activities, Inc., Activity Records.

Passover Singalong for Kids. Provident.

Raffi. *Everything Grows.* Troubador Records, Ltd.

———. *In Concert with the Rise & Shine Band.* Troubador Records, Ltd.

———. *More Singable Songs by Raffi.* Troubador Records, Ltd.

———. *One Light, One Sun.* Troubador Records, Ltd.

———. *Singable Songs.* Troubador Records, Ltd.

Raffi with Ken Whiteley. *Raffi with Ken Whiteley.* Troubador Records, Ltd.

———. *Rise and Shine.* Shoreline/Troubador/ Rounder.

Reuben, Steve. *Especially Wonderful Days: Sing Along Jewish Holiday Songs for the Primary Grades.* Published and distributed by A.R.E. Publishing, Inc.

Rosenthal, Margie, and Ilene Safyan. *Where Dreams Are Born.* Distributed by A.R.E. Publishing, Inc.

Schwartz, Stephen. *Prince of Egypt.* Dreamworks.

Sesame Street Series. Children's Television Workshop.

Shabbat Singalong for Kids. Provident.

Sharon, Lois & Bram. *Great Big Hits.* Elephant Records.

———. *Mainly Mother Goose.* Elephant Records.

Shiron L'Gan. Transcontinental Music Publications/ New Jewish Music Press.

Shlock Rock. *Shlock Rock for Kids Sing Together.* Shlock Rock.

Simon, Jon. *From Broadway to Hollywood.* Silver Lining Records. Distributed by A.R.E. Publishing, Inc.

———. *New Traditions.* Silver Lining Records. Distributed by A.R.E. Publishing, Inc.

———. *New Traditions 2.* Silver Lining Records. Distributed by A.R.E. Publishing, Inc.

———. *Shabbatjazz.* Silver Lining Records. Distributed by A.R.E. Publishing, Inc.

————. *Zoom Gali Boogie and Other New Traditions*. Silver Lining Records. Distributed by A.R.E. Publishing, Inc.

Solnik, Tanya. *A Legacy of Lullabies*. Distributed by Sounds Write Productions, Inc.

Taubman, Craig. *My Jewish Discovery*. Sweet Louise. Distributed by A.R.E. Publishing, Inc.

————. *My Newish Jewish Discovery*. Sweet Louise. Distributed by A.R.E. Publishing, Inc.

————. *Craig & Co.* series. Disney Productions.

————. *Rhythm, Rhyme, Music Time*. RRMT, Inc.

————. *Good Morning, Good Night*. Sweet Louise.

Today's Special. *Today's Special*. A & M Records of Canada.

Zim, Paul. *Kooky Cookie Kids*. Simcha.

————. *It's Jewish Holiday Time*. Paul Zim Productions.

Weber, Andrew Lloyd. *Joseph and the Amazing Technicolor Dreamcoat*. MCA Records Inc.

Wee Sing Series. Price/Stern/Sloan.

SOURCES FOR CASSETTE TAPES, CDS, AND SONGBOOKS

A.R.E. Publishing, Inc.
3945 South Oneida
Denver, CO 80237
(800) 346-7779
Fax: (303) 363-6069
www.arepublish.com
A good selection of those items especially appropriate for educational use.

Sounds Write Productions Inc.
6685 Norman Lane
San Diego, CA 92120
(619) 697-6120 or (800) 976-8639
Fax: (619) 697-6124
www.soundswrite.com
Produces, manufactures, and distributes high quality, contemporary Jewish music for people of all ages.

Tara Publications
P.O. Box 707
Owings Mills, MD 21117
(800) TARA-400
Fax: (800) TARA-403
www.jewishmusic.com
A comprehensive selection of Jewish music and videos, including the *Shalom Sesame* series.

GAMES

Brinn, Ruth E. *Jewish Holiday Games for Little Hands*. Rockville, MD: Kar-Ben Copies, Inc., 1995.
  Dozens of games for Shabbat and the Jewish holidays, with game boards and playing cards designed for reproduction. Features simple directions, holiday explanations, and a glossary.

Grundleger, Barbara. *Hands On! Teacher-made Games for Jewish Early Childhood Settings*. Denver, CO: A.R.E. Publishing, Inc., 1991.
  Descriptions of 85 games and activities for teachers to create. Each combines basic skills with Jewish themes.

Palatnik, Barbara. *Creative Activities for the Jewish Child*. Deerfield, IL: LaYeled, Inc., 1988.
  A handbook for preschool, kindergarten, and first grade educators. Includes songs, creative movement, and classroom games.

SCIENCE

Spanier, Elaine. *Science Adventures through the Year*. Deerfield, IL: B'nai Torah Pre-School, 1996. (Available from Congregation B'nai Torah Preschool, 2789 Oak St., Highland Park, IL 60035, 847-433-6900)
  A collection of science experiences tailored to concepts, skills, and symbols for each of the Jewish holidays.

COOKBOOKS

Nathan, Joan. *The Children's Jewish Holiday Kitchen*. New York: Schocken Books, 1995.

Introduces children to their Jewish heritage through the food associated with holidays. Here are 70 child-centered recipes and cooking activities from around the world. Covering the ten major holidays, each of the activities has a different focus — such as Eastern Europe, biblical Israel, contemporary America. Contains a vast array of foods, flavors, and ideas.

Rauchwerger, Lisa. *Chocolate Chip Challah and Other Twists on the Jewish Holiday Table.* New York: UAHC Press, 1999.

Using the Jewish calendar as a framework, both adults and children can cook up tasty treats all year long. Includes stories and an illustrated cooking dictionary. Each easy-to-follow recipe is designed for children ages 5-11, their families, and their teachers.

Stark, Mark. *Mark Stark's Amazing Jewish Cookbook for the Entire Family.* Los Angeles: Alef Design Group, 1997.

A delightful, hand drawn cookbook for the entire family. Includes recipes for traditional Jewish foods such as bagels, chicken soup, and *matzah* balls, as well as holiday treats such as potato *latkes* and Passover sponge cake.

Zalben, Jane Breskin. *Beni's Family Cookbook for the Jewish Holidays.* New York: Henry Holt & Company, Inc., 1996.

This sumptuous collection of Jewish holiday recipes gathers culinary treasures from the author's family and friends. Each section features a different holiday, and includes notes on the holiday's religious and cultural importance. Included are recipes for *matzah* ball soup, noodle *kugel,* and gefilte fish.

SECULAR CURRICULUM

Chenfeld, Mim Brodsky. *Creative Experiences for Young Children.* 2d ed. Fort Worth: Harcourt Brace College Publishers, 1995.

Learn to teach to the life of the children with "life themes," such as family and friends.

Hundreds of open-ended ideas and extensive resources.

Cook, Ruth E.; Annette Tessier; and M. Diane Klein. *Adapting Early Childhood Curricula for Children in Inclusive Settings.* Upper Saddle River, NJ: Merrill, 2000.

Updated to reflect the most recent developments in the field, this text presents the skills necessary for teachers to assist infants, young children, and their families to meet their special challenges and to develop to their fullest potential. The book takes a non-categorical approach that recognizes special needs, rather than special labels, and provides practical, developmentally appropriate, activity based curriculum adaptation.

Dombro, Amy L.; Laura J. Colker; and Diane Trister Dodge. *The Creative Curriculum for Infants & Toddlers.* Washington, DC: Teaching Strategies, 1999.

Provides a comprehensive, yet easy to use framework for planning and implementing a developmentally appropriate program. Designed for use in both day care centers and family child care settings, the book emphasizes that relationships between caregivers/teachers and children and families are the focus of curriculum for very young children.

Feidman, Jean R. *Wonderful Rooms Where Children Can Bloom.* Peterborough, NH: Crystal Springs Books, 1997.

Over 500 wonderful ideas and activities for making your classroom a warm and welcoming environment. This book will help teachers transform their rooms into inviting places where children will learn and grow.

A Guide to Children's Literature and Disability, 1989-1994
National Information Center for Children and Youth with Disabilities
(Address and phone on p. 372 below)
www.nichcy.org/pubs/bibliog/bib5.htm

A bibliography that identifies for parents and professionals books written about or including characters who have a disability.

Herr, Judy, and Yvonne Libby-Larson. *Creative Resources for the Early Childhood Classroom*. New York: Delmar Publishers, 1999.

The most complete guide to planning a developmentally appropriate curriculum for young children. This text focuses on the growth of the whole child and includes hundreds of activities that make education interesting and challenging for young children.

Starting Small: Teaching Tolerance in Preschool and the Early Grades
Available from the Southern Poverty Law Center (See p. 371 below for address)
(A teacher-training kit for early childhood educators consisting of a 58-minute video, "Starting Small: Teaching Children Tolerance," and five copies of a 250-page text that focuses on seven exemplary tolerance education programs. Free, one set per school, upon written request on a letterhead from elementary principal, day care director, or teacher education department chair.)

MATERIALS/SUPPLIES

A.O.S. Greenfield
66-15 Main St.
Flushing, NY 11367
(800) 263-6445
Fax: (718) 263-6447
www.jewish-education.com
Great Israeli source for posters and other curriculum materials.

The Learning Plant
P.O. Box 17233
West Palm Beach, FL 33416
(561) 686-9456
Fax: (561) 686-2415
www.learningplant.com
Jewish teaching resources and materials.

Discount School Supply
PO Box 7636
Spreckels, CA 93962
(800) 627-2829
Fax: (800) 879-3753
www.earlychildhood.com
Art, math, science and general classroom supplies at a discount.

"Kids on the Block" and "Glenn's Friends" Disability Awareness Programs
Bureau of Jewish Education
5700 Wilshire Boulevard, Suite 2710
Los Angeles, CA 90036
(323) 852-7702
Fax: (323) 761-8640
Puppet shows for elementary school children and preschoolers respectively, through the Promoting Disability Awareness Program.

Lakeshore Learning Materials
2695 E. Dominguez Street
P.O. Box 6261
Carson, CA 90749
(800) 421-5354
Fax: (310) 537-5403
www.lakeshorelearning.com
Materials and equipment for the early childhood and primary classroom. Strong focus on multi-cultural materials.

One World Poster Set
Eight 4-color 18" × 24" posters featuring artwork and text from *Teaching Tolerance* magazine. Includes teacher's guide for elementary and secondary classrooms. Free, one per individual teacher, upon written request on letterhead and faxed to Order Department at (334) 264-7310. (No bulk orders available)

TOYS

Childcraft Education Corp.
PO Box 3239
Lancaster, PA 17604

(800) 631-5652
Fax: (888) 532-4453
www.childcrafteducation.com
Materials and games for infant to grade three.

Chime Time
One Sportime Way
Atlanta, GA 30340
(800) 477-5075
Fax: (800) 845-1535
www.chimetime.com
Movement products for young children, such as movement and balance games and equipment, musical instruments, etc.

Community Playthings
PO Box 901 Route 213
Rifton, NY 12471
(800) 777-4244
Fax: (800) 336-5948
Excellent materials and equipment for the early childhood classroom.

Constructive Playthings
1227 E. 119th St.
Grandview, MO 64030
(800) 448-4115
Fax: (816) 761-9295
www.ustoy.com
Wide range of general supplies; also has a Judaic Resources catalog with good Jewish resources, puzzles, and toys.

PUBLISHERS

A.R.E. Publishing, Inc.
3945 South Oneida
Denver, CO 80237
(800) 363-7779
Fax: (303) 363-6069
www.arepublish.com
A great source for teacher manuals, curriculum, Copy Paks, cassettes, CDs, clip art, and more.

Behrman House
11 Edison Pl.
Springfield, NJ 07081
(800) 221-2755
Fax: (973) 379-7280
www.behrmanhouse.com
Publisher of Jewish curriculum material for preschool through adult.

CCAR Press
192 Lexington Avenue
New York, NY 10016
(800) 935-CCAR
Fax: (212) 689-1649
www.ccarnet.org
Books, prayer books, professional and scholarly works for adults and children for a liberal audience.

Feldheim Publishers
200 Airport Executive Parkway
Spring Valley, NY 10977
(914) 356-2282
Fax: (914) 425-1908
Jewish books for children and adults geared to a traditional audience.

Hachai Publishing
156 Chester Avenue
Brooklyn, NY 11216
(718) 633-0100
Fax: (718) 633-0103
www.hachai.com
Jewish children's books from a traditional perspective.

Jason Aronson Inc.
230 Livingston Street
Northvale, NJ 07647
(800) 782-0015
Fax: (201) 7674330
www.aronson.com
Publisher of books on prayer, history, spiritual issues, and more. Publishes *Jewish Book News*, a monthly Jewish book club catalog with articles and children's selections.

Jewish Lights Publishing
P.O. Box 237
Woodstock, VT 05091
(802) 457-4000 or (800) 962-4544
Fax: (802) 457-4004
www.jewishlights.com
Publisher of books for the Jewish soul. Wonderful children's selections as well.

Jewish Publication Society
1930 Chestnut Street
Philadelphia, PA 19103
(800) 355-1165
Fax: (703) 661-1501
www.jewishpub.org
Books for adults and children that further Jewish culture and education.

Kar-Ben Copies
6800 Tildenwook Lane
Rockville, MD 20852
(800) 4-KARBEN
Fax: (301) 881-9195
www.karben.com
Jewish children's books, including a large selection of board books.

KTAV Publishing House, Inc.
900 Jefferson St.
Hoboken, NJ 07030
(201) 963-9524
Fax: (201) 963-0102
www.ktav.com
Jewish textbooks and supplies.

The Melton Research Center for Jewish Education
Jewish Theological Seminary
3080 Broadway
New York, NY 10027
(212) 678-8083
Fax: (212) 749-8031
www.jtsa.edu/melton
Innovative curriculum and educational materials.

Pitspopany Press
1030 Fifth Avenue
New York, NY 10028
(800) 232-2931
Fax: (212) 472-6253
www.pitspopany.com
English language books from Israel for children up to age 12.

Redleaf Press
450 N. Syndicate Suite 5
St. Paul, MN 55104
(800) 423-8309
Fax: (800) 641-0115
www.redleafinstitute.org
Catalog of excellent early childhood resources for teachers.

Torah Aura Productions
4423 Fruitland Avenue
Los Angeles, CA 90058
(800) 689-0793
Fax: (213) 585-0327
www.torahaura.com
A plethora of educational materials, textbooks, instant lessons, and more for preschool through adult.

UAHC Press
838 Fifth Avenue
New York, NY 10021
(888) 489-UAHC
Fax: (212) 650-4119
www.uahcpress.com
Books for adults and children from the Reform movement. Includes some notable board books.

BOOK DISTRIBUTORS

The Bookvine for Children
3980 Albany Street
McHenry, IL 60050
(800) 772-4220
Fax: (815) 363-8883
www.bookvine.com
Distributor of children's books, with special listings of Jewish books and holiday titles.

Enjoy-a-Book Club
555 Chestnut Street
Cedarhurst, NY 11516
(516) 569-0324
Fax: (516) 569-0830
Distributor of Jewish children's books and provider of book fair services.

forWORDS Catalog of Jewish Books
P.O. Box 3761
Torrance, CA 90510.
(800) 44WORDS
Fax: (310) 784-0275
Comprehensive, annotated catalog of books for Jewish children, teachers and adults. An incredible resource. Also provides book fair services.

1-(800) JUDAISM
2028 Murray Avenue
Pittsburgh, PA 15217
www.Judaism.com
A catalog of books organized into "12 Paths to Judaism," each of which is introduced by a passionately committed author. One stop shopping for any current Jewish book, tape, video, or software.

PERIODICALS

Early Childhood Today
Child Care Information Exchange
Exchange Press Inc.
PO Box 3249
Redmond, WA 98073
(800) 221-2864
(425) 702-0678
www.ccie.com
Committed to supporting early childhood center directors in their efforts to craft early childhood environments where adults and children thrive.

Jewish Education News
Coalition for the Advancement of Jewish Education (CAJE)
261 W. 35th Street Floor 12A
New York, NY, 10001
(212) 268-4210

Fax: (212) 268-4214
www.caje.org
Contains both organizational news and excellent articles on Jewish educational issues.

Scholastic Early Childhood Today
2931 E. McCarty Street
PO Box 3710
Jefferson City, MO 65102
(800) 544-2917
Fax: (303) 604-7644
www.earlychildhoodtoday.com
The magazine for all early childhood professionals.

Teaching Tolerance
Southern Poverty Law Center
Morris Dees, Executive Chairman
400 Washington St.
Montgomery, AL 36104
(334) 264-0286
www.splcenter.org
A free semiannual 64-page magazine that provides educators with resources for promoting interracial and intercultural understanding. To subscribe, individual teachers and other educators should send a request on a letterhead.

Young Children
National Association for the Education of Young Children (NAEYC)
1509 16th Street, NW
Washington, DC 20036
(202) 232-8777 or (800) 424-2460
Fax: (202) 328-1846
www.naeyc.org
A professional journal on the education of children ages birth through eight years.

ORGANIZATIONS

Jewish Braille Institute of America
110 East 30th Street
New York, NY 10016
(212) 889-2525
www.jewishbraille.org
New Years cards in Braille; provides sheets of Genesis in Braille to schools free of charge.

Jewish National Fund
Department of Education
78 Randall Avenue
Rockville Centre, NY 11570
(800) 700-1312
Fax: (516) 678-3204
www.jnf.org
The JNF is the caretaker of Israel's trees. Order a tree to be planted in Israel. Educational posters, materials and curriculum also available.

National Information Center for Children and Youth With Disabilities
P.O. Box 1492
Washington, DC 20013-1402
(800) 695-0285 (Voice/TT)
www.nichcy.org

North American Conference on Ethiopian Jewry (NACOEJ)
132 Nassau St., 4th floor
New York, NY 10038
(212) 233-5200
www.circus.org/nacoej
Supplies education and aid for Ethiopian Jews in Israel and in Ethiopia, offers reading lists and other educational materials.

PROFESSIONAL ORGANIZATIONS

Coalition for the Advancement of Jewish Education (CAJE)
261 W. 35th Street Floor 12A
New York, NY, 10001
(212) 268-4210
Fax: (212) 268-4214
www.caje.org
Open to all Jewish educators across denominations and age levels.

National Association for the Education of Young Children (NAEYC)
1509 16th Street, NW
Washington, DC 20036
202-232-8777 or (800) 424-2460

Fax: (202) 328-1846
www.naeyc.org
An organization for early childhood teachers and directors

National Jewish Early Childhood Network
Helaine Groeger
11 Wonder View Court
North Potomac, MD, 20878
(301) 279-7505
Fax: (301) 279-7314
LAINEYG@aol.com
A caucus of Jewish early childhood teachers and directors that meets annually at the NAEYC conference.

RESEARCH

Kelman, Stuart L, ed. *What We Know about Jewish Education: A Handbook of Today's Research for Tomorrow's Jewish Education.* Los Angeles: Torah Aura Productions, 1992.
> An excellent summary of research on various topics. See especially "What We Know about . . . Early Childhood Education" by Ruth Pinkenson Feldman, pp. 81-87.

JEWISH ACCREDITATION

Jacoby, Emil. *Accreditation Manual for Jewish Schools.* Los Angeles: Bureau of Jewish Education of Greater Los Angeles, 1998.
> Includes an accreditation process designed to complement NAEYC accreditation. Provides a good, detailed breakdown of components of excellent Jewish early childhood education.

FINE JUDAICA

AllThingsJewish.com
214 W. Saint Paul Avenue
Chicago, Illinois 60614
(877) 613-5454
Fax: (707) 897-1645
www.allthingsjewish.com
Fine, unique Judaica and *Tribe*, an online magazine.

HaMakor Judaica, Inc.
P.O. Box 48836
Niles, IL 60714
(800) 426-2567
Fax: (847) 966-4033
www.jewishsource.com
Comprehensive source for all things Jewish.

J. Levine Co.
5 West 30th Street
New York, NY 10001-4421
(800) 5Jewish
Fax: (212) 643-1044
www.levinejudaica.com
Source for fine Judaica.

Rosenblum's
2906 W. Devon Ave.
Chicago, IL 60659
(773) 262-1700 or (800) 626-6536
Fax: (773) 262-1930
www.rosenblums.com
Great source for books and Judaica.

JEWISH SOFTWARE

DAVKA Corporation
7074 N. Western Avenue
Chicago, IL 60645
(800) 621-8227
Fax: (773) 262-9298
www.davka.com
Large distributor of Jewish software, including some good selections for preschool.

JeMM Productions
P.O. BOX 4167
Jerusalem 91041
Israel

972-2-6733372
In USA: (800) 871-6694
Fax: 972-2-673374
www.jemm.co.il
Jewish software, including *Portrait of Israel, The Interactive Haggadah,* and *Who Stole Hanukah?*

WEB SITES/WEB RESOURCES

Jewish Family & Life!
1001 Watertown Street Suite 3B
West Newton, MA 02165
(888) 1-LUV-JFL
Fax: (617) 558-9316
www.jewishfamily.com
Online magazine for Jewish parents, and more.

Following are several other Jewish web sites chosen from among the many extensive directories of such sites:

www.shamash.org – one of the largest and oldest collections of Jewish links

www.jewishnet.net – global Jewish information network

www.virtualjerusalem.com – includes a Jewish educator link with lots of information

www.mishpacha.org – a virtual community for real parents

www.jewishfamily.com – consists of more than 25 web sites and e-magazines